BTEC NATIONAL

D0997671

CHILDREN'S PLAY, LEARNING AND DEVELOPMENT

Student Book 1

REVISED FOR THE EARLY YEARS EDUCATOR CRITERIA

Penny Tassoni
Brenda Baker
Louise Burnham
Editor: Gill Squire

CP046006
CORNWALL COLLEGE

BTEC ALWAYS LEARNING

PEARSON

Published by Pearson Education Limited, Edinburgh Gate, Harlow, Essex, CM20 2JE.

www.pearsonschoolsandfecolleges.co.uk

Text © Penny Tassoni, Brenda Baker and Louise Burnham 2014
Edited by Gill Squire
Typeset by Phoenix Photosetting, Chatham, Kent, UK
Original illustrations © Pearson Education Limited and Katie Mac/NB Illustration Ltd 2012
Cover design by Pearson Education Limited and Andrew Magee Design
Picture research by Susie Prescott
Front cover photo © Mark Peter Drolet/Masterfile
Indexing by Catherine Harkness

The rights of Penny Tassoni, Brenda Baker and Louise Burnham to be identified as authors of this work have been asserted by them in accordance with the Copyright, Designs and Patents Act 1988.

First published 2014

17 16 15 14
10 9 8 7 6 5 4 3 2 1

British Library Cataloguing in Publication Data
A catalogue record for this book is available from the British Library

ISBN 978 1 447970 96 5

Copyright notice
All rights reserved. No part of this publication may be reproduced in any form or by any means (including photocopying or storing it in any medium by electronic means and whether or not transiently or incidentally to some other use of this publication) without the written permission of the copyright owner, except in accordance with the provisions of the Copyright, Designs and Patents Act 1988 or under the terms of a licence issued by the Copyright Licensing Agency, Saffron House, 6–10 Kirby Street, London EC1N 8TS (www.cla.co.uk). Applications for the copyright owner's written permission should be addressed to the publisher.

Printed in Italy by Lego S.p.A

Websites
There are links to relevant websites in this book. In order to ensure that the links are up to date, that the links work, and that the sites aren't inadvertently links to sites that could be considered offensive, we have made the links available on our website at www.pearsonhotlinks.co.uk. Search for the title, BTEC Level 3 National Children's Play, Learning & Development Student Book 1 or ISBN 9781447970965.

Weblinks in the Further Reading sections have been left in place for learners to access independently.

Copies of official specifications for all Edexcel qualifications may be found on the Edexcel website: www.edexcel.com.

A NOTE FROM THE PUBLISHER

In order to ensure that this resource offers high-quality support for the associated BTEC qualification, it has been through a review process by the awarding organisation to confirm that it fully covers the teaching and learning content of the specification or part of a specification at which it is aimed, and demonstrates an appropriate balance between the development of subject skills, knowledge and understanding, in addition to preparation for assessment.

While the publishers have made every attempt to ensure that advice on the qualification and its assessment is accurate, the official specification and associated assessment guidance materials are the only authoritative source of information and should always be referred to for definitive guidance.

BTEC examiners have not contributed to any sections in this resource relevant to examination papers for which they have responsibility.

No material from an endorsed book will be used verbatim in any assessment set by BTEC.

Endorsement of a book does not mean that the book is required to achieve this BTEC qualification, nor does it mean that it is the only suitable material available to support the qualification, and any resource lists produced by the awarding organisation shall include this and other appropriate resources.

The publisher would like to thank the following for their kind permission to reproduce their photographs:

(Key: b-bottom; c-centre; l-left; r-right; t-top)

Alamy Images: ableimages 269, Alan Edwards 291, Beverley Lu 17, FogStock 131, INSADCO Photography 173, Janine Wiedel Photolibrary 233, Jason Smalley Photography 107, PBWPIX 186, Picture Partners 221, 225, Profimedia.CZ a.s. 117, UpperCut Images 141; **BananaStock:** 77, Imagestate 14, 55, 103, 139, 323; **Corbis:** Ariel Skelley/Blend Images 247; **DK Images:** Howard Shooter 212, Vanessa Davies 7, 15l; **Fotolia.com:** Andrey_Arkusha 387, Blend Images 334, Warren Goldswain 319; **Getty Images:** Alistair Berg 238, Kidstock/Blend Images 404, Tim Platt 359; **Pearson Education Ltd:** Anna Marlow 185, Gareth Boden 80, 242, 321, 324, Ian Wedgewood 317, Jon Barlow 161, 277, 320, Jules Selmes 3, 4, 12tl, 12tr, 12bl, 12br, 21, 57, 92t, 121, 133, 241, 245, 275, 300, 332, 341, 369, 379, 383, 386, 391, Lisa Payne Photography 294, Lord and Leverett 114, 217, 409, Rob Judges 278, Roddy Paine 2, 124, StillVision 205, 208, Studio 8 18, 88, 92b, 110, 112, 126, 206, 218, 279, 282, 288, 289, 303, 329, 353, 366, Tudor Photography 95; **Science Photo Library Ltd:** Dr P. Marazzi 158, Lowell Georgia 65, Michelle Del Guercio 34; **Shutterstock.com:** auleena 164, Blamb 171, Diego Cervo 243, 246, emin kuliyev 81, 84, Ffolas 15r, Forster Forest 255, Greenland 250, Mariusz Szachowski 142, Masson 345, Matka Wariatka 171, MNStudio 125, 128, Monkey Business Images 231, 232, Oliveromg 193, 347, 350, stefanolunardi 111, StockLite 135, Suslik1983 137, Wavebreakmedia 163, 166; **SuperStock:** Ingram Publishing Alamy 401; **Veer/Corbis:** alexraths 244, Andresr 381, Elnur Amikishiyev 322, flashon 82, hunt 415, IKO 384, iodrakon 348, Ivonne 346, michaeljung 280, michel74100 204, rnl 78, Robert Kneschke 123, 382, Robert Marmion 162; **www.imagesource.com:** 203.

All other images © Pearson Education

Every effort has been made to trace the copyright holders and we apologise in advance for any unintentional omissions. We would be pleased to insert the appropriate acknowledgement in any subsequent edition of this publication.

The author and publisher would like to thank the following individuals and organisations for permission to reproduce their materials:

p.130 Table 3.1: How much sleep children need from *Information for parents: Sleep* at http://webarchive.nationalarchives.gov.uk/20130401151715/https://www.education.gov.uk/publications/eOrderingDownload/ES82.pdf, © Crown copyright 2010; **p.152** Table 3.8: How long to exclude children with infectious diseases adapted from *South East London Health Protection Unit (2010) School Health Matters: A guide to communicable diseases and infection control* (4th ed.), London: Health Protection Agency Publications, Used with permission; **p. 174** Table 4.3: The NHS vaccination schedule for babies and young children from http://www.nhs.uk/Conditions/vaccinations/Pages/vaccination-schedule-age-checklist.aspx, © Crown copyright; **p.210** Quote from The Effective Pre-School and Primary Education 3-11 Project: Final Report from the Primary Phase: Pre-school, School and Family Influences on Children's Development during Key Stage 2, https://www.gov.uk/government/uploads/system/uploads/attachment_data/file/222225/DCSF-RR061.pdf © Sylva, Melhuish, Sammons, Siraj-Blatchford & Taggart 2008, Used with permission; **p.325** Quote from The Children Act 1989 Section 47. © Crown copyright; **p.405** Quote adapted from Statutory Framework for the Early Years Foundation Stage. © Crown copyright 2012; **p.406** Quote from Statutory Framework for the Early Years Foundation Stage. © Crown copyright 2012;

p.411: Table 10.2 from *Mathematical Vocabulary Book*, Department for Education and Employment (2000) © Crown copyright 2000.

Every effort has been made to contact copyright holders of material reproduced in this book. Any omissions will be rectified in subsequent printings if notice is given to the publishers.

This resource is designed to help you through your BTEC National Children's Play, Learning and Development course, and is divided into ten units, which correspond to units 1 to 10 of the specification.

About your BTEC National in Children's Play, Learning and Development

Choosing to study for a BTEC National Children's Play, Learning and Development qualification is a great decision to make for lots of reasons. In recent years, there has been a growing understanding that children's earliest experiences shape their life chances and it is vital that children receive the best possible early education and care. As a future early years professional, you can play a significant part in making sure that the provision children receive is of the highest quality.

Your BTEC National Children's Play, Learning and Development qualification is a vocational or work-related qualification. This means that it will give you the opportunity to gain specific knowledge, understanding and skills that are relevant to your chosen subject or area of work. This new BTEC is a great foundation to build your skills for employment or further study.

What will you be doing?

The BTEC Nationals in Children's Play, Learning and Development are structured into **core units** and **optional specialist units**. How many units you do, and which ones you cover, depends on the type of qualification you are working towards. The different qualifications are Subsidiary Award, Award, Subsidiary Certificate, Certificate and Diploma. The following table shows you how the units in this book fit into each qualification.

Units		Core
Unit 1	Child Development	All levels
Unit 2	Play and Learning	All levels
Unit 3	Meeting Children's Physical Development, Physical Care and Health Needs	Certificate and Diploma
Unit 4	Health and Safety in Early Years Settings	All levels except Subsidiary Award
Unit 5	Working With Parents and Others in Early Years	Subsidiary Certificate, Certificate and Diploma
Unit 6	Supporting Children's Speech, Communication and Language	Certificate and Diploma
Unit 7	Supporting Children's Personal, Social and Emotional Development	Certificate and Diploma
Unit 8	Safeguarding in Early Years	All levels except Subsidiary Award
Unit 9	Observation, Assessment and Planning	All levels except Subsidiary Award
Unit 10	Supporting Children's Literacy and Numeracy Development	Certificate and Diploma

We will also provide a second resource (Student Book 2), which will contain an additional ten units for study. You can find details about this from your teacher/tutor or at www.pearsonschoolsandfecolleges.co.uk

About the authors

Best-selling author **Penny Tassoni** trained as an early years and primary teacher. Now working as an education consultant and trainer, she specialises in the whole spectrum of learning and play. Penny has written more than 30 books about early years, and frequently writes articles for national early years magazines. In addition to this, Penny is a well-known speaker both in the UK and internationally. She has in-depth knowledge of the BTEC Nationals in Children's Play, Learning and Development and uses her accessible and friendly style of writing to bring the information to life for learners on this course.

Brenda Baker has worked in early years settings and as a primary teacher. She then taught childcare and education in an FE college and, for a number of years, managed the Health and Social Care Department. In recent years she has contributed to textbooks and support materials for learners and teachers/tutors of early years, and for Teaching Assistant qualifications. She has extensive experience of BTEC qualifications.

Louise Burnham has worked as an early years and primary teacher and SENCO. She also led teaching assistant training and worked on childcare and teaching courses at a London FE college for a number of years. Louise has written or contributed to many books for early years and Teaching Assistant qualifications.

How to use this resource

This resource contains many features that will help you apply your skills and knowledge to work-related situations and assist you in getting the most from your course.

These introductions give you a snapshot of what to expect from each unit – and what you should be aiming for by the time you finish it.

How this unit is assessed

Learning aims describe what you will be doing in the unit.

A learner or early years professional shares their experiences related to the content of the unit.

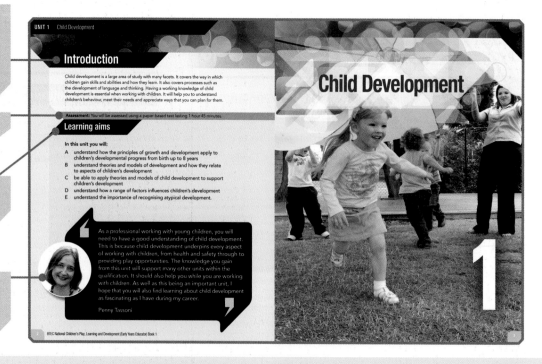

Features of this resource

There are lots of features in this resource to help you learn about what's included in each unit and to enable you to reflect on, or consider, key concepts. These pages show some of the features that you will come across when using the resource.

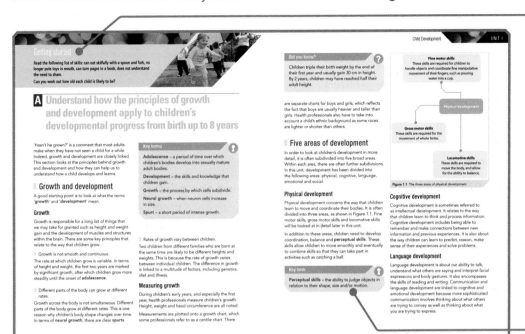

Getting started with a short activity or discussion about the subject of the unit.

Key terms boxes give definitions of important words and phrases that you will come across. These appear in bold blue text. Also see the Glossary for definitions of important words and phrases.

Assessment practice 2.1   3A.P1

Give a presentation to a group of new parents about the benefits of play to children's overall development.

Explain how play supports the physical, cognitive, language, social and emotional development of young children.

Activities that relate to the unit's assessment criteria. These activities will help you prepare for your assignments. They may include suggestions for tasks that help build towards your assignment, as well as helping you to develop your knowledge, skills and understanding. (For all units **except** Unit 1.)

Activity

Carry out an observation on a child during child-initiated play. How does the child's play relate to the social stages of play?

Activities will help you learn about key points.

Theory into practice

Sleep routines

Talk to three parents about how they settle their child for sleep and find out the following information.

- Does their child have a set bedtime?
- How do they manage the bedtime routine?
- Do they have, or have they ever had, any difficulties in getting their child to sleep?

Useful features that help you to understand how the theories and topics you are learning about relate to work with children.

Reflect

Many people decide to work with children because they wish to make a difference. Why might this viewpoint be considered behaviourist?

A regular feature that will challenge your own attitudes and beliefs, and encourage you to reflect on best practice.

Examples from real settings that focus on situations you could find yourself in when working in early years. These examples will make you consider how you might act in that situation and help you to improve your practice.

Case study

'Girls do not play football'

Anna is 7 years old. She has three older brothers, and her family is football-mad – her father takes them to support the local football team. Anna loves playing football, and she is quite good at it. However, her parents have noticed that since she went to school, she seems less interested in football. She has even started to refuse to go to football matches, saying that she cannot be a princess if she plays football.

1 What factors may have made Anna change her attitude towards football?

Ready for work?

Alison Davis Supervisor of a preschool

A lot of people think that working with young children is just about playing, but nothing is further from the truth. There is far more to play than people realise. Our staff have to know how to plan play that links to the EYFS and also how to build on children's interests.

One of the main things we look for when employing staff is whether or not they know how to support children as they are playing. This is a skill. Adults have to learn to closely observe children's responses and to know when to intervene or when to step back. Staff also have to know how to set out the environment so that it is ready for play. Children love coming in and seeing a home corner all laid out or something new in the sand tray. These are almost like little 'nudges' that help children get started. Finally, at the end of the day, when everyone is a little tired, staff have to tidy, clean and sort out ready for the next day. So child's play it is not.

Skills for practice

Setting out and maintaining role play
- Create a cosy area so that children think that they cannot be seen.
- Look out for as many real-life props as possible.
- Make sure the necessary props are ready.
- If a role-play situation is new to the children, be ready to join in and model what happens.
- Be ready to discreetly tidy up.

Maintaining sand and water
- Keep a dustpan and brush ready.
- Keep a cloth ready to wipe up water spills.
- Make sure aprons are clean and easy for children to put on.
- Sieve and rake through sand to keep it clean.
- Water needs to be changed daily or in some settings at the end of each session.
- Toys and objects for water and sand should be washed thoroughly and dried.

- Many settings have separate sand and water toys because sand scratches the surfaces.
- Sand and water are activities that need some supervision. Look out for children who are throwing sand and immediately intervene to prevent eye injuries. Wipe up spillages from both promptly.
- Be ready to do some discreet tidying away as too many objects in the sand and water trays can make them unattractive.
- If sand is outdoors, cover it when the outdoor area is not being used. Always check the sand for animal mess.

Creating a treasure basket
- Items have to be sufficiently large and robust so that a baby can mouth them safely.
- Avoid items that may break into smaller pieces or are small enough to swallow.
- Look out for items that are straightforward to wash afterwards.

123

Someone who works in early years explains how this unit of their BTEC helped them to develop as an effective practitioner. This feature gives you a chance to think more about the role that the person does, and whether you would want to follow in their footsteps once you have completed your BTEC.

Tips and guidance about the practical skills that you need to develop in order to work with children. In some units these tips link to the **Practical Evidence Portfolio** that you will need to complete while on placement if you are taking the BTEC National Award, Subsidiary Certificate, Certificate and Diploma in Children's Play, Learning and Development.

BTEC Assessment Zone

You will be assessed in two different ways for your BTEC National in Children's Play, Learning and Development. For most units, your teacher/tutor will set assignments for you to complete. These may take the form of projects where you research, plan, prepare, and evaluate a piece of work or activity. The table in this BTEC Assessment Zone explains what you must do in order to achieve each of the assessment criteria. Each unit of this resource contains a number of assessment activities to help you with these assessment criteria.

> The table in this BTEC Assessment Zone explains what you must do in order to achieve each of the assessment criteria.

> Assessment practice activities in this resource will help you to prepare for your assignments and to cover the criteria.

> You will be assessed against the different assessment criteria shown in this table.

For Unit 1, you will be assessed by a paper-based test. This BTEC Assessment Zone gives useful information about what the test may consist of and some general advice about how to approach the types of questions you will need to answer.

> Reading this sample case study will help you to prepare for your exam.

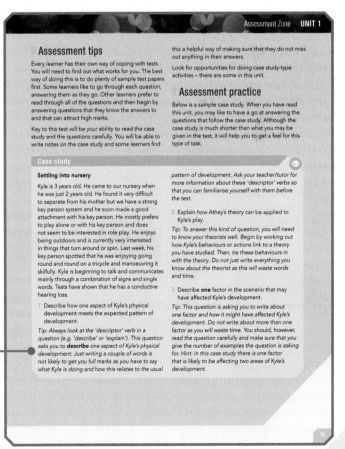

Introduction

Child development is a large area of study with many facets. It covers the way in which children gain skills and abilities and how they learn. It also covers processes such as the development of language and thinking. Having a working knowledge of child development is essential when working with children. It will help you to understand children's behaviour, meet their needs and appreciate ways that you can plan for them.

Assessment: You will be assessed using a paper-based test lasting 1 hour 45 minutes.

Learning aims

In this unit you will:

A   understand how the principles of growth and development apply to children's developmental progress from birth up to 8 years

B   understand theories and models of development and how they relate to aspects of children's development

C   be able to apply theories and models of child development to support children's development

D   understand how a range of factors influences children's development

E   understand the importance of recognising atypical development.

> As a professional working with young children, you will need to have a good understanding of child development. This is because child development underpins every aspect of working with children, from health and safety through to providing play opportunities. The knowledge you gain from this unit will support many other units within the qualification. It should also help you while you are working with children. As well as this being an important unit, I hope that you will also find learning about child development as fascinating as I have during my career.
>
> Penny Tassoni

Child Development

1

Read the following list of skills: can eat skilfully with a spoon and fork, no longer puts toys in mouth, can turn pages in a book, does not understand the need to share.

Can you work out how old each child is likely to be?

A Understand how the principles of growth and development apply to children's developmental progress from birth up to 8 years

'Hasn't he grown?' is a comment that most adults make when they have not seen a child for a while. Indeed, growth and development are closely linked. This section looks at the principles behind growth and development and how they can help us to understand how a child develops and learns.

Growth and development

A good starting point is to look at what the terms 'growth' and 'development' mean.

Growth

Growth is responsible for a long list of things that we may take for granted such as height and weight gain and the development of muscles and structures within the brain. There are some key principles that relate to the way that children grow:

1   Growth is not smooth and continuous.

The rate at which children grow is variable. In terms of height and weight, the first two years are marked by significant growth, after which children grow more steadily until the onset of **adolescence**.

2   Different parts of the body can grow at different rates.

Growth across the body is not simultaneous. Different parts of the body grow at different rates. This is one reason why children's body shape changes over time. In terms of **neural growth**, there are clear **spurts**.

> ### Key terms
>
> **Adolescence** – a period of time over which children's bodies develop into sexually mature adult bodies.
>
> **Development** – the skills and knowledge that children gain.
>
> **Growth** – the process by which cells subdivide.
>
> **Neural growth** – when neuron cells increase in size.
>
> **Spurt** – a short period of intense growth.

3   Rates of growth vary between children.

Two children from different families who are born at the same time are likely to be different heights and weights. This is because the rate of growth varies between individual children. The difference in growth is linked to a multitude of factors, including genetics, diet and illness.

Measuring growth

During children's early years, and especially the first year, health professionals measure children's growth. Height, weight and head circumference are all noted.

Measurements are plotted onto a growth chart, which some professionals refer to as a centile chart. There

Did you know?

Children triple their birth weight by the end of their first year and usually gain 30 cm in height. By 2 years, children may have reached half their adult height.

are separate charts for boys and girls, which reflects the fact that boys are usually heavier and taller than girls. Health professionals also have to take into account a child's ethnic background as some races are lighter or shorter than others.

Five areas of development

In order to look at children's development in more detail, it is often subdivided into five broad areas. Within each area, there are often further subdivisions. In this unit, development has been divided into the following areas: physical, cognitive, language, emotional and social.

Physical development

Physical development concerns the way that children learn to move and coordinate their bodies. It is often divided into three areas, as shown in Figure 1.1. Fine motor skills, gross motor skills and locomotive skills will be looked at in detail later in this unit.

In addition to these areas, children need to develop coordination, balance and **perceptual skills**. These skills allow children to move smoothly and eventually to combine skills so that they can take part in activities such as catching a ball.

Key term

Perceptual skills – the ability to judge objects in relation to their shape, size and/or motion.

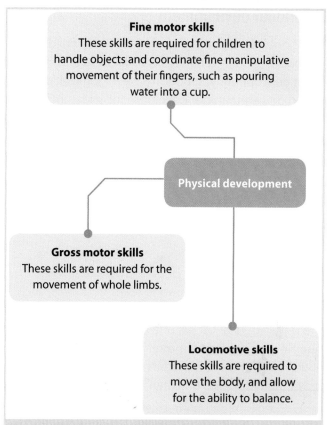

Fine motor skills
These skills are required for children to handle objects and coordinate fine manipulative movement of their fingers, such as pouring water into a cup.

Physical development

Gross motor skills
These skills are required for the movement of whole limbs.

Locomotive skills
These skills are required to move the body, and allow for the ability to balance.

Figure 1.1 The three areas of physical development

Cognitive development

Cognitive development is sometimes referred to as intellectual development. It relates to the way that children learn to think and process information. Cognitive development includes being able to remember and make connections between new information and previous experiences. It is also about the way children can learn to predict, reason, make sense of their experiences and solve problems.

Language development

Language development is about our ability to talk, understand what others are saying and interpret facial expressions and body gestures. It also encompasses the skills of reading and writing. Communication and language development are linked to cognitive and emotional development because more sophisticated communication involves thinking about what others are trying to convey as well as thinking about what you are trying to express.

Emotional development

Emotional development is about the way children experience feelings and learn to express and control them appropriately. Emotional development is linked closely to social development and it includes the development of self-esteem and our own sense of self (known as self-concept). It also includes the development of feelings towards others. Children's behaviour is complex, but it is often linked to their emotional and social development.

Social development

Social development refers to the ability to make relationships with other people. There are many skills that children will need to learn to do this, such as being able to adapt their behaviours in line with the behaviours of others and understanding other people's thoughts and intentions. Emotional and social development are often codependent, so you may find that they are written about together.

> ### Reflect
>
> Look at these examples. Can you see how emotional and social development are linked?
>
> - Anna is feeling happy. It is her birthday and her friends are celebrating it with her.
> - Dan is feeling miserable. His girlfriend has just dumped him.
> - Savi's friend has come round to show him his new car. Savi is impressed but he is also jealous.

▌Key principles of development

There is an old-fashioned phrase, 'don't run before you can walk'. This neatly ties up the idea that physical development and the acquisition of certain skills happen in a sequence.

Arnold Gessell (1880–1961), an American paediatrician, identified three principles of physical development, as follows.

1 Development follows a definite, orderly sequence.

As you watch children growing and developing, you see a pattern emerging that certain movements have to be in place before others can follow. For example,

the child has to be able to walk before he or she can skip.

2 Development begins with the control of head movements and proceeds down the body.

Babies gain control of their head and top of the spine before other parts of their body. This is thought to be a survival mechanism as it is important for babies to be able to turn their head to feed.

3 Development begins with uncontrolled large (gross motor) movements before movements become precise and refined.

At first, a young baby's arm and leg movements are uncontrolled. However, some control is quickly gained – first, control of the arms and then of the wrists and hands. By 6 months, most babies are usually able to take an offered toy reasonably easily. An adult may have had a similar learning experience if they have learned to use a computer with a mouse. Most people find that at first it is hard to keep the cursor visible on the screen, before gradually learning more refined movements that allow them to move the mouse and position the cursor more accurately.

4 Rates of development can vary between individual children.

In addition to Gessell's principles of physical development, we know that there can be significant variations between individual children's overall development, including their physical development. This is due to a number of factors including genetics and opportunities within the child's environment for stimulation.

> ### Theory into practice
>
> The principles of physical development must be applied in practice to make sure that activities we provide for children are appropriate. For example, there is little point in providing a sit-and-ride toy to a child who is not yet sitting independently, or giving a pair of scissors to a child who cannot control their hand movements.

Measuring development

To measure children's development, professionals look at the skills that children have acquired. These skills are sometimes referred to as milestones, or 'norms', and are linked to children's ages. These milestones have been determined by looking at development within large groups of children and considering what is typical or the norm for each age. This means that there will always be some variation, with some children showing development that is in advance of the milestones. Significant delays in development based on these milestones are likely to be monitored and investigated.

Link

Go to Unit 1: Section E for more information about monitoring delays in development.

The relationship between growth and development

Although we have looked at growth and development separately, in reality they are both vital and work together in supporting children's overall development.

Growth provides the background for development

Physical growth is essential to helping children's development as it makes certain movements possible. One example is that once a child can walk they see their environment from a new height. Another example is that children's hand movements are linked to the growth of the bones in their wrists. This in turn means that new opportunities for stimulation are available to the child.

Growth supports speech

The production of sounds and words is partly linked to the arrival of teeth and the building of muscles in the tongue. The easier it is for children to be understood, the more likely they are to keep on talking.

Growth can affect social and emotional development

As children begin to grow, they often start to feel more capable. Children who are taller than children the same age, for example, usually have higher

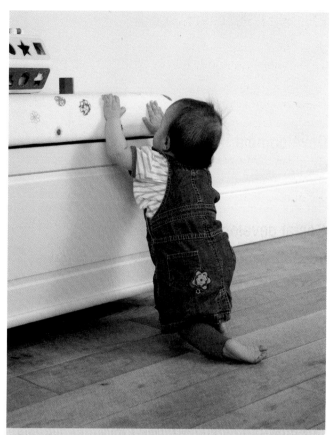

This child is able to pull herself up and see over the toy trunk.

self-esteem. The shape of a child's body can also affect how they feel about themselves.

Growth affects adults' responses

The size and shape of a child affects the way adults respond to them. For example, a tall child may be given more responsibility. Development as a result of growth also affects adults' responses. Adults may, for example, start to expect more of a child once they are able to dress themselves.

Bowel and bladder control

As well as the general ways in which we can see that growth and development are interlinked, there are some more specific ways. One example is bowel and bladder control. For children to move out of nappies, they need to understand what is happening when they wet or soil themselves. They also need the skills to move themselves to a potty and undress. These are developmental skills but growth also plays a significant part. The bladder has to be able to retain urine and expel it on demand. Interestingly, there is huge variation in when children are ready to move out of nappies.

Link

Go to Unit 3: Section C for more information about moving children out of nappies.

Development is also holistic and interrelated

We have seen that growth and development are interrelated, but so too are the different areas of development. Although it is convenient to break them down into specific areas, many developmental skills are interdependent. For instance, a child cannot sit and read a book if they do not have the physical skills to sit up and turn pages, or the language to decode the text. This codependency means that although you may find it helpful to focus on one area of a child's development, you must always remember that children are 'whole' people.

The importance of brain development

Over the past few years, **neuroscience** has helped us understand more about children's development. Neuroscience is a relatively new area of study and, over the next few years, it is likely that much more will be learned and revisions to current thinking will be made. What is known, however, is that brain development in babies and children underpins their overall development. Brain development is also referred to as **neurological development**.

Neurons

A good starting point when looking at the brain is to know a little bit about **neurons** and how they work. Neurons are the brain cells. A single neuron is of no use because what makes the brain work is the way that neurons connect together to transmit and receive electrical signals. It is these signals that operate and reflect our feelings, thoughts and actions.

Figure 1.2 shows a single neuron connecting to another. The connection is not a physical one as there is a tiny gap between the **axon terminals** and the **dendrites** of the other neuron. This gap is known as a **synapse**. Electricity seems to jump across this gap, almost like lightning. Although the diagram shows a single neuron, the reality is that there are billions of neurons and, at any given time, there will be millions of signals sent across the brain. Every new experience we have creates new connections between neurons within the brain.

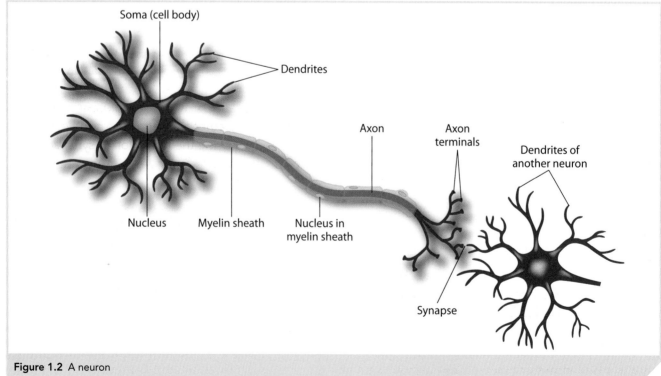

Figure 1.2 A neuron

Key terms

Axon – the part of the neuron where electricity travels.

Axon terminal – a part of the neuron involved in making a connection with another neuron.

Dendrite – a part of the neuron involved in making a connection with another neuron.

Myelin – the substance that coats the axon.

Myelination – the process of myelin coating.

Neural pathway – an established route for signals within the brain.

Neurological development – the growth and development of the brain, including the formation of new neurological connections.

Neuron – a brain cell.

Neuroscience – the study of how the brain grows and works.

Synapse – the gap between two neurons; electrical impulses pass across this gap from the dendrite of one neuron to the axon terminal of the other neuron.

At any time, there are millions of neurons firing off electrical signals, so the brain has ways of making sure that these signals can travel quickly.

Neural pathways

Repeated experiences create stronger and longer-lasting connections. These are known as **neural pathways** and have been likened to motorways because they allow the signals to move faster through the brain. Some neural pathways seem to be present at birth, but many others are formed as a result of repeated experiences.

Myelination

To prevent electrical pulses from straying, the **axons** of the neurons need to be coated with a substance called **myelin**. This process (**myelination**) begins at birth but is not complete until early adulthood.

Neural pruning

Many of the synapses or connections that neurons make will not be regularly used or needed. A process of pruning regularly takes place in the brain to remove these unused synapses. The first round of pruning takes place when children are 18 months old.

Early brain development

Brain development begins well before birth. Although we are born with approximately 100 billion neurons, most of these are formed between the tenth and twentieth weeks of pregnancy. This is one reason why it is important for pregnant women to take care of themselves during pregnancy. In the final two months before birth, the dendrites and axons of the neurons develop and begin to make some connections.

Link

Go to Unit 1: Section D to find more information about pregnancy and brain development.

From birth

There is a huge amount of growth and many processes taking place in a child's development from birth onwards. The brain triples in weight in the first two years. This is as a result of the axons and dendrites increasing in size, allowing an increasing number of synapses to be formed. Interestingly, the process of growth within the brain does not occur uniformly. Synapses that enable visual processes form earlier than synapses for language. It is not clear whether synapses follow a predetermined pattern, but the role of stimulation is definitely important. Babies' brains respond well to an environment that includes positive emotions, language and new sensations. Alongside the formation of synapses, the process of myelination begins and will continue until early adulthood.

Did you know?

Myelinisation plays a part in coordinating children's gross and locomotive movements. The myelinisation of neurons affecting gross motor development is usually completed by the time a child reaches 6 years old.

Additional growth spurts

In addition to the growth that takes place in a child's first couple of years, neurons also grow at other times. These growth spurts are thought to account for some astounding progress in children's development. Figure 1.3 shows the effects neural growth has on children's development.

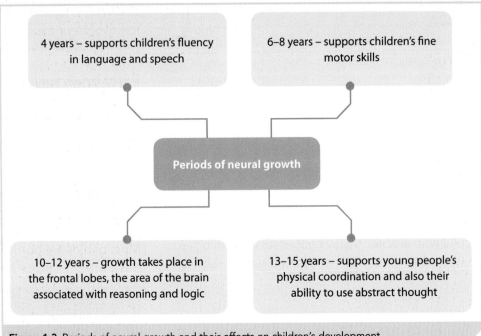

4 years – supports children's fluency in language and speech

6–8 years – supports children's fine motor skills

Periods of neural growth

10–12 years – growth takes place in the frontal lobes, the area of the brain associated with reasoning and logic

13–15 years – supports young people's physical coordination and also their ability to use abstract thought

Figure 1.3 Periods of neural growth and their effects on children's development

Theory into practice

The first two years of a child's life are thought to be quite important in terms of brain development.

This understanding has meant that frameworks such as the Early Years Foundation Stage (EYFS) now encourage early years professionals to spend time playing with and talking to babies and toddlers to ensure that there is sufficient stimulation.

- Make a list of the ways that babies and toddlers might be stimulated during the day.
- Why is it important that babies and toddlers spend time outdoors and in changing environments?

The effects of cortisol on the developing brain

Neuroscience is in its infancy but there is some speculation that children's developing brains can be affected by stress. When babies and young children are distressed, neglected or are in stressful situations (such as being in a chaotic or unpredictable environment), a hormone called cortisol is released in large quantities. If the stress is short-lived, and especially if the child is reassured, the production of cortisol is not thought to pose a problem and there is an argument that it actually helps the child to develop resilience.

On the other hand, there is some evidence that suggests babies' and young children's brain development is affected if they are exposed to long-term stress. It is believed that this exposure may affect their memory, ability to learn and level of resilience. In addition, there is also speculation that maternal stress during pregnancy may have an impact on an unborn child's developing brain.

How does an understanding of the principles of development help practitioners?

There are many reasons why it is important to understand the principles behind growth and development, and the usual patterns of development that children show at different ages.

1 To recognise a child's stage of development

It is always helpful to recognise a child's stage of development as we can then tailor our practice accordingly. For example, a child whose speech is still in the early stages will need us to point to things that we are talking about. Similarly, a child who is not yet able to travel up and down stairs unaided will need a helping hand. Recognising a child's stage of development also affects our practice in terms of keeping them safe. Children whose stage of development means that they are still impulsive will need more supervision than children who are more aware of risks and dangers in their environment.

2 To support development

Another important reason why practitioners need to have a good knowledge of child development is so that babies and children can be given the support they need. This is done in several ways, including by tailoring activities and resources to meet the interests and stage of development of the child. For example, a child who is able to play cooperatively with other children may enjoy short structured games such as 'What's the time, Mr Wolf?' as they understand the importance of rules.

3 To anticipate the next stages of development

By understanding a child's stage of development and the sequences of development, we can also plan for their next steps appropriately. This is an important part of a practitioner's role with children. There are a number of ways in which we can anticipate a child's next stage of development including using activities and resources, and providing children with a range of different experiences. By anticipating the next stages of development, we can also think about how best to prepare the environment. This may include the provision of appropriate equipment.

4 To recognise delays in development

Although children do have variable rates of growth and development, practitioners need to recognise when children are not making progress or their development is very atypical. Early recognition is linked to better outcomes for children as more support can be given.

Link

Go to Unit 1: Section E to find more information about how to recognise atypical development.

In section D we will look at the multitude of factors that can affect children's development. Understanding these factors can help practitioners to support children by providing a positive care and education experience.

Normative ages and stages of development

Birth up to 2 years

Babies at birth

Most babies are born at around 40 weeks **gestation**, although very few arrive on their due date! Growth and development have been ongoing since conception and by the time babies arrive, they are already able to recognise their mothers' voices.

Newborns have many survival reflexes that can be clearly seen. First, babies instinctively breathe, cry and suckle. They also have a 'rooting' reflex that allows them to search for a nipple or teat. Other **reflexes** that newborns show will disappear over time and be replaced by conscious movements. Well-known newborn reflexes include the moro reflex, where the baby flings out their arms if they sense a sudden downward movement; the palmar grasp reflex, where babies cling onto fingers tightly; and the stepping reflex, where a newborn moves their legs as if walking when held vertically. For the first few weeks, babies will develop a pattern of sleeping and feeding and, over time, they will increase the amount of time they spend awake.

Key terms

Gestation – the period of time between conception and birth.

Reflexes – automatic movements that do not require a conscious decision.

---

a The rooting reflex

b The moro reflex

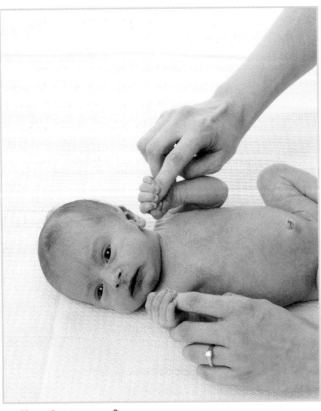

c The palmar grasp reflex

d The stepping reflex

The reflexes seen in a newborn baby.

3 months

At 3 months, babies' temperaments are beginning to show. Some babies will be easy-going and smiley, others will require more skilful and careful treatment as they may find it hard to settle or relax. Babies will show that they enjoy being with others by smiling, making eye contact and even protesting if they are not being given enough attention! Physically, the next few months will hail the gradual disappearance of the newborn reflexes, which will be replaced over time with controlled movements. At 3 months, babies can hold a rattle, but cannot yet control it, and they are less easily startled. Many babies have already started to recognise key elements in their routine by, for example, showing excitement when they see the bath water. Babies are also showing that they like to play and need adults or older children to play with them. Although they recognise their main carers' voices, they are still happy to be held by people that they don't know. This phase, when babies form **indiscriminate attachments**, is likely to last until babies reach 7 months or so when they will develop **specific attachments**.

6 months

At 6 months, babies are becoming increasingly strong and may, for example, be able to roll over. In the next three months, they will learn to become mobile, usually by crawling, although some will bottom-shuffle or develop a rolling technique. Most babies will also be close to sitting up, at first supported but, by around 9 months, without support. This gives babies new opportunities as they can sit and use their hands to play or touch things. Over the next few weeks, babies will be weaned and will be introduced to some new tastes. Weaning is a vital step in babies' development as their bodies now need a wider range of nutrients; especially iron. Some babies are quick to accept foods from a spoon but others will be slower, and patience will be required as foods may be spat out.

The amount of crying should also have decreased, with babies now using their voices to attract attention. They are likely to laugh, coo and also make some early babbling sounds and show that they enjoy being with adults. At 6 months, few babies cling to their main carers but over the next two months they will begin to have distinct preferences for being with familiar people. From 7 to 8 months, these specific attachments will be very obvious.

9 months

From 9 months, babies will start to look for an object if it is hidden in front of them. This concept is known as **object permanence**. Before this age, babies appear to accept something being taken out of their sight. The development of object permanence means that babies begin to enjoy games such as peek-a-boo.

With object permanence comes babies' unhappiness if their parents or key carers go out of sight. Babies will now have strong specific attachments to their parents and key people in their lives and they will develop other attachments too. This is known as the **multiple attachment** phase and is important in the socialisation process. Babies will be happy to be with the people they have formed attachments to, but they are likely to become very distressed when strangers approach and will try to hold onto their parents or key carers.

Many babies will now be crawling or otherwise mobile and they will be extremely active. This opens up new opportunities as they can now move towards what they can see and thus begin the journey to independence. Babies are usually also able to sit unsupported and this means that they can now

---

Key terms

Indiscriminate attachments – when babies and children do not seem to have formed special relationships with other people.

Multiple attachments – when babies and children have many specific attachments to other people.

Object permanence – recognition that when objects are out of sight, they have not disappeared.

Specific attachments – when babies and children have formed special bonds with other people.

see something, get to it and sit and play with it. They are able to play independently with toys, but will particularly enjoy being played with, especially where games are repetitive. They can now hold and manipulate objects easily and will start to pick up small things with a pincer grasp.

Babies at this stage will also be trying to communicate and over the next few weeks they will start to point to things to draw adults' attention. They now understand a few words and will enjoy looking at books. By 9 months, babies should be weaned and may be starting to feed themselves with simple finger foods such as soft bread. Routines such as feeding time and bathing time are now recognised, although some babies will try to roll away during a nappy change.

12 months

A baby's first birthday reminds us just how many skills they have developed. Most babies will be mobile and some may now be walking. Others will be able to walk by holding onto furniture in a movement that is sometimes called 'cruising'. Babies definitely have personalities at this stage and their families will know their strong likes and dislikes. They will also have favourite toys and people. Strangers and unfamiliar faces are likely to be a source of upset and the baby will immediately seek reassurance from people they know. At birth, babies were passive but by now they are truly active and trying to be independent. They point to things they want and will try to grab at things they see. Their physical coordination means that they can now hold things and pass them between their hands, although they will still have difficulty in, for example, using a posting toy or getting a spoon into their mouths. Over the next couple of months, the main carers should notice that, among the tuneful babbling, some words appear. First words are easily produced sounds, such as 'baba' or 'dada', and they will refer to a person or important object.

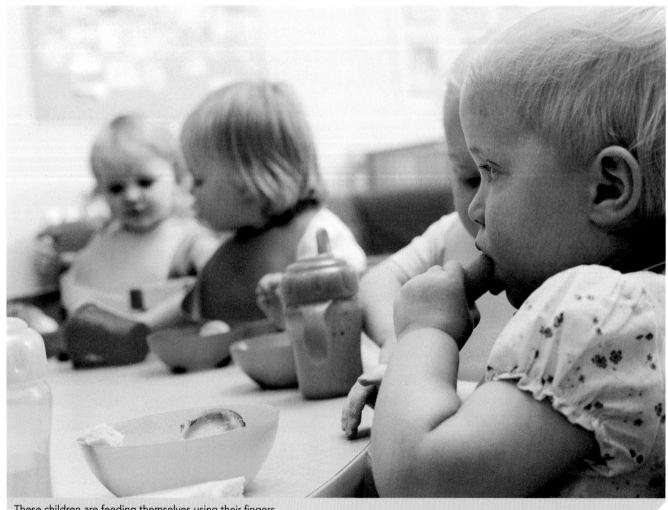

These children are feeding themselves using their fingers.

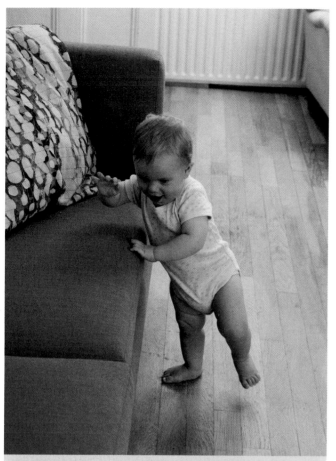

This baby is cruising – he is holding onto a sofa for help.

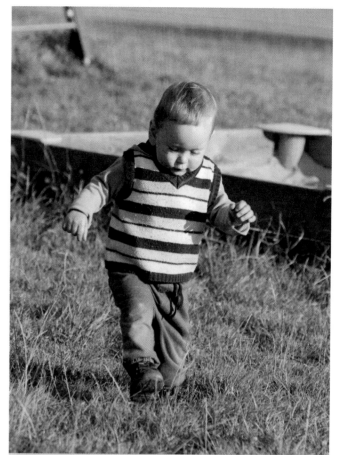

This child is exploring his surroundings.

15 months

At 15 months, many babies are walking, although they may be very unsteady on their feet. They often enjoy exploring from this new position and as a result they can be very restless. They may fall down and bump into things. At 15 months, babies are starting to explore items through touch and sight, rather than **mouthing**. They are also remembering routines and where things belong, although they can be easily distracted. The need to be near a familiar adult, especially a parent, is strong. These older babies will follow an adult or cry if 'their' adult is out of sight. At 15 months, strong communication skills are in place, with most babies knowing how to draw an adult's attention by either pointing or making loud noises. Many children at this age will also be starting to use just a few words. Even though they cannot say much, they will understand quite a lot of what is being said.

Table 1.1 shows a summary of children's typical development from birth to 15 months.

Theory into practice

Mouthing

Assessing whether children are still mouthing is important. If children are still exploring using their mouth, resources have to be carefully chosen in a setting. They will need to be large enough so that they cannot be swallowed, but also interesting enough for the child to learn from mouthing. Useful resources could include those with an interesting texture or taste.

Key term

Mouthing – exploring items by putting them in the mouth.

Table 1.1 Summary of children's typical development up to 15 months old

Age	Fine motor development	Gross and locomotive development	Cognitive and language development	Emotional and social development
0–3 months	• Reflexes including sucking, rooting, 'moro'		• At 1 month, turns head and may stop crying on hearing an adult and a familiar voice • Begins to coo at 6 weeks	• At 1 month, focuses on human faces with interest • Smiles from 6 weeks
3 months	• Watches hands and plays with fingers • Clasps and unclasps hands • Can hold a rattle for a moment	• Lifts head and chest up • Waves arms and brings hands together over body	• Recognises familiar routines such as bath time • Enjoys playing in water	• Cries when alone • Enjoys being held and spoken to • Indiscriminate attachments – is happy to be held by anyone
6 months	• Can reach for a toy • Can move a toy from one hand to another • Puts objects into mouth	• Moves arms to indicate that they want to be lifted • Can roll over from back to front	• Blends vowels and consonants together to make babbling sounds, e.g. 'ba', 'ma', 'da'	• Recognises emotions in others and responds • Likes being held and played with – indiscriminate attachments
9 months	• Can grasp an object with index finger and thumb • Can deliberately release objects by dropping them	• Can sit unsupported • Is likely to be mobile, i.e. crawling or rolling	• Begins to string syllables together to create tuneful babbling, e.g. 'dadada' • Understands some simple words such as 'no' and 'bye-bye'	• Wary of strangers • Prefers being with parents/key carers – specific and multiple attachments • Imitates others' actions such as clapping or peek-a-boo
12 months	• Uses index finger and thumb (pincer grasp) to pick up small objects • Can point to things with the index finger	• May stand alone briefly • May walk holding onto furniture (cruising) • Some children may walk unaided	• First words begin to appear alongside tuneful babbling • Understands simple instructions such as 'where's your hat?' • Knows own name	• Enjoys simple games with adults such as pat-a-cake or roll-a-ball • Stays close to familiar adults • Enjoys the company of familiar adults and siblings

continued

Table 1.1 (*continued*)

Age	Fine motor development	Gross and locomotive development	Cognitive and language development	Emotional and social development
15 months	• Can make precise movements with pincer grasp to pick up crumbs or small objects • Grasps crayons with palmar grip	• May be walking with hesitation • May fall and also bump into furniture • Crawls up stairs	• Communicates by pointing and vocalising • May have four to six words • Understands and responds to simple instructions	• Emotionally dependent on parents and key carers • Dislikes parents or key carers being out of sight • May follow adults out of rooms • Enjoys being played with

18 months

There is a significant shift in development at this age. Most babies have now become toddlers and are walking. Their style of walking may be unsteady, with a certain characteristic gait, but being mobile now provides them with new opportunities. They are able to see their world from a new angle and also to see things that were previously out of sight. As well as being able to walk, toddlers have learned to climb and have increased control over their hands. These newly developed skills mean that they may be quite determined and may show the first signs of becoming frustrated.

Emotionally, toddlers need to be with their main carers and will often check that they are still present even when busy playing.

express their needs. In terms of fine hand movements they may also know what they want to achieve, but struggle to get their hands to manage the task. They may, for example, want to do a jigsaw puzzle, but can't quite get the pieces to fit together. This leads to anger and frustration. Language is a key factor in resolving this and fortunately, over the next year, children's language will continue to develop. At the beginning of this year, they will have many words, but by the end of it, they should be able to put together a simple sentence and use it to express their feelings and desires.

2 years to 4 years

2 years

Life can be very frustrating for 2-year-old children as they are at a crossroads in their development. This shows in their behaviour as they may bite others and have strong temper tantrums. The source of their anger and frustration is often that they can see what they want, understand what is said, but have not yet developed the skills they need to control their impulses or to

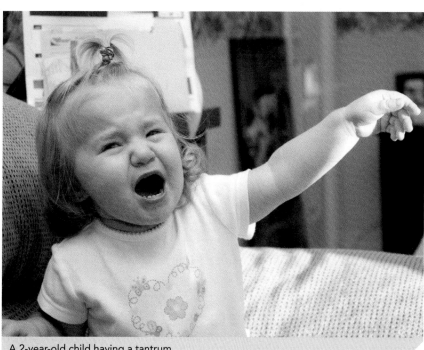

A 2-year-old child having a tantrum.

The physical skills of a 2-year-old child are relatively advanced, so they can climb on furniture and run. However, they will not be aware of the associated dangers. This often leads to adults stopping them doing things, which again causes frustration. This may seem a negative picture, but there are also many positives. Many 2-year-old children are extremely loving, as they now have strong bonds with their main carers and will want to spend time with them. They show positive emotions such as laughter and try to amuse adults, for example by pulling faces. They are also keen to be independent and will want to dress or feed themselves. Play is developing and can provide a good channel for their energies as well as a way in which they can practise skills and independence. They are not ready to **play cooperatively**, but they will at times play alongside other children. This is called **parallel play**. The beginnings of imaginative play can be seen, and many 2-year-old children will take out their frustrations on a hapless teddy, for example.

2½ to 3 years

At 2½ years, children are still pushing for independence. They are extremely active and restless and may want frequent changes of activities. Tantrums may still be a feature for some children, but if language is developing well and adults are thoughtful, these will decrease during the next few months. Children at this age still need reassurance from their main carer and will want to spend time being with them. Being afraid of strangers and being left with unfamiliar faces will still cause distress and anxiety. As children move closer towards 3, they will be increasingly interested in role play. Hand preference is usually established and children of this age begin to enjoy mark making on a large scale with paints and crayons.

At this age, children may start to be interested in other children of their age, although may not necessarily have the social skills to cope with waiting for their turn or the language for cooperative play. This means that children are still playing side by side or standing and watching older children play (**onlooker play**). Once children near 3 years old, play will become more cooperative. At around this time, many children will be toilet trained, but some children will be 3 before they are out of nappies. This development gives children great independence and enormous confidence.

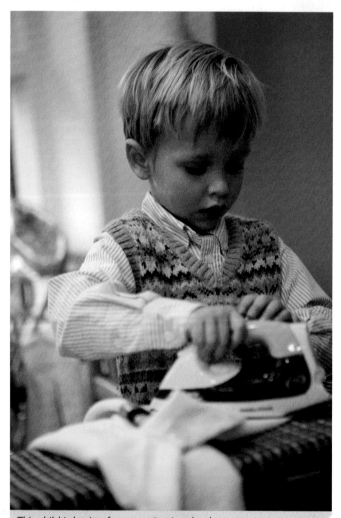

Key terms

Cooperative play – when children are playing with each other.

Onlooker play – when young children are watching other children play and are copying their actions from a distance.

Parallel play – when young children play next to each other using similar actions and materials. They are aware of each other but are not playing with each other.

This child is having fun engaging in role play.

Table 1.2 shows children's development from 18 months to 3 years.

Table 1.2 Summary of children's development from 18 months to 3 years

Age	Fine motor development	Gross and locomotive development	Cognitive and language development	Emotional and social development
18 months	• Can use a spoon to feed with • Can scribble • Can build a tower of three bricks • Uses palmar grasp to hold crayons and other long-handled objects	• Can walk unaided • Can walk upstairs with help (two feet to a stair) • Is restless • Can climb up onto a toy • Can squat to pick up a toy	• Is keen to explore and is very curious • Has around 15 words • Communicates wishes and understands simple requests • No longer mouths to explore objects and toys • Remembers where things belong	• Is emotionally dependent on parents and key carers • Imitates actions of adults • Plays alone, but enjoys being with adults and siblings • Wants immediate attention
2 years	• Can draw circles and dots • Can use a spoon effectively to feed with • Can put on straightforward items of clothing such as shoes (may be on wrong feet)	• Can run • Climbs onto furniture • Can use sit-and-ride toys	• May have 50 words • Is likely to be combining words, e.g. 'dada gone' • Is extremely curious • Remembers where things belong and can remember past experiences • Enjoys looking at books • Recognises self in mirror	• Can be distracted from some early tantrums • Has no understanding of waiting for needs to be met • Plays in parallel with others, but cannot share toys
2½ years	• Has a hand preference • Can do simple jigsaw puzzles • Can pour sand and water into cups • Is starting to develop a tripod grasp • Can pull down items of clothing such as trousers	• Runs quickly and confidently • Can kick a large ball • May begin to use a tricycle • Walks upstairs confidently, but may still use two feet to each step • Can jump with two feet together off a low step	• Has 200 words or so • Is making simple sentences • Enjoys asking questions • Is using personal pronouns such as 'I' instead of name • Enjoys looking at books and may have favourites	• Is highly dependent on adults • Can be jealous of other children gaining adult attention • Has tantrums when frustrated • Is impulsive and restless • Enjoys adult attention and praise

continued

Table 1.2 (*continued*)

Age	Fine motor development	Gross and locomotive development	Cognitive and language development	Emotional and social development
3 years	• Washes and dries hands with help • Holds a crayon and can draw a circle • Has established hand preference for most tasks • Tripod grasp is developing, using two fingers and thumb	• Can steer and pedal a tricycle • Can run forwards and backwards • Can throw large ball • Can walk upstairs on alternate feet • Can throw and kick with approximate aim	• Speech is clear enough for someone unfamiliar with the child to understand • Uses simple sentences • Asks many questions and may use questions as a way of getting attention • Enjoys books and turns pages • Understands difference between past and present	• Is starting to take turns and share for short periods • Enjoys being with other children and may have some friendship preferences • Finds it easier to wait and understand why it might not be possible for wishes to be granted • Will comfort another child

3 to 4 years

Unlike the younger age group, the milestones for expected development for older children become broader. This is because there can be wide differences between children on account of the many factors that affect children's development.

Link

Go to Unit 1: Section D to find more information about factors that affect children's development.

After the storm of being 2, the development of most 3-year-old children allows them to be calmer and more sociable. They begin to play well with other children of the same age and gradually start to share and learn to take turns. This type of play is known as cooperative play. Their language is one reason for this change as they can now express themselves fairly well. They can use questions and have a large vocabulary, although they are not yet fluent. They usually enjoy songs and rhymes and may well sing to themselves. Most of what a 3-year-old child says should be intelligible to someone who does not know the child.

They enjoy playing and are now able to play independently, although they still enjoy being with adults. Another significant shift is the way in which 3-year-old children begin to cope when separated from their main carer. Though they are still wary of strangers, most 3-year-old children will happily leave their main carer for someone they know, such as their key worker. At 3 years old, children have again increased their physical skills. They can now pedal and steer a tricycle and enjoy the sensation of speed and control.

4 years to 8 years

4 to 5 years

During this year, most children will begin school. This is a huge transition and means that they will be with many more children than before. For most children, this is not a problem as their social skills have developed and they enjoy playing with others, particularly of the same sex. Most children will also have developed one or two close friendships and although the odd squabble may break out, they have usually learned how to do some simple negotiating. This skill does of course link to their overall language development. It also links to the development of **theory of mind** – the ability to work out what

Key term

Theory of mind – children recognising their own conscious mind and understanding that other people will have different thoughts to them.

other people might be thinking in a given situation. At around 4 years old, most children are able to recognise that other people may not have the same thoughts or knowledge as them and that this in turn might influence their behaviour. A good example of this is the way that a 4-year-old child may offer a banana to an adult even though the child does not like bananas. He does this because he knows that the adult does like bananas.

Most 4-year-old children are now able to use language well and fairly grammatically, although there will be some speech immaturity and mispronunciations.

These children have just started school. Can you see how their development of social skills has helped the transition?

Most 4-year-old children's behaviour is cooperative, although they do need plenty of reassurance and praise from adults and, as with the younger age group, they need play activities that interest them.

Physically, children are now able to manage many tasks that give them increasing pleasure and independence. They can, for example, eat with a knife and fork and dress themselves, and they are able to catch and throw a large ball. Their hand–eye coordination means that they can draw more representational pictures and make items such as a simple necklace by threading beads onto a string.

5 to 8 years

In previous years, development in all areas has been rapid. From this point through until puberty, development might be described as steady. The key changes that take place are the refinements of existing skills. A good example of this is using scissors. Previously children were able to cut out shapes roughly, but in these years, children should refine this skill so they are able to cut along a line. In the same way, children show increasing coordination of the larger movements so that they can run, swerve and dodge more easily than before, such as during chasing games.

Most children will be established in school and, as part of their schooling, will be developing their literacy skills, including reading and writing. This is a long process and most children will need to put considerable effort into decoding simple words. As well as learning to read and write, children will also be exposed to new concepts such as learning about number.

Socially, most children in this age group have developed some strong friendships. These are based mainly on shared interests, although it is interesting to note that most children will choose same-sex playmates. Children are starting to ascribe reasons to the behaviours of others as they have a developing understanding of theory of mind. For example, a child may say, 'I think he did that because he was missing his mummy.'

Table 1.3 shows children's development from 3 to 8 years.

Table 1.3 Summary of children's development from 3 to 8 years

Age	Fine motor development	Gross and locomotive development	Cognitive and language development	Emotional and social development
3–4 years	• Buttons and unbuttons own clothing • Cuts out simple shapes • Draws a person with head, trunk and legs	• Walks along a line • Aims and throws a ball • Hops on one foot	• Recognises and names a few colours • Knows names of numbers and can count aloud up to ten • Talks in sentences and, by 4 years old, is fluent although there are some speech immaturities in certain sounds such as 'th'	• Comforts children who are in distress • Will now have clear friendship preferences, many of which will be same-sex
4–5 years	• Forms letters and writes own name • Colours in pictures • Completes 20-piece jigsaw	• Skips with a rope • Runs quickly and is able to avoid obstacles • Throws a large ball to a partner and catches it	• Can count objects accurately up to ten • Can make simple patterns • Sentences are well constructed but some speech immaturities remain • Speech is used to argue with others	• Understands the need for rules • Is starting to develop theory of mind • Begins to enjoy sharing with others • Enjoys having friends and is upset if friends are not available • Is able to separate more easily from parents/carers
5–8 years	• Cuts out shapes accurately • Produces detailed drawings • Ties and unties shoelaces • Can colour in shapes	• Hops, skips and jumps confidently • Can balance on a beam • Chases and dodges others • Can use a bicycle and other wheeled toys such as roller skates	• Is able to understand and enjoy jokes and riddles • Can use language to reason and explain ideas • Is able to do simple calculations although may need to use fingers or counters • By 7 years old, has mastered early reading and writing skills	• Enjoys having rules and reminding others of rules • Is starting to understand the difference between behaviours that are accidental rather than done on purpose • Is protective towards young children • Has strong friendships that are likely to be same-sex • Is able to stay overnight with relatives and friends

The cultural environment

In section D, we will look at how children's development is influenced by a range of factors, including cultural ones. In this section, it is worth being aware that children's development is never entirely a product of their genetic make-up, but that it is also influenced by the environment in which they are being brought up. When the subject of how children developed was first studied by biologists, theorists and philosophers, there was significant debate about whether children's development was a product of nurture (their upbringing) or nature (genetics and human instincts). Today, most researchers agree that there is interplay between individual genetic dispositions, evolutionary instincts and where and how a child is raised.

Activity

Read the following details about 4-year-old Jodie.

Jodie enjoys playing with other children. Her favourite activity is playing in the home corner. She washes her hands and face, but she is in nappies. She talks in full sentences and loves listening to stories. She enjoys simple jigsaw puzzles with six or so pieces. Jodie insists that her mother stays at playgroup with her and cries when she leaves.

1 Write down the parts of Jodie's development that are typical for her age group.

2 Explain the parts of Jodie's development that are atypical for her age group.

B Understand theories and models of development and how they relate to aspects of children's development

For many years, psychologists have been considering the processes by which young children learn and develop. In this section, we are going to consider some of the classical theories of child development and how they have influenced practitioners' understanding of children. The classical theories of child development provide a starting point, but much research has been carried out since these theories were developed so some more modern perspectives are also covered.

Issues when looking at theories of development

A good starting point before looking at theories of development is to consider some of the issues that psychologists have found when looking at child development.

Nature or nurture?

Is children's development tied closely to human instincts and genetics, or could it be that what happens to children shapes their learning and development? These are fundamental questions in psychology. Many of the early theories of development were influenced by the idea that we inherit skills, abilities and behaviours. Subsequent research has since shown that our behaviour can also be shaped. The issue for many psychologists is to define how much of our skills, personalities and so on is inherited and how much is influenced by our environment. Increasingly, the view that is being taken is that both cases apply, although we may be born with certain **predispositions**. This is sometimes called the nature versus nurture debate. Theories that come down in favour of nature can be described as **nativist**, and theories that come down in favour of environment can be thought of as **behaviourist**.

Key terms

Behaviourist – the belief that development is shaped by the environment.

Nativist – the belief that development is predetermined.

Predisposition – an increased likelihood of showing a skill, trait or developing a condition as a result of genetic inheritance.

Reflect

Many people decide to work with children because they wish to make a difference. Why might this viewpoint be considered behaviourist?

Is development continuous or does it occur in stages?

Some of the theories we will look at in this unit are 'stage' theories, such as Erikson's stages of personality or Piaget's stages of cognitive development. These theories are based on the idea that development passes through defined and separate stages and that each stage will have recognisable features. For example, in language development children babble before they speak words, so babbling is seen as a stage in itself. Other psychologists feel that development is more gradual and that it is a continuous process. This means that development in stages versus continuous development is another area of debate for psychologists.

Theory into practice

Is development stage-like or continuous?

Many early years professionals may feel that children don't jump from stage to stage, but that development is gradual. It can be hard to see sudden jumps on a day-to-day basis, although over a few weeks they can see that children's development has progressed.

- In your placement, ask the staff what they think. Do they think that children's progress fits into stages or do they see that their development is continual?
- You may like to ask if there are any areas of development that seem particularly stage-like.

Limitations of research

Unlike theories in some 'hard' sciences such as physics, it can be difficult to prove beyond doubt how children learn and develop. This is because there are many **variables** such as culture, parenting style, environment and genetic influences. Even research studies on identical twins do not give a consistent picture. Add to this the difficulty of communicating with babies and very young children and it becomes clear why theories of development are constantly being revised and adapted. Having said this, such research does help practitioners to work in ways that are likely to be advantageous to children.

Theories and models of development

Table 1.4 summarises some of the theories and models of development that are covered in this unit. Each has influenced the view of children that adults have when working with them. In the case of some of the theories of how children learn, the impact has been seen on day-to-day teaching practice as well as on the curriculum.

Theories that consider how children learn behaviours

For a number of years, people have wondered how children and even adults learn behaviours. Why do some children have repeated tantrums while other children of the same age do not?

We will now look at some of the theories that consider how children learn behaviours. Some of these theories are controversial when applied to work with children, for example, 'behaviourist' models and particularly those of Pavlov and Skinner. They are controversial because they look at how the environment and external influences shape children's learning and development as if children were passive recipients.

Interestingly, theories of behaviour are in some ways also theories of learning, so they have been used to encourage children to learn new skills.

The first theory we will look at is that of Albert Bandura.

Key term

Variables – factors that may be involved in development.

Table 1.4 Major theories and models of child development

Area of development	Theorist/researcher	Theories/findings
Physical	• Arnold Gessell	• Development follows a pattern
Learning behaviours	• Albert Bandura • Ivan Pavlov • B. F. Skinner	• Social learning theory: children learn from observing others • Classical conditioning: children learn through association • Operant conditioning: children's learning and responses are dependent on reinforcement
Models of cognition	• Jean Piaget • Chris Athey • Lev Vygotsky • Jerome Bruner • Information processing theories	• Stage model of cognitive development: children use experiences to create their own thoughts and logic • Suggested several schemas that children explore on different levels using play in order to learn • Social constructivism: children learn by being with, and supported by, adults and other children • Scaffolding and spiral curriculum: adults can support children to learn quite complex concepts • Learning is a process of handling and retrieving information
Language	• Noam Chomsky • B. F. Skinner	• Babies are primed to learn language – they have a Language Acquisition Device (LAD) • Language can be learned through a reinforcement model (this is now seen as a flawed model)
Personality and self-esteem	• Erik Erikson • Susan Harter • The Big Five • Charles Cooley	• Life stage model: personality is affected by our interactions with others • Self-esteem is the product of self-concept and our ideal self • Research looking at personality being defined into five traits • The 'looking-glass self' theory – children develop self-image as a result of how others react to them
Pro-social and moral	• Jean Piaget • Lawrence Kohlberg • Albert Bandura	• Stages of moral development are linked to cognitive stages • Stages of moral development: young children are amoral • Children are influenced by what they have seen
Development in relation to environment	• Urie Bronfenbrenner	• Children's development is influenced by their immediate family, friends, community and society
Attachment	• John Bowlby • Harry Harlow • Mary Ainsworth	• Maternal deprivation can cause long-lasting mental health issues: stages of separation anxiety • Harlow's monkeys (1958): an experiment that showed food alone is not sufficient to form a mother–child bond – the monkeys needed security, care and reassurance as well • The 'strange situation' study (1970) – an experiment used to identify and measure babies' types of attachment

Bandura's social learning theory

The social learning theory is a widely accepted theory that originated in America in the 1940s. The key figure among social learning theorists is Albert Bandura (born 1925). The social learning theory is sometimes called 'observational learning'. More recently it has been renamed the social cognitive theory. Social learning theorists are particularly interested in looking at the moral and social behaviour that humans display.

Learning by watching others

Social learning theorists suggest that children learn through **conditioning** and by observing others. This is sometimes referred to as observational learning. It is an interesting theory and many early years professionals will have seen children learn from the behaviour of other children or the behaviour of adults around them.

One of the features of observational learning is that it is spontaneous – children will learn through watching others rather than being shown or taught to do something. For early years professionals and parents/carers, this means that children may copy some aspects of our behaviour that we are unaware of! Though some children will directly copy behaviours, observational learning also means that some children learn not to do something by watching others' experiences.

> **Key term**
>
> **Conditioning** – learning to act in a certain way because past experiences have taught us to do, or not to do, something.

Terms used in social learning theory

It is useful to understand two terms that are used in observational learning:

- **model** – the person whose behaviour is being imitated/learned from
- **modelling** – the process by which learning takes place.

Bandura's bobo doll experiment

The bobo doll experiment is a famous experiment carried out by Bandura, which showed that children can learn behaviour by watching adults. In the experiment, Bandura showed a film to three groups of children. The film showed an adult in a room with a bobo doll (a large inflatable doll). The three groups of children each saw a different variation of the behaviour of the adult.

- Group A saw the adult acting aggressively towards the doll.
- Group B saw the adult being aggressive towards the doll but at the end of the film, the adult was rewarded with sweets and lemonade by another adult.
- Group C saw the adult being aggressive towards the doll but at the end of the file, a second adult appeared and told off the adult.

After the film, each child was taken in turn into a playroom that had a variety of toys, including the bobo doll. The reactions of the children were recorded. Group C children were the least aggressive towards the doll but there was little difference between groups A and B. This suggested that the children were less influenced by the reward that had been offered to the adult than they were by the behaviour of the adult that they observed.

As a follow-up to the experiment, the children were asked if they could demonstrate how the doll had been attacked and they were rewarded for doing so. There was little difference between the three groups of children. This showed that they could all imitate the behaviour they had seen.

> **Research**
>
> Search on video-sharing websites such as YouTube for freely available videos showing Albert Bandura talking about the bobo doll experiment.

The social cognitive theory

Since his original work on social learning theory, Bandura has explored further the elements that are required in order for observational learning to take place. Children do not seem to learn everything that is modelled so it is clear that certain elements must be present. Indeed, Bandura suggests that there are several conditions that are required in order for children to be able to learn from watching others. We will now look at these in some detail.

Attention

First, children need to be interested enough to pay attention and to notice what the adult or other child is doing. In addition, they have to focus on the right elements and avoid distractions or anything irrelevant. For example, an adult might stop and blow their nose while logging on to the computer, but the blowing of the nose is irrelevant to the process. Being able to filter out the irrelevant and focus attention is a skill that develops over time.

Encoding and retrieving information

In order for us to learn, information has to be encoded into the long-term memory so that it can be retrieved. The processes that allow us to **encode** and **retrieve** memories are still developing during childhood. Situations that are very complex to understand are, therefore, more difficult for children to learn from.

> ### Key terms
>
> **Encode** – the process by which information gained by the brain is stored.
>
> **Retrieve** – the process by which memories can be activated.

Opportunity to reproduce actions

Children also need to be in the position where they can replicate what they have seen. For instance, a child sees an adult tidying away toys – but they need an opportunity to join in.

Physical skill

A sufficient level of physical skill might also be necessary. For example, a 2-year-old child may see an adult cut a piece of paper along a line, but the child's fine motor skills may not have developed sufficiently to allow them to learn from this.

Motivation

Children need to be interested and motivated to try out what they have learned. They may also have seen that an action results in a reinforcer, such as admiration from others. For example, a 6-year-old child may notice during a PE lesson that other children laugh at a boy who makes silly sounds and be motivated to try this out in order to provoke a similar response.

Pavlov's classical conditioning theory

Ivan Pavlov (1849–1936) is famous for his work with dogs. He developed a theory about how learning might take place based on experiences. His approach is referred to as behaviourist and it is a very different model of learning from constructivist approaches such as Piaget's. The behaviourist approach suggests that our learning is influenced by rewards, punishments and environmental factors. The term 'conditioning' is often used by behaviourists. Conditioning means that we learn to act in a certain way because past experiences have taught us to do, or not to do, something. We may know this as learning by association – for example, not touching a flame because we were once burnt.

The idea of conditioning was born out of research into dogs' digestive systems. Ivan Pavlov was a physiologist who, while studying dogs, noticed that they always started to salivate before food was put down for them. He came to the conclusion that the dogs were anticipating the food and were salivating because they had learned to associate the arrival of food with other things such as the sound of footsteps or the sight of buckets.

To show this more clearly he devised an experiment in which he fed dogs while a bell was sounded. Normally dogs do not salivate when hearing bells, but the dogs began to associate the bell with food and would salivate simply on hearing the bell.

The learning process by which the dogs learned to salivate when hearing a bell can be shown diagrammatically, as in Figure 1.4.

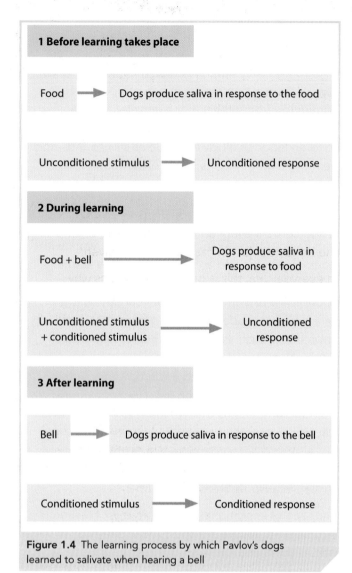

Figure 1.4 The learning process by which Pavlov's dogs learned to salivate when hearing a bell

Extinction

Pavlov also looked at what would happen if the bell rang repeatedly and no food was offered to the dogs. He found that gradually the conditioned response (dogs salivating) became weaker until finally the dogs did not react to the bell. The term used by behaviourists when this happens is 'extinction'.

Applying classical conditioning to humans

Pavlov's work was subsequently built on by John B. Watson, who showed that it was possible to use classical conditioning on humans. In a famous experiment Watson was able to make a baby of 11 months afraid of a white rat. The young child had previously shown no fear of rats, but by pairing the rat with something that did frighten the child, the child was conditioned to be afraid of the rat.

Theory into practice

Classical conditioning can help us to understand how some children might develop seemingly irrational fears, such as suddenly being afraid of the dark or particular foods or animals. Look at the following example.

Alana was 5 years old and had always gone to bed without being afraid of the dark. One night she was violently sick and her room was in darkness. Afterwards Alana cried if no light was left on at night.

B. F. Skinner's operant conditioning theory

Burrhus Frederic Skinner (1904–1990) believed that all learning could be shaped by controlling the environment. His work was based originally on that of Edward Thorndike (1874–1949). He had shown that when cats were put in a maze they could learn the skills to escape and gain a reward. If they were put in a similar box again, they could then use the skills they had developed to escape once more.

Skinner's research developed Thorndike's work further. His behaviourist theory is known as **operant conditioning**. The basis of the operant conditioning theory is that learning occurs through behaviour being rewarded or punished. In other words, an association is made between a behaviour and a consequence of that behaviour. Consequences – known as **reinforcers** – can be either negative or positive, and primary or secondary. A reinforcer is anything that strengthens the behaviour it follows.

Negative reinforcers are likely to make us repeat behaviour, but this is in order to stop something negative from happening to us. For example, we may continue to wear oven gloves to stop us from being burnt.

Key terms

Operant conditioning – a theory that suggests that the environment 'operates' on and thus influences a child's learning using reinforcers.

Reinforcers – positive or negative experiences used to strengthen children's behavioural responses.

Punishers are often confused with negative reinforcement. They are another type of reinforcer but are likely to stop us from repeating behaviour. For example, we may learn to stay away from an electric fence after receiving a shock.

Positive reinforcement is when a behaviour is strengthened by praise or reward.

Unexpected positive reinforcers

Skinner found during his experiments that it was often hard to predict what would act as a primary reinforcer, and that it was sometimes only after the event that this became clear. An example of this is when children sometimes deliberately behave badly in order to attract their carer's attention. If they manage to attract attention they are more likely to show the behaviour again, although they might be told off. Gaining the carer's attention in this case is the positive reinforcer even if the child is being told off.

Primary and secondary reinforcers

There are some reinforcers that give us instant pleasure, satisfaction or meet a need. These are referred to as primary reinforcers. Chocolate is a primary reinforcer because most people find that once they put it into their mouth, they enjoy the taste.

Secondary reinforcers are different because they do not give us satisfaction in themselves, but we learn that they symbolise getting primary reinforcement. A good example of secondary reinforcement in our daily lives is money. Coins and notes in themselves do not reward us, but we learn that they can be used to buy something that will give us primary reinforcement, such as food. (The learning used when making the association between money and being able to get something in return is classical conditioning.)

Theory into practice

Young children and money

Young children do not understand the value of money because they have not made the association between money and pleasure. Toddlers, for example, are often more interested in the size, colour and shape of coins than in their value. This means that offering money as a reward to young children is not very effective.

Schedules of reinforcement

Skinner looked at the effect that giving positive reinforcement at different intervals would have on behaviour. How long would behaviour continue to be shown without a positive reward before extinction takes place?

Interestingly, he found that unpredictable reinforcement works better than continual reinforcement. This would seem to work because it teaches the learner not to expect a reward or reinforcement every time – so they keep on showing the behaviour just in case a reward is given!

In everyday life, this is one of the reasons why gamblers find it so hard to stop playing. They know that they will not win every time, but carry on just in case they get lucky.

Delaying reinforcement

Delaying positive reinforcement, such as saying to a child that they can have a sticker at the end of the week, weakens the effect of the reinforcement. Immediate positive reinforcements are the most effective, partly because the behaviour is then more strongly linked to the reinforcement.

Applying conditioning theory to practice

Conditioning is a very powerful form of learning. It means that children can be encouraged to show wanted behaviour through positive reinforcement, i.e. through giving praise, attention, stickers and so on. However, it also means that if you give positive reinforcement in response to unwanted behaviour, for example, giving a child a packet of sweets to stop them from whining – you may encourage the unwanted behaviour.

In some cases it might be better to ignore a child's behaviour if it is not dangerous. Giving children attention may lead to them being positively reinforced and in doing so help them to learn the unwanted behaviour.

Summary of Skinner's theory

Conditioning, especially operant conditioning, seems to explain in part why, in certain situations, children may learn and demonstrate certain behaviours. As such, operant conditioning is involved in some popular behaviour modification strategies such as star charts or ignoring behaviours, as we have seen. It is also used commercially by retailers. For instance, a reward card is effectively a star chart for adults!

Criticisms of the theories of conditioning

The model of conditioning, especially when applied to child rearing and development, has many limitations. It does not properly address the issues of free will, creativity and temperament. Skinner's work in particular attracted many critics, including Noam Chomsky (born 1928), who disagreed not only with Skinner's approach to how language was learned, but also with Skinner's argument that a controlled environment could totally shape human behaviour for the better.

Research

Read Noam Chomsky's article 'The Case against B. F. Skinner', which appeared in the *New York Review of Books* in 1971. You can access this article by going to www.pearsonhotlinks.co.uk and searching for this ISBN: 9781447970965.

Theories that consider the development of cognition and language

For years, parents/carers and teachers/tutors have been fascinated by the questions that children ask and the peculiar comments they make. Most people who have worked with children of different ages can clearly see that the way in which children think and understand changes as time goes by. There are several models that try to explain how children's logic and reasoning is developed. Later on in this section, we will also consider theories that attempt to explain the development of language.

Piaget's theory of cognitive development

A good starting point is to look at Piaget's work, as it has been very influential and has provided other researchers with insights and ideas that they have developed further.

Jean Piaget (1896–1980) was a zoologist who became interested in children's cognitive development as a result of working on intelligence tests. He noticed that children consistently gave similar 'wrong' answers to some questions and began to consider why this was. Piaget used his own children to make detailed observations and gradually developed a theory that has been influential in education in many countries. It has also acted as a starting point for other theories and research.

Although Piaget's theory is based on children's cognitive development, he also used it to explain the way that children play and their moral development.

His theory of learning is sometimes referred to as a **constructivist approach**, as he suggested that children construct or build up their thoughts according to their experiences of the world around them. Piaget used the term **schema** to mean a child's conclusions or thoughts. Piaget felt that the development of thoughts was an ongoing process, with children needing to adapt their original ideas if a new piece of information seemed to contradict their conclusions (to describe this, he coined the term 'adaption'). For example, a toddler may come to believe that milk is served in blue beakers, because their experience of having milk is linked with it being served in a blue beaker. If one day the toddler is given juice in the blue beaker instead of milk, they will need to consider their theory, so coming to the conclusion that milk and other drinks come in blue beakers. Piaget used specific vocabulary to describe the process of children learning in this way. Figure 1.5 outlines Piaget's theory.

Why children think differently to adults

Piaget's belief that children develop schemas based on their direct experiences can help us to understand why young children's thinking is sometimes so different to ours. Piaget also suggested that, as

Key terms

Constructivist approach – a model to explain children's cognitive development, which considers that children develop their own ideas based on experiences and interactions.

Schema – a repeated action, way of doing something or way of thinking/reasoning that can be specific or generalised.

Assimilation
The child constructs a theory or schema

Equilibrium
The child's experiences to date seem to fit the schema (everything balances)

Disequilibrium
An experience occurs that casts doubt on the effectiveness of the schema (things don't add up any more!)

Accommodation
The child changes the original schema to fit the new experience or piece of information

Figure 1.5 Piaget's theory of learning

children develop, so does their thinking. He grouped children's cognitive development into four broad stages. Table 1.5 outlines these four stages and they are described in more detail in the following paragraphs.

Sensorimotor stage (birth to 2 years)

This is the first stage of children's lives. It begins at birth with babies using their reflexes to survive. Babies are also very reliant on using their senses in the first two years, especially taste and touch. Babies' first schemas are physical ones, as they learn to repeat and then control their movements.

Development of object permanence

One of the tests that Piaget used to show the development of thought in babies was object permanence. In the first few months, a baby will appear to accept the disappearance of an object. Piaget suggested that this is because babies have not learned the idea that an object is still in existence somewhere, even if it is not visible. At around 8 or 9 months, babies seem to understand this concept and we can test it by taking an object from a baby and hiding it under a cushion near them. The baby should lift up the cushion to find it.

Table 1.5 Piaget's stages of cognitive development

Stage	Ages (approx)	Features
Sensorimotor	0–2 years	• Moving from physical reflexes to coordinated movements • Development of object permanence • Development of the general symbolic function (child begins to use symbols, e.g. language)
Pre-operational	2–7 years	• Child uses symbols in play and thought • Egocentrism • Centration • Animism • Inability to conserve
Concrete operations	7–11 years	• Ability to conserve • Children begin to solve mental problems using practical supports such as counters and objects
Formal operations	11–15 years	• Ability to think and manipulate ideas abstractly, e.g. calculate without the need for counters • Start of deductive logic

Development of the general symbolic function

Towards the end of the sensorimotor stage, the child begins to use symbols. Language is symbolic as we use words to represent objects. The child also uses objects to stand for things in their play such as a piece of dough to represent a cake. Piaget felt that being able to use language is a breakthrough as schemas can become internal rather than physical. Piaget believed that language developed from thought. Others, such as Vygotsky, believed that thought developed from language.

Pre-operational stage (2 to 7 years)

During this stage, children develop their skills in using symbols, i.e. language. Many early years professionals will find that children in this stage are using a lot of imaginative play, for example using objects in a representational way: sticks may become guns, or cardboard boxes may become cars. Piaget did divide this stage into two further sub-stages – preconceptual and intuitive – but there are four main features that run through both of these sub-stages:

- egocentrism
- difficulty with conservation
- centration
- animism.

Egocentrism

According to Piaget, children in the pre-operational stage tend to see things from their own perspective and thus their logic is different from that of adults. Piaget called this egocentrism and this is a strong feature of the whole of the intuitive stage. Piaget designed several tests that showed the way in which children were seeing problems – one of the most famous being the Swiss mountain scene test (see Figure 1.6). In this test children were shown a model of a mountain range. A doll was put in the scene and the children were shown a series of photos and asked which of the views the doll would be able to see. Children under

7 years consistently chose a photo that corresponded to the view they were seeing themselves. Piaget argued that this was because they could not 'decentre', i.e. take themselves out of their bodies and see something from another perspective.

Difficulty with conservation

In the pre-operational stage, children find it difficult to understand that things can remain the same, even though their appearance may change. Piaget suggested that the inability to 'conserve' was an important feature of the pre-operational stage. He designed many tests to show whether children could conserve in different ways.

Table 1.6 shows some of the tests that are commonly used with children. You might like to try these with children on your placement.

Centration

In this stage, children are beginning to classify objects and make associations. However, they are often doing this by looking at only one attribute at a time, such as sorting objects according to size, but not size and colour. Piaget called this centration. This may be why children are unable to conserve, i.e. in the mass conservation test described in Table 1.6, they concentrate on the shape of the clay rather than its quantity.

Figure 1.6 The Swiss mountain scene made famous by Piaget

Table 1.6 Tests commonly used with children to show whether they can conserve

Name of test	Method used
Number	Two parallel rows with equal numbers of counters are shown to the child. The counters in one of the rows are then put closer together so that one row appears longer than the other. Children are asked, 'Are there the same number of counters in each row?'
Length	Two pencils of identical length are put side by side. One pencil is then moved diagonally so that its point is no longer alongside the other pencil. The child is asked, 'Are they the same length?'
Volume	Two identical beakers are filled with the same amount of water. The contents of one beaker are poured into a narrower but taller beaker. The children are asked, 'Is there still the same amount of water?'
Mass	Two balls of clay or dough are rolled out to exactly the same size. The child is asked to pick them up to check that they are the same. One of the balls is rolled into a sausage shape. The children are asked, 'Is there the same amount of clay in each ball?'

Animism

Many children show signs of animism: believing that because they have feelings, other objects must also have feelings. Many early years professionals see this when children say things such as 'that dog's mummy will be cross with her' or 'that wall is bad, it hurt me'.

Reflect

Animism in children's drawings

We can see animism in children's drawings. Many children, even after the preconceptual stage, will draw animals and objects that smile, such as a sun with a smiling face.

- Look at several drawings done by children between the ages of 4 and 8 years.
- Can you see any signs of animism in the drawings?

Concrete operations stage (7 to 11 years)

The concrete operations stage marks a great leap in children's logical abilities. They begin to use rules and strategies to help their thinking. Piaget called this the concrete operations stage because children's understanding is aided by the use of practical tools, for example, using counters to find the answer to 15 minus 9.

Children in the concrete operations stage are also able to conserve and decentre (they see things from the point of view of others – for example, they understand that the view the doll sees in the Swiss mountain scene test will be different to their own view). Piaget also suggested that these children would understand the concept of reversibility. An example of reversibility is when clay is rolled into a ball, then into a sausage and back into a ball, it will still have the same mass. In mathematical terms, it means that children are able to understand that there is a link between division and multiplication. For example, they will understand that $7 \times 5 = 35$ and $35 \div 7 = 5$.

Formal operations stage (11 to 15 years)

The main difference between the formal operations stage and the concrete operations stage is that children are now able to manipulate thoughts and ideas to solve problems without needing practical props. This means that in theory, tasks such as map reading can be done without having to turn the map around to work out whether a turning is on the right or left. This is an interesting example of a formal operations task, as many adults may have difficulty reading maps!

Piaget suggested that thinking at the formal operations level would not be an automatic step and that in some areas of learning we would not all achieve this level all of the time; and in some areas this would depend on the training and experiences that we were given. In the case of map reading, we might be able to manage to read a map without turning it around given enough experience and training.

Another feature of the formal operations stage is that children are able to **hypothesise** about situations in a realistic way – for example, what would you do if someone broke into your home? The ability to hypothesise means that children can speculate on outcomes. Piaget described this feature of thinking as hypothetico-deductive reasoning.

Summary of Piaget's theory

Piaget's work on the theory of cognitive development was so influential that it is perhaps useful to summarise some of its main features.

- Children develop their thoughts according to their experiences.
- Children's learning passes through distinct stages, although attaining formal operations seems to depend on training and experiences.
- Children's language is used to support their cognitive development.

Criticism and further developments of Piaget's theory

Though Piaget developed a comprehensive theory about how children might learn, his work also acted as a springboard for other theorists, many of whom have found flaws in his theory.

Piaget's research methods may have been biased

Piaget used clinical interviews as the major research method with children. This method is open to bias. Piaget carried out hundreds of interviews and the type of data that was collected is **qualitative**. Despite this, the data is very informative. Piaget also used experiments, but the tests he constructed have also been criticised.

Does cognitive development really happen in stages?

This is one of the criticisms of Piaget's early work. However, from the 1970s Piaget suggested that

---

Case study

Piaget and early years practice

Although Piaget had no particular recommendations about how his theory should be used to teach children, his work did have an effect on educational practice. There are two main strands: readiness and learning by discovery. Both of these strands were used to suggest that an individual approach to children's learning should be taken.

Readiness

If children's thought processes cannot be fast-tracked this means that we can only work at the child's pace. If a child does not have the concept of conservation of number, this would mean that there is no point in teaching children addition or multiplication, for example.

Learning by discovery

The way that children develop their thinking is by reviewing their schemas and adapting their ideas (accommodation) to new information. In order to do this, children will need a wide range of experiences.

Think about your work placement setting:

1 Is there an assumption that children need to work at their own pace? Are children grouped according to their stages of development or according to their ages?

2 What types of activities are chosen that encourage learning through discovery? For example, children using beakers and water to find out about the properties of water.

---

cognitive development was a spiralling process and considered that at times children will show features of more than one stage at once. This he referred to as *décalage*. Despite this, he maintained that children would not be able to skip whole elements of the stages and progress to another stage.

Piaget underestimated children

One of the most widely accepted criticisms of Piaget's work is that the ages he gave for children's thinking are inaccurate. He underestimated children's level of thinking. One of the reasons given for his inaccuracies is the type of tasks that he used with children. Margaret Donaldson, who worked with Piaget at one point, was a particular critic. With a colleague, she showed that results could be very different if the task made sense to children and linked with their experiences. Their use of a 'naughty teddy' to manipulate counters showed that children as young as 4 could 'conserve'. In a famous book called *Children's Minds*, Donaldson outlined that children could be logical thinkers when they were able to make 'human sense' of the situation.

Babies' abilities

More recent research studies are now showing that Piaget underestimated babies' abilities, particularly in reference to object permanence. Several researchers, including Elizabeth Spelke at Harvard University, have carried out tests showing that babies express surprise if a number of items are shown, disappear and then a different (either decreased or increased) number of objects reappear.

Piaget underestimated how training and practice can help children

Piaget suggested that the cognitive development of children was heavily linked to maturation and, therefore, children could not be fast-tracked through the stages. There has, however, been some research suggesting that children can achieve tasks if they are given experiences to help them.

Chris Athey

Piaget's use of the term and concept of schemas has been developed further in the UK, notably by Chris Athey (1924–2011) and Tina Bruce (who at one time was Chris Athey's research assistant). Athey took Piaget's early work on schemas and developed it further. She suggested that schemas develop from actions and experiences and that children develop them to make sense of their world. By working closely with parents, observing children and looking at their paintings and drawings, Athey and Bruce started to identify a number of schemas that children frequently used. These schemas have since been developed and are often used to support children's learning through play.

Link

Go to Unit 2: Section C to find more information about learning through play.

In addition to identifying schemas, Athey suggested that children could explore and make progress at four different levels. Table 1.7 shows Athey's levels of schema.

Lev Vygotsky

Another key constructivist model was produced by Lev Vygotsky (1896–1934). His theory is known as a **social constructivist** model as it focuses on the role that adults and other children play in a child's learning. Unlike Piaget, Vygotsky did not provide a stage model of cognitive development, but focused instead on how children might learn with others.

Key terms

Hypothesise – to speculate or propose an idea or theory.

Qualitative data – information that is collected by informal methods and cannot be scientifically replicated.

Social constructivist – a model that explains children's cognitive development by suggesting that their logic and reasoning is developed through experiences, but also by interactions with and questions from adults and older children.

Table 1.7 Athey's levels of schema

Level of development	Description and use	Example
Motor level	Children explore through physical movements	Twirling around
Symbolic representational level	Children start to ascribe meaning to the schema	Pretending to be a dancer
Functional dependency relationship	Children start to see the relationship between the schema and other things	Stopping a clockwork mouse from turning
Thought	Children are able use the schema to think about things	Talking about how the washing machine is not working because it cannot spin round and that if a clock is not working the hands might not go round

Vygotsky's work was not published in English until the early 1960s, even though his work was known in Russia in the 1920s and 1930s. He believed that children's social environment and experiences are very important. He considered that children were born to be sociable and that, by being with their parents and then with their friends, they acquired skills and concepts. Vygotsky saw children as 'apprentices', learning and gaining understanding through being with others. In support of Vygotsky's work, researchers looked at the ways mothers worked with their children on a construction task. They saw that although techniques varied, mothers were able to encourage their children by either demonstrating or by praising movements that would help the children to complete the task.

Vygotsky also suggested that maturation was an important element in children's development and that we need to extend children's learning so that they can use their emerging skills and concepts. He used the term 'zone of proximal development' to define this idea.

Zone of proximal development

The zone of proximal development is the gap between what a child is currently able to do and what they might just be able to achieve if an adult provides some support. For example, a child might have the fine motor skills that allow them to untie a shoelace and make a simple knot. If an adult takes time to guide the child in tying their shoelaces, the child might with practice be able to tie a bow. It is highly unlikely that without the adult's input, the child would be able to master tying shoelaces. For the child to be able to achieve tying their shoelaces it is essential that the adult initially judges the child's skill level accurately. If the child's fine motor skills are not sufficiently developed, they will not be able to cope with the task.

Jerome Bruner's modes of thinking

Jerome Bruner's (born 1915) work was influenced by Piaget, but more particularly by the work of Vygotsky. Bruner does not have a stage theory as such but he suggests that children gradually acquire cognitive skills, which he refers to as 'modes of thinking'. Before looking at Bruner's modes of thinking, it is useful to look at Piaget's and Vygotsky's influences on his work.

Piaget's influence

Bruner, like Piaget, believes that children are born with a biological structure, which means that thinking and cognitive development are linked to maturation. He also believes that children are naturally curious and that children learn at first through being active. Abstract thought develops from action.

Vygotsky's influence

Bruner particularly stresses the social aspect of learning and the link between thought and language. Bruner also suggests that the role of the adult is important in helping the child to develop as a thinker. Bruner coined the term **scaffolding** to explain the role that adults could play in developing children's thinking. The idea is that adults can find ways to support children's thinking by, for example, simplifying a task/action or asking questions so that little by little, children can understand a concept.

Key term

Scaffolding – a term used to describe a style of working with children in which the adult helps the child to acquire information.

Table 1.8 shows Bruner's three modes of thinking in children's development and skill acquisition.

Table 1.8 Bruner's three modes of thinking

Mode	Description and use
Enactive	Learning and thought take place because of physical movements
Iconic	Thoughts are developed as mental images
Symbolic	Symbols including language are used in thinking

Enactive mode

Through repeating physical movements we often learn a skill such as tying our shoelaces or learning to drive a car. This is the first type of cognitive skill that Bruner suggests babies are able to use. This fits in with Piaget's sensorimotor stage where children repeat movements and learn about their world through their physical movements.

Iconic mode

An icon is something that is visual and Bruner suggests that the iconic mode involves building up a picture of things we have experienced in our minds. We may, for example, be able to shut our eyes and imagine the room that we are in. The iconic stage does relate to Piaget's pre-operational stage as children concentrate more on appearances than adults and this is what often confuses them during Piaget's tests of conservation.

Symbolic mode

Like Piaget, Bruner believes that children's thinking drastically changes at around 7 years. Bruner links this change to the child's ability to use symbols but particularly to the use of language. In symbolic mode, thinking can take place without us having direct experience. For example, we may listen to the news on the radio and retain this information, even though we have not directly witnessed the events mentioned.

Information processing theories of cognitive development

Information processing theories of cognitive development consider the mental processes that allow us to learn. There are several different researchers associated with this approach to cognitive development, including Robert Kail (born 1950), Robert Siegler (born 1949) and David Klahr (born 1939). This is very much an area of ongoing research with some suggesting a stage-like model of development, but others suggesting that development is continuous. Information processing theorists also draw on the language and concepts used in computing to help talk about cognitive development. A major focus for all information processing theorists is the role that memory plays in helping us to process new information.

Memory

Memory is an important component in our ability to process information and so is at the heart of information processing theory.

At its simplest, there are three processes involved in memory:

1 Encoding

This is about organising information so that it can be stored. Poorly encoded information sometimes results in us not quite remembering something, for example, recognising the tune but not knowing the words of a song. Complex information seems to be harder for children to encode than simple information.

2 Storage

This is about keeping the information and not losing it.

3 Retrieval

This is about being able to recall information.

Multi-store model of memory

The most influential work carried out on memory was done by Richard Atkinson (born 1929) and Richard Shiffrin (born 1942). They proposed a multi-store model that has formed the basis for further work on memory. You can see an outline of their model in Figure 1.7. Today, most work on memory suggests that it is made up of different components through which information can be transferred. A filtering process is also in place, which explains why we do not remember every detail of every experience we have had.

Sensory memory

This is at the start of the process. Information received from the five senses can be stored temporarily, rather like a pause button. The information will either be transferred to the short-term memory (in which case it needs to be interpreted or encoded very quickly), or it will be lost.

Short-term memory

Information moving to the short-term memory will be held temporarily. The short-term memory is extremely short – this is why you may forget a phone number unless you keep repeating it or write it down. Work done on memory suggests that only about seven or so items can be held in the short-term memory at any time. You can try this out by seeing how many random numbers or names your friends can remember. As children get older, they seem to be able to use strategies to hold onto information in the short-term memory.

Long-term memory

Unlike the short-term memory, the long-term memory can hold information for a few minutes or even a lifetime. The long-term memory is seen as having unlimited capacity. This may come as a surprise if you are someone who has difficulty remembering things, but storage capacity is completely different from the process of retrieving information.

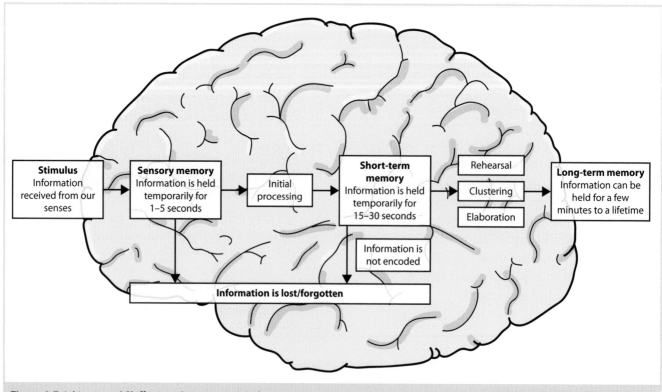

Figure 1.7 Atkinson and Shiffrin's multi-store model of memory

Strategies for boosting the capacity of short-term memory

1 Rehearsal

Repeat to yourself what you want to remember, for example, repeat a telephone number or practise actions to a song.

2 Clustering or chunking

Clustering involves grouping pieces of information. For example, rather than remembering a telephone number as 0-1-3-3-6-6-0-6-7-9-9-7, you would remember it in clusters or chunks: 01-33-66-06-79-97. In the same way, rather than remembering each item that you need when shopping in a supermarket, you might think about all the dairy items that you want or all the ingredients you need to make a cake. Children as young as 2 years old can begin to chunk information.

3 Elaboration

Elaboration means finding connections between things that need to be remembered. If you find a person's name difficult to remember, you might think about one feature about that person to help you. Mnemonics such as *Never Eat Shredded Wheat*, to remember the points of the compass, are forms of elaboration.

4 Language and memory

It is worth noting also that there are strong links between language and children's ability to process information. Where children's language is still developing or is atypical they will find it harder to encode information that is presented to them as speech. This is one of the reasons why we have to show and do things to young children. It is also one of the reasons why children who seem to have listened to a story may not afterwards be able to tell us anything about it.

Key points from information processing theorists

1 Information processing appears to improve with age

There have been quite a few experiments showing that children's ability to process information improves with age. One experiment asked children of different ages to name familiar objects as they appeared out of a bag. Younger children, although they knew the names of the objects, were consistently slower. Children also seem to acquire more strategies as they become older.

2 Experience enhances information processing

Information processing theorists suggest that part of the reason that children think differently from adults is that they are processing the information in different ways. At the heart of this processing is our ability to use our memories. As we get older we use our past experiences to help us solve new problems; when presented with several pieces of information, we also become more skilled at holding them until we need to use them.

3 Information processing may be at the heart of intelligence

There has been some thought that the speed at which information is processed is at the heart of intelligence, with some children of the same age seeming to be faster at solving problems. Children with high IQs seem to be good at remembering things and solving problems by applying existing knowledge to a new situation.

Theories of language development

Language helps children to communicate and understand more about the world around them. It is also the basis for developing literacy skills. Language is an important developmental topic and so is looked at again later.

Link

Go to Unit 6: Supporting Children's Speech, Communication and Language to find more information about language development.

Understanding the structure of language

It is important to have some understanding of the structure of language. All languages have rules, which are understood and used by both the speaker and listener. These rules are often referred to as grammar. By following the rules of grammar, speakers and listeners can understand each other. Linguists who study the structure of language use the term grammar to describe the package of a language. This consists of three key elements: phonology, semantics and syntax.

Phonology

Languages have a sound system, known as phonology. When we hear someone speaking, we may recognise the language that they are using, even if we cannot speak it. This recognition may be based on listening to the sounds that are being used. The sounds that are used in a language are called **phonemes**. Some languages use fewer phonemes than others. There are 44 phonemes used in English, as opposed to 11 in Rotokas, an East Papuan language.

> **Key term**
>
> **Phonemes** – the smallest units of sound in a language that help to distinguish one word from another. In the English language, for example, 'p' and 'b' are separate phonemes because they distinguish words such as 'pit' and 'bit'.

Semantics

Languages are composed of words, or units of meaning. When we learn a language we also have to learn what these units are and how they can be changed. An example of a unit is adding '-less' onto the end of a word, which changes the meaning of the original word.

Syntax

Finally, we have to learn the rules for using the words and how their place in a sentence can change their meaning. For example, 'the cat ate the mouse' has a different meaning from 'the mouse ate the cat' even though the same words have been used.

The sequence of language development

A good starting point when considering language development is to look at the pattern of how children learn to speak. It is interesting to note that babies and children, in whichever country they are born, all follow a similar pattern. The first year of a baby's life is spent trying to tune in to the language that they are hearing and learning the skills of communication, i.e. making eye contact and responding to other people's facial expressions and words. This first year is often known as the prelinguistic phase and is now considered to be vital in children's overall language development.

Table 1.9 outlines the major stages in language development.

Table 1.9 Stages in language development

Stage	Age	Features	Comments
Prelinguistic			
Cooing	6 weeks	Cooing	Babies make cooing sounds to show pleasure. These early sounds are different to sounds made later on mainly because the mouth is still developing.
Babbling (phonemic expansion)	6–9 months	Babies blend vowels and consonants together to make tuneful sounds, e.g. 'ba', 'ma', 'da'	Babbling has been described as learning the tune before the words. The baby seems to be practising sounds. Babies increase the number of sounds or phonemes. This is sometimes called phonemic expansion. All babies, even deaf babies, produce a wide range of sounds during this period. During these months babies also learn some essential communication skills. These include making eye contact, recognising some emotions in others and responding to them.

continued

Table 1.9 (*continued*)

Stage	Age	Features	Comments
Prelinguistic – *continued*			
Babbling (phonemic contraction)	9–10 months 11–12 months	Babies babble, but the range of sounds is limited Babies seem to repeat the same sounds in long strings, e.g. 'babababa' (echolalia)	The range of sounds or phonemes that babies produce becomes more limited and reflects the phonemes used in the language that they are hearing. At this stage, it would in theory be possible to distinguish between babies who are in different language environments. At 10 months babies understand 17 or more words. Babies' communication skills have also developed further. They now know how to attract an adult's attention by pointing and raising their voice. They can also understand a lot of what is being said to them either through word recognition, but also by reading faces.
Linguistic			
First words	Around 12 months	Babies repeatedly use one or more sounds, which have meaning for them	The first words are often unclear and emerge gradually. They are often one sound, but are used regularly in similar situations, e.g. 'baga' to mean drink and cuddle. Babbling continues.
Holophrases	12–18 months	Toddlers start to use one word in a variety of ways	Toddlers use holophrases to make their limited vocabulary more useful for them. One word is used in several situations, but the tone of voice and the context helps the adult understand what the toddler means. Most toddlers have between 10 and 15 words by 18 months. By this time toddlers have often learned how to get an adult's attention and how to make them laugh.
Two-word utterances (telegraphic speech)	18–24 months	Two words are put together to make a mini sentence	Toddlers begin to combine words to make sentences. They seem to have grasped which are the key words in a sentence, e.g. 'dada gone' or 'dada come'.
Language explosion	24–36 months	A large increase in children's vocabulary combined with increasing use of sentences	This is a period in which children's language seems to evolve rapidly. Children learn words so rapidly that it becomes hard for parents to count them! At the same time the child uses more complicated structures in their speech. Plurals and negatives begin to be used, e.g. 'no dogs here'.

continued

Table 1.9 (continued)

Stage	Age	Features	Comments
Linguistic – *continued*			
Language explosion – *continued*	3–4 years	Sentences become longer and vocabulary continues to increase	Children are using language in a more complete way. Mistakes in grammar show that they are still absorbing the rules and sometimes misapplying them! Mistakes such as 'I wented' show that they have learned that '-ed' makes a past tense. These types of mistakes are known as 'virtuous' errors. By this time, children are able to use their communication skills in order to socialise with others in simple ways, e.g. they may repeat a question if they think that they have not been understood.
Fluency	4–6 years	Mastering the basic skills of the language	Children have mastered the basic rules of English grammar and are fluent, although will still be making some 'virtuous' errors.
Speech maturity	6–8 years	Mastering the reproduction of most sounds	During this period, children's speech becomes clearer as their tongue, teeth and jaw develop. Children begin to use language to get their point of view across to others, although some do this by simply raising their voice! In this period, children's level of language is key to acquiring the skills of reading and writing.

Theories of how children acquire language

The nature versus nurture debate appears once more when we look at the theories of how children learn language.

Skinner's operant conditioning theory

We have already looked at Skinner's operant conditioning theory in relation to how children learn behaviours. This is a nurture theory. Skinner suggests that we learn language mainly because our first efforts at communicating as a baby are rewarded or reinforced in some way. For example, a baby may get a smile from a parent if they gurgle or a toddler saying 'more' and pointing at food will learn that by using language they can get what they want. Skinner used this idea of reinforcement to explain why babies stop making some sounds. He reasoned that when babies made sounds that parents did not recognise they would not receive any attention, whereas sounds that were recognisable were noticed and reinforced. He called this process selective reinforcement.

This approach would explain why children often speak in similar ways to their parents, using familiar phrases and intonation.

Criticisms of Skinner's theory

Skinner's theory does not explain why all babies and children follow the same pattern of learning language. If Skinner's theory was correct, you would expect to see that children's language develops very differently depending on the amount and type of reinforcement that adults and others give. This is not the case however, as most children seem to pass through the same stages.

The theory does not explain why young children speak in different ways to adults around them – for example, 'dada gone'. If children learn by imitating what they hear and by incorrect sounds or sentences not being reinforced, why do they say things such as 'wented' or 'swimmed'?

Nor does the theory explain how children learn the rules of a language in such a way that they are quickly able to make up their own sentences. Learning through imitation and reinforcement would mean that children would only be repeating what they have heard, rather than being able to invent their own sentences.

Theory into practice

Praise and acknowledgement

Although Skinner's model of how language develops has many limitations, we do know that it is important for children to be encouraged so that their language develops. Children who are acknowledged learn that adults are pleased when they talk and so are more likely to interact.

- Look at an experienced member of staff in your setting.
- How are they giving babies positive reinforcement when they try to communicate?

Noam Chomsky

Noam Chomsky's (born 1928) work on language is based on the idea that our ability to learn language is instinctive. This is a nature, or nativist, theory. His theory has been widely accepted as it is comprehensive and, unlike Skinner's ideas, explains why all babies' language development follows a pattern. He is famous for suggesting that humans have a Language Acquisition Device (LAD). This is not an actual physical part of the brain, but a structure within our brains that allows babies to absorb and understand the rules of the language they are being

exposed to. The brain is able to analyse the language and work out the system that the language uses. This is a complex process, but explains why children can quickly understand and then use their language creatively and correctly without ever being formally taught or knowing the rules.

The LAD would explain why all babies can learn any language they are exposed to and why all babies follow the same pattern of development even though their abilities may be very different.

Reflect

Is there a critical period for learning language?

The idea of a critical period is an attractive one. It has been suggested that if children are not exposed to language in the first ten years of their lives, they would not be able to learn to speak. There is some evidence both for and against this idea.

Teenagers and adults who have been brain damaged as a result of an accident find it harder to regain language they have lost, whereas children with similar injuries find it much easier. This would support the idea of a critical period.

Children who have suffered severe deprivation have still managed to acquire some language. One of the most famous of these children is Genie. Genie was 13 years old when she was rescued in 1957. She had spent her childhood in appalling conditions. She was punished for making any sounds and was strapped down. When she was found she could understand a few words, but essentially had no speech. Although she made progress in learning to speak, she struggled with the rules of speech. This would cast doubt on the idea of a 'critical period' because speech was still gained. Having said this, cases such as this are complicated because of the abuse that the children have suffered. It could be argued that the effects of physical and emotional abuse play a part in any difficulty that children have with learning.

Theories that consider personality and the development of self-esteem

Are we born with our personalities or are they the result of our experiences? This is a key question in personality development. The way we act and how we face different situations is also part of our personality and is linked to our self-esteem. We will now look at theories of personality and also self-esteem.

Erik Erikson's life stages

Some psychologists were influenced by the well-known work of Sigmund Freud (1856–1939) and developed his theories further. One of these psychologists was Erik Erikson (1902–1994), who considered that the social environment, for example parenting and friendships, affects our personalities. He accepted Freud's theory of the structure of the personality being divided into three (the id, the ego and the superego) but he did not feel that Freud's work went far enough.

Erikson's work is interesting because he considered that our personalities are not fixed, and instead we keep on changing during the course of our lives. Erikson's stages of personality development are life stages and are linked to social stages. He considered that at each stage, we face a dilemma or conflict. Like Freud, he believed that the outcome of each stage would determine our personality.

It is worth noting that work on infant development in relation to brain development and the production of cortisol, a stress hormone, supports Erikson's theory that children need unconditional love and acceptance.

Research

For more on Erikson's work, visit the *Illinois Child Welfare Journal* and download an article called 'Cortisol Changes and the Quality of Child Care in Australian Preschool and Kindergarten Children'. You can access this article by going to www.pearsonhotlinks.co.uk and searching for this ISBN: 9781447970965.

Table 1.10 shows details of Erikson's life stages and the effects on a child's personality if a stage is not completed successfully.

There have been many attempts since Erikson to describe what makes each of us different and whether these differences are innate or whether we are shaped by our childhood and later experiences. It is a fascinating area and no doubt one that will be under continual review. Defining personality is quite difficult in the first place. Is it just about our social skills with others, or is it about the way in which we approach problems or new situations?

The Big Five

Current research into defining and understanding personality considers five **traits** and suggests that these make up our personality. The term 'the Big Five' is widely used to describe this model.

The idea is that we all share five traits, but at different levels. One person might score highly on three traits, while someone else might be low on four.

Many studies suggest that when the five traits are measured in adults they are seen to be reasonably stable over time, although how effectively they can be used to measure children's personality is not yet clear. Some researchers believe that they can be used from middle childhood and into the teenage years but this is an area of ongoing work. Figure 1.8 shows these five traits.

Did you know?

Some employers are now profiling prospective employees' personality using a test based on the work of leading personality researchers Paul Costa and Robert McRae.

Key terms

Empathy – the ability to feel or understand the emotions of others.

Trait – a set of characteristics.

Table 1.10 Erikson's life stages and their effects on a child's personality

Age	Stage	Description	Effects on personality if stages are not completed successfully
0–1 year	Basic trust versus mistrust	Babies have to decide whether the world and the people around them are safe and friendly, or hostile.	If babies do not have their emotional and physical needs met, they may decide that the world is hostile. This might affect later relationships.
2–3 years	Autonomy versus shame	Children are exploring their environment and trying to do things for themselves. They are also moving out of nappies.	If children are not given encouragement or are made to feel guilty, they may doubt themselves. This may cause them to be less independent in the future.
4–5 years	Initiative versus guilt	Children are increasingly able to plan and carry out activities. They also need to learn about their gender role.	Children need to feel independent, but also have boundaries on their behaviour. Too much control of the child can result in a fearful and dependent child, but no limits or boundaries can leave the child without any guilt or conscience.
6–12 years	Industry versus inferiority	Most children are in school at this point. They are starting to compare themselves to others.	Children who experience failure and notice that they are not as competent in some areas as their peers may lose confidence and feel inferior. Children who only meet with success during this phase may become over-confident and lack **empathy**.
13–18 years	Identity versus confusion	Adolescents need to forge an identity separate from their parents' identities.	Ideally at the end of this stage adolescents have a firm idea of who they are and what they want to go on to do. During this process, Erikson suggested that some young people may have a crisis of identity.

Temperament in babies and toddlers

Research that focuses on the temperament of babies and toddlers looks at their characteristics. By looking at babies from birth, researchers can see that even at that stage, babies respond differently. Measurements of the frequency of crying, activity level and interest in others, as well as how easily babies are soothed or become irritable, have shown that babies' temperaments do vary. Researchers Stella Chess (1914–2007) and Alexander Thomas (1914–2003) famously categorised babies into three types:

- Easy

The majority of babies seem to fall into this category. Babies feed and sleep well, cry little and are easily soothed. They adapt well and show that they are happy.

- Slow to warm up

These babies are more passive than others, reluctant and do not show their emotions. They take time to adapt to new foods, people or routines but are then happy.

- Difficult

The minority of babies fall into this category. These babies cry more than others, are hard to settle and have irregular feeding and sleeping patterns. They are more unpredictable and are harder to please and keep happy.

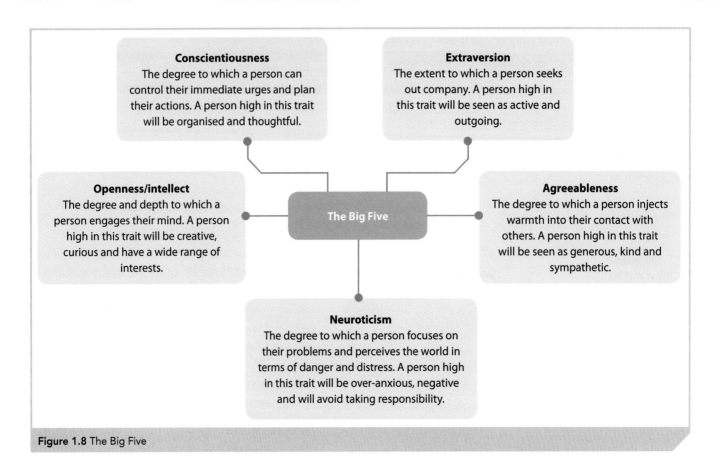

Conscientiousness
The degree to which a person can control their immediate urges and plan their actions. A person high in this trait will be organised and thoughtful.

Extraversion
The extent to which a person seeks out company. A person high in this trait will be seen as active and outgoing.

Openness/intellect
The degree and depth to which a person engages their mind. A person high in this trait will be creative, curious and have a wide range of interests.

The Big Five

Agreeableness
The degree to which a person injects warmth into their contact with others. A person high in this trait will be seen as generous, kind and sympathetic.

Neuroticism
The degree to which a person focuses on their problems and perceives the world in terms of danger and distress. A person high in this trait will be over-anxious, negative and will avoid taking responsibility.

Figure 1.8 The Big Five

Subsequent follow-up work found that the characteristics that babies showed early on remained into later childhood, although it has also been found that some babies who were 'difficult' had parents who were able to respond positively and thus mitigate their behaviours.

Difficulties with temperament approaches

There are many difficulties with, and criticisms of, using a temperament approach when describing babies and young children. First, there are practical issues as to who is reporting on babies' and young children's behaviours. Parents are notoriously inaccurate as they are highly subjective. Then we know that parents' responses to their baby can also have an influence on the baby's reactions. Calm, confident, prompt and warm responses to a baby are likely to decrease a baby's fretfulness and so parents may report the baby's temperament as 'easy'. Other factors such as birth, stress during pregnancy and substance misuse may also explain differences in temperament and so cast doubt on a genetic disposition towards temperament. In addition, labelling a baby may also change parents' responses towards their child.

The development of self-concept

Who are we? What are we like? These are fundamental questions for children, almost like being able to place oneself on a map. In some ways, the development of self-concept is the process by which we gather information about ourselves. It is important because it is closely linked with self-esteem. It is useful to understand the differences between the terms used when talking about self-concept.

- Self-concept – this is our vision of our whole selves. It includes our self-esteem, our self-image and our ideal self.
- Self-image or self-identity – this is the way that we define ourselves, for example, who we are, where we live, our gender etc.
- Ideal self – this is our view of what we would like to be.
- Self-esteem – this is also referred to as self-confidence. Self-esteem is a global evaluation of how we feel about ourselves.

Susan Harter's model of self-esteem

Susan Harter's model suggests that our self-esteem is related to how close our self-image and ideal self are. The closer our self-image and ideal self are to each other, the higher our self-esteem. This is shown in Figure 1.9. It is worth noting that it is considered normal for there to be some difference between an individual's self-image and their ideal self.

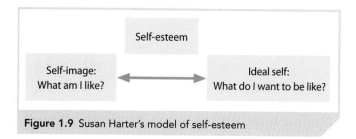

Figure 1.9 Susan Harter's model of self-esteem

How children develop self-image

Children gradually develop self-image. The first step for children is to be able to recognise themselves. A well-known test for this is to put a touch of red lipstick on a baby's nose and then put the baby in front of a mirror. A child who is beginning to recognise themselves will touch their nose, rather than the nose in the reflection. Many babies are doing this by the time they are 18 months old and nearly all by the age of 2 years.

The reaction of others

Children also develop self-image as a result of how others react to them. Children may listen to what their parents say about them or notice how carers talk to and treat them. This is sometimes known as the 'looking-glass self' theory. It was first described by Charles Cooley (1864–1929) and has been widely adopted as a popular theory of how self-image is formed. Cooley speculated that this process begins as babies.

If children perceive that they are wanted, liked and loved they will have positive self-regard. If they are constantly criticised they will come to the conclusion that they are not good enough or naughty. Children may also link performance to praise – believing that they must always achieve if they are going to be liked or loved by their parents and carers. This means we must be careful to make sure that we give children 'unconditional praise' to show them that we like them for themselves, as well as praise for their achievements and efforts.

Learning about yourself from others is also thought to contribute to children learning gender expectations. A famous study showed that adults reacted differently towards baby boys than they did towards baby girls.

We also notice the reaction of others to our achievements. If we are good at a skill that is valued, we are likely to feel positive, but if we are good at a skill that others do not value, it does not become a positive part of our self-image. This becomes an issue particularly when children reach school age. For example, a boy who is an excellent dancer will not necessarily have a high self-esteem if dancing is not valued by his friends and peers.

Comparison to others

From around 5 or 6 years, children begin to compare themselves to others. They may notice that they are not running as fast as others in their class or that they are not able to read as fluently. The process of comparison helps children to work out 'their place' but it can also lead children to feel that they are not as good as others. Increasingly children also look at some children whom they perceive as being popular and make comparisons. It is interesting to note that sometimes children who are doing well at school may still have low self-esteem, simply because they are comparing themselves to their friends whom they may perceive as doing better.

The development of the ideal self

The development of the ideal self is complex. Children will start to pick up messages from teachers, parents, carers and other children about what is valued. We also know that as they grow older children pick up messages from media such as the television. These sources and experiences start to give children ideas of what the 'perfect' child is like.

Case study

'Girls do not play football'

Anna is 7 years old. She has three older brothers, and her family is football-mad – her father takes them to support the local football team. Anna loves playing football, and she is quite good at it. However, her parents have noticed that since she went to school, she seems less interested in football. She has even started to refuse to go to football matches, saying that she cannot be a princess if she plays football.

1 What factors may have made Anna change her attitude towards football?

2 How could the school help to make Anna feel that football can be a girl's game?

Theories that consider children's moral development

We will now look at pro-social and moral behaviour. These are hot topics because the media often suggests that children are not as well behaved as in previous generations.

Pro-social behaviour

Pro-social behaviour is the type of behaviour that we tend to encourage in young children, such as comforting another child or sharing equipment. Psychologists have studied this behaviour to consider whether pro-social behaviour is instinctive or learned. The conclusions reached by some of their studies are interesting, though at times also uncomfortable.

Universal egoism

It is debated among psychologists and social scientists whether pure altruistic behaviour (helping others for no obvious gain) exists. Many believe that all acts of pro-social behaviour are in some way selfish – hence the term 'universal egoism'. If we consider this idea carefully, we may be able to see the logic. Do we stop and give someone a hand when they drop their bag because if we don't we may feel guilty later? Do we sympathise when our friends have problems so that one day they will do the same for us?

If we think about these sorts of questions, it is possible to see the logic of universal egoism. It is suggested that universal egoism is actually one way that the human race ensures its survival and continued existence. For example, a mother might starve herself in order to be able to feed her children.

Reflect

How do you feel about the concept of universal egoism?

Can you think of any acts of goodwill, kindness or self-sacrifice that show this theory to be false?

Social learning theory

Bandura's social learning theory supports the idea that children learn pro-social behaviour from their parents. Children who grow up seeing adults sharing and helping are more likely to show this type of behaviour themselves.

Theory into practice

The social learning theory approach to pro-social behaviour would suggest that we can help children to show caring behaviour by being good role models. We can also take a behaviourist approach and make sure that caring behaviour is reinforced by praising or rewarding 'wanted behaviour'.

- Give some examples of how you might model pro-social behaviour in your setting.
- Does your setting have a code of conduct about how adults must behave in the presence of children?

Moral development

At what age are children able to tell right from wrong? In England and Wales the age of legal responsibility – 10 years old – is one of the lowest in Europe.

The development of moral reasoning in children is complex because it involves children's own experiences of being treated fairly, their ability to understand a situation and their ability to empathise with others. One of the most famous approaches to understanding moral development is through a cognitive, i.e. stage, model. This cognitive approach was put forward by Jean Piaget and then later built on by Lawrence Kohlberg.

Piaget's theory of moral development

In line with his view that cognitive development followed a stage process, Piaget suggested that moral development did the same. Piaget used a clinical interview approach with children, asking them to explain how they were playing games and also by telling them stories. He suggested that children's moral development was a three-stage process. Table 1.11 outlines these three stages.

Piaget also felt that during the three stages, children gradually move away from the concept of morality and fairness being imposed by others (heteronomous morality) to a state of understanding that we can be in control of our moral reasoning (autonomous morality).

Kohlberg's theory of moral development

Lawrence Kohlberg's (1927–1987) work on moral development is well known. He built on Piaget's descriptions of moral development. He suggested that, as with other cognitive areas, moral reasoning is linked to stages of development. He suggested that there are three levels of moral development, which are then subdivided into stages. Table 1.12 shows these levels and sub-stages.

Case study

Paint on clothes

Daniel is 4 years old. He loves painting at nursery. Children are encouraged to put on aprons before they start painting, but these aprons do not have any sleeves. One day Daniel did not put an apron on and his mother was angry with him because the new shirt he was wearing got paint on it. Today Daniel is busy painting, but accidentally gets paint on the cuffs of his jumper although he is wearing an apron. He tries to wipe off the paint, but his hands have paint on them as well. More paint gets on the jumper. Daniel starts to cry. He tells the supervisor that he has been naughty.

1 Why might Daniel think that he has been naughty?

2 Is Daniel likely to know the difference between an accident and a deliberate act?

3 Why is it important for adults to consider their reactions to such situations?

Table 1.11 Piaget's stages of moral development

Stage	Age	Comments
Pre-moral	0–4 years	Children in this stage are learning about right and wrong through their own actions and by considering the effects on adults around them.
Moral realism	4–7 years 7–11 years	In this period children's moral development is greatly influenced by the adults in their lives. Their judgements very much depend on what they think the adults' expectations would be. Children are preoccupied with justice and following rules. This means that children have developed a concept of fairness.
Moral relativism	11+ years	In this stage children understand the concept of equity, i.e. that treating people in exactly the same way may not result in fairness. For instance, a child who does not understand their homework may need more of a teacher's time than a child who does. The motive for people's actions is also considered by children.

Table 1.12 Kohlberg's levels of moral development

Age	Level	Sub-stages
6–13 years	Pre-conventional	• Punishment and obedience • Individualism, instrumental purpose and exchange
13–16 years	Conventional	• Good boy/nice girl • Law and order orientation
16–20+ years	Post-conventional/ principled	• Social contract • Universal ethical principles

Preconventional

This level is divided into two stages. At this level, children are not being guided by their own moral reasoning, but are following their parents or carers. They are doing this to either seek reward or to avoid punishment, as follows.

- Stage 1 – punishment and obedience

The child finds out about what is wrong and right through seeing the consequences of their actions.

- Stage 2 – individualism, instrumental purpose and exchange

The child is learning that some actions and behaviours are rewarded. The child is also learning to avoid behaviours that might mean punishment. By the end of this stage the child is also beginning to enjoy helping people and has learned the 'if I help you, you might be able to help me' approach.

Did you know?

Kohlberg identified that at first children learn moral development through the behaviourist approach, i.e. being positively reinforced for wanted behaviour and being punished for unwanted behaviour.

Conventional

The next level of moral development consists of an awareness of group behaviour and the idea of what is, and isn't, acceptable in society, as follows.

- Stage 3 – mutual interpersonal expectations, relationships and interpersonal conformity (often known as the 'good boy/nice girl' stage)

In this stage children come to believe that good behaviour pleases other people, for example friends, teacher/tutors and parents/carers. Children are also becoming aware of the motive factor, i.e. 'he meant to help really'.

- Stage 4 – social system and conscience (also referred to as law and order orientation)

This is a widening-out stage. Before, children wanted to show good and correct behaviour to please people they knew. In this stage, they become more aware of society's needs and interests and what is deemed by society to be right or wrong. People in this stage are keen to obey regulations and laws.

Post-conventional/principled

This level of morality is very different to the others. At this level, people are not accepting the morality of the group or society unquestioningly. Demonstrators who break laws, for example animal rights campaigners who illegally set animals free, would be demonstrating this level of morality. This encompasses the following stages:

- Stage 5 – social contract

At this stage rules and regulations are seen as useful tools to make sure that there is some protection and fairness in society. People working at this level are prepared to tolerate rules being broken, if they do not see that they are fair or just rules.

- Stage 6 – universal ethical principles

This last stage was in some ways an unclear one for Kohlberg and a difficult one to test. People working at this stage would be extremely ethical people who are not swayed by society and have inner principles that they have developed. People in history who may have reached this level are often killed or persecuted – they are seen as troublemakers who are unwilling to compromise their position. You may like to consider who you think falls into this category – for example, Martin Luther King, Gandhi or Mother Theresa?

Reflect

If Piaget and Kohlberg are correct, young children are essentially amoral. They are learning about morality from the actions and reactions of the adults that they are with. They are, therefore, not making judgements for themselves. If children are with adults who have very different moral codes from the setting, this might create difficulties for the child, for example believing it is acceptable to hit another child.

- How does your setting communicate its values to parents?
- Why might it be difficult for a child where the setting and parents have very different codes?

Activity

Jed is 3 years old. His parents have noticed that over the past few months his speech has really come along, although they laugh when he says things such as 'we goed to the shops'. They have also noticed that he learns things that they have not taught him. At mealtimes with his grandparents, he always rolls up his napkin just like his grandfather. Jed's parents have also noticed that for the past month or so, he becomes very upset and frightened when he sees a dog. This is surprising, because he always used to love looking at and touching dogs when they went to the park. They wonder if his new fear is to do with an incident that happened a few weeks ago when they were having a picnic and a dog snatched a sandwich out of his hand.

Think of theories that explain Jed's development in terms of his:

- language development
- learning to do things without being taught
- fear of dogs.

Theories that consider children's development in relation to their environment

We have seen at the start of this unit that there is an interplay between 'nature' and 'nurture' in terms of children's development. An interesting theory that looks at children's development in terms of their social environment has been proposed by Urie Bronfenbrenner.

Urie Bronfenbrenner's ecological systems theory

Urie Bronfenbrenner (1917–2005) proposed that children's development has to be seen in the context of the overall environment that the child experiences, or the 'ecological system'. He proposed five systems that are usually represented in concentric circles to demonstrate how they interrelate.

Microsystem

This is a child's immediate family and home environment. This is the centre of a child's world and forms an essential part of what a child learns and how they learn to relate to others.

Mesosystems

These are the child's immediate experiences beyond the immediate home and family. These include preschool, nursery and school, as well as visiting family members or going to an afterschool activity.

Exosystems

These are one step beyond the child's immediate experiences, but have an impact on what happens in the mesosystems and microsystem. The example commonly given is the parent's workplace. The threat of redundancy is likely to impact on the child's home, even though the child is not directly linked to the workplace.

Macrosystem

This is a further layer outwards and something that is out of the control of the child and their family, but it still has an influence on the other systems. It is about the economic and cultural situation of the community and society in which the child and their family is living – for example, a new government decides to cut the funding for preschool places. This in turn affects whether the parent can work and also whether the child can spend time in education.

Chronosystem

This is the final layer and provides the context in terms of the 'history' of both the society and the child's life. A family feud may have influenced generations of attitudes towards trusting others with money or, taking a larger view, the development of telecommunications has influenced how some work is carried out. For example, some parents may now be able to work from home.

The influence of Bronfenbrenner's theory

Since Bronfenbrenner's theory has emerged, greater consideration has been given to seeing child development as interrelated to the cultural and social context in which the child is raised. It has also influenced policies with a view to supporting children and their families.

Theories that consider attachment

The study of children's early relationships and their importance in overall development did not really start until the 1950s when John Bowlby (1907–1990) published *Maternal Care and Mental Health*. The results of this and subsequent research have had noticeable and continuing effects on childcare practice. This means that adults working with babies and children need to have a good understanding of the stages of **attachment** and attachment theory, as well as the effects of separation.

> **Key term**
>
> **Attachment** – a special relationship or bond between a child and people who are emotionally involved with them.

What is meant by attachment?

The term 'attachment' is widely used by psychologists studying children's early relationships. An attachment can be thought of as a unique emotional tie between a child and another person, usually an adult. Research has repeatedly shown that the quality of these ties or attachments will shape a child's ability to form other relationships later in life. Psychologists have also studied the effects on children when attachments are not made in infancy or when they have been broken, for example, through separation.

Attachment as a process

Psychologists have studied the ways in which babies form early attachments. It is generally accepted that unlike geese, which immediately start to follow the first creature they see after hatching, babies form attachments gradually. There seems to be a general pattern to the way children develop attachments and Table 1.13 summarises these stages.

Bowlby's theory of attachment

The work of John Bowlby has greatly influenced social care policy, childcare practices and research into early relationships. After the Second World War he was asked to investigate the effects on children who were being brought up in orphanages or other institutions. In 1951 his findings were published. He showed that meeting children's physical needs alone was not sufficient: children were being psychologically damaged because of the absence of their mothers. He reached this conclusion by looking at the life histories of children who had been referred to his clinic. He noticed an overwhelming trend: most of these children had suffered early separation from their mothers and families.

Table 1.13 The stages of forming attachments

Age	Stage	Features
6 weeks–3 months	Pre-attachment	Babies begin to be attracted to human faces and voices. First smiles begin at around 6 weeks.
3 months–7/8 months	Indiscriminate attachments	Babies are learning to distinguish between faces, showing obvious pleasure when they recognise familiar faces. They are happy to be handled by strangers and prefer to be in human company rather than left alone, hence the term 'indiscriminate attachments'.
7–8 months	Specific attachments	Babies begin to miss key people in their lives and show signs of distress such as crying when a carer leaves the room. Most babies also seem to have developed one particularly strong attachment, often to the mother. Babies show a wariness of strangers even when in the presence of their key people. This wariness may quickly develop into fear, if the stranger makes some form of direct contact with the baby, e.g. by touching them.
From 8 months	Multiple attachments	After making specific attachments, babies go on to form multiple attachments. This is an important part of their socialisation process.

Separating babies and children from their main attachments

Most early years professionals will notice that as children become older, they find it easier to separate from their parents. This is because they have formed other attachments to staff and, as they get older, to other children. They have also learned that although their parent is absent, they will return. However, babies and toddlers find it difficult to cope with the absence of their main attachments and will show signs of distress.

Bowlby noted that there seemed to be a pattern to the way children reacted if they were separated from their main attachments. This pattern is often referred to as **separation anxiety**.

Key term

Separation anxiety – a set of behaviours and actions that occur when a child is distressed as a result of the person or people they are attached to being absent.

Separation anxiety is clearly seen in babies from around 7 months and seems to reach a peak at around 12 to 15 months. Older children will show separation anxiety if they are separated for long periods, for example, if a parent dies or goes away for a period of time.

There seem to be three distinct stages of separation anxiety. These stages are described in Table 1.14.

Table 1.14 The stages of separation anxiety

Stage	Features
Protest	Children may cry, struggle to escape, kick and show anger.
Despair	Children show calmer behaviour, almost as though they have accepted the separation. They may be withdrawn and sad. Comfort behaviour such as thumb sucking or rocking may be shown.
Detachment	Children may appear to be over the separation and start to join in activities. The child is actually coping by trying to forget the relationship, hence the term 'detachment'. The effects of detachment may be longer-lasting, as the child may have learned not to trust people they care for.

Features of Bowlby's theory of attachment

1 Monotropy

Bowlby believed that babies need to form one main attachment that would be special and of more importance to the child than any other. Bowlby suggested that in most cases this relationship would be formed with the mother, but that it could be formed with the father or another person.

2 Critical period

Bowlby was greatly influenced by **ethologists** such as Konrad Lorenz (1903–1989) and therefore he believed that babies need to have developed their main attachment by the age of 1 year. Bowlby also believed that during a child's first four years, prolonged separation from this person would cause long-term psychological damage.

Key term

Ethologist – a person who studies patterns of animal behaviour.

3 Children need 'parenting'

Bowlby showed through his findings that simply meeting a child's physical and care needs is not enough for healthy growth and development. Children need to have a main attachment in their early lives to give them consistent support. His early papers suggested that the mother should play this role, although his position changed in later years.

4 Children show distress when separated from their main attachment

Bowlby outlined a pattern of distress that babies and children show when separated from their carers (separation anxiety). He made links to show that when adults had been separated from their mothers in infancy, they would not form deep and lasting relationships. He called this effect 'maternal deprivation'.

Criticisms of Bowlby's work

There are many criticisms of Bowlby's work and it has been superseded by other pieces of research. When looking at the criticisms of his work it is, however, important to remember the political, economic and social climate of the time.

Did you know?

Bowlby's work on separation anxiety changed the way that hospitals worked with young children. Before his findings were published, most institutions had a policy of not allowing contact between parents and children. They found that children were invariably upset after seeing their parents, whereas if there was no contact the children appeared to recover more quickly from the separation. It is ironic that this was the absolute opposite of what was actually happening – children were in fact detaching from their parents. As a direct result of Bowlby's work, hospitals began to allow more contact between parents and children and today it is common practice for parents to be able to stay overnight with their children.

The role of the mother was over-emphasised

This has been a major criticism of Bowlby's early work. At the time of writing, women were the traditional care-givers. For economic reasons, after the Second World War, the government was keen for women to return to their traditional roles within the home. Bowlby's later work did emphasise that babies could form an attachment with someone other than the mother.

Attachments to more than one person were not explored

Bowlby placed a lot of emphasis on the importance of one single attachment. Subsequent research has shown that as children get older, they can develop equally strong attachments to other figures such as their fathers and siblings. These are known as multiple attachments.

The quality of the substitute care was not taken into consideration

Bowlby did not take into consideration the effect of being in poor-quality care. This means that it is hard to be absolutely sure that the psychological damage done to the children was only the result of maternal deprivation.

Later studies have suggested that children's development may not be affected if there is a substitute person acting as an attachment figure. This is the concept behind the key person system that is used in early years settings today.

Attachment behaviour

It is important for adults working with children to be able to identify when babies and children have made attachments. This can generally be observed through looking at their behaviour. There are four broad indicators that babies and children might show. What is interesting about attachment behaviours of young children is that they are active. Babies and young children show clear responses to a person they have made an attachment to, as follows.

1 They actively seek to be near the other person.

2 They cry or show visible distress when that person leaves or (for babies) is no longer visible.

3 They show joy or relief when that person appears.

4 They show an acute awareness of that person's presence, such as looking up at them from time to time, responding to their voice or following their movements.

The quality of attachments

There has been some research that has looked at the quality of babies' early attachments. It would seem that, where babies and children are 'securely' attached, they are able to explore and develop their independence. Babies and children whose attachment is less secure seem to show either indifference or clingy types of behaviour.

Why is this child upset that her mother is leaving the nursery?

Harlow's monkeys

An experiment often referred to as 'Harlow's monkeys' looked further at the way in which a group of monkeys in different conditions formed attachments. Monkeys were used because it would have been unethical to use babies. (Animal rights campaigners might also say that it was just as unfair to use monkeys.) In the late 1950s, Harry Harlow (1905–1981) raised a group of rhesus monkeys from birth. The monkeys were put in a cage with two man-made substitute mothers. One mother was made of wire and the other was covered in terry towelling. Half of the monkeys were fed by the wire mother and half by the cloth mother. They found that, regardless of which mother was feeding them, the monkeys 'attached' themselves to the cloth monkey. They clung onto her when they were frightened and turned to her for comfort. This study showed that providing food alone does not mean that attachments will be formed.

A few years later, Harlow developed the experiment further to see what would happen if the cloth mothers 'rejected' the monkeys. One group of monkeys was randomly blasted with compressed air by their cloth mothers. As a result these monkeys tended to spend more time clinging to their cloth mothers than those in the other group who were not blasted. This seemed to show that rejection or abuse made the monkeys insecure and try more often to gain some comfort even though there was a chance that they would be 'rejected' again.

Research

Search on video-sharing websites such as YouTube for freely available videos showing Harlow's experiment.

'Strange situation'

The quality of attachments was also looked at by Mary Ainsworth (1913–1999) who is considered, alongside Bowlby, to be a key figure in this area of psychology. Mary Ainsworth created a scenario that she used to measure babies' reactions to being left with a stranger and then reunited with their mothers (or fathers). This scenario is now widely used to study attachment behaviour.

The scenario is known as the 'strange situation' and it is divided into eight parts with each part lasting about 3 minutes. During the experiment, the baby (a 1 year old) has some time by itself as well as with a stranger, as follows.

1. Parent and baby enter room.
2. Parent remains inactive, baby is free to explore room.
3. Stranger joins parent and infant.
4. Parent leaves room.
5. Parent returns, settles baby and stranger leaves.
6. Baby is alone in the room.
7. Stranger returns and interacts with baby.
8. Parent returns again and stranger leaves.

Ainsworth and her colleagues were particularly interested in the reactions of the baby to the parent when they left or returned and the way in which the parent interacted with the baby.

They categorised the behaviour into three types.

- Type A – anxious–avoidant

Baby largely ignores parent and shows little sign of distress when parent leaves, continuing to play. Baby ignores or avoids parent on their return. Baby dislikes being alone, but can be comforted by stranger.

- Type B – securely attached

Baby plays while parent is present, but shows visible distress when parent leaves, and play is reduced. Baby is easily comforted on return of parent and carries on playing. Cries when alone because the parent is not there but can be partly comforted by the stranger. Reactions towards stranger and parent are markedly different.

- Type C – anxious–resistant

Baby is wary and explores less than other types. Very distressed when parent leaves and actively resists stranger's attempts to comfort. Wants immediate contact with parent on return but is ambivalent, showing frustration and anger alongside clinginess, for example wanting to be held but then immediately struggling to get down.

Research

Search on video-sharing websites such as YouTube for freely available videos showing Mary Ainsworth's 'strange situation' experiment.

Why are some children more securely attached than others?

Ainsworth came to the conclusion that the quality of attachment depended on the parenting that the baby received. Where parents were able to sense and predict their babies' needs and frustrations, the babies showed type B behaviour, i.e. securely attached. This meant that they were able to explore and play, knowing that their parent was a safe base.

Theory into practice

Research findings on the need for babies and young children to have surrogate attachments in order to cope with separation from their parents or key carers has changed practice in early years settings. It is now good practice for settings to have a key person or key worker system in place. This is a member of staff who will take special responsibility for developing a strong relationship with a particular child.

- How does your placement setting help children to settle in?
- Why is it important that children have a strong bond with their key person?

C Be able to apply theories and models of child development to support children's development

One of the reasons for considering the theories and models of child development is that it can help us to understand what is happening to a child in relation to normative development. In addition, we can use some of the theories and models of development to influence our own practice, where this is appropriate. Tables 1.15 to 1.20 show how the theories and models of development we have already looked at can influence our practice.

Theories that consider how children learn behaviours

In Section B, we looked at theories and models of how children learn behaviour. Two of these theories are often used in practice when working with children, as shown in Table 1.15.

Theory of social learning: Role-play activities can be set up to encourage children to learn new skills and behaviours.

Table 1.15 How theories that consider how children learn behaviours can influence practice within settings

Theory	Description	How the theory could influence practice	How to apply the theory to practice
Theory of social learning (e.g. Bandura)	Suggests that children learn skills and attitudes, but that they also learn behaviours from watching adults	• To help children learn manners, thoughtfulness and turn taking • To help inspire children to try out a new activity or skill • To help children learn a new skill from observing an adult (if the skill is developmentally within their grasp)	• Make sure that you are role modelling the attitudes and behaviours you wish children to repeat • Recognise that children can pick up unwanted behaviours after observing adults • Set up role-play activities following a visit or outing • Remember: the later version of this theory also considered the factors that are required for this to take place. We have looked at these factors in the text. When developing practice based on this theory, remember that the age of the child will affect the skills they are able to learn.
Theory of operant conditioning (e.g. Skinner)	Suggests that adults can reinforce children's wanted behaviour	• To help children learn wanted behaviours such as manners, tidying up after an activity and turn taking • To encourage children to persist at an activity • To consider whether some behaviours have been learned because young children have had reinforcement for showing unwanted behaviours, e.g. children may tip out toys onto the floor because an adult always reacts	• Remember that positive reinforcements work better when they are provided at the time of the wanted behaviour or very shortly afterwards • When providing positive reinforcements, explain to a child why the reinforcement is given so that the child understands the link • Use intermittent schedules of reinforcement, e.g. reinforcements that are not regular • Recognise that the strongest positive reinforcement is usually adult attention and that if a child is showing an unwanted behaviour it is sometime best to ignore it • Make sure that you do not use secondary reinforcers, such as star charts, with children whose cognitive development means that they do not understand the concept • Make sure that expectations of wanted behaviour are age/stage appropriate • Understand that some unwanted behaviours are not linked to getting adults' attention but because the behaviour itself is pleasurable, e.g. children run rather than walk because it is more fun to run • Remember: in the long term, children's internal motivation is key to their later success, e.g. children who learn to feel pride in their own efforts will enjoy an activity for its own sake. Another example is a child who chooses to help another child because they wish to, rather than because they want praise from adults. Both of these examples demonstrate internal motivation.

Theories that consider the development of cognition and language

There are several theories that have been influential in early years practice relating to the development of cognition and language. Interestingly, many of them complement each other quite well, as Table 1.16 shows.

Table 1.16 How theories that consider how children develop cognition and language can influence practice within settings

Theory	Description	How the theory could influence practice	How to apply the theory to practice
Piaget's theory of cognitive development	Jean Piaget suggested a stage-like approach to cognitive development. He focused on the child as an 'active learner', believing that children construct their own ideas and logic about their immediate world based on the experiences they have had.	• To recognise that children learn at their own pace • To provide plenty of opportunities for exploration and play so that children can develop their own thinking	• Provide opportunities for children to explore a range of materials, particularly those that lend themselves to concepts, e.g. sand, water and dough • Provide opportunities for children to take part in a wide range of practical skills so that they can develop schemas • Provide opportunities for role play as children use this to play out their experiences with other children, using their own 'rules' • Do not mock children who say things such as, 'Where is your mummy?', as this is a logical statement to them • Be aware of a child's stage of development in respect to their ability to conserve, as this is a requirement before children can explore some areas of number work
Vygotsky's zone of proximal development	Lev Vygotsky suggested that interaction with adults and older children plays an important part in children's development. He suggested a model known as the zone of proximal development, whereby a child can develop a new skill or level of complex thinking, extending them beyond their current level, with the support of an adult.	• To help children develop new skills, knowledge or level of reasoning	• You need to accurately identify a child's current level of skill, knowledge and reasoning. This is done through careful and sensitive observation • Plan for the next steps for individual children • Work closely with children, using sensitive interaction and questioning so that children can be supported to acquire a new skill, level of reasoning or piece of knowledge

continued

Table 1.16 (continued)

Theory	Description	How the theory could influence practice	How to apply the theory to practice
Athey's schema theory	Chris Athey based her work partly on Piaget's concept of children developing schemas or patterns of thinking. She suggested that patterns of thinking could be identified through children's play.	• To identify schemas that children are using and to provide further opportunities for children to use them • To help parents and practitioners recognise that a child's activity is not meaningless, but may be supporting their cognitive development	• Observe children at play and identify the schema they may be exploring • Consider resources and activities that may support children's exploration of common schemas • Take film clips of children engaged in play with schemas and talk about their significance to parents • Talk to parents about their child's play interests at home and plan activities around these interests
Bruner's theoretical framework	Jerome Bruner suggested that children process information in different ways according to their age. He also suggested that children learn through play and exploration, especially when adults play an active role in questioning or engaging with the child. He used the term 'scaffolding' to explain this process.	• To help children learn concepts and develop their reasoning and logic	• Provide plenty of opportunities for meaningful interaction with children that follow the format of a 'discussion' rather than instruction • Refer children back to their previous experiences so that they can make the connection between them and their new thoughts, experiences and ideas • Revisit topics and activities with children every few months so that they can experience them again and gain new insights • Plan challenging but enjoyable activities so that children gain new experiences – learning through play • Talk to parents about the importance of active learning that is supported by adults in helping their child's cognitive development
Information processing theory	This theory considers the role of memory and language in the way that children interpret, store and retrieve memories. Theorists who looked at this include Kail, Siegler and Klahr.	• To help adults and parents support young children's learning and understand why children may not always process information in the way we might have expected	• Recognise that young children process information when there is a visual or active component • Use props and puppets, and make sure that children can see pictures when reading stories • Show children what you want them to do rather than just telling them • Allow children plenty of time to respond to you when asking a question. They need time to process what has been said

continued

Table 1.16 *(continued)*

Theory	Description	How the theory could influence practice	How to apply the theory to practice
Information processing theory – *continued*		• To provide activities that are sensory, active or visual to make processing easier for young children	• Use photographs to help children remember things they have experienced in the past • Use play and sensory opportunities as a way to support learning • Expect that children of the same age may have different 'processing speeds' • Keep instructions short • Use visual timetables so that children can understand what is going to happen next • Expect to give children reminders as 'words' are easily forgotten
Chomsky's Language Acquisition Device theory	Noam Chomsky proposed that humans have an innate sense of language and a device that allows babies and young children to acquire language if they are sufficiently exposed to it.	• To ensure that there are sufficient opportunities for meaningful and age/stage appropriate interaction • To support the language development of children who have an additional home language	• Think about whether children have sufficient opportunities to interact with you • Make sure the length of interactions with children allow them to acquire language • Speak in a way that is grammatically correct and clear • Do not correct children's language, but instead repeat it back to them in a corrected format • Reduce the level of background noise that may be acting as a distractor • Encourage parents to use their home language while their children are young so that it can be acquired. Learning a language later in life can be more difficult

Link

Go to Unit 2: Section C to find more information about supporting children's exploration of common schemas.

Theories that consider children's personality and the development of self-esteem

In Section B, we looked at the theories and models that discuss the development of children's personality and self-esteem. Two theories are influential in early years practice, as Table 1.17 shows.

Table 1.17 How theories that consider the development of children's personality and self-esteem can influence practice within settings

Theory	Description	How the theory could influence practice	How to apply the theory to practice
Erikson's psychosocial theory of personality	Erik Erikson suggests that personality is stage-like and that in the different stages, certain reactions and attitudes of parents and other adults can influence children's personality.	• To create nurturing environments in which children are given opportunities to explore, and given some responsibility • To ensure that adults working with children understand the importance of sensitive working	• Ensure that children have opportunities to try to be independent and to take risks • Do not over-criticise children if they make mistakes, but do have sufficiently high expectations • Provide some unconditional and positive acknowledgement of children for their own sake, e.g. 'I love your smile' • Help parents be aware that unconditional support and love at home is essential and that although they may wish for their child to achieve, over-focusing on this may make the child insecure
Harter's model of self-esteem and the 'looking glass' theory of self-concept	Susan Harter suggests that young children are developing their self-image. A strong self-image is important in the later global evaluation that leads to self-esteem. The 'looking glass' theory suggests that self-image is developed partly in response to the way that adults and other children react to the child.	• To help practitioners develop strong, nurturing relationships with children • To ensure that settings are happy places where adults are positive about children and their families	• Think about how often positive comments are made to children • Show positive body language such as smiling and making eye contact • Avoid talking negatively about children when they are within earshot • Give unconditional praise and acknowledge children's attempts and efforts • Be interested in what children are doing • Challenge unkind remarks made by children to each other • Make sure when talking to children about unwanted behaviour that there is a distinction between disapproving of the behaviour rather than the child

Theories that consider children's moral development

Both Piaget's and Kohlberg's theories of moral development can impact on our practice. Table 1.18 shows you how.

Table 1.18 How theories that consider children's moral development can influence practice within settings

Theory	Description	How the theory could influence practice	How to apply the theory to practice
Kohlberg's and Piaget's stages of moral development	Both Piaget and Kohlberg came to the conclusion that children are essentially amoral. Piaget, however, did recognise that children are influenced by adult reactions.	• To make sure that expectations of children's moral behaviour are age/stage appropriate • To make sure that adults understand that children's early learning about pro-social and moral behaviour is dependent on their reactions	• Recognise that children are likely to follow the examples set by the adult • Make sure that your reactions to incidents and unwanted behaviour are proportional and provide explanations of why it is good to behave in certain ways, e.g. if a child has forgotten something, do not react as if aggressive behaviour has been shown • Expect that although children may be able to tell you the setting's rules, they will not necessarily be able to resist temptation!

Theories that consider children's development in relation to their environment

We discussed Urie Bronfenbrenner's ecological systems theory in Section B. Table 1.19 shows how his theory can be applied to our practice in settings.

Table 1.19 How theories that consider children's development in relation to their environment can influence practice within settings

Theory	Description	How the theory could influence practice	How to apply the theory to practice
Bronfenbrenner's ecological systems theory	This theory suggests that the child's immediate environment, community and wider society can influence their development.	• To understand the importance of working in partnership with parents • To find ways of working closely within and with the local community	• Aim to build strong relationships with parents • Provide plenty of information about what the child is doing within the setting • Talk to parents about their child and what they feel their child's strengths and weaknesses are • Involve parents in the planning for their child and, if appropriate, provide advice about activities they could do at home • Create opportunities for parents to participate within the setting • Look for ways of lending resources and materials to parents • Take an interest in what children enjoy doing at home and with their family and friends • Create links with the local community, e.g. the allotment society, local faith groups and health services • Organise visits to the local community

Theories that consider attachment

John Bowlby's attachment theory has been influential on the key person system that operates in settings today. It has also been useful for improving our practice in other ways. Table 1.20 outlines these ways.

Table 1.20 How theories that consider attachment can influence practice within settings

Theory	Description	How the theory could influence practice	How to apply the theory to practice
Bowlby's attachment theory and Ainsworth's research into the security of attachment	The work of John Bowlby and Mary Ainsworth suggests that children need strong attachments to their parents, but also to the adults who are with them when their parents are not available. This has resulted in the introduction of the key person system to settings.	• To ensure children are not distressed when separation from their parents takes place • To ensure the smooth transition between home and the setting • The provision of a key person system within settings	• Make sure that each child in the setting has a key person and has time to become settled – settling-in procedures must be flexible • Find out about the child's previous experiences of separation, recognising that children who have previously been distressed may take longer to settle in and build a relationship with you • Build a relationship with children before their parents leave them for the first time • Consider the routines of the day and whether there are enough opportunities for key children to spend time with you • Work closely with parents to provide continuity of care and act to reunite the child with their parent if there are signs of separation anxiety • Make sure that you show unconditional care for the child

D Understand how a range of factors influences children's development

There are many different factors that can shape children's development. In this section, we look at these and also at how they might contribute to children's uniqueness.

negatives such as abuse and poverty. Though these can certainly influence a child's development, it is also important to be aware of positive factors, such as having caring parents or good schooling.

Positive and negative factors

Earlier in this unit, we looked at the expected patterns of development for children at different ages but there are many factors that can influence a child's pattern of development. It is important to note that delayed development in one or more areas of development can impact on a child's overall development. Often, when people think about factors affecting a child's development, they focus on

Children are unique

We have seen that children's development often follows a similar pattern but that children are in themselves unique and special. We know that all of our experiences affect the shaping of the brain but that we also seem to have some innate dispositions. A combination of positive and negative factors and experiences is, therefore, likely to provide a good explanation for why each child is so unique even when following typical patterns of development. It also explains why some children in disadvantaged circumstances can still do well, as the effects of positive factors can outweigh the disadvantages of the negative factors.

▍ Prenatal and postnatal factors

There are a number of factors that can influence a child's development before they are born.

Preconceptual care

How healthy parents are before a baby's conception is now recognised as playing a part in a child's later development. Smoking, drugs and also alcohol can all affect the eventual health of a baby.

Lifestyle during pregnancy

It is well known that expectant mothers should take care during pregnancy. This is because the baby's overall health and later development can be affected by the following factors.

Poor diet

Ideally, expectant mothers should eat a balanced diet throughout the pregnancy. In the first 12 weeks, it is important for mothers to take folic acid supplements and eat plenty of green vegetables. This can help to prevent a baby being born with spina bifida.

Smoking

When a pregnant woman smokes, the amount of oxygen available to the unborn baby is reduced. This seems to have significant and possibly long-term effects on the health of children. As with many areas of child development, research is still ongoing, but a clear link between cot death (sudden infant death syndrome) and smoking while pregnant has been established. Babies are also likely to be born preterm and lighter in weight.

> **Did you know?** ❓
>
> The first trimester, or first three months, of a pregnancy is when most of the baby's development takes place. It is also when the baby is most vulnerable.

Alcohol

Over the past few years, women have been advised not to drink while pregnant, especially in the first three months of pregnancy. This is because alcohol can cause a condition known as fetal alcohol syndrome. Babies born with this syndrome are likely to develop learning and behavioural difficulties. Alcohol interferes with the development of healthy brain cells and so affects brain functioning.

Drugs

If you read the packaging of most prescribed and over-the-counter drugs, there will be a warning for pregnant women. This is because the chemicals in drugs can interfere with the healthy development of an unborn baby.

Stress

There is ongoing research looking at the effects of stress on pregnant women and on their children's later development. There is some speculation that high levels of stress during pregnancy may have an impact on children's cognitive and motor development.

Infection

Some infections, such as rubella (German measles), chickenpox and influenza can affect an unborn baby's development and, in some cases, cause a miscarriage.

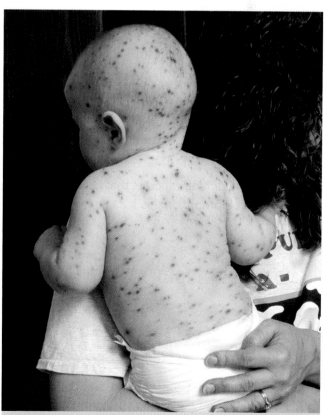

Chickenpox can be more harmful to unborn babies than to young children.

Antenatal checks

Women who are pregnant are advised to attend antenatal checks. As part of an antenatal visit, the baby's development and the mother's health will be checked. This is important because pregnancy can cause problems for women's health, including diabetes and high blood pressure. Antenatal visits are also opportunities for women to gain information, support and advice.

Birth

Children's development can also be influenced by what happens during birth.

Birth itself can be tricky for a few babies. A baby may not breathe straight away or may be injured during the birth. Lack of oxygen (hypoxia) or oxygen starvation (anoxia) can affect brain function and may result in learning difficulties.

Premature or preterm births

Most pregnancies last around 40 weeks, but a few babies are born too early and this can play a part in their later development. A baby that is born before 37 weeks is usually considered to be preterm or premature. Today, with medical advances, babies born at 25 weeks are often able to survive, but early births can cause many complications, as the breathing and other systems within the body are not sufficiently mature. This is one reason for the higher incidence of hearing, sight and learning difficulties in babies born before the final 12 weeks of a pregnancy.

When babies are born preterm, their progress is usually measured according to the date they were due rather than their actual birth date. It can take some babies born preterm several years to reach their 'birth' age norms.

Biological factors

Biological factors come into play once children are born.

Inherited and genetic dispositions

First of all we have to consider genetic disposition. Children will inherit two sets of genes: one from each of their parents. This genetic information will determine many of the physical characteristics of a child and in some cases will be responsible for certain diseases, such as cystic fibrosis. Alongside things that we clearly inherit, research also seems to show that our complex genetic make-up will give us some predispositions that might affect all areas of our development including personality, cognitive abilities, and also illness. This is the point at which nature and nurture come together. A child who has a predisposition towards asthma may only go on to develop it when living in an area where the air quality is poor, or in damp housing. In the same way, it is thought that a child who has a predisposition towards music may only go on to develop a talent fully if given sufficient opportunity to do so.

Sleep

Lack of sleep can create significant problems in children's development. It is thought that most children under 5 years old should be sleeping between 10 and 12 hours per night, with babies sleeping significantly more. Figure 1.10 shows how ongoing insufficient sleep may affect a child.

Diet

We have seen that diet is important during pregnancy, but it is also important during childhood. A diet lacking in sufficient nutrients is likely to affect children's growth and development. Children who are overweight (note that it is possible to be both overweight and malnourished) are more likely to have atypical physical development. Their emotional and social development might also be affected in later childhood.

Disability

Early in this unit we saw that each area of development is codependent on others – for example, a 6-year-old child who is playing skittles is using both cognitive and physical skills. This codependency can mean that a child who has specific difficulties may be disadvantaged in other areas of development. Disadvantage is not inevitable if the child is properly supported, as the case study shows.

Long-term medical conditions

Some long-term medical conditions have the potential to affect children's overall development. There are many reasons for this. First, some illnesses

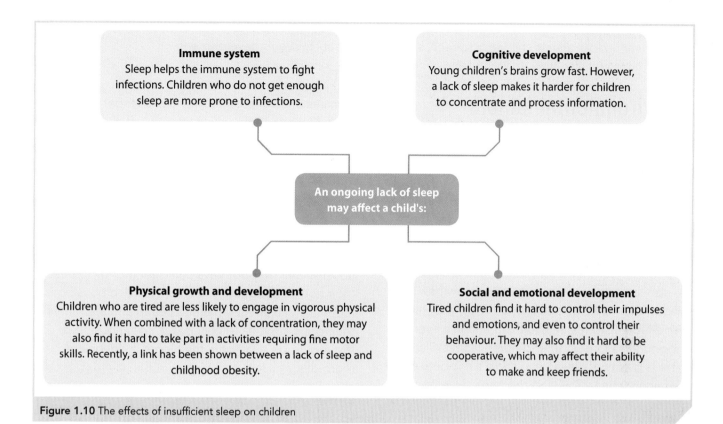

Figure 1.10 The effects of insufficient sleep on children

Case study

Joining in activities

Michael was born without sight. He has just changed school and now attends a primary school where a special needs assistant supports him. In the playground some of the children want to play with a ball. In his last school, he could not join in and so did not have many opportunities to be physically active. In this new school, the playground lines are raised slightly and there are balls that have bells in them. His special needs assistant is also at hand and she encourages him to join in.

1   Why might Michael's social development be affected if he cannot join in with other children's play?

2   Explain how Michael's special needs assistant is making a difference to his overall development.

---

or the drugs that a child takes may reduce the child's energy level or capacity to take in information. Second, some long-term medical conditions require time away from nursery or school settings. This can affect the child's learning. Finally, as with disability, a medical condition that affects a specific developmental area might impact on other areas if practitioners are not sensitive. For example, a child with asthma might not be able to run around and so will miss out on playing with other children.

Short-term illnesses

While children may miss out on play and learning if they have a long-term medical condition, the same can be true of some short-term illnesses. This is particularly true if children have repeated episodes of illness. This may result in several absences, with the same effects that we saw earlier. In addition, medical conditions such as conductive hearing loss or glue ear can also cause problems for children.

Conductive hearing loss

Conductive hearing loss (sometimes known as glue ear) is a common childhood condition, but its effect on development can be significant. Children with conductive hearing loss have a build-up of fluid in their Eustachian tubes. This results in fluctuating and partial hearing loss, with children's hearing being better at some times than at others. This type of hearing loss affects children's speech, social development and also their ability to learn.

Environmental factors

Where children grow up, and in what circumstances they grow up, can affect development both positively and negatively.

Socioeconomic factors

Some children are lucky. They grow up in well-heated and safe homes with parents who have sufficient income to meet their basic needs. Some children are also lucky because their parents know how to support their children's education. They may read their children stories, talk to them and use everyday opportunities to help their children learn skills. There is plenty of research to show a link between socioeconomic factors and children's development. It is thought that growing up in poverty can harm children's life chances.

Poverty

Poverty affects children and their families in a variety of ways. Poverty in the United Kingdom is categorised as relative rather than absolute, i.e. children are not starving, but the effects of growing up in poverty are still very marked in terms of many children's life chances. This plays out in many respects, including children's health outcomes. Health statistics indicate that there is a higher incidence of **infant mortality** as well as a higher rate of **morbidity**. This is the incidence of ill health. In addition, a child growing up in poverty is likely to have a lower life expectancy.

Children growing up in poverty are also statistically likely to perform less well in terms of educational attainment and so may leave school with few qualifications. This in turn can affect their prospects

Key terms

Infant mortality – the rate of death in the first year of life.

Morbidity – the rate of incidence of ill health within a population.

of finding work. Figure 1.11 shows how poverty can affect children's development.

Diet

Families on low incomes may buy cheaper foods, and often foods that are manufactured, which have lower nutritional value. This may be a contributing factor in terms of later life expectancy and also in the rate of morbidity, as poor nutrition is linked to a weaker immune system.

Housing

Families on lower incomes may live in poorer quality housing and may not have sufficient money to heat their homes adequately. Damp, crowded housing is more likely to affect children's health and also limits their opportunities to play freely. Poor housing is thought to be a factor in the higher incidence of morbidity.

Stress

Parents managing on low budgets are more likely to show signs of depression and develop stress-related illnesses. This in turn can affect how much energy they have to parent effectively.

Education

Children from low-income households are less likely to do well academically because they may not attend the best schools or have the same access to educational tools and resources such as books or the Internet. This is considered to be a factor in lower levels of academic attainment and qualifications.

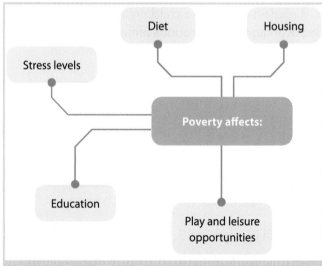

Figure 1.11 How poverty can affect children's development

Play and leisure opportunities

Stimulation is important for children's cognitive development and other areas of their development. Play is one of the ways in which this takes place, but as children become older it also occurs through leisure activities such as swimming, playing an instrument or joining clubs. Low-income families may not have transport or the financial resources to allow their children to access play and leisure opportunities. Lack of opportunities for stimulation is also thought to be a factor in lower attainment in schools.

Research

Find out more about the effects of poverty on children's wellbeing. A good starting point is to read a report written by Frank Field and commissioned by the government in 2010 to provide an independent review on poverty and life chances. The report is called 'The Foundation Years: Preventing poor children becoming poor adults'. You can access it by going to www.pearsonhotlinks.co.uk and searching for this ISBN: 9781447970965.

Factors that may reinforce or counterbalance the effects of poverty

Though the statistics paint a negative picture in terms of outcomes for children living in poverty, there are some factors that might either reinforce or mitigate some of the effects of poverty. This is interesting as it explains why some children from seemingly disadvantaged backgrounds are able to do well and their own outcomes are positive.

Wider family and friends

We saw from Bronfenbrenner's theory that children's interactions with others beyond their immediate family can influence development. This can be both positive and negative. If family and friends have high expectations and, using their contacts, provide children with opportunities for learning and stimulation, some of the effects of poverty may well be counterbalanced. If, on the other hand, there is little support for the child, there is a likelihood that the effects of poverty may be compounded.

Carers and teachers/tutors

Carers and teachers/tutors can have a significant impact on children's self-belief, both positively and negatively. If carers, including early years professionals, and teachers/tutors have low expectations of children, they are less likely to provide them with stimulation and opportunities to learn. On the other hand, carers, practitioners and teachers/tutors who have high expectations of children, regardless of their family background, are more likely to support children's achievement.

'Pygmalion in the classroom'

The effects of raising expectations were studied by researchers Robert Rosenthal and Lenore Jacobson in the 1960s in an experiment that was later dubbed 'Pygmalion in the classroom'. The researchers randomly picked some children's names from a class register at the start of the academic year, but told the class teacher that these children had been identified as having potential and this would show itself during the year. At the end of the school year, those children whose names had been given to the teacher had indeed made significant improvements.

Wider society

Societies that are materialistic and in which the differences between rich and poor are significant may reinforce the negative effects of poverty. Where this is the case, there are likely to be negative and even prejudiced attitudes towards those who are not wealthy. This in turn can affect services for families as well as individuals' sense of self-worth. On the other hand, in societies that are more egalitarian and where there is more social mobility, a child living in relative poverty is less likely to be disadvantaged.

Research

Find out how the UK compares to other countries in terms of social mobility by visiting the website for the Organisation for Economic Co-operation and Development (OECD). You can download a useful article from the website by going to www.pearsonhotlinks.co.uk and searching for this ISBN: 9781447970965.

How the family experience of education can affect the child's development

There is some statistical evidence that the level of parental education can have a determining effect on children's educational attainment. This was reaffirmed by the Effective Provision of Pre-School Education (EPPE) project. The EPPE project, which began in 2003 and tracked a group of children from the age of 3, suggests that the level of education of a child's mother influences academic outcomes. This is interesting and research is ongoing to explain why this should have such an effect. There is some thinking that a more educated mother may interact more with her child and may also engage in activities such as reading.

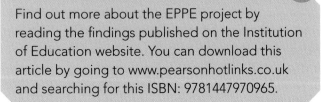

Research

Find out more about the EPPE project by reading the findings published on the Institution of Education website. You can download this article by going to www.pearsonhotlinks.co.uk and searching for this ISBN: 9781447970965.

On the other hand, it may be that if parental levels of qualification are high, this gives them access to higher-paid employment. This in turn may allow for better housing and choice of schools. Interestingly, there is a link yet again to poverty and social mobility, as education is claimed by some researchers to be the key to improving outcomes for children.

In addition, a family's experience of education and its benefits may also affect the parents' attitudes and interest in their own child's education. Parents who have had positive experiences of education and correlate this with their employment prospects are more likely to value it and thus become involved. On the other hand, parents whose own experience of education has not been positive or feel that they have not derived any direct benefit are less likely to be actively involved in their child's education, and this can lead to underachievement.

Social/political factors

There are a number of social and political factors that are sometimes used to explain differences in children's development.

Social class

Defining 'social class' is increasingly difficult. It is related to levels of education, employment status and also levels of income. As we have seen, children from more affluent backgrounds or those whose own parents have higher levels of education are statistically more likely to have positive outcomes in terms of child development.

National policies, strategies and services

It may seem a long way removed for individual children and families, but policies made by governments can have an effect on children. A good example of this would be the policy to ensure that nursery education was made available for all children aged 3 years. This was not a local policy, but a national one. From this policy, strategies were put in place to ensure that services could be delivered. In England, the strategy also included having a mandatory national early years curriculum, which is known as the EYFS. In terms of the individual child, this national policy meant that children were able to access nursery education. Similarly, a government may have a policy to improve the health of children under 5 years, which may result in a strategy to improve vaccination rates. In turn, this could mean that money will be allocated locally so that vaccinations can be delivered by local services.

The numbered list below shows the relationship between national policy, strategies and services.

1 Government elected on the basis of its manifesto

The manifesto is an outline of the policies that, if elected, the government would implement.

2 Policies

Policies that are often a reflection of the manifesto are put into action by the relevant government department, for example the Department of Health or the Department for Education. To do this they create strategies.

3 Strategies

Strategies are developed so that services can be organised or existing services can be amended to reflect the new priorities.

4 Services

These are the 'face' of the policies. Though the types of services available will be determined nationally, they will often be run locally.

Local policy, strategies and services

We have seen that children and families will be influenced by what happens at the national level, but there will also be impacts at the local level. Though the general picture is set nationally, services are usually run locally. A good example of this would be children's centres. Where children's centres are placed and what services they offer depends on local policy. This in turn means that different areas adopt different strategies based on what they think would be best for the communities they serve. This means that in some areas, children's centres have drop-in baby clinics and offer day care, but others do not. This might mean that two children living just a few miles from each other, each having the same level of speech delay, can have quite different experiences. In one area, there may be drop-in clinics, as this has been prioritised, but in another area, the priority might be the provision of play parks and so there may be a long waiting list to see a speech and language therapist. Such differences in local policies can therefore result in different outcomes.

Cultural factors

The culture in which children grow up can have an effect on their development in a variety of ways. These ways include the value that is put on education and also attitudes towards gender.

Value put on education

When children are growing up in a community where education is valued, this might mean that the school is well supported by parents and that children are encouraged to do well. On the other hand, if parents and the immediate community do not value education, there is a likelihood of less parental engagement. Levels of parental engagement with education seem to play an important role as, for example, a child whose parent hears them read the school book that has been brought home is likely to have a higher level of attainment than one whose parent doesn't hear them read. The value placed on education by the local community can also affect older children, so that if their peer group does not value doing well in school, individual children who wish to succeed may find it hard to 'be different'.

Gender expectations

In some communities, children's gender can play a part in their development. If children are in communities where boys are valued highly, girls may not do as well, as they may not be given the same levels of attention and encouragement. There are also some persistent attitudes about which subjects are suitable for boys or for girls. This can make it hard for individual children to excel or even take up subjects that do not conform to gender stereotypes. In practice, this means that some boys who could do well in languages or girls who could well in science may not fulfil their potential.

How education affects children's development

Children's development is affected by education. This is one reason why it has been government policy over a number of years to provide some free hours of early education for young children. It has been demonstrated by projects such as Highscope in America, but also the EPPE research (see earlier in this section) that outcomes for children who have access to high-quality provision can be strengthened.

How education supports children's development

By having structured, carefully thought through activities and adult interactions, each area of a child's development can be structured. This is because those providing opportunities are able to recognise what stage of development a child has reached and what types of opportunities and activities would benefit the child further.

Physical development

While parents can support children's physical development at home, educational opportunities might present the child with a wider range of equipment and resources structured to meet their developmental needs as well as interests.

Cognitive, language and intellectual development

Many parents are able to talk to their children and provide activities that stimulate reasoning and problem solving, but some parents find this easier than others for a variety of reasons, not least time. Professional environments can be set up so that the adult focus is on interaction and on providing a range of resources and activities that develop concepts such as number, shape and interest in early science. This additional stimulation can support children's cognitive development, speech and literacy as well as helping children to gain mathematical and early scientific concepts.

Emotional and social development

High-quality provision that has a strong key person system can support children's emotional and social development. In these settings children learn the skills of socialisation, turn taking and sharing. They also learn self-care skills and, providing that they have strong relationships with their key person, can develop a sense of independence and thus confidence.

▌ Emotional factors

What is happening or has happened to a child's family can make a difference to a child's development. First of all, as we have seen earlier, children benefit enormously from strong attachments to their parents. Strong attachments seem to support children's language and also their cognitive development. Children also benefit from attachments to other family members such as siblings and relatives. This underlies the idea of a secure family for a child.

Unfortunately, many children will experience family stress during childhood and this can affect their development.

Divorce and separation

Children with divorced parents or those of lone parents seem to fare less well academically at first sight, but a closer inspection reveals a more complex picture. First, divorce may result in a lone parent having a lower income. As we have seen earlier, poverty seems to make a significant difference to development. In addition, it would seem that it is the way that parents separate and/or divorce that matters. Children whose parents stay on reasonable terms and find ways to ensure that contact is maintained are likely to fare better.

Parental depression

Any type of depression is likely to have an adverse effect on children. Parents who are depressed find it hard to give their children attention in ways that reinforce the attachment. Postnatal depression, for example, is of particular concern because it can hinder the establishment of attachment, which is why midwives and health visitors try to be vigilant in looking for its signs in new mothers. Figure 1.12 shows events that can be linked to depression.

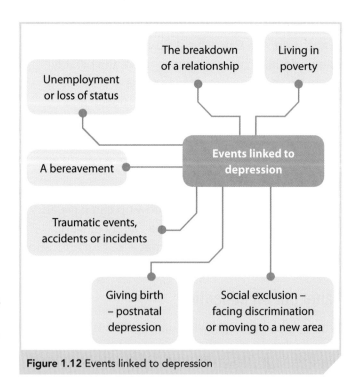

Figure 1.12 Events linked to depression

Addiction

Drug and alcohol abuse can significantly affect parenting ability. This is why parents who are addicted to either drugs or alcohol are likely to be supported by a social worker.

Sibling rivalry

It would seem that conflict between siblings may have a negative effect on children's self-esteem. Contrary to popular opinion, it may be better to be an only child than to live in a family in which there is significant sibling rivalry.

Stresses on children

There are some stresses that can affect children's short- and long-term development, as we will now see.

Separations and transitions

We have seen that secure attachments play an important role in children's development. So what happens when children attend nursery, go to a childminder or have a change in au pair or nanny? The answer depends very much on whether children are settled in a setting, and on how transitions are managed when there are changes. Figure 1.13 shows some examples of separations and transitions.

Link

Go to Unit 7: Section B to find more information about managing transitions.

Abuse

It is a sad fact that some children are subject to abuse. Abuse in all its forms affects children's emotional and social development. It can affect their self-worth into adulthood.

Link

Go to Unit 8: Section B to find more information about different types of abuse.

Bullying

Bullying has been a hot topic for some time now. It is well known that long-term bullying can affect children's development; particularly their emotional and social development. In terms of very young children, it is important to realise that true bullying is quite rare. Having said this, toddlers can find themselves being dominated or physically targeted by other toddlers and this can temporarily affect their social development unless adults respond sensitively.

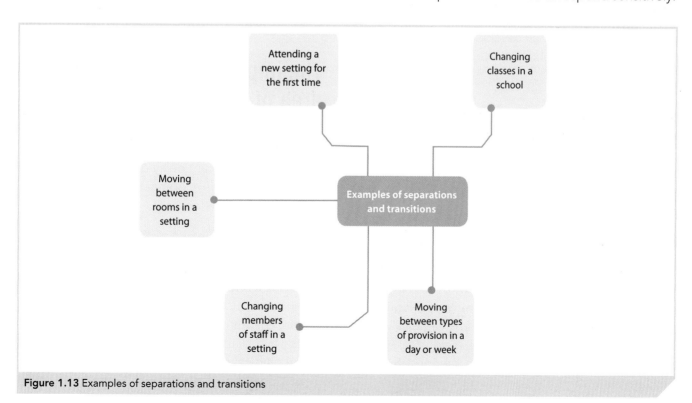

Figure 1.13 Examples of separations and transitions

E | Understand the importance of recognising atypical development

In Section A, we looked at the usual patterns of development associated with different ages of children, but it is also worth noting that some children's development shows very different patterns and rates of progress. In some cases, these children will need additional support. This section looks at the importance of recognising atypical development.

What is atypical development?

While no two children of the same age will show exactly the same rate of development, the term 'atypical development' is used to refer to children whose patterns and rates of normative development are unusual and are significantly different from those expected within their age range.

Delayed global development

There are some children whose rate of progress across all areas of development is significantly lower than that associated with normative development for their age range. The term often used to describe this type of atypical development is 'delayed global development'. Thus if a child aged 4 years has the overall development profile of a 2 year old, their development may be described as being 'globally delayed'.

Specific delay

Some children may have delay across several areas, but it is more common to find that children have a specific delay within an area of development. A good example of this would be a child who cannot pronounce certain speech sounds, but who is otherwise communicating and understanding well.

Gifted

It is important not to assume that all atypical development is related to children who may have a delay or specific need. Some children's development is atypical because their development, especially in relation to cognition and language, is significantly advanced and thus very different to the normative development within their age range. Over the past few years, there has been some debate about defining 'gifted', especially in view of a recent government initiative that encouraged schools to identify the highest 10 per cent within a cohort. Many organisations that support gifted children and their families argue that this is an inflated number.

Research

Find out more about giftedness by visiting the websites for the National Association for Gifted Children, the National Association for Able Children in Education and Potential Plus UK. You can access these websites by going to www.pearsonhotlinks.co.uk and searching for this ISBN: 9781447970965.

Talented

Some atypical development may relate to a specific skill that a child has acquired within or across an area of development. The term often used is 'talented'. For example, if a 3-year-old child can play tennis, his or her development in relation to this skill could be described as 'talented'.

The impact of delay in one area of development

A key reason in favour of early recognition of atypical development is that areas of development are interrelated. A significant delay or unrecognised need in one area of development is likely to impact on other areas of development.

The potential impact of a delay within social development

Children who have a delay within their social development may not be able to socialise and play with other children. As young children's play often requires physical movement, there can be a knock-on effect on physical development as the child may not be practising physical movements. Children whose social skills are limited may also not seek or respond to opportunities for interaction both with adults and other children and may, therefore, be excluded from play or bullied. This can have an impact on their acquisition of communication skills, their self-esteem and the development of speech and language. In addition, children who are not developing social skills and engaging in play may also find it hard to meet the behaviour expectations within settings.

The potential impact of a delay within cognitive development

Children's cognition and speech is closely linked. This means that some children who have a delay with cognition may struggle to cope with the abstract use of language and so may only understand what is said when there are visual cues and props. Cognition is also an element in learning to read and write, as print is an abstract concept. Shapes of letters correlate with sounds and so a child who has difficulty in processing in the abstract is more likely to have difficulty in understanding the link. In addition, children with cognition difficulties may not play in the same way as their peers and this can affect their social development. It can lead to feelings of low self-esteem and may impact on their behaviour if they are excluded from play.

The potential impact of a delay within language development

Being able to talk and communicate is essential for children to express their feelings and also respond appropriately to those of others. Some children with a delay in their language development may find that it has a knock-on effect on their emotional and social development, as they will experience fewer opportunities to interact and play with other children. In addition, children's behaviour can be affected by language delay as they may become frustrated by being unable to join in other children's play or upset as they are not being understood.

Language is closely associated with cognition as words are a tool for information processing. Children with lower levels of language development are thus likely to find it harder to talk about what has happened and also to use language to organise and express their thoughts.

The potential impact of a delay within emotional development

Emotional development includes the skills of being able to recognise feelings in others and create relationships with them. Children who show atypical development in this respect may miss out on opportunities to play with other children and develop a whole range of social and physical skills as a result. Children's emotional development is also linked to their ability to manage their behaviour appropriately. This in turn may mean that other children are less likely to want to interact with them. In addition, emotional development is linked to concentration and attitudes towards learning. Children who are emotionally secure, confident and happy will find it easier to concentrate and thus learn.

The potential impact of a delay within physical development

Children who have a delay in physical development may find it hard to explore new materials and their environment. This may mean that they have fewer opportunities for interaction with adults and other children as they may not talk about what they are doing and seeing. This can impact on speech and cognitive development. In addition, most play has an element of physical movement. Depending on the type of delay, children may have restricted opportunities to join others in play and this may result in social isolation and bullying. Children may also become aware of their limitations in respect of self-care and mobility and this in turn can impact on their behaviour, self-esteem and self-concept.

Children who show atypical advanced development in cognition and language

Genuinely gifted young children may need additional support because their advanced cognition and linguistic development makes it harder for them to form relationships with their peers. They may not be able to sustain interest in the play of their peers. As a result of increased cognition, some children are also self-aware and so are able to realise that they are in some way 'different' to other children of a similar age. This can result in a lowered self-esteem. In addition, some children may show unwanted behaviours as a result of a lack of stimulation or frustration.

CORNWALL COLLEG
LEARNING CENTRE

The impact on children's outcomes where atypical development is not recognised

We have seen how development that is in some way atypical may have a knock-on effect in other areas of a child's development. This may result in a child not being able to access all areas of learning at the level of need. A major implication of unrecognised delay that is reported by children and their families is the effect on their self-esteem. This may be because of bullying, their recognition of being 'different' and their difficulties in making strong and equal friendships with other children. In addition, for children with communication and language and/or cognition difficulties, there is a likely impact on their literacy.

Reasons for early recognition of atypical development

In order to meet children's needs, it is important that we recognise them first of all. Children whose development is atypical are likely to need additional support or resources. In some cases, early recognition followed by professional support can lessen the impact of any delay or disability. Early recognition will also help adults and parents to respond in ways that support the child. This is particularly important where atypical development creates unwanted behaviours either through frustration or, in the case of gifted children, boredom. In addition, early recognition can sometimes lead to the diagnosis of medical conditions, which if left unchecked could further impact on a child's development.

The importance of involving parents

Working in partnership with parents is essential. It is not uncommon for parents to be the first to notice that their child's development in one or more aspects is unusual. Some parents report that their comments and thoughts were not properly listened to and acted on. In other cases, it might be the adults working with children who pick up some aspects of atypical development. In these cases, it is essential that concerns are shared with parents at the earliest opportunity. (It is worth noting at this point that adults working in settings do not have the right to refer children to specialists without the consent of parents, except where abuse is suspected.) It is good practice for adults working with children to create systems whereby parents and settings can share observations and comments as well as family history.

Link

Go to Unit 5: Section A2 to find information about working in partnership with parents.

Building a picture of development

Observing and assessing children's development is fundamental in recognising atypical development and ensuring the right support and services are provided. To recognise atypical development, it is usual to build up a picture of the child's overall development. The idea is to avoid jumping to conclusions based on a few minutes spent with a child. By observing the child over time and also gaining information from parents, a more accurate picture can be gained. This can be added to by seeking the advice and expertise of outside agencies. This might include health visitors, speech and language teams and SEN teams.

Further reading and resources

Athey, C. (2007) *Extending Thought in Young Children: A Parent–Teacher Partnership* (2nd ed.), London: Sage Publications.

Donaldson, M. (1986) *Children's Minds*, London: HarperCollins.

Gerhardt, S. (2004) *Why Love Matters: How Affection Shapes a Baby's Brain*, Oxford: Routledge.

Lindon, J. (2010) *Understanding Child Development: Linking Theory and Practice* (2nd ed.), London: Hodder Education.

Lindon, J. (2012) *What Does It Mean To Be Two?* (3rd ed.), London: Practical Pre-School Books.

Thornton, S. (2008) *Understanding Human Development: Biological, Social and Psychological Processes from Conception to Adult Life*, Basingstoke: Palgrave Macmillan.

Ready for work?

Debra Collinson   Nursery manager

I have been the manager of Little Angels nursery for six years and I cannot emphasise strongly enough how important it is to have a good knowledge of child development when working with children. A lot of parents want to know what normal behaviour is and whether their child is doing well. Being able to reassure parents, especially when it comes to the behaviour of their 2 year old, is very important.

An understanding of child development also helps us plan. We do everything to make sure that children make good progress and, for that to happen, we have to know what the next steps are for each child. As well as knowing about the stages of child development, knowledge of child development theories can be very useful. Understanding that children learn from copying, for example, means that staff often sit and do an activity, knowing that children will come over, watch them and then join in.

When it comes to managing behaviour, knowing about why children are likely to keep on doing things allows us to manage the situation effectively. We often deliberately do not react to a child's behaviour so that they learn not to do things just to get attention.

Having a good knowledge of child development also helps us to work out when children may not be making the type of progress that we would expect for their age. Sometimes, there are short-term factors that explain this, such as a change in the family, but at other times, we work with parents and may suggest a referral. The good news is that, in this area, children who need some additional help are well supported, and early intervention seems to make quite a lot of difference.

Skills for practice

Sustained shared conversations

One of the ways that practitioners can affect children's cognitive and language development is by talking to them and interacting with them. This is quite a skill, but one that a theorist such as Vygotsky suggested would be key to a child's development. It takes a while to learn how to talk to children in ways that enable you to have a shared conversation. Here are some tips.

- Look carefully at what a child is doing.
- What seems to be of interest to them?
- Go down to the child's level and spend some time doing the activity they are engaged in.
- Allow a little time to pass and then make a statement about the activity, for example 'The spider is very busy.'
- Be aware of the child's reaction and allow enough time for a response.
- If the child makes a response, follow their conversational direction.
- If appropriate, ask for their thoughts about what is happening, e.g. 'Do you think the spider gets tired?'

Assessment Zone

How you will be assessed

This unit is externally assessed in the form of a test. This will provide employers, universities, other professionals and parents with reassurance that you have been taught about child development, and have a good knowledge of it.

The format of the test

You will be given a case study based on children in an early years setting. You have to think about and use the information in the case study when answering a series of questions. Questions will cover all the knowledge requirements of the unit, including:

- the principles of growth and development for children aged from birth up to 8 years, and how they apply to the five developmental areas – physical, cognitive, language, social and emotional
- theories and models of child development, and how they apply to your work in supporting children's development
- factors affecting a child's development, the reasons why development may follow an atypical pattern, and recognising when development is atypical.

There are two test dates every year and your teacher or tutor will decide when to enter you for the test. It is possible to resit the exam. You are allowed 1 hour and 45 minutes to complete the test and this includes the time it will take you to read the case study. If you have any special needs you will need to talk to your teachers/tutors in advance of the test date so that they can make special arrangements for you.

Revising for the exam

You will need to have a good knowledge of children's normative development in each of the five developmental areas. This often requires repeated practice and revision.

By the test date you should be able to recall what children at each age/stage of development should be able to do.

In order to help you revise, you could set true or false quizzes for yourself and your peers or play games where someone describes what a child is doing and you have to say what age the child is.

You also need to be able to identify when a child is portraying atypical behaviour. This might be a 3-year-old child who is not able to talk at all, or even a 3-year-old child who is able to read a book fluently.

Some of the questions test whether you can apply the information given in the case study to theories of and approaches towards development.

The specification that you may be given, or that you can download from the Edexcel website, lists theorists and models of child development that you may be tested on. It is important that you familiarise yourself with the specification well before the test, and make sure that you revise all aspects of it.

To help you revise theories of development:

- make a series of cards that give you some brief information about the main points of each theory and how they relate to what children do. Then, test your peers on the name of a theorist and the main points of their theory
- look at what children are doing while you are on placement. Think about their actions and how these actions relate to a theorist.

In the test you will need to read the case study carefully and think about what may have affected the children's development. Remember that factors can either have a positive or negative effect on children's development.

Think about the children in your setting. What positive factors are influencing their development? In what way is their development being negatively affected?

Assessment tips

Every learner has their own way of coping with tests. You will need to find out what works for you. The best way of doing this is to do plenty of sample test papers first. Some learners like to go through each question, answering them as they go. Other learners prefer to read through all of the questions and then begin by answering questions that they know the answers to and that can attract high marks.

Key to this test will be your ability to read the case study and the questions carefully. You will be able to write notes on the case study and some learners find this a helpful way of making sure that they do not miss out anything in their answers.

Look for opportunities for doing case study-type activities – there are some in this unit.

Assessment practice

Below is a sample case study. When you have read this unit, you may like to have a go at answering the questions that follow the case study. Although the case study is much shorter than what you may be given in the test, it will help you to get a feel for this type of task.

Case study

Settling into nursery

Kyle is 3 years old. He came to our nursery when he was just 2 years old. He found it very difficult to separate from his mother but we have a strong key person system and he soon made a good attachment with his key person. He mostly prefers to play alone or with his key person and does not seem to be interested in role play. He enjoys being outdoors and is currently very interested in things that turn around or spin. Last week, his key person spotted that he was enjoying going round and round on a tricycle and manoeuvring it skilfully. Kyle is beginning to talk and communicates mainly through a combination of signs and single words. Tests have shown that he has a conductive hearing loss.

1 Describe how one aspect of Kyle's physical development meets the expected pattern of development.

*Tip: Always look at the 'descriptor' verb in a question (e.g. 'describe' or 'explain'). This question asks you to **describe** one aspect of Kyle's physical development. Just writing a couple of words is not likely to get you full marks as you have to say what Kyle is doing and how this relates to the usual pattern of development. Ask your teacher/tutor for more information about these 'descriptor' verbs so that you can familiarise yourself with them before the test.*

2 Explain how Athey's theory can be applied to Kyle's play.

Tip: To answer this kind of question, you will need to know your theorists well. Begin by working out how Kyle's behaviours or actions link to a theory you have studied. Then, tie these behaviours in with the theory. Do not just write everything you know about the theorist as this will waste words and time.

3 Describe **one** factor in the scenario that may have affected Kyle's development.

Tip: This question is asking you to write about one factor and how it might have affected Kyle's development. Do not write about more than one factor as you will waste time. You should, however, read the question carefully and make sure that you give the number of examples the question is asking for. Hint: in this case study there is one factor that is likely to be affecting two areas of Kyle's development.

Introduction

Play is a major part of childhood. Children can be seen playing all over the world – either in groups, by themselves or alongside adults. In this unit we will look at the benefits for children as they play, different approaches to organising play and the role of the adult in play. The knowledge that you gain in this unit will support your work while you are on placement.

Assessment: You will be assessed by a series of assignments set by your teacher/tutor.

Learning aims

In this unit you will:

A   understand the links between play and children's development

B   understand how a range of play activities and opportunities can support children's learning and development

C   understand how theoretical and philosophical approaches to play and learning influence current practice in early years settings

D   understand early years professionals' involvement in children's purposeful play opportunities, activities and learning.

I love watching babies playing with objects in the treasure basket. They are often fascinated by the simplest things that as adults we take for granted.

Harriet, *a student on placement in a baby room*

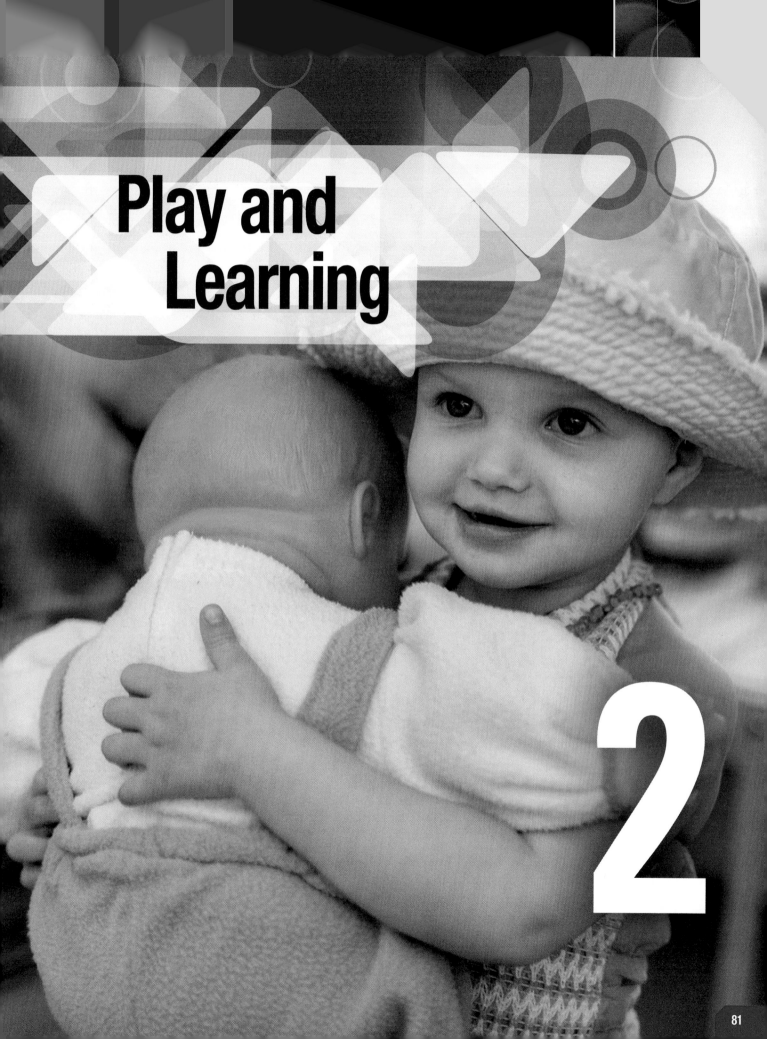

Play and Learning

2

⁘BTEC
Assessment Zone

This table shows what you must do in order to achieve a **Pass**, **Merit** or **Distinction** grade, and lists activities that relate to each learning aim.

Assessment criteria

Pass	Merit	Distinction
Learning aim A: Understand the links between play and children's development		
3A.P1 English Explain how play supports the physical, cognitive, language, social and emotional development of young children. **Assessment practice 2.1** **Assessment practice 2.2** **3A.P2** I&CT Explain how children play at different stages of development. **Assessment practice 2.3**	**3A.M1** Discuss the role of play in supporting the physical, cognitive, language, social and emotional development of a child at different stages. **Assessment practice 2.2** **Assessment practice 2.3**	
Learning aim B: Understand how a range of play activities and opportunities can support children's learning and development		
3B.P3 Explain how types of play support the learning and development of young children to include: • physical play • imaginative play • sensory play • creative play • construction play. **Assessment practice 2.2** **3B.P4** Explain how resources can best support different types of play and learning activities and opportunities in early years settings. **Assessment practice 2.2**	**3B.M2** Analyse how selected types of play and learning activities and resources meet the needs of a child and support the child's holistic development. **Assessment practice 2.3**	**3B.D1** Evaluate the extent to which different examples of play and selected resources support the holistic development of children from birth up to 2 years and children from 2 up to (but not including) 8 years. **Assessment practice 2.3**
Learning aim C: Understand how theoretical and philosophical approaches to play and learning influence current practice in early years settings		
3C.P5 Describe how theoretical, philosophical and other approaches to play and learning influence provision in early years settings. **Assessment practice 2.4**	**3C.M3** Analyse the extent to which an early years curriculum/framework has been influenced by theoretical, philosophical or other approaches to play. **Assessment practice 2.4**	**3C.D2** Evaluate the success of the application of a theoretical, philosophical or other approach to play in an early years setting. **Assessment practice 2.5**

continued

Assessment criteria (*continued*)		
Pass	Merit	Distinction
Learning aim D: Understand early years professionals' involvement in children's purposeful play opportunities, activities and learning		
3D.P6 Explain the benefits to babies' and children's development of adult involvement in play and learning activities. **Assessment practice 2.6** **3D.P7** Explain how early years professionals can effectively support learning and development: • in child-initiated play with individual children • in adult-initiated and directed activities with groups of children. **Assessment practice 2.6**	**3D.M4** Analyse the skills that are required by early years professionals to effectively support children's learning and development in play and learning activities, with examples. **Assessment practice 2.6**	**3D.D3** Evaluate how skilled early years professionals in early years settings can contribute to effective child-initiated play and adult-led play and learning activities. **Assessment practice 2.7**

English   English Functional Skills signposting

I&CT   Information and Communication Technology Functional Skills signposting

How you will be assessed

This unit will be assessed by a series of internally assessed tasks set by your teacher/tutor. They will include practical tasks that will need to be carried out in placement, and that link to your Practical Evidence Portfolio*. Throughout this unit you will find assessment practice activities that will help you work towards your assessment. Completing these activities will not mean that you have achieved a particular grade, but you will have carried out useful research or preparation that will be relevant when it comes to your final assignment.

In order for you to achieve the tasks in your assignment, it is important to check that you have met all the Pass grading criteria. You can do this as you work your way through the assignment.

If you are hoping to gain a Merit or Distinction, you should also make sure that you present the information in your assignment in the style that is required by the relevant assessment criterion. For example, Merit and Distinction criteria will require you to analyse and evaluate.

The assignment set by your teacher/tutor will consist of a number of tasks designed to meet the criteria in the table. This is likely to consist of a written assignment but may also include activities such as the following:

• producing a transcript for a presentation

• providing evidence of information gained through further reading, examples from practice or discussion with relevant professionals working in the sector

• using evidence from case studies or observations to support your recommendations

• creating a leaflet for parents and carers.

* For students taking the Subsidiary Award, there is no requirement for any assessment in the workplace.

A Understand the links between play and children's development

The importance of play

Play can form a significant part of children's overall development. It naturally prompts children to practise and develop skills and knowledge. This is why in recent years it has become the foundation of all the early years curricula in the UK.

The United Nations Convention on the Rights of the Child states that all children have the right to be able to relax and play, and to join in a wide range of cultural, artistic and recreational activities. There is also general agreement that children need opportunities within their play and times when adults (including early years professionals) support them. Though play can support children's development, it is important to note that children tend to benefit more fully when there is a range of different resources and also when there is a good balance between **adult-directed play** and **child-initiated play**.

Key to providing and monitoring play is making it pleasurable. The pleasure that children get from play means that they are likely to repeat movements and activities and so gain knowledge and competence. Children are also more likely to learn if their play is **purposeful**.

How play can support children's physical development

One of the challenges that babies and young children face is to be able to control their movements. This is linked partly to the process of maturation but also to practice. As well as physical control of the body, children also need to develop strength and stamina. From early on, play provides the motivation for this to take place effortlessly. Babies, for example, will try to move cot toys or grab a rattle, while toddlers will push a brick trolley around a room.

Table 2.1 gives examples of how common toys and play activities support physical development.

Table 2.1 How play activities support physical development

Toy or activity	What physical development it supports
Treasure basket play	• Fine motor skills, as objects are handled • Hand–eye coordination, as objects are taken to the mouth for exploring • Gross motor movements, as whole-arm movements are needed to reach out and select an object
Swing	• Balance, as the child has to maintain an upright position • Fine motor movements, as the child grabs the sides
Wheeled toys such as sit-and-ride items or tricycles	• Gross motor movements, as legs are strengthened • Spatial awareness and general coordination, to avoid obstacles • Stamina, as children keep moving
Water and sand play	• Fine motor skills, as children scoop, pour and use their hands to play • Hand–eye coordination, as children scoop and pour, splash and dig • Muscle tone, as children are standing

Link

Go to Unit 3: Section B to find more information about treasure basket play and other activities to support physical development.

Key terms

Adult-directed play – when adults take a role in planning, organising and leading play.

Child-initiated play – when children choose what to play with and how to play.

Purposeful play – play that allows children to concentrate and also may permit the learning or practice of new skills or concepts.

Sustained shared thinking – sensitive interactions between adults and children over a period of time that support children to develop their thoughts about a topic or concept.

Treasure basket play – a collection of natural materials and objects put in a basket to support babies' play.

Although children can gain a lot of knowledge from play, adults have an important role while children are playing. They may point out to a child that their favourite train is blue, and in this way the child learns about colour. As well as learning about specific concepts such as colour and shape, children will gain other skills such as concentration and memory skills. In addition, through play – especially when an adult is involved – children may have the opportunity to develop their thoughts about a skill or concept further. This is sometimes known as **sustained shared thinking** and is important because, through interactions with adults, children are able to explore a concept or skill in more depth. An example of this would be when an adult helps children to build a den and together they talk through the types of materials they could use and the advantages of each material. During the play, with the adult's support, the children would keep thinking about how best to construct the den. This type of adult interaction helps children to progress their thinking as well as their language. For sustained shared thinking to work well, adults have to spend sufficient time with children, hence the term 'sustained'.

Table 2.2 gives examples of how common toys and play activities support cognitive development.

How play can support children's cognitive development

Play gives children first-hand experiences of touching and doing things and so supports their understanding of the world through a process that is often referred to as 'active learning'. A baby, for example, learns that a spoon falls, and a 4-year-old child learns that a torch may have batteries.

How play can help children's communication and language development

Play is a great vehicle for children to learn to communicate and also to use language. Children are able to hear the structure of language as they play with each other and also with adults.

Table 2.2 How play activities support cognitive development

Toy or activity	What cognitive development it supports
Shape sorter	Shape recognition, although an adult or older child will need to name the shapes so that a child can acquire the language
Jigsaw puzzle	Problem solving, through sorting pieces
Water play	Learning about volume, although an adult will have to give children the language of 'full' or 'empty'
Games such as snap, noughts and crosses or picture lotto	Matching, sorting and recognising numbers as well as developing strategies for winning

They can also join in conversations, especially during role play where dialogue between children is a key way of interacting. Interestingly, children also use language to organise their play and so it is not uncommon to hear 2-year-old children talk to themselves as they play. Children cannot learn language without having interaction with adults or older children, and play provides opportunities for this to happen. An adult may play Humpty Dumpty with a baby and the baby will learn to recognise new vocabulary (key words) such as 'fall down'. The interaction during play also stimulates the baby so that later on the baby is likely to babble and vocalise more.

Rich play opportunities give children a reason for learning words and so extending their vocabulary – a new item in the home corner is likely to prompt a 'what's that?' question from a child. Once children are starting to talk, they tend to vocalise as they are playing. A 2-year-old child playing alone is likely to be talking and older children tend to talk to each other. Table 2.3 lists some examples of how certain activities support children's language development.

Table 2.3 How play activities support language development

Toy or activity	What language development it supports
Toy telephone	Babies and toddlers talking aloud
Home corner and **small-world play**	Children talking to each other and aloud
'I spy' and other language games	Older children thinking about sounds in words

How play can support children's social development

Most children begin to play in their first year of life when an adult is with them. The early skills of play begin as babies learn to respond positively and to take turns; for example, when an adult plays peek-a-boo or roll-a-ball games. It is interesting that from quite early on, babies will prompt an adult to play with them. They may pull a hat over the face as a signal that they want to play peek-a-boo or crawl with a ball that they put in the adult's lap. These early experiences of play help children's social development and pave the way for playing with other

Key terms

Attachment – a special relationship or bond between a child and someone who is emotionally involved with them.

Key person – a practitioner designated to take responsibility for a child's emotional wellbeing by having a strong attachment with them and a good relationship with their parents.

Small-world play – play with toys such as sets of farm animals, trains, cars and play people.

children. By the time most children are 3 years old, they want to play with other children and so will learn to share, take turns, respond to others' reactions and negotiate.

Adults can also support older children to learn skills such as playing fairly and playing games with rules by introducing games such as snap or physical games such as hide and seek. Once children have learned these games and the social skills, they can then go on to use them independently.

How play can support emotional development

Play is a pleasurable experience for children and so it has immediate effects on their sense of wellbeing. It also supports other aspects of their emotional development. First, play is important in helping to form **attachments**. When adults and babies play together, they are likely to be spending time together that is pleasurable and intense for both of them. This helps create, but also sustain, bonds. This is one reason why encouraging parents to play with their children is so important. It also is a reason why early years professionals should play with children in their settings: especially during settling-in periods, so as to support children's transitions when they need to develop bonds with their **key person**.

Through play, children also learn that we are all different. They may learn this by seeing other children choosing to play with resources that are different to the ones they normally choose to play with. For example, a child may see children playing with items in the home corner that they would not normally play with. This would help the child to understand that people use different objects to cook with than the ones used in their own home. Learning that other people are different is a significant step for children and one that is important as they learn to respect others.

Play to help children who have experienced trauma

In addition to play being used in early years settings, it is also used in therapy to help children who have experienced trauma. Play therapists will often set up play opportunities that will help children express what has happened to them, for example in cases of abuse. As well as using play to understand what has happened, it also enables children to express their anger and fear as part of the therapeutic process.

Play also helps children to understand their role and that of others in the world. This often comes through role-play opportunities. A young child will often imitate what they have experienced and put themselves into different roles; for example, 'I'm the mummy today and you have to do what I tell you.' This benefit of play is one reason why it is used to support children who have been in traumatic situations: quite often children will play out what has happened to them in a safe environment.

Some materials used in play also help children to release emotions, imagination and creativity – a 2-year-old child may enjoy furiously hitting a drum, or a 6-year-old child may create an intricate model.

Play should also give children a sense of control and freedom. This in itself is empowering for them, especially where young children have little real control over their lives. Babies handling objects in the treasure basket are able to choose for themselves what to touch, what to drop and what to bang together. The great thing about treasure baskets and many other play opportunities for children is that there are no real rules, only the ones that they choose to establish.

Play is also liberating for children because they can make mistakes. For example, a sandcastle may disintegrate because the sand was not damp enough, but this may not matter to the child.

The benefits of child-initiated play to overall development

The role of adults in supporting and providing play opportunities for children is interesting and something that we will explore further in Section D. However, there are clearly times when adults need to teach children skills, knowledge and concepts using play as a vehicle. This is known as adult-directed play. There are also benefits to children playing as and how they please. This is known as child-initiated play, but may be referred to in some settings as 'free play'.

Child-initiated play has many features. In its simplest form, it means that children can choose what to play with, who to play with and what form the play takes. Many children will experience child-initiated play in their own homes because they will take out toys and bits and pieces, and make up their own play. However, it is also important that children get opportunities for child-initiated play in our settings. This is because child-initiated play supports many aspects that are central to children's development. Table 2.4 shows the benefits of child-initiated play.

> ### Assessment practice 2.1   3A.P1
>
> Give a presentation to a group of new parents about the benefits of play to children's overall development.
>
> Explain how play supports the physical, cognitive, language, social and emotional development of young children.

How children's play might change according to age

As children develop, so does the way in which they play. It is important to be aware of how children's play changes so that you can plan for their play. If you work with children of very different ages, it is also important to make sure that you are providing for their varying needs.

Table 2.4 Benefits of child-initiated play

Area of development	Benefits of child-initiated play
Imagination and creativity	When children are involved in their own play, they often make unusual and interesting connections. They may, for example, mix together different resources such as dough, balls and farm animals. Adults can find it hard to be as imaginative.
Confidence and agency	By learning that they can control the play part of their lives, children gain in confidence. They also gain 'agency', which means that they learn internally that they are people who can do things.
Independence	It is very easy for adults to help children, but when children are playing for themselves, they are also learning to be independent. They may, for example, wipe up a spill or manage to do up an item of clothing while dressing up.
Concentration and perseverance	Babies and children are able to concentrate for longer periods during child-initiated play. They are also able to persevere and overcome setbacks, e.g. if a piece of jigsaw puzzle does not fit or if a tower of bricks has fallen down. The same level of concentration and perseverance is not usually associated with adult-directed play and activities.
Memory and learning	Children seem to remember and therefore learn more when they have been involved in a child-initiated activity.

Social stages of play

In the 1930s, Mildred Parten looked at young children's play and noticed that as children become older, they tend to play more cooperatively. Her work has been widely accepted as it showed that children's social development was reflected in the way they played. Her work has since been built on and ages have been added alongside the different stages. This can be helpful as a guide to planning play and provision for groups of children.

Table 2.5 shows the different social stages of play. It is important to note that the ages listed in the table are only a guide. Repeated and careful observation of children in different situations is always the best way to assess the changes in children's play.

Activity

Carry out an observation on a child during child-initiated play. How does the child's play relate to the social stages of play?

Although being aware of the stages of play is very helpful in terms of planning for groups of children, it is worth remembering that older children may sometimes choose to play by themselves or alongside each other, and therefore it is important to provide for this. It is also worth noting that the social stages of play relate to children playing with their peers (children of the same or similar age). Babies do not usually play with each other cooperatively but we may see them playing with adults.

These children are engaged in parallel play – they are aware of each other but they are not interacting.

Table 2.5 The social stages of play

Age	Stage of play	Characteristics
0–2 years	Onlooker	Babies are fascinated by what others are doing but may not be engaged in play. Onlooker behaviours are also found in older children when they are new to a group or unsure.
0–2 years	Solitary	Babies may be aware of others but will engage in their own play.
2–3 years	Parallel	Children will be aware of other children. They play side by side. At times they may notice what each other are doing and copy each other's actions (or try to take what the other child is using).
3–4 years	Associative	Children will be very interested in others. They may be engaged in the same play and share materials but not actually coordinating their actions, e.g. if a child is dancing, another child may copy the actions, smile and make eye contact.
4 years and onwards	Cooperative	Children are playing with each other without the support of an adult. They interact and engage in the same play, e.g. pretending to be a family in the home corner.

B Understand how a range of play activities and opportunities can support children's learning and development

In the previous section we saw that children's development could be supported through play, but only when children had rich and diverse play experiences. In this section we will look at different types of play and opportunities that can support children's learning and development. Play and learning activities provide babies and children with valuable opportunities to interact with each other and with adults. They also allow children to explore the world around them and, in doing so, to develop their physical skills. This section is important because in your placement you will need to show that you can plan for different ages of children and that you understand the benefits of different types of play.

Types of play

To make it easier to talk about play and resources, they are often grouped into five different types. Each type of play has particular benefits to children's development and an understanding of these benefits is necessary in order to plan for play. These play types often best describe the play of children aged

between 2 and 8 years old rather than babies and very young children. Later we will look at play for babies and children under 2 years. Figure 2.1 shows five broad play types.

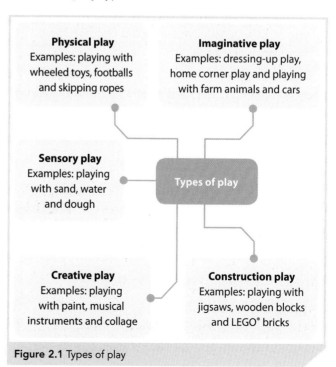

Physical play
Examples: playing with wheeled toys, footballs and skipping ropes

Imaginative play
Examples: dressing-up play, home corner play and playing with farm animals and cars

Sensory play
Examples: playing with sand, water and dough

Types of play

Creative play
Examples: playing with paint, musical instruments and collage

Construction play
Examples: playing with jigsaws, wooden blocks and LEGO® bricks

Figure 2.1 Types of play

Physical play

This refers to any type of play where the main focus is some sort of physical activity. This might be play where children are running, climbing, kicking or throwing. It supports the development of physical skills, confidence and social skills.

Link

Go to Unit 3: Section B to find more information about the different types of resources that can be used to support physical play.

Imaginative play

Imaginative play involves children pretending in some way and is sometimes referred to as 'pretend play'. It helps support the development of children's communication and language skills, their social skills and helps them understand identity as they take on different roles. There are many forms and levels of imaginative play:

- **Pretend play** – where children use an object in their play and 'make' it into something else, for example, a stick becomes a sword.
- **Role play** – where children take on a role, often an adult one, and incorporate props to make it more lifelike.
- **Socio-dramatic play** – where children come together to play out scenes from adult life, for example, the family going to a restaurant. This type of play is usually seen when children have good language skills.
- **Superhero play** – where children enjoy dressing up and acting out a hero role. This can be influenced by what children have seen on screen. Spiderman, Batman and various Disney characters have long been popular.
- **Small-world play** – this is where children create their own small worlds and direct the action. Popular resources include farm animals, dinosaurs, play people and trains.

Key term

Gloop – a sensory mixture made by mixing cornflour with water.

Reflect

Have you seen different ways in which the children in your training placement engage in imaginative play?

Do particular children have favourite ways of playing imaginatively?

Sensory play

Sensory play involves children playing with tactile materials such as dough, sand and water to help them develop their fine motor skills and hand–eye coordination, explore concepts of volume and shape and explore the textures and properties of different materials. Over recent years, many settings have begun to use a wide range of materials that includes cornflour and water (**gloop**), mashed potato, cold cooked spaghetti and gravel.

Creative play

Creative play involves children using resources freely in a creative way. Resources may include collage materials, junk for modelling, paints, crayons and also musical instruments. Note that creative play is only genuinely creative for children when they have freedom to explore the resources rather than being directed to make something that the adult has in mind. It helps children develop their fine motor skills and hand–eye coordination and allows them to express and release their emotions.

Construction play

Construction play involves children using resources to build things or join things together in some way. This may include jigsaws and train tracks as well as bricks, both large and small. It helps children develop spatial awareness and improve their hand–eye coordination. They are also able to explore how things work.

Play types can come together

Although it can be useful for planning purposes to separate play into different types, it is important to recognise that children will often combine types of play, especially as they become older. They may, for example, use wooden blocks (construction play) to design and build a train (creative play) that afterwards they use for socio-dramatic play (imaginative play).

Activity

1 Consider the following different types of play:
- physical
- imaginative
- sensory
- creative
- construction.

2 How do these types of play link to the early years curriculum of your home country?

Here is an example: creative play links well to Expressive Arts and Design in the Early Years Foundation Stage in England (EYFS).

Play and learning opportunities for children from 2 to 8 years

Earlier on we looked at play types for children from 2 to 8 years. Table 2.6 shows some specific play opportunities that can be created for the play types and also by combining play types.

Play and learning opportunities for babies and children from birth to 2 years

Babies and very young children need play opportunities that are different from those needed by older children. This is partly because they need more adult interaction, but also because they are likely to be mouthing until they are 18 months or so. Playing with an adult is essential for babies and very young children as, through play, they learn the skills of interacting with others.

As an adult, playing with babies and toddlers requires great sensitivity. Adults have to be ready to stop a game if a child becomes bored but equally need to seize the moment if the child shows that they want to play. We will now look at some popular play opportunities for children under 24 months.

Treasure basket play

This type of play is easy to prepare, and very beneficial to babies. Thirty or so objects made from natural materials (**not** toys) are placed in a low basket. The baby is then free to explore the items as they choose. The role of the adult is to supervise for safety

Table 2.6 Play opportunities for different types of play

Play opportunity	What to do	Play types
Delivering 'shopping'	Outdoors, children can use wheeled toys to deliver shopping. Put out boxes or shopping bags and create an outdoor home.	• Imaginative play • Physical play
Farm animals in the leaves and straw	Using a large container such as a builder's tray, put out farm animals with leaves and some straw.	• Imaginative play • Sensory play
Painting with brushes and water	Put out buckets of water and grown-up paintbrushes. Children can practise mark making by pretending to paint.	• Imaginative play • Creative play • Sensory play
Making 'cakes' in the home corner	Put out dough, muffin cases and baking trays in the home corner. Children can pretend to cook.	• Sensory play • Imaginative play
Hiding jigsaw pieces in dry sand	Hide jigsaw pieces in dry sand. See if the children can find all the pieces and make up the puzzle. You could also do the same with construction blocks.	• Sensory play • Construction play

and to be close by as a reassuring presence. The aim is not to direct the play. This is a form of child-initiated play for babies who can sit up and so are able to select their own resources, but who may not be mobile.

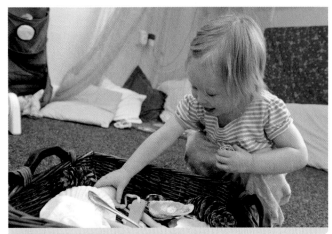

This baby is playing with a treasure basket.

Heuristic play

Heuristic play has many similarities to treasure basket play. It is used with older babies and toddlers. Children play with an assortment of objects that they can explore. The key difference is that items made of plastic can be introduced – although not toys.

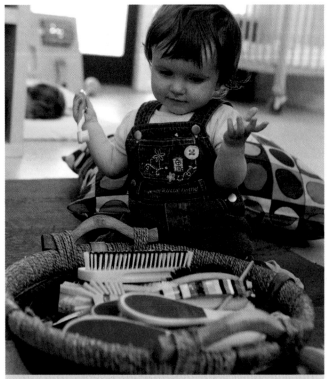

This child is engaging in heuristic play.

Everyday items work the best and, because toddlers enjoy repetitive movements, it is usual to put out collections of small items, for example, several shells or several wooden rings. As with treasure basket play, children need a wide range of objects in sufficient quantity to provide a multitude of combinations.

When providing for heuristic play, make sure that none of the items included are toys. The child should be in front of a pile of materials, which can include tins of different sizes (e.g. biscuit tins, cake tins, cylindrical tins), wine corks, shells, hair curlers, chains, plugs, wooden dolly pegs, pompoms or cardboard tubes. Make sure that an adult is not engaged with the child and that the child is able to explore freely.

Peek-a-boo and hide and seek

From around 6 months, babies begin to enjoy simple games of peek-a-boo. At first they are interested in watching as adults hide behind their hands and then reappear, but by 8 months they join in. Toys and puppets can also be used to support this type of play, e.g. Jack-in-the-box or pop-up puppets.

Once babies and toddlers are moving, try creating small spaces where they can go and hide. Part of the fun for older babies and toddlers is to hear the adult saying in a pretend voice that they cannot see the child. Although these games can be planned, it is important as well for this type of play to be spontaneous. For example, you could play at bath time with a towel or after a nappy change with a clean item of clothing.

Table 2.7 gives some more examples of games you can play with children under 24 months old.

Activity

Choose one of the activities in Table 2.7 and try it out with a baby or toddler.
- Think about how the child responds.
- Does the child want to repeat the play?

Table 2.7 Games to play with young children

Play opportunity	Description
Action rhymes	Action rhymes such as 'Humpty Dumpty' and 'Row, row, row your boat' are play opportunities for babies and toddlers.
Building and knock-down play	Babies and toddlers love knocking down towers of bricks and stacking beakers. With young babies, the adult has to build up the tower but, by around 8 months, most babies are trying to help too.
Roll-a-ball	From around 6 months or so, most babies enjoy having a ball rolled over to them. As they develop, they begin to be able to roll it back. With toddlers, expect to find that they sometimes hog the ball or tease you.
Water play	Whether it is part of a bathing routine or put out as an activity, babies and toddlers love playing with water. Water play can be provided in paddling pools or baby baths, but also with toddlers in buckets. Look out for scoops and buckets as well as fabric. Always supervise water play.
Sensory play	Sensory play includes water, but also other materials that babies and toddlers can handle. Cold cooked spaghetti, gloop and even mashed potatoes are popular sensory materials.

Resources to support play and learning

In order to create rich play environments for children it is important that they are well resourced. The majority of resources that are used day in, day out with children are fairly inexpensive, but there are some key items of equipment that most large settings will invest in. As an adult working with children, it will be your responsibility to make sure that resources that support children's play and development are available or set out for them.

The importance of providing for indoor and outdoor play

There has been much concern that many children no longer spend time outdoors. To reverse this trend, early years settings have been encouraged to use resources and equipment both indoors and out. Most things that can be done indoors can also be done outdoors. This means that some resources are taken outdoors or duplicated, or similar materials are provided and kept outdoors.

There are many advantages for children in playing outdoors – these include greater freedom, the possibility of having larger quantities of things such as sand and water and the opportunity to combine play types. This means that it is usual now to find role-play areas outdoors as well as resources for mark making and painting.

Treasure basket play outdoors

Treasure basket play can be used indoors and outdoors. Outdoors, it may be important to put out a rug or set the treasure basket on a comfortable surface. Key resources include a low basket and a large range of natural objects and materials. For treasure basket play to remain stimulating, it is essential for new objects to be introduced and others taken out. A rotation of objects works well.

Heuristic play outdoors

Heuristic play can be used indoors and outdoors. A large collection of containers, small objects and everyday items needs to be provided. See the earlier section on heuristic play for details of the types of objects that should be included.

Resources for different ages of children

When planning for children's play it is important to provide resources that support each of the different types of play. As children's play interests and skills develop, it is usual to provide slightly different resources according to children's age and stage of development. Table 2.8 gives some examples of popular resources that are used to support all areas of children's play.

Table 2.8 Examples of resources that can be used indoors and outdoors for children of different ages

Age	Type of play				
	Physical play	Imaginative play	Creative play	Sensory play	Construction play
0–24 months	• Swings • Sit-and-ride toys • Balls • Low climbing frame	• Puppets • Toy telephones • Dolls • Cuddly toys	• Treasure basket play • Heuristic play	• Cold cooked spaghetti • Jelly • Water play: baby baths, paddling pool • Gloop	• Pop-up toys • Stacking beakers • Post-it toys • Lift-up puzzles • Heuristic play
24 months–4 years	• Tricycles • Balls (different sizes) • Stilts • Tree stumps • Climbing frames • Scooters • Hoops • Slides	As above, but also: • Small-world toys such as farm animals, dinosaurs, play people, cars and garage • Dressing-up clothes • Props for dressing up: hats, belts, shoes, notepads • Home corner props, e.g. kitchen, bed, cot	• Dough: rolling pin, shape cutters, plates • Paint: rollers, sponges, brushes • Mark making and drawing: felt-tips, crayons, stampers, charcoal • Collage materials: glue sticks, sequins, ribbons, feathers • Junk modelling materials: staplers, masking tape, boxes, tubes, double-sided tape	As above, but also: • Sand • Gravel • Pasta • Rice • Tea leaves • Can be used with: bottles, scoops, sieves, tubes • Digging (outdoors)	• DUPLO® • Wooden blocks • Jigsaw puzzles • Interlocking tubes and guttering
4–8 years	As above, but also: • Bicycles • Skateboards • Roller skates • Skipping ropes	As above, but also: • A puppet theatre • A dolls' house	As above, but also: • Kits and more intricate materials	As above, but combined with small-world play.	As above, but also: • Construction kits with more intricate components, such as LEGO® and MECCANO®

Theory into practice

Look at the equipment and resources in your work placement setting. Are there resources and equipment for each of the following play types?

- Creative
- Physical
- Construction
- Sensory
- Imaginative

Can you see how the resources reflect different types of play and play opportunities, but also the needs and interests of the children? An example would be a home corner that supports children's imaginative play but into which practitioners have added a changing mat and some nappies because one child is interested in babies.

Buying and finding resources

Most practitioners will find that they are sometimes given opportunities to add to their existing resources. It is important that new resources are chosen carefully. Figure 2.2 shows some of the important points to consider when choosing new equipment.

Figure 2.2 What to consider when choosing resources

Stage of development

Resources have to be matched to children's stages of development, otherwise they may be unsafe. This means that small items are unlikely to be suitable for children under 2 years. Thinking carefully about stage of development also means that the toys you choose are likely to meet children's play needs and interests.

Storage

Storage is an issue for many settings. Think carefully about how easily the resources can be stored.

Duplication

Children need a wide range of resources. Check that you do not already have something similar.

Balance between toys and resources

Toys have their place, but sometimes too many toys can reduce opportunities for challenge. General resources such as shells, wooden blocks and sand are often what is needed. Supplement these with everyday objects (not toys) such as saucepans with lids, serving spoons and rotary whisks.

Safety marks

All toys and resources provided for children must be safe for them to play with and handle. Look out for marks that indicate toys conform to certain standards. There are three marks that you should look out for: the CE mark, the Lion Mark and the Kitemark. The CE mark is a declaration by toy manufacturers that their products are safe; the Lion Mark indicates that toys have been tested; and the Kitemark indicates that safety requirements have been met.

This fabric book shows the CE mark and Lion Mark.

How play opportunities and types support development

One of the reasons why children need a varied diet of play types is that each type provides different developmental benefits. Part of providing a rich environment for children is to ensure that there is a range of different activities, resources and materials for them to play. It is also about providing children with new challenges and, in the case of physical play, giving them opportunities to understand and manage risk. This is considered important as it provides children with confidence and also experience that will help them later to judge the safety of environments or actions.

As children get older, they sometimes become interested in certain resources or themes. One of the skills of the adult is to find ways in which, by building on their interests, children can still access different types of play.

Table 2.9 shows how the five main types of play may support children's overall development. It also shows how some of the key play opportunities that are used with babies and toddlers can be useful.

Respecting cultural differences

When we provide opportunities for play, it is important that we make sure they reflect children's own lifestyles. This might include reflecting cultural nuances as well as different family circumstances in the environment. We may, for example, think about providing props and resources in home corners that reflect what children use and see in their own homes. This might include providing for a range of cooking utensils, decorations and ornaments. If children do not have their cultures and lifestyles reflected in their play environment, it makes it harder for them to play in a meaningful way.

Case study

Cultural differences

Vedat's family is Turkish. Each day at home he sees coffee being made in the traditional way, using a very small saucepan. One day, Vedat's key person sees him in the home corner. She sees that he is very agitated and keeps throwing items onto the floor. When asked why he is upset, he tells her that he can't play properly because there is nothing to play with. She asks him what he wants to do. He replies that he wants to make coffee. She points to the toy kettle but Vedat simply shakes his head. Later she tells his mother about what happened and finds out that coffee is made very differently in Turkey compared to in the UK.

1 Why is Vedat frustrated?

2 Why is it important to work closely with parents to understand individual children's play needs?

3 What are the next steps that the nursery needs to take to help Vedat play?

Table 2.9 The main types of play that support children's overall development

Type of play	What aspects of development it supports
Physical play	• Fine and gross motor movements • Balance and general coordination • Stamina • Allows children to explore risk and challenge • Confidence and feelings of competence • Spatial awareness and understanding of the world • Social skills (in situations where children are playing cooperatively), e.g. games such as hide and seek

continued

Table 2.9 (*continued*)

Type of play	What aspects of development it supports
Imaginative play	• Language • Exploration of roles • Confidence and feelings of competence • Expression and release of emotion • Social skills (in situations where children are playing cooperatively)
Sensory play	• Fine motor movements • Hand–eye coordination • Use of tools and equipment • Exploration of early mathematical concepts such as volume and shape • Expression and release of emotion • Curiosity and interest in materials and textures • Confidence and feelings of competence
Construction play	• Fine and gross motor movements • Hand–eye coordination • Spatial awareness • Curiosity and interest in structures and how things work • Problem solving and challenge • Confidence and feelings of competence • Social skills (in situations where children are playing cooperatively)
Creative play	• Fine motor movements • Hand–eye coordination • Expression and release of emotions • Confidence and feelings of competence • Curiosity and interest in learning
Treasure basket play for babies	• Fine motor movements • Hand–eye coordination • Spatial awareness • Confidence and feelings of competence • Curiosity and interest in learning • Independence • Exploration of materials • Challenge
Heuristic play for older babies and toddlers	• Fine and gross motor movements • Hand–eye coordination • Spatial awareness • Confidence and feelings of competence • Curiosity and interest in learning • Independence • Exploration of materials • Challenge

continued

Table 2.9 *(continued)*

Type of play	What aspects of development it supports
Peek-a-boo/hide and seek play	• Social skills – learning to take turns • Greater attachment to adult and hence emotional security • Eye contact • Curiosity and increased understanding of their world • Language development
Building and knock-down play	• Hand–eye coordination • Fine gross motor movements • Greater attachment to adult and hence emotional security • Curiosity
Action rhymes	• Social skills – learning to take turns • Greater attachment to adult and hence emotional security • Curiosity • Language development

Assessment practice 2.2   3A.P1 | 3B.P3 | 3B.P4 | 3A.M1

1 Write an information pack for parents that explains how different play and learning activities and opportunities might support babies' and children's development.

2 For each play type and for each play and learning opportunity, give suggestions of resources that might be used.

Use case studies or examples from your work placements to support your explanations.

How children's play and interests may change

As children develop, we often see that what they play with and how they play changes. This is often linked to their cognitive and language development. A good example of this is imaginative play. Most 3-year-old children enjoy taking on roles. You will probably see them pretending to cook and have 'grown-up' conversations in the home corner. A 2-year-old child in the home corner will enjoy opening and closing all the cupboards, but will not necessarily be in role. Table 2.10 shows how children's play interests may change and develop. Note that these are broad characteristics and so may not apply to individual children.

Table 2.10 How children's play interests may change according to their age/stage of development

Age	Characteristics	Examples of play interests and activities
0–18 months	• Babies enjoy playful activities with adults. • Play with adults is closely linked to communication and relationship building. • Repetitive simple movements combined with adults' facial expressions seem to be important, e.g. peek-a-boo and shake-a-rattle. • Babies can spend time playing and exploring objects independently. • Everyday routines can become playful opportunities for babies, e.g. dropping a spoon for the adult to pick up, and bath time. • A key feature of babies' play is mouthing. They will often explore objects by taking them into their mouth. At around 18 months, this usually reduces or disappears.	• Treasure basket play • Heuristic play with older babies • Water and sensory play • Games with adults such as roll-a-ball, building and knocking down beakers • Pop-up toys and musical games • Swings for babies who are starting to sit up
18 months –3 years	• Children needing to play near or with adults. This seems to be for reassurance. Children may break off their activity if they cannot see 'their' adult. • May have moments watching or copying other children, but are likely to need an adult to support play with others. • Sensory play enjoyed and is likely to engage children without adult involvement for long periods, i.e. 30 minutes. • Play is often exploratory, repetitive and involves gross motor movements, e.g. opening and closing doors. • Small-world play is of interest, particularly cars, trains and play characters from around 2 years. • Interest in role play from around 2½ years. • Adult supervision required for safety reasons but adult involvement required to support children's engagement in play.	• Transporting – moving items from one place to another, e.g. filling up a pushchair with items • Dropping and posting activities, e.g. pushing a ball down a tube, dropping a puzzle onto the floor • Sensory materials, especially water • Simple puzzles and construction toys, with adult encouragement

continued

Table 2.10 (continued)

Age	Characteristics	Examples of play interests and activities
3–4 years	• Beginning to show cooperation during play, but adult involvement is required to sort out sharing of equipment between different groups of children. • Children enjoy opportunities to play with each other independently of adults and may seek to be out of sight. • Simple games enjoyed when played in a small group with an adult. • Sensory materials tend to be particularly popular and played with independently of adults. • Small-world and role-play starting to reflect children's ability to pretend and be imaginative.	• Wheeled toys • Paint • Sensory activities such as dough, water and sand • Small-world play • Dressing up and home corner play • Construction sets and opportunities to make things such as dens and houses
4–8 years	• Generally cooperative, with children being able to sustain play without an adult's involvement. • Children often able to sustain play that is of interest to them for more than an hour. • Wide play interests including activities that require fine motor skills and patience. • Same-sex play becomes more common. • Increased complexity in role-playing, with characters being assigned. • Board games and games with specific rules enjoyed. • Children may enjoy completing activities or kits by themselves.	• Bicycles • Ball games • Dressing up • Small-world play • Construction play – often intricate play such as using LEGO®, as well as block play • Sensory play combined with small-world play • Games such as snap, pairs and snakes and ladders

Assessment practice 2.3

3A.P2 | 3A.M1 | 3B.M2 | 3B.D1

Observe two children of different ages from the following age bands: 0–2 and 2–7 years. Write a brief description of how they play and whether this play is typical for their age. Then:

1 describe how children play at different stages of development

2 explain how you might use play to meet each of the children's developmental needs

3 discuss how play might support the physical, cognitive, language, social and emotional development of a child at different ages

4 give examples of the types of play and learning activities that you would provide for each of the children and the resources that you would provide

5 analyse how the chosen types of play and learning activities and resources will meet the needs of the children and support their holistic development

6 discuss the suitability of the resources to support play and play opportunities in early years settings and to meet the different stages of development

7 evaluate the extent to which the chosen examples of play and resources would support the holistic development of children across the age groups 0–7 years.

C Understand how theoretical and philosophical approaches to play and learning influence current practice in early years settings

Children have enjoyed playing in similar ways over a number of years but the way play is viewed by adults and also the way play has been provided has changed. In this section we look at how a range of attitudes and perspectives towards children's play have influenced what you will find in many early years settings today.

Definitions of play

It may seem hard to believe, but defining what is and isn't play is quite controversial and potentially difficult. Most people would agree that two children digging enthusiastically in the sand on a beach were playing, but not everyone would describe it as play if there was an adult telling the children how best to do it.

Tina Bruce's features of play

Professor Tina Bruce has been very influential in the field of early years education, with particular reference to play and learning. Bruce looked at play and considered the features that it might have. She came up with the following 12 features of play.

1 Play is an active process without a product.

2 Play is intrinsically motivated.

3 Play exerts no pressure to conform to rules, goals or tasks or to take definite directions.

4 Play is about possible, alternative worlds that involve the concepts of 'supporting' and 'as if' and that lift the player to the highest levels of functioning. This involves being imaginative, creative, original and innovative.

5 Play is about wallowing in ideas, feelings and relationships, and becoming aware of what we know (metacognition).

6 It actively uses first-hand experiences.

7 It is sustained and, when in full flow, helps us to function in advance of what we can actually do in our real lives.

8 In play we use technical prowess, mastery and competence that we have previously developed. We are in control.

9 Children or adults can initiate play but each must be sensitive to each other's personal agenda.

10 Play can be solitary.

11 It can be with others, who are sensitive to fellow players.

12 Play integrates everything we learn, know, feel, relate to and understand.

Free-flow play

The term 'free-flow play' is used by Tina Bruce to consider the way that children bring together their experiences, skills and relationships to create play. Famously, Bruce talks about children 'wallowing' in play.

Interestingly, although acknowledging their value in feeding into free-flow play, Bruce does not believe that experiences such as exploring gloop or being shown a game by an adult can be counted as play.

Recent use of the term

Bruce is known for using the term free-flow play to describe children playing freely and combining the features above. This term has now been absorbed into the general vocabulary of early years education and has a much broader sense.

At the time of writing, it is taken to mean that children can move freely from one play opportunity to another, both indoors and outdoors. Free-flow play also means that children can help themselves to resources and also choose to mix resources if they wish. The idea is that they are free to explore and take play in the direction that they choose. Most preschool group settings are likely to have some periods of free-flow time built into their routine, although whether this allows for what Bruce originally described is questionable in some settings.

Reflect

Find out whether your placement setting offers free-flow play. Consider how close it is to Tina Bruce's model of free-flow play.

Structured play

Structured play is also referred to as 'adult-directed play' or 'adult-initiated play'. Structured play puts emphasis on helping children to learn while they are playing and so it is sometimes called 'purposeful play'. When you are on your placements in different settings that care for children of similar ages, you may find that their approach to structured play varies. This is because play can be structured at many different levels. Note that many would question whether very structured play is indeed play at all.

Table 2.11 provides some examples of how play can be structured at different levels.

Table 2.11 Different ways that play can be structured

Level of structured play	Description	Examples	Advantages and disadvantages
Highly structured – adult-directed	Children are told what they will be doing. The adult explains how to play and use the resources. The adult joins in or supervises the play. The adult discourages children from using the resources in ways different from the planned objective. Note: This level of structure is unlikely to work well with younger children.	• Drama productions and plays • Board games such as snakes and ladders • Games of cards • Structured cooking	Advantages: • Children may learn new skills • Parents may be reassured that their child is 'learning' Disadvantages: • If play is not of interest to children, there will be few benefits • Reduces options for creativity and independence and is not empowering
Structured – adult-directed	Children are asked if they are interested in taking part. Play is based on children's interests or something that the children are likely to enjoy. Children are free to leave at any time. Other children may come and join in. Adult takes the role of a play partner rather than director.	• Building dens • Collecting leaves • Making a conveyor belt for the home corner shop • Seeing who can make the largest sand castle • Going on a 'sound' walk	Advantages: • Children are given opportunities to learn new skills or to do something that is different from their usual play or experiences • Interaction levels are high • Concentration levels are high • Children feel part of process Disadvantages: • Children are not leading the play

continued

Table 2.11 (continued)

Level of structured play	Description	Examples	Advantages and disadvantages
Structured play opportunities where children are directed to play in certain ways	The environment is set up ready for play. Children are directed to play with different materials and may be given specific tasks, e.g. 'You two, go to the jigsaws.' Children are not encouraged to deviate from the 'adult' purpose of the play.	• Play is set up in different areas, e.g. mark making, jigsaws, cars, dough table	Advantages: • Children experience different types of play • Adult can make sure that the curriculum is covered Disadvantages: • Children cannot be creative or explore materials • Concentration levels can be low
Structured play opportunities that children can choose to use and deviate from	Resources are put out by adults in ways that may prompt children to play in certain ways or take their play interests forward. Children are free to ignore the prompts or use them in other ways as part of their play.	• Play is set up in different areas but in ways that might encourage children to learn or experience something new, e.g. coins are hidden in the sand tray, blocks of ice are put in the water tray	Advantages: • Children may gain new experiences from the resources provided and this may support the curriculum objectives • Children are more likely to concentrate Disadvantages: • Children may be diverted from their original play interests

Where do you think this structured activity would sit in Table 2.11?

The playwork principles

In many early years settings and at the heart of current early years curricula, play is about learning and development, but playworkers have a slightly different approach to providing play, and also to the role of the adult. This vision is set out in what is known as the 'playwork principles'. This set of principles came from the Playwork Principles Scrutiny Group in Cardiff in 2005.

Playwork is mainly found in out-of-school settings such as after-school clubs and holiday schemes, but it is worth looking at each of the playwork principles and considering both the differences and similarities to the way play is approached in early years settings. You may see that what is known as child-initiated play in early years is at the heart of playwork (see principle 2). Structured play as described previously would not be considered as play. It is worth visiting a playwork setting and watching how playworkers approach their work.

Below are the eight playwork principles.

1 All children and young people need to play. The impulse to play is innate. Play is a biological, psychological and social necessity, and is fundamental to the healthy development and well-being of individuals and communities.

2 Play is a process that is freely chosen, personally directed and intrinsically motivated. That is, children and young people determine and control the content and intent of their play by following their own instincts, ideas and interests, in their own way for their own reasons.

3 The prime focus and essence of playwork is to support and facilitate the play process. This should then inform the development of play policy, strategy, training and education.

4 For playworkers, the play process takes precedence and playworkers act as advocates for play when engaging with adult-led agendas.

5 The role of the playworker is to support all children and young people in the creation of a space in which they can play.

6 The playworker's response to children and young people playing is based on a sound up-to-date knowledge of the play process and reflective practice.

7 Playworkers recognise their own impact on the play space and also the impact of children and young people's play on the playworker.

8 Playworkers choose an intervention style that enables children and young people to extend their

play. All playworker intervention must balance risk with the developmental benefit and wellbeing of children.

Philosophical approaches to play and learning

In some ways the definitions of play have come about because of different views about childhood and the nature of child development. Here, we will look at the impact that different philosophical approaches to play have had on today's early years practice.

Friedrich Froebel

Friedrich Froebel (1782–1852) was born in Germany. Through his own schooling, he learned about the natural world and this influenced his later thoughts about the importance of children spending time playing outdoors. Here, there was much philosophical interest in the nature of childhood. Froebel believed that children were essentially born good, but that adults need to provide the right care and environment to protect them from evil. He also recognised that play was essential for learning, but that adults might support it by giving children objects for them to explore. These 'gifts' would help children to learn concepts, for example, learning about texture by giving them a hard ball and a soft ball. Froebel also used rhymes and music as a way of helping children learn about concepts and he is thought to be responsible for rhymes such as 'Round and round the garden, like a teddy bear'. In addition, Froebel gave children wooden blocks to use so that they could build and make structures with them.

Links to early years practice

Froebel's belief that children should learn through nature and the outdoors is still of major importance. His use of blocks to help children learn through play is also reflected today in the 'block play' that is used in many early years settings. Rhymes are also a major feature of early years practice with babies and older children.

Key term

Block play – play using large wooden bricks of different shapes and sizes.

Research

Find out more about the differences between the ways that early years professionals may approach play compared to the approach of playworkers. Visit a playwork setting or go to the SkillsActive website for more information. You can access this website by going to www.pearsonhotlinks.co.uk and searching for this ISBN: 9781447970965.

Theory into practice

Does your work placement setting have block play? How is it used to support children's play and development?

Margaret and Rachel McMillan

Margaret McMillan (1860–1931) and her sister, Rachel (1859–1917), were social reformers, and founded a nursery school in a deprived part of London in 1914. The McMillans recognised that children's physical needs were important for their learning, and food and medical checks were included in the nursery's day-to-day practice.

Margaret McMillan was influenced by the work of Maria Montessori, but particularly by that of Friedrich Froebel. The nursery was the first open-air nursery and imaginative play was seen as an essential tool for learning. In addition, the McMillan sisters thought that a nursery should be an extension of the home and so were thoughtful about involving parents and also making sure that children felt secure.

The McMillans should also be remembered for their successful campaign to give children from poor families free school meals.

Links to early years practice

It is now accepted that physical health and wellbeing are important to children's learning. The McMillans' thoughts about nursery being an extension of home have links to today's key person system. Both outdoor play and imaginative play are recognised as being fundamental to early years practice.

Maria Montessori

Montessori (1870–1952) was a doctor who worked in a psychiatric clinic with children who had learning difficulties. In 1896 she was appointed director of an institute where she was able to explore her ideas about how to help children with learning difficulties. A structured approach that was based on the children's own pace of learning had notable success and this formed the basis of her later work with young children in a school called the Casa de Bambini (Children's House).

Montessori believed that up until the age of 6 years, children had the capacity to learn easily and quickly. She called this phase the 'absorbent mind' and believed that their ability to learn should be capitalised on rather than wasted. This belief meant that Montessori saw that the role of the adult was to guide children in their play or 'work' and provide them with the equipment and an environment from

which they would be ready to learn. Figure 2.3 shows some examples of Montessori equipment. This means that although she saw children as active learners, she also felt that play without a clear purpose would be wasting valuable time.

Montessori had great confidence in children's abilities and felt that they could concentrate for long periods and be independent in their learning. This means that the role of the adult is to be there as a guide for the child, but to allow children to learn for themselves. Montessori also believed that children's independence and skills could be fostered by mastering everyday skills such as dressing, cooking and even gardening. Montessori's philosophy is still in use today and there are many Montessori nursery schools in the UK and throughout the world.

Links to early years practice

As well as in Montessori nursery schools, some elements of the Montessori approach can be seen in the general early years curricula. Practitioners are used to the concept of play with a purpose and also adults acting as facilitators. The importance of children learning everyday skills such as dressing and cooking can also be seen.

Research

Find out more about Montessori education at the Montessori UK website. You can access this website by going to www.pearsonhotlinks.co.uk and searching for this ISBN: 9781447970965.

Figure 2.3 Montessori settings still use the equipment that Maria Montessori designed to help children learn concepts.

Rudolph Steiner

Born in Austria, Rudolph Steiner (1861–1925) was an academic with numerous interests including social reform, religion, science and architecture. He is particularly known as being the founder of a spiritual movement known as anthroposophy. His ideas on education were published in 1907 in a book entitled *The Education of the Child*. In 1919, a school was opened for the employees of the Waldorf Astoria cigarette factory and Steiner was asked to lead it. The school proved popular and further schools were created.

Central to Steiner's **pedagogy** were his spiritual beliefs. He believed in reincarnation and hence thought that children were especially in need of protection as they were literally 'finding their way'. In terms of practice, this meant that the role of the adult was to allow the child to develop their own imagination and explore the senses at their own pace. Sensory and natural materials were important and no toys were given as Steiner believed that the child has to develop their own sense of self. Handwork, such as crochet and knitting, was felt by Steiner to be important for development, but encouraging a child to learn to read or look at books early on was, on the other hand, damaging.

> **Key term**
>
> **Pedagogy** – an approach to the teaching of children.

Links to early years practice

The Steiner approach to education is now known as Steiner Waldorf and there are many schools both internationally and in the UK. The past links to anthroposophy are acknowledged, but few schools endorse or teach it. Today, Steiner Waldorf is very popular with parents who want their children to experience an unhurried, artistic and imaginative childhood. Reading and writing are not taught until children are around 6 or 7 years old, as the focus is on children being able to listen and retell stories

first. Though direct elements of the Steiner Waldorf approach have not been integrated into mainstream early years education, activities such as music, cooking, group time and play with natural objects can be found in some settings.

> **Research**
>
> Find out more about the Steiner Waldorf approach to early education at the Steiner Waldorf Schools Fellowship website. You can access this website by going to www.pearsonhotlinks.co.uk and searching for this ISBN: 9781447970965.

Theoretical approaches to play and learning

In the twentieth century, there was much interest in researching children's play and coming up with theories of how play influenced development. Here, we will look at how some of the key theories of play have influenced today's early years practice.

Jean Piaget

Jean Piaget believed that children learn by doing and that their cognitive development was reflected in their play. He described children's development in a series of stages of play. Table 2.12 outlines these stages. Piaget spent time watching children play and noted that as children developed, their play became more complex and they started to create rules. He felt this was connected to their ability to deal with abstract concepts – rules being something that you cannot see. He believed this showed a high level of cognitive development.

> **Link**
>
> Go to Unit 1: Sections B and C to find more information about Piaget's theory of cognitive development.

Table 2.12 Piaget's stages of play

Age	Type of play	Common features
0–2 years	Mastery play	Children are gaining control of their bodies. Play allows them to explore their environment. Play in this age group tends to be repetitive – as if the child is trying to master their movements and understand the world.
2–7 years	Symbolic play	Children are using language as a means of communicating and this is reflected in their play. Children are using symbols in their play, e.g. a stick becomes a spoon.
7–11 years	Play with rules	Children are developing an understanding of rules and find them fascinating and fulfilling. Children may make rules, but then break them.

Links to early years practice

Piaget's stages of play as well as his stages of cognitive development have been important for early years education. His stages of play and the importance of children learning through discovery have helped support the idea of children's learning and play being interconnected.

Lev Vygotsky

In Unit 1, we looked at Vygotsky's view of cognitive development, but here we look at his thoughts about play. He was particularly interested in imaginative play, which he suggested began when children were 3 years old. In 1933 he gave a lecture entitled 'Play and its role in the mental development of children' in which he examined the nature and purpose of play in children. He suggested that play was essential to the development of preschool children rather than just a characteristic that young children shared. He also suggested that imaginative play allowed children to explore thoughts, rules and roles beyond their current level of competence and so was effectively the child's zone of proximal development. In the lecture, Vygotsky also looked at the way in which imaginative play develops and, in turn, how this develops the child. He noted that at first, imaginative play starts with a re-creation of what children have seen first-hand, but that children quickly begin to explore beyond this. This, he suggested, helps children to make the move into abstract thought –

These children have devised a game where one has to follow the other along the lines – whoever 'falls' off the line is out.

and so higher mental function. Vygotsky, like Piaget, was also interested in the way that children develop rules in their play and how these allow play to become more challenging and enjoyable. Vygotsky was also clear that it was not just children's cognitive development that was developed through play, but also their emotional and social development.

Link

Go to Unit 1: Section B and C to find more information about Vygotsky's zone of proximal development.

Links to early years practice

Most early years settings provide opportunities for role play and small-world play, although many include this for children younger than 3 years. It is also good practice for adults to introduce new experiences to children so that these can feed into their role play. Vygotsky's thoughts about cognitive development and the way in which children learn from adults and older children have also meant that adult-directed activities, including playing games, are included in most settings' routines.

Jerome Bruner

Jerome Bruner has been very influential in early years practice. He is famous for coining the term 'scaffolding' to explain the way in which adults can support children learning by asking questions, guiding or breaking information down into small steps. For Bruner, like Vygotsky, play is essential for development. In the 1970s, with other researchers, he investigated play in preschools. The results proved interesting, as it was noted that children's play was richer and more sustained in the presence of sensitive adults who engaged with them. It was also noted that children played for longer periods and more richly when they were engaged in construction-type activities rather than those with no 'end', such as sand and water.

Key term

Scaffolding – a term used to describe a style of working with children in which the adult helps the child to acquire information.

Research

Read an article entitled 'Play, thought and language', which is based on Bruner's address to the Preschool Playgroup Association of Great Britain in 1983. You can access this article by going to www.pearsonhotlinks.co.uk and searching for this ISBN: 9781447970965.

How does the article relate to the practice that you have seen in nurseries or preschools?

Links to early years practice

Bruner's research has been influential in many ways. First there is the idea that adults should engage with children at times as they play and that adult-directed activities can feed into child-initiated play. Children who have been cooking with an adult in the morning might then use this experience to enrich their play later. The Oxford Preschool Project also showed that construction-type activities provided rich play and, as a result, block play is provided in many settings.

Chris Athey

In Unit 1 we looked at Chris Athey's development of Piaget's theory in relation to schemas. Here, we look at how you might see her schema theory in action in early years settings. In her work, Chris Athey identified several schemas that seem to occur in children's play and suggested that these were linked to the child's cognitive exploration. Since her original work, the idea of using schemas to make sense of children's play and also to use them as a way of planning for individual children has become popular. As we saw in Unit 1, Athey suggested that children could explore schemas on different levels, but this information has not yet filtered down to all settings. Table 2.13 shows Athey's schemas and others that have since been added, as well as examples of resources that might be used to support a child's interest.

Links to early years practice

Observing children, noting their patterns of play and from this, identifying the schemas present, has become a key way that many settings work. Once schemas are identified, many settings will then plan activities or put out resources that may support children's exploration further. This approach has been particularly successful in helping practitioners (and parents) understand what otherwise might look like unwanted behaviour, for example, taking sand out of a sand tray (transporting).

Table 2.13 Resources that may support a child's interest

Schema	What you may observe	Opportunities/resources that can be put out to support play
Transporting	Children who are interested in moving things from one place to another, e.g. putting objects in a pushchair and taking them across the room or pouring water from the water tray into a bucket.	• Pushchairs • Wheeled toys • Brick trolleys • Bags • Buckets
Enveloping	Children who enjoy covering things or themselves, e.g. putting a blanket over the whole of a dolly.	• Blankets and fabrics • Wrapping paper
Enclosing/containing	Children who enjoy putting things in and out of containers or spaces, e.g. sitting in a tent.	• Russian dolls • Boxes with lids • Stacking boxes • Tents
Trajectory	Children who are interested in the way things move through the air, e.g. throwing and dropping.	• Balls • Beanbags • Sticks
Rotation	Children who are interested in circles and things that spin round, such as washing machines.	• Salad spinner • Spinning tops • Rotary clothes line • Chair that swivels
Transforming	Children who enjoy watching things change, e.g. mixing paint, dropping food colouring into water.	• Opportunities to mix things, e.g. sand and water
Connecting	Children who are interested in putting things together, e.g. lines of cars or tying string from a chair leg to a table leg.	• Construction materials • Opportunities to tie things together
Positioning	Children who take time to place objects and themselves in a particular order or position, e.g. enjoying laying a table with accuracy.	• Ice cube trays and small objects that can be put inside • Peg boards • Opportunities for children to group objects and not be disturbed by others
Orientating	Children who are interested in seeing things from different positions and viewpoints, e.g. trying to climb to be up high.	• Climbing equipment • Balancing equipment, e.g. seesaws • Looking through binoculars

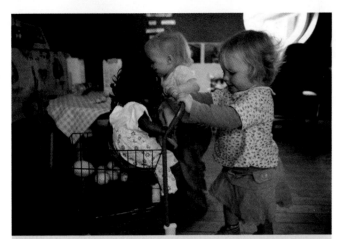

This child is busy pushing a shopping trolley in the role-play area. Can you identify a link to a schema?

Activity

Find out if your work placement identifies schemas in children and plans resources and activities as a result.

Theory into practice

Observe a 2-year-old child at play. Can you identify any repeated patterns of behaviour? (Ignore a behaviour that only occurs once.) Does this fit any schema from Table 2.13?

Other approaches to play and learning

Over the years, there have been many different approaches to play that have influenced current practice and thinking about how best to provide and plan for play. Here, we will look at some other approaches to providing play, all of which have their roots in other countries, and therefore cultures.

Reggio Emilia

Reggio Emilia is a province in Northern Italy that has become famous for its approach to preschool education, which began with a collaboration between parents and practitioners after the Second World War. This collaboration is very much at the heart of practice in the Reggio preschools and is one of the many features that have influenced practitioners from other countries who have visited them. Unlike many early years programmes, there is no curriculum

to follow – children and adults follow their interests and the role of the adult is to be a supporter for the children, but also a learner. Adults also take the role of being the recorder of children's work and play. Photographs and notes are displayed so that children can refer to them and reflect on their projects. Another feature of Reggio Emilia's preschools is that they see children as being competent learners and individuals. A well-known phrase is 'the hundred languages of children', which refers to the idea that children will have many different ways of expressing their ideas and learning and that practitioners have to be ready to recognise and provide for them. Thus music, drawing and sculpture are genuinely valued forms of expression.

Benefits of Reggio Emilia's approach

This approach has the following benefits:

- children are seen as competent learners
- parents and early years educators work closely together
- adults and children explore ideas, problems and play together
- children are able to reflect back on their play, experiences and learning as photographs and recordings are made by adults.

Links to early years practice

Many settings work closely with parents and talk to them about their children's interests. Photographs and other ways of recording children's work and play are often used. As a result of Reggio Emilia's influence, many early years settings are also trying to create **ateliers**, or areas where children can create things.

Key term

Atelier – a workshop.

Highscope

Highscope, an approach to early years education, has grown out of a project in America that ran in the 1960s. It started life as a small research project that was trying to improve the life chances of young children from vulnerable families. The project quickly showed through its research that children who attended were benefiting from its approach compared to children in the control group, who were in other settings. Several features of Highscope are famous.

Plan–do–review

Highscope is perhaps best known for its 'plan–do–review' approach to play. The idea is that children spend time talking about what they want to do before getting out the materials and resources. Afterwards in small groups they talk about what they have done or how their plan changed.

Daily routine

Highscope is a structured approach and a daily routine is followed. The routine consists of small and large group times and also times for transition. The aim of this routine is to give children a sense of order and security. This perhaps reflects the origins of Highscope's work with disadvantaged children.

Role of the adult

Again, perhaps reflecting the needs of vulnerable children who may not have opportunities to interact, Highscope has a clear vision of the role of adults. Adults are seen as key to children's learning and support children through sensitive interactions, which in turn are based on a careful assessment of children's development. This role links to the work of Vygotsky.

Benefits of the Highscope approach

This approach has the following benefits:

- children are seen as competent
- adults work in partnership with children
- children are given opportunities to reflect on what they have been doing and have learned
- adults are thoughtful about children's development and needs
- children who may be from homes where there is little predictability can gain a sense of security through the daily routine.

In addition, Highscope showed the benefits of research-based practice and set a trend in measuring outcomes for children.

Links to practice

Some of the approaches of Highscope can be seen in many settings, for example, the presence of different

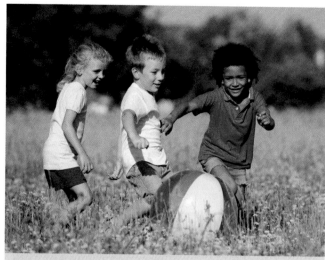
Being outdoors encourages children's sense of wellbeing.

areas or environments from which children can learn and the need for adults to observe children's development carefully.

Forest Schools

Forest Schools have their origins in Scandinavian countries, which have vast woodlands. The idea of integrating playing outdoors with early education has long been part of the Danish education system and it is this model that has been adapted by some early years settings in the UK. The idea behind Forest Schools is that by playing out in the woodlands and also learning skills such as building a campfire, children's all-round development is enhanced. Children seem to develop more confidence and social skills while also benefiting physically. The ideal, as seen in Denmark, is that an early years setting is based in or within walking distance of a forest, but for many settings in the UK this is not possible. This means that many settings will take children out for sessions in a local woodland or will build some of the principles, such as children having opportunities for risk and challenge, into their outdoor play.

Benefits of the Forest School approach to play

This approach has the following benefits:

- children have feelings of freedom
- there are opportunities for children to express themselves
- children gain confidence and independence
- children gain practical skills and knowledge

- social skills improve as children make and do things with others
- children learn awareness of, and respect for, nature including temperature, seasons and wildlife
- children gain physical skills including balance, coordination and fitness
- there are genuine opportunities to explore risk and challenge
- access to a rich environment with plenty of spontaneous learning opportunities.

Links to practice

Over the past few years, there has been widespread concern that children are not spending time outdoors. This has been linked to an upward trend in childhood obesity and a downward trend in children's emotional wellbeing. As a result of this, early years curricula require that children spend time outdoors. This fits very well with the ethos of Forest Schools.

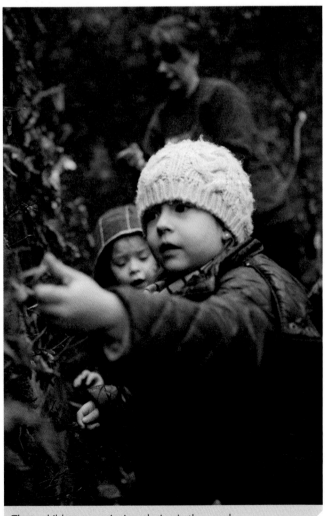

These children are enjoying playing in the woods.

New Zealand Te Whāriki

Te Whāriki is the early years curriculum framework of New Zealand. The term means 'woven mat' and comes from the idea that many strands are important in the education and nurture of children, including their parents, the community and children's interests. It covers ages 0 to 6 years and is based on four key principles.

- Empowerment – children need to be empowered in order to grow and learn.
- Holistic development – children's development is seen as holistic (and includes spiritual development) and so is key to all of their experiences.
- Family and community – children's family and community are seen as central to their development.
- Relationships – children learn through relationships.

As well as these principles there are five strands or areas of development that are seen as being crucial to children's learning and development. Each strand has goals. It is worth noting that these goals are focused on what practitioners might try to achieve for the child. The strands are:

1 wellbeing – Mana Atua
2 belonging – Mana Whenua
3 contribution – Mana Tangata
4 communication – Mana Reo
5 exploration – Mana Aotūroa.

Research

Find out more about Te Whāriki by visiting the Early Childhood Education website. You can access this website by going to www.pearsonhotlinks.co.uk and searching for this ISBN: 9781447970965.

Benefits of the Te Whāriki approach

This approach has the following benefits:

- parents, family and community are seen as vital in children's education
- families' cultures and languages are genuinely respected

- practitioners are expected to reflect on practice
- daily observations of children are used as a tool for planning and reflection
- children are seen as competent, individual learners
- play and exploration led by children is seen as important.

Links to early years practice

There is a strong emphasis on adults spending time **reflecting on practice**. This has also become a feature of recent early years practice in the UK. As a way of creating partnerships with parents and involving them in their child's education, practitioners create '**learning journeys**' or '**learning stories**' that they can share with parents. These include photographs and comments from parents and children. 'Learning journeys' as a way of observing and assessing children's development has been adopted/adapted in many UK settings.

Key terms

Learning journey/learning story – a way of assessing and planning for children's development using a narrative approach that can easily be shared and constructed with parents and children.

Reflecting on practice – thinking about the way one works in order to make changes, build on strengths and stay up to date with developments.

Understanding the early years framework relevant to your setting

Play underpins most early years curricula or frameworks in the United Kingdom at the moment. In England practitioners use the EYFS. As an early years professional, you will be expected to know about the curriculum in your setting and to be able to use it to create activities and play opportunities. A good starting point when looking at the curriculum is to read carefully to find what is meant by play – as we have seen, there are many definitions of what this might mean.

Key features of the EYFS

The EYFS has the following features:

- The EYFS is statutory and all settings working with children aged 0 to 5 years must use it.
- Reception classes are part of the EYFS.
- Play is the key way in which the curriculum is delivered.
- The definition of play includes adult-directed activities as well as child-initiated activities.
- Targets for children's development are outlined. These targets are known as Early Learning Goals.
- The curriculum is divided into three prime areas of development and four subsidiary areas. The three prime areas of development are seen as central to supporting children's overall development and the idea is that these feed into the other areas of development.
- Settings have to show that they are providing opportunities for children to work towards the Early Learning Goals using the areas of development outlined in Table 2.14.

Table 2.14 Areas of development in the Early Learning Goals

Prime areas of development	Subsidiary areas of development
Personal, social and emotional development	Mathematical development
Communication and language	Knowledge and understanding of the world
Physical development	Literacy
	Expressive arts

Activity

Find out how your setting plans play and activities linked to the EYFS or other curricula.

Plan a play activity for a specific child or group of children and link it to the EYFS or other curricula.

Assessment practice 2.4

3C.P5 | 3C.M3

Write an essay that shows how different approaches to play have shaped the curriculum and practice in your work placement. Make sure that you refer to at least two of each of the following: theoretical, philosophical and other approaches to play.

Assessment practice 2.5

3C.D2

An early years setting is deciding whether to change its practice by adopting another approach, for example, theoretical or philosophical, but first it would like to find out how successful a change might be.

You have been asked to choose one approach and then consider how successful it is in practice. The early years setting that has commissioned this work is keen to have a written report that evaluates your findings.

Which area of development outlined in the Early Learning Goals are these boys working towards?

D Understand early years professionals' involvement in children's purposeful play opportunities, activities and learning

Children benefit from adults who know how to plan a range of play types and opportunities, but can also engage in different ways in their play. In this section we look at the ways in which adults might plan, organise and be involved in children's play in order to support children's overall development.

The benefits of adult involvement in play to babies' and children's development

There is plenty of research into the area of adult involvement in play as well as in learning activities and opportunities, including that provided by the Effective Provision of Pre-School Education Project (EPPE), which suggests that the role of the adult is important in children's play. Learning to support children's play is a skill that comes with experience. Here, we will look at the ways in which adults might be involved in children's play and also some practical tips that you can use while on placement.

Research

Read the findings of the EPPE project that, in 2003, began following the progress of a cohort of 3-year-old children for 8 years. You can access the findings by going to www.pearsonhotlinks.co.uk and searching for this ISBN: 9781447970965.

Babies and children can gain a lot from playing independently and together, but adults can significantly enhance their experiences, for example by helping children to build relationships, extend their communication and social skills and acquire higher-level thinking skills. Table 2.15 shows ways that adults can be involved in babies' and children's play and the potential benefits of their involvement.

Table 2.15 Ways that adults may be involved in play

Area of development	Adult involvement	Example of an activity involving an adult
Physical	<ul><li>Put out suitable equipment based on children's interests and developmental stage.</li><li>Encourage and reassure babies and children so that they attempt movements.</li><li>Model or join in with children to help them learn or practise a skill, e.g. holding a toddler's hand as they walk on a wall.</li><li>Plan play activities to develop specific movements or skills.</li></ul>	Skipping ropes are put out for a small group of 6-year-old children to play with. The adult thinks that this will develop their coordination further and that it will be a new skill. The adult joins in so the children can see how to use a skipping rope. Some children find it hard, but the adult encourages them.
Cognitive	<ul><li>Put out new materials or different combinations for babies and children to explore and play with.</li><li>Use naturally occurring opportunities to draw babies' and children's attention to things.</li><li>Draw babies' and children's attention to different features while joining in with their play.</li><li>Take an interest in what babies or children are doing – listening to them, chatting to them and watching them.</li></ul>	A group of 4-year-old children have enjoyed playing with glitter. The adult makes dough with glitter in it. The children are very excited. They make lots of comments and ask questions about where glitter comes from. The adult joins in and the next day they spend time looking at mirrors and things that reflect light.
Language	<ul><li>Put out new materials or different materials so that babies and children have something new to talk about.</li><li>For children from around 2 years onwards, put out small-world and role-play props for children to play with and encourage use of language.</li><li>Take an interest in what babies and children are doing and spend time questioning, chatting and listening to them.</li></ul>	An adult puts out a collection of hats for a couple of 2-year-old children to play with. The adult puts a small hat on the head of one and the child giggles and says 'liddle'. The adult says 'It is too little. Can you get me a bigger one?'

continued

Table 2.15 (continued)

Area of development	Adult involvement	Example of an activity involving an adult
Emotional	<ul><li>Plan play activities that will allow children to express their feelings using resources such as musical instruments, puppets or paint.</li><li>Join in with babies and children as they play. This can help develop closer bonds between you.</li><li>Observe children as they play to help you understand how they may be feeling.</li><li>Encourage babies and children as they are playing to help develop their self-esteem.</li></ul>	A 1-year-old baby has just come into the nursery. The baby is still settling in. The adult takes out a puppet and plays peepo with it. The baby smiles and comes towards the adult. The adult makes the puppet clap its hands. The baby copies the action and the adult smiles. The baby comes to sit on the adult's knee and together they carry on playing with the puppet.
Social	<ul><li>Plan play activities that will prompt children to play alongside or with other children.</li><li>Join in with children to model how to take turns or how to support an individual child.</li><li>Help babies and toddlers develop social skills by playing with them.</li></ul>	An adult gets out a fishing game. Three children want to play with it. The adult sits with the children and joins in. The adult reminds the children to take turns and praises them for playing well together.

The skills that early years professionals need to engage with babies and children in play

One of the key ways in which we can support children's development is to engage directly with them during play. Engaging with children is quite a skill – if adults are not sensitive, there is a danger that opportunities for children's learning and development can actually be decreased.

Skills for child-initiated play

The key to engaging with children during child-initiated play is that ownership and direction of the play must stay with the children. This means that if children are happily creating a boat using wooden blocks, the adult should not come along and suggest that they build a tower. The Theory into practice box gives some tips about how to engage with children who are already playing and involved in an activity that they have initiated themselves.

Theory into practice

How to engage with children who are already playing:

- Observe what children are doing – stand near them or sit with them. Do not interfere but show that you are interested.
- Make interested comments about what children are doing such as: 'Wow, you are busy' or 'I used to love doing that when I was your age.'
- Monitor children's reactions to your presence. Do they want an adult present? Do they turn or move away? Do they respond and want you to be involved?

Link

Go to Section C in this unit to find more information about Chris Athey and the schemas she identified for children's play.

This child wanted a practitioner to pretend to be a customer at her grocery shop.

Skills for adult-initiated play

Adult-initiated play is where adults set up play in ways that allow children to take control and explore for themselves. With babies and toddlers, treasure basket and heuristic play would be a good example of this. With both of these types of play, the adult puts out materials that they believe would be of interest to the children but then allows the children to explore and use the materials in their own way.

In some ways, adult-initiated play is quite a clever way of working – it allows children to play and explore, but also allows the adult to introduce new materials and concepts to children and to model new skills.

Key term

Adult-initiated play – where adults put out toys and resources in ways that may prompt children to play in specific ways.

Building on children's interests

Adult-initiated play can also build on children's existing interests. You may, for example, observe that a toddler is walking around with a shopping bag, picking up bits and pieces, moving them to the other side of the room and then tipping them out. Your conclusion might be that the child is exploring the transporting schema. To support the child further you may decide to put out a pushchair.

Using the early years curriculum

Sometimes the starting point for adult-initiated play will be the curriculum. A practitioner might identify a learning experience that children need to have and then think of a way of setting up the play accordingly, e.g. setting up a shop so that children handle and talk about money, or creating a darkened space and putting torches inside so that children can play with light.

Supporting children's development

Some adult-initiated play will arise to support children's development. This might include setting up a play opportunity, or modelling play – for example, an adult might start to make marks on a whiteboard to encourage a couple of children to practise their mark-making skills.

Setting up play environments

Adult-initiated play is used a lot to set up play environments. Table 2.16 shows some of the ways that adults can set up play for children aged 3 to 5 years and the benefits this play has for children.

The learning potential in unplanned events

One of the wonderful things about working with children is the way that unplanned learning can take place in a very spontaneous way. This is more likely to happen outdoors and also during open-ended play activities such as building a den or playing with sensory materials. For example, children might lift up a tarpaulin and notice some earwigs under it. It is important not to waste these unplanned learning opportunities as you have the ability to build on children's captivation and the experience to encourage further discussion or exploration.

Table 2.16 Play activities for children aged 3–5 years

Area	Aims and benefits	Resources
Role-play area: a souvenir shop	• To help children learn new vocabulary • To help children talk and learn about holidays	• Postcards • Buckets and spades • Souvenirs • Real money • Till
Water tray: a seabed	• To help children see how sand and water mix/separate • To help children think about the seabed	• Sand to go into the bottom of the water tray • Sticks for stirring • Treasure – glass beads, coins
Sand play: at the beach	• To build on a child's recent experience of going on holiday and spending time on a beach	• Tarpaulin sheet that sand will be put onto • Buckets • Spades
Small-world play: road building	• To build on children's interests in tunnels and cars	• Cars • Cardboard tubes • Masking tape
Mark making: at the office	• To encourage children to make marks by creating a 'grown-up' environment	• Calculator • Briefcase • Diaries • Envelopes • Stampers • Headed paper

Activity

The role-play area is often set up by adults to support children's play and give them different play opportunities.

Make a list of ways in which a role-play area might be set out to allow children to use different vocabulary or learn about different materials.

Promoting adult-initiated play

There are many ways that adult-initiated play can be promoted when working with children. Sometimes we might tell children what is available – so that they know what is new – but other times we might just leave children to spot what is there. It can also be helpful to model some play as this helps children to know what to do – modelling play is a very effective way to kick-start an activity, for example, pretending to be a shopper in the role-play shop or making a card in the creativity area. As with child-initiated play, the aim should be to keep ownership of the play with the children and though we might aim to enrich the play by showing an interest, it is important that it remains enjoyable for the children.

Skills for adult-directed play

As described in Section C, adult-directed play is often linked to structured play. When planning adult-directed play, it is important to be aware of its possible limitations. If it is overly directed and/or not carefully planned, there is a danger that children will lose interest and concentration. Adults should understand why they are using this style and make sure the play will be interesting and challenging for the children. Adults also have to make sure that children will be able to participate. This means being aware of children's interests and stage of development. Finally, we know that children learn best when they have good relationships with adults.

In some settings, adult-directed play is used to teach children particular concepts, games or vocabulary, but the aim afterwards is for children to be able to use/adapt what they have learned into their own play.

Planning adult-directed play: five questions

Before you plan adult-directed play, think about the following five questions.

1 Why is an adult needed?
2 How do you intend it to be pleasurable for children?
3 How do you intend to ensure that children can participate fully?
4 Will children be able to use/practise the skill or concept in their own play?
5 How do you know that each child is ready for this?

Encouraging children to participate

In order to benefit from play activities, children need to join in. In terms of adult-directed activities, children are more likely to participate if they have a strong relationship with the adult, the activity looks interesting and the activity matches their development level. Young children are likely to be put off if the activity is passive or if they have to listen to a very long explanation of the activity first.

In terms of child-initiated activities, it is important that the activities build on children's known interests or on resources that we know are likely to be of interest to the age and stage of the child. When using materials and resources that children have already explored and played with, it may also be important to enrich them with other resources or lay them out differently. In addition, some children may need an adult to stay and play with them. This is particularly the case with babies and children under 3 years old.

Ensuring a balance between adult-directed and child-initiated activities

As we have already seen, both child-initiated and adult-directed activities are important to children's development and learning. It is, therefore, important to check that there is a balance of each type of activity during a session. The balance between adult-directed and child-initiated play also needs to reflect children's age and stage of development. Children who have particular developmental needs are likely to need more adult-directed activities. There is also an expectation in the EYFS that older children will benefit from more adult-directed activities that focus on literacy and numeracy.

Case study

Adult-directed play

Annie has seen that two children have been filling up beakers with sand and making sandcastles. She realises that this might form the basis of a good game that she can play with the children while teaching them how to recognise their numbers. She asks the children if they would like to play a game in the sand tray with her. She shows them the game and together they play it. After a few minutes, Annie leaves the children. They carry on playing the game, but then start to adapt it. Another child comes and wants to play with them.

They explain the rules and happily play together. Annie watches from a distance. She sees that although the game has changed, the children are still throwing a dice and then counting out.

1 Explain why Annie's adult-directed play was successful.
2 Why is it essential to be aware of children's stage of development and interests?
3 Why is it helpful for adult-directed play to be used as a starting point for child-initiated play?
4 Explain why adult-directed activities might be used to help children socialise together.

Supporting children's group learning and socialisation

Play is a way for children to develop social skills including turn taking, and learning to follow instructions and rules. These are important skills for children as they learn to be a part of a group and thus learn to socialise. Adult-directed play can be a good starting point for children to learn these skills. You could start with games such as parachute play and 'What's the time, Mr Wolf?', which have simple rules, before introducing other games where children need to be able to sit or stay still for longer periods.

How to respond to individual needs and ensure that play is inclusive

We have seen that play can contribute to children's development. For this to take place, we need to ensure that it is inclusive. This means that the resources, play opportunities and the way that we support children during play meets their individual needs.

In order to ensure that play is inclusive and that we recognise children's individual needs, the role of the adult is to gain as much information as possible and to understand what is appropriate for each child's age and stage of development. There are many ways of doing this.

Parents

Parents often know what their children enjoy playing with and also what support they may need. Talking to parents may also help us understand children's culture and ensure that this is reflected in the materials and props that we provide. In the case of children with additional needs, parents may also give us advice about how they adapt resources at home.

Other professionals

To ensure that provision for play and learning is inclusive, we may also need to work with other professionals. Some children will need particular support in order that they can play. They may have a learning difficulty or a physical or sensory impairment. To support these children, we will need to talk to their parents, but may also find it useful to seek advice from professionals such as a physiotherapist or a professional from the sensory impairment team.

In addition, there are organisations that lend out specialist equipment.

Research

Find out about the work of Play England, an organisation that campaigns for play. You can access the Play England website by going to www.pearsonhotlinks.co.uk and searching for this ISBN: 9781447970965.

Observing during play

We can learn a lot about children while they are engaged in play. We can see what interests them, how they interact with other children and also whether they have any specific difficulties. We can also see whether the current opportunities are sufficiently challenging for children.

Tips for watching babies and children at play

Think about the following questions when you are observing children at play.

- How interested is the child in the play?
- How long does the child stay engaged with the play?
- How are they using the resources and toys?
- Are they interacting with adults or other children?
- Are there any other resources that might be more suitable for the child?
- Does the child need more/less adult support to be able to use the resources/toys or to access the play?
- Is the play sufficiently challenging for the child?
- Is the play sufficiently pleasurable for the child?

Listening to children

Even very small children can let us know what it is that they would like to be able to do or play with. Trying to engage with children is very important even if they are not yet talking. A scrapbook with photos of toys and activities can help children to point to things that they would like to do.

Responding to children's needs

Once you have recognised children's needs it is important to respond to them promptly. The following scenarios show how practitioners have responded effectively to a range of children's needs.

- Harry, aged 1 year, has a visual impairment. Staff have spoken to Harry's parents and also taken advice from the sensory impairment team. They have made sure that toys and resources are put out on light-reflecting surfaces so that Harry is able to find them more easily. They have also looked for toys that make sounds.
- Jasmine is 3 years old and is new to the setting. Her father has dropped her off at nursery today and mentioned that at home she loves playing with her brother's train set. Her key person decides to get this out to help Jasmine settle in.
- Yannick is 2 years old. He is trying to join the older children on the climbing frame, but is not quite tall enough. His key person notices his efforts and asks him if he would like some help. Yannick nods and lets the key person lift him up to the first rung. Yannick grins with pleasure.

The role of the early years professional in keeping children safe

Play needs to be enjoyable for children. One of the things that makes play enjoyable for children is excitement. Children gain excitement in many ways, but key among these are exploration and challenge. Where adults are overly concerned with safety, there is a real danger that the environments that children find themselves in will be dull, predictable and lacking in stimulation. Having said this, adults working with children do have a legal duty to provide a reasonable standard of care, which includes keeping children safe.

Identifying potential hazards

A key way in which we can keep children safe is to carry out ongoing risk assessment. You should be aware of how resources and materials might be used in potentially hazardous ways. Ropes, for example, often find their way around children's necks, and a heavy item such as a rock might fall on a child's toe. A swing can easily catch a child in the face.

Once you have thought about what might happen, the next step is to think about ways of preventing or reducing the impact of an accident. You might talk to children about how they should use the resources, supervise the area more closely or join in with the play. For some items such as swings, you might move

them to a particular spot where children can still access them, but there is less likelihood of another child passing by being injured. In settings where children are of different ages, it can be that items are fine with certain age groups, but become risky with younger children. Marbles are a good example of this – they are great for 6- and 7-year-old children, but dangerous for babies and toddlers.

Supervision

Good supervision is a fantastic way of allowing children to explore and try out challenging activities. Adults can provide children with reassurance, practical advice and also words of caution where necessary. Good supervision does not just mean standing like a prison guard watching children – it should be about taking a genuine interest in what the children are doing, by chatting or being an unobtrusive presence.

Knowing and understanding the children

If you get to know individual children well, it becomes easier to manage potential risks and find a good balance between safety and exciting play.

Developing children's thinking and learning during play

One role of the early years professional during play is to develop and extend children's thinking and learning. This can happen during both child-initiated and adult-directed activities. The role of the early years professional is often to draw children's attention to features of what they are doing. An adult might comment, for example, that 'the sand is dry today' and so 'it is hard to make sandcastles'. From this comment, a conversation might develop about how

Although this outdoor area is probably safe, what might you need to think about?

much water should be added in order to make the perfect sandcastle or about the difference between dry and wet sand. The skill of the adult is to engage children in this thinking and learning without spoiling the children's enjoyment of their play.

Helping children to develop positive attitudes towards others

During play, there are often opportunities for early years professionals to help children develop positive attitudes towards others and learn to respect others. There are many ways in which we might do this.

Role modelling

During play, adults can role model caring and thoughtful behaviours. We can show children how to take turns, share resources and help out others.

Explanation

Where a range of culturally-rich resources are on offer, especially in the home corner, adults can model their use and talk to children about how and why they are used. This can help children to learn about differences and similarities, and develop respect.

Case study

Preparing food

Ayse and Jaden are playing at the dough table. Ayse takes the rolling pin and starts pounding the dough with it. Jaden shouts out that Ayse is stupid and that rolling pins are not used in that way. Ayse starts to cry. Lisa, the room leader, comes across and sits down at the table. She tells Jaden that there are many ways of using a rolling pin and that sometimes families use them to soften meat in the way that Ayse was using the rolling pin. She tells Jaden that the way he spoke to Ayse was not very friendly or respectful. She stays with the children and plays alongside them for a while, talking to them about the many different ways in which food can be prepared.

1 Why was it important for Lisa to intervene in the play?

2 How did Lisa help the children to learn about differences?

3 Why is it important that children learn about differences through play?

Direct intervention

Sometimes, adults might intervene in play to help children respect others or help them understand that there are differences between people. The case study: Preparing food shows an example of this.

Assessment practice 2.6 — 3D.P6 | 3D.P7 | 3D.M4

Create an information pack for a newly qualified childminder. The childminder will be working with babies, toddlers and children in a home environment. The information pack should explain the role of the early years professional in child-initiated and adult-initiated play and learning activities and the benefits of this involvement to babies' and children's development. It should then contain an analysis of the skills needed by early years professionals to support children's learning and development during play and learning activities, giving some examples. It should also include guidance as to how early years professionals can initiate and direct play sensitively and effectively. Make sure to cover activities with both individual children and groups of children.

Assessment practice 2.7 — 3D.D3

A training college has asked you to give a presentation to learners that evaluates the importance of child-initiated play and how adults can contribute to its effectiveness.

Further reading and resources

Bruce, T. (1991) *Time to Play in Early Childhood Education*, London: Hodder Arnold.

Moyles, J. (2010) *The Excellence of Play* (3rd ed.), Oxford: Oxford University Press.

Tassoni, P. and Hucker, K. (2005) *Planning Play and the Early Years*, Oxford: Heinemann.

Tassoni, P. (2008) *Penny Tassoni's Practical EYFS Handbook*, Oxford: Heinemann.

Website

Playwork Principles Scrutiny Group (2005) *The Playwork Principles*: www.playwales.org.uk

Ready for work?

Alison Davis Supervisor of a preschool

A lot of people think that working with young children is just about playing, but nothing is further from the truth. There is far more to play than people realise. Our staff have to know how to plan play that links to the EYFS and also how to build on children's interests.

One of the main things we look for when employing staff is whether or not they know how to support children as they are playing. This is a skill. Adults have to learn to closely observe children's responses and to know when to intervene or when to step back. Staff also have to know how to set out the environment so that it is ready for play. Children love coming in and seeing a home corner all laid out or something new in the sand tray. These are almost like little 'nudges' that help children get started. Finally, at the end of the day, when everyone is a little tired, staff have to tidy, clean and sort out ready for the next day. So child's play it is not.

Skills for practice

Setting out and maintaining role play

- Create a cosy area so that children think that they cannot be seen.
- Look out for as many real-life props as possible.
- Make sure the necessary props are ready.
- If a role-play situation is new to the children, be ready to join in and model what happens.
- Be ready to discreetly tidy up.

Maintaining sand and water

- Keep a dustpan and brush ready.
- Keep a cloth ready to wipe up water spills.
- Make sure aprons are clean and easy for children to put on.
- Sieve and rake through sand to keep it clean.
- Water needs to be changed daily or in some settings at the end of each session.
- Toys and objects for water and sand should be washed thoroughly and dried.

- Many settings have separate sand and water toys because sand scratches the surfaces.
- Sand and water are activities that need some supervision. Look out for children who are throwing sand and immediately intervene to prevent eye injuries. Wipe up spillages from both promptly.
- Be ready to do some discreet tidying away as too many objects in the sand and water trays can make them unattractive.
- If sand is outdoors, cover it when the outdoor area is not being used. Always check the sand for animal mess.

Creating a treasure basket

- Items have to be sufficiently large and robust so that a baby can mouth them safely.
- Avoid items that may break into smaller pieces or are small enough to swallow.
- Look out for items that are straightforward to wash afterwards.

Introduction

If children are fit and healthy, their learning and development is encouraged and they are more likely to be happy. In this unit, you will learn about the principles of children's development and how to provide for children's physical needs. You will also learn how to recognise when children are unwell and how to support children who have long-term medical conditions.

Assessment: You will be assessed by a series of assignments set by your teacher/tutor.

Learning aims

In this unit you will:

A   understand the physical needs of children for their development and health

B   understand the role of the early years professional in supporting children's physical development

C   be able to meet a child's physical care needs

D1   know how to recognise and respond to children who are unwell

D2   understand the role of the early years professional in supporting children with ongoing health conditions.

> Some people think that working with children is all about play. Yes, that is part of the job, but you also have to know how to keep children healthy and care for those with long-term medical conditions such as asthma.
>
> Penny Tassoni

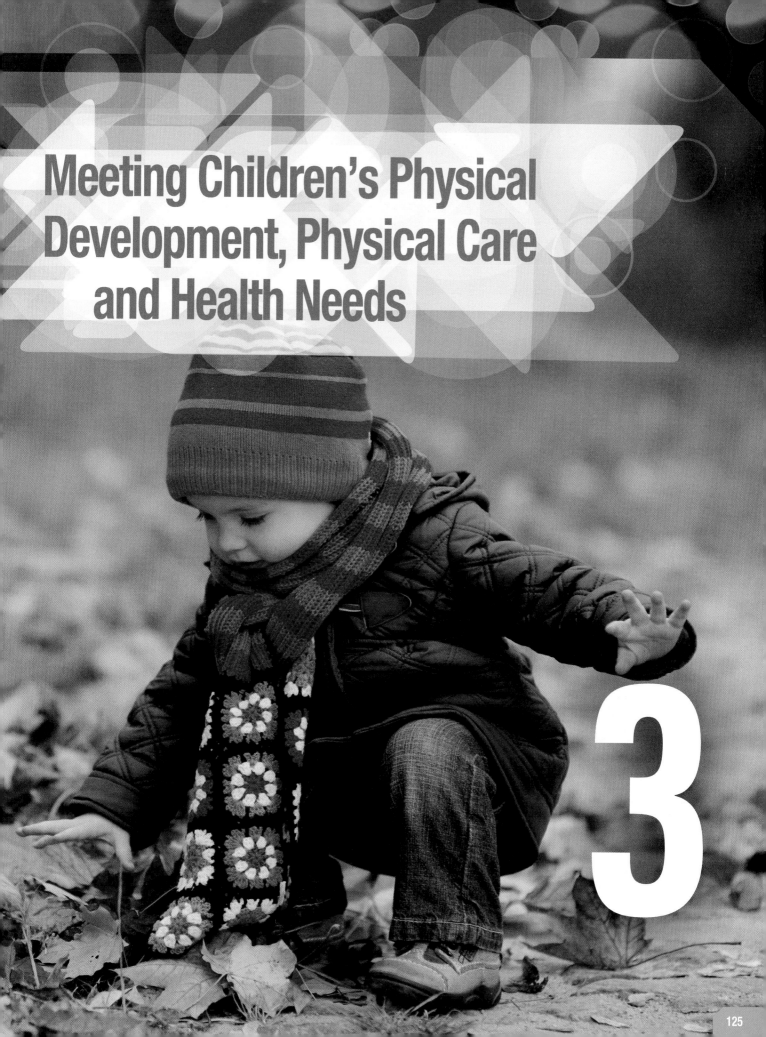

Meeting Children's Physical Development, Physical Care and Health Needs

3

BTEC
Assessment Zone

This table shows what you must do in order to achieve a **Pass**, **Merit** or **Distinction** grade, and lists activities that relate to each learning aim.

Assessment criteria		
Pass	**Merit**	**Distinction**
Learning aim A: Understand the physical needs of children for their development and health		
3A.P1 Explain why it is important to children's health and holistic development to provide: • a nutritious diet • exercise • sleep. **Assessment practice 3.1**	**3A.M1** Discuss the relationship between how children's physical needs are addressed and their holistic development. **Assessment practice 3.1**	
Learning aim B: Understand the role of the early years professional in supporting children's physical development		
3B.P2 English Explain how different types of indoor and outdoor activities and resources are used in early years settings to support the physical development of babies and children from birth up to 8 years. **Assessment practice 3.2** **3B.P3** Explain ways in which early years professionals can provide inclusive, risk-managed activities that support varied physical development of children. **Assessment practice 3.2**	**3B.M2** Assess the contribution of early years professionals to inclusive provision in physical activities, using examples. **Assessment practice 3.2**	**3B.D1** Evaluate how early years professionals can support a child's unique needs at different stages of their physical development. **Assessment practice 3.2**
Learning aim C: Be able to to meet a child's physical care needs		
3C.P4 Plan, record and carry out safe and hygienic physical care routines to meet the age, stage and needs of a selected child and promote a healthy lifestyle. **Assessment practice 3.3**	**3C.M3** Analyse the extent to which the implemented care routines contributed to the child's holistic development and promoted a healthy lifestyle. **Assessment practice 3.3**	**3C.D2** Assess the effectiveness of the planning and implementation of the care routines, making recommendations for improvements. **Assessment practice 3.3**

continued

Assessment criteria (*continued*)		
Pass	**Merit**	**Distinction**
Learning aim D: 1 Know how to recognise and respond to children who are unwell 2 Understand the role of the early years professional in supporting children with ongoing health conditions		
3D1.P5 Describe how to recognise signs of illness in babies and children. **Assessment practice 3.4** **3D1.P6** Explain procedures to follow in early years settings when babies and children are unwell. **Assessment practice 3.4**	**3D1.M4** Assess how partnership work with parents could meet the health needs of babies and children. **Assessment practice 3.5**	**3D.D3** Evaluate the role of the early years professional in early years settings in meeting the needs of children who are unwell and those who need ongoing support, using examples. **Assessment practice 3.5**
3D2.P7 Explain how early years professionals in early years settings support children with: • asthma • eczema • diabetes. **Assessment practice 3.5**	**3D2.M5** Discuss how early years professionals in early years settings can best support children with an ongoing health condition. **Assessment practice 3.5**	

English   English Functional Skills signposting

How you will be assessed

This unit will be assessed by a series of internally assessed tasks set by your teacher/tutor. They will include practical tasks that will need to be carried out in placement, and that link to your Practical Evidence Portfolio. Throughout this unit you will find assessment practice activities that will help you work towards your assessment. Completing these activities will not mean that you have achieved a particular grade, but you will have carried out useful research or preparation that will be relevant when it comes to your final assignment.

In order for you to achieve the tasks in your assignment, it is important to check that you have met all of the Pass grading criteria. You can do this as you work your way through the assignment.

If you are hoping to gain a Merit or Distinction, you should also make sure that you present the information in your assignment in the style that is required by the relevant assessment criterion.

For example, Merit and Distinction criteria will require you to analyse and evaluate.

The assignment set by your teacher/tutor will consist of a number of tasks designed to meet the criteria in the table. This is likely to consist of a written assignment but may also include activities such as the following:

• producing a reference document for new employees about the importance of meeting children's physical development and physical care needs

• providing evidence of information gained through further reading, examples from practice or discussion with relevant professionals working in the sector

• using evidence from case studies or observations to support your findings or recommendations

• developing a procedures handbook for staff in an early years setting.

Babies and children's physical care is important to their overall development. Make a list of five things that you think are involved in caring for children.

A Understand the physical needs of children for their development and health

It is easy to forget that babies and children cannot learn, relax and play if their basic physical needs are not met. Figure 3.1 shows the physical needs of babies and children.

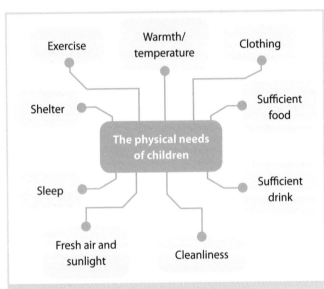

Figure 3.1 The physical needs of babies and children

In addition to these basic physical needs, we also have to think about temperature and ventilation when providing an environment for children. Ideally, indoors the temperature should be 18–21°C, with babies' sleeping spaces at 16–18°C.

Ventilation is important indoors to prevent airborne illnesses and to make sure that the air is sufficiently oxygenated.

The importance of meeting children's basic needs

When any of children's physical needs are not met, their development, health and wellbeing are likely to

be affected. If, for example, children are too hot or too cold, they may find it hard to concentrate and if they do not have enough sunlight, they may develop **rickets**, which is a bone disease. Children should also live in good housing because when they are exposed to damp or live in unsafe homes, they are more likely to develop a **respiratory disease** such as **asthma** or have accidents.

Key terms

Asthma – a long-term lung disease that inflames and narrows the airways causing difficulty in breathing.

Respiratory disease – a condition that affects the lungs or a person's ability to breathe.

Rickets – a bone disease caused by lack of vitamin D.

Maslow's hierarchy of needs

Abraham Maslow (1908–70) was a psychologist who was interested in understanding people's behaviour and motivation. He studied people who were high achievers and came to the conclusion that it was only possible to reach high levels of personal and career fulfilment if other needs were met first. Maslow showed this through a hierarchical model similar to the one shown in Figure 3.2. The idea is that the basic physiological needs on the bottom layer have to be met before the next layer of needs can be met. When Maslow's work was published in 1943 it was influential in many areas, and notably for large employers. Maslow's model is useful in reminding us that children cannot learn or benefit from settings unless their physical and emotional needs have been met.

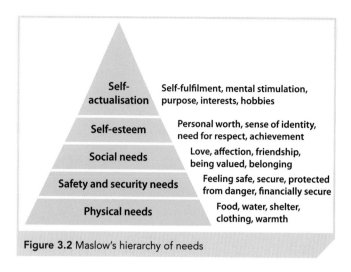

Figure 3.2 Maslow's hierarchy of needs

The need for a nutritious diet

The development of babies and children is also affected by what, and how much, they eat. Food and drink intake supports the physical and brain growth of babies and young children and also provides them with sufficient energy to move. It therefore helps to develop their physical skills. Food and drink are also important for good health, and children who are **malnourished** or **undernourished** are more likely to have periods of ill health. On the other hand, babies and children who have too much food and drink and insufficient exercise, even if the food is otherwise healthy, are likely to develop health problems later in life that are associated with being overweight, such as heart disease.

Key terms

Malnourished – having a lack of proper nutrients.

Undernourished – having insufficient food/nutrients.

What is a healthy diet?

It might seem easy to suggest that children should have a healthy diet, but recognising what and how much children should eat is actually quite complex. This is because children's needs change according to their age and level of activity. A good starting point is to understand that food and drink provide us with nutrients. A healthy diet is, therefore, one in which children have the right balance of nutrients for their age/stage in order to support exercise, growth and development.

Nutrients are often grouped into the following food groups:

- protein – good for growth and repair of cells
- carbohydrates – good for energy
- fats – good for energy and to absorb some vitamins
- minerals – necessary for a range of different functions, such as calcium for bone development
- vitamins – necessary for a range of different functions, such as vitamin C for healthy skin.

Changing needs

It is important to understand that babies and young children have different nutritional needs than adults. Adults have larger stomachs and so they need to eat less often than babies and children. The proportion of fat and protein in an adult's diet in comparison to other nutrients is also lower than the proportion in a child's diet. Children's nutritional needs change during childhood and they can vary according to the child's activity level. When planning meals, knowing what babies and children need at different ages is, therefore, essential.

Activity

Find out about what babies and children need in terms of nutrition by visiting the Caroline Walker Trust website. You can access this website by going to www.pearsonhotlinks.co.uk and searching for this ISBN: 9781447970965.

Then, create a chart that shows sample menus for children of three different ages.

The role of sleep

Sleep is vital to children's health and wellbeing. This is because sleep is needed for healthy brain function and growth and to enable the body's cells to repair themselves. It is also needed to regulate the hormones that are responsible for growth and even appetite. Sleep is needed for other reasons, as we will now see.

Concentration

Brain function is helped or hindered by sleep. When children are tired they will find it harder to concentrate.

Memory/learning

During sleep, the brain reviews the day's events and this seems to be important in terms of putting down memories. Children who are not sleeping sufficiently are likely to find it harder to learn because they will not remember as much.

The immune system

Sleep plays a part in supporting the immune system. During sleep the body repairs cells and fights infection. Children who are not sleeping sufficiently are more likely to have colds and other infections.

Controlling emotions and impulses

Young children tend to be impulsive and **emotionally labile**. A lack of sleep exaggerates this and so children who are not sleeping sufficiently are more likely to show impulsive behaviour. Linked to this is sleep's ability to provide children with a sense of wellbeing.

Key term

Emotionally labile – having emotions that may be strong and fluctuate quickly.

Obesity

There has recently been a study into the relationship between how long a child sleeps and their weight. It would appear that children who are not getting sufficient sleep run the risk of becoming overweight and even obese. Scientists are still working on the correlation between sleep and weight gain, but it is thought to be related to the hormones that are responsible for appetite and metabolism. Also related is the fact that being tired increases lethargy and so decreases interest in physical activity.

Research

You can find out more about the latest research into the links between childhood obesity and sleep by looking at the FLAME study on the British Medical Journal website. You can access this study by going to www.pearsonhotlinks.co.uk and searching for this ISBN: 9781447970965.

How much sleep?

Although children vary in how much sleep they need, there are some useful guidelines that we can follow. Table 3.1 shows the guidelines for children aged 3 months to 5 years.

Table 3.1 How much sleep children need at different ages

Age	Naps	Night-time	Total
3 months	5 hours	15 hours	20 hours
4–12 months	3 hours	11 hours	14 hours
1–3 years	2 hours 15 minutes	11 hours	13 hours 15 minutes
3–4 years	1 hour 30 minutes	10 hours 30 minutes	12 hours
5 years	None	10–12 hours	10–12 hours

Source: Department for Education (2010) © Crown copyright 2010

Activity

Download an early support booklet that has been provided by the Department of Education for parents about the importance of sleep for children. You can access this booklet by going to www.pearsonhotlinks.co.uk and searching for this ISBN: 9781447970965.

Read the booklet and make a poster that gives advice to parents about the importance of sleep and bedtime routines.

Signs that a child is tired

Babies and children will show us when they are tired. Look out for the following signs:

- irritable behaviour
- crying for no clear reason
- a lack of concentration
- dark rings around the eyes
- having tantrums or becoming whiny and uncooperative.

Helping children to sleep

You can only fall asleep when your body relaxes and feels safe. This means that children who are tired may find it hard to sleep in an environment that is noisy or unfamiliar. We can help babies and children to sleep by providing them with familiar objects such as their own sheet or cuddly toy, and by making sure that the environment feels calm.

▌The importance of exercise

Babies and children need exercise, among other things, to improve their lifelong health. This does not mean formal movements or PE lessons, but

These children all have their own beds and sheets, and an adult will stay with them so they feel safe.

opportunities to move around or, in the case of non-mobile babies, to be able to kick and move their arms. Figure 3.3 shows the benefits of exercise to children's overall development.

How much exercise?

Over the past few years, there have been concerns that young children are not having sufficient opportunities for vigorous exercise. At the time of writing, the recommendation is that young children should spend an hour over the course of the day engaged in physical activity. This might be walking, running, using wheeled toys or generally engaging in some form of play. When planning for children's physical activity, it is worth knowing that young children need a stop–start approach. Their lung and heart capacity means that they will find it hard to maintain vigorous activity for long periods. This is why toddlers are in and out of their pushchairs, for example – one moment they will be sitting down and the next they will be up walking or having a run about.

▌How health impacts on growth and holistic development

Being healthy helps children to feel good about themselves and so it supports children's confidence and sense of competency. This means that health and wellbeing are often linked together when we consider their impact on children's development. Interestingly, children who have continued poor health are more prone to depression because of this link and so steps to promote children's health will have an effect on their wellbeing.

Figure 3.3 The benefits of exercise

Good health is important for babies' and children's all-round development. When babies and children are poorly, they are less likely to want to play with others, interact and explore their environment. This lack of stimulation will, in turn, delay their cognitive and social development as they will not be gaining new experiences or interacting well with others. Feeling poorly also means that babies and children are less likely to cope with the trials and tribulations of the day and so are more likely to have tantrums, cry or become frustrated.

For children of school age, taking time off school due to illness may mean that they fall behind with learning to read as well as other aspects of the curriculum.

For children with medical conditions, care has to be taken to support them, because their long-term development can be affected for the reasons just described.

Assessment practice 3.1   3A.P1 | 3A.M1

Make an information pack that shows the physical needs that children have and why they are important for children's holistic development. Be sure to include coverage of the following topics in your pack:

- why a nutritious diet, exercise and sleep are important to children's health and holistic development
- the relationship between how children's physical needs are met and their holistic development.

Use case studies and/or observations from your work placements as evidence to help you create the information pack.

B Understand the role of the early years professional in supporting children's physical development

Children's physical development is linked to the type of environment and resources that adults provide. This section looks at how practitioners can support children's physical development.

The role of observation

Observation plays an extremely important role in supporting development. By looking carefully at babies' and children's physical development, we can work out what their developmental needs are. We can also think about whether children are showing any signs of developmental delay that may need further investigation. For observation to be of any use, we do need to know what typical development looks like for most children. This means that it is worth revising your knowledge of normative development. We also need to talk to parents, as children often show some aspects of their physical development outside of the setting.

Case study

The importance of observing children

Purmina is 18 months old. She loves playing with her sit-and-ride toy. Her **key person** has spotted that she is coordinating her feet movements to push the toy along with both feet. She is also moving quickly and knows when to stop and turn the toy. Her key person talks to Purmina's mother who tells her that, at home, Purmina tries to get on her brother's tricycle. They agree that it is time for Purmina to try out a simple tricycle that requires pushing rather than pedalling, but which she can steer.

1 Why is it important for Purmina's key person to observe her development?

2 Why is it helpful for the key person to talk to Purmina's parents?

3 How will this observation help Purmina's development?

By observing children, we can also think about other areas of their development – such as their confidence levels and whether they are keen to try out new experiences. We can also begin to identify children's interests and plan activities that take these into account.

Link

Go to Unit 1: Section B to find more information about how children develop.

Key term

Key person – a practitioner designated to take responsibility for a child's emotional wellbeing by having a strong attachment with them and a good relationship with their parents.

The importance of physical development

The importance of physical development to children's overall or holistic development is increasingly being recognised. It is not only important in keeping children healthy, but it has other benefits too. Children who have opportunities for physical development are likely to gain in confidence as they master a range of skills, for example the ability to walk, climb and run and skills associated with self-care, such as feeding and dressing. Opportunities for physical development also help children to develop a range of skills associated with coordination and spatial awareness, such as being able to avoid obstacles or place a cup back onto a table. Opportunities for physical development are also associated with the development of early problem-solving skills as children move objects or explore resources in order to find things out.

Selecting appropriate and safe resources and activities

There are many different resources that can be used to support children at different ages and stages in acquiring skills. Choosing resources requires thought about the ages/stages of children, and also their interests. This is why observing children's individual needs is so important. Table 3.2 shows some examples of skills that children should develop and the type of resources that might be useful to encourage this.

Link

Go to Unit 2: Section B and Unit 4: Section B to find information about toy safety marks and instructions.

This child is developing physical skills by playing on a sit-and-ride toy.

Table 3.2 Examples of resources to help children practise skills

Fine motor movements 0–2 years		Fine motor movements 2–8 years	
Skill	**Activity**	**Skill**	**Activity**
Hand coordination: grasping; moving objects from one hand to the other	• Rattles • Self-feeding • Play with sensory materials such as gloop (from 6 months) • Activity mat	Pincer grip	• Tweezers, pipettes • Sewing, pegboards
		Strengthening hand preference	• Routine activities that require an active hand and a stabilising hand, e.g. dustpan and brush, drying a beaker
Hand–eye coordination	• Pointing to pictures in books • Turning pages in books • Self-feeding • Baby gym • Pop-up toys • Playing with water	Hand–eye coordination	• Turning pages in books • Self-care skills such as dressing, eating • Sewing • Construction toys, e.g. LEGO® • Drawing and painting • Playing with malleable materials, sand and water • Junk modelling
Gross motor movements 0–2 years		**Gross motor movements 2–8 years**	
Skill	**Activity**	**Skill**	**Activity**
Strengthening of limbs and muscles	• Baby gym • Activity mat • Bath time • Playing with water • Playing in ball pool • Throwing soft balls	Locomotive skills and balance	• Climbing frames • Running • Obstacle courses • Movement to music
Locomotive movements and balance	• Baby swing • Brick trolley • Sit-and-ride toys • Climbing frame	Hand–foot coordination	• Tricycles, bicycles, pushchairs and other wheeled toys requiring steering • Ball games involving catching and throwing • Games such as 'The hokey cokey'

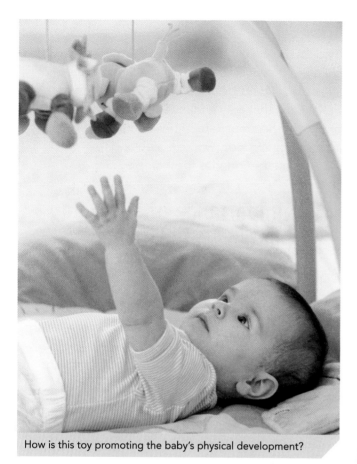

How is this toy promoting the baby's physical development?

Reflect

Resources and activities

Make a list of toys, resources and activities that your work placement uses to promote children's fine and gross motor movements.

Approaches to providing challenge and helping children manage risk

Part of growing up includes learning to manage physical risks. This may include deciding when to cross a road or whether it is safe to climb up a ladder.

For babies and children, learning about their environment is the first step on the way. Until a few years ago, there was a focus on total risk elimination in early years and play settings. This has now been revisited because it has been shown that children did not benefit from this approach – they did not learn the skills needed to keep themselves safe. For example, children who have not walked on an uneven surface

will not know that they need to moderate their speed when doing so. Today, it is accepted that children need physical challenges in their environments and opportunities to explore and experience risk management. It is also recognised that where settings totally eliminate risk and, therefore, challenge for children, there is a greater likelihood of accidents taking place because children become bored and use toys and resources inappropriately. Figure 3.4 shows the benefits of providing risk and challenge in settings.

Figure 3.4 The benefits for children of providing opportunities for risk and challenge in settings

Most settings have to work out how to balance risk against their legal duty to take reasonable steps to prevent accidents. The test of what is reasonable or not is linked to what a 'reasonable person' thinks is acceptable. This, in turn, is likely to link to the age of the child and how significant the risk is. An example of an unreasonable level of risk would be giving a marble to a baby – however, it would be reasonable to let a 6-year-old child play with marbles.

Deciding on the level of risk

When deciding how much risk and challenge is acceptable, we have to consider several factors.

The age/stage of the child

Babies and toddlers have little awareness of safety and are very impulsive. We also know that until 18 months or so, babies and toddlers put things in their mouths. However, the majority of older children are often more aware of their surroundings and have more self-restraint.

Risk assessment

It is important to identify the risks in order to make a decision about what is appropriate. As part of the risk assessment, you should consider what the physical impact/injury for the child would be if an activity went wrong. A slight bump or bruise is likely to be acceptable for an older child but the possibility of concussion or a serious wound is not.

Group size and composition

When young and older children are together and sharing the same space, it is important to think about what resources can be used and what activities can take place. A toddler can easily stumble into the path of an oncoming bicycle or football, for instance.

Did you know?

Learning to manage risk is now seen as important in children's development, even by those involved in child safety. Look at the vision and values of the Child Accident Prevention Trust (CAPT), a leading organisation in preventing accidents involving children. You can access the CAPT website by going to www.pearsonhotlinks.co.uk and searching for this ISBN: 9781447970965.

Adult support and supervision

If adults are on hand to support and supervise children, the levels of risk and challenge can be increased. This is because adults can stop risky behaviours that may endanger the child or other people in the area. Remember to discuss the importance of safety with children and to set appropriate boundaries for their play.

The importance of managing risk in physical activities

We have seen that there are many factors to take into consideration when thinking about risk. Where we have identified that there are potential risks involved in an activity, we need to think about how these risks can be managed. Table 3.3 shows how risk can be managed in a range of situations so that learning opportunites are not stifled.

Table 3.3 How to manage risk in a range of situations

Situation	Physical benefits	Risks	Managing the risks
Bath time	Helps babies' fine and gross motor coordination	• Danger of drowning • Danger of scalding	• Check water temperature • Do not leave the baby unattended • Have all equipment ready
Playing on a climbing frame	Increases confidence and improves gross motor movement	• Children could fall • Children could stand on another child's hands	• Supervise younger children • Make sure the climbing frame is the right height for the age/stage of the child • Do not allow climbing when it is wet • Limit the number of children allowed on the climbing frame
Sewing	Helps children's hand–eye coordination and pincer grasp	• Child could swallow a needle • Child could prick skin • Child could poke another child in the eye	• Supervise and give children advice • Use needles that are appropriate for the children's ages, e.g. large blunt-ended ones for younger children • Space children out in the room
Playing on tricycles	Helps children's hand–foot coordination	• Children could fall off • Children could hit each other or younger children	• Check that tricycles are appropriate for the child • Create separate areas for riding or have rules about where tricycles can go

Managing risk

Make a list of ways that adults in your setting manage risk when children are engaged in physical activities.

Using the environment to support physical development

When planning the layout of a setting and specific activities, always think about covering a range of physical skills both indoors and out. Many resources and activities that will support fine and gross motor movements can be set up in both environments. Tables 3.4, 3.5 and 3.6 show activities and resources that can be used indoors and outdoors.

Babies

In cold or damp weather, babies will need to be dressed warmly but they should still spend time outdoors.

Table 3.4 Resources to support fine and gross motor movements: babies

Babies	
Fine motor movements	**Gross motor movements**
Treasure basket play	Paddling pool
Sensory play	Baby gym
Shakers	Swings
Rattles	Roll-a-ball games
Looking at books	Knock-down bricks and beakers
Activity mat	Tree stumps to allow babies to cruise

Toddlers aged 1 to 2 years

Toddlers are very active and so need opportunities to move around.

Table 3.5 Resources to support fine and gross motor movements: toddlers aged 1 to 2 years

Toddlers aged 1–2 years	
Fine motor movements	**Gross motor movements**
Heuristic play	Climbing frames
Mark making	Some wheeled toys – sit-and-rides
Paint	Soft play cushions
Playing in water and sand	Throwing (beanbags and soft balls indoors)
Sensory play, e.g. gloop	Swings

This child is being helped onto a climbing frame. How is the activity helping his physical development?

Children aged 2 to 8 years

As children develop, their need for space increases when playing with wheeled toys or during other vigorous activities. Some settings, such as schools, have large indoor spaces that are helpful in this respect.

Table 3.6 Resources to support fine and gross motor movements: children aged 2–8 years

Children aged 2–8 years	
Fine motor movements	**Gross motor movements**
Construction, e.g. block play	Parachute games
Mark making, chalking and drawing	Moving to music
Painting	Throwing and catching (beanbags in limited spaces)
Role play (this may include elements of gross motor movements)	Soft play
Sand and water play	Circle games, e.g. 'The farmer's in the den', 'The hokey cokey', musical statues

Theory into practice

Observe what activities are available to promote the development of children's fine and gross motor movements in your setting. Create a chart like the one below and fill it in to show whether these opportunities are indoors or outdoors.

Fine motor movements		Gross motor movements	
Indoors	**Outdoors**	**Indoors**	**Outdoors**

How to ensure inclusive provision

Inclusive provision is about making sure that children of all ages benefit from physical activities. This includes children who may have physical needs, mobility needs or learning difficulties. It may also include children who are not confident and need reassurance and encouragement from adults.

In order to ensure inclusive provision, the adults in a setting should have a positive and can-do attitude. The next important thing is to identify the needs of each child. There are many ways that you can do this, including observing the child and talking to parents and other professionals who may be involved with them. Once individual needs have been identified, the next step is to consider how to adapt, change or add in new resources to meet them. Many voluntary organisations will be able to provide advice or even equipment to support children with additional needs.

Gender and culture

In addition to supporting children who may have additional needs, we also have to ensure that our provision is inclusive for children regardless of their gender and culture. This is important, because if children are not taking part in the full range of physical activities and play there is a danger that their development will be restricted. To check that all children are able to access provision it is worth observing children over a period of time as they play. It may be that you spot that some equipment is only used by certain children. Some settings report that some of their girls choose not to play with wheeled toys or take part in ball games as they get older. If this is the case, consider whether the equipment itself could form part of a wider activity – for example, setting up a role-play shop outdoors and using the tricycles to do 'online delivery'. The involvement of adults can also influence children's play preferences – so, if an adult starts off a skipping game and invites children to come and join in, wider participation is more likely.

Involving parents

It is good practice to involve parents in all aspects of our work. Helping parents to understand the benefits of all types of physical play, including fine motor movements, is particularly helpful when it comes to gender and culture.

The involvement of the practitioner has encouraged more children to experiment with the sand.

Children with additional needs

Some children with additional needs will need extra support so that they can be included, and participate fully, in physical activities. With careful thought, many activities can be adapted to ensure that all children can take part. For example, rather than standing up to play a parachute game, children could sit down in order to accommodate a child with mobility difficulties. In some cases, special equipment or resources will be needed and it is good practice for early years settings to work with other professionals and parents to identify what these resources may be. Children with sight problems, for example, may require the use of a fluorescent ball with a bell inside. Alternatively, the environment may need to be adapted to help children with additional needs. This might mean putting in additional handrails so that children can hold onto them to move from area to area, or carrying out work to make sure all of the outdoor spaces in a setting are accessible. As well as adaptations to the environment, resources and equipment, some children will need more adult support. Adults might be used to coach children or to be on hand to steady them when necessary. In some cases, adults might also assist children onto and off equipment.

Case study

Making adaptations for children with additional needs

Jaydee is 3 years old and has mobility needs. A number of staff have seen that she is keen to play on the climbing frame. They talk to her parents and physiotherapist, who agree that it would be good for her development to experience being up high. One member of staff is interested in abseiling and they have the idea of creating a rope-and-pulley system so that Jaydee can be put in a sling and experience the climbing frame. Jaydee is very excited and uses her arms to touch each of the rungs. Her friend is waiting for her at the top. They hug each other and laugh.

1 How have the staff team embraced a can-do approach?

2 Why is it important to talk to parents and other professionals before adapting equipment?

3 What are the benefits to Jaydee's development?

You have been asked by an early years setting to create an information pack for parents. The early years setting covers children aged 0 to 4/5 years old. The pack is to help parents understand the activities and resources that will be used in promoting and supporting their children's development. It should include information about the different types of activities and resources that are used with babies, toddlers and older children indoors and outdoors.

The manager of the setting also feels it would be useful for staff to have an information sheet about their overall role in promoting children's physical development. She is particularly keen for her staff to understand the importance of inclusive practice and

their role in providing inclusive provision, as well as how adults can support children at different stages of their physical development. She is also keen for staff to understand the role of adults in allowing children to manage risks while maintaining their overall safety.

Create an information sheet that evaluates how early years professionals can support a child's unique needs at different stages of their physical development.

Use case studies and/or observations from your work placements to help you create the information pack and information sheet, as well as further reading.

C Be able to meet a child's physical care needs

As part of your role in working with babies and children you will need to know how to meet their physical care needs. Although older children can often manage many of their own physical care needs, babies and younger children will need a lot of support.

The importance of routines that respect and empower children

Good care routines are respectful of babies and children and help them to understand the process, and where possible to be involved in it. In practical terms, this means always talking to babies and children when you are with them and finding ways to involve them in a routine. For example, babies can hold items during a nappy change or start the process of wiping their own faces during a cleaning routine. Finding ways of involving children means

that they can start the process of learning to care for themselves. It also makes the experience more pleasant for them and can reduce their anxiety. The following tips are useful when carrying out care routines.

- Let babies and children know what is going to happen.
- Always talk to babies and children during physical care routines, using a warm and sensitive voice.
- Explain the importance of what you are doing as soon as children can understand.
- Find ways of involving the child and, if possible, giving them choices.
- Look for ways in which the child can do some parts of the process.
- Try to find ways to ensure some privacy during toileting.
- Look for ways of making physical care routines fun.

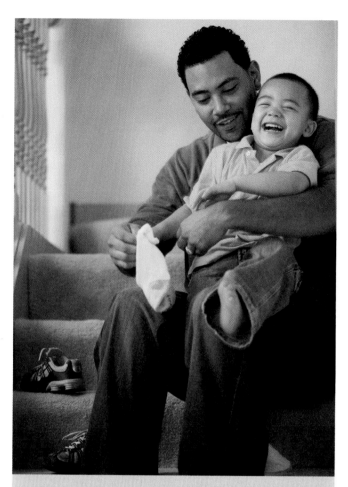

You can see that this parent is making the routine of putting shoes and socks on fun.

How to work with parents to provide for individual needs

Meeting children's individual physical care needs should be done in close consultation with parents.

Children may have ongoing health conditions, such as eczema or dietary needs, and these will need careful management and/or additional support. It is important to work with parents to find out all of the information you need about children's needs when they first come in to a setting. In turn, you will need to regularly share information with parents about their children. Children's needs may change over time but by discussing them on a regular basis with parents or carers, and by recording the information carefully, practitioners can ensure these needs are met.

Parents are likely to have preferences about what should happen when their child sleeps, which nappies and skin products to use and also what their

child should wear. Parents will also know about any allergies that their children may have or particular needs that may affect the child's health and comfort, such as ongoing health conditions or special dietary needs. Many aspects of babies' and children's routines need to be continued when children are with us, particularly their sleeping and feeding routines, so it is important that we make sure we consult with parents about these things.

It is also important to remember that parents' wishes may be linked to cultural and religious practices. An example of this would be people of the Muslim faith, who would prefer any washing to be done under running water. This means that their children will need to be showered rather than bathed.

Reporting to parents

As well as gaining information from parents, we also need to share information. It is important for parents to know how much their child has slept, what they have eaten and also details about their bladder and bowel movements. Many settings will either exchange information orally at the end of a session or write something to go home with the child. Exchanging information is particularly important with babies and younger children.

The role of the key person

The key person plays a vital role in meeting children's physical care needs and it is a requirement of the Early Years Foundation Stage (EYFS) that the key person works with children's parents and carers. The key person should talk to parents about how they meet their children's needs for sleep, rest and food, as well as toileting at home. Wherever possible, the aim is to ensure that settings try to meet children's needs in the same way so that there is some continuity of care between a child's home and the setting. It is also good practice for early years settings to exchange information with parents about how children's care needs have been met in the session. This is particularly important with babies and toddlers who are not able to talk to their parents about what they have been doing. Most early years settings, therefore, use daily diaries or home–setting books in which parents and early years professionals can record information about food intake, general health and also toileting.

Health and safety during physical care routines

The process of making sure that the physical care needs of children are met involves some tasks that carry a potential risk. It is important that early years professionals are aware of these risks so that they can ensure their own health and safety and also the health and safety of the child. For example, lifting a baby or toddler up onto a raised surface in order to change a nappy can potentially put a strain on the early years professional's back unless it is done properly. There is also a risk to the child of falling from the raised surface. During each physical care task, you should carefully evaluate the risks to both you and the child and then take the necessary steps to minimise them.

Infection control

As well as the potential for physical risks during physical care routines, it is essential to avoid the possible risk of infection, especially from tasks related to nappy changing or toileting. It is for this reason that disposable gloves and aprons are provided in early years settings. Good hand-washing procedures should also be in place. These procedures protect both the child and the adult.

Theory into practice

Find out the following things during your placement.

- How does your placement setting work with parents so that babies' and children's physical needs are met?
- What specific information does the setting ask parents or carers when a child first joins the setting? For example, do they ask for information about their skin care or naps?
- How does the setting share information with parents? Is information shared on a daily basis?
- How does the setting make sure that information about a child's specific needs, such as skin allergies or conditions, is shared with those who will be directly working with the child?

Good hand-washing procedures must be in place at every childcare setting.

Table 3.7 Supporting development during everyday activities with babies and children

Activity	Good practice	Developmental benefits
Nappy changing	• Interaction between child and adult • Opportunities for the baby or child to contribute, e.g. holding the clean nappy	• Supports language development • Helps baby or child to build an attachment towards their key person • Helps baby or child to feel part of the process
Feeding a baby a bottle	• Close physical contact • Eye contact • Interaction	• Helps baby to build an attachment • Gives baby pleasure • Helps promote baby's receptive language
Mealtimes	• Interaction between child and adults • Talk about food, e.g. colour, size, shape • Encouragement for serving themselves and self-feeding	• Supports language development • Gives child a healthy attitude towards food • Helps child develop concepts of number, size and colour • Promote social development • Helps child's fine motor skills
Getting dressed	• Interaction between child and adult • Talk about features of clothes, e.g. colour, shape, number of buttons • Encouragement for child to dress themselves	• Supports language development • Helps child to build an attachment • Helps child learn concepts of colour and number • Develops fine motor skills • Helps child to develop self-care skills and confidence
Going for a walk	• Interaction between child and adult • Encouragement for children to get dressed and go out • Talk about what children see during the walk	• Supports language development • Helps child to learn about their surroundings • Develops gross motor skills • Supports development of healthy bones and muscles • Promotes a healthy lifestyle

Using care routines as learning and development opportunities

Years ago, care and education were seen as separate activities. Now we know that it is good practice to use everyday care routines as a way of supporting children's overall development. With babies and very young children, it is good practice for the key person to undertake the majority of physical care activities, such as nappy changes, with their key children and to work closely with the children's parents to share information.

Table 3.7 shows some ways that adults might use everyday activities as learning and development opportunities with babies and children.

Supporting children and families to make healthy lifestyle choices

Increasingly, early years settings have a role in supporting children and their families to make healthy lifestyle choices. This is done in a variety of ways, including by having a healthy food policy at the setting. As a result of this policy, foods served in the early years setting will be healthy and children will be encouraged to try new fruits and vegetables. Many early years settings also provide nutritional information for children and their families by putting out leaflets and using wall displays.

How to provide sleep routines

Falling asleep is easier for babies and children when there is some sort of routine. Sleep routines allow babies and children to feel safe and, therefore, to relax. The ability to relax is key to falling asleep. To help babies and children fall asleep, it is important that adults spend time with them beforehand so that they feel emotionally secure. It is also helpful if adults choose things to do with children that are calming. There is little point in expecting children to fall asleep immediately after they have been running around.

Bedtime routines

The following bedtime routine for the home is recommended by many health visitors to help babies and children get into the habit of sleeping:

1. Mealtime
2. Give the child time to play and relax with you
3. Bath or shower the child
4. Change the child into nightwear
5. Child cleans teeth
6. Take the child into the bedroom, which is darkened slightly
7. Put the child into bed/cot
8. Share a story with the child
9. Reassure the child
10. Leave the bedroom

Theory into practice

Sleep routines

Talk to three parents about how they settle their child for sleep and find out the following information.

- Does their child have a set bedtime?
- How do they manage the bedtime routine?
- Do they have, or have they ever had, any difficulties in getting their child to sleep?

Creating an environment for naps

Bedtime routines are also important in group-care settings, where it is important to create both a routine and an environment that help children to take naps.

It is good practice to have a separate area for children to sleep in. This area should feel calm, tidy and homely. Children should also have their own bed, which is always in the same place. Ideally, the room should be darkened. As with the home routine for bedtime, children benefit from a strong routine in group care.

As some children struggle after waking up, it is a good idea to have a routine to help them. A story and a hug while a child is waking up can work well. Also consider offering children a drink of water, as some children will be dehydrated.

Research

Should children be woken up if they are napping? This is a contentious issue. Find out what your setting's policy is on this.

Comfort objects

Some children will be used to having comfort objects such as a dummy, special blanket or toy with them in order to sleep. You should find out from the child's parents what they need and also how the comfort object is usually used.

Preventing sudden infant death syndrome

If you are responsible for putting babies down to sleep, you should follow the latest guidelines to prevent sudden infant death syndrome (also known as cot death). At the time of writing, these guidelines include preventing the baby from overheating by making sure the room is cool and not using cot duvets or bumpers. You should also place babies on their backs with their feet touching the end of the cot. This is known as 'feet to foot'. It is important to know that smoking plays a part in cot deaths. You should not handle a baby for 20 minutes after you have last smoked because the baby will breathe in your exhaled air, which will be low in oxygen.

Research

Find out about the latest guidelines for putting babies safely to sleep from the Lullaby Trust website. You can access this website by going to www.pearsonhotlinks.co.uk and searching for this ISBN: 9781447970965.

How to care for skin

Skin is an organ that has many purposes, one of which is to protect the body from infection. This means that keeping skin clean and healthy is essential. As children have different types of skin and many children may have skin conditions, it is essential for early years professionals to find out from parents how they should look after children's skin. For example, a child with severe eczema may not be able to use soap on their hands or face, and children with dry skin may need to use moisturisers or oils.

Hand washing

Developing good hand-washing routines with children is important to prevent infections and stop germs spreading. It also gets them into a habit for when they are older. Remember the following guidance.

- Keep nails short.
- Wash hands after going to the toilet, after playing outside and after touching animals.
- Wash hands before eating or drinking.
- Use a nail brush if there is dirt under the nails.
- Dry hands thoroughly – each child should have his or her own towel or paper towel.

Washing the face and body

Bath or shower time is usually a source of great pleasure for children and is often part of a bedtime routine at home. If you are employed in a child's home, it may become your responsibility, although many parents enjoy this part of the day with their children. Remember never to leave children unattended in a bath or bathroom as young children can easily drown or be scalded by hot water.

The bottom and genital areas of children need to be washed each day, although older children should be encouraged to wash these parts themselves. Each child should have their own towel and flannel to prevent the spread of any infection. After the bath or shower, the skin needs to be thoroughly dried to prevent soreness. Younger children have folds of skin under their arms and neck that need to be patted dry.

Although many children have a bath or shower before going to bed they will still need to have their hands and face washed in the morning, and younger children will need to have their faces and hands washed after meals.

Changing nappies

Changing nappies will be part of the role of most early years professionals. It is extremely important for babies and children because skin infections and nappy rash may occur if it is not done properly. Ideally, nappy changes should be done mostly by the child's key person. Figure 3.5 outlines how to change a nappy.

Nappy rash

Nappy rash is common in babies. It comes up in the genital area as a bright red rash, which often starts as a spotty rash. If left untreated it may turn into sores. It is painful and so early years professionals must do everything they can to prevent babies and toddlers from developing it. This means changing soiled nappies promptly, having frequent nappy changes and keeping an eye out for any changes to the skin. You should also let parents know as sometimes a change in diet or skin product can be a trigger. Many parents and practitioners also find that babies who are teething are more prone to nappy rash.

One of the best treatments for nappy rash is to leave the nappy off so that the skin can dry and heal. With parents' permission, barrier cream can be used, but the most important thing is that the skin is kept as clean and dry as possible.

Bathing babies

As well as being a key aspect of the routine for caring for babies, bath time is often great fun for them. Most babies love being in the bath and benefit from playing in the water. They learn from the sensory experience of touching the water and also develop muscles while kicking and splashing around.

Making sure that bath time is safe

Although bath times can be fun, they can also be dangerous – some babies drown or are scalded. The following safety advice must always be followed when bathing babies and young children.

- Never leave babies or young children alone when they are near or in water.
- Always check the temperature of water. It should be around 38°C: warm, but never hot.
- Make sure that any toys for the bath are suitable for the age of the baby.

1 Wash and dry your hands. Get everything that you need to hand and put on disposable gloves. Remember to tell the child what you are going to do, and keep communicating with them throughout.

2 Lift the child onto a changing mat and remove the dirty nappy. Place it out of reach of the child.

3 Clean the area carefully, making sure that you wipe from front to back. Use a clean wipe or piece of cotton wool for each wipe.

4 Dry the area and apply barrier cream, if requested by parents. Put on a new nappy and fasten. Take the child down from the mat.

5 Safely dispose of the dirty nappy and disinfect the changing area. Dispose of your gloves.

6 Wash your hands thoroughly.

Figure 3.5 A step-by-step guide to changing nappies

Preparing for bath time

Good preparation and organisation is essential when bathing a baby. Everything should be laid out before starting to undress the baby. The room needs to be warm – 20°C – as babies chill quickly. Adults also need to check they are not wearing anything that might scratch babies' skin – for example, a watch or jewellery. An apron is often useful, as babies tend to splash. Figure 3.6 outlines how to bathe a baby.

Sun protection

Although children and adults need some sunlight because it is a major source of vitamin D, babies' and children's skin burns easily in the sunlight. We also know that UVA rays from the sun can cause cancers. This means that most settings will have a policy relating to sun protection that should be based on the latest guidelines.

Research

Find out about protecting children's skin from the sun by visiting the NHS website and/or the Cancer Research UK website. You can access these websites by going to www.pearsonhotlinks. co.uk and searching for this ISBN: 9781447970965.

At the time of writing, the following is recommended for the summer months.

- Shade – make sure you put babies and children in the shade whenever possible.
- Sunglasses – provide sunglasses that will protect eyes against UVA rays.
- Sun cream – use a high-factor sun cream, and use it generously. Use non-allergenic creams and be ready to apply according to the manufacturer's instructions.

1 Put the baby on a flat surface. Undress them and take off the nappy. Clean the nappy area.

2 Wrap the baby gently but securely in a towel so that the arms are tucked in.

3 Hold the baby over the bath and wash the head and hair.

4 Take off the towel. Holding the baby securely under the head and round the arm, lift them into the water.

5 Use your spare hand to wash the baby.

6 Lift the baby out of the bath, supporting the baby under the bottom. Quickly wrap them in a warm towel.

Figure 3.6 A step-by-step guide to bathing babies

- Clothing – whenever possible, keep children covered up in loose, long-sleeved cotton clothes.
- Hats – use sunhats to protect babies' and children's heads from the sun.

Looking after children's hair

In recent years, there has been an increase in outbreaks of head lice in preschool settings and in schools. Head lice are parasites that live close to the scalp. They are also sometimes known as nits, which is the name given to the eggs that they lay. Regular combing with a fine-toothed comb can prevent and kill head lice. The comb pulls the lice out and damages the eggs.

Brushing and combing hair

If you are responsible for washing and combing hair, you need to follow parents' wishes. For example, children of African Caribbean descent may need oil rubbed into their hair and some children may have braids or dreadlocks that should not be brushed. Remember the following advice.

- Hair should be combed or brushed twice a day.
- Make sure that you check for head lice or nits.
- If hair is tangled, start with a wide-toothed comb and then use a brush.

To make brushing hair more enjoyable for children:
- give toddlers a doll of their own with hair to brush
- encourage older children to brush their own hair
- let children look in the mirror while you are brushing.

Supporting children's progression out of nappies

There is no set time when children should be ready to move out of nappies. Anywhere between 18 months and 3 years is fairly typical. It is important that parents understand this age range and do not feel pressurised to start toilet training their children until they are physically and emotionally ready. A successful process requires the child to recognise they need the toilet and to get there in time. If children need constant reminders or are having accidents, the full process has not been achieved.

Signs of readiness

When children are ready to move out of nappies, the process can be very quick. Most children are clean and dry within three or four days and no longer have accidents or require constant reminders. Children's physical maturity, their individual motivation and their language development will all have an effect on their readiness to move out of nappies. You should look out for the following things to help you decide whether or not a child is ready and work closely with parents to make sure the time is right.

- Children's physical maturity:
  - Is the child's nappy dry for a long period, e.g. two hours?
  - Can the child walk upstairs on alternate feet?
  - Can the child manage simple undressing?
- Children's motivation:
  - Is the child keen to move out of nappies?
  - Is the child interested in potties/toilets?
- Children's language:
  - Does the child have sufficient language to signal that they need to use the toilet?

Starting off the process

When you think the child is ready to progress out of nappies, it is worth removing the nappy and having a potty or two strategically placed in the room. Let the child know where they are but do not keep reminding them. A low-key approach, which is calm, relaxed and matter-of-fact, works well. Too much emphasis on the child being a 'big boy' or 'big girl' can make it harder to put the child back into nappies if required. Too much pressure can also mean that the child becomes anxious and this anxiety can, in turn, prevent the child from relaxing sufficiently to pass urine.

If the child has an accident, simply clear it up without comment. When the child manages to get to the potty and perform, it is worth praising the child, but not over-reacting. When the child goes to sleep or, if staying near a potty in this way is not possible, put a nappy back on the child. Within a day or so, it will soon become clear whether the child is ready. If a child is not ready, it is better to return to nappies for a few more weeks and then try again.

You have been asked to do some training for work experience students who are spending time in a day nursery. Their teacher/tutor has asked you to look at all aspects of providing physical care and promoting a healthy lifestyle.

Your training should include:

- why it is important that care routines are planned and carried out with attention to safety and hygiene
- why it is important to ensure that physical care routines take into account the age, stage and needs of individual children
- the role of the adult in providing physical development and care needs, and the impact this has on children's lives

- how adults use care routines to support children's physical needs
- how care routines can contribute to children's holistic development and can be used to promote a healthy lifestyle.

To provide an illustration of how best to provide safe and hygienic physical care routines for children, you must also provide one example of how you have created a routine for a child in your setting which can be used for discussion. To lead the discussion on why the care routine meets the child's developmental needs, you should analyse the routine that you have developed and implemented. You should also prepare notes that analyse the effectiveness of the planning and care routines in your setting and include suggestions for improvements.

D1 Know how to recognise and respond to children who are unwell

There will be times when you will need to deal with a baby or child who is unwell. Recognising that the child is poorly and knowing what to do will be very important, especially in the rare event of a life-threatening disease. This section looks at how to recognise and respond to babies and children who are unwell. While this section provides information about how to respond to illness, it cannot take the place of a valid, recognised first aid qualification. Until you have been on a first aid course, you should be very careful about any actions you take in an emergency, because the wrong action could cause more harm to the casualty. If in doubt, you should summon help first.

Signs of illness

It is important to recognise the signs that babies and children are either becoming ill or are poorly. Babies and very young children rely on us to notice that they are becoming, or are, unwell as they cannot tell us. Some symptoms can be very obvious, however,

others – particularly behavioural signs – require that we know children well to spot them. Figure 3.7 shows some of the key signs that might alert us to a baby or child being unwell or incubating an illness. Some of these signs, as we will see, are indicators that emergency attention is required.

Symptoms requiring urgent attention

There are some symptoms that are important to notice and then act on immediately. Most childhood illnesses are mild but there are some, notably meningitis, that have sudden onset and can be fatal if not treated quickly. All of the following symptoms indicate that a baby or child should be seen immediately by a doctor. Some of these symptoms are associated with meningitis and septicaemia. Remember if you notice a baby or child's skin looks blotchy or a rash is appearing, press a glass to it. If the rash does not fade under pressure, you should immediately summon emergency help.

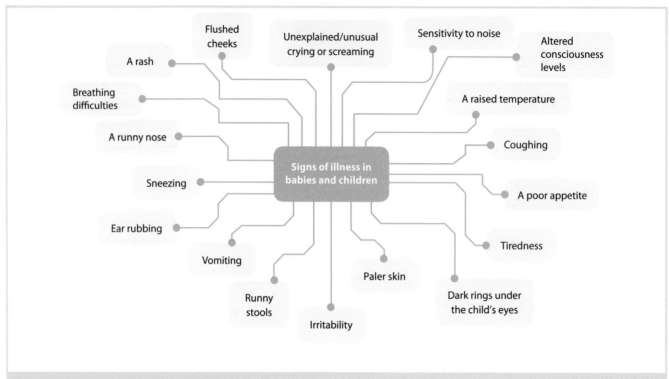

Figure 3.7 Signs of illness in babies and children

Link

Go to Unit 4: Section B to find more information about how to summon emergency help.

Babies

All of the following symptoms indicate that a baby should be seen immediately by a doctor:

- raised temperature above 38°C if the child is under 3 months
- raised temperature above 39°C if the child is over 3 months
- child has a fever (above 38°C) with cold hands and feet
- child displays unusual crying or screaming
- convulsions
- the child is floppy and unresponsive
- pale, blotchy skin
- blueness of skin
- an intense response to light
- drowsiness
- refusal of food
- vomiting
- vomit that contains blood
- fast breathing or difficulty in breathing.

Children

All of the following symptoms indicate that a child should be seen immediately by a doctor:

- temperature above 40°C
- fever with cold hands and feet
- child complains of headache
- child complains that their eyes hurt
- unresponsiveness
- child screams and dislikes light
- drowsiness
- pale blotchy skin
- blueness of skin
- child complains of stiff neck
- violent and prolonged vomiting
- vomit containing blood
- fast breathing or difficulty in breathing.

Research

Find out more about childhood meningitis at Meningitis Now's website. You can access this website by going to www.pearsonhotlinks.co.uk and searching for this ISBN: 9781447970965.

Procedures for reporting and recording illness

An essential aspect of your role is to know about and follow your setting's policy for reporting and recording illness in children.

Reporting signs of illness promptly is important as procedures to stop the spread of infection will need to be implemented. Parents may need to be contacted and, in serious cases, medical help sought.

It is important to record illness. It is usual to write down the date and time of the illness, the child's name, the symptoms and the actions that were taken. Where a baby or child has a temperature, you should record the temperature, how it was taken and the time it was taken, and keep doing this until the child leaves your responsibility. You should also do this with episodes of diarrhoea and vomiting.

There are some illnesses that settings may need to report to authorities. These are known as **notifiable diseases**. In England, all notifiable diseases have to be reported to Ofsted and, in addition, if two or more children have food poisoning, this also has to be reported.

Key term

Notifiable disease – a disease that has to be reported to authorities.

Research

You can find a list of notifiable diseases on the Public Health England website. You can access this website by going to www.pearsonhotlinks.co.uk and searching for this ISBN: 9781447970965.

Informing parents about illness

Parents need to know if their child is unwell. This is one reason why it is important to maintain up-to-date contact details for parents. Parents should also, as part of the admissions process, have given written consent for emergency medical treatment.

It is usual for settings to contact parents immediately it is recognised that the child is unwell. Where a child has a slight complaint, such as not eating as much as usual, this may be noted, and the parents informed when they arrive to collect the child. When contacting a parent, remember the following.

- Check that you are talking to the child's parent.
- Clearly explain the symptoms to the parent.
- Clearly explain what measures have been taken.
- Let the parent know whether their child needs immediate collection or, in the case of an emergency, where their child is.

If a child has been hospitalised, a member of staff should have accompanied the child and should meet the parents at the hospital.

When parents arrive, let them know if there are restrictions on when their child can return to the setting. This is particularly important for infectious diseases (see Table 3.8).

To prevent the spread of infections such as chickenpox or gastroenteritis, early years settings will have policies in place to prevent children from returning to the setting too early after being infected. The exclusion policy does vary from setting to setting, but many early years settings will follow the guidance from Public Health England.

Research

Download the guidance on infection control in schools and other childcare settings from the Public Health England website. You can access this website by going to www.pearsonhotlinks.co.uk and searching for this ISBN: 9781447970965.

Table 3.8 How long to exclude children with infectious diseases

Disease	Exclusion period
Chickenpox	For 5 days from the onset of rash
Diarrhoea and/or vomiting	For 48 hours after the last episode of diarrhoea or vomiting
Flu (Influenza)	When recovered
Impetigo	Until lesions are crusted and healed or 48 hours after commencing antibiotic treatment
Measles	For 4 days from the onset of rash
Mumps	For 5 days from the onset of swelling
Whooping cough	For 5 days from commencing antibiotic treatment

Source: Public Health England (previously Health Protection Agency) (2010)

Reporting communicable diseases

There are some diseases that are serious and can be a threat to public health. When children are diagnosed with these diseases, family doctors and also early years settings are required to notify Public Health England.

At the time of writing, the following are included among the list of diseases that doctors are required to report.

- Measles
- German measles
- Whooping cough
- Typhoid (pertussis)
- Scarlet fever
- Tuberculosis
- Diphtheria
- Hepatitis A, B and C
- Meningococcal meningitis
- Septicaemia
- Mumps

Supporting children who are unwell

Being poorly is distressing for babies and children. Many babies and children will want the reassurance of being with their parents. While waiting for parents to arrive, it is important to give the child reassurance. Babies and children should not be left alone, not only because they could take a turn for the worse but also because they need this reassurance from you. Remember to:

- make the baby or child as comfortable as possible
- explain to them what is happening to their body and what is going to happen next
- offer a comforter, if a child has one
- stay calm and positive
- follow the baby or child's mood, e.g. recognise if they do not want to communicate
- observe the child closely and be ready to get emergency help if the child's condition deteriorates or you see any of the symptoms described earlier.

Steps to take if a baby or child has a temperature

If a child has a temperature, you should:

- remove layers of clothing
- keep the room cool and well ventilated
- take the child's temperature and record it. Repeat every hour or earlier if symptoms change
- offer a paracetamol- or ibuprofen-based medicine, if permission has been gained from parents
- offer the child sips of cooled boiled water
- get emergency help if the temperature rises to the temperatures given earlier in this section.

Research

Find out how to take a child's temperature using the following instruments:

- a fever strip
- a digital thermometer in the mouth/under the armpit
- a digital thermometer in the ear
- a traditional thermometer in the mouth/under the armpit.

Find out the advantages and disadvantages of using different methods to take a child's temperature.

Preventing the spread of infection

It is essential that we take precautions to prevent the spread of infection when children are unwell.

Isolate the baby or child

The first step to take if illness is suspected is to keep the baby or child separate from other children. Being in close contact is a sure way for infection to be passed from one child to another, either through contact or through the air. Some large settings, such as schools, will have a designated room for unwell children.

Ventilate

It is a good idea to keep the setting well ventilated by opening a window to disperse/dilute airborne infections.

Wear disposable gloves and aprons

Disposable gloves and aprons should be worn if a child has diarrhoea or has vomited. Gloves and aprons should be worn to clean the toilet or area affected. It is important to dispose of the gloves and aprons immediately. If the child's clothing needs changing or the child needs washing, a new set of gloves and aprons should be used.

Use disinfectant to clean areas affected

Toilets and any areas affected by faeces or vomit need to be cleaned immediately with disinfectant. Items used to clean the areas should be disposed of or disinfected. Items that the child handled before becoming ill should also be disinfected. In addition, where vomiting and/or diarrhoea has occurred, the whole setting should be thoroughly cleaned, with particular attention paid to door handles, toys and food utensils.

In cases where babies and children show other symptoms such as tiredness or headaches, the area where they have been isolated should be cleaned thoroughly after they have left.

Hand washing

It is essential that adults who have been with the child wash their hands frequently, especially after coming into contact with the child. Other children who have been playing, or in contact, with the child should also have their hands washed.

Procedures for giving medicines

Every setting should have policies in place for the administration of medicines. In England, these policies have to be based on the **statutory** EYFS framework. Policies for settings in England will require parents to provide written consent for each medicine that is to be administered. Policies will also state that all medicine that is being administered must be recorded and reported. Early years settings will, therefore, have procedures in place to keep records of medication that has been given to children. In the case of medications that are occasionally given to children because of a known medical condition such as asthma, or because of a severe allergic reaction, settings will have procedures in place to make sure parents know that these medications have been given to their children.

Most settings will also refuse to give children medicines that are not in their original package, for example, cough syrup in a clear bottle.

Key term

Statutory – required by law (statute).

Research

Find out the statutory obligations for settings providing medicines in the country in which you work.

Find out the policy and procedures of your placement setting.

Can you see how the policy and procedures relate to the legal requirements?

- Record the date, time and dosage, and sign your name.
- Check that the baby/child does not have any adverse reactions.
- Store the medicine as per the manufacturer's instructions and also in a place that is out of reach of other children.

Remember to check the following when giving medicine.

- Check that there is written parental consent in place for the medicine that you are administering.
- If possible, find out what the medicine is for.
- Make sure that the medicine is labelled with the child's name and that you are giving it to the right child.
- Make sure that the medicine is in date and has been stored correctly.
- Follow the dosage instructions and the methods of administration.

Assessment practice 3.4   3D1.P5 | 3D1.P6

A leading workplace nursery that has an after-school club has asked you to attend a conference for their staff.

You have been asked to give a presentation and provide handouts for staff, which provide information about the procedures to use when children are unwell and how to recognise the signs that children are unwell.

You should also give an overview of the role of the early years professional, which analyses the features of their work with children who may be unwell.

D2 Understand the role of the early years professional in supporting children with ongoing health conditions

Many babies and children will have ongoing health conditions. These conditions can be anything from eczema and asthma through to sickle-cell anaemia. This section looks at some of the most common health conditions and the principles behind working with children who have health issues.

Working with parents and carers to meet children's individual needs

It is easy to find out about the common conditions that affect many children in the UK, but every child will still have different needs, triggers and even medication. This is why it is essential to work closely with parents to make sure that we are meeting the child's needs and not doing anything that might make the child's condition worse or put the child in danger.

Listening to parents carefully, taking notes and making sure that you understand the condition, how it is managed and what you need to do are essential. The following list shows some of the kinds of questions that you may need to ask parents.

- What is the name of the medical condition?
- What are the symptoms/effects?
- How long has the child had the medical condition?

- Are there any triggers that we need to be aware of?
- How will we know when the child is getting worse, needs medication or emergency help?
- What should we do in case of emergency?
- How can we reassure your child?
- How is the medication used?
- When should the medication be used?
- Where should the medication be stored?

Keeping records of medication requirements

It is a requirement of the EYFS that records are kept every time medication is given to children by adults. The type of medicine, the dosage and the time and date have to be recorded, as well as the name of the person who gave the medicine to the child. It is important to keep accurate records and record details promptly for several reasons. Firstly, it enables adults to check that medication has been given to the child and that this has been done at the correct time. Secondly, it means that if there is a medical emergency, there is a record showing what medicines have already been administered. Thirdly, it prevents any confusion about exactly what has been given to the child and when.

Ensuring inclusive provision

Years ago, settings often refused to take children with serious ongoing medical conditions or would insist that parents come onsite to give medication to their children themselves. This meant that some children could not access education and services. Today, under anti-discrimination legislation, this is no longer the case. However, simply admitting a child with an ongoing medical condition does not necessarily mean that the setting is being inclusive. Settings must be aware of individual children's physical and emotional needs. Good practice means that children who have ongoing medical conditions should not be made to feel different in a setting and that, wherever possible, thought is given to making sure the child feels fully part of the setting, for example by adapting routines.

The Inclusive provision case study shows how two settings have each managed a child with diabetes very differently.

Case study

Inclusive provision

Gregory and Rajeet are both 4 years old. They attend different preschool settings but they both have type 1 diabetes. This means that they both need injections of insulin before they eat and need to eat regular snacks. Read each case study and answer the questions that follow.

The staff team at Farmhouse Nursery spent a long time with Gregory's parents discussing Gregory's needs. The team and his parents wanted to find ways to make sure that Gregory did not feel isolated or miss out in any way. The preschool made some plans and asked what Gregory's parents felt about them. The suggestion was that they would introduce a rolling snack time, but that Gregory would be prompted to have his at a certain time. This way his condition would be managed, but he would not sit and eat alone.

The manager at Minnows preschool was horrified when Rajeet's mother said that he had diabetes. She asked his mother to send in a factsheet explaining what the condition was and what it meant for the setting. The manager decided that it was unfair on the other children if the routine of the setting was disrupted. She told Rajeet's mother that she should send in a box of snacks for Rajeet and that he could sit out in the cloakroom to eat them.

1 Which setting is working in an inclusive way, and why?

2 What effects might the settings' approaches have on each of the children?

3 What effects might the settings' approaches have on each child's parents?

Meeting the needs of children with asthma

Asthma is a respiratory condition that affects one in eleven children in the UK. During an asthma attack, the airways are narrowed and mucus can form, which further prevents air from reaching the lungs. Asthma can be fatal and so it is important to know what you should do if a child has an asthma attack. You should also know what can trigger an individual child to have an asthma attack, and how their asthma affects them. As we saw earlier, working with parents will be important to gain this knowledge.

How asthma as a condition is managed

When a child is diagnosed with asthma, a decision will be made about whether the condition should be managed by giving the child a **preventer inhaler**. Many people refer to this type of inhaler simply as a preventer.

Preventer inhalers are used daily and are unlikely to be taken into settings unless a child is going on an overnight stay. Preventers reduce, but do not eliminate, the possibility of a child having an asthma attack. They are of no use during an asthma attack.

Reliever inhalers are used during an asthma attack. They work by enlarging the airways, so helping to facilitate breathing. Reliever inhalers are usually blue. Parents and others may call them Ventolin inhalers. Reliever inhalers can save a child's life during an attack.

If you are caring for a child with asthma, make sure that you have a reliever inhaler for them that is in date and remember the following information.

- Reliever inhalers must always be kept near or with the child.
- Reliever inhalers must not be locked away.
- Take the child's reliever inhaler with you if you go outdoors, on a trip or leave the building.

Nebulisers

Nebulisers are used in hospitals and in emergencies. They are machines that create a mist containing the same drugs as a reliever inhaler. The child will wear a mask to breathe the mist in. The fine mist helps the drugs work more effectively.

Key terms

Preventer inhaler – an inhaler that is used to control the symptoms of asthma with the aim of preventing or reducing attacks.

Reliever inhaler – an inhaler that is used during an asthma attack. It works by enlarging the airways, so helping to facilitate breathing.

Spacers

Spacers are often given to children to help them take their inhalers more easily. They are effectively plastic tubes. At one end there is a mouthpiece and at the other end there is a hole to slot the inhaler into. The inhaler is depressed and then the child breathes in. Figure 3.8 shows you what a reliever inhaler looks like when it has a spacer attached to it.

Reliever inhaler

Volumatic spacer

Mouthpiece

Figure 3.8 This reliever inhaler is attached to a spacer, which makes it easier for the child to breathe in the drug.

Recognising the signs of an asthma attack

It is important that you find out from a child's parents what the signs are that their child is likely to have, or is having, an asthma attack. This is because although there are some common signs such as wheezing, not all children will present with these. The following list shows the common signs associated with an asthma attack. Some, but not all, of these signs are likely to be present:

- wheezing
- difficulty in catching breath
- chest pains
- persistent coughing
- difficulty in talking
- rapid breathing
- anxiety and panic.

What to do if a child is showing signs of an asthma attack

If a child is showing signs of an asthma attack, you should do the following.

1 Reassure the child and stay calm.

2 Get the child to sit down and discourage onlookers.

3 Get the child's reliever inhaler. This should always be kept with or near the child.

4 Give the inhaler a quick shake. Attach the inhaler to the spacer if provided.

5 Encourage the child to take one or two puffs while breathing in.

6 If the child does not start to feel better, the inhaler should be taken again at a rate of two puffs over 2 minutes – one puff at a time. The child should take up to a maximum of ten puffs.

7 If the child is not feeling better, call an ambulance.

8 After 10 minutes of waiting for the ambulance, and if the child is still unwell, use the inhaler again as in Step 6.

When to get emergency help

Asthma can be fatal, so it is important to summon emergency help if:

- a child is not responding to their reliever inhaler
- a child's lips or fingernails are turning blue.

Common triggers

Table 3.9 shows some common triggers of asthma and ways of preventing or minimising them. This is not an exhaustive list and you will need to find out from parents what triggers their individual child.

Table 3.9 Common triggers of asthma and ways of preventing/minimising them

Trigger	Steps to reduce/minimise
Dust and associated dust mite droppings	<ul><li>Keep the setting clean</li><li>Wash cuddly toys</li><li>Wash bedding at 60°C</li></ul>
Strong perfumes	<ul><li>Do not wear strong perfumes</li><li>Do not use cleaning products, soaps or sensory materials that contain heavy perfumes</li></ul>
Pollen	<ul><li>Keep children indoors if the pollen count is high or be ready with an inhaler</li></ul>
Mould and fungi	<ul><li>Make sure that any problems with damp in buildings are dealt with</li><li>Do not have rotting fruit and vegetables lying around</li><li>Keep rooms well ventilated</li></ul>
Exercise	<ul><li>Although children do need to take exercise, some children will need a puff of their inhaler beforehand</li><li>Children may need time to rest</li><li>Be aware of children's breathing</li></ul>
Colds	<ul><li>Be aware that a child is more likely to have an attack</li></ul>
Change of weather	<ul><li>Sudden changes of weather can create problems</li><li>Wrap children up – if children are going from warm to very cold, see if they wish to pull a scarf up over their mouth to start with</li></ul>
Stress and emotion	<ul><li>Some children have asthma attacks when they are very upset</li><li>Make sure that time is spent settling children in</li><li>Make sure that you prepare children for any changes that may cause distress</li></ul>

Research

Find out more about asthma by visiting the Asthma UK website. You can access this website by going to www.pearsonhotlinks.co.uk and searching for this ISBN: 9781447970965.

Meeting the needs of children with eczema

Eczema is very common in childhood. According to the NHS, one in five children has eczema, with most children having it in early childhood. Eczema causes the skin to become itchy, dry, red and cracked. There are many types of eczema but the most common form is atopic eczema.

Areas of the body often affected by eczema include:

- wrists
- back of knees
- crook of arms
- neck
- around eyes and ears.

This child suffers from eczema on the back of her legs. Are there any other parts of the body where you think eczema is more likely to be present?

Eczema triggers

Although it is unclear what causes eczema, we do know that it tends to follow a pattern of flaring up and then calming down – although children's skin may well be dry in the periods when the eczema is not present. Flare-ups can be caused by triggers, although what will trigger an episode for an individual child will vary. Some common triggers are:

- soaps/detergents
- rough clothing
- food allergies (especially in babies)
- overheating
- a skin infection
- dust mites (and their droppings)
- pet fur
- pollen.

Remember that if you are working with a child, you should find out from the child's parents if there are any identified triggers.

Treatments and ways of managing eczema

Babies and children with eczema are likely to need treatment at some point. In order to manage eczema, parents are likely to give specific instructions regarding the use of certain things, such as using soap when washing hands or playing in the sand. It is good practice to ask parents whether their child is allowed to come into contact with particular items before trying out new activities that involve the skin being in contact with something, for example, mark making in shaving foam.

Treatments

Below are typical treatments for eczema.

- **Emollients** are often suggested or prescribed for babies and children with eczema. These are applied constantly as a cream to the affected areas even when there are no flare-ups.
- Topical corticosteroids in cream form are often prescribed during a flare-up and need to be applied sparingly. If you are asked to apply a **topical corticosteroid**, follow the manufacturer's instructions and make sure that you wash your hands thoroughly.
- Antibiotics may also be prescribed if the skin becomes infected.

Reducing the risk of infection

Eczema causes the skin to be very itchy and this means that babies and children will find it hard not to scratch. If the skin is broken as a result of the scratching, there is a danger that it may become infected. To prevent this from happening:

- try to make babies wear mitts or special sleepsuits
- keep babies' and children's nails short
- keep the skin clean and dry after washing
- make sure babies' and children's hands are washed.

Key terms

Emollients – special moisturisers designed to prevent skin from drying.

Topical corticosteroids – prescribed creams that are used in the treatment of eczema.

Effects of eczema on the child and family

Eczema prevents babies and children from sleeping well because it is so itchy and can become very sore. This means that it is likely to impact on their behaviour and development. It can also impact on children's feelings about themselves as they often recognise that their skin is different to others'.

Eczema can also have an impact on the family. It is very distressing for parents to see their children suffering and many parents will find that they have to reassure and comfort their children in the night. This means that the whole family can become sleep deprived. In addition, parents need to take extra care when washing their children, and give extra time for applying emollients.

Recognising the impact of eczema is important as it could mean that children may want to have a daytime nap or need reassurance when their skin is particularly itchy.

Research

Find out more about eczema by visiting the website for the National Eczema Society. You can access this website by going to www.pearsonhotlinks.co.uk and searching for this ISBN: 9781447970965.

Meeting the needs of children with diabetes

Diabetes is a potentially fatal condition that is caused by the body not producing sufficient insulin. Insulin is produced by the pancreas. It is needed by the body to control the amount of glucose in the blood. Glucose is important as it gives cells energy. Too much or too little insulin can create problems for the body.

Diabetes is a lifelong condition. There are two types of diabetes: type 1 and type 2. Most children under 8 years old who suffer from diabetes will have type 1.

Type 1 diabetes occurs when the body is unable to produce any insulin. This means that the body cannot process glucose and so it is a very serious condition. Signs that a young child has type 1 diabetes include lack of weight gain, thirst and extreme tiredness.

Once a diagnosis has been made, parents are shown how to check their child's blood glucose level and how to inject insulin. The child will also need to follow food guidelines or a diet to start with.

Controlling diabetes

Diabetes is a condition that has to be controlled carefully. There is a balancing act between how much insulin the child will need and how much food (which in turn creates glucose) the child eats.

This means that, if a child is diabetic, you will need to follow parents' instructions carefully. You may also need training as to how to inject the child with insulin and check the child's glucose level. As soon as children are old enough, most consultants will encourage the child to do this for themselves so that they are more involved in the management of their disease. In addition to insulin injections, food intake has to be regulated. The modern approach is to avoid giving children a strict diet, but to make sure that they eat within guidelines, which may limit the intake of certain foods, such as sugar.

How much food a child needs to eat and how much insulin they need will vary day-to-day according to the child's activity level.

What happens if there is an imbalance between glucose and insulin?

Where there is an imbalance between glucose levels and insulin, a child may develop **hypoglycaemia** (often known as a 'hypo') or **hyperglycaemia** (often known as 'hyper'). Hypos are very serious and have to be responded to immediately.

Key terms

Hyperglycaemia – when there is too much glucose and insufficient insulin.

Hypoglycaemia – when there is too much insulin and insufficient glucose.

Signs of hypoglycaemia

Hypoglycaemia can have a sudden onset and so it is important to be observant. It is also a good idea to keep something sugary, such as a sweet, on hand. If hypoglycaemia is not treated quickly, children can lose consciousness. As children become older, they are able to recognise the signs of hypoglycaemia themselves.

Signs include:

- shakiness
- sweating
- hunger
- difficulty seeing
- lack of concentration
- headache
- change in temperament, e.g. being moody
- loss of colour
- drowsiness.

Note: If a child loses consciousness, emergency help must be called.

Dealing with hypoglycaemia

As there is not sufficient glucose in the child's body, the priority is to give the child something high in sugar. This might be a sweet or sugary drink, or sugar in a glass of water. Chocolate is not ideal but if nothing else is available, use it.

Once the child becomes more responsive, check their blood glucose levels. If necessary, give a slow-burning carbohydrate-rich food such as a sandwich or banana.

Signs of hyperglycaemia

Hyperglycaemia occurs when blood glucose levels are too high. Although serious, it is not as serious as a hypo. There are several causes, including the child having too much sugary food or too much that is high in carbohydrates. It may also be a sign that the child has not had sufficient insulin. Symptoms include thirst, tiredness and passing urine more frequently.

Responding to hyperglycaemia

The child's glucose level will need checking and parents will need to be informed. It may be that the child will need to go to the doctor for a reappraisal of the condition.

Reporting and recording

In order to control diabetes, information has to be accurately shared between the setting and parents. It is important to know how the child is, what has been eaten and what dosages of insulin have been given.

Balancing children's diet

You should find out from the parent what the child needs in terms of their diet. It is usual for children to need frequent snacks and smaller meals so that food intake is spread across the day. It is also essential to know which foods are restricted. It is also important to find out from parents what to do if the child is likely to be engaging in more physical activity than normal.

Assessment practice 3.5 | 3D2.P7 | 3D1.M4 | 3D2.M5 | 3D.D3

A children's centre is keen to make sure that new staff members understand how to work with children (and their parents) who have ongoing medical conditions, health needs or who are unwell. You have been asked to provide an information pack that has useful advice and information, but also encourages new staff to think about the wider issues. To support the information in your pack, you should provide examples from case studies or observations.

Your pack should include the following information:

- how to support children with eczema, diabetes and asthma
- the importance of partnerships with parents
- how early years professionals can best support children with ongoing health conditions
- how to work with parents to ensure inclusive and sensitive provision in meeting children's individual needs
- the overall role of early years professionals in meeting the needs of children who are unwell or need ongoing support.

■ Further reading and resources

Crawley, H. (2006) *Eating Well for Under-5s in Child Care: Practical and nutritional guidelines* (2nd ed.), St Austell: The Caroline Walker Trust.

Department for Education (2010) *Information for Parents: Sleep*, Nottingham: DCSF Publications.

Duffy, A., et al (2006) *Working with Babies and Children Under Three*, Oxford: Heinemann.

South East London Health Protection Unit (2010) *School Health Matters: A guide to communicable diseases and infection control* (4th ed.), London: Public Health England Publications (previously Health Protection Agency).

Virgilio, S. J. (2005) *Active Start for Healthy Kids: Activities, Exercises, and Nutritional Tips*, Illinois: Human Kinetics.

Website

The Lullaby Trust: www.lullabytrust.org.uk

Ready for work?

Anna Rogers   Full-time nanny

I have been working as a nanny for five years now and in that time I have been with three different families. At the moment I look after two lovely children called Poppy and Joey. As a nanny, you have to work closely with parents and make sure that you follow their care routines, especially their way of putting children to bed. Routines vary enormously from family to family and so it is important to be able to adapt your way of working. I have also worked with one child who had diabetes and this required me to be very organised around testing the child's glucose levels and making sure that meals were on time. I was worried at first about having this level of responsibility but it soon just became part of the overall routine.

Skills for practice

Creating physical care routines

There are many practical tips to bear in mind when creating a plan for physical care routines for children.

- Find out about a child's individual needs from their parents or carers, or existing key person.
- Based on the information you gained from parents, work out a daily routine for meal and snack times, sleep time, and nappy changes or opportunities to visit the toilet. Think about timings.
- Think about each child's need for exercise and time spent outdoors.
- Record the proposed daily routine and talk to parents and colleagues about whether it is suitable.

Once you have created a physical care routine and you are starting to follow it, you can then think about how effective it is. A good routine that will provide a child with a healthy lifestyle should not feel rushed or pressured. It is also worth remembering that as children grow and develop, their physical care needs change and so new routines will need to be created.

Changing cot bedding

It is important that cot bedding is kept clean and fresh. To help you with this, remember the following things the next time you change cot bedding.

- Wear disposable gloves if sheets or blankets are soiled.
- Remove cot bedding carefully. Fold sheets and blankets inwards.
- Wipe down the mattress according to the setting's procedure. Allow the mattress to air.
- Wash hands before touching clean sheets and blankets.
- Put a base sheet over the mattress, making sure that there are no creases.
- Fold the top sheet and blanket down the cot so that they will only cover the baby's chest. Firmly tuck the sheet and blanket in at the base and in on one side. This should prevent the baby from being able to slip down underneath the covers and cuts the risk of cot death from overheating.

Introduction

Keeping children safe from accidents and disease is an important part of our work. For parents to be able to trust us, they need to know that their babies and children will be safe in our hands. Health and safety is one area in which there can be no compromises or poor practice. It is also an area where it is important to keep up to date with the latest health and safety guidelines as well as those relating to emergencies and medical incidents.

Assessment: You will be assessed by a series of assignments set by your teacher/tutor.

Learning aims

In this unit you will:

A   understand prevention and control of infection in early years settings

B   understand how to keep children safe and secure in early years settings

C   be able to assess health and safety risks in early years settings.

> Sometimes health and safety is seen as unimportant. However, in my mind, nothing could be further from the truth. As a nanny, parents need to know that their children are safe with me.
>
> Divya, *nanny to a 3- and 6-year-old*

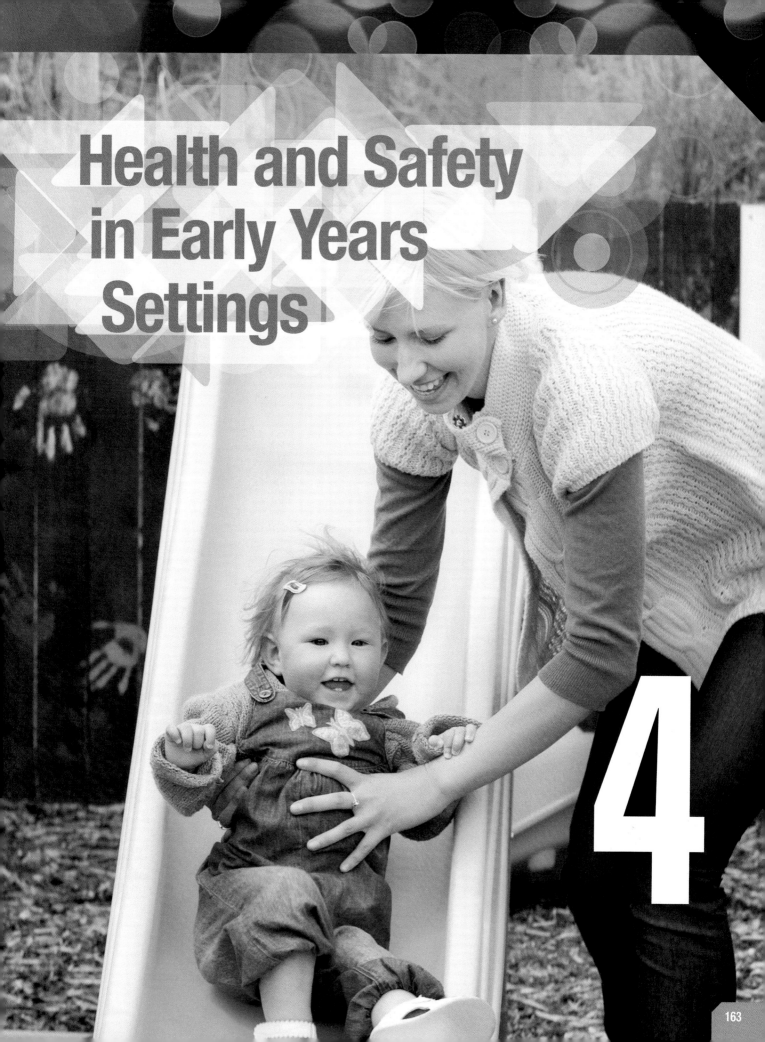

Health and Safety in Early Years Settings

4

BTEC Assessment Zone

This table shows you what you must do in order to achieve a **Pass**, **Merit** or **Distinction** grade, and lists activities that relate to each learning aim.

Assessment criteria		
Pass	**Merit**	**Distinction**
Learning aim A: Understand prevention and control of infection in early years settings		
3A.P1 Explain why it is important to prevent and control the spread of infection in an early years setting. **Assessment practice 4.1**	**3A.M1** Analyse how procedures in early years settings prevent and control the spread of infection. **Assessment practice 4.1**	
3A.P2 I&CT English Describe how infection prevention and control is influenced by legislation, regulations and guidance, using examples of procedures in early years settings. **Assessment practice 4.1**		
Learning aim B: Understand how to keep children safe and secure in early years settings		
3B.P3 Explain common hazards and how early years professionals could prevent accidents to babies and children in one early years setting to include: • understanding children's capabilities • hazard recognition. **Assessment practice 4.2**	**3B.M2** Discuss how policies and procedures contribute to children's safety and security in a selected early years setting. **Assessment practice 4.3**	**3B.D1** Assess methods to keep children safe and secure in early years settings. **Assessment practice 4.3** **Assessment practice 4.6**
3B.P4 Describe how procedures for keeping children safe and secure are influenced by legislation, regulations and guidance, using examples from early years settings. **Assessment practice 4.3**		
3B.P5 Explain the responsibilities of early years professionals in early years settings in: • responding to an accident • responding to a missing child • evacuating the setting • calling for emergency help • taking children on an outing. **Assessment practice 4.4**		

continued

Assessment criteria (*continued*)		
Pass	Merit	Distinction
Learning aim C: Be able to assess health and safety risks in early years settings		
3C.P6 Present a risk assessment of health and safety hazards for a play and learning activity for children of a selected age in one early years setting. **Assessment practice 4.5**	**3C.M3** Make adjustments to a risk assessment of a play and learning activity to include children at different stages of development. **Assessment practice 4.5**	**3C.D2** Evaluate the extent to which risk assessment contributes to effective early years practice in a selected early years setting. **Assessment practice 4.6**

 English Functional Skills signposting   Information and Communication Technology Functional Skills signposting

How you will be assessed

This unit will be assessed by a series of internally assessed tasks set by your teacher/tutor. They will include practical tasks that will need to be carried out in placement, and that link to your Practical Evidence Portfolio. Throughout this unit you will find assessment practice activities that will help you work towards your assessment. Completing these activities will not mean that you have achieved a particular grade, but you will have carried out useful research or preparation that will be relevant when it comes to your final assignment.

In order for you to achieve the tasks in your assignment, it is important to check that you have met all of the Pass grading criteria. You can do this as you work your way through the assignment.

If you are hoping to gain a Merit or Distinction, you should also make sure that you present the information in your assignment in the style that is required by the relevant assessment criterion. For example, Merit criteria require you to analyse and discuss, and Distinction criteria require you to assess and evaluate.

The assignment set by your teacher/tutor will consist of a number of tasks designed to meet the criteria in the table. This is likely to consist of a written assignment but may also include activities such as the following:

- creating a section for an early years setting's health and safety procedures file containing information about safety and security
- reviewing and analysing case studies of an accident or incident in an early years setting
- analysing case studies, observations or examples from settings.

Getting started

Health and safety practices help us to keep children safe. Write down a list of ways that you can keep children safe in settings. When you have completed this unit, see if you can add some more ways to your list.

A Understand prevention and control of infection in early years settings

As part of keeping children safe, it is important to prevent them from becoming unwell. In Unit 3 we looked at ways of recognising and responding to illness. In this section we will look at how to prevent and control the spread of infection in an early years setting.

The importance of infection prevention and control

Infection control is about managing the spread of infection and preventing bacteria, parasites, viruses and fungi from infecting others. Although a common cold is usually harmless, other diseases such as **norovirus**, E. coli and influenza can be fatal for babies and young children. This is because their immune systems are still developing. In addition, we may care for children who have ongoing health problems and whose immune systems are not very strong as a result.

Key term

Norovirus – a common stomach bug that causes severe diarrhoea and vomiting.

Ways that infection might be spread

Before looking at how infections are spread, a good starting point is to understand how they can enter the body. There are three main ways that this can happen: by breathing in, by swallowing or via a wound, as shown in Figure 4.1.

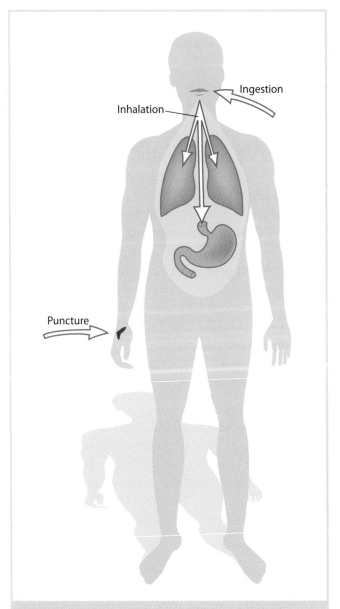

Figure 4.1 The three main ways that infection can enter the human body

Reflect

Puncture wounds

Think about the following.

- Have you ever had a small cut that has become infected?
- How did the injury occur?
- Was any treatment necessary? If so, what was it?

There are some specific ways that infections can spread, as we will now see.

Airborne

Some **microorganisms** that cause disease are spread by tiny droplets in the air when someone who is infected coughs or sneezes. The droplets are then breathed in or swallowed by another person, causing that person to become infected. Airborne droplets are extremely fine and can travel considerable distances. Colds, norovirus and measles travel this way.

Key term

Microorganisms – living organisms, including viruses and bacteria, that are too small to be seen with the naked eye.

Some microorganisms, for example influenza, form in heavier droplets and so closer contact with the infected person is needed to pick up the disease.

You can pick up microorganisms including influenza by touching an object that has been touched by an infected person. The influenza virus lasts for up to 48 hours on hard surfaces. It is, therefore, important to regularly clean objects such as door handles and light switches.

Direct contact (skin-to-skin and head-to-head)

Some diseases and parasites can be passed between people by skin-to-skin contact, for example, scabies. Others can be transmitted by head-to-head contact, for example, head lice.

Faecal/oral transmission

Infections, especially food poisoning, can spread when someone has passed faeces, wiped themselves and then not washed their hands thoroughly. The faecal microorganism is then on their hands and can be ingested or spread to others by touching other people or objects.

Blood/body fluid transmission

Serious diseases such as HIV and hepatitis can be transmitted through the transfer of blood and bodily fluids from one person to another, although this is rare in early years settings.

Common childhood infections

Table 4.1 shows some common infections and how these can be prevented from being spread.

Table 4.1 Common infections, how they are spread and steps that can be taken to minimise them

Infection	How it is spread	How it can be minimised
Chickenpox	Airborne particles and close contact	- Ventilation of rooms - Hand washing - Prompt recognition that a child has the infection - Quarantine of the child and exclusion for five days
Influenza	Airborne particles and close contact	- Ventilation of rooms - Hand-washing procedures for adults and children - Prompt recognition that a child has the infection - Quarantine of the child and exclusion until child is fully recovered

continued

Table 4.1 (continued)

Infection	How it is spread	How it can be minimised
Diarrhoea and vomiting caused by food poisoning	Bacteria spread in food and also by touch	• Hand-washing procedures for children and adults • Good food hygiene at all points during food preparation and cooking process including storage of food • Prompt recognition that a child has food poisoning • Quarantine of the child and cleaning of everything that they have been in contact with • Use of paper towels rather than general towels • Cleaning of toilets and bathroom areas
Diarrhoea and vomiting caused by norovirus	Virus spread through touch and close contact	• Hand-washing procedures for children and adults • Sterilisation and cleaning of toys and resources • Cleaning of toilets and bathroom areas • Use of paper towels rather than general towels • Quarantine of the child • Exclusion of the child for 48 hours after the last episode of vomiting or sickness
Common cold	Virus spread through airborne particles and close contact	• Good ventilation • Hand-washing procedures for children and adults • Use of disposable tissues

Legislation and regulations that apply to infection prevention and control

There are many different pieces of legislation that will impact on day-to-day practice within settings and in this unit we will look at those that affect, in particular, health, safety and security. A good starting point is to look at some of the language used in health and safety legislation.

- **Acts** – these are written laws that parliament has put in place.
- **Regulations** – legal requirements that have to be followed. They have their origins in **European Community Directives** and the Health and Safety Executive.
- **Statutory guidance** – the **statutory guidance** for the early years sector has special legal status and has to be taken into consideration by all providers. If an accident or incident occurs and it is shown that statutory guidance was not followed or

complied with in other ways, the person or setting would be at fault.

- **Approved Codes of Practice** – these codes of practice have similar legal status to statutory guidance.
- **Practice guidance** – this is guidance that may be followed, but it is not legally binding.

Key terms

European Community Directive – a legislative act that countries in the European Union are required to implement in their home country. A directive does not specify the method that should be used to implement the act, so countries are given a certain amount of freedom to decide how they achieve the intended outcome of the act.

Statutory – required by law (statute).

Statutory guidance – a legal term that means that settings or an individual have to follow or pay regard to advice.

Legislation that applies to early years settings and is designed to reduce infections includes the following.

Food handling regulations

England, Scotland, Wales and Northern Ireland have food handling regulations that came into force in 2006 as a result of several European directives. As each home country has its own regulatory powers, you will need to find out about the food handling regulations for your home country. The regulations are similar across all of the home countries as they incorporate European directives. Therefore, in this section, we will look at the regulations solely for England.

> **Research**
>
> Visit the Food Standards Agency website to find out about the food handling regulations in your home country. To access this website go to www.pearsonhotlinks.co.uk and search for this ISBN: 9781447970965.

The Food Safety and Hygiene (England) Regulations 2013

Some of the key points in the Food Safety and Hygiene (England) Regulations that affect practice in early years settings are:

- early years settings and schools may need to register with, or gain approval from, the local authority if they are providing food to children
- early years settings are required to keep premises where food is prepared clean and hygienic (see Figure 4.2)
- equipment should be kept in good working order, clean and disinfected
- a food management system has to be in operation and records should be kept to show that food is stored, handled and disposed of hygienically and safely
- settings are required to train and supervise staff who are involved in the preparation and handling of food
- food has to be kept and stored at a safe temperature, which will depend on whether it is being frozen, chilled or kept warm
- precautions have to be taken to prevent pests and insects coming into areas where food is prepared and stored.

Figure 4.2 Would you want your meal to be prepared here?

Early years settings are also required by law to keep up-to-date records to show that food safety management is taking place. As well as good record-keeping, staff members should make sure that they report anything that might cause a spread of infection, such as an accident in the toilet, if a child is vomiting or if a child is not feeling well. In addition, staff must report if they have had diarrhoea or vomiting. If they are responsible for food preparation or serving of snacks, they should not return to work until they have been free of the symptoms for 48 hours.

Safeguarding and welfare requirements

The safeguarding and welfare requirements of the early years foundation stage (EYFS) state that settings have a duty to maintain hygiene procedures in order to keep children safe and healthy. While no specific procedures are given for early years setting to follow, it is still a legal requirement to prevent infection.

Infection prevention and control procedures

There are many steps we can take to reduce or eliminate the source and transmission of infection in early years settings, starting with our own personal hygiene. Personal hygiene is important as we touch food, resources and, of course, the children. Figure 4.3 shows how we can make sure our personal hygiene is as good as it can be.

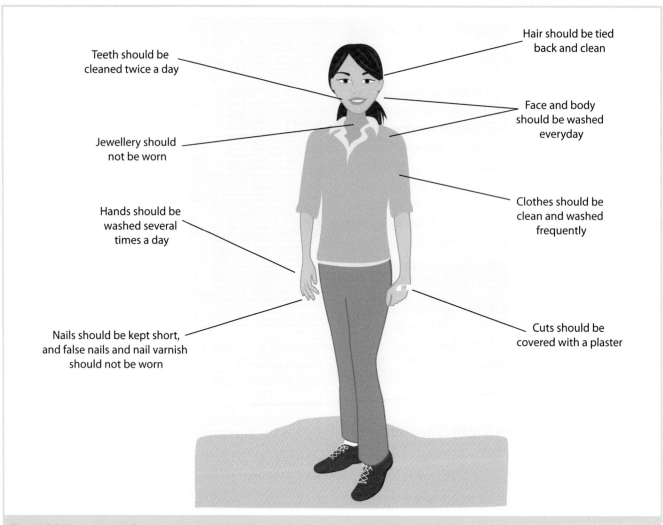

Teeth should be cleaned twice a day

Hair should be tied back and clean

Face and body should be washed everyday

Jewellery should not be worn

Clothes should be clean and washed frequently

Hands should be washed several times a day

Nails should be kept short, and false nails and nail varnish should not be worn

Cuts should be covered with a plaster

Figure 4.3 It is important that our own personal hygiene is good so that we do not spread infection.

Hand-washing routines for adults and children

If there is one message that is universal about infection control, it is the importance of hand washing. As practitioners, we need to be role models for hand washing. From very early on, children need to be taught to wash their hands and this activity has to be supervised until adults are sure that children are doing it properly every time. In order for us to teach children to wash their hands properly, it is important that we know how, and when, to wash our own hands. The step-by-step guide in Figure 4.4 shows the correct routine for washing hands thoroughly. It is advised that liquid soap and disposable paper towels are used in early years settings.

Adults and children should wash their hands thoroughly:

- after going to the toilet
- before eating or drinking
- after touching any animals
- after going outdoors
- after playing with sensory materials
- when hands look grubby.

Additionally, adults should wash their hands:

- before preparing food
- after touching raw meat or fish
- before and after a nappy change
- after changing children's clothes
- after dealing with waste.

Figure 4.4 A step-by-step guide to hand washing

1. Palm to palm
2. Backs of hands
3. Interdigital spaces
4. Fingertips
5. Thumbs and wrists
6. Nails

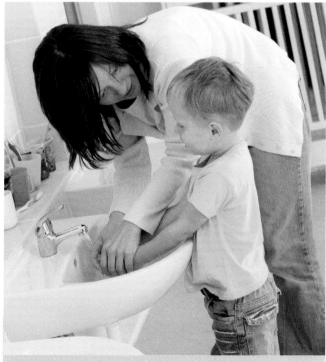

This child is learning about hand washing by doing it with an adult.

Disposable gloves and aprons

In order to prevent the spread of infection, you will need to follow the policies and procedures of your setting and also use the equipment provided.

You should use disposable gloves and aprons for nappy changing, dealing with toileting accidents, cleaning and dealing with waste. It is important that you dispose of the gloves each time you have finished an activity with them. For example, gloves should be changed each time you change a child's nappy.

Safe handling and disposal of waste

Settings will follow the arrangements for recycling and waste collection set up by their local authority, but they should also have their own waste disposal procedures. It is usual for group-care settings and schools to have separate bins for paper waste, food waste and hazardous waste. Hazardous waste includes anything that has been in contact with bodily fluids, such as plasters, nappies and dressings.

In addition, if there are children with medical conditions that require injections, a specially designed 'sharps' bin is needed for needles and syringes. Bins for hazardous waste are normally colour coded. They should be kept away from children and instructions from the waste contractor must be followed. You should not flush waste down the toilet.

Managing spillages of blood and bodily fluids

It is likely that you will be handling bodily fluids on a regular basis if you work with babies or young children. To avoid the spread of infection, you should always wear disposable gloves and disposable aprons when there is blood, vomit, urine or faeces involved. It is important to note that wearing disposable gloves and aprons gives some protection, but it is still essential to wash your hands thoroughly afterwards. You should also change or wash your clothes if there is any possibility that there has been contamination. Anything you use when dealing with bodily fluids, such as cloths, should be thrown away after use. All items that have been used to deal with bodily fluids should be correctly disposed of in a colour-coded hazardous waste bin.

In your work with children, you are likely to have to wipe children's noses. Disposable tissues are needed for this task and again, to avoid spreading infection, you should wash your hands afterwards.

Waste bins

As we have seen earlier, you will find that there are special bins in group-care settings and schools that should be used for disposing of waste that has been in contact with human bodily fluids, such as blood, urine and faeces. These bins are usually yellow and nappies, wipes and plasters should be put inside. Nappies are usually wrapped before being disposed of in the bin.

Decontamination and cleaning procedures

Environments that children are in should be cleaned regularly, as well as areas where the children do not usually enter, such as the kitchen. This applies to resources too. In some settings, cleaners will come in after the children have left, but the staff team must still take responsibility for the cleanliness of the environment during the day. If you work as a nanny or childminder, you will need to take responsibility for keeping the environment clean and hygienic. Table 4.2 shows recommended cleaning procedures for early years settings.

Table 4.2 Recommended cleaning procedures in early years settings

Area or equipment	How often should it be cleaned?	Cleaning method
Basins and taps	• Daily and whenever needed	• Hot water and detergent
Bins	• Daily	• Hot water and detergent
Carpets	• Daily	• Vacuum daily • Steam clean every six months in group-care settings
Floors	• Daily	• Hot water and detergent • Only use disinfectant if there has been a toileting accident, or if blood and vomit are present
Tables and chairs	• Daily	• Wipe with disposable cloths
Nappy changing mats	• After use	• Wipe with disposable antibacterial cloths
Bedding	• Every few days or immediately if soiled	• Soiled washing should be handled wearing disposable gloves and apron. Solid waste should be flushed down the toilet. Linen should then be put into a plastic sack and tied until ready for washing at 60°C • Each child should be allocated their own bedding
Soft toys	• Weekly	• Hot water and detergent, and then rinse

continued

Table 4.2 (continued)

Area or equipment	How often should it be cleaned?	Cleaning method
Plastic toys	• Weekly or preferably after use where they have been mouthed by babies	• Hot water and detergent, and then rinse
Water trays	• Water should be changed after use	• Tray should be dried if not in use
Water toys	• Wash and dry after use	• Hot water and detergent, and then rinse
Sand tray indoors	• Sand should be sieved regularly • The tray should be washed and dried when the sand is changed	• Sand needs changing every month • Wash tray with hot water and detergent
Sand outdoors	• Rake the sand on a daily basis	• Keep covered when not in use • Check for animal faeces • Change when discoloured
Play dough	• Children should wash hands before and after use • Play dough should be replaced after every session (ideally)	• If an outbreak of gastroenteritis occurs, use of play dough, water and sand play should be stopped

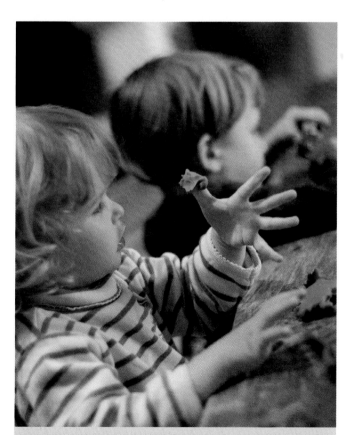

These children are enjoying handling dough – but are their hands and the dough clean?

Cleaning equipment

Separate cleaning equipment is needed for toilets, bathrooms, kitchens and play areas. The cleaning equipment can be colour coded for identification or can be stored separately.

This is to avoid cross-contamination. Disposable wipes are recommended, otherwise cloths should be changed daily. Mops should be washed through with hot water and detergent, and left to dry.

Did you know?

Food and kitchen hygiene

There are specific measures that, if followed, make sure kitchens are kept clean and areas for food preparation are hygienic. You can find out about these measures by visiting the Food Standards Agency website. You can access this website by going to www.pearsonhotlinks.co.uk and searching for this ISBN: 9781447970965.

Activity

Find out how your work placement prevents the spread of infection.

Look at their policy and procedures.

1 Who manages the day-to-day cleaning in the setting?

2 Who is responsible for ensuring that kitchen areas are kept clean?

The immunisation programme for children

Many serious childhood infections can now be prevented through children receiving a **vaccine**. This is known as vaccination. When children are vaccinated against a disease, the body creates the necessary antibodies so that if they are exposed to the disease, they are **immune** to it. When most children are vaccinated against a disease, the bacteria or virus responsible for it have fewer opportunities to infect and, therefore, reproduce. Vaccination is considered to be a key way in which diseases can be controlled and potentially wiped out.

Key terms

Immunisation – the process by which someone is protected against an infectious disease.

Vaccine – a very weak dose of an infectious organism that is injected into someone in order to prevent a disease.

Table 4.3 details the immunisation programme that is offered to children at the time of writing and is detailed on the NHS website. However, it is worth noting that some children who have pre-existing medical conditions, such as cancer or epilepsy, may not be able to be vaccinated.

Table 4.3 The NHS vaccination schedule for babies and young children

Age	Vaccine
2 months	• 5-in-1 (DTaP/IPV/Hib) vaccine against diphtheria, tetanus, whooping cough (pertussis), polio and Hib, which can cause pneumonia • Pneumococcal (PCV) vaccine (a bacteria that can cause pneumonia and meningitis) • Rotavirus vaccine (an infection that causes diarrhoea and sickness)
3 months	• 5-in-1 (DTaP/IPV/Hib) vaccine (second dose) • Meningitis C • Rotavirus vaccine (second dose)
4 months	• 5-in-1 (DTaP/IPV/Hib) vaccine (third dose) • Pneumococcal (PCV) vaccine (second dose)
12–13 months	• Hib/Men C booster, given as a single jab containing meningitis C (second dose) and Hib (fourth dose) • Measles, mumps and rubella (MMR) vaccine, given as a single jab • Pneumococcal (PCV) vaccine (third dose)
2 and 3 years	• Annual flu vaccine
3 years and 4 months, or soon after	• Measles, mumps and rubella (MMR) vaccine (second dose) • 4-in-1 (DTaP/IPV) pre-school booster, given as a single jab containing vaccines against diphtheria, tetanus, whooping cough (pertussis) and polio

Maintaining accurate records and reports

It is good practice for early years settings to keep accurate records and reports of all matters relating to infection control and cleaning schedules.

Records and reports should include risk assessments linked to food hygiene and to cleanliness in relation to the maintenance of environments and resources. There is a duty for early years settings to report any outbreak of food poisoning to Ofsted and also, where appropriate, to the local Health Protection Team. Although there is no requirement for early years settings to keep immunisation records, some may decide to collect this information from parents as part of the admissions system.

Assessment practice 4.1   3A.P1 | 3A.P2 | 3A.M1

A childminder is thinking about setting up a business. She has asked for an information sheet that explains how infections can be prevented and what her role would be in preventing the spread of infections. She works with babies and children up to the age of 8 years.

She also needs to know how legislation and regulations will influence the procedures she needs to set up for controlling the spread of infection in her setting.

Produce an information sheet that will explain the importance of preventing and controlling the spread of infection in an early years setting and give her the information she needs to do so. This should include some practical ways of preventing the spread of infection. You should discuss nappy changes, cleaning routines and the disposal of waste.

Include examples of procedures commonly used in early years settings showing how they follow guidance from the relevant infection control regulations.

B Understand how to keep children safe and secure in early years settings

It is impossible to prevent children having the occasional bump or bruise, but most accidents, especially serious ones, can be prevented. This section looks at how you can prevent accidents in an early years setting.

Common types of injuries

Sadly, thousands of children are admitted to hospital every year as a result of injuries sustained in accidents. Table 4.4 shows some common accidents with examples of how they may have occurred.

Table 4.4 Common accidents

Accident/Injury	Possible cause of the accident/injury
Poisoning	A child finds some medicine lying around.
A bite or sting	A child is bitten by a dog in the park.
A chemical burn	A child touches some bleach that has been put in a bucket and left unattended.

continued

Table 4.4 (continued)

Accident/Injury	Possible cause of the accident/injury
A cut	A child finds a penknife that has been dropped and left on the floor.
Crushing	A child is in a car park and is not seen by a driver.
Electrocution	A child pushes their finger into a lamp fitting.
A fall	A child falls from an open window.
Introduction of a foreign body	A child swallows a nail.
Suffocation	A child puts a plastic bag over their head, pretending it is a mask.
Drowning	A child is playing in a paddling pool and slips face forward.
A burn	A child finds some matches and lights one.
A scald	A child tries to move a mug of tea as it is on their book.

How to avoid injuries

Later in this section, we will discuss the importance of following a process of identifying hazards and carrying out risk assessments in order to prevent accidents from happening. However, accidents may still happen to children while in group care in an early years setting or while being looked after by a childminder or nanny in home-based care. Many of these accidents are due to adults failing to supervise children properly or to act on risk assessments.

Supervising and being alert

A key way that we can keep children safe is to know what they are doing and what and who they are playing with. This means being alert at all times. Most early years settings will have a **key person** system. If

you are a key person, you need to take responsibility for your children and keep an eye on what they are doing.

New equipment, resources and activities

When we introduce new equipment, resources and activities into a setting, it is important that we are particularly vigilant. Although we may think a resource is safe, a child may do something with it that is unexpected.

Ages and stages of children

The ages and stages of children and understanding their capabilities should have an impact on our risk assessments, the level of supervision we provide and our choice of resources and equipment. Table 4.5 outlines some key characteristics and behaviours of babies and children at different ages/stages that may be hazardous and the implications these characteristics have for our practice.

> **Key term**
>
> **Key person** – a practitioner designated to take responsibility for a child's emotional wellbeing by having a strong attachment with them and a good relationship with their parents.

Table 4.5 Key characteristics of babies and children and the implications they have for our practice in terms of risk assessment

Age/Stage of children	Key characteristics/behaviours	Implications for our practice
Non-mobile babies	• They will wriggle and roll so may fall off raised surfaces. • They will take any object to mouth.	• Do not leave babies on raised surfaces. • Babies should be supervised closely unless they are asleep.
Mobile babies	• Mobile babies can move very quickly. • They will explore and touch everything in their range. • They will mouth any object found on the floor or at their height. • They will pull themselves up onto furniture and other items that may not be stable. • They will attempt to climb stairs. • They have no sense of danger.	• Keep floors vacuumed and free of objects that could be choking hazards. • Remove tablecloths and furniture or equipment that is unstable. • Use stair gates. • Babies should be supervised closely unless they are asleep.
Toddlers	• They are restless and exceedingly active. • They will copy the actions of older children and adults. • They are determined. • They love climbing. • They love throwing. • They may still be mouthing. • They can move fast. • They may climb out of their cot or bed to play and explore. • They have no understanding of danger. • They are impulsive.	• Make sure there are plenty of activities that will engage them, especially climbing and throwing. • Keep medicines out of reach. • Create child-friendly areas. • Provide close adult supervision at all times. • Do not leave toddlers unsupervised unless they are asleep.
3–4 year olds	• They will play with others but may squabble or become very excited. • They may engage in superhero play and try to hit each other or jump from heights. • They may copy what they have seen adults do, e.g. attempt to use lighters or feed a baby. • They have limited understanding of danger and may forget instructions.	• Be ready to step in if play becomes very boisterous or children are getting cross with each other. • Be aware of your actions in terms of giving children ideas. • Be ready to keep repeating rules and expectations. • Increase adult awareness and close supervision for some activities. • Children need close supervision when they are very excited or tired.

continued

Table 4.5 (continued)

Age/Stage of children	Key characteristics/behaviours	Implications for our practice
4–8 year olds	• They will play cooperatively, but may show off to peers or become excited by ideas. • They may engage in superhero play. • They may engage in risky behaviours if they are bored or the environment is not stimulating enough. • They have more awareness of safety, but still need reminding of rules. • They enjoy having some responsibility and independence. • They are starting to understand the concept of 'rules'.	• You should recognise that children's behaviours can change according to who they are with. • Make sure that the play environment continues to be stimulating and physically challenging outdoors. • Talk to children about rules and the reasons behind them. • Close adult supervision will be required for some activities. Adults need to be aware of what children are doing at all times.

Recognising and reporting hazards in the indoor environment

There are some areas, resources or activities in particular that have the potential to be hazardous for children in early years settings. Table 4.6 shows some key ones, the risk(s) they pose and ways the risk(s) can be minimised.

Table 4.6 How to manage potential hazards in the indoor environment

Area/Activity/Resource	Risk	Ways of minimising the risk
Water	• Danger of children drowning • Danger of children slipping	• Do not leave children playing alone with water. • Tip water out after use. • Make sure that spills are wiped up promptly.
Sand	• Danger of sand going into children's eyes • Danger of children slipping	• Do not use sand with babies and toddlers. • Make sure that children know they must not throw sand. • Be ready to intervene if children are throwing sand. • Make sure that spills are wiped up promptly.
Play dough	• Danger of children eating the play dough – salt is harmful to babies and young children • Danger of infection	• Do not give to babies and children who are still mouthing. • Make sure that dough does not smell like food as children may be encouraged to eat it. • Change dough frequently. • Make sure that children wash their hands.

continued

Table 4.6 (*continued*)

Area/Activity/ Resource	Risk	Ways of minimising the risk
Mark making: pens, pencils, paintbrushes	• Danger of children poking themselves in the eye with the resources	• Do not give pencils to babies and toddlers. • Prompt intervention if older children are using the resources inappropriately.
Scissors, hole punchers and staplers	• Danger of children getting puncture wounds and cuts	• Make sure resources are out of reach of babies or toddlers. • Show children how to use the equipment correctly. • Provide child-safe scissors.
Dressing up clothes – belts and similar items	• Danger of strangulation if children engage in play using belts, e.g. pretending to take a 'dog' for a walk – one child may put a belt around another child's neck to act as the dog lead • Danger of belts hitting children's eyes or face	• Explain to children that belts and similar items can cause children injury. • Be aware of how children are playing with items.
Bathrooms and toilets	• Danger of children drowning • Danger of cross-infection	• Directly supervise babies and toddlers. • Supervise and intervene if children are using either area as a play area. • Make sure that children wash and dry their hands properly.
Physical care routines/bathing and nappy changing	• Danger of children drowning in the bath • Danger of children being scalded by hot water • Danger of children falling off a changing mat	• Do not leave any young children unattended during bathing. • Adults only should supervise children during bathing – do not give older children this responsibility. • Run cold water first, then add hot water into the bath. • Check temperature of the water before putting babies into baths. The water should be lukewarm at around 36–37°C. • Be organised when nappy changing so you do not have to leave the child alone. • Consider changing older babies and toddlers on a mat that is placed on the floor.

continued

Table 4.6 *(continued)*

Area/Activity/Resource	Risk	Ways of minimising the risk
Entrances and doorways	• Danger of children escaping onto the road • Danger of children going home with strangers or parents who do not have custody of them	• Set out clear procedures for the collection of children. • Keep entrances and doorways locked or secure. • Make sure that staff and parents understand the importance of security.
Windows	• Danger of children falling out	• Make sure that windows above ground floors can only be opened slightly. • Make sure windows that have tables/cots/other climbable objects under them are kept locked.
Cooking activities	• Danger posed by the use of knives, hot stoves and ovens	• Keep babies and toddlers away from the kitchen. • Show children how to use knives properly. • Explain to children about hazards present in the kitchen. • Make sure cupboards that contain dangerous items are locked. • Do not leave children in the kitchen unattended. • Use saucepan guards.
Toys and objects scattered on the ground	• Danger of children falling over the resources	• Keep 'walkways' clear. • Pick up objects that are likely to be a hazard. • Explain to children the importance of not leaving things on the floor. • Encourage children to tidy resources away.
Adult behaviours: hot drinks and handbags	• Danger of scalding children if hot drinks spill onto them • Danger of children taking medicines and/or lighters out of adults' handbags	• Keep hot drinks out of reach and out of sight of children. • Put lids on hot drinks. • Put handbags out of reach or locked away in a cupboard.

Specific hazards in home settings

In home settings there are some specific hazards that you need to be aware of.

Pets

Pets need to be kept away from food preparation areas. When you first meet parents, you will need to ask whether the presence of a pet is likely to cause any allergic reactions in their children. In addition, cats and dogs should not be left alone with babies and young children.

Kitchens

Many homes will have a kitchen–diner arrangement, which means that children are eating in the kitchen or going in and out of it to use a table. Great care needs to be taken to make sure that objects such as knives and kettles are kept out of reach. Children should never be left in the kitchen without supervision.

Mixed-age groups

In many ways it is wonderful for settings to allow babies to play alongside toddlers and older children, but it does create some challenges. First of all, remember that toddlers are likely to want to hold, cuddle or even hit a baby. This means that babies should never be left alone with toddlers or even young children. The other challenge is around the provision of equipment and resources. What is safe for a 4-year-old child may not be suitable for a baby. This means that planning is very important; settings should think about having set areas where certain toys belong.

Recognising and reporting hazards in the outdoor environment

Today, it is recognised that babies and children need to spend time playing outdoors. Being outdoors is very beneficial for their health and wellbeing, but it also raises safety issues. We will now look at how to ensure children are safe outdoors.

The importance of checking the outdoor area for hazards

Before babies and children are taken to an outdoor environment, it is usual for the area to be checked. This is because incidents could have occurred overnight, boundaries may have been broken or damaged and litter or dangerous objects could have been dropped. In addition, animals such as foxes and cats may have been in the area and **defecated**.

> **Key term**
>
> **Defecate** – excrete faeces (solid waste) from the body.

What to look out for

Here are some key points to check in the outdoor areas.

- Is the area secure? Check fences and gates.
- Are there any signs of debris, broken glass or litter – sweep up if necessary.
- Is the equipment in a good state? Remove old or broken equipment if necessary.
- If there is a sandpit area, is it clean? Rake and replace the sand if necessary.
- Is equipment such as slides and climbing frames dry? Dry the equipment if necessary.

Common outdoor hazards

Babies and children should spend some time each day playing outdoors. This means that we need to be aware of common outdoor hazards. Table 4.7 shows potential hazards and how the risk caused by the hazard can be minimised and managed.

Table 4.7 How to manage potential hazards in the outdoor environment

Area/Piece of equipment	Hazard	Ways to minimise the risk
Ice on paths	• Child falling	• Have salt ready for cold weather.
Slides/climbing frames	• Child falling off the equipment • Child being pushed off	• Make sure rungs/steps are dry and clean. • Supervise and check that children are using the equipment safely. • Make sure clear rules are in place for turn taking on the equipment.
Swings	• Child falling • Child banging his/her head	• Locate swings in specific areas away from where children may be walking. • Supervise children and make sure clear rules are in place for turn taking.

continued

Table 4.7 (continued)

Area/Piece of equipment	Hazard	Ways to minimise the risk
Wheeled toys such as tricycles	• Child falling • Collisions with other children	• Provide cycle helmets. • Create specific areas where wheeled toys can be used.
Fencing/Gates	• Children escaping if gates are left open or if there are gaps in fencing • Strangers entering if gates are left open or if there are gaps in fencing	• Check fences thoroughly. • Make sure that gates are securely fastened. Do not rely on parents to remember to close them.
Water activities	• Danger of child drowning • Danger of child slipping	• Do not leave children playing alone with water. • Tip water out after use. • Make sure that spills are wiped up promptly.
Sand	• Danger of sand going into children's eyes • Danger of children slipping • Possibility of contamination from animal faeces	• Do not use sand with babies and toddlers. • Make sure that children know they must not throw sand. • Be ready to intervene if children are throwing sand. • Make sure that spills are wiped up promptly. • Make sure that sand is covered when not in use. • Before children play, check sand for possible contamination such as animal faeces or urine.
Plants	• Poisoning • Children being poked, or poking themselves in the eye with sticks	• Check that you have no poisonous plants in reach of children. • Make sure there are rules about how children can use sticks – they are not for fighting.

Research

Poisonous plants

Few plants are poisonous, but find out which ones are by visiting the website for the Royal Horticultural Society. You can access this website by going to www.pearsonhotlinks.co.uk and searching for this ISBN: 9781447970965.

Assessment practice 4.2   3B.P3

You have been asked to create an information pack that will help staff in an early years setting to identify and recognise common hazards in the indoor and outdoor provision. Your information pack should explain how staff in the setting can take steps to reduce the possibility of accidents and injuries to children. You should include information about the different capabilities of children at different ages.

Reporting hazards

Whether the hazards are found indoors or outdoors, you have a legal duty to report them under the Health and Safety at Work Act 1974, but also a separate legal duty of care towards children. It is important that you report any hazards promptly to your supervisor, manager or the health and safety officer. Most settings have a procedure for this and so you will need to find out what this is in your work setting. Most settings will also have a health and safety book in which hazards can be reported. Following the report on a hazard, the risk assessment will need to be updated.

If you feel the hazard is too dangerous to leave in the area while you report your concern, you should remove the item of equipment if it is safe to do so. Failing that, you should make sure that children are kept away from the area and then report the hazard.

Research

Find out what you should do in your current work placement if you come across something that could be a potential hazard.

The role of risk assessment in identifying hazards

By knowing what dangers there are in the setting, early years professionals can take appropriate steps to eliminate or minimise them. The process of identifying hazards and minimising or eliminating them is called 'risk assessment'. Good risk assessment also involves carefully evaluating the level of risk and deciding on the necessary precautions to take. This process is vital when working with babies and children. It can prevent accidents from occurring. In addition, it is a legal requirement as we have a duty of care towards children, which includes keeping them safe. If an accident occurs and insufficient risk assessment has taken place, you may be prosecuted.

Section C of this unit looks in detail at the risk assessment process, including how to identify hazards, how to assess infection and safety risks, as well as the procedures you need to follow to ensure that findings are accurately recorded.

Equipment and resources to minimise hazards

There are some pieces of equipment that can prevent accidents. They are only useful if they are used consistently and in accordance with the manufacturer's instructions. They are never an alternative to supervision or good health and safety practices. Table 4.8 lists some examples of useful safety equipment.

Table 4.8 Useful safety equipment

Equipment	Features
Safety gates	Restrict children's access to areas such as stairs and kitchens
Cupboard locks	Restrict children's access to cupboards where cleaning equipment or medicines are kept
Safety corners	Cover sharp edges on furniture, preventing eye and head injuries
Cycle helmets	Provide protection against head injuries when children are on scooters or bicycles
Smoke detector	Signals that there is smoke in the environment and so can save lives
Fire blanket	For use in kitchens to throw over items that are on fire
Fire extinguishers	A number of different types; used to put out small fires

continued

Table 4.8 (continued)

Equipment	Features
Harnesses	Prevent babies and toddlers from falling out of highchairs and pushchairs – make sure that children can be released quickly if needed
Reins	Prevent toddlers from wandering off or into traffic
Window and door locks	Prevent toddlers and young children from falling out of windows or 'escaping'
Car seats	Required by law in cars to transport children under 13 years. They can prevent serious injuries in the event of an accident. Car seats have to be properly installed and be of the right design for the age/weight/height of the child.

Did you know?

In the past, safety plug covers would have been included in Table 4.8 as an example of a useful piece of safety equipment. Although they are still widely used, they have been subject to some debate in the media in recent years and they are now considered unnecessary and unsafe.

Find out the latest thinking about safety plug covers by carrying out your own research.

Current safety and security legislation and regulations

It is easy to think of health and safety legislation as being boring or something that is of no interest. The reality is that it forms the skeleton for safe working practices in early years settings. We will now look at the importance of health and safety legislation, what it means in practice and also where to find out more information about it. We will look at the legislation that covers all parts of the United Kingdom (UK) and go on to consider legislation that affects early years settings in particular.

The importance of complying with relevant legislation

Every setting and every practitioner within it needs to make sure that they comply with the legislation relating to health and safety practices. This legislation underpins safe working practices and prevents many accidents and deaths each year.

Compliance is, therefore, essential because it has potential life-saving effects. Non-compliance, even out of ignorance, is illegal. It is considered to be an act of negligence. Prosecutions are fairly rare, but nonetheless, you have a duty of care to both yourself and the children you work with.

Current health and safety legislation

Health and safety legislation is the same in all countries across the UK but there are regulatory differences relating to early years settings in various home countries. For example, there are different adult-to-child ratios in place across countries. It is important to be aware of the legislation that relates to the country in which you work.

Health and Safety at Work Act 1974

Everyone who is in employment is covered by protection that ensures their workplace is healthy and safe. This protection is in the form of the Health and Safety at Work Act 1974. This piece of legislation is the reason why you may be asked to wear disposable gloves when changing nappies; by wearing them, the risk of picking up or spreading an infection is minimised.

This legislation covers any workplace and places responsibilities on employers as well as employees.

Employers' responsibilities

Employers have to take reasonable steps to maintain the health and safety of their employees and also other people, such as learners, while they are on the premises.

Employers with more than five employees have to have a health and safety policy and make sure that employees are aware of it. Every employer's health and safety policy will be different, but in childcare settings it is likely that policies will have a section about the importance of eliminating cross-infection and subsequent procedures relating to using disposable gloves and putting waste in specific bins. In addition, a section of the health and safety policy will probably have a section about keeping employees and children safe.

Employees' responsibilities

As an employee, you have to cooperate with your employer in relation to health and safety. Employees' responsibilities can be summed up as follows. Employees must:

- follow health and safety policies and procedures
- use equipment and means of protection that have been provided by the setting
- report any hazards or dangers promptly
- make sure your actions do not put others at risk.

Theory into practice

The Health and Safety at Work Act 1974 is the reason why you are likely to have an induction period when you start work. It is also the reason why you will be instructed to wear disposable gloves, keep fire exits clear, carry out risk assessments and report any incidents promptly.

The Management of Health and Safety at Work Regulations 1999

These regulations require employers to carry out risk assessments on activities and equipment that might pose a serious risk to individuals' health or safety. These regulations require settings to:

- make a particular staff member responsible for health and safety
- carry out risk assessments on work activities and equipment, and take measures to minimise the risks
- have emergency procedures in place and ensure that employees know about them, e.g. by carrying out regular fire practices
- provide adequate information, supervision and training for employees
- carry out specific risk assessments to protect the health and safety of expectant mothers.

The Workplace (Health, Safety and Welfare) Regulations 1992

These regulations look at the physical conditions provided for employees. They include the number of rest breaks they are entitled to, the level of lighting that is required in the setting, toilet arrangements and the provision of water.

The Manual Handling Operations Regulations 1992 (as amended)

These regulations are designed to protect employees if they have to lift or handle objects or people. Employees have to carry out risk assessments for these activities. Wherever possible, employers should provide equipment that would avoid an employee doing any lifting, but if this is not possible, they should develop policies and procedures in order to make the activity safe.

In early years settings, this may result in staff going on training courses, or being given clear instructions about what they should, and should not, do in terms of lifting children or equipment.

It is easy to forget how often we pick up babies and toddlers and it is important to follow health and safety guidance when doing so.

Reflect

Why are the Manual Handling Operations Regulations 1992 important in early years settings?

Hint: Think about times when staff may need to lift children or equipment in the course of their work.

The Reporting of Injuries, Diseases and Dangerous Occurrences Regulations 2013

These regulations, known as RIDDOR, state that employers are responsible for reporting any injuries, diseases or other incidents that have seriously affected their employees to the **Health and Safety Executive**. As the full implications of an accident or incident may not be known at the time, employers will provide a health and safety accident book, which has to be filled in if there is an accident or incident.

Key term

Health and Safety Executive – an independent national body that regulates health, safety and illness in the workplace.

Health and Safety (First Aid) Regulations 1981 (as amended)

These regulations require that employers provide a first aid box and have sufficient staff trained to deal with first aid incidents and to contact the emergency services.

Note: Early years settings also have to comply with separate legal requirements that require them to employ first aiders who have been trained in paediatric first aid. Settings also have specific health and safety policies that you must follow.

The Regulatory Reform (Fire Safety) Order 2005

This piece of legislation states that whoever is in charge of the setting must carry out a risk assessment relating to fire, making sure that there are clear ways of escaping the building, including ways for people who may be vulnerable, such as children or people with mobility needs. The workplace also has to be equipped with fire-fighting equipment and smoke alarms, and a person has to be appointed to be in charge of fire safety. In many settings, this will be the person in charge of health and safety.

The Control of Substances Hazardous to Health Regulations 2002

These regulations are known as COSHH. They require employers to make sure that risk assessments and procedures minimise the dangers of hazardous chemicals. COSHH regulations apply to cleaning products as well as industrial chemicals. As part of the regulations, hazardous products have to be managed in ways that will keep children safe. This is why many settings will have locked cupboards or rules that prevent children from going into the kitchen.

Look out for this symbol, known as the 'running man'. It is required by law to indicate how to get out of a building in the event of a fire.

Legislation affecting the organisation of early years settings

There are pieces of legislation that affect the way early years settings are run and inspected. The legislation is different in each of the home countries. You will need to find out about the following things in the country in which your setting is based.

* What are the required adult-to-child ratios?
* How should outings be staffed and organised?
* How should settings carry out risk assessment for toys and resources?

Statutory Framework for the Early Years Foundation Stage

In England, early years settings have legal requirements to follow with respect to health and safety. These requirements include a duty to keep children safe. For example, settings are required to take steps to prevent unauthorised persons from entering the premises and also to check the identity of visitors. In practice, this means that most settings have secure fences around the premises and have a system in place for checking the identity of anyone coming into the setting. It also means that the external gates are kept locked during session time.

> **Research**
>
> You can find out about the legislation that affects the organisation of early years settings in your home country by going to the following websites.
>
> - If you work in England, read the Statutory Framework for the EYFS (2014) or visit the Ofsted website.
> - If you work in Wales, go to the Care and Social Services Inspectorate website.
> - If you work in Northern Ireland, go to the Department of Health, Social Services and Public Safety website.
> - If you work in Scotland, go to the Care Inspectorate website.
>
> You can access all of these websites by going to www.pearsonhotlinks.co.uk and searching for this ISBN: 9781447970965.

The importance of keeping up to date

As you can see from the years in which the regulations we have covered were passed, health and safety legislation does change. It is important to be aware of changes to legislation and their possible effects on your working practices.

Where to find current information

There are many agencies that have responsibility for health and safety. As part of this they are charged with providing information that is up to date. It is, therefore, fairly straightforward to keep on top of the changes that affect your practice.

In addition, there are many organisations that have been set up to improve health and safety. Table 4.9 lists some key sources of information that you may find helpful.

Table 4.9 Key sources of information about health and safety legislation

Agency/ Organisation	Role
Health and Safety Executive	A government agency responsible for health and safety in the workplace across Great Britain.
Food Standards Agency	A government agency responsible for food health and safety across Great Britain.
Public Health England	A government-funded agency that provides independent advice about health.
Health Protection Scotland	An agency that provides independent advice about health.
Health in Wales	A section of the National Health Service in Wales that provides advice about health issues.
Public Health Agency (Northern Ireland)	An agency that provides advice about health issues.
Department of Health, Social Services and Public Safety (Northern Ireland)	A department in Northern Ireland that deals with health, social services and safety.

> **Research**
>
> You can access the websites for the agencies listed in Table 4.9 by going to www.pearsonhotlinks.co.uk and searching for this ISBN: 9781447970965.

Create an information sheet that outlines the legislation that affects practice in early years settings. Your information sheet should give the correct names of the various pieces of legislation and also examples of how each one affects procedures in early years settings. You should go on to explain how the policies and procedures of a setting help to ensure the safety of children.

Finally, discuss with a partner the extent to which children can be kept safe and secure in early years settings. Can we prevent accidents from ever happening? Make sure you consider all the arguments for and against and that you reach your own conclusion.

Policies and procedures of the setting

Fortunately, serious accidents, emergencies and illnesses are relatively rare, but it is still important to know what you should do if you are ever faced with any of these situations. We will now look at what to do if you should find yourself faced with the need to evacuate a building, respond to a first aid situation or contact the emergency services. Although the following information covers how to respond to emergencies, it cannot take the place of a valid, recognised first aid qualification. Until you have been on a first aid course, you should be very careful about any actions you take in an emergency, because the wrong action could cause more harm to the casualty. If in doubt, you should summon help first.

Whatever the emergency or situation, it is important that you stay calm at all times and reassure the children in your care.

Every setting needs to have policies and procedures in place that explain to staff, parents and others what they should do in a range of emergency situations. This means that if there is an emergency, it can be dealt with quickly and correctly without anyone panicking. Policies and procedures will need to be reviewed and updated if circumstances change or following an emergency or incident.

Evacuating premises

Every setting will need to have a policy in place that states in what circumstances the building should be evacuated. For example, as the result of a fire, gas leak or bomb threat. As well as a policy for evacuation, settings will also need to have procedures in place for staff to follow if an evacuation is required. For example, the procedures will explain in detail what adults need to do and where they need to go. We will look again at the practicalities of evacuating a setting later in this section.

Reporting accidents and incidents

It is important that all accidents and incidents are recorded and reported to parents. In the case of serious incidents or accidents, they should also be reported to organisations such as the Health and Safety Executive or to the inspectorate of your home country.

As part of its health and safety policy, each setting will have procedures dealing with how to report accidents and incidents and you will need to follow them. Information that needs to be filled in promptly after an accident or incident includes:

- the date
- the time of the accident or incident
- the location of the accident or incident
- the name of the child/adult involved
- the name of the adult in attendance
- a description of the incident/accident and cause
- the injuries, if any, to the child
- the first aid treatment, if any, that was given and by whom
- a signature.

Minor accidents

However minor an accident, parents will need to know what has happened to their child. Most settings will let parents know at the end of the session if a child has had a bump, bruise or a fall. Most settings will have a slip that contains details of the accident for the parent to take home with them so that, if necessary, they can take it to the hospital.

Actions to take if a child is missing

Parents expect us to keep their children safe and we should take every precaution to prevent children from going missing. The reasons why children might go missing include:

- a gap in a fence
- a child being picked up by another adult
- a child getting out through open doors or windows
- a child wandering off from others during an outing.

It is also important to recognise that some children can be thought to be missing when they are actually still on the premises or a parent has collected them early. This might happen because:

- a member of staff has asked the child to come and do something without letting other staff members know
- the child has gone to the toilet
- the child has gone home without staff realising or the register being amended
- the child has gone to play outdoors without staff being aware
- staff have forgotten that another adult is with the child.

What to do if you suspect a child is missing

Settings should have a policy that deals with what to do in the event that a child goes missing as part of their child protection or safeguarding policies, and it is important that you follow this. This policy is likely to be informed by local or national policies.

If you suspect that a child is missing, it is essential that you stay calm. Panicking means you are less likely to be logical and methodical. The list below gives the usual procedures that settings follow both indoors and outdoors, but you will need to check if procedures differ in your setting.

What you should do indoors

- Act quickly. Check whether the child is really missing – call their name, look properly for them in the room. If you are with a colleague, ask them to help you.
- Alert your supervisor or senior team.
- Carry out a thorough search of the building and outdoor area, including cupboards and sheds.
- While this search is happening, another adult should take a register of the remaining children and they should be kept safe.

- If the child is not located, call the police on 999/112.
- Parents must also be contacted by a senior member of staff.

What you should do outdoors

- Act quickly. Check whether the child is really missing – call their name and check if other adults have seen the child.
- Search the immediate area and call the child's name regularly.
- At the same time, another adult should keep all of the other children together and take a register or head count.
- If the child is not found, call the police on 999/112 and wait for advice. Be ready to give a description of the child including their name, age and what they were wearing.
- Call the setting and speak to a senior member of staff. They, in turn, should contact the child's parents.
- If the setting is close by, other adults from the setting could search beyond the immediate area.

Case study

Missing child

Tom works at a large day nursery. The nursery has free flow in and out of doors. There are 34 children in the setting. Tom is responsible for an activity and decides to look out for Carla, who he thinks will enjoy this activity. Tom looks around the room, but cannot see her.

1 What should Tom's next actions be?

2 Why is it important that Tom acts quickly?

3 What should happen if, after an initial search, Carla is not found?

Reporting the incident

If a child has gone missing, even if only for a short amount of time, the incident has to be recorded and also reported. The setting will do this according to the requirements of the inspectorate in the home country, for example, a missing child incident in England should be reported to Ofsted.

A review of policies and procedures will also need to take place in the setting. In some cases, there may be disciplinary actions if a staff member is thought to have been negligent.

Preventing accidents and incidents on outings

Taking children out and about, whether it is just for a walk to a postbox or a day out, is great for their development. The term 'outing' is usually used in this context to mean any time you leave your setting's premises with children.

A good starting point when planning an outing is to check the advice and statutory requirements given by the appropriate **inspectorate** in your home country.

Key term

Inspectorate – a body that makes sure regulations relating to a particular activity are obeyed.

Table 4.10 lists potential hazards that may be present on an outing and steps that can be taken to minimise them.

Table 4.10 How to deal with potential hazards on outings

Danger/Hazard	Steps to minimise/deal with potential hazards
Traffic	• Babies and toddlers should be wearing reins. • The ratio of adults to children must be sufficient. • What is going to happen on the outing and the 'rules' children must follow should be explained. • Adults and children should consider wearing fluorescent jackets so that motorists can see them. • Use all crossing points. • Visit the route and assess risks before the outing.
Abduction by strangers (very rare)	• The ratio of adults to children must be sufficient. • Children should be closely supervised at all times. • Adults should take responsibility for particular children.
Children wandering off	• The ratio of adults to children must be sufficient. • Children should be closely supervised at all times. • Adults should take responsibility for particular children.
Bites and stings	• Take a first aid kit. • Keep children away from litter bins. • Teach children not to touch dogs or cats that are not their own pets.
Dehydration	• Take plenty of drinking water. • Monitor children's intake of water in hot weather.
Sunburn/sunstroke	• Follow sun protection guidelines.

continued

Table 4.10 (*continued*)

Danger/Hazard	Steps to minimise/deal with potential hazards
Children with ongoing medical conditions	• Take children's medicines with you on the outing. • Take a mobile phone. • Take emergency numbers and appropriate records for the children with medical conditions. • Observe children for signs that medication is needed, e.g. inhalers, insulin.
Motion sickness (on cars, buses, trains)	• Find out from parents beforehand whether their children suffer from motion sickness. • Allow sufficient time to stop during the journey. • Take a bucket, disposable gloves, an apron, disposable wipes and plastic bags to put soiled clothes in. • Take a spare change of clothes.
Toileting accidents	• Give children plenty of opportunities and reminders to go to the toilet. • Take a bucket, disposable gloves, an apron, disposable wipes and plastic bags to put items in. • Take a spare change of clothes.
Accidents	• Risk assess the outing beforehand. • Closely supervise children. • Ratio of adults to children must be sufficient. • Make sure that adults take responsibility for individual children. • Take a first aid kit. • Take emergency contact numbers. • Take a mobile phone.
Rainy, cold weather	• Check the weather forecast and postpone if possible. • Ask parents to bring in warm, waterproof clothes. • Take plenty of spare clothes with you. • Use all possible shelters. • Change timings of the outing so you can spend more time indoors.
Food poisoning/ allergies	• Make sure that children wash their hands before eating. • In hot weather, bring ice packs to keep food cool. • Give parents information about how to avoid food poisoning in packed lunches. • Make sure that adults know which children have food allergies. • Supervise children at mealtimes.

Planning outings

Moving children anywhere is like a military operation. Good planning and organisation are required if you are thinking about taking children on an outing.

You should always try to visit places ahead of an outing so that you can carry out a risk assessment and familiarise yourself with where you are going – especially if it is an all-day trip.

Before you leave the childcare setting you will need to have:

- consent forms from parents – they must be signed and dated for each trip
- insurance for going on trips
- insurance for any drivers taking children (as well as a valid driving licence)
- assurance that booked minibuses and coaches have seat belts
- carried out a risk assessment
- sufficient adults for safety and to comply with the required adult-to-children ratios
- a first aid kit
- registers
- emergency contact details for every child
- a mobile phone
- spare change/money
- changes of clothes for every child
- medication for children with ongoing health conditions
- comforters (for babies and toddlers)
- sun cream, hats and sunglasses
- disposable gloves, aprons and wipes
- drinking water.

During the outing

It is important that you are very organised, calm and vigilant at each stage of the outing. Keep checking that you have the right number of children in the group and consider using fluorescent jackets so that they can see you and you can see them. Make sure that all adults with you are fully briefed about which children they are responsible for and each of the children's individual needs.

It is important to have planned the outing carefully so that you are not rushing – this is not good for children or for adults.

Policies and procedures for taking children on outings

Every setting will have its own policy and procedure for taking children on outings. This will be based on the requirements or advice from the inspectorate in your home country. Not following the policies and procedures may mean that you are liable for prosecution in the event of an accident or incident.

Happily, there are few problems with the vast majority of outings because most adults understand the risks and potential hazards.

Most procedures will cover:

- whether a written risk assessment is required
- how a risk assessment should be written if it is required
- what information needs to be given to parents before they give their consent
- what the requirements are for insurance
- what the requirements are for staff-to-child ratios
- what the procedures are if a child goes missing
- what equipment/resources should be taken on the outing, e.g. mobile phones.

Research

1 Find out about your home country's requirements for outings with children younger than school age and the requirements for outings with children of school age.
2 Look at your work placement's policy for organising outings.

Activity

Find out what the procedures are in your setting for:

- a fire
- reporting accidents and injuries
- a serious accident requiring medical assistance
- a missing child
- preventing accidents and incidents on outings.

In addition, you may like to find out how your setting deals with unforeseen events, such as heavy snow.

The role of early years professionals in keeping children safe and secure

As early years professionals we have a responsibility to keep children safe. We have already seen that supervision is central to this, but so are good organisation skills and increased awareness of what children are doing. Make sure that the level of supervision is correct for the age and stage of children. In general terms, babies and toddlers need very close supervision, but as children become older the level of supervision required may change depending on what they are doing.

Close supervision and engagement

Close supervision requires adults to be alongside children. Babies and toddlers will need this level of supervision most of the time, but children aged 5 to 8 years will only need it during certain activities, such as going on an outing or when cooking.

Is this level of supervision appropriate for the age of the children and the type of play they are engaged in?

Supervision within sight

There are times when it is safe for children to play within sight of adults, but not necessarily in close proximity to them. Being away from adults is good for increasing children's independence. This level of supervision is useful once children are 3 or so years old and are engaging in low-risk activities.

Awareness

Children from 4 to 8 years will not need close supervision all of the time, but they will need an adult to know where they are and what they are doing. There are many ways of doing this. Adults can watch children at a discreet distance or go over and chat to them from time to time about what they are doing.

Keeping up-to-date registers

One of the requirements of the EYFS, but also of schools, is to keep accurate and up-to-date registers. Registers have to be completed at the start of each session and if children leave before the end of a session, this should be indicated. Registers are needed to ensure safe evacuation of children in the event of a fire or other emergency.

Role-modelling safe behaviour

Children can learn about staying safe by watching the way that adults behave and also by hearing their reasoning about why certain things keep us safe. For example, an adult may tell a 4-year-old child that they are going to check that the door is closed so toddlers cannot get out. This, combined with the action of closing the door, is likely to help the 4-year-old child remember to close the door.

The power of role modelling also means that you need to think hard about what children see you do. Smoking is a good example. Smoking is banned in early years settings, but if you go outside to smoke, children must not see you.

Observing children to understand their stage of development

It is important to observe individual children as this will help you to understand their stage of development and also how they may play with objects – relying on milestones alone is not a good idea.

Selecting equipment and resources

The equipment and resources you choose for children must be right for their stage of development. Children under 18 months will, for example, play with objects by mouthing them. Therefore, small objects that are fine for older children to play with will be dangerous for babies and toddlers.

The appropriateness and safety of resources and equipment must be regularly checked through a rolling programme of inspections. A tricycle that was safe a year ago may have moving parts that have become loose. Anything that is found to be unsafe should be put out of reach of children immediately. Table 4.11 describes some of the dangers you should check for.

Table 4.11 Dangers you should check for in equipment and resources

Items	Danger
Toys and resources made from plastic	• Plastic can become brittle with age and snap.
Toys and resources with moving parts, e.g. wheeled toys	• Toys with moving parts, including wheeled toys, need checking. Moving parts can become weakened over time. • Screws can become loose.
Toys with batteries	• Batteries can leak. When toys are not in use, batteries should be removed and stored in a locked place.
Resources or equipment that require electricity	• These resources should be checked every year. • Any wear and tear or malfunctioning, e.g. flickering lights, will mean that the resource or piece of equipment should be removed.

Safety marks and instructions

Toys should only be bought if they conform to European standards and have the safety marks in place. Sadly, there are some toys that will have fake stamps on them, so you should still look carefully and assess whether they look and feel safe.

The instructions that come with toys and resources must be read and kept safely. Reputable manufacturers will often offer spare parts and so this is another reason why it is worth keeping the instructions.

Link

Go to Unit 2: Section B to find more information about toy safety marks and to see examples of what the marks look like.

Understanding the principles of first aid

Accidents can happen and it is important to know what you should do when they occur. The main aim of first aid is to keep someone alive so that they can receive medical treatment.

As well as understanding the principles of first aid, it is essential that you attend paediatric first aid training. Ideally, only first aiders should give children first aid, including mouth-to-mouth resuscitation. The exception to this is when there is no first aider available and a child's life is in danger.

DR ABC

The acronym 'DR ABC' has been adopted to help people remember the priorities when there is an accident.

D is for Danger

You should always assess the danger to you and to others before taking any action.

R is for Response

See if you can get a response from the child. Try speaking loudly or gently shake the child's shoulders. If there is a response, but the injuries seem significant, call an ambulance immediately by ringing 999 or 112. Stay with the child, treating the injuries if you know what to do. Keep talking to the child and monitoring their responses.

A is for Airways

If there is no response from the child, shout for help and make sure that someone calls 999 or 112. Then, you should open the child's airway. This will help them to breathe.

Did you know?

112 is the European emergency number that can be used everywhere in the European Union. Like 999, ringing it is free of charge.

If no one is around, you should open the child's airway and then follow the guidelines for breathing and circulation/compressions before calling emergency services.

To open a child's airway, tilt the child's head back by placing one hand on the child's forehead and two fingers underneath the child's chin. Figure 4.5 shows this action in practice. If you are trying to open a baby's airway, you should only tilt the baby's head back slightly as babies have narrow airways.

Note: you should not tilt a child's head back if you have any suspicions that the child's neck is injured, for example, if the child has fallen from a height or has been in a road traffic accident.

Figure 4.5 Opening up the airway of a child is important to help their breathing. Place your hand on the child's forehead, put two fingers under the child's chin and tilt their head back.

B is for Breathing

Quickly check that the child is breathing. Put your head close to their face and see if you can feel the child's breath on your cheek. While listening and looking for breathing call out for help.

C is for Circulation/Compressions

If you cannot feel any breath, you will need to give the child five rescue breaths. You should then check for signs of life, for example, swallowing, movement, breathing and speech. If there are no signs of life, you should carry out 30 chest compressions. If you are alone, carry out chest compressions and rescue breaths at a ratio of 30:2 for one minute and then dial 999 or 112.

Afterwards, if the child is not responding by showing any sign of life, give them two breaths and then

30 chest compressions. Keep doing this until the ambulance arrives.

Note: You are more likely to do harm by not giving chest compressions to a child that needs them than giving chest compressions to a child that does not need them.

Giving rescue breaths (children over 1 year)

- Make sure the child's airway is open.
- Pinch the child's nose.
- Put your mouth around the child's mouth to create a seal.
- Breathe steadily into the child's mouth. Each breath should be delivered slowly (over 1–1.5 seconds). Make sure the child's chest rises and falls with each breath.

Giving chest compressions (children over 1 year)

- Press down on the lower half of the child's sternum with the heel of one or two of your hands depending on the size of the child. It is important to avoid pressing down on the child's abdomen.
- Press the chest down to one-third of its depth.
- Do this at a rate of 100 to 120 times a minute.

Giving rescue breaths (babies under 1 year)

- Make sure the child's airway is open.
- Place your mouth around the baby's mouth and nose to create a seal.
- Blow gently into the baby's mouth. Each breath should be delivered slowly over (1–1.5 seconds). Make sure the baby's chest rises and falls with each breath.

Giving chest compressions (babies under 1 year)

- Use two fingers to press down sharply on the lower half of the child's sternum. It is important to avoid pressing down on the baby's abdomen.
- Press down at least one-third of the depth of the chest.
- Do this at a rate of 100 to 120 times a minute.

Serious injuries

Table 4.12 shows how accidents and serious injuries can be responded to. Note that you should only respond if you have been trained in first aid, unless there is no one else around and the situation is life-threatening.

Table 4.12 How to respond to different serious injuries

Type of injury	How to respond
Burns and scalds	<ul><li>Put the affected area under the cold tap for 10 minutes.</li><li>If skin is broken, wrap the affected area in cling film and call 999 or 112.</li></ul>
Severe bleeding	<ul><li>Check if anything is embedded in the wound – if there is, do not attempt to remove it.</li><li>If nothing is in the wound, press firmly down using a clean cloth if one is available.</li><li>Lift up the wounded area so that it is higher than the child's heart.</li><li>If something is in the wound, press on each side of the wound to apply pressure to minimise bleeding.</li><li>Call 999 or 112.</li></ul>
Suspected fractures – legs and arms	<ul><li>Suspected broken leg or back injury: Do not move the child. Call 999 or 112. Keep the child warm with a blanket.</li><li>Suspected broken arm: Sit the child up. Put a pad between the child's arm and the chest. Support the arm with a sling or scarf. Go straight to hospital.</li></ul>
Choking baby (under 1 year)	<ul><li>Lie the baby face down along your arm with your hand supporting the baby's head. Using the heel of your hand, give five firm back blows between the baby's shoulder blades. Figure 4.6 shows this in action.</li><li>Stop after each blow to check if the obstruction is cleared from the baby's mouth.</li><li>If the obstruction is not clear after five back blows, lie the baby along your forearm on their back, keeping their head low and supporting their back and head.</li><li>Using two fingers, give up to five chest thrusts. To do this, push inwards and upwards (towards the baby's head) against the baby's breastbone. The area you should push is one finger's breadth below the baby's nipple line.</li><li>Check if the blockage has cleared after each thrust.</li><li>If the blockage is still not clear after three cycles of back blows and chest thrusts, dial 999 or 112 and continue the cycle of back blows and chest thrusts.</li></ul>
Choking child (over 1 year)	<ul><li>Stand behind the child and make sure the child is bending over forwards. Using the heel of your hand, give five firm blows between the child's shoulder blades. After each blow, check to see if the blockage has cleared.</li><li>If the blockage has not cleared after five blows, give up to five abdominal thrusts. Stand behind the child, place your arms around their waist and bend the child over forwards. Make a fist and place it directly above the child's belly button. Then, place your other hand on top and thrust both hands backwards into the child's stomach with a hard, upward movement.</li><li>Stop after each thrust to check if the blockage has cleared.</li><li>Note: do not use abdominal thrusts on pregnant women or people who are obese.</li><li>If the blockage is still not clear after three cycles of back blows and abdominal thrusts, you will need to call for help.</li><li>If you are with other people, ask one person to dial 999 or 112.</li><li>If no one is around dial 999 or 112 yourself.</li><li>Then, continue with the cycles of back blows and abdominal thrusts until help arrives.</li></ul>

continued

Table 4.12 (*continued*)

Type of injury	How to respond
Severe allergic reactions, e.g. a rash, swelling of the lips and/or tongue, noisy breathing or difficulty breathing	• If the child has an EpiPen®, administer it if you have been trained and have permission to use it. • Call 999 or 112. • Keep the child upright.
Electrocution	• Check that the child is not still in contact with the source of the electrocution – if so, push the child's body away from the source with a wooden pole or another object that is not made of metal. • Check for a pulse and breathing and follow DR ABC, as necessary. • Call 999 or 112.

Figure 4.6 Babies often choke when weaning. To stop this, lie the baby along your arm and using the heel of your hand give a firm back blow to the baby between the shoulder blades. Repeat if the obstruction is not cleared.

For minor injuries where children's lives are not in danger, you should reassure the child and other children who may be around the area, and make them comfortable while waiting for a first aider.

When to call for an ambulance

There are some signs that indicate a child will need immediate medical attention following an accident or an incident. Note that some of these signs are the same as those that indicate a child may have a serious illness. They include the following:

• no pulse
• if the child is not breathing
• if the child is unconscious
• if the child is having difficulty in breathing
• if a child's lips and fingertips are turning blue
• heavy bleeding
• a limb that sticks out at an awkward angle
• a head injury
• if a child has concussion
• a burn or scald
• face and/or neck swelling (may indicate an allergic reaction/poisoning)
• cold and clammy skin
• a fever
• a convulsion or fit.

Concussion

If a child has had a blow to the head it is important to keep an eye on them even if they seem fine at the time. Concussion can occur later. If you notice any possible loss of consciousness, even if it is only momentary, then you must call 999 or 112 for an ambulance. Look out for dizziness, dilation of pupils, confusion, vomiting and drowsiness, as well as a child complaining of a headache. If any of these signs occur after a child has had a knock to the head, act quickly. Make sure that parents know the signs of concussion as well.

The importance of first aid training

Although we have looked at the principles of responding to accidents and incidents, it is not a substitute for paediatric first aid training leading to a recognised qualification. If you intend to go directly into employment, you may be required to have this training anyway as part of the requirements of the inspectorate in your home country.

Once you have had first aid training, it is important to revise the principles from time to time and also to attend regular training to keep your knowledge up to date. This is because the advice and techniques given do change over time. It is also easy to forget some of the advice.

Carrying out an emergency evacuation

There are several reasons why you may need to evacuate a building. Evacuation may need to take place because of any of the following.

- A bomb threat: evacuate to the fire assembly point unless otherwise directed.
- Flooding: move to a higher floor in the setting or to high ground.
- A gas leak: do not turn any electrical appliances on or off, or let anyone in the area smoke or use lighters or matches. You should also keep doors and windows open.
- A person who is being violent or threatening: if safe to do so, you should evacuate the building and take the children to a safe place – this may not be the designated fire assembly point. If this is not possible, you should try to find a room or place in which you can lock yourselves away.
- An explosion: evacuate the building. This may mean moving to somewhere other than the designated fire assembly point.
- A fire: evacuate to the fire assembly point.

General principles for evacuating children safely

Your setting should have a comprehensive evacuation and fire plan and you should familiarise yourself with it. You should also check that you know where the nearest doors are and the escape route for the part of the building in which you are working. It is important to follow procedures within the setting as this can avoid confusion; it also means that every adult knows what they need to do and which children they need to take responsibility for.

If you are working with babies, you may have an evacuation crib. Make sure that this is always available and that you know how to use it.

Table 4.13 is a list of 'Dos' and 'Don'ts' when evacuating children.

Table 4.13 General principles for safely evacuating children

Do	Don't
Raise the alarm immediately.	Panic or scream.
Leave by the nearest exit.	Waste time by picking up personal possessions or getting coats.
Give clear instructions to the children.	Ignore the alarm because you think it is a practice.
Take a register with you.	Forget to take the register.
Respond to an alarm immediately even if you think it might be a practice.	Run.
Remember to check all areas of the setting, e.g. the toilets if you are with older children.	Let the children out of your sight.

continued

Table 4.13 *(continued)*

Do	Don't
Close doors behind you if there is no one following you (in the event of a fire).	Go back into the building until the all-clear is given.
Go straight to the assembly point if it is safe to do so.	Block fire exits under any circumstances.
Keep the children with you.	Lock fire exits under any circumstances.
Let the appointed fire officer know if anyone is missing.	

Calling for emergency help

To call for the emergency services in the UK, you are required to ring 999 or 112. Calls to these numbers should only be made in the event of an emergency that requires the presence of an ambulance, the police or fire services. For gas leaks, you should contact the emergency number for the gas services, which is 0800 111 999.

Emergency help should be called for in the following situations:

- if there is a fire or explosion
- if a child is trapped
- if there has been a traffic incident
- if there is a bomb threat
- if someone is using violence or threatening violence
- if serious damage is being caused or could be caused to property
- if a criminal has been disturbed or apprehended
- if there is danger to life
- if there is a serious injury
- if someone has chest pains
- if someone is having difficulty in breathing
- if someone has a severe allergic reaction
- if someone is bleeding heavily
- if someone is fitting or has a concussion
- if someone is drowning
- if someone has been poisoned.

Making a call

If you have to call the emergency services, it is important that you do so promptly, but also calmly. Under stress, it is very easy to forget information and so remaining as calm as you can is essential. The emergency services are used to taking calls and will ask you a series of questions in a set order, as follows.

1 The service that you require:

This allows the call to be handled by the correct service.

2 The address and, if possible, the postcode or a nearby landmark:

This allows the emergency vehicles to be dispatched.

3 The number you are calling from:

This allows them to call back if the connection is broken. It also helps them to eliminate hoax calls.

4 What has happened:

This allows the dispatcher to send the correct emergency service. If an incident involves a child you should let the operator know this.

Do not waste time by trying to talk about what has happened before the operator has taken down the address as this can slow down the dispatch of the emergency vehicle.

Fire and rescue service

In the event of a fire or explosion, you should only call 999 or 112 once you are out of danger yourself. You should give the location of the fire and say if the building has been evacuated or anyone is trapped. You should not go back into the building.

In the event that a child is trapped, you may consider calling an ambulance as well. You should give clear details of how the child is trapped and what parts of their body are trapped.

Ambulance

If a child is unwell or there is an accident, you should give the age, sex and any medical history of the child or adult. You should also give information about the symptoms and what has happened to cause the accident. You should also say what has been done so far and what is happening to the child at the time. Ideally, you should try to make the call close to the child so that you can pass on any instructions to them or follow instructions with them.

Police

If someone is being violent or is threatening violence, you should try to call the police from a safe place. You should make it clear why you need immediate help, for example, by explaining the level of the threat and the type of actions that are taking place.

If you see criminal activity, you should not confront the perpetrator.

Maintaining accurate records and reports

Maintaining accurate and coherent records and reports is a duty of anyone working with children. This includes records of medication, accidents and incidents. How and by whom they should be completed will depend on the policies of the setting in which you work. The policies will be based on the statutory requirements, which are in turn inspected by Ofsted, the regulatory body. Ofsted states that any serious incidents or accidents should be reported to them within 14 days of the incident.

Assessment practice 4.4 3B.P5

You have been asked by the head of an early years centre to be an acting health and safety officer. Some staff members are not taking health and safety very seriously so you have decided to give a presentation focusing on the responsibilities that early years professionals have in keeping children safe and secure.

Prepare a presentation that explains the role of the early years professional in the following areas:

- what to do in the event of a serious accident
- actions to take if a child goes missing
- how to safely evacuate the setting in case of emergency
- how to call for emergency help
- actions to take to ensure the safety of children before and during an outing
- reasons why these actions help keep children safe.

C Be able to assess health and safety risks in early years settings

The risk assessment process

Risk assessment is a process that can be done informally as well as formally. Formal risk assessments are needed when the risks are thought to be significant. The risk assessment should be written down but you will need to follow the specific risk assessment procedure for your setting. This will be based on the requirements of the country in which you work.

The process of risk assessment is quite straightforward.

1 Look at an area, activity or resource and consider what hazards or risks may be associated with it. Think about what the consequences of an accident may be. It can be worth thinking about common types of accident while doing this. (Some settings use a rating scale to identify the level of risk.)

2 Identify to whom the risk might apply and how they could be harmed. Remember, something that is safe for older children may be dangerous for younger ones.

3 Evaluate the risk and identify how it will be managed (what precautions will be put in place), e.g. supervising children more closely or putting equipment away after use.

4 Record this information accurately and coherently on a sheet.

5 Sign and date the sheet.

6 Make sure the precautions are implemented.

The same process applies to assessing both indoor and outdoor provision, but assessments for outdoor provision may need to take account of the weather. This is because each type of weather may create new hazards. A slide in dry weather is a different proposition to a slide that is wet because it has been raining. A surface that is safe in dry weather may become hazardous in icy conditions.

Figure 4.7 shows an example of what a risk assessment form might look like.

Activity/ equipment	Risks	Risk to whom?	Strategies to minimise risk
Feeding the fish	• Fish food could be swallowed • Contamination	• Children	• Adult will supervise • Adult will hold fish food container • Adult and children will wash their hands after the activity
Making soup	• Cuts from knives • Potential cross-infection • Burns and scalds	• Children • Adult	• Adult will supervise • Vegetables will be washed • Adult will teach children how to use knives safely • Only two children will take part at a time • Adult and children will wash their hands before and after the activity • Children will be kept away from the stove • Protective clothing will be worn • Knives will be put out of reach when they are not being used

Date: Carried out by:

Signature:

Figure 4.7 A sample risk assessment form

Reviewing assessments

As well as carrying out risk assessments for individual 'one-off' activities, settings will also need to do regular risk assessments on areas within their setting. These risk assessments will need to be reviewed and updated when necessary. Most settings will review them annually but they will need to review them more often if there are changes made to the areas. Changes may include intakes of younger children or a larger number of children. It is important that risk assessments are also reviewed in the light of any accidents.

Research

Find out what the requirements are for risk assessment in your home country.

• In England, you should look at the Statutory Framework of the EYFS or visit the Ofsted website.

• In Scotland, you should look at information provided on the Care Inspectorate website.

• In Wales, you should look at information provided on the Healthcare Inspectorate Wales website.

• In Northern Ireland you should look at information provided on the Department of Health, Social Services and Public Safety website.

You can access all of these websites by going to www.pearsonhotlinks.co.uk and searching for this ISBN: 9781447970965.

Assessment practice 4.5   3C.P6 | 3C.M3

Ask your placement supervisor if you can carry out a risk assessment of the health and safety hazards for a play and learning activity for a child in the setting. Make sure you include all possible hazards, who may be affected by them and then record how each hazard could be minimised.

Ask your placement supervisor to review your risk assessment to check that it is accurate and sufficiently thorough.

After your supervisor has looked at it, make adjustments to your risk assessment to show how you would manage the same hazards if children at different stages of development were involved in the activity.

Assessment practice 4.6   3B.D1 | 3C.D2

Write an article for an early years magazine that counters the claim that health and safety is a waste of time. Your article should evaluate:

• the methods used in early years settings to keep children safe and secure

• the extent to which risk assessment is key to early years practice and how this can be shown by giving examples from a chosen early years setting.

Assessing infection and safety risks

In this unit, we have looked at the steps involved in a risk assessment, the risks and hazards that may be present in an early years setting and how these risks and hazards can be prevented or the effect minimised. To complete this unit you need to show evidence of your ability to assess health, infection and safety risks in a variety of situations.

Indoor and outdoor play and learning

A good starting point for assessing infection and safety risks is to revisit Tables 4.6 and 4.7. Use these tables to recap the hazards that can be found in the indoor and outdoor play environments. Then carry out a risk assessment for the setting in which you are working. You should think about the age of children that will be using the environments and the resources that will be present. The age of a child can make a difference to how safe an environment or resource is. For example, an object that is safe for a 4-year-old child to use could be a hazard for a baby.

Personal care routines

Personal care routines, such as nappy changing, need to be carefully assessed. We learned in Section A that infection control must be a high priority in a setting. For example, this means using protective clothing, such as gloves and aprons, and disposing of waste safely. Revisit Section A to help you assess the risk of infection that is involved in personal care routines you carry out. Also think about the physical dangers to children during their personal care. For example, the danger of a baby falling from a raised surface during a nappy change or children slipping over on wet floors. Look back at Table 4.6 to help you further assess the risks associated with physical care routines.

Providing food

You will need to show a good understanding of the risks associated with food handling. Revisit Section A that looks at how infection is spread and then consider how you could minimise the risk of infection when you handle, prepare and serve food. In addition, think about the safety risks involved in preparing food, such as scalding, cuts and potential falls. As food handling is important, consider attending a food handling hygiene course.

Cleaning and maintaining the environment, equipment and toys

In Section A we looked at the importance of cleaning and maintaining the environment and any equipment and toys. We also looked at how often this work might be done. It is important that you make sure cleaning is carried out in a safe manner. This includes using gloves to prevent cross-infection and ensuring that cleaning products are used according to manufacturer's instructions. Cleaning products are also likely to contain hazardous chemicals and so should be stored carefully.

Taking children on outings

In Section B we looked at risks and hazards associated with taking children on outings. Revisit this section as well as Table 4.10 to help you minimise or prevent these risks and hazards. If you intend to take children on an outing, you should be aware of the possible risks and hazards and be vigilant at all times.

Recording findings accurately

You will need to show that you can record your risk assessment findings accurately and coherently. As paperwork varies from setting to setting, ask your placement supervisor for the correct paperwork you should be using. It is also worth asking for a duplicate form so that you can practise filling it in using the principles we looked at in Section B.

Further reading and resources

DK Publishing (2014) *First Aid Manual* (10th ed.), London: Dorling Kindersley.

Parker, L. (2011) *The Early Years Health and Safety Handbook* (2nd ed.), Oxford: Routledge.

Websites

Cancer Research UK SunSmart: www.sunsmart. org.uk *Information about sun safety.*

GOV.UK: www.gov.uk/government/publications/ fire-safety-in-the-home *Information about fire safety in the home.*

Health and Safety Executive: www.hse.gov.uk *Guidelines and advice about health and safety including latest legislation.*

Ready for work?

Liz Williams Deputy manager of a day-care centre

I've been working with children for nine years and over this period I have come across so many people who think that working with young children is just about changing nappies and playing with them. They do not realise the level of responsibility that we have to keep children healthy and safe. When I show people the number of written policies that we have to follow and also the level of ongoing training that we do to keep staff up to date with first aid they are amazed.

People, especially those in training, are also surprised to hear that we expect everyone to clean equipment as well as bathrooms if these are needed during the day. We do have cleaners, but if a child has an accident or is sick, we cannot leave an area unclean. So everyone in my setting, including me, rolls up their sleeves and puts on the gloves from time to time.

Skills for practice

Risk assessing a play activity

It is important to be able to risk assess a play and learning activity. Here are some simple tips to help you do this.

- Look at the age and stage of the child's development.
- Think about the implications for how they might use any of the equipment or resources, such as babies putting things in their mouths.
- Think about the implications for their behaviour, for example, 2-year-olds are impulsive, whereas babies do not follow instructions.
- Think about each part of the play and learning activity and consider where the hazards might be, such as getting dressed or tidying up.
- Finally, for each hazard that you identify, work out how to minimise the danger. In some

cases this might mean adapting the play and learning activity.

A matter of life and death: first aid questions

If a child is not breathing, should I call an ambulance or give them rescue breaths?

- If you are alone, you should start by giving five rescue breaths and 30 chest compressions. If you are not near a phone, carry the baby or child to the nearest phone after you have given rescue breaths.
- If you are with someone else, one of you should call an ambulance while the other person starts compressions. The operator will give you further instructions.

Should I give any first aid if I do not have a first aid certificate?

- If the child's life is at stake, you should do whatever you can.

Introduction

Babies and children are surrounded by people who play an important part in their lives. These people may be the child's parents or carers, grandparents or other family members. In addition, many families have other professionals who support them and their children. For example, children may go to more than one setting, such as a childminder and a preschool, or may be supported by health professionals, social workers or outreach workers. As early years professionals, it is important that we understand all of the different roles that are played by adults in children's lives and also that we work with parents, colleagues and other professionals in a cooperative way.

Assessment: You will be assessed by a series of assignments set by your teacher/tutor.

Learning aims

In this unit you will:

A1   understand the impact of parental rights, views and experiences on partnership work with parents and/or carers in early years settings

A2   understand how to work cooperatively with parents and/or carers

B   understand how to work cooperatively with colleagues and other professionals in early years settings

C   be able to work with parents and/or carers and others in early years settings to meet the needs of children.

When I started my course, I thought it would be all about working with children. However, after starting my placement, I began to see just how important it is to know how to work with parents too.

Yasar, *a learner on an early years course*

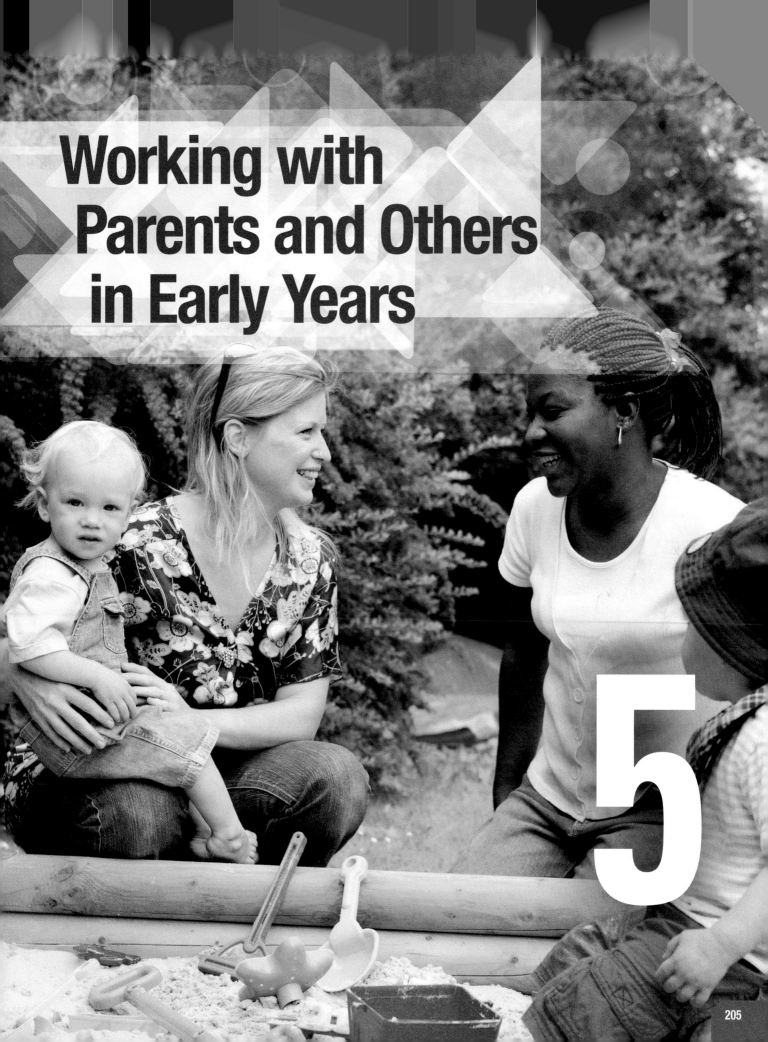

Working with Parents and Others in Early Years

5

::BTEC
Assessment Zone

This table shows you what you must do in order to achieve a **Pass**, **Merit** or **Distinction** grade, and lists activities that relate to each learning aim.

Assessment criteria

Pass	Merit	Distinction
Learning aim A1: Understand the impact of parental rights, views and experiences on partnership work with parents and/or carers in early years settings **Learning aim A2: Understand how to work cooperatively with parents and/or carers**		
3A1.P1 Describe how concepts of parental rights and responsibilities affect the care of children in early years settings. **Assessment practice 5.1** **3A1.P2** Explain how partnership work with parents in early years settings may be affected by parental views, experiences and parenting styles. **Assessment practice 5.1**	**3A1.M1** Discuss the impacts arising from parental rights and parenting for the care of children in early years settings. **Assessment practice 5.1**	**3A.D1** Evaluate how effective partnership work with parents and/or carers in early years settings can impact on outcomes for children. **Assessment practice 5.2**
3A2.P3 Explain the importance of building a professional relationship for partnership work with parents and/or carers in early years settings. **Assessment practice 5.2** **3A2.P4** English Examine how effective communication affects partnership working with parents and/or carers in early years settings. **Assessment practice 5.2** **3A2.P5** Explain, using examples from early years settings, the limitations of the role of the early years professional when giving advice to parents and/or carers. **Assessment practice 5.2**	**3A2.M2** Analyse how different ways of building professional relationships with parents and/or carers can be used effectively to support partnership work in early years settings. **Assessment practice 5.2**	
Learning aim B: Understand how to work cooperatively with colleagues and other professionals in early years settings		
3B.P6 Explain the role of other professionals in the lives of families with babies and children. **Assessment practice 5.3** **3B.P7** Review the purpose of working collaboratively with other professionals for work in early years settings. **Assessment practice 5.3** **3B.P8** Explain how cooperative work is managed to contribute to children's health, wellbeing, learning and development. **Assessment practice 5.3**	**3B.M3** Discuss, using examples, ways in which working collaboratively with other professionals benefits children and families. **Assessment practice 5.3**	**3B.D2** Evaluate the extent to which collaborative work with colleagues and other professionals in early years settings could impact on outcomes for children. **Assessment practice 5.3**

Assessment criteria (continued)

Pass	Merit	Distinction
Learning aim C: Be able to work with parents and/or carers and others in early years settings to meet the needs of children		
3C.P9 Work with parents and/or carers when meeting the needs of children. **Assessment practice 5.4**	**3C.M4** Demonstrate confidence when working with parents and/or carers and colleagues. **Assessment practice 5.4**	**3C.D3** Assess the extent to which own work with parents and others in early years settings contributed to meeting the needs of children. **Assessment practice 5.5**
3C.P10 Demonstrate cooperative work with colleagues. **Assessment practice 5.5**		

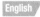 **English** English Functional Skills signposting

How you will be assessed

This unit will be assessed by a series of internally assessed tasks set by your teacher/tutor. They will include practical tasks that will need to be carried out on placement, and that link to your Practical Evidence Portfolio. Throughout this unit you will find assessment practice activities that will help you work towards your assessment. Completing these activities will not mean that you have achieved a particular grade, but you will have carried out useful research or preparation that will be relevant when it comes to your final assignment.

In order for you to achieve the tasks in your assignment, it is important to check that you have met all of the Pass grading criteria. You can do this as you work your way through the assignment.

If you are hoping to gain a Merit or Distinction, you should also make sure that you present the information in your assignment in the style that

is required by the relevant assessment criterion. For example, Merit and Distinction criteria require you to discuss, analyse, assess, demonstrate and evaluate.

The assignment set by your teacher/tutor will consist of a number of tasks designed to meet the criteria in the table. This is likely to consist of a written assignment but may also include activities such as the following:

- producing a guidance document for new learners about to start a work placement in a setting
- writing case studies or giving examples from a placement to demonstrate your understanding
- using observations you have carried out on children in your placement
- creating materials that could be used to train new staff.

Getting started

How many professionals who work with children can you name? Do you know what they do and how they work to support families? At the end of this unit, come back to this task and see if you answer the question differently.

A1 Understand the impact of parental rights, views and experiences on partnership work with parents and/or carers in early years settings

The term 'parent' should be viewed as a very broad one. Although some children do live with both natural parents, many live with a carer who is not their parent. This could include step-parents or others who have parental responsibility for them or who are looking after them. It might also include foster carers, grandparents or staff in residential homes. This section looks at the important role that parents and carers play in children's lives.

Parental rights and responsibilities

The importance of parents or other carers in children's lives was established and set out in the Children Act 1989 (revised in 2004). It was stated that, wherever possible, children should remain with their parents. Under the Act, parents and others who have parental responsibility have the right to make decisions for and about their children in the following areas:

- the name of the child
- the child's religion
- the child's education
- the child's medical treatment
- where and with whom the child should live
- money and property belonging to the child.

Although not stated in the Children Act 2004, there is also an expectation that parents and carers will protect their children and keep them healthy and safe. Parents also have to ensure that children receive education from 5 years of age until the end of **statutory** schooling. If parents do not manage

to do this, they may face prosecution and/or lose their powers of parental responsibility under separate legislation.

Key term

Statutory – required by law (statute).

Research

Find out school leaving ages in the United Kingdom (UK) by going to the Gov.uk website. Then find out more about the expectations that are associated with parental responsibility by visiting the 'Parental rights and responsibilities' page on the Gov.uk website. You can access this page by going to www.pearsonhotlinks.co.uk and searching for this ISBN: 9781447970965.

Link

Go to Unit 8: Section A, Table 8.1 where you will find out more information about the Children Act 2004.

Children's welfare is paramount

Although we have seen that parents and carers have the right to make particular decisions when it comes to their children, if their actions are not in the interests of the child, such as refusing medical treatment on their behalf, these rights can be suspended. This is because the guiding principle of the Children Act

2004 is that the **welfare** of the child is paramount. When the child's welfare is compromised, parents' or carers' wishes can be overruled.

> **Key term**
>
> **Welfare** – holistic needs including health and wellbeing.

Parental responsibility

The term 'parental responsibility' has legal status and it may apply to people who are not a child's birth parents.

Parental responsibility is given automatically to:

- the child's birth mother
- the child's father, if he is married to the child's mother
- the child's father, if he is named on the birth certificate.

Otherwise legal steps will need to be taken for parental responsibility to be accorded to the father. The father can acquire parental responsibility if:

- a Parental Responsibility Agreement is made with the mother
- he obtains a Parental Responsibility Order from the court
- he obtains a Residence Order from the court
- he becomes the child's guardian.

Step-parents can also acquire parental responsibility if:

- a Parental Responsibility Agreement is made with the agreement of those who have parental responsibility
- a Parental Responsibility Order is given by the court when the step-parent is married to the child's mother.

In addition, the local authority can gain parental responsibility if the child is taken into care or there are concerns about the child's welfare.

Other people, such as family members and foster carers, can also gain parental responsibility. Again, this happens through the court and is often given in cases when the child is considered at risk or where the child's parents have died.

Adoption

Where a child has been adopted, all parental responsibility is transferred to the child's adoptive parents.

It is important when working with children to know who has parental responsibility and whether there are any Residence Orders or Care Orders in place.

> **Research**
>
> **How strong are parental rights?**
>
> Find out about Victoria Gillick's challenge to her local health authority in a case known as Gillick v West Norfolk and Wisbech Area Health Authority. The case centred on the parental right to prevent a local health authority from giving contraception to underage young people.

The importance of enduring relationships

Professionals, practitioners and teachers come and go, but most parents or carers are a constant presence in their children's lives. It is the parents/carers who know their child well and who support them through happy and sad times. This is why the phrase 'enduring relationship' is used when describing the bond between parents and their children. Parents act as role models and, therefore, children will often develop similar attitudes and values to their parents. Figure 5.1 shows the ways that parents help and support their children.

The bond between parents or carers and children is usually strong, but it is also complex. Many parents will say that they have both strong positive and negative emotions when it comes to their own children. Parents need to be reassured that strong feelings of love, but also anger, are normal.

The recognition that parents play such a pivotal part in children's lives should be shown in every part of our work with parents. It is good practice to listen to their ideas and feelings, and involve them in the provision of their child's education.

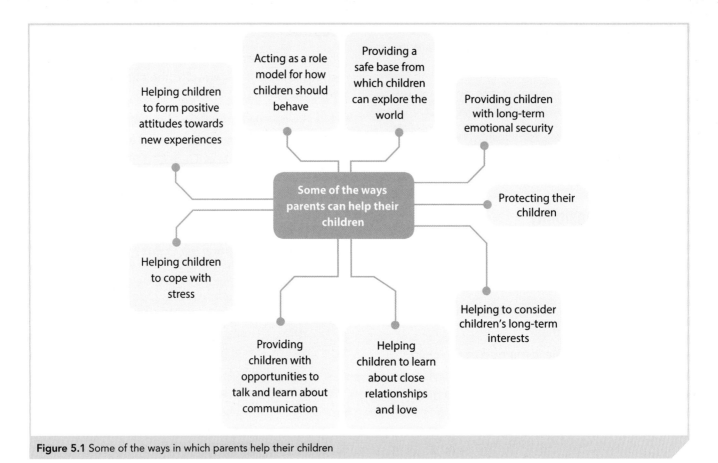

Figure 5.1 Some of the ways in which parents help their children

The parental effect on children's learning

Children learn a variety of attitudes and practical skills from their parents. Parents, therefore, play a huge part in supporting children's emotional development and later in their academic achievements. This has been recognised by educators for a long time but more recently, it has been demonstrated by a piece of research known as the EPPE Project.

The EPPE Project

EPPE stands for the Effective Provision of Pre-School Education (although over time this name has changed to Effective Pre-School, Primary and Secondary Education – EPPSE). Between 1997 and 2005 the project tracked a group of 3,000 children who were 3 years old at the start of the project. The children and their families were selected from a range of socio-economic groups. Many of the children attended some type of preschool education but some stayed at home.

The researchers carried out in-depth studies of the children's histories and then evaluated the home environment and also the preschool environment in cases where children were attending a preschool.

There were many findings from the EPPE project as it reported year on year. A major and quite famous finding was that 'what parents do is more important than who they are'. It found that 'while parent's social class and levels of education were related to child outcomes, the quality of the early years home learning environment (HLE) was more important'.

The Home Learning Environment

The EPPE project evaluated what the researchers called the 'Home Learning Environment'. They found that where parents did some or all of the following activities, the benefits for children were strong:

- sharing stories
- singing songs and nursery rhymes
- painting and drawing
- taking children on visits, e.g. to the library or park
- letting children play with friends at home
- teaching children numbers and the alphabet
- playing with numbers and letters.

Effects of the EPPE Project

The EPPE Project has helped professionals realise the importance of parents' involvement in early education. This in turn has meant that more settings are starting to see parents as 'partners' in children's learning. It is now good practice for practitioners and settings to look for ways of encouraging and supporting parents by explaining the type of activities that can help their child.

> **Research**
>
> Find out more about the EPPE Project. For an overview of the research, download an article produced by the Teaching and Learning Research Programme. You can access this article by going to www.pearsonhotlinks.co.uk and searching for this ISBN: 9781447970965.

The study of the same 3,000 children continued until 2008 under the new name of Effective Pre-School, Primary and Secondary Education (EPPSE).

▮ Parental views about childhood

Parents are not all the same. Often, they have very different views about what they think is right for their child and also how children, in general, should be brought up. These views may be based on their culture, lifestyle or own experience of being parented. We will look more at different parenting styles later in this section.

Recognising that parents will have very different views is important because it is easy to fall into the trap of making assumptions. Children coming from different families will have had a range of experiences.

It is worth exploring some typical areas where there are differences in parenting style and looking at the opposing views. Note that many parents will sit somewhere in the middle on some, or all, of these issues. When looking at these areas, it is important to remember that parents like to either be in control or give an amount of control to their children.

Education

Parents are likely to have different attitudes towards the importance of education. For some parents, formal learning and education in schools is of paramount importance, yet others, for a variety of reasons, may feel differently. For example, some parents feel that schools do not stress the importance of being an individual and others may feel that learning to read, write or study is a waste of time as practical skills are more important.

> **Research**
>
> A growing number of children are being educated by their parents at home. Find out more by visiting the website for a charitable organisation called Education Otherwise, which supports home education. You can access this website by going to www.pearsonhotlinks.co.uk and searching for this ISBN: 9781447970965.

Television/DVDs

Some parents may restrict television viewing or not allow it at all. Other parents may install a screen in their child's bedroom and will be happy for them to watch it.

Mealtimes

Some parents will want their children to sit down at the table at set mealtimes. Others will be happy for their child to eat in front of the television or when they are hungry.

Some parents will have strong feelings about what their child should eat (for example, a vegetarian diet), whereas others will follow their children's own food preferences and may even provide alternative meals.

Bedtimes and routines

Some parents will have set bedtimes for their children. Other families may not prioritise bedtime, allowing children to set their own. In some families, routines are not always established and there may not be fixed times for doing everyday activities such as washing and dressing.

Some parents will have a bedtime routine with their children, which may include reading a story.

Gender roles

Some parents choose toys according to the gender of their child. They may be uncomfortable with play that breaks gender stereotypes, for example, boys playing with pushchairs and girls playing with construction toys.

Some parents actively try to make their children play with toys that are not traditionally associated with their gender.

Some parents also choose clothes that reinforce traditional gender stereotypes, for example, camouflage clothes for boys and pink fairy dresses for girls.

However, some parents actively dislike clothes that reinforce gender stereotypes.

Attitude to risk

Some parents have a relaxed attitude to health and safety. They may let their children play out of sight or not use safety equipment as long as the child is happy.

Meanwhile, other parents are conscious of health and safety and may not let their child play out of sight or take risks.

Parents' or carers' own experience of being parented

All of us have had an experience of childhood and being parented. This means that parents will be affected by what has happened to them as children. This experience may have been positive, mixed or even difficult; whatever the experience, it will affect their conscious and subconscious behaviours.

Some parents deliberately try to use different strategies or take a very different approach from that of their parents. Others will find that they parent in a very similar fashion to their own parents.

Three broad styles of parenting are traditionally described: authoritarian, permissive and authoritative. If parents do not follow the authoritative style, they often alternate between authoritarian and permissive. This is particularly common where a parent's own parent was authoritarian.

Authoritarian

This style of parenting is one where parents may be distant and attempt to limit and control their children. They may not provide explanations for rules and may punish children if they do not conform.

Permissive

This style of parenting is one where children are given freedom and there are few boundaries on their behaviours or actions.

Authoritative

This style of parenting is one where the parent feels comfortable with their role and is ready to set boundaries, but also negotiate with the child. The parent allows the child some freedom and choice, but only in areas that will not impact on the child's health and wellbeing.

Although parents are often inconsistent in their own style of parenting, it is thought that overall, children benefit when parents are authoritative.

Mixed styles in families

Of course, when there are two parents and sometimes step-parents involved in parenting, there can be conflicts and differences in approach. This can be a source of conflict for some parents and, in turn, can lead to children not gaining the stability they need.

Parental confidence and education

A parent's confidence and education may influence their parenting approach and indeed it is thought that authoritative parenting yields the best results. Many early years settings and organisations in the community offer parenting classes. These classes are run to help parents feel more confident about their parenting skills. Parents who are confident and equipped with some knowledge about child development often find it easier to cope with the stresses of parenting. The effects on children's development are also positive when parents feel comfortable and confident about their own ability.

Children's outcomes are also believed to be linked to parents' levels of education. The EPPE Project is clear that children's home learning environments play an important role in children's early development, and where parents have knowledge about the type of activities that benefit their child, outcomes are often better. As home learning environments are important to children's development, early years settings often focus on supporting and advising parents about the types of activities they can do with their children at home. In England, this is a requirement of the EYFS.

Parenting classes are sometimes seen as something only for 'failing parents', but many settings now offer these information sessions on activities to support the home learning environment in addition to topics such as sleep, feeding and behaviour. These subjects are often the top issues for parents.

Activity

1 Find out what is available for parents in your local area who wish to learn more about parenting.

2 What does your setting do to help parents?

Visit mumsnet, a well-known website that is regularly visited by parents. Why do you think that this website is so popular? You can access the website by going to www.pearsonhotlinks.co.uk and searching for this ISBN: 9781447970965.

Factors that may make parents and/or carers emotionally unavailable

Most parents form strong attachments with their children and are able to cope with the stress of being a parent. However, there are some things that may interfere with establishing this security and strong attachment. It is worth remembering that being a parent or carer is not just about providing for children's physical and care needs. It is also about being able to be **emotionally available.**

Key term

Emotionally available – the capacity to be able to respond, support and deal with the emotions of others.

There are many factors that prevent parents from being emotionally available and responding appropriately to their children. For some parents, not being able to respond to their children will be a short-term difficulty, but for other parents, this may be a longer-term issue. We will now look at these factors.

Depression

Depression changes a parent's state of mind as there is a chemical imbalance in the brain. When a parent is depressed, it is hard for them to create the conditions for strong attachment. They may not 'feel' the full range of emotions and so give the warmth, love and energy that babies and young children require. The effects of this on babies and children can be significant, particularly in terms of speech and language and also emotional development.

There are many causes of depression, including relationship breakdown and postnatal depression. Depression is often something that people find difficult to talk about or get help for. As depression is very common, some settings provide information about mental health services so that parents can seek appropriate help.

Mental health issues are still seen as **taboo** and some parents are scared that social services will remove their children. This is highly unlikely, but it remains a perception among parents.

Figure 5.2 shows the common signs of depression.

Key term

Taboo – a custom that prevents discussion of a particular practice or association with a person, place or thing.

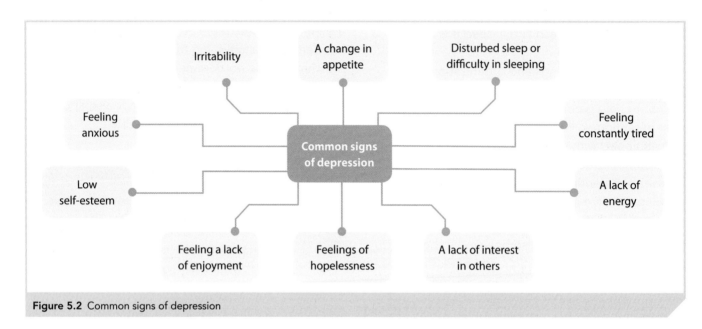

Figure 5.2 Common signs of depression

Postnatal depression

Postnatal depression can occur in women in the weeks following birth. Many women know that they are not feeling 'right' but do not seek help. They may go through the motions of caring for their baby, but struggle to bond. This will cause difficulties with attachment for both the child and the mother.

Once recognised, postnatal depression responds well to treatment, but if left unchecked it can have long-term effects on the child and parent.

Substance misuse and addiction

Alcohol and drugs affect the chemical reactions in the brain. This means that parents who are substance misusers and/or addicts may not be able to parent their children effectively. In the case of addiction, the parent's focus may not be on the child, but on securing the substance or alcohol. Substance misuse and addiction is often the reason why children will be removed from a parent.

Relationship breakdown

Where there is a relationship breakdown between parents, especially one that is bitter and contested, it is likely to create stress, tension and, in some cases, depression. Parents may also be so involved in their own emotions that they may overlook or not be able to respond to their children.

In addition, there can be effects on the relationship between the absent parent and the child. If children do not have regular contact with a parent, there is a danger that the period of absence will result in the child 'detaching' from the parent.

Research

Find out what help is available to support families where there is relationship breakdown by visiting the website for the National Association of Child Contact Centres. You can access this website by going to www.pearsonhotlinks.co.uk and searching for this ISBN: 9781447970965.

Illness

A serious illness, such as cancer, can mean that parents, however much they wish to, may not be physically well enough to give their children sufficient time and energy. Where there is serious illness in the family, this may also mean that the physically fit parent may be preoccupied in caring for the parent who is unwell. They will probably also be coping with their own emotions.

Other factors, including low income

Any event or situation that puts stress on parents, especially over a long period, may mean that parents may not have the energy or the emotional stamina to be available for their children. This includes the stress of living on a low income, which in turn is associated with depression. Parents who have had a close bereavement may again not be in a position to be available for their children. Although the effects of stress can be short-term, it should be recognised that stress is a trigger for depression.

The impact of differing approaches on a child's learning and development

Later in this section we look at some of the barriers that can affect **cooperative** working. In addition to these, it is important to recognise that there may be times when the approach of an early years setting is different to the approach taken by the parent. As we have seen, parents will have a variety of different views and approaches to things such as television, mealtimes and risk. In some cases, parents may look at the approach that an early years setting takes to working with their child and feel less confident in their own parenting ability. This could impact on the relationship between the early years professional and the parent, which in turn could affect a child's progress in terms of their learning and development.

For example, a parent who struggles to get a child to eat at the table may question her parenting skills when she finds out that her child happily eats at the table in the nursery. Similarly, a pre-school may report that a child in the setting never has tantrums, but when at home with the parent, the child often has tantrums. It is important, therefore, to be aware that parents' and carers' confidence can be affected by your actions. Make sure you look for ways in which parents can be supported, if they so wish. They could be invited to spend time in the setting so that some of the strategies that early years professionals in the setting use can be shown and explained.

Assessment practice 5.1   3A1.P1 | 3A1.P2 | 3A1.M1

You have been asked to give a presentation and also write a short article that considers the impact of parental rights, views and experiences on cooperative working. Your article should include information about the following.

1 How the concept of parental rights and responsibilities affects early years practice and the care of children.

2 How partnership work with parents in early years settings may be affected by the views and experiences of parents or carers, as well as the parenting style used at home.

3 The importance of understanding and respecting parenting views and styles and how this is one of the roles of the early years professional in early years settings.

Key term

Cooperative – produced by two or more people/groups working together to achieve something.

A2 Understand how to work cooperatively with parents and/or carers

Good relationships with parents and carers do not just 'happen'. They require thought, skill and reflection. In this section, we will look at practical ways in which we can work and communicate with parents. Note that parents can be anyone with parental responsibility or who has a special role in the child's life. This may include grandparents or foster carers.

The importance of building relationships

When parents or carers have strong relationships with their child's **key person** and other practitioners within the setting, they are likely to feel more confident about leaving their child with us. This will also help when settling the child in and supporting separation. They are also more likely to share information with us, which can be used to ensure that the child's individual needs are met. This allows for continuity of care between the home and childcare setting. Parents who have strong relationships with staff are also more likely to feel comfortable about asking questions. Finally, many early years curricula, such as the Early Years Foundation Stage (EYFS) in England, now expect early years professionals to provide information to parents so that they can support their child's development at home. This is difficult to achieve unless parents and practitioners have a good working relationship.

> **Key term**
>
> **Key person** – a practitioner designated to take responsibility for a child's emotional wellbeing by having a strong attachment with them and a good relationship with their parents.

The importance of respecting the emotional attachment of parents and carers

When looking at how to work with parents and carers, a good starting point is to understand the deep emotional attachment that most of them have with their children. Many of their actions, choices, behaviours and concerns are influenced by this attachment. Here we look at attachment from a parent's perspective.

> **Link**
>
> Go to Unit 1: Section C and Unit 7: Section A to find more information about the importance of attachment.

Separation

Parents are instinctively wary of being separated from their children. This is particularly true when children are under 4 or 5 years old. The actions outlined below show some of the behaviours rooted in attachment that parents may exhibit.

Goodbye rituals

Some parents need to know that they are doing the best for their child right up until the point that they leave them at a setting. They may take the child's coat off and hang it up for them before being ready to hand the child over. Other parents may need their child to give them a certain number of kisses or goodbyes. Goodbye rituals are important to parents and should be respected.

Rushing off

Some parents cope with separation by rushing off quickly. This is not a sign that they do not care, but is usually because they want the separation to be over quickly. Show parents that you understand this is important before you suggest that their child needs a slightly longer goodbye.

Staying behind

Some parents cope with separation by staying for as long as they can or even not leaving the premises. Although this might not be helpful for the child, it is an attachment behaviour and you will need to be empathetic if you feel that this behaviour needs moderating. Some settings support parents who are finding separation difficult by organising coffee mornings or encouraging parents to take voluntary roles in the setting.

Settling in

As parents will often find it hard to cope with separation, it is good practice for early years settings to work closely with parents during the settling-in process. If settings are sensitive to, and respect, parents' or carers' emotional needs, then settling in is a negotiated process that remains focused on the child.

Provision of food

Parents need to feed their children. This is instinctive and universal. Parents, therefore, will want to know if their child has eaten enough and may be concerned if their child has not eaten at all.

Providing warmth and safety

Another concern of parents is whether their children are warm and safe. This is why some parents resist their children playing outdoors when it is cold or damp, or notice if their child's coat is not properly done up. It is also why some parents over-dress their children. Understanding these concerns and also sharing information with parents about the benefits of outdoor play is important.

Friendships and loneliness

Parents need to know that their child will not be alone or have no friends. As children become older, the issue of friends becomes important to parents. They may ask their child who they played with. Making sure that you greet children when they first come in and take care of them before they settle in will reassure parents. It can also be worth taking photographs of them playing with other children or noting this activity down in a home book.

Can you tell that these children are enjoying playing with each other?

The importance of communicating effectively with parents and carers

Communicating well with parents and carers is central to developing a genuine partnership with them. Every practitioner needs to have strong communication skills, not just the individuals who regularly work with specific children. This is because parents may ask a question to a member of staff who is not the child's key person. It is important that communication is seen as an ongoing process as it is needed for relationships to be maintained.

The benefits of effective communication are significant and include the following.

- Parents will find it easier to trust the staff and so separation may be easier.
- Parents are more likely to exchange and share significant information with us that may help us to meet children's needs.
- Good communication will help parents and staff to discuss children's development and allow parents to play a part in the tracking of their child's development.
- Staff and parents can find it easier to ask questions or make comments without being misunderstood.

- Parents are able to become engaged with the care, learning and development of their children. This can have a positive effect on children's achievement.
- Good communication reduces the likelihood of misunderstandings and allows for quick clarification if they do arise.
- The setting is more likely to receive honest feedback that can inform its work and policies.
- Parents are more likely to access information that has been signposted.
- Everyone benefits from having a more harmonious environment.

The features of good communication

There are some universal features that are important for good communication and **interpersonal skills**. Table 5.1 shows the key features and the reasons for them.

> **Key term**
>
> **Interpersonal skills** – the skills required for building relationships.

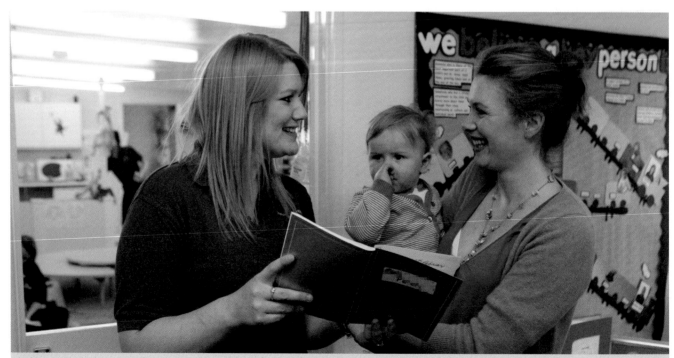

This practitioner is showing warmth and interest. How can these things help us to build and maintain a professional relationship with parents?

Table 5.1 The key features of good communication skills

Feature	Why is it important?
Warmth/ **empathy**	It encourages parents to talk to us and develop a relationship with us.
Sincerity/ honesty	It encourages parents to trust us.
Interest	It is essential if parents are to share information with us.
Active listening	It is essential if parents are to feel that their ideas, emotions and comments are being taken on board. It is also important as it helps us to understand parents' needs and feelings.

Key term

Empathy – the ability to feel or understand the emotions of others.

Communicating appropriately and with empathy

There are many ways that we can communicate with parents. Table 5.2 shows some of these ways. Note that the 'comments' column shows things that you need to be aware of when using the different types of communication.

Table 5.2 Ways to communicate with parents

Communication methods	Comments
Face-to-face interactions	• Useful for sharing and giving information as it is possible to see the other person's reaction. • May not be best for conveying complex information that someone else needs time to consider or see written down, e.g. in order to make decisions.
Phone	• Can be difficult to interpret the other person's reactions and is also hard to assess if they have understood the meaning. • Choice of words and tone becomes very important. • Phone conversations allow for quick responses. • In some situations, notes should be taken at the time of a call so that a record can be made. If this is appropriate, remember to record the date and time of the call.
Sign language	• British Sign Language is a recognised language and allows someone to communicate fully if they are not able to hear.
Letters and memos	• Useful as they allow the reader to take time and absorb the information. • They are likely to be kept. • The style and tone of the letter or memo has to be thought about to avoid misunderstandings. • It is important to check for spelling mistakes.
Emails	• Useful if a more relaxed style is needed. Be aware that not everyone will have access to a computer or will store/print out emails. This can mean that no records will be automatically kept by the other person.
Text messages	• Useful for an instant update for parents. • It is important that the tone and language is professional. • Only a dedicated work mobile should be used to send text messages.
Audio-visual recordings	• Audio-visual recordings can be used to help parents 'see' or 'hear' their children and so provide a way of sharing information with them.

Face-to-face communication and body language

The majority of communication with most parents happens face to face. Most parents will come and look around a setting before joining, for example, and many, but not all, will drop off and collect their children. Parents are also likely to come in if they have any issues. Understanding active ways in which you can communicate effectively is therefore important, as is your body language and attitude. We will now look at specific ways that help you to communicate effectively.

Proximity, orientation and posture

Proximity is about the distance between you and the person you are communicating with. If you are too far away from another adult it will be hard to demonstrate interest and warmth, but if you are too close it may be uncomfortable. Note that there are cultural differences as well as personal differences that affect how much space should be left between you and another person. You need to be observant and notice when you are too close or too far away from someone. For example, the person you are talking to may try to move back a little bit from you or they might move a bit closer.

Orientation relates to your body's position. Standing or sitting slightly at an angle when communicating with adults is helpful as it means that both of you can break off eye contact if you want to and it allows the communicating style to be less direct.

Posture is also important, whether you are standing or sitting. Leaning forwards slightly in a chair shows, for example, that you are interested, while leaning backwards may make the other person think that you are bored.

Smiling

It is important to smile when you are communicating with parents as this is usually seen as a sign of warmth and interest.

Facial expression

Facial expression is a strong element in communication. People can show a lot of feelings through their faces and a good communicator will not only notice other people's facial expressions, but will be aware of their own. Facial expressions can show warmth, empathy, interest and signs of listening.

Eye contact

Eyes are powerful tools when interacting with someone and they can show interest, sincerity and warmth. Eye contact is powerful, so it is important not to stare or be too intense as this can feel threatening. The level of eye contact that is appropriate can vary from culture to culture and it is important to be sensitive to this.

Tone of voice

Tone of voice is stronger than the words that are actually said, both in face-to-face interactions and in communication over the phone. Tone can say a lot about what someone is really thinking. Good communicators use warm tones and do this by thinking warm thoughts. Smiling as you talk on the telephone will also give you a warmer tone.

Active listening

The term 'active listening' is often used to describe the way in which good communicators do not just listen, but they think about what they are hearing. They also closely observe body language, gestures and other signals that are sent out by the child or adult. Active listening requires that you give your full attention to the other person and focus not just on what they are saying, but *how* they say it. Active listening is essential when encouraging young children's speech and also when dealing with potentially difficult situations with other adults.

> **Reflect**
>
> How good a listener are you? Try spending some time listening to a friend without interrupting or changing the topic of conversation.

Barriers to communication

Although the principles of communication are straightforward, there are many potential barriers to communication. It is important that you are able to recognise these barriers and find ways of overcoming them. Figure 5.3 shows some of the key barriers.

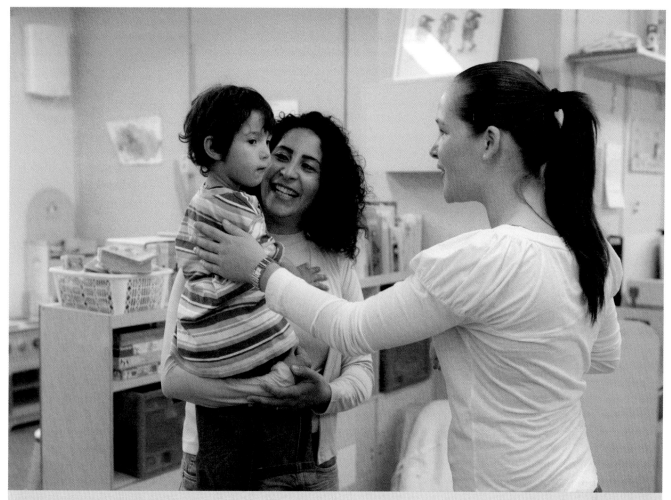

Parents will often drop their child off at the setting. What is the practitioner on the right doing to communicate effectively with this mother and her child?

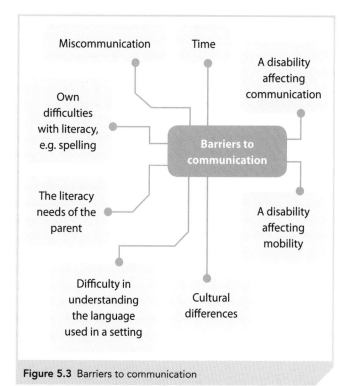

Miscommunication

Time

A disability affecting communication

Own difficulties with literacy, e.g. spelling

Barriers to communication

The literacy needs of the parent

A disability affecting mobility

Difficulty in understanding the language used in a setting

Cultural differences

Figure 5.3 Barriers to communication

How to overcome barriers

It is important that when we identify possible barriers to communication, we look for ways to overcome them. This needs everyone in the setting to have a can-do approach. In particular, it is important to avoid making assumptions about a parent's level of understanding. We must always be respectful and we should be prepared to be flexible in our approach. It is also important to consider the individual needs of parents and/or carers and we should take time to reflect on our interactions with them to consider whether the ways in which we communicate could be improved.

Table 5.3 shows the common barriers to communication listed in Figure 5.3 and the ways in which they may be overcome.

Table 5.3 Strategies for overcoming communication barriers

Barrier	Strategies for overcoming the barrier
Limited time with the parents and/or carers or they do not drop off and pick up their children.	• Use home setting books. • Email parents and/or carers. • Phone parents and/or carers. • Hold information sessions at flexible times, e.g. on Saturdays or in the evenings. • Update the setting's website with news, if relevant.
The parent(s) and/or carer(s) has/have a disability affecting communication.	• Invite a signer to support the parent and/or carer. • Find out how to meet the parent's/carer's needs, e.g. better lighting, larger print or speaking more clearly. • Check that the setting complies with the Disability Discrimination Act 2005.
The parent(s) and/or carer(s) has/have a disability affecting mobility.	• Choose a place that suits the needs of the parent and/or carer. • Find out how to meet the parent's/carer's needs, e.g. adjust the height of chairs, help with doors, provide ramps. • Check that the setting complies with the Disability Discrimination Act 2005.
The parent(s) and/or carer(s) may have difficulty in understanding the language used in a setting.	• Provide an interpreter or invite the parent and/or carer to bring a friend to act as interpreter. • Translate key documents. • Use I&CT, such as translator pens or welcome cards. • Look for local support to help you, e.g. local authority teams with ethnic and minority support.
The literacy needs of the parent(s) and/or carer(s).	• Do not assume that all parents and/or carers are comfortable reading and writing. • Offer to fill in forms without embarrassing parents/carers. • Look for ways of presenting information orally.
Own difficulties with literacy, e.g. spelling.	• Ask a sympathetic colleague to check documents such as letters. • Use a dictionary/spellcheck. • Consider getting further help with your literacy.
Cultural differences in communication style, e.g. choice of language proximity eye contact.	• Respect that people communicate in different ways and use different styles. • Be sensitive, and if and when appropriate, adapt your own style of communication to reflect that used by the parent and/or carer.
Miscommunication	• Clarify meaning as soon as possible. • Apologise for any misunderstanding, if appropriate. • Reflect on how miscommunication can be avoided in future, e.g. by avoiding educational jargon or thinking about the tone of your writing.

The importance of parental consent, confidentiality and data protection

We already know that parents have a set of parental rights, but they also have expectations that their privacy and wishes will be respected. It is important that all adults working with parents understand these rights and expectations.

Parental consent

Parental consent is needed for children to be taken out of the setting on outings, and also before you can pass on information or refer children or parents to other services. The only exception to this is when there is a child protection issue and informing parents could endanger the child.

Confidentiality

If we are working well with parents, they are likely to share information that is quite personal. This may be written information, such as admission forms, but also comments on a day-to-day basis.

Unless there is a child protection issue, such information has to be treated as highly confidential. If you gossip about what parents have said or talk about it to others in the setting who do not need to know, you are likely to endanger your relationship with the parents. You are also likely to make the parents mistrustful of other professionals in the future. Most settings will also have a policy on confidentiality and you should always follow it. Breaching confidentiality is usually a disciplinary matter.

The Data Protection Act 1998

The keeping of records, storing of data and passing on of information is strictly regulated by the Data Protection Act 1998. The act covers both paper-based and electronic records. The Act is designed to prevent confidential and personal information from being passed on without a person's consent.

This Act originally applied only to information that was stored on computers, but it has been updated to include any personal information that is stored, either on paper or on screen. Under the Act, organisations that collect and store information must register with the Data Protection Commission. Anyone processing information must also comply with the eight enforceable principles of practice shown in Figure 5.4. In terms of working with children and their families, this means that most information that is collected and held in an early years setting will be confidential. It also means that you need to have systems in place to make sure that information is up to date and that access is secure.

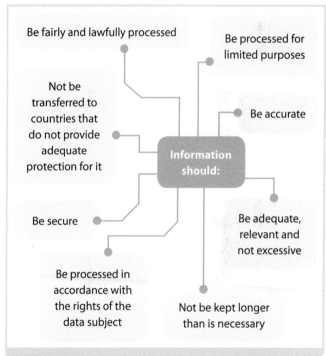

Figure 5.4 The eight enforceable principles of data protection

Research

For more information about the Data Protection Act 1998 visit the website for the Information Commissioner's Office. You can access this website by going to www.pearsonhotlinks.co.uk and searching for this ISBN: 9781447970965.

Case study

Maintaining confidentiality

Erdem's mother wants to invite a child to Erdem's birthday party. She cannot find the phone number of the child although Erdem and the child have played at each other's houses before. Erdem's mother asks Janice, the nursery assistant, whether she could just pop into the office and get the phone number for her. Janice can see that this is a genuine request as Erdem's mother does know the other parent's address.

1 What should the nursery assistant do?

2 Explain why it is important that confidentiality is upheld.

3 Consider what Janice should say to Erdem's mother.

Partnership working with parents and carers

Partnerships with parents will vary from setting to setting according to the type of setting and ages of the children. However, the following approaches are often used.

Shared working

Shared working is the concept of parents and settings working closely together. This approach is considered to be best practice in early years. Many settings will do the following things to achieve shared working.

Key person approach

A key person is someone who has responsibility for the emotional wellbeing of a child and will have a close relationship with them. They should also develop a strong relationship with parents. When using the key person approach, the key person should greet the parent and the child, and pass on any important information to the parent. In the past, the key person in some settings took on a record-keeping role, but it is now understood that in order to prevent babies and young children from being harmed by separation, they need a strong substitute relationship.

Sharing information

Many settings will have systems in place whereby parents can send in, or talk through, information and observations that can contribute to the child's records. This system is useful because children do have different opportunities and experiences when they are with their parents. It also helps in supporting children's development at home.

Settings will share other information with parents in a variety of ways. These include home-setting diaries and notebooks, face-to-face conversations at the beginning and end of the session and also phone calls and emails.

Open-door policy

Many settings operate an open-door policy. This means that parents can come into the setting at any time to be with their child or discuss anything they wish with staff members.

Progress reports

Most settings will have times when they meet with parents to talk about their child's progress. This might be during the day or in the evening.

Stay and play

Some settings offer stay-and-play sessions where parents with younger children can get to know the setting or where parents who have a little time can stay and play with their children before leaving them.

Parental involvement

It is also good practice to look for ways of involving parents as much as possible in the running or direction of the setting. The following activities are common ways to do this.

Volunteer opportunities

Many settings encourage parents to act as volunteers. For some parents, being a volunteer helps them to develop a new career. Volunteer opportunities may include cooking with children, helping out in the office or fundraising.

Parent committees

Some settings are managed and run by parents and others will have a parent committee that supports the work of the setting by giving feedback and/or raising funds. Parent committees help early years settings to stay in touch with parents and ensure that the setting is genuinely meeting children's needs.

Social events

Social events can be linked to fundraising or they can simply encourage families and staff to get to know each other. It is important to vary the type of events and hold them at a range of times so that more families can join in.

'Bring a grandparent or friend' day

Parents are important in children's lives and so too are many grandparents. An event that encourages grandparents into the setting can help practitioners to meet and talk to children's extended family and friends.

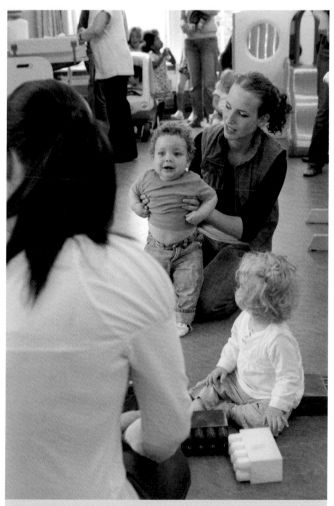

Stay and play sessions are great opportunities for parents to see what their children are doing. They also help staff and parents to get to know each other.

Supporting children's development at home

Parents play an important role in their children's lives. The EYFS builds on this by requiring early years settings to encourage parents to support their child's development and learning at home. Early years settings do this by telling parents about the types of play and activities that their child has enjoyed and by giving them ideas of how they can build on these at home. Some early years settings also put up displays and leaflets that have suggestions about books and games that will be helpful for children's development.

Support must be provided sensitively so that parents do not feel that they are being judged or criticised. This is one reason why strong relationships and good communication with parents is important. There are several other ways that settings can support the child's development at home.

Information sessions

Many settings will hold sessions where parents can learn about aspects such as managing sleep, choosing schools or the early years curriculum.

Lending toys, resources and books

Some settings lend parents toys, games and books to use at home. This helps parents who may not know what to buy to support their child or who may not have the money to do so.

Leaflets, DVDs and other articles

Many settings will put out a range of information that parents can take home or borrow.

Discussions

It is a requirement for settings using the Early Years Foundation Stage framework in England, and also good practice in other countries, for the key person to discuss with parents ways of supporting their child's progress at home. They might share activities that the child has enjoyed and benefited from in the setting.

Theory into practice

Find out what initiatives your work placement setting has introduced to support working with parents.

Factors that might affect the participation of families in settings and how these can be overcome

There are many reasons why not all parents will wish to work in partnership with us. Although this may be disappointing, it is important to remember that it is totally within parents' rights not to engage.

Understanding the reasons why parents are not always able to participate can sometimes help to overcome the barriers. Usually this occurs, as we have seen, through good communication skills and stronger relationships between parents and staff, especially the key person–parent relationship.

Case study

Coping with learning difficulties

Alessie is a single parent with learning difficulties. Social services have been supporting her since the birth of her son, Jamie, two years ago. Over the past few months, Alessie has found it hard to care for Jamie who is an active and impulsive 2-year-old child. Concerns have been raised about his welfare.

At a recent case conference, it was decided that Alessie could continue to have care of Jamie as long as he continued to attend nursery regularly. Alessie is worried about taking Jamie to the nursery. She has told her social worker that everyone is bound to think she is a bad mother. She is also worried that she will not understand or cope with forms that have to be filled in. Her own experiences of education were not good as she was bullied at school. The social worker goes with Alessie and Jamie to the nursery for the first time.

1 What are the key factors that might affect Alessie's participation in the setting?

2 Explain what the setting will need to do in order to help Alessie participate.

3 Why will it be important for Jamie's key person to establish a trusting relationship with Alessie?

Time

Today, many parents work, which means that they may not be able to drop off and collect their children from settings. They may not have time to read books or diaries that are sent between home and the setting or to volunteer to help. It is important not to assume that parents are just not interested.

If time is the issue, we may have to work around parents' needs and times. This may mean more flexible meeting times or more communication using phone and email.

Theory into practice

Many day-care nurseries have working parents who may not have much time. Find out the strategies that nurseries use to communicate and work in partnership with parents.

For example, you could ask a key person how they maintain contact with parents and whether they do things such as using a home setting book.

Confidence

Some parents may not feel confident in early years settings. This might be because they do not feel welcome or because they have had a previous poor experience. Some dads in particular can feel that they do not belong in what is sometimes an all-female environment.

It is useful to make sure that parents who come for the first time are warmly greeted and time is taken to put them at ease. It is also important for all-female settings to look for ways to make dads feel welcome. Some settings have 'dads' days' or run social events and information sessions aimed at dads.

Literacy

It is important always to remember that not all parents can read and write easily. Some parents may worry that they may be asked to do something they are not comfortable with, for example, fill in a form or read a book to their child.

Think about how you communicate information in your placement setting – is all of the information written down? Could you use photos or video clips as well? Think also about involving outreach workers who may be able to signpost basic skills classes.

Expectations

We cannot assume that parents always have the same expectations as us. Some parents may not understand that the setting does want to involve them. They may think that only 'favourite' parents are able to participate. They may also be new to the area or have joined the setting during the year and may not know anyone. Some parents do not think that they 'belong', as settings are run by professionals. They may also not know what is expected of them and so unless settings make an effort to regularly talk to parents about how they can become involved, the participation of some parents in the setting may be low.

Settings should be a welcoming environment. Think about the signs in your placement setting. Are there many 'do not' notices around? Good key person relationships can help parents feel more welcome and key persons can personally invite a parent to join in with activities.

Reflect

How friendly and welcoming is your placement? What makes it welcoming? Are there any ways that you feel the environment could be improved?

Signposting services for parents

It is good practice to help parents and carers find information easily. There are many ways that we can do this.

Referrals

If you are working closely with a children's centre, outreach teams or health professionals, you may help parents by asking if they would like a referral. Note that you cannot refer parents to services unless they give their consent.

Leaflets

Most settings look out for leaflets that they can put out for parents to pick up about services, organisations and groups in their local areas. Good links with other professionals and organisations should make it easy to keep the leaflets and information up to date.

Websites

Many organisations have web addresses. These web addresses can be displayed clearly for parents somewhere in the setting, or you can write the addresses down for individual parents. It is important parents understand that you are not responsible for the content of the information on websites or the advice given.

Drop-in sessions

In some settings, drop-in sessions are organised so that other professionals and services can meet parents in the setting. This is particularly true of children's centres, which may have job advisers and provide access to health professionals.

Recognising your limitations when giving advice

Although it is important to signpost parents to services and to give advice about child development and other similar topics, it is important that we understand the limitations of our role. Unless you are being employed as a counsellor or benefit adviser, you should not provide advice other than to signpost the availability of information. There is a danger that you may give inaccurate information to parents by mistake. This could prevent families from gaining the correct support they need and potentially cause harm to a child. This could lead to a breakdown in trust between the family and the setting or a service to which they have been referred.

Friendly, not friends

We should be friendly with parents but we cannot become their friends. This is because it clouds our relationship with them and may mean that the needs of children stop being our main focus. This is particularly important to remember if a parent tells you that they are not coping.

Case study

Friendly or friends?

Alun is working as an assistant in a nursery. He has good relationships with the children's parents. He gets on particularly well with one parent who is having personal relationship problems. After listening to the parent's problems, Alun gives her advice about what she should say to her partner. The following week, the parent complains to the nursery manager, saying that because of Alun's advice, her partner has now left.

1 How has Alun crossed the line between being friendly and friends?

2 Why was it inappropriate for Alun to give the parent relationship advice?

3 Find out the name of an organisation that specialises in relationship counselling.

Challenging discriminatory behaviour and promoting respect

All early years professionals have a duty, not only to protect children from **discrimination**, but also to actively promote respect for others. Discrimination can be institutional (where the policies or procedures within an institution discriminate against certain groups of people) or individual. Discrimination can be practised by adults working in a setting, by people from outside organisations, or by others such as parents and carers. Discrimination can have a negative effect on children's lives because it can mean that they are denied the care and education to which they are entitled. By challenging discriminatory behaviour and promoting respect you are dealing with the immediate effects that discriminatory behaviour can have on children. This will, in turn, improve their long-term outcomes.

Key term

Discrimination – not giving equality of opportunity to groups or individuals because they belong to a particular group.

Discrimination should always be challenged. If you ignore it, it could be assumed that you condone discriminatory language or behaviour. Consider how a child or their family might feel if they experience discrimination that is ignored. They may feel that you share the same views or believe that the discriminatory treatment is normal practice.

It can be difficult to challenge discrimination, particularly if it is institutional within an early years setting. In this case, you will need to raise it with a senior manager or Ofsted, the official body for inspecting and regulating settings. To be able to challenge discrimination you will need to have a good understanding of legislation and the policy, procedures and practice in your own setting. If you feel confident that you know what good practice is, you will be able to deal more effectively with concerns about discrimination.

Link

Go to Unit 8: Safeguarding in Early Years to find more information about child protection.

Assessment practice 5.2   3A2.P3 | 3A2.P4 | 3A2.P5   3A2.M2 | 3A.D1

You have been asked to prepare a discussion paper outlining current views and evidence about the importance of working cooperatively with parents. You should present information that considers the following:

- the importance of building professional relationships with parents

- ways that settings can contribute to partnership working by using effective communication

- the limitations placed on practitioners for providing advice to parents and why understanding the limitations are essential

- how effective professional relationships with parents can impact on outcomes for children.

B Understand how to work cooperatively with colleagues and other professionals in early years settings

Many children and their families will have contact with, and be supported by, other professionals. For example, children may go to more than one early years setting or their families may be supported by services provided by a children's centre. For some families, social workers have a leading role in coordinating services if they need support caring for a child with disabilities or if they have been identified as needing additional support. This section looks at the responsibilities that other professionals have and the role they play in children's lives.

Professional responsibilities of early years professionals

All staff working in early years settings have a range of general responsibilities. These start with a duty of care towards children. This means that children's welfare and safety have to be viewed as being of prime importance. Whenever decisions are made, anyone working in early years must consider the impact that decision will have on children's welfare and safety. In addition, early years professionals have a contractual duty to work cooperatively and follow all of the policies and procedures of the setting in which they work. This will include following the setting's health and safety policy and the safeguarding and behaviour policy.

Roles and responsibilities of colleagues in early years settings

Within early years settings where there are teams, it is likely that there will be a range of professional roles. It is useful to understand the different roles and responsibilities of each role.

Special Educational Needs Coordinator (SENCO)

The term SENCO stands for Special Educational Needs coordinator. A SENCO is someone who oversees the support of children within a setting who have additional needs. There is a legal requirement for all early years and school settings to have someone in this role. Their key responsibilities are to liaise with parents and other professionals, to ensure that the special needs policy of the setting is adhered to and to help colleagues meet and support the needs of children.

Key person

The role of the key person is to provide additional support and develop a special relationship with individual children and their families. There is a legal requirement within the EYFS for every child to have a key person. The EYFS also states that in addition to helping the child feel secure, the key person must encourage parents to support their children's learning at home. The key person will also coordinate the planning and observations for each of their key children.

Early years teachers

Some settings have an early years teacher on their staff team. Early years teachers provide additional knowledge and expertise about the education and development of children. In some settings the early years teacher will take the lead in planning activities and will be supported in this role by other staff.

Early years professionals

Early years professionals are staff who have additional knowledge and training in early years. They are likely to be on the management team of the setting and may be the decision maker in terms of the educational direction of the setting.

Teachers

Where early years teams are based in schools or are part of a school's early years provision, there will be some liaison with the primary teachers in key stage 1. The role of teachers is to lead and be responsible for class teaching.

Roles and responsibilities of professionals who may work with families

Some families will need additional support and so a range of professionals will be working with them. In some cases, families will have referred themselves to these services and professionals. In other cases, there may be a statutory obligation for a local authority to support families where children are identified as being **in need**.

The definition of 'in need' in terms of local authority statutory obligations is a child who:

- needs local authority services to achieve or maintain a reasonable standard of health or development
- needs local authority services to prevent significant or further harm to health or development
- is disabled.

It is worth noting that children with disabilities are categorised as 'in need' by the Children Act 1989, and local authorities have an obligation to allocate a social worker to assess the child's and the family's needs regardless of the financial or social situation of the family.

> **Key term**
>
> **In need** – refers to children who are unlikely to maintain, or be given the opportunity to maintain, a reasonable standard of health or development, or children whose health could be impaired without the support of local authority services. It also includes children who are disabled.

Social workers

Social workers can work for organisations such as the NSPCC as well as for local authorities. As social work is a large area, most social workers will work in different specialisms or in different teams. There may, for example, be social workers who specialise in fostering and adoption and others who work with vulnerable families.

Social workers are likely to spend time assessing the needs of the child and the family, organising services and meeting with other professionals who are involved with the family.

Family support workers

Family support workers work with families and provide practical support and advice. They are usually employed by local authorities and will work closely with social workers. Family support workers will often work with families as a result of referrals from social workers or from other agencies involved with the family.

Police liaison officers

Police liaison officers often work closely with social workers and other professionals when abuse is suspected and needs investigating. In addition, some police liaison officers work to support families where crimes have been committed or there are incidents such as road traffic accidents that impact on the family.

Outreach workers

Outreach workers often work closely to support families who may otherwise not access advice and services. Some outreach workers are based in children's centres and may help parents with parenting, life skills and also child development. Outreach workers often meet parents in other early years settings or in the local community and build up a relationship with them. Some outreach work is done as a result of referrals from social workers, early years professionals and health visitor teams.

Home-Start volunteers

Home-Start is an organisation that supports families with young children. Volunteers, often experienced parents, will visit families once a week. They provide practical as well as emotional support. Families can self-refer or parents can be offered a referral from health visiting teams, early years settings and social workers.

Research

Find out more about Home-Start by visiting the organisation's website. You can access the website by going to www.pearsonhotlinks.co.uk and searching for this ISBN: 9781447970965.

Roles and responsibilities of health professionals

Midwives

Midwives play an important part in families' lives. They provide antenatal care, help to deliver the baby and also visit the baby in the ten days following birth. In some areas, mothers will have the same midwife for antenatal, delivery and postnatal care. In other areas, mothers will see community midwives for most of the antenatal and postnatal care, but will see hospital midwives for some antenatal checks and delivery. Midwives provide support and advice for new mothers, but they also have a role in child protection. They may recognise signs of postnatal depression as well as other strains on the family and will pass this information to other health professional and social services if appropriate.

Health visitors

Health visitors have an important role in all families' lives. Health visitors visit families in the weeks following a child's birth. They provide advice and information to parents about topics such as weaning, behaviour and sleep. Health visitors also have a role in monitoring children's development. They may carry out developmental checks as well as weigh and measure children. These activities are often carried out in health clinics, children's centres and also in children's homes. Health visitors also have a role in child protection. They may spot signs that parents or carers are not coping with their role or that children are failing to thrive. Depending on the assessment of families' needs, health visitors may regularly visit families where there

are concerns. The health visitor role is now often supplemented by a community nursery nurse who will visit families to do routine checks.

Speech and language therapists

In Unit 1 we saw the usual patterns by which children learn to communicate and talk. Speech and language therapists will work with children and their families where a child's speech is delayed or they need support in order to communicate. Speech and language teams have an important role in providing information to other professionals. They may run courses or visit settings to advise on how to increase opportunities for adult–child interaction. Referrals to speech and language therapists can be made by a variety of professionals and in some cases by the parents themselves. Early years professionals can also make a direct referral with parents' consent or parents can be advised to talk to their family doctor (GP) or health visitor.

Dieticians

Dieticians work with children and their families where information and support is needed about children's diet. This may be because a child is not gaining sufficient weight or is overweight. Dieticians will also be involved in supporting families whose

Health visitors play a key role in families' lives. What do you know about their role?

children have diabetes, coeliac disease or food phobias. Given that increasing numbers of children have weight problems, dieticians may also provide information about healthy eating to the community and to early years settings.

Referral to a dietician is usually provided by a GP, paediatrician or other health professional.

Paediatricians

Paediatricians are qualified doctors who specialise in the health of babies, children and young people. Many paediatricians are based in hospitals. Babies and children who are unwell, or have problems including sleep, bowel control or other medical conditions, are likely to be referred to a paediatrician by the child's GP or health visitor. Paediatricians may also be involved in child protection issues as they may examine the child following an unexplained injury or suspected abuse.

Portage

Where children have identified disabilities or learning needs, parents may be offered 'portage'. Portage is where children are visited in their homes by a portage worker who will work with them and their parents. Portage workers are often volunteers. Together with parents, they will set small goals and work towards them. Portage workers usually work with children under 5 years old. Close involvement and collaboration with parents is important to the scheme's success because parents will need to carry on exercises with their children after the visits. Referrals to portage are usually made by social workers and health professionals.

Physiotherapists

Physiotherapists will work with children who need support with their physical development and movement. Their aim is to maximise children's

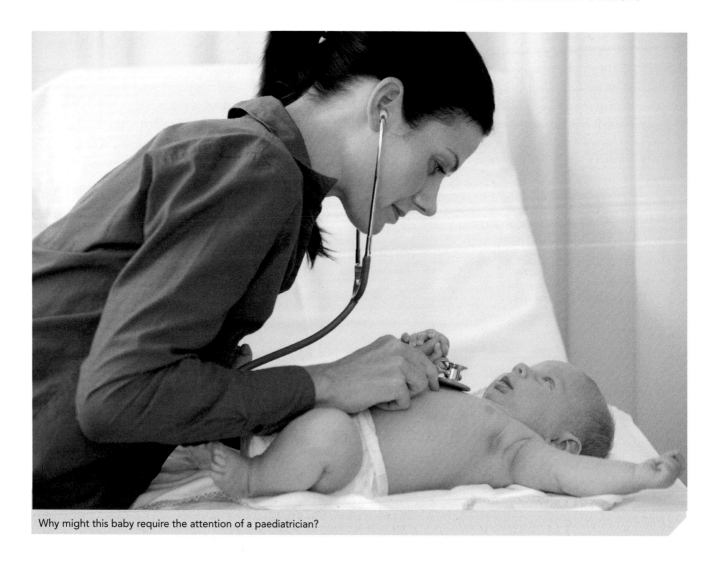

Why might this baby require the attention of a paediatrician?

movements. Physiotherapists work closely with parents and may also work with early years staff. They may provide exercises, equipment and advice as well as suggest modifications that might be needed in order for children to access the provision. Children may be referred to physiotherapists by paediatricians, family doctors and other health professionals.

Sensory impairment team

Children with sensory impairment such as hearing or sight problems are usually supported by members of the sensory impairment team. They will work with parents and early years settings to help children maximise their senses or be able to access provision. The sensory impairment team may visit a setting to suggest modifications, tips and equipment that will help children learn.

Roles and responsibilities of educational psychologists, child psychiatrists and counsellors

Educational psychologists

Educational psychologists look at children's learning and behaviours. Children may be referred to them when they are not reaching expected developmental goals. They usually assess children and recommend strategies that other professionals and parents can use to progress children's development and behaviour. Most referrals will be made as a result of early years settings or schools raising concerns, but family doctors and other health professionals may also refer children.

Child psychiatrists

Children can have depression and other mental health issues such as phobias. Psychiatrists will work with children and often their families to talk through issues and, in some cases, provide medication. Referrals to child psychiatrists are usually made through a family doctor or paediatrician.

Counsellors

Counsellors can play an important part in helping children and their parents cope with a range of situations. Counsellors tend to specialise in different areas such as bereavement, relationships and trauma. They help children and their parents talk and work through their problems. Counselling can be arranged privately, but many children and families will be referred by health and other professionals.

Play therapists

Play therapists help children to talk and work through traumas including bereavement, accidents and abuse. This is done through the medium of play. Play therapy can also help other agencies find out what has happened to children and so there are often close links with police teams. Children in need of play therapy are likely to be referred by a variety of professionals including police, paediatricians and health professionals.

Through play, this child is being helped to talk about what is happening in her life.

Why cooperative working is needed

Most adults working with children will find that they will need to work together with other people. This begins with the parents or carers, but is also likely to include work colleagues and professionals from a range of disciplines. We will now look at the importance and principles of cooperative working.

Cooperative working is primarily about good communication between different professionals, colleagues and also parents and carers. It means that services and individuals work together in order to provide services, meet families' needs and also keep children safe in child protection cases.

Victoria Climbié and Peter Connelly

Sadly, in the past, cooperative working and subsequent communication was often not in place. This was a contributory factor in many high-profile deaths of children. A recent high-profile case was the Peter Connelly case, and before this the case of 8-year-old Victoria Climbié, who was tortured and then killed by a great-aunt. After the Climbié killing, an inquiry was held, led by Lord Laming. The enquiry found that doctors and social workers were not sharing information. The Laming inquiry made a number of recommendations, many of which have been acted on and turned into legislation in England, for example, in the Children Act 2004. In the other home countries, similar approaches have been taken.

Since the Laming inquiry, there has been a renewed focus on ensuring that services for children and young people are more coordinated to improve children's life chances and outcomes. This is one reason why children's centres often provide a wide range of services, including speech and language therapy, employment advice and health care. The new focus on **multi-agency** and partnership working has also meant that there are more multi-agency approaches towards child protection. A good example of this is the local safeguarding children

boards that have been set up in England. These boards work with local early years settings and schools and consist of police, social services and health professionals. One of the positive benefits of multi-agency work has been more opportunities for early years professionals to meet and learn more about other professions and, in some cases, gain knowledge and further skills.

> ### Link
>
> Go to Unit 8: Section C to find more information about the role of local safeguarding children boards, the Laming inquiry and the Children Act 2004.

> ### Activity
> Find out about the Peter Connelly case by carrying out an Internet search.
> - Why was the public shocked by this case?
> - Why was this case a good example of a breakdown in cooperative working?

The benefits of working cooperatively

If professionals work effectively with colleagues in their own setting and with professionals from other agencies, children's life chances will be improved. Child abuse can also be prevented when different agencies work together and share information. Abuse, if not prevented or quickly recognised, can damage children for life and so working together can make a real difference. There are also other important benefits for children and families.

One of the most important outcomes is the potential for children and families to have efficient support that is organised and tailored around their needs. Information sharing also means that parents do not have to repeat pieces of information about their children every time a new professional works with them. Additionally, collaborative working creates a climate of trust between parents and professionals because parents can feel that everyone is working in

> ### Key term
> **Multi-agency** – activities that involve staff from different agencies working together.

the best interests of their children. Close working also prevents misunderstandings, miscommunications and again this contributes to the climate of trust.

Figure 5.5 shows many more of the benefits of working cooperatively. Key benefits for parents are that services are coordinated and they feel listened to.

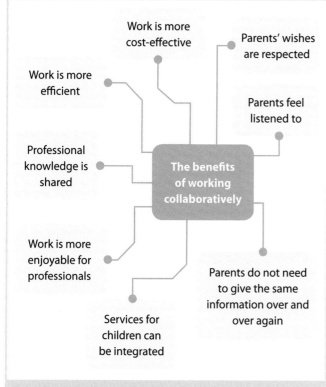

Figure 5.5 The benefits of working collaboratively

Although children and their parents benefit from cooperative working, so too does everyone involved. For example, professionals can learn skills and information from each other and, in some situations, knowing what others are doing with the child and family complements professionals' own work, so improving outcomes for the child.

Teamwork

If teams in a setting work cooperatively, it usually makes work more enjoyable and reduces stress in the workplace. This, in turn, is likely to rub off on children and their families because a happy workplace is more likely to be positive and welcoming. Where staff are unhappy or do not understand their roles and responsibilities, misunderstandings can occur, which means that the needs of children are less likely to be met.

Challenges of cooperative working

Although it is easy to say that cooperative working should take place, the reality is that it requires significant effort and organisation. When people are not sharing the same physical environment, and do not have the same roles, experiences and knowledge, cooperative working becomes more challenging. Even colleagues in some large settings find that they do not always know what is happening.

Understanding the potential difficulties in cooperative working is, therefore, a good first step. Once you are aware of the potential difficulties you can start to look for ways to overcome them.

Time

Most people working with children are busy. Professionals in different disciplines may not work the same hours or be able to attend meetings.

Case study

Cooperative working

Maisy is 3 years old. She was born with significant health problems and also a learning difficulty. Her social worker has organised support for her and the family, which means that she has portage, **respite care** and also a place at a local nursery. Maisy's key person is in frequent contact with her parents, social worker, physiotherapist and also other health professionals. Maisy's parents are relieved that she and they are getting this support.

1 Why is it important that Maisy's needs are met promptly?

2 What are the benefits to Maisy's family when professionals are working cooperatively?

Key term

Respite care – short-term care with the assistance of professional carers.

The different priorities of professionals

Professionals working in different fields will have slightly different priorities. A physiotherapist will look at supporting and improving children's range of movements while a speech and language therapist might focus on listening skills. In addition, caseloads for health professionals and social workers may mean that they have to prioritise treatments, visits or consultations.

Different priorities can sometimes be a source of tension. A social worker who has a role in preventing child abuse might organise respite care for a family, while an early years professional who has seen that the child is not coping well with different transitions and changes might feel that stability is more important for the child.

Parental priorities

Parents may have very different priorities from professionals. They may be concerned about getting their child out of nappies, whether the child is sleeping through the night or whether their child has friends. It is important therefore, when working with parents, not to make any assumptions that their priorities are the same as those of professionals.

Different approaches and ethos

As well as having different priorities, different professionals will have their own procedures, policies and ways of working. Information systems and administrative processes are also likely to be different. Simple things such as making contact may require going through an administrator first or decisions might need to be approved by managers. A 'quick turnaround' for one professional might mean an hour; however, for another it might mean a week. This can lead to frustration and miscommunication if other professionals do not know how the other services are set up.

Relationships and trust

As with many areas of life, relationships and trust are key factors in collaboration. It is important that we show respect for parents, colleagues and other professionals. Small exchanges that show respect and interest can make all the difference to the smooth running of cooperative working.

Sharing information

Sometimes, professionals and parents may not know that a piece of information they have is important to another service or person. For example, a professional may assume that a parent already knows about and is claiming housing benefit when they are not. Different professionals and organisations will have different views on what information can be shared. Fear of breaching the Data Protection Act 1998 and, therefore, failing to share important information was noted in the Laming report following the death of Victoria Climbié.

Overcoming difficulties

There are some strategies that can help professionals to overcome difficulties in cooperative working. These strategies include:

- finding out about the roles and responsibilities of other professionals and colleagues
- finding out if anyone is acting as the '**named person**' for a child's family
- taking time to build up a working relationship with others – be friendly and show respect for their work and ideas
- not making assumptions about the way others might work or the timescales they use
- not making assumptions that others have the same information as you.

> ### Key term
>
> **Named person** – a person who is the main point of contact.

Issues around information sharing

Cooperative working requires good communication and the sharing of information. On the other hand, families have a right to expect that information they share about their family is treated in confidence. This means there are issues around how, with whom and when information should be shared. A good starting point when thinking about information sharing is to look at your own setting's policies and procedures in relation to the sharing of information. The following principles are usually embedded in policies.

- The welfare of the child is paramount and so in cases where a child's life or welfare is at risk, or likely to be so, parental consent is not required to share information.

  Example: A 4-year-old child comes into the setting with burn marks on the back of her legs and knees. The child's social worker is immediately contacted.

- Parental consent is required before making referrals to other services. If you refer children or talk about them to others without parental consent, you are likely to be in breach of the Data Protection Act 1998. Remember that you can only share information with other services when you have reasonable concerns that the child's welfare is in jeopardy.

  Example: Jason's key person is concerned that he has difficulty in making a 'g' sound. She asks Jason's mother if she can make a direct referral to the speech and language team. Jason's mother says that she thinks he will grow out of it. The key person respects this decision, but instead finds out more about speech immaturities in general from the speech and language team.

- Only relevant information should be shared with others. This means that when there are complex family needs, only information that will impact on another professional's ability to do the work should be shared.

  Example: Hannah's key person knows that Hannah's brother has been convicted of theft. She does not share this information when talking to the physiotherapist about Hannah's fine motor movements.

- Information is only passed to those who have a direct need or involvement with the child and the family. This is sometimes called the 'need to know' approach. Although it might be important for information to be shared, it should only be passed on to those who have a direct need or reason to have it. In settings, this might mean that only the key person and the manager may hold certain information that will not be shared with the rest of the team.

  Example: It is suspected that Harry may have been physically abused by one or both of his parents. The investigation is in its early stages. Social workers have only told the manager of the setting and Harry's key person.

- Information is accurate and up to date. If necessary, check whether this is the case with parents or other individuals before passing it on. If you are not sure of the accuracy, you should indicate this.

  Example: Greta is 5 years old. She is finding it hard to settle in at school. With the parent's consent, the school phones Greta's preschool. Greta's key person at the preschool says that Greta used to get very anxious about going to the toilet, but the key person stresses that this might have changed since.

- Information is kept secure. You should think about how information is shared and how it is likely to be kept secure. Everyone 'handling' personal information has this duty under the Data Protection Act 1998.

  Example: A social worker has asked to see a child's developmental records. She gives the setting assurances that the records will not be passed on to any other service, but if she thinks the information will be useful to another service, she will refer the other service directly back to the early years setting.

How to ensure data protection in cooperative work

We have seen earlier that the Data Protection Act 1998 sets out clear requirements regarding personal information. It is, therefore, important that you ask parents before you share information with other professionals, except where the child's welfare is seriously at risk. It is also important to pass on only information that is needed and to do so securely so that other people with no interest in the child or the family do not see it. Most settings will have policies and procedures in place and you should always follow them.

Multidisciplinary meetings

There are times when it is important for professionals from a range of services to meet together to develop a strategy or plan for the child and their family.

Meetings may be called because of child protection issues, because children need a wide range of support due to complex disabilities or medical conditions, or because a family is in need of additional support. These meetings are sometimes called 'case conferences'.

There will also be times when a review of what has already been put in place is required. As multi-agency meetings are difficult to organise, they are usually kept to a minimum and some information sharing and decision making may sometimes be done without face-to-face meetings.

Before the meeting

It is usual for the service convening the meeting to organise the arrangements – time, date and place. They should also state the purpose of the meeting and give clear indications of any background reports that need compiling or any pre-reading that is needed. Meetings should be held with the consent of parents unless the child's welfare is at risk.

The convening service should also nominate the chair and draw up the agenda.

It is also good practice for parents to attend meetings so that they can provide information, but also because decisions should not be made without them. This includes meetings in respect of child protection. Some parents may not be able to attend, but they should be given the opportunity to nominate someone to attend for them.

At the meeting

If you are attending a **multidisciplinary** meeting, make sure you arrive punctually, have read any background documents or have prepared information to share.

Key term

Multidisciplinary – a team of people from different areas of speciality.

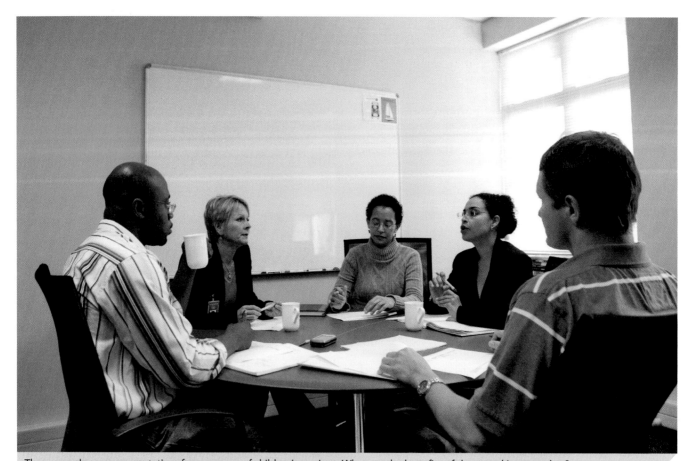

These people are representatives from a range of children's services. What are the benefits of them working together?

At the start of the meeting it is good practice for the chair to outline what is going to happen during the meeting. This is particularly important when parents are attending. Apologies for those who are absent should also be read out. It is also usual for everyone to introduce themselves and their roles. Minutes or notes from the meeting should be kept. This allows anyone who was not present to know what conclusions were reached in the meeting.

The usual pattern of many meetings is first to consider the current situation and what has happened since the previous meeting (if there has been one) before deciding on a plan of action. The plan of action should be clear and everyone should know what actions they are individually responsible for. Before the meeting ends, times and dates for a follow-up meeting (if needed) should be set.

After the meeting

The service that convened the meeting should circulate the minutes of the meeting promptly. If a formatted action plan has been written, this should also be sent out. Everyone involved should then try to complete the actions or tasks that have been agreed. Any difficulties should be promptly shared with others if this is likely to affect their input.

Theory into practice

Find out about the type of meetings that your placement settings are involved in. Involvement could include coverage of the following areas:

- special educational needs
- child protection
- supporting children with disabilities.

Assessment practice 5.3   3B.P6 | 3B.P7 | 3B.P8   3B.M3 | 3B.D2

You have been asked to give a presentation about cooperative working at a local training centre. Your presentation should last 20 minutes. You have been asked to evaluate the impact of cooperative working on children's health, wellbeing, learning and development. To prepare for this presentation, you should write a speech that includes:

- what is meant by cooperative working and the range and roles of professionals that might support children and their families (e.g. health professionals)
- an evaluation of the concept and benefits of cooperative working on children's health, wellbeing, learning and development
- the extent to which cooperative working is in place, including any barriers, practical issues and conflicting ideologies.

C Be able to work with parents and/or carers and others in early years settings to meet the needs of children

An important part of completing this unit is to put into practice the knowledge you have gained in Learning aims A and B. Your teacher/tutor will explain exactly what you need to do to demonstrate competence when working with parents and/or carers and other early years professionals. Assessment practice 5.4 and 5.5 contain two suggested activities you could do independently to prepare yourself for working effectively in partnership with parents in an early years setting.

Ask your placement supervisor if you can carry out an activity, take photographs of it and write about what the child has done in order to share it with a parent.

When preparing the information to share with the parent, think about the child's needs and interests, and also how you might find out more about the parent's view of their child's development. Make sure that you work within the settings' policies, procedures and guidelines about data protection and information sharing.

After you have shared the information with the parent, ask for feedback from either the parent or your placement supervisor about how well you interacted, listened and showed that you valued the parent's views.

Find out which other professionals your setting currently works with to support children's needs. Bearing in mind that some information might be confidential, find out why the other professionals are involved and what their roles and responsibilities are.

Using evidence from your work placement, assess how your own work with parents and cooperative work with colleagues in the setting have each contributed to meeting children's needs. Make sure you review all the evidence and information and then draw conclusions about the impact of your work with parents on children's developmental outcomes.

▌ Further reading and resources

Crowley, M. and Wheeler, H. 'Working with Parents in the Early Years' in Pugh, G. and Duffy, B. (2013) *Contemporary Issues in the Early Years* (6th ed.), London: Sage Publications.

Gasper, M. (2009) *Multi-agency Working in the Early Years: Challenges and Opportunities*, London: Sage Publications.

Sylva, K. et al. (2004) *The Effective Provision of Pre-School Education (EPPE) Project: Final Report*, London: Institute of Education.

Whalley, M. (2007) *Involving Parents in their Children's Learning* (2nd ed.), London: Sage Publications.

Website

Department for Education: www.gov.uk/government/organisations/department-for-education
Information about multi-agency working, including leaflets.

Ready for work?

Althea Suvari   Manager of a children's centre

I have been working in a children's centre for five years now. It is a very exciting place and I have enjoyed working with colleagues from a range of professions. Our children's centre offers a range of services to children and their families. There are first aid courses, baby massage, parenting classes and information and advice sessions with a range of professionals including GPs, health visitors and speech and language therapists. The team includes outreach workers and we liaise closely with other childcare providers in the town. To make sure that everyone knows what is available and what is happening within the centre, we have regular catch-up sessions. This brings us together as a team and although we may not always be working alongside each other, it is important to understand each other's roles and responsibilities. We also have strict policies and procedures about confidentiality and every new member of staff has to read and understand these as part of their induction. A careless word would mean the end of the trust that parents have in us.

Skills for practice

Tips for working effectively in partnership with parents

- Always greet the child and parent warmly. However busy you are, try to smile or wave to them.

- Give information to parents promptly and make sure you are always honest with them. For example, tell the parents if their child has missed them during the day or if their child has not eaten.

- Reassure parents. Let them stay at the setting for longer if they need to or take photographs of their child throughout the day.

- Show interest in the child. Ask parents questions about what the child enjoys doing at home and what the child likes to eat, and find out tips on how to settle the child.

- Show interest in the parent. Ask about their weekend or previous evening when the parent drops their child off at the setting or ask how their day has been when they pick up their child.

Tips for working in partnership with colleagues and other professionals

- Try to understand the role of the colleague or professional in the setting or when working with a child.

- Recognise that you may have different priorities, but find ways of respecting what they do.

- Be friendly, show respect and be ready to learn from colleagues and other professionals.

- Promptly follow up on discussions and any areas on which you have agreed to work.

Introduction

Do you remember learning to talk? The chances are that you have no particular memory of it. This is because most children have mastered talking by around the age of 4 years. Being able to communicate ideas and emotions, and understand those of others, is a gateway into many other aspects of development. In this unit we will look in detail at how children acquire language, or in some cases more than one language, as well as how adults can support children at all stages of their journey.

Assessment: You will be assessed by a series of assignments set by your teacher/tutor.

Learning aims

In this unit you will:

A1 understand the role of speech, communication and language in children's overall development

A2 understand how research into language development supports good practice

B   encourage and develop children's speech, language and communication

C   understand how to support children with varied language needs.

I work with toddlers, and one thing that never ceases to amaze me is the way that they progress between the ages of 2 and 3 in terms of language development. They love hearing and using new words.

Dawn, *a nursery nurse*

Supporting Children's Speech, Communication and Language

6

BTEC Assessment Zone

This table shows what you must do in order to achieve a **Pass**, **Merit** or **Distinction** grade, and lists activities that relate to each learning aim.

Assessment criteria		
Pass	**Merit**	**Distinction**
Learning aim A: 1 Understand the role of speech, communication and language in children's overall development 2 Understand how research into language development supports good practice		
3A1.P1 Explain how communication and language development can affect social and emotional development. **Assessment practice 6.1**	**3A1.M1** Analyse how communication and language development affect the overall development of children using examples from early years settings. **Assessment practice 6.1**	**3A.D1** Evaluate the contribution of a theory of language development in relation to the overall development of children. **Assessment practice 6.2**
3A2.P2 I&CT English Explain how theories of language development apply to early years practice. **Assessment practice 6.2**	**3A2.M2** Discuss how theories of language development have contributed to effective practice in an early years setting. **Assessment practice 6.2**	
Learning aim B: Encourage and develop children's speech, language and communication		
3B.P3 Describe how to provide an environment in an early years setting that promotes speech, communication and language. **Assessment practice 6.3**	**3B.M3** Analyse the role of the early years professional in providing appropriate environments that support children's speech, communication and language, using examples. **Assessment practice 6.3**	
3B.P4 I&CT Use observations and assessments of children to plan and record learning activities that support and promote speech, communication and language in the early years. **Assessment practice 6.4**	**3B.M4** Provide consistent and effective support to promote children's speech, communication and language. **Assessment practice 6.4**	
3B.P5 Use effective command of the English language to support children's speech, communication and language in learning activities. **Assessment practice 6.4**		

continued

Pass	Merit	Distinction
Learning aim C: Understand how to support children with varied language needs		
3C.P6 **I&CT** Explain how to support children in an early years setting who are developing more than one language. **Assessment practice 6.5**	**3C.M5** Discuss how to plan for and give support to children with varied language and communication needs. **Assessment practice 6.5**	**3C.D2** Evaluate the extent to which early years professionals contribute to the speech, communication and language development of children with varied needs. **Assessment practice 6.5**
3C.P7 Explain how to support children in an early years setting who have additional language needs. **Assessment practice 6.5**		

English   English Functional Skills signposting   **I&CT**   Information and Communication Technology Functional Skills signposting

How you will be assessed

This unit will be assessed by a series of internally assessed tasks set by your teacher/tutor. They will include practical tasks that will need to be carried out on placement, and that link to your Practical Evidence Portfolio. Throughout this unit you will find assessment practice activities that will help you work towards your assessment. Completing these activities will not mean that you have achieved a particular grade, but you will have carried out useful research or preparation that will be relevant when it comes to your final assignment.

In order for you to achieve the tasks in your assignment, it is important to check that you have met all of the Pass grading criteria. You can do this as you work your way through the assignment.

If you are hoping to gain a Merit or Distinction, you should also make sure that you present the information in your assignment in the style that is required by the relevant assessment criterion. For example, Merit and Distinction criteria will require you to analyse and evaluate.

The assignment set by your teacher/tutor will consist of a number of tasks designed to meet the criteria in the table. This is likely to consist of a written assignment, but may also include activities such as the following:

- writing an article for an early years journal
- using evidence from case studies or observations to support your findings or recommendations
- producing a good practice guide for early years professionals containing guidance about how to support speech, communication and language development.

Many children in the United Kingdom communicate in more than one language. Write down ideas for how children can be supported to do this. At the end of this unit, look back at what you have written and see if you can add any more information.

 A1 Understand the role of speech, communication and language in children's overall development

Most people take the ability to talk and understand what others are saying for granted. For babies and young children, communication and language skills are still being learned. This section looks at the importance of communication development to children's overall development, as well as factors that might affect it.

The range of skills associated with communication

We often think of speech when we talk about communication and, indeed, it is a key way that we communicate. However, we also use other skills to communicate. We have already looked at some of these skills in the context of working with parents, colleagues and other professionals.

Eye contact

Eye contact is one of the earliest skills to develop in babies as it is fundamental to most communication. Babies are quickly able to gaze into the eyes of an adult. Eye contact is needed to show that we are listening, to be able to register others' feelings and to assess the impact of communication.

Contact

Babies and young children often use physical contact as a tool to aid communication. They may tap our back to get our attention or hug us to show that they are happy.

Gesture

One of many skills that babies learn is to use gestures. From around 9 months, babies will often start to point to things in order to draw our attention to them. Babies and children will also clap their hands to show that they are pleased and will also learn some early gestures, such as waving to indicate goodbye.

Body language

Babies and children use body language as a key way of expressing how they feel. They may clench their fists when angry, quiver when excited and show us that they want to be picked up by opening their arms.

Active listening

Children are active when they listen. Up until 6 or 7 years, they are likely to ask questions and blurt out ideas and thoughts when they are listening. This means that listening is quite a 'loud' activity, as children seem to need to talk in order to process information and make new connections with it.

Theory into practice

Observe a group of children between the ages of 3 and 5 who are having a story read to them. Note how many children seem to need to talk as they are listening. See how many of their comments are related in some way to what they have just heard.

Components of speech and language

In order for children to speak and understand speech, they have to master three key elements. Figure 6.1 shows these three elements.

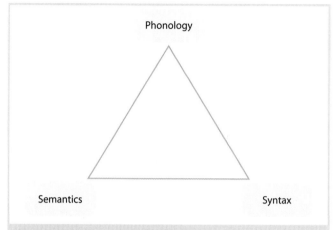

Figure 6.1 The key elements of speech

Phonology

Phonology is the study of speech sounds used in a language. Speech sounds are often known as **phonemes**. Some languages have more sounds than others. English has around 44 (this count does vary depending on the way that the language is being analysed). Note that speech sounds can be written in a variety of ways. For example, 'ee' as in feed is the same sound as 'ea' as in bead!

Children have to 'tune in' to the phonemes and then make the phonemes of the language that they are exposed to. Babies begin this process before they are born. From around the 26th week of pregnancy, they are already recognising the speech patterns of their mother. However, producing the sounds is a gradual process and is dependent on the growth and development of teeth and muscles in the mouth, including muscles in the tongue. It is, therefore, normal for many children at 3 years to say 'dat' rather than 'that'.

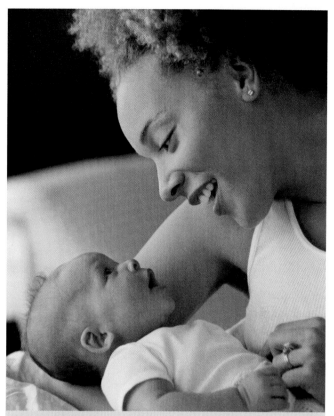

This baby is listening to the sounds of his mother's voice. This will help the baby 'tune in' to the phonemes of her language.

Key term

Phonemes – the smallest units of sound in a language that help to distinguish one word from another. In the English language, for example, 'p' and 'b' are separate phonemes because they distinguish words such as 'pit' and 'bit'.

Semantics

Semantics is about understanding the meaning of words. At first, babies learn the meaning of words by associating sounds with objects or actions. A parent may say, 'where's your hat?' and touch the child's hat. After a while the child will associate the sound of the word 'h-a-t' with the object.

Syntax

Syntax is about the grammar of a language, or the way that words are put together to make sentences. Children seem to be primed to work out the structure of a language and, although they may simplify a sentence, they rarely get the word order of a sentence wrong.

Activity

Look at the simple sentence below:

The **cat** ate the **mouse**.

1 Swap the position of the two words that are bold.

2 How does swapping the position of the words affect the meaning of the sentence?

3 Are you able to explain the grammar behind the change in meaning or do you 'just know'?

Receptive language

Receptive language is the term used to describe the ability to listen to, and understand, what is being communicated. Children may show that they understand something even though they are not able to say the words. For example, a child may be able to point to an object when asked to do so. Children develop receptive language in the first phase of language development. The first phase of language development is known as the **prelinguistic phase**.

Expressive language

Expressive language is the term used to describe the ability of a child to communicate actively using sounds and, over time, words. In the first year of a baby's life, most expressive language takes the form of babbling or cooing, but in a child's second year, linguistic development starts to occur and they are able to begin using words.

Link

Go to Unit 1: Section B to find more information about the prelinguistic and linguistic phases of language development.

How communication links to emotional and social development

Communication and language are interlinked with children's emotional and social development, and their behaviour.

Emotional development

Children who have strong attachments to their parents and **key persons** are likely to develop language more easily. This is because there is a strong link between attachment and language. Babies who are held and cuddled start to 'read' their parents and other carers and this in turn helps them to understand body language in others. Babies and young children who have strong attachments are also motivated to babble and communicate with their parents as they have learned that they will gain a positive response.

Key terms

Atypical behaviour – behaviour that is not usually associated with a specific age range.

Key person – a practitioner designated to take responsibility for a child's emotional wellbeing by having a strong attachment with them and a good relationship with their parents.

Prelinguistic phase – the first phase of language learning, which comes before the production of first words.

Social development

There is a strong link between language and social development. Children who can read other people's body language and can communicate with them are more likely to be accepted by others and engage in playful situations. The acquisition of language also makes a difference to the way that children can play together, as language seems to help children interact. It can also help them to be less impulsive and more thoughtful.

Behaviour

There is a significant link between children's behaviour and language. This is very noticeable in children between the ages of 2 and 3 years whose speech is developing well. At 2 years, children are likely to be impulsive, have difficulties in waiting and sharing and become frustrated. Once children are able to talk in simple sentences, their behaviour changes. They start to become less impulsive, more aware of the needs of others and more cooperative. However, when children's language does not follow the typical pattern of development, they may show behaviour that is equally **atypical**.

Theory into practice

- Are there any children in your placement settings whose language is atypical?
- Does this affect their behaviour?
- If so, what behaviours do they show?

Links to cognitive development

Speech, communication and language seem to play an important part in children's cognitive development. This is because language helps children to process information and is linked to recall and memory. As children's language develops, they are more likely to use it to explore new ideas, explain their thinking and also solve problems. The development of language is one reason why children become less impulsive and are able to understand explanations. Interestingly, the link between thought and language also means that for the first five or six years or so, many children will talk aloud as they play and as they think.

Link

Go to Unit 1: Child Development to find more information about cognitive development.

Recognising links to other areas of development

It is very helpful to be aware of the impact that language can have on other areas of development, and also vice versa. A child who does not have a strong relationship with their key person is less likely

to talk in the setting and a child who has difficulty in feeding might not be developing the groups of muscles in the mouth that will help sound production. The link between language and development means that it is good practice to carry out specific observations on different areas of development. It also emphasises that it is important to be aware of the way that many areas of development are interlinked.

The importance of communication and language to academic achievement

Although it is easy to focus on speaking and listening, we need to be aware that children will learn to read and write as they develop. This usually begins when children start school. Both reading and writing require that children are fluent speakers first. In the case of children learning to read, speech is needed in order for children to make the connection between the sounds they hear or make and the written symbols on a page, but also for children to make sense of what they are reading.

Good language skills are also needed in order for children to write. This is because writing is about putting words down on paper or screen. If children do not have words or cannot form sentences, they will have nothing to write.

Reading and writing are essential for children's academic achievement and, therefore, children who start school without being fluent in English (or the language of their home country) will struggle to cope.

Factors that may affect speech, communication and language development

There are many practical factors that can affect a child's ability to communicate, speak and understand others. Figure 6.2 shows these factors.

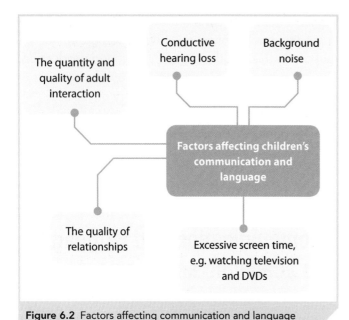

Figure 6.2 Factors affecting communication and language

The diagram shows "Factors affecting children's communication and language" connected to:
- The quantity and quality of adult interaction
- Conductive hearing loss
- Background noise
- The quality of relationships
- Excessive screen time, e.g. watching television and DVDs

Background noise

Background noise affects children's speech. First of all, babies have to 'tune in' during their first year. This process can be disrupted if there is a lot of background noise, especially from the radio and television. This is thought to be because these other human voices make it harder for the baby to focus on their parent or key person.

Background noise doesn't just affect babies. Toddlers and older children are less likely to talk when it is noisy and this includes times when music is being played. It would seem that when there is noise, there is a reduction in the amount of **vocalisations** that take place.

Theory into practice

Many settings create quiet corners and spaces where children can go to talk.

- Look out for quiet spaces in your setting. The spaces can be indoors or outdoors.
- Do they make a difference to how much children talk?

Excessive screen time

Watching television and DVDs or using computers for a number of hours each day can have an impact on children's speech and language. Some screen time is fine but children who spend too much time looking at

a screen, particularly by themselves, are more likely to have a delay in speech and language development. This is because learning language is an active process and requires face-to-face interactions. When children are spending time in front of the screen, they are not getting the same level of interaction.

Excessive time watching television can impact negatively on children's language development.

Children need to have strong relationships with their parents and adults who are looking after them. This is because children vocalise and talk more to people that they like being with.

Key terms

Conductive hearing loss – a hearing loss often caused by glue ear.

Glue ear – a condition in which fluid builds up in the auditory (Eustachian) tube in the ear, preventing sounds from being heard properly.

Vocalisations – sounds that are made by babies either for communication or as a means of exploration. Sounds may include words.

Theory into practice

The importance of relationships to children's language development is one of the reasons why it is vital that an effective key person system is in place.

- Find out how your setting's key person system works to support children's language.

Quantity and quality of adult interaction

Language development is closely linked to how much interaction a child has with adults, particularly parents and key carers. Babies and young children who have plenty of opportunities to talk are likely to acquire language quickly. It is also important that adults are good at listening to children and allowing them to respond. As children develop, they need increasing opportunities to talk and also to hear specific words in order to improve their vocabulary, for example, 'sandals' rather than 'shoes'.

Conductive hearing loss

Conductive hearing loss is very common, particularly between the ages of 2 and 6 years. Conductive hearing loss is usually caused by '**glue ear**', which is a build-up of fluid within the ear, preventing sound from travelling into the inner ear.

Conductive hearing loss affects children's ability to hear sounds clearly. This in turn makes it hard for them to speak clearly or to understand what others are saying. How badly children are affected depends on the severity of the condition. A child might have a conductive hearing loss if they:

- have muffled speech
- stare intently at adults' lips
- have varying levels of responsiveness
- are slow to react to instructions
- show a lack of interest in watching television
- appear withdrawn
- are aggressive due to frustration.

Helping children with known hearing loss

The following actions will help children who have a known hearing loss:

- keep background noise to a minimum
- position the child so that they are not picking up additional noises – this is important for children with hearing aids
- make sure that children can see your face before you start talking
- allow children to sit or stand close to you
- identify the subject of the conversation at the start, for example, 'Look at the daffodils. Today we are going to draw the daffodils.'
- allow children plenty of time to process information
- do not raise your voice – speak clearly instead
- watch carefully to check for children's responses – repeat the sentence again if necessary
- use high levels of facial expression
- point and use gestures.

Working with children with speech delay

There are many reasons why children might have a speech delay and so the starting point when working with children with a speech delay is to find out the possible cause(s). Sadly, today, some speech delay is down to a lack of interaction with adults. If this is the case with the children that you are working with, it will be important to consider the length, as well as the frequency, of your interactions.

Remember to:

- work with children by themselves or in pairs
- make sure that you give children sufficient time to respond
- do things that are interesting for them
- crouch down to their level to make good eye contact
- avoid activities where children only have to listen – think about activities where children are able to talk spontaneously and in a natural way

- monitor children's word count – how much are they talking?
- monitor how many times the child interacts with adults in the session and how long the interactions last
- record children's language to check for progress
- work with parents so that you are sharing important information
- work closely with speech and language teams.

Research

Find out more about the signs of conductive hearing loss. You could start by visiting the NHS website. You can access this website by going to www.pearsonhotlinks.co.uk and searching for this ISBN: 9781447970965.

Learning difficulties

Some children have difficulty in learning and using language because they may have particular learning difficulties. Speech is abstract and this means that some children with learning difficulties struggle to understand that sounds can have meanings. Other children may find it hard to understand the 'rules' of the language they are being exposed to.

Early detection and referral

As language plays such a significant role in children's development, it is important that all adults working with children recognise when a child's pattern of language is atypical. Early referrals often result in better long-term outcomes for children and the effects of the language delay can be reduced.

For children who have learning difficulties, being referred early on is essential as they may need to be supported using systems such as **Makaton**. Without Makaton, children may not be able to make the links between the words and their meaning.

The importance of early detection is why many local areas have drop-in sessions for parents as well as online referral processes. Although many referrals will be to speech and language teams, some children will need to be referred for an **audiology test**. The referral is usually done via a health visitor or GP.

Link

Go to Unit 6: Section C to find more information about Makaton.

Key terms

Audiology test – a hearing test carried out with a machine called an audiometer.

Makaton – a language programme used to help children with specific difficulties understand the spoken word.

Theory into practice

Find out how speech and language referrals are made in your local area.

Assessment practice 6.1   3A1.P1 | 3A1. M1

You have been asked by a childminding network to give a presentation and produce a handout that focuses on the links between communication and language and children's overall development. You also need to cover factors that might affect a child's communication and language development. The group of childminders work with children from birth to 8 years and would like specific examples wherever possible to illustrate your thoughts.

A2 Understand how research into language development supports good practice

How children learn language and how adults should support them to best effect has been the focus of research for a number of years. In this section, we look at some theories and ideas of language and consider how they impact on current early years practice.

The impact of theories and ideas of language development

There are several theories of how children acquire language. These can be divided into three categories: **innate**, **behaviourist** and **social interactionist**.

> ### Key terms
>
> **Behaviourist theory** – a theory of learning that states that development and behaviour can be conditioned and shaped by the environment.
>
> **Innate theory** – behaviours/actions that children do instinctively.
>
> **Social interactionist theory** – behaviours/actions that children learn to do as a result of gaining information and feedback during interaction with adults and other children.

Noam Chomsky

In Unit 1, we learned that Noam Chomsky (born 1928) suggested that children's language development is innate. He suggested that a specific structure in the brain, known as the Language Acquisition Device (LAD), allows children to break into a language code and use it. His model suggests that children can pick up more than one language at an early age without being formally taught, although he does speculate that there may be a 'critical period' for language learning. Chomsky's theory is sometimes criticised for not addressing factors in language development such as the role of the parent or key person interacting with the child.

Chomsky's work has helped to explain why all children learn language, regardless of the particular language they are exposed to. His theory makes it clear that children should be able to pick up more than one language at a young age.

Critical period

Many linguists, including Chomsky, wonder whether there might be a period in which babies and children are primed to learn language and that beyond this period, learning a language without studying it becomes difficult. In rare cases, children have been found in abusive situations where they have not been spoken to and, therefore, are unable to interact. The most famous of these cases was a girl known as Genie. Genie was rescued at the age of 13 from a household in which she was rarely spoken to. At the time of her rescue she had only a few words. She was given intensive support and her number of words increased dramatically, but she did not manage to acquire the rules of language (syntax).

> ### Link
>
> Go to Unit 1: Section B to find more information about Noam Chomsky.

Impact on early years practice

The notion of a critical period is one reason why practitioners working with babies and toddlers are encouraged to work in ways that will help children learn to talk and communicate. The presence of a critical period also means that learning more than one language should be done early in a child's life. This is particularly relevant in the United Kingdom as many children have parents whose first language is not English and, therefore, they should be able to learn two or more languages simultaneously.

Roger Brown

Through his research, Roger Brown (1925–97) outlined five stages of language development in young children. He is known for the term 'telegraphic speech', meaning that children use sentences that are stripped back but still grammatically correct, for example, 'daddy gone'. Brown used **longitudinal observations** to record children's emerging speech and to classify different types of telegraphic speech. He noted that children often made '**virtuous errors**' as their language was emerging, for example, 'goed' or 'wented', but that the word order they used was correct. He also noted that the length of children's sentences (**mean length utterance**) increased as their language developed. Table 6.1 summarises the five stages that Brown identified.

Key terms

Longitudinal observations – information gained about a child from a series of observations that are carried out over a period of time.

Mean length utterance – the average number of words used in a sentence.

Virtuous errors – logical mistakes made by children that suggest they have some understanding of sentence structure, for example, 'I runned' and 'I wented'. Although the tenses are used incorrectly, the errors are logical.

Table 6.1 A summary of Roger Brown's five stages

Stage	Mean length utterance	Age	Some examples of stage
1	1.75	15–30 months	Two-word sentences, e.g.: • 'No want' • 'Go car' • 'Teddy sleep'.
2	2.25	28–36 months	Use of the following: • 'ing': 'Daddy going' • 'on': 'Hat on now' • 'in': 'Duck in water' • regular plurals using 's', e.g. 'sheeps there'.
3	2.75	36–42 months	Use of the following: • some irregular past tenses, e.g. 'Me fell down' • possessives, e.g. 'Mummy's hat'.
4	3.5	40–46 months	Use of the following: • 'a' and 'the': 'I want the book' • 'ed' on regular verbs, e.g. 'Charlie chased the squirrel' • third-person present tense, e.g. 'He works', 'Daddy likes books'.
5	4.0	42–52+ months	Use of the following: • third person (he, she) irregular, e.g. 'he has' (rather than 'he have').

Impact on early years practice

Brown's work has been helpful to those studying children's language as he outlined a clear sequence by which children learned to use grammar in their speech. Although other researchers have looked at his work and questioned whether his model can be applied to all languages, the stages he identified have helped early years professionals understand the sequence by which children learn English. His work has also helped adults realise that children are quite logical in their speech from an early age and that they often preserve correct word order.

B. F. Skinner

As we saw in Unit 1, Skinner (1904–90) felt that the role of the adult was key to children's language learning. He suggested that adults pay more attention to babies when the babies produce sounds that are similar to the language that the adult is using, and also when they encouraged children to talk correctly by using praise or **positive reinforcement**.

Impact on early years practice

Skinner's focus on the role of the adult in helping children to acquire language is probably significant, but his hypothesis has been disputed. First, parents seem to be very accommodating of children's grammatical errors and so will not ignore a child who says 'Me want dat' instead of 'I want that'. These days Skinner's theory is not thought to be strong in terms of explaining the acquisition of language, but it is known that adults do play a part in language development by talking to their children and acknowledging their speech. In terms of the impact on our practice, Skinner's work suggests that adults need to respond positively and quickly to babies and children in order to encourage them to vocalise more.

Key term

Positive reinforcement – an action or object that acts as a reward to reinforce a desired behaviour.

Link

Go to Unit 1: Section B to find more information about B. F. Skinner, praise and positive reinforcement.

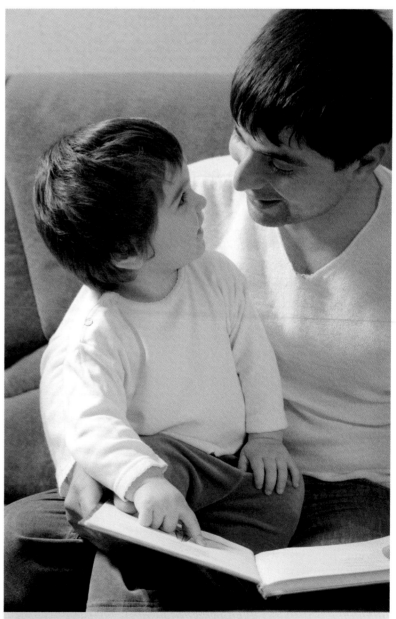

This baby and parent are sharing a book. Look at how well they are interacting.

Jerome Bruner

Jerome Bruner (born 1915) has focused on the role of adults, particularly parents, in supporting young children to learn language. He is famous for using the term 'Language Acquisition Support System' (LASS) to describe the way that a parent or key carer works sensitively with the child to help them understand and break into speech. The baby or child is like an apprentice and the adult helps the child to join in by interacting with them. Bruner's suggestion is that a biological model, as proposed by Chomsky, is not sufficient for language learning.

Impact on early years practice

The importance of relationships in language development and also in other areas of development is seen as key in early years practice. We know that it is helpful if children and adults have good relationships, but also if adults modify and use their language to help the child.

The importance of not over-correcting and using positive reinforcement

There are a couple of important practical points that we can pull out from the different theories of language to apply to our practice with babies and young children.

Avoid over-correcting

Assuming that Chomsky and Brown's work gives a credible account of how children learn language, there are dangers associated with over-correcting children. Many of children's 'mistakes' will be as a result of their attempting to detect the underlying grammar. As English has grown out of many languages, there are several different rules that children will acquire over time. A good example of this is the different rule that applies to the pluralisation of the following common words: 'dog' becomes 'dogs' but 'sheep' do not become 'sheeps'. Instead of overtly correcting children, which may reduce their motivation to communicate, the

suggested approach is to repeat the sentence back to the child using the correct form, for example, 'so you saw sheep in the field'.

Positive reinforcement

Children are more likely to communicate when they feel happy and comfortable with the adult. They also need to feel that they are listened to and that their communications are valued. Smiling, responding to a child and showing interest are all ways that children's attempts at communication can be positively reinforced. However, bear in mind that there is no point or any benefit in overtly praising children for how well they are speaking.

The importance of 'motherese'

We know that some researchers have looked at the process by which children learn to talk. However others, such as Bruner, have also considered the style of language that adults, particularly parents, use with their children.

The term '**motherese**' was originally used in the 1970s to describe a style of language that was noted when mothers spoke to their babies. As fathers also play a part in talking as well as other carers, the term **child-directed speech** (CDS) is often used instead.

There are several features of child-directed speech that we can see when adults talk to babies and young children. These features seem to help babies and children understand what is being said and will eventually help babies and children to talk.

> ### Key terms
>
>
>
> **Child-directed speech** – speech patterns used by parents speaking to their children, usually involving slow and simplified vocabulary, a high-pitched voice and the use of repetition and questions.
>
> **Motherese** – the language patterns of parents speaking to their children, which are often simplified and repetitive. The term is usually used in reference to mothers.

A higher-pitched voice

Adults use a higher pitch of voice than usual when talking to babies and children. This is thought to appeal more to babies and children and so draw their attention to what is being said.

Slower pace

Adults use a slower pace than usual when talking to infants. This is thought to help babies and children distinguish between words and help them to 'tune in'.

Shorter sentences

Adults use shorter sentences with fewer words than usual. This helps the baby or child to work out what is being said.

Simplified sentences

Adults use simple grammar and vocabulary such as 'look at the ball'. This helps the baby or child to pick up grammatical constructions.

Did you know?

Most parents are able to use child-directed speech without any training or knowledge of language development.

Assessment practice 6.2   3A2.P2 | 3A2.M2 | 3A.D1

A group of trainee health visitors have asked you to provide information in the form of an article about theories of communication and language development and how these might affect current practice in early years. Use evidence from work placements/observations and further reading when writing the article. They have requested practical examples of how two theories might be used in practice.

B Encourage and develop children's speech, language and communication

As we have seen, the way that parents, carers and key persons use language in their day-to-day communication with young children can have a positive influence on children's language development. In this section, we will look at the different opportunities that adults have to communicate with children and how these opportunities can be used to promote the development of children's language skills.

Assessing babies' and children's language and communication development

At all stages of babies' and children's language development, it is important to observe and assess their progress. This is because early detection and referrals can make a significant impact on children's later development. It is also important to keep assessing children even if their language

development has been good, as sometimes children fail to continue making progress for a variety of reasons. A good example of this is children who develop conductive hearing loss or babies who vocalise well but then fail to produce words. Recording babies' and children's vocalisations can be helpful as we are able to look back at previous recordings and check that language has progressed.

Here are some things to look out for at different ages.

- At around 3 months – does the baby seem to recognise people and enjoy being held and spoken to?
- At around 8 months – is there a change in how the baby vocalises, i.e. do they now babble?
- At around 10 months – does the baby point to objects?
- At around 11 months – does the baby respond to certain words, e.g. if babies hear the word 'bye-bye' do they start to make a gesture?

- At 18 months – does the child say a few words even if they are not clear?
- At 2 years – does the child understand much of what is said?
- At 2½ years – is the child putting two words together, e.g. 'daddy gone'?
- At 3 years – is the speech fairly clear? Are children talking easily?
- At 4 years – is the child speaking fluently although with some grammatical errors and speech immaturities?
- Around 5 years – is the child starting to enjoy jokes and word games?
- At 6 years – is the child able to say all of the speech sounds, i.e. 'that' not 'dat'?

The importance of sufficient adult interaction

The way that adults talk to babies and children should change according to the child's stage of language development. At all ages, babies and children benefit from sustained interactions with adults. This does not mean that adults have to 'teach' children to talk, but more that adults should engage in a chatting style of conversation, acting as a language partner.

The length of interactions

The length of interactions is just as important as the quality of interactions, as children need time to think, explore concepts and develop ideas. Where research has been carried out into group care, it would appear that some children do not get sufficient interaction and in England this has prompted several initiatives, such as 'Every Child a Talker', to help practitioners reflect on their skills and the length of time they spend interacting with children.

Research

Find out more about the 'Every Child a Talker' initiative by going to the Department for Education website. You can access this website by going to www.pearsonhotlinks.co.uk and searching for this ISBN: 9781447970965.

Activity

The length of interaction between adults and children and providing opportunities for children to talk are important for children's language development.

Ask your placement supervisor if you can make a sound recording. Record yourself working with a child aged between 2 and 5 years, and then reflect on the following questions.

- How many opportunities do you provide for the child to talk?
- Does the conversation seem warm and natural?

As with other types of observation methods, you should treat sound recording as confidential information. If you want to play the recordings outside of the placement setting, or keep them, you will need to gain the permission of the placement supervisor/parents.

As children's speech develops, it is important for adults to be good listeners and allow children to do most of the talking.

Verbal interactions with babies

For babies to 'tune in' to the language or languages that they are meant to be learning, it is essential that they spend time with adults who are directly interacting with them. This is important because in the prelinguistic phase babies learn about the sounds and tune of the language, as well as communication techniques such as making eye contact and recognising others' emotions.

There are some important ways that adults can help babies break into what is otherwise a code made from sounds.

Holding babies

The starting point and the motivation for babies to break into the 'code' is often linked to their need for love and attention. Simply holding a baby and talking to them makes a significant difference. Babies who spend long periods on the floor away from adults or in forward-facing pushchairs will find it hard to connect what they are hearing with any meaning.

Eye contact

Making eye contact is a key communication skill. Babies seem to want to make eye contact very early on as they will often gaze into the adult's eyes when they are being fed. Making eye contact with a baby when you are with them is key to helping them feel included in the conversation – albeit a one-sided conversation at first.

Drawing babies' attention – using gesture

Often and without realising it, adults who communicate well with babies point things out to them. This is important as it helps babies to focus on an object, person or action. This in turn means that babies are more likely to understand what the accompanying words are about.

Drawing babies' attention – using facial expression

Babies can also have their attention drawn to language through our facial expressions. Babies need strong facial expressions to help them be interested in what is happening. Eyebrows and mouths are of particular interest to babies as they help them 'read' the human face more easily. If you have a fringe, think about clipping it back so that babies can see your whole face.

Theory into practice

A common facial expression that adults use with babies is one of mock surprise or shock. The adult pretends to be shocked or surprised by the baby. The adult's eyebrows are raised and the mouth is often open. Babies love this expression and will often giggle.

- Try to notice when an experienced adult who is working with babies uses this expression. Does it engage the baby?

Running commentary

As well as directly pointing out things to babies, adults also need to keep chatting to them, even when they are busy doing other things. This means, for example, that while an adult is setting the table, the baby should still be spoken to. This style is sometimes called 'running commentary'. Some adults find it difficult to do this as the baby does not reply, but it is essential as it allows the baby to hear direct communication.

Theory into practice

Ask if you can spend a few minutes observing an experienced adult working with a baby. Watch how the adult carries on a conversation with baby even when the adult is doing a task such as feeding or nappy changing.

Acknowledging babies' vocalisations

Babies are not silent! They cry, moan and will also make babbling sounds. It is important, therefore, to respond to babies' sounds by talking to them, picking them up or, if necessary, comforting them. This helps babies to practise vocalisations and to help them feel that they are understood.

See if you can pinpoint specific techniques used by the practitioner in Figure 6.3 to engage the baby and encourage their language development.

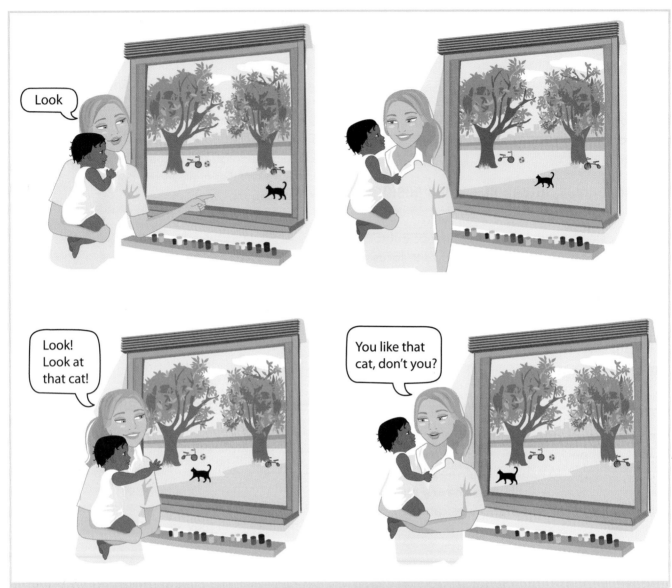

Figure 6.3 What communication techniques is this practitioner using to help the baby's language development?

The importance of appropriate adult support

There are some basic things that adults can do to help children's language development. These things are shown in Figure 6.4.

Time to respond

One of the most important things to remember when working with babies and children is to remember that they will need time to respond to what you say. This is because it takes time for them to process information or, in other words, they require thinking time. In recordings of adults talking to children, this is one of the most common mistakes that are made.

Acknowledging attempts to communicate

We saw that acknowledging vocalisations is important with babies, but this remains important throughout children's early childhood. You can show that you are acknowledging that children are communicating by making eye contact and getting down to the child's level. Squatting down to properly acknowledge a 2-year-old child shows them that you are listening and that you are interested.

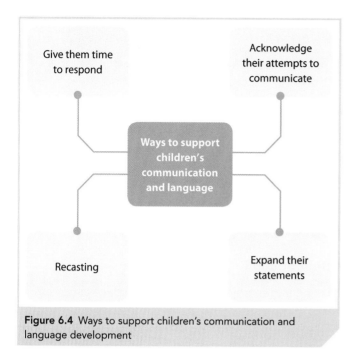

Figure 6.4 Ways to support children's communication and language development

Reflecting back

When children are starting to talk, they are likely to make mistakes. You should not correct children, but you should repeat the word or phrase back correctly, as in the following example. For example:

- Child: 'Look. I'm a mermelaid.'
- Adult: 'A mermaid. How exciting!'

Expanding statements

Babies and children need adults to acknowledge what they are saying, but also to expand their statements. Expanding a child's statement in a sensitive way helps them make connections to things that they have already experienced. For example, an adult and child may have the following conversation:

- Baby at 11 months: 'Dadada.'
  Adult: 'Can you hear Daddy coming down the stairs?'
- 2-year-old child: 'All gone now.'
  Adult: 'Have you finished everything? You were very hungry, weren't you?'
- 4-year-old child: 'I've got new shoes.'
  Adult: 'They're lovely new shoes. And they've got very smart buckles too.'
- 6-year-old child: 'We're going on holiday and I am going on a plane!'
  Adult: 'That's exciting. I wonder if you will fly over France where Josh now lives.'

The importance of having a good command of English

Most of children's language learning comes from interactions with adults. This is why it is important for adults working with children to have a good command of the English language. Early years professionals should talk clearly to children, use grammar and vocabulary accurately, and pronounce words correctly.

Ways of promoting speech and language development

As well as using the language techniques that we saw earlier, adults can help develop children's language in other ways.

Drawing children's attention to detail

To develop children's language, it is important that adults draw their attention to detail. This helps build children's knowledge of the world around them and also gives them descriptive vocabulary. This might mean pointing out the bark or the buds on a tree. It may also mean pointing out to a child that their jumper has stripes on it.

Active listening

It is essential to listen carefully to children and use the active listening skills that we saw in Unit 5 when working with adults. These skills include making good eye contact, showing interest and acknowledging what a child is saying. When interacting with children, the active listening skills you use need to be more exaggerated; for example, your facial expression might be stronger or you might allow more time for a child to think and reflect.

> **Link**
>
> Go to Unit 5: Section A2 to find more information about active listening skills and face-to-face communication.

Accurate naming

Once children have understood and are using general words such as 'shoes' or 'dogs', it is important to give them more accurate words such as 'sandal' or 'terrier'. This helps them to develop a more sophisticated vocabulary, which in turn, will help their **cognitive processing**.

Key term

Cognitive processing – the way in which the brain processes, retains and makes links between existing and new information.

Helping children to sequence

When children first start talking, they can find it hard to sequence what they have done. Adults can help children talk about things that they have done by asking prompting questions such as, 'and what happened next?'

Children can also be helped to sequence through the use of visual prompts such as photographs. A series of photographs taken while out shopping can help the child remember what happened first. Learning how to sequence their talk is an important skill for children to learn as it is something that links to their later literacy and ability to read.

Theory into practice

Listen to the way that an adult in your setting helps a young child to sequence and talk about something they have done.

- How does the adult show interest?
- How does the adult help the child to get the sequence right?

Creating an environment that encourages communication and language

Babies, children and adults need things to talk about. This means that the environment we create, including the development of routines and activities, becomes very important. New things seem to attract babies' and children's attention and although at some level routine is important, the environment needs to be of sufficient interest to encourage communication and speech.

Reflect

Think about times when you have been in an environment that was not stimulating.

- How did it make you feel?
- How easy was it to maintain an exciting conversation?

How to create a language-promoting environment

Small spaces

Many children enjoy being in small spaces such as tents, dens or role-play areas. Small spaces are often places where children sit and enjoy talking. It is good practice in settings with children over 1 year old to create small spaces where children can sit and talk. Older children might talk to each other but adults working with younger children need to use these small spaces to interact with children or tell a story.

Background noise

Children interact and vocalise less in noisy environments. In group-care settings where there might be a large number of children, strategies to cut down background noise are important. They include the following:

- changing the layout of the setting to create smaller areas
- making sure that adults do not call out across the room to children
- using all available space at all times, including outdoors
- avoiding the use of continual background music
- using sound-absorbing materials such as carpets in some areas
- moving games and activities that might be noisy to other areas
- modelling quiet talking to children.

Getting children interested

Children need things to talk about. This is why when children go on outings, they often have plenty to say because they are seeing new and interesting things. As there is a link between the development of communication and language and stimulation, it is important that we provide new and exciting things for children to look at. This might mean bringing in new objects that children may not have seen before such as a star fruit or a small suitcase full of different sized and coloured socks. We should also think about new activities for children. These activities can include everyday activities such as washing up, raking leaves or cleaning the toys.

Where there are regular routines for children, they can become a source of stimulation if small changes are made, for example, by using placemats on one day and tablecloths on another.

Being aware of the need to provide stimulation is particularly important in settings where children may spend a lot of time each year or, in the case of day-care settings, for a number of years.

Group size

The amount of interaction a child has with an adult is closely linked, as we have seen, to their communication and language development. This means that when children are in group care, we need to think carefully about group size and also the composition of the group. When children are talking well, they are likely to dominate conversations. This is not their fault and they should not be reprimanded, but it means that a younger child in a group or a child with delayed speech may not have as many opportunities for interaction.

Wherever possible, it is good practice for settings to organise their routines to minimise group sizes. Some examples of how this may work are as follows.

- Two children help an adult to set the table for lunch while the rest of the nursery carries on playing.
- An early years professional shares a story with a baby on her lap while another baby explores a treasure basket.
- A nanny has made a pretend tent for a 4-year-old child and then she does a jigsaw puzzle with a 6-year-old child.

Theory into practice

Have you seen any strategies used in your work placement setting designed to minimise the number of children in one area?

How background noise affects speech, language and communication development

We saw in Section A1 that background noise, especially television and radio, can affect babies' ability to tune in. It also affects toddlers' and older children's speech, as they are less likely to talk when there is speech in background noise. This is the case even when the children are not actually engaging in watching the television or radio.

The importance of stories and rhymes

Babies and young children benefit from all types of rhymes. The rhythms and alliterations in rhymes seem to help children with **auditory discrimination** and so they become aware of the sounds. The development of auditory discrimination seems to help children later when they learn to read and spell and this is why rhymes are part of most early years curricula.

Rhymes also help children with speech production, as children will often be repeating the same sounds during a rhyme. This repetition helps children to develop mouth movements and strengthen muscles in the tongue and cheeks. Where children have difficulties in producing specific sounds, it is likely that speech and language therapists will recommend certain rhymes for children to practise.

Key term

Auditory discrimination – the ability to hear and pick out particular sounds amid others.

It is also good for children to hear stories. Storytelling is an important skill to master, as it appears to help children learn about vocabulary and sentence structure. It is also likely to encourage older children to make up their own stories, which is good preparation for writing stories later on in life. Table 6.2 provides some tips for using stories and rhymes with children.

Table 6.2 Tips for using stories and rhymes with children

Age range	How you could use rhymes and stories
0–1 years	• Use finger rhymes and action rhymes when holding babies • Popular rhymes include 'Humpty Dumpty', 'Pat-a-cake' and 'Round and round the garden'
1–3 years	• Use finger rhymes and action rhymes every day • Allow sufficient time for the child to respond • Be ready to slow down or repeat rhymes so that the child can join in • Expect to hear children saying rhymes aloud to themselves • Make up short, simple stories based on children's activities
3–5 years	• Use all types of rhymes, including counting rhymes • Use props for counting rhymes so that children start to visualise numbers • Tell children classic stories and also stories that are based on activities they have been doing • Encourage children to re-tell or act out stories
5–8 years	• Plan rhymes based on sounds that children are learning to support their reading programme where phonics are being taught • Encourage children to make up and tell stories using props

Table 6.3 Tips for exploring books with children

Age range	How you could explore books
0–1 years	• Use simple picture books with this age group • Encourage the baby to touch pictures and turn pages • Share the same books several times so that the baby starts to recognise pictures and react to words
1–3 years	• Look for picture books that tell a very simple story • Look out for books that rhyme or repeat sentences • Let the child hold the book and turn the pages • Expect that children will have favourite books
3–5 years	• Look out for picture books that tell stories • Ask children questions about the stories • Encourage children to turn pages, make comments and look at the words • Read books by running your finger under the text • See if children can 'guess' what the next phrase or word will be in their favourite books
5–8 years	• Look out for books that have a good story • Let children look at the pictures and encourage them to do some reading with you • Expect that children will have favourite books and topics

The importance of books

Books are wonderful for children's language development at all ages. They introduce babies and children to new words and ideas, and also help them to learn about the printed word. Children who are regularly read to at a young age are more likely to show good speech and language development. They are also more likely to be interested in learning to read. Table 6.3 provides some guidelines for using books with different age groups.

Assessment practice 6.3

3B.P3 | 3B.M3

You have been asked to give a presentation to parents and volunteers in a preschool about the benefits of stories and rhymes. In your presentation you should give examples of:

- the type of books and rhymes that might be used with children from 0 to 8 years
- how these books may help children.

The preschool manager has also asked you to write an article for a newsletter that analyses the role of early years professionals in providing environments that effectively support children's speech, communication and language. Use examples from three different settings to show how activities and resources are used across the 0 to 8 age ranges.

Activities that promote language development

There are some activities that are particularly good at promoting children's language development. They seem to engage children and naturally prompt them to respond and to talk.

Imaginative play: 1–3 years

The start of imaginative play can be seen in children under 3 years. Putting out props such as telephones, cups and saucers is likely to encourage children to talk. They may do this alone but it is better if adults join them in the play as this should encourage longer interactions. You might, for example, pretend to talk into a phone and then pass it to a 15-month-old child who is likely to grin and chatter. Children also love to play little games whereby they offer a cup of tea or play food to an adult.

Imaginative play: 3–5 years

In this next phase, children are likely to enjoy playing with other children cooperatively. They may do this using role-play areas or with small-world play. Children can talk together but there are times when it is helpful for adults to join children or provide the starting stimulus. This is because an adult can introduce new vocabulary and phrases that children can then absorb and start to use, as shown in the case study that follows.

When introducing new role-play areas it is good practice to base them on children's direct experiences. You could also help children learn more by going on outings, reading books or inviting visitors into the setting. This helps children to know how to role play different situations. Ideally, role play should be offered in and out of doors.

Figure 6.5 shows some different role-play areas that work well.

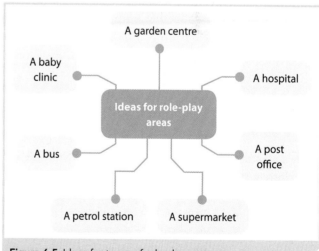

Figure 6.5 Ideas for types of role-play areas

Imaginative play: 5–8 years

As children get older, their imaginative play changes. It can become more intense and also scripted. In terms of role play, children tend to like having accurate props and dressing-up clothes. The role of the adult is often that of being a receptive audience and also a **facilitator**. However, for small-world play, children like adults to be interested in what they are doing and sometimes will welcome an adult to take part or help them construct items for the play.

Key term

Facilitate – the action of supporting children rather than leading their actions and play.

Puppets

Puppets can be used at any age to encourage babies and children to talk. Puppets, if handled well, can make babies smile and babble and with toddlers, they are likely to prompt interest and sometimes questions. It takes quite a while before children have the skill to manage a puppet for themselves, but finger puppets and hand puppets are great for the 5 to 8 years age range. They can use the puppets as part of their imaginative play and some children choose to put on little puppet shows.

Link

Go to the 'Skills for practice' section at the end of this unit to find more information about how to use puppet shows.

Case study

The post office

The team at Little Acorns preschool set up a post office in the role-play area. They decided to visit the post office in the village so that the children could learn more about it. The postmaster was the father of one of the children. He showed groups of the children around and gave the preschool some forms, a stamper and a few signs that were no longer needed. The staff videoed the postmaster pretending to serve a customer who had a large parcel. Back at the preschool, and with the help of the children, the team set up the role-play area and for a couple of sessions took it in turns to pretend to be the postmaster. The role-play area was a great success and the children quickly started to use appropriate language.

1 Why was it a good idea to take the children to the post office?

2 Why did staff need to join in the role play at first?

3 What were the benefits to the children of this approach?

Story sacks

Story sacks have been very popular in the United Kingdom in the past few years. They are usually carried out with children from around 3 years or so. The idea behind a story sack is that children and adults talk and read a story book that is accompanied by props. You can buy commercial story sacks but they can also be made. Most story sacks comprise a well-known story, puppets or props and some suggestions for follow-up activities. In many settings, parents will be encouraged to take story sacks home with their child.

Using a story sack is simple. You need to let the children explore the props and then read them the story. The key is to make sure that children have plenty of time to absorb the story and to look at the pictures. When the story is finished, you can then encourage children to re-tell the story using the props. In addition, other activities can be carried out, such as counting the characters or making further props.

Research

Find out more about using and making story sacks from the National Literacy Trust website. You can access this website by going to www.pearsonhotlinks.co.uk and searching for this ISBN: 9781447970965.

Assessment practice 6.4   3B.P4 | 3B.P5 | 3B.M4

Produce activity plans and collect witness statements from your placement settings to show that you have provided appropriate support for developing the speech, language and communication of children in the settings in which you have worked.

Make sure that the activity plans cover children within all of the age ranges from 0 to 8 years (i.e. from birth up to 2 years, 2 years to 4 years and 4 years to 8 years).

C Understand how to support children with varied language needs

Children who are developing more than one language

Today in the United Kingdom, many children are learning English alongside another language or even languages. Many people think this is a recent development, but that is not true. For many centuries, parts of the United Kingdom have spoken other languages alongside English, such as Celtic and Welsh. Indeed, English itself is a mixture of several languages! This section looks at the importance of supporting children to acquire another language alongside English, although the principles apply to the support of any combination of languages, for example, Welsh and English.

The benefits of multilingualism

Children who are lucky enough to be exposed to more than one language may benefit in many ways. First, being able to think in more than one language allows greater flexibility of thought and is often associated with creativity and problem solving. It is also thought to help children to acquire further languages more easily.

The cognitive benefits are thought to be significant and so are the emotional and social benefits. Most children who are learning more than one language are doing so because they are with one or more family members who speak the language. The languages spoken will have a strong association either with a religion or another culture. Being able to communicate in these languages will allow children to be part of their family's culture or religion. This in turn gives children a strong sense of cultural or religious identity and self-concept. In many cases, having access to their family's language will also mean that children can communicate with extended family who in some cases may be living in other countries.

There are other benefits of multilingualism in terms of parenting and **attachment**. Parents need to communicate with their children in a language that allows them to express genuine but sometimes subtle emotions and this tends to mean the parents' first language. Trying to parent a child in a language that is not a first language can be very difficult.

Key term

Attachment – a special relationship or bond between a child and someone who is emotionally involved with them.

Case study

Learning two languages

Martina is 4 years old. Her parents work for an international company and they were posted to the United Kingdom two years ago. She attends a preschool and is learning English there as her parents speak Polish. Every week Martina speaks to her grandmother and her cousins in Poland. She is doing well in both languages.

1 How is Martina benefiting from having Polish spoken at home?

2 Why is it important for Martina's grandparents and family that she can speak Polish?

The context in which languages are being learned at home

When you are working with children who may have more than one language, it is important to begin by finding out which languages are spoken and by whom. The following questions can be used to understand children's language use.

- What language or languages does your child hear at home?
- Who speaks these languages?
- Which language or languages are directly spoken to your child?
- If you speak more than one language to your child, how do you do this? For example, one language in the house, another language out of the house.
- Has your child heard English before? If so, how much?
- Does your child speak any English?

These questions should help you to establish whether children are learning English alongside another language or whether they are learning English 'from scratch'. It will also help you to know whether children are hearing the languages in a consistent way, which, as we will see, can make a difference to the acquisition of them.

Gaps in vocabulary

The questions should also help you to learn about whether children are likely to have any 'gaps' in vocabulary. For example, it is common for children who have a different home language to the setting only to know the names of household objects in the home language. This might mean that a child who speaks Punjabi at home may not have the English for words such as 'sheet' or 'sofa'. Recognising where possible gaps might occur is useful because we can then plan specific activities for children in English.

The impact of being introduced to English in the setting

When children come into the setting with an established home language, they may feel unsettled at first. This can be quite daunting for them.

When children join the setting, it is important that parents realise the impact that learning English may have on the child's home language or languages. The impact will very much depend on how much time the child spends being exposed to English, and at what age. A baby in day care, for example, may spend ten hours a day being exposed to English. The same baby may only hear one or two hours a day of the parents' language. This lack of exposure to the parents' language may lead to the baby growing up able to understand the parents' language, but not being able to speak it. On the other hand, a child who is 3 years old and has been immersed in the parents' language for three years with minimum exposure to English is likely to pick up English quickly but still retain their home language, providing that parents continue to use it.

Recognising the emotional impact on a child

When children are able to communicate easily in their home language, it is a great shock for them to come to a setting and find that other children and adults do not understand them when they talk. It is also hard for children to understand why, all of a sudden, they no longer understand what is being said to them by other children and adults in that setting. For some children, this can be very distressing and can cause **regression**. It is, therefore, important to make sure that the settling-in process is done carefully and that children have a strong relationship with a key person before being separated from their parents.

Link

Go to Unit 5: Section B to find more information about how adults encourage language development in babies.

Key term

Regression – to move backwards developmentally to a previous stage.

The importance of the key person

Whether children arrive in a setting with some or no English, the key person has an essential role in settling children in and also establishing a relationship with the child and their parents. Many children will want to stay near the key person at all times to make them feel safe. This relationship will be an important factor in helping the child to acquire language.

Working with children

The principles of helping children to acquire English when they join a setting at 2 or 3 years old is similar to helping babies to talk. The key person needs to build up a good bond with the child and then use the simplified language that characterises adult speech with babies. This will include facial expression, gesture and plenty of pointing.

Language routines

Key persons should also help children by creating little language routines with them. For example, they may go with a child to set beakers out on a snack table. If these little moments are done every day with the same child it will mean that the child will start to 'break in' to some key words that are used each time. In this example, the key words may include 'beaker' and 'table'.

This key person is using facial expression and gesture to draw the child's attention to the word 'fish'.

The importance of children tuning in to the sounds of the setting's language

When many children come into the setting without having any English, they are likely to spend time 'tuning in'. In some ways this could be compared to a baby's prelinguistic phase. Although it might take a baby several months to tune in, young children who have already begun to talk in another language will tune in much quicker. As we have seen earlier, when tuning in it is helpful for children if similar phrases are used each time a routine event happens – this way the child begins to tune in more quickly.

As many children do need tuning in time before they will be ready to talk, it is important not to pressurise them into speaking. Interestingly, children will often be able to join in with songs and rhymes before they start to talk. This is because songs and rhymes are processed differently in the brain.

Valuing home languages

We saw earlier that bilingualism or multilingualism can have some important benefits to children's emotional, social and cognitive development. Sadly, these benefits can be negated when adults working with children and the wider community do not value the home language. Children who feel they are different because they use more than one language, or that they feel there is disapproval of them using a home language, can develop lower levels of confidence and self-esteem and this in turn can affect their overall development.

As well as being important for children's development, showing parents that we value the language they use with their child will help our relationship with them. This is because it can be hard for parents to be partners with us or to feel confident and relaxed in our company if they feel that we disapprove of them using a different language.

There are also benefits for other children, as they can learn words in another language and develop an awareness of other cultures and religions.

Figure 6.6 shows some simple ways to show children and their parents that their languages are valued.

Ensuring consistency in the way languages are used

All children learn language by being exposed to its sounds and structures. Children with more than one language should not automatically develop a speech delay, but sometimes this can happen when a baby or young child is being spoken to in a mixture of languages by the same person. For example, a mum may start to tell her child to go to bed in English but then may switch into Turkish. Inconsistent language use means that children are often slower to break in to the different sounds, words and meanings of the two languages being used.

One person, one language

Interestingly, if two adults are talking to a child, each using a different language, there are unlikely to be any problems. This approach is sometimes called 'one person, one language' as the child can very

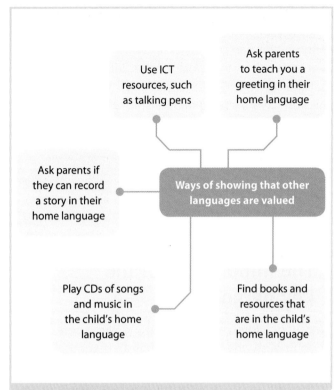

Use ICT resources, such as talking pens

Ask parents to teach you a greeting in their home language

Ask parents if they can record a story in their home language

Ways of showing that other languages are valued

Play CDs of songs and music in the child's home language

Find books and resources that are in the child's home language

Figure 6.6 Ways of showing that other languages are valued

quickly come to expect to use one language with one adult and another language with the other adult in this situation. See Figure 6.7 for an example of this approach.

In some families, children may acquire three languages as each parent may speak a different language directly to their child and then at school or preschool they may acquire English from adults who talk to them in English.

'Très bien. T'as fait ça tout seul'.

'Wow! That's a tall tower.'

Figure 6.7 This child is being exposed to English and French. He associates the different languages with each adult.

One person using more than one language in consistent situations

Some parents use more than one language with their children but do this in a consistent way. For example, a dad may speak in Spanish to his child, but may switch to English when his partner comes home from work. This way of teaching two languages can work, but parents need to make sure that children are spending sufficient time using each language so that the child can become fluent in both languages. For example, a toddler who is only hearing one hour of Spanish a day but ten hours of English is likely to understand Spanish but not necessarily be able to speak it.

Inconsistent language when children are fluent

For older children who have established fluency in two or more languages, a person switching between languages in the same sentence or conversation is not problematic. This is because the child has already worked out the meanings, sounds and words of each language.

Theory into practice

Find out what advice your setting gives to parents with more than one language. Do they suggest that parents should speak in their first language to their children?

Case study

Hearing multiple languages

Baran's father is Turkish. Whenever he talks directly to Baran he uses Turkish. When he is talking to someone who does not know Turkish, he speaks in English. In these situations he still keeps talking to Baran in Turkish. Baran's mother is German. She has always spoken to Baran in German, but she talks to her husband in English because they met in England. She cannot speak Turkish and her husband's German is pretty basic. Baran is due to start nursery next year when he is 3 years old.

1 At this point in time, which languages would you expect Baran to use for talking?
2 Why is Baran likely to know some English, but not be able to use it yet?
3 Which languages will Baran be able to use when he is 5 or 6 years old?

Children who have additional language needs

Some children will need additional support in order to be able to communicate and use language. There are a variety of reasons why a child might need additional support, including if they have hearing loss, learning difficulties or speech delay. This section looks at some of the principles involved in supporting children with additional communication and language needs.

The importance of visual cues and props

Many children who have language and communication needs are helped when visual cues and props are provided in settings. The visual information helps them to understand or process the spoken language more easily. All babies and children benefit from having visual cues and props, but they are particularly helpful for children who find it hard to convert spoken words into meaning.

Figure 6.8 gives some examples of the type of cues and props that are commonly used in settings.

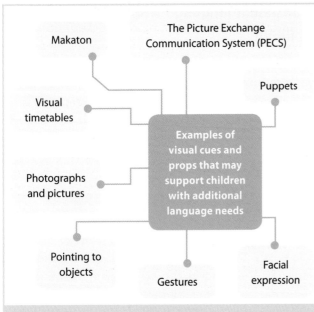

Figure 6.8 Examples of visual cues and props that may support children with additional language needs

Puppets

Puppets can help to motivate children to communicate. They can be used to act out actions alongside the words being spoken by adults and therefore they can help children to understand the meanings of words.

Facial expression

All children benefit from high levels of facial expression – for example, smiling, frowning and pretending to look shocked. Facial expression helps children to enjoy communicating and also helps them to understand the meaning of words.

Gesture

Using gestures helps children to understand the meaning of what is being said by adults. Children can also copy gestures to help them to be understood by others.

Pointing

Pointing to objects or people at the start of a conversation helps children know what is being talked about. Pointing is usually accompanied by facial expression and also the word 'look!' to help draw children's attention to the object.

Photographs and pictures

Many early years settings will use photographs. These are key to helping children remember what they have been doing or to help them understand what is being spoken about.

Visual timetables

Visual timetables are usually photographs or pictures arranged in a way that helps a child to know what is going to be happening throughout a session. This helps them to feel secure. Figure 6.9 shows an example of what a visual timetable may look like.

Figure 6.9 An example of a visual timetable

Makaton

Makaton is used to support children's communication skills. It is not a language and it is generally introduced on the advice of a speech and language therapist. In the UK the signs used in Makaton are from British Sign Language and give children a 'picture' of what the words mean. For example, as Figure 6.10 shows, the sign for a man is stroking the chin to indicate a beard. It is important that Makaton signs are done alongside speech.

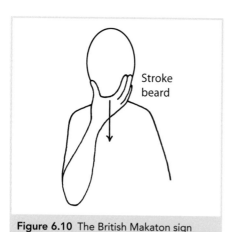

Stroke beard

Figure 6.10 The British Makaton sign for 'man'. It carries the sign note 'stroke beard'.

Key terms

Makaton – a language programme where signs and symbols are used to help children with specific difficulties understand the spoken word.

Picture Exchange Communication System – a system that helps children with communication difficulties to learn about the two-way nature of communication through the exchange of pictures.

Picture Exchange Communication System

The **Picture Exchange Communication System (PECS)** will be suggested and implemented in settings by the speech and language team. The system is based on the idea that children and adults exchange cards to communicate. For example, at its simplest, if a child would like a drink, they pass a card with a picture of a drink to an adult, who then responds by giving the child a drink. This is done alongside speech and is often used with children who need help understanding the concept of interaction and turn taking or with children who have communication difficulties.

Providing quality interaction

All children benefit from quality interaction with adults, but it is particularly important when working with children who have a speech delay or additional needs. Below are some key areas that it is essential to get right when interacting with children.

The environment

- Avoid distracting environments with a lot of background noise.
- Make sure that there is something to trigger children's interest and allow you to communicate together.
- Think about where the child seems to communicate most and where they like spending time.

Your relationship

- Make sure that your relationship with children is good and positive.
- Consider whether you are fun to be with.
- Observe the child's body language when you are with them – is the child relaxed and pleased to be with you?

Your communication skills

- Speak clearly and moderate your style according to the age/needs of the child.
- Use high levels of facial expression, gesture and note children's reactions.
- Give children sufficient time to answer or respond to you. Be patient!
- Acknowledge their communication positively – smile, show interest and, if appropriate, ask further questions.
- Expand what they are trying to communicate to you.
- Use props, photographs or pictures if needed.
- Do not overtly correct children's speech – rephrase correctly instead.

Case study

Quality interaction?

Chara, a practitioner, is meant to be supporting Jonas's communication and language. Jonas is happily playing with some building blocks in the corner of the room. Chara goes up to him and tells him to come with her. Jonas is not happy. She takes him to a table in the centre of the busy room and gets out some cards with pictures on them. Jonas does not seem interested. Chara becomes irritated, partly because Jonas is not interested and also because she is frequently interrupted by other children. She is also frustrated because when she asks Jonas a question, he does not seem to respond. After five minutes, she tells Jonas that he can go.

1 Where should the interaction have taken place?
2 Why might Jonas's responses be being influenced by Chara's style?
3 What suggestions could you give to Chara for the future?

Following advice and programmes from speech and language therapists

Many children who have additional communication and language needs will be referred to speech and language therapists. Speech and language therapists may work with the child directly but they are also likely to suggest activities that need to be carried out at home by parents and also in settings. The type of activities will very much depend on the nature of the child's difficulty. For children who are not producing certain sounds, a therapist may suggest games and rhymes that strengthen the muscles in the mouth and teach the child new mouth movements.

For children who have difficulty in processing the meanings of words, therapists may suggest the introduction of Makaton or PECS.

Following the advice and programmes suggested by the speech and language therapist is essential because otherwise children are not likely to make progress. In addition, inconsistent or incorrect use of programmes such as PECS can create more problems for the child.

If you know that a child is working with a speech and language team, it may be worth asking the parent for permission to contact the team so that you can find out more about the child's programme.

Working closely with parents and carers

It is always good practice to work closely with parents, but it is essential if we are to support children with their language development. Some parents have found particular ways of communicating with their children that are useful for us to know about. This enables us to share our knowledge with parents about particular ways we may work with their children.

Gaining information for assessment

As children can behave and communicate differently at home, it can also be useful for parents to share information and, if possible, recordings of their child at home. Recordings can be taken on a mobile phone or on a recording device such as an MP3 player. If recordings are kept, of course with parents' permission, we can go back to them at a later date and see if children have made progress.

Children's interests

Building up a picture of what the child is interested in talking about can also be helpful. For example, if a child has been taken to see steam trains at the weekend, we could follow this interest up with the child by getting out a train set or a book about trains to encourage the child to communicate.

This practitioner found out that a child in her setting loves puppets. She uses them to encourage the child to communicate.

Understanding children's body language

It is important to find out from parents how their child communicates their feelings if they are not talking. Parents may be able to tell us about their child's body language in certain situations. For example, if a child is nervous they might touch their ear. Being able to interpret a child's body language is particularly important when settling children in.

Working with children with hearing loss or language delay

Many young children are likely to have some hearing loss at one time or another. There are different types of hearing loss but the most common type in children is known as conductive hearing loss or 'glue ear'. The other type of hearing loss is usually permanent and is, fortunately, relatively rare. This type of permanent loss is known as sensorineural loss and is likely to be picked up in the few months after birth. Children with sensorineural loss require hearing aids or, in some cases, a cochlear transplant.

Link

Go to Unit 6: Section A1 to find more information about hearing loss in children.

The role of the SENCO

If children are not making expected progress in their speech, communication and language, or in other areas of development, additional plans and activities should be drawn up. To help practitioners with this, every early years setting should have a SENCO. The term 'SENCO' stands for Special Educational Needs Coordinator. A SENCO is someone who coordinates the provision of special needs in a setting. They help draw up plans with practitioners and parents and carers, provide advice and guidance and make sure support is implemented. They also coordinate referrals to other professionals, when needed.

Who to approach for additional help

It is important that we recognise when children need additional help with their speech, communication and language. There are a range of professionals and services who work with children who may have communication needs. However, the usual referral route is to speech and language therapists as communication and language is their area of expertise.

For children who may have difficulty with hearing, it is usual for referrals to be made either to audiology teams or teams that support hearing loss, often known as sensory impairment teams.

Children who have identified learning difficulties or complex needs may be supported by a range of other professionals from whom you can gain ideas and support. These professionals include educational psychologists, physiotherapists and portage workers.

Link

Go to Unit 5: Section B to find information about the roles these professionals play.

You are working at a local children's centre. The centre has children from a wide variety of backgrounds with a range of different needs, including children with speech delay and children who come to the centre without knowing English. The children's centre works with children from birth through to 8 years as it runs out-of-school provision and works closely with the primary schools in the area.

You have been asked to make an information sheet that outlines ways in which adults might work to support children who have:

- English as an additional language
- additional language needs.

The information sheet should provide practical strategies as well as background knowledge.

In addition, the head of the children's centre has asked you to write a professional article that considers the early years professional's role in promoting communication and language across the age ranges. The head has asked that you include the early years professional's role in providing an effective environment for the promotion of communication and language and discuss how to plan for and give support to children with varied language needs.

Use evidence from observations or further reading to show the extent to which early years professionals contribute to children's language and communication development.

Further reading and resources

Brock, A. and Rankin, C. (2008) *Communication, Language and Literacy from Birth to Five*, London: Sage Publications.

Brown, R. (1973) *A First Language: The Early Stages*, London: George Allen & Unwin Ltd.

Callander, N. and Nahmad-Williams, L. (2010) *Communication, Language and Literacy*, London: Continuum.

Fisher, S. (2009) *Puppets, Language and Learning*, London: Featherstone Education.

Tassoni, P. (2012) *Penny Tassoni's Practical EYFS Handbook* (2nd ed.), Oxford: Pearson.

Website

The National Literacy Trust:
www.literacytrust.org.uk

Ready for work?

Louise Williamson Reception class teacher

I have been a reception class teacher for three years. The level of speech that children come with into the reception year affects how well they do with their reading. We see this time and time again. In theory, at 4 years old all children should be talking well, but that is not always the case. In the reception class, we can have as many as 30 children and although I do have a nursery nurse with me, it still means that our adult–child ratio is 1 : 15, which means that long conversations with individual children are fairly rare. We do, however, work hard at providing small group opportunities, and in the first couple of school terms most of our activities are linked to promoting language. We do rhymes and stories every day and as part of our play provision we set up a range of different role-play areas. Some of these areas are based around children's interests, but others are about building children's vocabulary by introducing them to new experiences. Last school term, we set up a takeaway restaurant, which was very popular, where children pretended to use the phone for ordering. They also had to learn their addresses in order to place the order.

Skills for practice

Supporting speech, communication and language during activities

- Remember to speak clearly.
- Use a chatty style but allow children time to talk too.
- Avoid asking question after question.
- Expand children's statements so they have the opportunity to hear a detailed vocabulary.
- Remember that children often talk if they have heard something of interest.
- Do not correct children's speech, instead respond back using phrases correctly.
- Remember, talking should be fun.

Choosing books and reading stories

1. What should I do if a child shouts out when I am reading a group story?

Shouting out is common in children under 6 years. This is because listening involves thinking and young children are often thinking aloud. This is one reason why children benefit from being read to individually or in very small groups. The best strategy is often to nod, but carry on reading.

2. What books should I choose for 2-year-old children?

They should be well illustrated and have a short, simple story with plenty of repetition. Stories with animals are often popular.

3. How many children should be in a group for story time?

The fewest number possible! Children always benefit more from being able to see the pictures, talk about the story and answer questions.

Using a puppet

- Choose a puppet that you like and which fits your hand well.
- Bring the puppet close to you and cross your wrists – this will mean that children will not see that you are using your hand.
- Make slow, repeated movements.
- Make good eye contact with your puppet as if it were real.
- Do not take the puppet off while you are with children – instead take it off when you are out of sight.

Introduction

For babies and children to thrive, they need love, attention and careful support. This helps them to make relationships, express their feelings and emotions appropriately, and also gives them the confidence to try out new skills. The term 'personal, social and emotional development' is used to describe the skills and support needed by babies and children. When children have the support that they need, they go on to make friends, cope with strong and sometimes conflicting thoughts and emotions, and are able to show qualities such as perseverance. As an early years professional, understanding how to support children of all ages in this area will be key to your day-to-day work.

Assessment: You will be assessed by a series of assignments set by your teacher/tutor.

Learning aims

In this unit you will:

A   understand how the key person approach supports effective attachments

B   understand how to prepare and support children through transitions and significant events in their lives

C   understand the role of the early years professional in supporting children's personal, emotional and social development

D   support and promote children's positive behaviour.

Understanding how to promote children's behaviour and how this links to their development has really helped me on placement.

Joseph, *a student on an early years course*

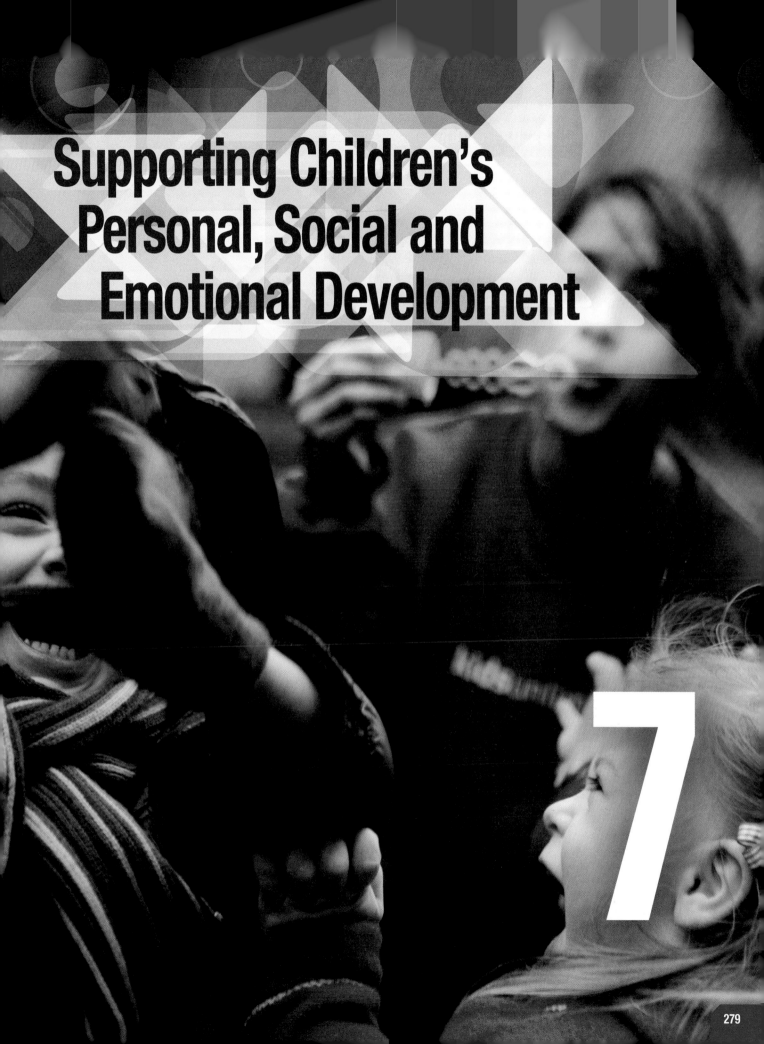

Supporting Children's Personal, Social and Emotional Development

7

Assessment Zone

This table shows what you must do in order to achieve a **Pass**, **Merit** or **Distinction** grade, and lists activities that relate to each learning aim.

Assessment criteria		
Pass	**Merit**	**Distinction**
Learning aim A: Understand how the key person approach supports effective attachments		
3A.P1 Explain how the key person approach supports effective attachments. **Assessment practice 7.1**	**3A.M1** Discuss the influence of attachment theory on the key person approach in early years settings. **Assessment practice 7.1**	
3A.P2 Explain the role of the key person in early years settings in meeting children's personal, emotional and social development needs. **Assessment practice 7.1**		
Learning aim B: Understand how to prepare and support children through transitions and significant events in their lives		
3B.P3 Explain how children may be affected by different transitions and significant events. **Assessment practice 7.2**	**3B.M2** Assess the contribution of early years professionals in supporting children through different transitions and significant events. **Assessment practice 7.2**	**3B.D1** Evaluate the extent to which early years professionals can support children through transitions and significant events. **Assessment practice 7.2**
3B.P4 I&CT English Explain how to prepare children in early years settings for different transitions and significant events. **Assessment practice 7.2**		
Learning aim C: Understand the role of the early years professional in supporting children's personal, emotional and social development		
3C.P5 Explain how to develop relationships with children in early years settings that support their personal, social and emotional development. **Assessment practice 7.3**	**3C.M3** Assess the success of particular techniques or approaches being used to support a child's personal, social and emotional development in relation to early years practice. **Assessment practice 7.3**	**3C.D2** Evaluate the techniques and approaches that early years professionals take in supporting a child's personal, social and emotional development. **Assessment practice 7.3**
3C.P6 Explain why discriminatory behaviour and attitudes should be challenged in early years settings. **Assessment practice 7.3**		

continued

Pass	Merit	Distinction
Learning aim D: Support and promote children's positive behaviour		
3D.P7 Describe different factors that may affect children's behaviour. **Assessment practice 7.4**	**3D.M4** Consistently and effectively promote and support children's positive behaviour appropriate to children at different ages and stages of development. **Assessment practice 7.4**	
3D.P8 Model and promote positive behaviours expected of children in the early years. **Assessment practice 7.4**		
3D.P9 **I&CT** Support children to manage their own behaviour and develop positive attitudes in relation to others. **Assessment practice 7.4**		

English English Functional Skills signposting

I&CT Information and Communication Technology Functional Skills signposting

How you will be assessed

This unit will be assessed by a series of internally assessed tasks set by your teacher/tutor. They will include practical tasks that will need to be carried out on placement, and that link to your Practical Evidence Portfolio. Throughout this unit you will find assessment practice activities that will help you work towards your assessment. Completing these activities will not mean that you have achieved a particular grade, but you will have carried out useful research or preparation that will be relevant when it comes to your final assignment.

In order for you to achieve the tasks in your assignment, it is important to check that you have met all of the Pass grading criteria. You can do this as you work your way through the assignment.

If you are hoping to gain a Merit or Distinction, you should also make sure that you present the information in your assignment in the style that is required by the relevant assessment criterion. For example, Merit and Distinction criteria will require you to discuss, assess and evaluate.

The assignment set by your teacher/tutor will consist of a number of tasks designed to meet the criteria in the table. This is likely to consist of a written assignment but may also include activities such as using case studies or observations from your placement setting.

Getting started

Make a list of **transitions** that are likely to happen in the first five years of children's lives, for example, starting school.

At the end of this unit, see how many more transitions you can add to your list.

A Understand how the key person approach supports effective attachments

All babies and children need to feel loved, reassured and nurtured. This usually comes from their parents or primary carers, but children also need this to continue when they are separated from their parents or primary carers. In this section we will look at the importance to children's overall development of receiving the love, reassurance and nurturing that they need. We will also look at how practitioners can 'step in' to support children when their parents are not with them.

The importance of strong attachments

There is something very interesting about the nature of child–adult **attachments**. It would seem that they give babies and children confidence that allows them to go out and explore, but also to develop further attachments and relationships. Children with secure attachments seem to find it easier to trust and accept the care and attention of other adults as well as other children. They also seem better placed to give care and attention, and show empathy.

> ### Key terms
>
>
>
> **Attachment** – a special relationship or bond between a child and someone who is emotionally involved with them.
>
> **Transitions** – changes in children's lives, especially in relation to adults who may be looking after them.

> ### Link
>
> Go to Unit 1: Section B to find more information about how attachments are formed.

The earliest attachments between parents and children seem to be the most significant, as they are often intense and enduring. Attachments with other adults who spend frequent and long periods with babies and children (such as in day care) are also important to children's overall wellbeing, as we will go on to see. It is worth noting that as well as the psychological effects of attachment, such as confidence and ability to control emotions, there are also physiological ones. These are only starting to be understood, but it is thought that when children do not have a strong attachment, they are likely to have higher levels of the stress hormone, cortisol. This is thought to be associated with a suppressed immune system and so children are more likely to have episodes of illness.

How strong attachments contribute to development in other areas

In Unit 1, we looked at attachment theory and how babies and children need to develop strong bonds with their parents or primary carers. When children are separated from their parents, even for a few hours, they need to have strong attachments with those looking after them. Strong attachments help babies and children to feel secure, loved and understood. This helps them to feel confident so that they can explore and try new things and also cope better in stressful situations. They are also more likely to relax and this in turn helps them to sleep. Table 7.1 gives practical examples of how strong attachments can influence development.

Factors that might affect parental attachment

Parents or a child's primary carers are key to children's wellbeing and it is important that strong attachments are made. There are, however, many factors that can affect parents' ability to attach.

Table 7.1 How strong attachments can influence development

Social and emotional development	
Making relationships	Children who have strong attachments find it easier to make relationships with others. They learn to trust other people and also to understand others' needs and feelings. Children who have poor attachments may find it harder to make meaningful relationships. As children learn a lot by playing with other children, this can be problematic.
Confidence	Children need a degree of confidence so that they can try out new things. Children are more likely to have confidence if they feel loved and nurtured.
Showing consideration for others: behaviour	Where children have strong attachments, they find it easier to show appropriate behaviours for the situation they are in. This comes over time, but children will find it easier if they have been shown consideration and warmth at an early age.
Controlling emotions	Everyone at all ages can feel angry, irritated, sad or react impulsively. Being understood can help children to manage these feelings as they develop.
Physical growth and development	
Sleep	Children are more likely to relax and find it easier to sleep.
Feeding (babies)	Children are more likely to feed well and so thrive.
Gross and fine motor skills	Children are more likely to develop new skills and to explore their environment. Their confidence will allow them to try to do things for themselves.
Cognitive development	
Concentration and perseverance	When babies and children are insecure or worried, they cannot focus their attention on what they are doing. They may be easily distracted or give up quickly. This reduces how much learning they can gain from what they are doing, e.g. if a child gives up after 2 minutes of a looking at a jigsaw puzzle, they will have missed out on learning about shapes and problem solving.
Confidence	Trying out new games, play or tasks will help a child learn new skills or think differently. If children are insecure, they are less likely to try out new things and hence miss out on learning.
Language development	
Developing receptive and expressive speech	Children who are strongly attached will often spend time listening and talking to the people to whom they are attached. They may spend time with them chatting and listening to stories and so acquire more language.
Practising speech with other children	Children practise language by playing with other children, especially from 3 years onwards. As attachment affects children's ability to make and maintain friends, some children may miss out if they cannot form good relationships with others.

Postnatal depression

For some mothers, a chemical imbalance affects their ability to attach to their baby. This can prevent the mother from demonstrating usual maternal behaviours such as gazing, eye contact, cuddling and soothing the child. Fortunately, postnatal depression can be treated and it is important that anyone working with new mothers looks out for the signs of depression.

Link

Go to Unit 5: Section A1 to find more information about the signs of depression.

Drug and alcohol abuse

As we saw in Unit 5, drug and alcohol abuse can affect the usual responses and feelings that parents have towards their children. They may not spend time holding, cuddling or appropriately responding to them. In some cases, parents may also harm their children as their mental balance is disturbed.

Child health

A child's health, particularly at birth, may affect parental attachment. Babies born prematurely, or with health issues, are likely to need care away from home. Physical contact between parent and child may be reduced by distance, the fragility of the child or physical barriers such as incubators. However, parents are now advised to spend as much time as possible with their child, including physical contact and talking to their child. Where their baby is cared for in an incubator, parents are encouraged to stroke and talk to them.

How research on attachment has influenced current practice

The importance of secure attachments and the need for children to have a substitute attachment when their parents are temporarily unavailable has shaped early years practice in many ways. Today, much of the good practice we see in early years settings relating to settling in children and preparing them for significant events in their lives has come about through an understanding of the work of attachment theorists such as John Bowlby, Mary Ainsworth and James and Joyce Robertson.

Recognising separation anxiety

Before attachment was fully understood, distressed children who were crying because their parents were no longer there were often seen as showing unwanted behaviour. Today, we know that distress is indicative of a child having a strong attachment and needing reassurance. We also know from Bowlby that separation anxiety is harmful for children and so steps should be taken to avoid children being distressed, for example preparing them for transitions. This is why settings should have settling-in policies that help children to feel comfortable with at least one member of staff before separation takes place.

Supporting parents

The work of Mary Ainsworth (1913–99), which we looked at in Unit 1, shows that children's attachments to their parents may not always be secure. The need to support parents with babies and young children is now a focus for early years. Attempts are made to recognise those mothers and families who, for a variety of reasons, may find it hard to form an attachment. This recognition is done by a variety of services including midwives during pregnancy and shortly after birth, health visitors and also family doctors. Groups such as baby massage, often held in children's centres, can help to support parents and carers in developing good attachments with their children. Early years professionals are also encouraged to offer support and identify when parents may need to access further help.

Link

Go to Unit 5: Section A1 to find more information about the reasons why families may find it hard to form an attachment to their child.

Substitute attachment

James Robertson (1911–88) and his wife, Joyce Robertson (1919–2013), were concerned that the effects of separation on young children were not recognised. James Robertson began filming children's behaviour when they were separated from their mothers, who were going into hospital. James Robertson made eight films showing children of different ages and receiving a range of care. In some of the films, the children are staying with the

Robertsons, and Joyce Robertson takes time to soothe, comfort and meet children's emotional as well as physical needs. In other films, children are staying with responsive foster carers. Outcomes for children who could form substitute attachments were considerably better than for those who had no adult supporting them. The idea behind offering children a substitute attachment is the basis of the **key person** system that is used now in early years settings.

Research

Find out more about the Robertsons' work, by reading about the films that were made at the time. You can access the Robertson Films website by going to www.pearsonhotlinks.co.uk and searching for this ISBN: 9781447970965.

The role of the key person in establishing attachments

To help babies and children cope with the otherwise detrimental effects of separation from their parents, it is now good practice for every child to be allocated a key person. (In some early years frameworks, such as the EYFS in England, this is also a legal requirement.)

A key person is someone who takes particular responsibility for a child's emotional needs and does this by encouraging the child to make an attachment with them. This special relationship helps the child to gain comfort and reassurance in their parents' absence. As well as working intensely with the baby or child, it is also the role of the key person to develop a relationship with the child's family. In this way, the child's physical and emotional needs can be closely met. From 2012, in England the key person also has a role in supporting parents to engage in learning activities at home that will complement those in the early years settings.

Why babies and children need an emotional bond with a key person

We know from research done over a number of years, including that of Bowlby, Ainsworth and the Robertsons, that children become distressed if they

are separated from their parents and no substitute attachment is available. When we are stressed, a hormone called cortisol is released. Though all of us secrete cortisol, high levels of cortisol that are sustained over a period appear to be associated with poorer health. Research has shown that children who are separated from their parents without a substitute attachment are more likely to have raised levels of cortisol. The effects of this are thought to put children at increased risk of illness and may also affect their ability to learn.

In addition to these **physiological effects** of stress, there are **psychological** ones, too. It would appear that children who are separated from their parents and have no substitute attachment may find it hard to cope with separations in the future, as the distress is in some way remembered.

Key terms

Key person – a practitioner designated to take responsibility for a child's emotional wellbeing by having a strong attachment with them and a good relationship with their parents.

Physiological effects – changing or influencing normal bodily functions.

Psychological effects – changing the pattern of behaviour or thinking.

How the key person approach is applied in different types of settings

Though it is good practice for all babies and children to have a key person, the systems used can vary in different settings, depending on the size of the setting, the age of the children and, crucially, the number of hours that children are spending in the setting.

Day care

Most day-care settings will take children from 6 months, or sometimes earlier, through until they start school. It is usual for day care to operate for at least ten hours per day and for 50 weeks a year. As staff are likely to be working a 37- to 40-hour week with holidays and time off for lunch breaks, it is rare for one person alone to act as key person to a particular child. A way of working known as a 'buddy' system is therefore often used.

Buddy systems

A buddy system means that the key person role will be shared between two staff members. The idea is that when one key person is not available, the other member of staff can step in. This allows for continuity of care and means that children do not suffer separation anxiety because their 'key person' is not there.

Sessional care

Many children in preschools and maintained nurseries will attend sessions of around three hours each day. In many preschools and nurseries, the child is likely to be allocated a single key person, but another member of staff may frequently step in to support the child in their absence.

Home-based care

Most, but not all, childminders and nannies work alone and so act as the sole key person for children. Childminders may have children for sessions or children may come for 40 or 50 hours a week. Where children are looked after by more than one childminder, it is more common for the child to develop special bonds with both adults and so both people may become key for the child.

Crèches

There are many different models of crèches, ranging from those that only see children for very short periods to those that see children for regular sessions. It is good practice for children who attend regularly, but for short sessions, to have a sole key person, but also to become familiar with other staff. When children attend 'one-off' sessions, they may be allocated a key person who will reassure and comfort them, but in such a short time, it is unlikely that an attachment can be made.

Reception classes

In many reception classes, the teacher will be the key person for all of the children as they have the responsibility to work with and share information with parents. In some schools, teaching assistants or nursery nurses may act as key persons in terms of building close relationships but then pass on information about the child to the teacher so that they, in turn, can report to parents.

Theory into practice

There has been much debate as to whether a teacher with 25 or so children can make genuine attachments to children given the pressures of time.

Find out how schools in your area operate a key person system.

How the key person system supports effective relationships with parents

The key person role is not just about working with children. When key person systems work well, they are the starting point for effective relationships with the setting. Parents and carers become used to and enjoy meeting the person who is directly looking after their child. From this starting point, parents can develop a wider relationship with the setting. The benefits of effective relationships with parents include:

- strong involvement and interest in the care and education of the child
- confidence and trust in what the setting is doing
- effective information sharing.

In addition, effective relationships can benefit families who need additional support. Using the relationship with the key person, parents can be signposted to other services and advice, including those run in children's centres such as dads' clubs, job clubs and 'stay and play' sessions.

Communication with parents

Good communication with parents and carers is essential to the key person role. It helps us to work in partnership with parents and, as part of this, to provide continuity of care and approach. Key persons should therefore be good at talking and building a relationship with parents so that information can be easily shared.

As we have seen in Unit 4, we may need to talk to parents about subjects such as diet or skin products or their approach to helping their child fall asleep. We may also need to work with parents to provide consistent approaches to managing unwanted behaviour. This requires good communication skills and active listening, as well as **empathy** and warmth. Where relationships between key persons and parents are strong, children seem to find the transition between home and setting easier.

In England, key persons are also expected to take a role in supporting parents with learning activities at home, such as teaching children to read, cook and play games. Many will share resources and ideas with parents and tell them what their child has enjoyed within the setting.

Key term

Empathy – the ability to feel or understand the emotions of others.

How children's language and social development benefit from the key person system

Babies' and children's early language development is closely linked to the relationships they build with adults. A strong key person relationship helps babies and children in many ways.

- **Amount of exposure** – When babies and children have strong attachments to their key person, they spend time interacting with them. This exposure and strong attachment helps them gain language, and makes the learning fun.

- **Tuning in** – For babies and toddlers, it is essential that they spend time with their key person. This is because they are 'tuning in' to the tones and meanings of words. As we all speak using different tones and may also use different expressions, a baby who is being handled and spoken to by several different people may not be as quick to 'tune in' to the meanings of words.

- **Acknowledging and responding** – It can be difficult to understand what babies and toddlers are trying to say. This is because of speech immaturities. If you spend time with the same children, it becomes easier for you to understand them. A strong relationship with the children's parents also means that you may know what

children's home words are for things and also what they have been doing. If children repeatedly find that their vocalisations are not being responded to, they are likely to talk less.

Providing age-appropriate physical contact

Babies and young children need physical contact with their key person, particularly if they spend long periods of time away from their parents. Holding a child's hand or allowing a child to cuddle up to you while you share a story sends out reassuring signals to a child. Physical contact has been shown to reduce anxiety, and hence cortisol levels, so it is important when children are upset.

Safe working practices

Although it is important to offer children physical contact, you need to be aware of doing so in a way that is appropriate and empowers them.

Appropriate contact is very much dependent on the age of the child and the setting that you are in. You will need to find out and follow your setting's policy, but it is likely that the policy will state that physical contact will only occur when you are in sight of other adults. Of course, this will not be the case if you are working in home-based care.

Offering contact

It is good practice to offer physical contact and to observe a child's immediate reaction – if you offer a hand, the child may indicate that they are not interested by shaking their head or moving away slightly. Insisting on physical contact is highly inappropriate unless a child's life is in danger.

Recognising children's wishes

Babies and toddlers will often indicate that they need a cuddle by reaching out to you. It is important that you follow their wishes as this helps them to learn that they are in control of what happens to their bodies. It is also important to let a child's hand go or put a toddler back on the floor at the first indication that they have had enough.

Is the level of physical contact between the practitioners and children acceptable here?

Examples of appropriate physical contact

Table 7.2 shows some examples of appropriate physical contact with children of different ages.

Recognising that a child has made a good attachment with their key person

When children have a strong attachment with their key person, they are likely to show several attachment behaviours.

Eye contact

Babies and children make eye contact with people they are attached to. Toddlers will, for example, glance up from a play activity to check that 'their' adult is still there.

Table 7.2 Appropriate physical contact with children

Age of children	Type of contact
Babies	Should be picked up and cuddled. May be kissed (subject to parental wishes) but never on the lips. Sitting on adult's lap.
Toddlers	Picked up and cuddled at a toddler's request. Sitting on adult's lap.
Preschool children	Hand holding, snuggling in next to an adult – in some settings sitting on adult's lap is allowed. Cuddled if the child requests it.
School-age children	Hand holding. Hugging, but only if the child is seriously upset.

Proximity

Babies and toddlers will often want to stay close to their key person and if they play out of sight, they will quickly come back into 'range'.

Seeking behaviours

When there are strong attachments, children will seek out their key person. They may want to show them something that they have done or ask or demonstrate that they want their key person to play with them.

Reassurance

A good test of attachment is whether a child looks for reassurance from their key person if they are feeling upset. Children may also only be ready to separate from their parents if they know that they can be cuddled by their key person.

Physical contact

Babies and young children need physical contact. It helps them feel reassured and is good for their emotional wellbeing. Having said this, babies and children will only accept physical contact from people that they are comfortable with and with whom they have a bond.

Noticing and objecting to absence

Where a child has a key person, they should notice whether or not that person is present. Older children may be disappointed if the key person disappears, but younger children may cry or even show signs of separation anxiety unless there is a 'buddy system' in place. Key persons with strong bonds are likely to find that their key children will wait by the door if they go out of the room.

Can you see how comfortable this child looks with his key person?

body language, style of interaction and also how you are showing interest in the child, for example, by getting down to their level. You should also think about how you are working with parents to gain information from them about how best to form a relationship with the child.

> ### Link
>
> Go to Unit 1: Section B to find more information about separation anxiety.

> ### Theory into practice
>
> In your work placement, ask if you could observe a toddler or a 3-year-old child to see if they are showing signs of attachment to their key person.

Observing attachment behaviours

If you are a key person to a child it is important that you check that your key child has attached to you. If this has not happened, you should reflect on your

Assessment practice 7.1

3A.P1 | 3A.P2 | 3A.M1

You have been asked to review how effective the key person system is in your setting. As part of this work, you need to write a report that looks at the principles behind the key person approach. Your manager has also asked you to look at how the key person approach supports effective attachments.

Use observations or examples from your work placements, as well as further reading, as evidence to help you write the report.

Your background report should cover the following:

- the importance of attachment to children's overall development
- the role of the key person in supporting effective attachments and in meeting children's personal, social and emotional development needs
- how attachment theory has influenced the key person approach in early years settings.

B Understand how to prepare and support children through transitions and significant events in their lives

At some time or another babies and young children are likely to face a change of carer or setting. When this is managed well, children's anxiety levels are lower and they will find it easier to adapt. This section looks at ways in which we can help children cope with the move from one carer to another and from one setting to another. The term used for these changes is 'transition'. Almost all children will experience transitions between different settings and between an early years setting and a school. However, some children will experience other significant events in their lives outside of a setting, such as the birth of a sibling, moving house, a family breakdown or even the death of a family member.

Types of transitions

There are a number of different transitions that occur in children's lives. Recognising the many transitions that children make, including those on a day-to-day basis, can help us to plan for them and also find ways of lowering children's anxiety.

Day-to-day transitions

Moving from home to setting is a transition for children. In addition, there will be many children who may be moving from home to setting and then to another setting later in the day. An example of this would be a child who goes to a childminder who then takes the child on to nursery or school.

As well as 'formal care and education', it is also important to recognise that many families use friends and relatives. This is known as **informal care**. This might mean that as well as seeing a childminder and a teacher, the child might be picked up by a friend of the family for the rest of the afternoon.

Key term

Informal care – when parents make childcare arrangements with friends or family who are unregistered.

Day-to-day transitions within settings

As adults we often forget that even relatively small transitions within the same setting can be stressful for children. In school, children make transitions between classrooms, playtime, assembly and hall time. In some nurseries and preschools, children may go to particular areas for certain periods of the day or to certain staff members for some activities. These are all transitions.

These children are all ready to go outside for PE. This is a transition from the classroom.

Moving from one family to another

Some children will be moving from one family to another as well as managing day-to-day transitions. This may happen because parents have shared custody and children stay with one parent for some of the time and then move to another.

Moving from one setting or practitioner to another

As children grow, they are also likely to experience a change in their key person. They may move from a preschool into a school or from a childminder into a preschool. It is also worth remembering that transition does not have to be a physical change of environment – for example, children who are looked after at home will face a transition if their au pair or nanny leaves. In day care it is usual for children to change rooms as they become older. This again is a significant transition.

Changes in friendship groups

As children grow, they are likely to develop strong friendships with peers. When children change settings, early years professionals or groups, it is worth remembering that they may be changing friendship groups as well. As children develop attachments to other children, this can be stressful for them.

Looked-after children

Looked-after children are likely to experience multiple transitions. First, they will be in the care of the local authority and have left the family home. They are also likely to be in **foster care** placements and these may not last long, depending on the child's and the foster family's situation. Some children may then go on to be adopted.

Key terms

Foster care – temporary care in foster families for looked-after children who are not with their parents.

Looked-after children – when the local authority has responsibility for the care of children.

Changes to family structures

Some children may face a change to their family structure. This may be through divorce, relationship breakdown or bereavement. There may also be additions to a child's family such as the birth of a sibling or the arrival of a parent's new partner and their children. For children, change to their usual family structure is likely to be very stressful.

Changes in environment

Children also make transitions when they move home or even when we take them on outings.

Case study

How many transitions?

Andrea is 4 years old. Her parents work full time, but they have managed to organise childcare for her every day. Before school on Mondays, Tuesdays and Wednesdays, she goes to a childminder who has children in the same school. She also goes to an after-school club on those days. On Thursdays, before and after school, she goes to her grandmother's house and her grandmother takes her to a swimming class. On Friday, she is sometimes taken to school by her father if he is free; otherwise, she goes to a neighbour's flat and the neighbour takes her to school with their own children. On Friday afternoon her aunt picks her up.

1 How many different transitions is Andrea experiencing in the week?

2 How many adults will she be with over the course of a week?

3 Why is informal care a major part of many children's lives?

Effects of transitions and significant events on children

Each type of transition may affect children, although the effects may be relatively short-lived if there is otherwise consistency in attachments with the important adults in their lives. This means that moving home may be problematic, but if children are still in the same setting, in the same friendship group and with the same family and practitioner attachments, it would be unusual for children to remain stressed. On the other hand, a child whose parents have separated and is now moving between two family units is likely to need longer-term support.

Table 7.3 shows some of the possible effects on children. Note that some of those listed apply only to transitions that are causing the child enormous levels of stress, such as a bereavement.

Discussing transitions and significant events with parents and children

Table 7.3 shows the many effects that transition can have on children. As transitions can create stress for children, our role is to look for ways of minimising stress and also supporting children through it. The starting point for this is to work closely with parents so that we know what is happening in children's lives and also how they are reacting.

We know that children do remember stressful separations and so when talking to parents about current transitions, it is important to find out if children have already experienced other transitions and how these worked out. Below are some points that may be useful when discussing events and transitions with parents.

- What is currently happening, and how is the child feeling or reacting?
- What does the child know about what is due to happen?
- How does the parent feel about the transition?
- Has the child had past experiences of transitions – what were they and how did the child react?
- How does the child normally react to stress?
- What helps the child to cope with stress?

Strategies to prepare children for transitions and significant events

There are many strategies that we can use with children to prepare them for planned and unplanned transitions or significant events. How we will support

Table 7.3 Possible effects of transition on children

Type of transition	Possible effects
Physical	• Disturbed sleep and sleeping patterns, including waking in the night, refusal to go to bed • Disturbed eating habits, including over-eating or becoming anxious about food • Toileting accidents when they had been clean and dry in the day, bedwetting (enuresis) • Attempt to go back into nappies – by young children who were just toilet trained • Frequent illnesses such as cold, flu • **Regression** or refusal in self-care tasks such as feeding and dressing • Repetitive movements, e.g. head banging, sucking and rocking
Communication and language	• Stammering • **Selective mutism** • Withdrawal • Lack of interest in communicating with others, including peers
Cognitive	• Difficulty in concentrating • Forgetfulness • Difficulty in following instructions • Lower interest in activities
Emotional	• Increase in temper tantrums for children under 4 years • Temper tantrums in older children • Increase in impulsivity • Crying and tearfulness • Outbursts of anger often directed at those with whom the child has a strong attachment • Clinginess sometimes combined with angry gestures, such as hitting
Social	• Attention-seeking through unwanted behaviours • Antisocial behaviours that are unusual for the child and not age-appropriate, e.g. biting, spitting • Withdrawal or lack of interest in joining other children for play • Solitary play activities

children will depend on our discussion with parents, the type of transition and also the children's age and stage of development.

Discussion with children

Discussing what is going to happen can help children to prepare. How much information we give them may depend on the type of transition, as some things may be quite overwhelming and children may need time to digest information and ask questions. A useful strategy can be to ask general questions to find out children's current knowledge and understanding of the transition.

The timing of any discussion is important too. Telling young children too far in advance can make them anxious, but leaving things until just before they happen can be equally problematic. That is why it is helpful to work with parents so that timescales and messages are agreed.

Key terms

Regression – to move backwards to a previous stage.

Selective mutism – where a child is unable to talk although they have the ability to do so.

Books

There is a range of books that can help children understand more about a transition that is about to take place. Books can sometimes be used to help children make connections and as a way of allowing them to raise questions. A book about the arrival of a baby brother might prompt a child to say that their mother has a big tummy and she is going to have a baby too! Books can also be used after a transition to help children explore their emotions and feelings. This can be particularly helpful for transitions such as bereavement, divorce and separation.

Photographs

As well as books, photographs can be helpful. A child who is anxious about going on holiday may be interested to see photographs of an airport, while a child who is going to a new nursery might be interested in seeing a photograph of their new key person.

Storytelling

Simple stories can also be used to help children prepare for changes in their lives. Stories may be about a character of a similar age and situation so that a child understands the connections.

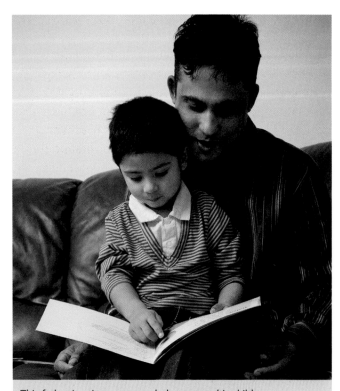

This father is using a story to help prepare his child for school.

How to support transitions

Wherever possible, we should be looking for ways for children and their families to get to know us before they start in the setting. This is why, in most early years settings, time will be spent with children before they join us. Ideally, the key person should focus on playing and building a relationship with the child. The following activities are very popular and seem to be effective.

Visits to the setting

Children and parents need to visit before they start at the setting to look around, explore and meet children and staff. It is also helpful for children to know where things are on a visit, especially toilets and changing rooms as well as toys and resources. It is helpful if visits are done when the setting is working smoothly so that parents and children can see a calm setting. It is good practice for the key person to spend time with the child and the parents on these visits. This allows the child to start building a relationship with the key person. Many children will need more than one visit to the setting and it can be helpful to give parents instructions on what they should do at each visit with the aim that, little by little, the child becomes used to spending time with the key person while the parent is close by but not heavily involved.

Home visits

Many early years settings will carry out home visits. Ideally, they should be made by the child's key person. The idea is to see the child in their own home, where they and their parents may feel more relaxed. Home visits often allow parents to ask questions or share information that they might not have wanted to raise when surrounded by other adults. During the home visit, the key person should interact and play with the child. It can be helpful to take a photograph of the visit so that the child has a memory of this when they start at the setting.

Visits to other settings or colleagues

Sometimes we may need to help children make the transition to another setting or to another staff member. We may support this by taking the child to visit the new setting or staff member they will be working with. This will require parental consent. It is important when doing this to allow the future key person to spend time with the child. We may stay next to the child so that they feel safe, but keep a 'low profile' so that the future key person can get to know the child. This can be a good time to share information and answer questions about the child.

Welcoming a child's future key person

It is common for reception teachers and other people such as childminders to visit early years settings to see their 'future' children there. It is important that we are welcoming to visitors and that we help them get to know children. Often this is a good time to share information informally with them. As with other aspects of sharing information, it is important to gain parental consent before doing this.

Working with colleagues and other professionals to support transitions

For some types of transition, we will need to work with colleagues or other professionals in order to help the child and the family. We may need to seek information from another service or professional. All information sharing that is specific to the child and the family requires parental consent, unless there is a child protection issue. If no consent is given, general information about the structure of the service and advice about supporting transitions can be given but no specific information about the child or the family can be shared.

The type of information that we may need or others will need from us will very much depend on the type of transition the child will be experiencing. It can be worth preparing questions or information in advance of having a conversation with a colleague or other professional so that you can focus your discussion on the key points. The following are some general points that might be raised when sharing information:

- structure and role of the service or setting
- specific policies or **ethos** within the setting
- how long the child has been coming
- what the child enjoys doing
- how the child reacts to stress
- how you can comfort or reassure the child.

Key term

Ethos – the philosophy or approach used by a setting that affects the practice.

Remaining in contact

Where children and their families are using several settings or services, it will be important to have ways of staying in contact. This requires parental consent, but it is worth seeking, as when a child is moving from one setting to another it is important for the various key persons to keep in contact. This is sometimes done using a notebook that travels with the child in which activities, incidents and thoughts are jotted down. It is good practice to do this with the child.

Research

Find out about Winston's Wish, an organisation that supports children who are facing or have suffered a bereavement of someone close to them. You can access the organisation's website by going to www.pearsonhotlinks.co.uk and searching for this ISBN: 9781447970965.

Support the settling-in process

Settling in at a new setting needs to be viewed as a process. We have seen that babies and young children are likely to have separation anxiety if they have not made a substitute attachment before their parents leave them at the setting. This means that the focus of settling in should be on facilitating this attachment. As children do not make immediate attachments, a series of visits either to the setting or to the child's home will need to be made so that the child becomes used to seeing their key person and interacting with them.

Once this process is under way, it can be useful to check whether the child is starting to feel comfortable with their key person. Parents can be asked to withdraw their attention little by little. They may start by picking up a magazine while the key person and child are playing. Then they may wander across to the other side of the room. If the child is happy to keep on playing, the parent might be able to tell the child that they are popping out for a couple of

Collecting information

Asia is due to start at a new childminder's on Thursday. She was previously at a nursery, but she was unhappy. The childminder has asked if she could gain some information about Asia from the nursery, but the parents have not given consent. They have not yet told the nursery that Asia will be leaving. The childminder believes that it would be helpful to find out more about the nursery's routines and ethos and so she prepares some questions and makes a phone call to the nursery. She tells the manager that she is a childminder and she may at some time in the future be minding one of the children. She does not reveal the name of the child or any information that might allow the nursery to identify her. She asks the manager if she can ask a few quick questions. She asks about the opening times of the nursery, how they help children to fall asleep and other questions relating to the routine and care of children.

1 Why couldn't the childminder ask questions about Asia?

2 Why was it still important that she found out about the day-to-day running of the nursery?

3 How might she use the information to help Asia make the transition?

minutes. When the child is able to cope with this and be reassured by the key person, it is likely then that longer periods of separation can begin to take place. It is good practice to go at the child's pace wherever possible, but key to this is that the child and the key person need to develop a relationship.

Activities to build relationships

There is no single way of building a relationship with a child, but it is important that during the settling-in process, the key person finds a way of 'befriending' the child. This requires responsiveness and acute observational skills. If you rush a child by, for example, touching them before they are ready, they are likely to become fearful.

Puppets

Puppets can help young children form a relationship with their key person. This is because they are intriguing for young children and so temporarily deflect the child's focus away from their parent onto the key person. Children will often touch a puppet, make friends with the puppet and then with you.

Blowing bubbles

Children of all ages seem to enjoy bubbles. Blowing bubbles so that a child can catch them can be very engaging and can encourage a child to approach you and ask you to blow some more.

Cooking

Older children often find it easier to make relationships when they are involved in an activity with other children. Cooking is a great activity as children are busy and there is likely to be plenty of talk.

Checking that a child has settled in

The starting point for settling in is whether the child can separate from the parent without immediate distress. It is important though to recognise that this in itself is only one facet of settling in. Figure 7.1 shows other things that we should be looking out for. Note that if you do not observe these, it may be that the child needs longer with their key person or, in rare cases, that the child needs a different key person.

Recognising signs of concern or distress

Table 7.3 showed how stress caused by transitions might affect a child. It is important to keep an eye out for these and also to find out from a child's parents about the child's behaviour at home. Finding out how a child is doing at home is important, as this way we can build a picture of their overall reaction to the current transition. Though it is usual for children to take a while to adapt to new situations, if a child appears to be showing serious signs of distress, it is important that careful thought is given as to how to help the child.

It may be that in extreme cases, such as food refusal or selective mutism, referrals are made to other services. These can be arranged through a family

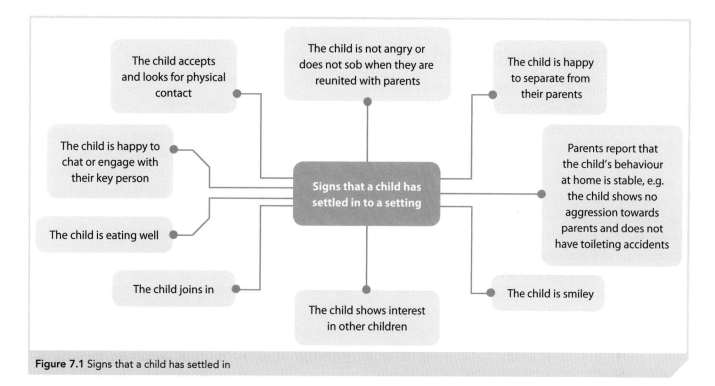

Figure 7.1 Signs that a child has settled in

doctor or sometimes a children's centre, but would need parental consent. In the case of looked-after children, the child's social worker should be informed in addition to the person with the direct care of

the child. Recognising that children's distress is not temporary and that the symptoms are significant is essential to prevent the child experiencing further distress and potentially worsening symptoms.

Assessment practice 7.2   3B.P3 | 3B.P4 | 3B.M2 | 3B.D1

The staff of a children's centre work with many children who experience a range of common transitions and some significant life events. A training guide is being written to support new staff. You have been asked to contribute several sections, including:

- the effects of transitions and significant events on children

- ways that early years professionals can work to help children with transitions and significant events.

Use observations or examples from your work placements as well as further reading as evidence to help you write the guide.

C Understand the role of the early years professional in supporting children's personal, emotional and social development

Early years professionals have an important role to play in supporting children's social and emotional development. Babies and children need to have very positive experiences in their early years so that they

can go on to make strong relationships and manage their emotions. It is always important to remember that this takes time and is also linked to a child's overall development.

Theories and models of self-esteem development

In Unit 1, we looked at the development of self-concept and self-esteem. We saw how children learn about themselves mainly through the way that others respond to them. This is often referred to as the 'looking glass' effect. It has major implications for the way that adults respond to and work with children. If children frequently see and hear that adults are not positive about them, they are likely to come to the conclusion that they are not likeable people. On the other hand, children who gain genuine warmth, respect and high regard from adults are more likely to develop a positive self-concept. In Susan Harter's model of self-esteem the development of a strong self-concept is essential as it means that when the child becomes older, they are more likely to develop strong self-esteem.

Link

Go to Unit 1: Section B to find more information about the development of self-concept and self-esteem.

Praise

Children need to be praised for their achievements, but not all praise should be conditional on success. Children need to feel liked and valued for 'just being'.

Warmth

Children can tell when adults really like them and feel warm towards them. Adults who are warm towards children listen to them, are interested in what they are doing, but also offer appropriate physical contact and are often playful.

Acceptance

It is impossible for children to show positive behaviours every minute of every day. Accepting that children will sometimes forget to say 'thank you' or may not feel like being cooperative is therefore important. Children who are repeatedly made to feel guilty are less likely to become confident.

Avoiding comparisons

As part of children feeling that they are cared for and accepted unconditionally, it is important not to keep making comparisons between children. 'I've just asked James to do the same thing and he didn't make a fuss' is the kind of comment that can be quite damaging if used repeatedly.

Encouraging self-efficacy

It is useful if children, even as babies and toddlers, feel that they are involved but also able to do things for themselves. This might be simple tasks such as feeding and helping with dressing themselves but also choosing what to play with. This is sometimes known as **self-efficacy** and helps children to feel that they are capable and competent. This in turn supports a strong self concept.

Key term

Self-efficacy – the understanding that you are able to do things for yourself.

Theory into practice

In your work setting look out for different ways in which children are given opportunities to do things for themselves to promote their self-efficacy.

How understanding Theory of Mind helps adults to support children to develop social skills

Link

Go to Unit 1: Section A to find more information about theory of mind.

It is thought that children's ability to understand what others might be thinking is a key skill in their social development. This ability is sometimes referred to as 'theory of mind' and it is thought that children who may have an autism spectrum disorder have difficulties in this specific area.

Theory of mind allows a child to work out what others might be feeling and why, even if the other's thoughts are different to theirs. There is a well-known test that can be used to see if a child has developed theory of mind, known as the Sally Anne test. It would seem that most children have acquired this by 4 or 5 years old.

Understanding that it takes a while for children to develop theory of mind is useful for practitioners. It means that we cannot always expect very young children to interpret the reasons why others are doing things or to understand the impact of their own actions on others.

While it is thought that theory of mind is linked to children's cognitive development and so cannot be 'fast tracked', we can help children by explaining what others might be thinking and feeling, e.g. 'Sarah hasn't got anyone to play with. Do you think that she might be feeling sad?'

Theory into practice

In the Sally Anne test, a child is shown two dolls, Sally and Anne, and a story is told and acted with the two dolls. The child sees Sally put some marbles in her basket and then go out to play. The child then sees 'naughty' Anne take Sally's marbles from the basket and put them in a box. Then Sally is brought back in. The child is asked where Sally will go to find her marbles. Children who are starting to acquire theory of mind will point to the basket as they understand that Sally does not know that the marbles have been moved to the box.

- Try out the Sally Anne test with children of different ages and see which children are starting to develop theory of mind.

The role of observations

One of the ways in which adults can support children's personal, social and emotional development is to be aware of their needs, but also their next steps.

Transitions and significant events

It is essential to observe children during transitions and significant events. Being in a new place and potentially being separated from a parent or carer is stressful for children. Observing a child will mean that any nervousness or uncertainty shown by the child can be picked up and the adult can immediately offer reassurance. As part of observing

children during transition, we need to be able to recognise that children have genuinely developed strong relationships with their key person, with older children and their peers.

Assessing progress

We have seen that children's social and emotional development usually changes over time. Although toddlers find it hard to play with other children, it is usual that by 4 years they will have developed some friendships. It is therefore important to recognise the progress that children have made so that they are given more opportunities to further develop their skills, or thoughts can be given as to why they may not have made the expected progress.

Monitoring behaviour

Children's behaviour needs to be observed for several reasons. First, we need to think about whether children are showing behaviours typical of their age/ stage of development. This should help you to think about ensuring that activities and expectations are appropriate. How children are feeling and coping with stress often plays out in their behaviour. It is therefore helpful to monitor behaviour, as it might be a sign that a child is finding it difficult to cope with a change within the family such as the birth of a sibling, the separation of parents or change of setting. Finally, another reason for monitoring behaviour is to consider whether a child is showing any behaviours that may indicate that they have been or are being harmed.

Professional boundaries with children

While it is important that we build strong relationships with children and their parents, we have to understand that there are certain professional boundaries that we need to keep. Children and their parents do rely on us and this requires us to remain professional though friendly.

Physical contact

As we saw earlier, it is important that physical contact and use of language remain appropriate and in line with a child's age and stage of development. You must also ensure that you are working within your setting's policy and in line with parents' wishes.

Details of own personal life

Children and parents do like to hear some details about our lives but it is important that we are careful how much we say about our personal lives. This is a sensitive area, but overall nothing you say should cause any concern to either a child or a parent; our focus is to work with them and so parents should not feel they need to care for us or have concerns about our suitability.

Case study

Too much information

Jaydee is 4 years old. Her mother noticed that she was unusually quiet when she picked her up. That night at bedtime, Jaydee asked what happened if someone was 'off their head'. Her mother asked her who had said this and Jaydee replied that one of the staff had told a group of children to be quiet because she had a headache and another member of staff had called over that she shouldn't have 'got off her head' the night before.

1 Why was this language and conversation inappropriate in the setting?

2 Why was Jaydee's mother upset on hearing that this had been said?

3 How might this comment affect the trust between Jaydee's mother and the staff in the setting?

Skills to develop trusting relationships with children

It is essential that we create the right conditions for children to develop strong relationships with us. This is vital if you are a key person to a child, as your role is to create a strong attachment. There are many skills that contribute to this, some of which we looked at in Unit 6, as part of how to communicate with children.

Eye contact

Babies and children are primed to notice our eyes, and strong eye contact is linked closely to building relationships. Often with children that we do not know well, it is a good idea to 'gaze' and then look away. This is because sustained eye contact with someone you do not know well can feel uncomfortable.

Sensitive communication, listening and showing empathy

Sensitive communication requires a number of skills including being able to listen carefully, showing interest in what a child is saying or, in the case of babies, being interested in what they are pointing at. Sensitive communication is also about our tone of voice and whether we sound warm, interested and kind. Children also need us to be empathetic, which is about the way that we show our understanding of how they are feeling. It is good practice, for example, if a child is looking sad after waving goodbye to a parent, to acknowledge this rather than 'chivvying' the child along. It may be that we ask the child if a cuddle is needed as well as reassuring the child that the parent will come back later.

Playfulness

Babies and children often have a strong sense of humour. This means that it is helpful if adults have a playful style when this is appropriate. This may mean smiling or pretending to do something that makes a child laugh. Playfulness does need to be appropriate, as children may copy your actions.

See how this adult and child are having fun together!

Supporting children's emotional wellbeing and resilience

There are several ways in which adults can work with children to help them feel secure and also develop independence. Having a sense of independence will in turn help to make children more **resilient**.

> **Key term**
>
> **Resilient** – being able to recover quickly from different or difficult situations.

Providing choices

Providing choices for children can help them to develop self-efficacy. This is because they learn to make decisions for themselves. How much choice children should be given and over what, needs to be tailored to the child's stage of development. It is not fair for children to be given a choice only for the adult to intervene because their choice was inappropriate – choices have to be genuine ones! Child-initiated play is one of the key ways in which most early years settings give opportunities for children to make choices. In addition, there are other simple ways of giving children choices, for example:

- cooking activities – choosing what to put into a salad or how to bake a cake
- books – choosing which books to share with an adult
- mealtimes – choosing where to sit and even the colour of plates or beakers.

Encouraging independence and praising effort

As well as providing opportunities for choice, from the earliest age children need opportunities to show some independence. This may be through child-initiated play rather than just adult-directed activities, but also through day-to-day activities such as dressing, serving their own food, pouring drinks and choosing when to go to the toilet. It often takes more time for a child to feed and dress themselves, but it is extremely important for children's emotional development and, as we have seen earlier, it supports children's sense of self-efficacy. In order to support

children's independence, it can be helpful to make sure that children have sufficient time, but also that their efforts are noticed, praised and acknowledged. This may be in the form of praise, but also through making a commentary of what the child can now do for themselves.

Routines

Most babies and young children thrive on a little bit of predictability. This means that having some routines is important for children. Not every moment of the day needs to be regulated as this can be stifling and unstimulating, but there are some key points each day where establishing a routine can be helpful. Figure 7.2 shows these routines. Mealtimes and snack times should be opportunities when babies and children can develop some skills for independence, such as feeding themselves.

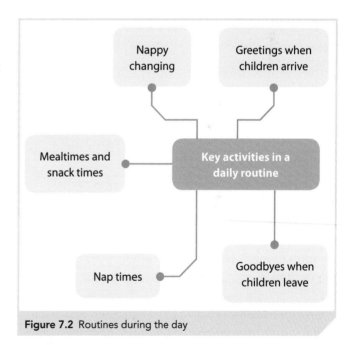

Figure 7.2 Routines during the day

Realistic boundaries

Children seem to need boundaries in order to become secure. They need to know what is and is not acceptable behaviour within the setting. Boundaries should relate closely to the children's age and stage of development, so while we might expect a 4-year-old child with typical development to wait to take their turn when playing a game, we may need to remind a younger child or accept that a toddler will struggle to wait.

Setting boundaries

Boundaries should be set with a clear rationale, such as health and safety, fairness and being considerate towards others. The rationale should be explained calmly to children. With older children, it is good practice for them to be involved in some boundary setting as this is good for their own development. They may, for example, be able to provide rules for where a ball game should be played or how they will ensure that everyone can join in an activity.

The importance of friendships

Friendships are very important to children as they develop. This starts early on with babies being very excited by looking at other babies. Toddlers will often enjoy copying and playing alongside other toddlers. **Reciprocal** and **cooperative friendships** begin when children are around 3 years old.

Key terms

Cooperative friendship – when children negotiate, play or agree what to do with each other.

Reciprocal friendship – when children take equal or similar pleasure in being in each other's company.

Friendships help children in a variety of ways. First, they are the bedrock of many play activities, which in themselves can support children's overall development. Children's self-concept is developed through friendships as they note how their peers respond to them. Children who have positive responses from peers are likely to become more confident in dealing with others. Children who have a shaky start may, on the other hand, have less confidence about approaching and playing with other children. By the age of 5 years, most children should have at least one strong friendship. If not, it is worth looking at ways of supporting the child.

Observing friendships

It is helpful to note whether children are starting to make friends from around 3 years or whether any child is being regularly excluded from play. This is important because a child who is regularly excluded may be missing out on gaining confidence and the developmental benefits that having friends brings.

Theory into practice

Ask your placement if you can observe a group of children aged 3 years or over for an hour.

- Do any of the children have reciprocal friendships?
- What are the observable signs that children are friends?

How to support children to develop social skills

Children need a variety of social skills in order to develop relationships and friendships. There are some features that other children look for in choosing a playmate. Figure 7.3 shows these features.

Figure 7.3 Social skills that children need to acquire

Empathy

It is probably not possible to 'teach' empathy, but it is possible to create conditions for children that will support its development and encourage them to make friendships. First, children who have strong attachments will find it easier to be empathetic. They have been 'cared for' and 'understood' and this in turn helps them to show these qualities towards others. This is why children having a strong attachment to their key person is so important in early years settings.

In addition, children learn from watching adults' responses to others. If they see adults being kind and thoughtful towards others, they are more likely to adopt these behaviours. If, on the other hand, they see adults who seem unsympathetic or, even worse, laugh at or mock others, this behaviour is likely to be copied.

As well as seeing role models, as children become older they can benefit from adults who point out how others might be feeling. They may read a book and ask a child about how the character in the book might be feeling and see if the child can relate this feeling to a time in their own lives.

time, which is one reason why toddlers are often not developmentally ready to play cooperatively with others. Having said this, it is important to help toddlers with this process and we may begin by looking for opportunities for them to pass things to each other or take turns.

Plenty of praise and encouragement is needed when children show these positive behaviours. The need for adults to do small activities and games in which children take turns, learn to be patient and sometimes allow others to win will carry on until most children are around 5 years old or so. Even then, the odd reminder is still needed from time to time.

Friendliness and playfulnesss

Friendliness is characterised by relaxed body language, open gestures and often a lot of smiling. Children who are very anxious about being with other children often give off closed and fearful body language and this in turn sends out negative messages to other children. This can develop into a vicious cycle in which the child becomes less confident about joining in with other children. We can support children to show friendliness by helping them to feel confident. We may do this by organising activities in which they have particular responsibilities and also planning activities that are naturally 'fun' so that children are likely to smile and giggle. Helping children to smile and giggle often helps them to connect with each other.

Being cooperative

As children's friendships develop through mutual play and activities, it is important that we help them to learn the skills of being cooperative. Children who try to dominate games or want only their ideas to be used by the group are likely to be unpopular playmates, as are children who always want to be first or sulk if they lose. These are not easy skills to acquire and they do take

How is this adult supporting these children to make friends?

The style that adults use when reminding children about being cooperative is important too. If adults become cross or make the child feel guilty, they may associate being cooperative and thus thoughtful with feeling uncomfortable.

Supporting children's group learning and socialisation

For many children, friendships develop fairly easily if they have acquired social skills and the confidence needed to interact with others. If you observe that a child does not appear to have friends, consider why this might be. It may be that the child has lower levels of language and so is not able to join in or is over-boisterous or just shy. If any of these are the case, the first step is to work on the underlying reasons. In addition we can do some of the following.

Playing alongside

It can be helpful to play alongside a child while they are with others so that you can model play behaviours such as listening to others, joining in and taking turns.

Giving hints

With children from around 5 years, it may also be appropriate to give them hints about how to join in children's play. They may, for example, try to dominate a game or just ask children to change what they are doing. A quiet reminder about being a 'follower' rather than always trying to 'lead' a game might be in order.

In addition, we may also have to collaborate with children's parents. Many parents of children once they get to 4 or 5 years old also become concerned if their children are not making friends. It might be useful to share strategies and also to find out how the child reacts at home. Some children, for example, may have made good friends with older children outside of the setting and it may be that they prefer playing with older children where games might be more demanding or exciting.

Some children who are used to getting their own way at home and who are not given opportunities to be thoughtful and flexible can find it harder to make friends in a setting. If this is the case, it may be a good idea to discuss it with the parents and suggest that they work on this at home as well.

Preventing bullying

Happily, bullying is rare in the early years, although children may be dominated by other children or unhappy because they do not have a friend to play with. With children of school age, bullying can occur and so it is important to be aware of it and take steps to prevent it.

All schools will have policies designed to prevent bullying and will also pick up on bullying. The policies will have procedures that identify steps to take if you notice that a child might be being bullied or if you are told about a bullying incident.

As well as following procedures, it is also important for adults to model cooperative behaviours and to praise these when they see them in children. It is also important to be aware of children who are unhappy in their home lives, perhaps because of changes to the family structure. Supporting these children is important, as such children are at risk of being bullied or alternatively using bullying as an outlet for their own emotions.

Signs that a child might be bullied include the following:

- appearing quiet or withdrawn
- angry outbursts
- difficulty in sleeping
- tearfulness
- bedwetting when previously dry.

The effects of prejudice and discrimination on children's life chances

All forms of prejudice and discrimination have a negative effect on children's lives. Indeed, prejudice can lead to discrimination. When discrimination occurs, it means that children are being denied the care and education to which they are entitled.

Discrimination, for any reason, can seriously affect children's social and emotional development. Even very young children can pick up on the attitudes and actions of adults or, in some cases, of other children. This can make children feel as if they do not belong, which can have a long-term effect on their ability to build friendships. Children who are excluded or feel that an activity is 'not for them' will easily lose confidence in their own ability. It will affect how they view themselves, which can lead to low self-esteem and possibly lower levels of achievement in their learning and development. It is, therefore, important to challenge discriminatory behaviour and promote respect for others.

Communicating effectively with parents and carers

We saw in Unit 5 that it is essential to work in partnership with parents and carers. In particular, we looked at the skills that are needed in order to communicate with parents and carers. These include positive body language, sensitive communication and also the need for confidentiality. When it comes to communicating with parents or carers about children's emotional and social development, it is worth recognising that this area is a sensitive topic. Most parents and carers are anxious to ensure that their child has friends and is settled within the setting. It is, therefore, important that we listen to parents' and carers' concerns and also use the knowledge gained from observations to talk through with them how their child is doing. It may be that their child needs additional support or that their responses are typical for their age.

Assessment practice 7.3 — 3C.P5 | 3C.P6 | 3C.M3 | 3C.D2

A local radio show has been running a series about childhood. You have been asked to go on a live chat show to talk about the importance of supporting young children's personal, social and emotional development. In preparation for this show, the producer has asked you to provide some background information for the interviewer. The material should cover:

- the importance of practitioner relationships to children's personal, social and emotional development
- ways in which practitioners may support children's wellbeing and resilience
- ways in which practitioners may support the development of children's social skills, including friendships
- why it is important to challenge discriminatory behaviour and attitudes in early years settings.

In addition, to give the story a more human feel, the radio show would like you to discuss and assess different types of techniques or approaches that are being used where you work to support a child's individual social and emotional development.

D Support and promote children's positive behaviour

As babies and children develop, so too does their behaviour. During this process, adults have an important role in helping children to show positive behaviour that is appropriate for their stage of development and that reflects the context they are in. In this section we will explore how you might work with children to support their positive behaviour and consider what factors you should take into account and strategies that might be used.

Cultural and social perspectives

Working out what is appropriate behaviour for children is very interesting and also quite complex. First of all, our behaviours change according to whom we are with, where we are and how we are feeling. This means that you would probably behave differently with your friends at a party than you would if you were studying in a library.

In addition, people have different cultural and social expectations of what is appropriate behaviour, many of which they have 'inherited' from their own upbringing. It is important to reflect and be aware of different perspectives in relation to behaviour because you will need to work with parents, colleagues and other professionals, and we know that children benefit from consistency. Three areas in particular are interesting when it comes to expectations of children's behaviour.

Views and beliefs about childhood

People have very different views and beliefs about how children should behave. Some are based on spiritual beliefs such as reincarnation and others on social traditions. Here are some questions that may make you think about your own values and beliefs.

- Should there be strict boundaries set by adults or should children be free to explore and set their own boundaries?
- How much respect should children pay to adults? Should children be free to ignore them?
- Are children competent and independent learners or do adults have to teach children everything?

Social norms and values

Every society will have its own values and these become linked to social codes of behaviour. These are based on tradition as well as other things such as religion. As the United Kingdom is very diverse, we may expect to find that there is a range of social norms and values. Look at the following statements and see what you think about them.

- Children should be made to sit at the table at mealtimes.
- Saying please and thank you is important.
- Taking your shoes off when you enter a home is essential.

Gender expectations

The way that cultures, individuals and society expect boys and girls to behave can be different. This can be reflected through the type of play and resources that are provided, but also through the clothing that is given. Look at the following statements and see if you recognise them.

- Boys are more active than girls.

- Girls are better than boys at sitting down.
- Boys like being outdoors.
- Girls try to please adults.

The influence of cultural and social perspectives on adult responses

As well as recognising that there are different cultural and social perspectives, it is important to understand that these are likely to shape adults' responses towards children's behaviour. An early years professional may insist that a child sits at the table until the end of the meal because this was the norm in their childhood. Gender expectations are also interesting: it is sometimes thought that adults subconsciously curb girls' exuberant behaviours while not doing this with boys, saying 'boys will be boys'.

It is important for you to be aware of your own thoughts about children's behaviour and, where necessary, make sure that they do not lead to discrimination. It is also helpful to think about whether another adult's reaction to a child's behaviour is based on their own cultural and social perspective.

Avoiding conflict

The different opinions that people have about 'socially acceptable' behaviour can lead to conflict among adults unless they are explored and some clear expectations are established. This is why early years settings have behaviour policies that are shared with new staff, but these policies should also be shared with parents.

Links between behaviour and both language and cognitive development

We have seen that what we expect of children is linked to social and cultural perspectives, but it is important to understand that children's behaviour is also closely linked to their cognitive and language development. This means that even with encouragement and a positive environment, there are some things that children do that are simply 'normal' for their stage of development.

Effect of language on behaviour

Most children between the age of 2 and 3 years take an incredible language journey. At the start of this journey, they are likely to be highly impulsive and find it difficult to share attention or possessions with others. If their language develops well, we should see quite a change after their third birthday. This is linked to language development, which in turn seems to help their cognitive development. From around 3 years, most children seem to be able to wait a little and do some simple sharing. Parents will find that they are more cooperative with simple tasks and that they have fewer tantrums.

Language delay

Where children have language delay and so are not able to express themselves, the usual milestones for positive behaviour are unlikely to be met. This is because language helps children to manage their behaviour and be less impulsive. Thus a 4-year-old child whose language level is similar to that of a 2-year-old child is likely to show many of the behaviours that characterise a child who is 2 years of age.

Theory into practice

With permission, talk to staff in your setting about children whose behaviour is atypical.

Is there a link to their use of language?

Realistic expectations

Although all children are unique, it is worth knowing the usual patterns of behaviour for the age group of the children you are working with. This should help you to establish fair expectations. Table 7.4 shows examples of what we might expect at different ages, goals for behaviour and also the role of the adult. Note that this is a guide only and that an individual child's behaviour might be affected by levels of language and other factors.

Link

Go to Unit 1: Child Development to find more information about how a child's behaviours may be affected by language and a range of other factors.

Table 7.4 Expectations at different ages, goals for behaviour and the role of the adult

Age	Stage of development	Goals for behaviour	Role of adult
1–2 years	• Actively explores environment • Imitates adults in simple tasks • Repeats actions that gain attention • Alternates between clinginess and independence • No understanding that toys or other objects may belong to others	• To play alongside other children (parallel play) • To carry out simple instructions such as 'Can you find your coat?'	• **Good supervision** is necessary as children of this age do not understand the dangers around them. • **Distraction** works well in stopping unwanted behaviour, as children often forget what they were doing, e.g. if a child wants another child's toy, offer a different one instead. • **Praise** is needed for children to understand how to get adult's attention in positive ways and to develop good self-esteem. • **Being a good role model** is important as children learn behaviour through imitating those around them.

continued

Table 7.4 (*continued*)

Age	Stage of development	Goals for behaviour	Role of adult
2–3 years	• Easily frustrated and may have tantrums • Dislikes adult attention being given to other children • No understanding of the need to wait • Finds sharing difficult • Rapid physical and emotional learning • Tries to be independent	• To wait for needs to be met, e.g. at mealtimes • To share toys or food with one other child with adult help • To play alongside other children • To sit and share a story for 5 minutes • To say 'please' and 'thank you' if reminded • To follow simple instructions with help, such as 'Wash your hands'	• **Good supervision and anticipation** are the keys to working with this age range. Children are trying to be independent but lack some of the physical and cognitive skills they need. This makes them frustrated and angry. Adults need to anticipate possible sources of frustration, and support children either by offering help or by distracting them, e.g. a child who is trying to put their coat on may need an adult to make a game of it so the child does not become frustrated. • **Praise and encouragement** are needed for children to learn what behaviour adults expect from them. Some unwanted behaviour that is not dangerous should be ignored so that children do not learn to use it as a way of getting adult attention. • **Consistency** is needed as children will try to work out what the limits are on their behaviour. • **Being a good role model** helps children as they model their behaviour on others around them. This is especially important as children act out their experiences through play.
3–4 years	• Follows simple rules by imitating other children, e.g. collects aprons before painting • Able to communicate wishes • Enjoys activities such as painting • Enjoys being with other children • Can play cooperatively • Enjoys helping adults	• To follow rules in games when helped by adult, e.g. playing lotto • To say 'please' and 'thank you' often without reminder • To take turns and share equipment • To follow adults' instructions most of the time, e.g. 'Let Simon have a turn' • To help tidy away	• **Praise and encouragement** builds children's confidence and makes them more likely to show desirable behaviour. • **Explanation** of rules should be given, as children are more likely to remember and understand them. • **Good supervision** is still needed, as although children are able to do many things for themselves, they remain unaware of the dangers around them. Most of the time children will be able to play well together, but squabbles will break out. • **Being a good role model** will help children learn the social skills they need to resolve arguments and express their feelings.

continued

Table 7.4 (*continued*)

Age	Stage of development	Goals for behaviour	Role of adult
4–5 years	• Plays with other children without help from adults • Is able to communicate feelings and wishes • Understands the need for rules	• To ask permission to use other children's toys • To comfort playmates in distress • To say 'please' and 'thank you' without a reminder • To tidy up after activities	• **Providing stimulating activities and tasks** that allow children to develop confidence is important. Children are keen to help adults and enjoy being busy. Tasks such as setting the table allow children to feel independent. • **Praise and encouragement** help children feel good about themselves, which is important as they are often starting school. Children need to feel that they can be 'good'. • **Explanation** helps children to remember and understand the need for rules or decisions. • **Being a good role model** helps children to learn social skills – they will copy what they see.
5–8 years	• Has strong friendships • Can argue back • Copies behaviour of other children, e.g. may swear or spit • Understands the need for rules and plays games that have rules • Understands the difference between right and wrong • Has many self-help skills, e.g. getting dressed, wiping up spills	• To follow instructions from adults • To apologise to others • To listen to others **From 6 years:** • To work independently and quietly in educational settings • To be helpful and thoughtful	• **Praise and encouragement** avoids children looking for other ways of gaining attention. Praise is needed as children become more aware of others and compare themselves critically. • **Explanation** helps children to understand the reasons for rules and decisions. They also need to consider the effect of their actions on others. As children become older, they are likely to argue back and clear boundaries need to be enforced. • **Being a good role model** is important, as children try to understand more about adults. Speech and actions are modelled increasingly on adults whom children admire. • **Providing activities and responsibilities** helps children 'mature' and learn more about their capabilities. Small responsibilities help independence and confidence, e.g. ask them to pour drinks for other children.

Short-term factors that may affect behaviour

Children's behaviour is not constant. Like adults, they become tired, hungry and have days when they do not feel like interacting or sharing. This means that while we may have some ideas about what is usual in terms of expectations of behaviour, adults have to be aware of short-term factors that will influence a child's behaviour at any given time.

Tiredness

All children and adults need sleep. Children who are feeling tired or have not slept sufficiently are likely to show the behaviours outlined in Figure 7.4.

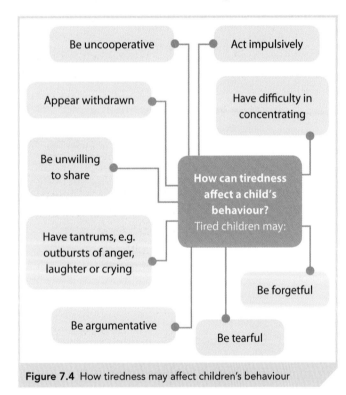

Figure 7.4 How tiredness may affect children's behaviour

Hunger

When we are hungry, our blood glucose levels drop. This affects the brain's capacity to function. As impulsivity and emotions are governed by our neural activity, this can mean that children will show behaviours that are otherwise unusual for them. When children eat diets that are high in sugar, their blood glucose level is likely to fall suddenly – this can account for quite dramatic mood swings.

Reflect

Look at the characteristics that children may show when they are tired.

How many do you recognise when you are feeling tired?

Boredom

The brain likes to be stimulated. When children are bored and lacking stimulation, they are likely to do things that will literally give their brains a boost – they may run around, do things that make sounds and do things that feel exciting for them. It is therefore essential that you are thoughtful about what type of activities and resources are available for children and whether they are sufficiently fascinating, exciting and stimulating. The likelihood of children showing unwanted behaviours is therefore high during periods when they are waiting around for things such as meals, snacks or lining up.

Illness

When children are feeling poorly, they are more likely to show behaviours that are uncharacteristic. Often it is only after the child's symptoms begin to show that we recognise that the child was probably not well, so it is important to be observant and take note of uncharacteristic behaviours.

Bullying

As we have seen in the previous section, bullying is rare in early years, but can occur with school-age children. It is important that we are thoughtful about whether a child might be experiencing friendship difficulties or being bullied. Look out for children who become withdrawn, are angry or seem to be intent on hurting others, especially younger children. If you suspect that a child is bullying or is being bullied, you should raise this as an issue with the child's key person, who will need to talk to the child's parents.

Abuse

We know that some children are victims of abuse. Ongoing abuse and the consequences of abuse can change children's behaviour. In Unit 8, we look at the signs that might indicate that a child is being abused and you will see that as well as physical indicators there are often things that can be noticed in a child's behaviour. If you spot a change in a child's behaviour towards other children or in their general demeanour, it will be important to follow this up. It may be that other circumstances, such as a family problem, are causing the difficulty, but it is essential not to rule out the possibility that there might be abuse. You should report any concerns to the lead person named in your setting's child protection policy.

Link

Go to Unit 8: Section B to find more information about the signs of abuse.

Long-term factors that may affect behaviour

There are some long-term factors that might affect children's behaviour. Understanding these can help us to support children more effectively.

Chronic illness

Children with **chronic illnesses** may struggle at times to show positive behaviour. There are many reasons for this, including tiredness and the effects of drugs, but also the condition itself. Eczema, which is common in children, can prevent a child from sleeping properly, but during a flare-up, the itching itself can be unbearable and may result in a child becoming frustrated and angry.

Anxiety

There are multiple reasons why children may be affected by anxiety including home circumstances, transitions or trauma. Children who are anxious may show a variety of behaviours including attention seeking, withdrawal and impulsiveness.

Not settled

We have looked at the importance of key persons and supporting children with transition. When a child is not fully settled in, they will find it harder to show positive behaviour. It may be that the child will

Key term

Chronic illness – a long-term medical condition.

not share, or show anger, but they may also exhibit attention-seeking behaviour.

The effect of transitions and other significant events on behaviour

Many children will be looked after by several adults over the course of a week. While some children can manage a number of transitions, it is not always ideal and sometimes can create disturbances in children's behaviour. It is worth remembering that every transition brings a new environment or a different relationship as well as different expectations from adults. As we will see later on in this section, children thrive on consistency and so changes can be problematic.

Some children navigate this well, but other children will struggle to 'belong' or to remember the routine and expectations of each setting. In addition, if there are any difficulties within the child's own family, this will make it particularly hard for the child to show positive behaviour. Figure 7.5 outlines how children's behaviour can be affected if they find transition difficult.

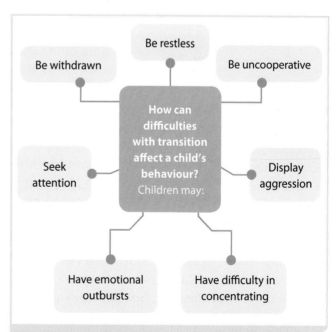

Figure 7.5 How difficulties with transition may affect a child's behaviour

Supporting children

If you feel that a child is struggling because of the transitions they are making or because of a significant event that has affected them, you should try the following.

- Talk to parents about where the child goes and how things are working.
- Gain suggestions from parents about how to support the child.
- Find out more about the routines and expectations of other settings.
- Spend more time with the child so that a strong attachment can be built.
- Try to create a special routine for when the child arrives, e.g. hang up their coat, share a story and then lay the table together.

Social cognitive theory and positive behaviour

Albert Bandura's work on social cognitive theory, also known as social learning theory, has many implications for helping children to show positive behaviour. First, his work shows the importance of children learning from adults, simply by observing them. This is why many settings' policies will have clear guidelines for staff conduct such as showing respect and manners and not shouting or being aggressive towards children.

Link

Go to Unit 1: Section B and C to find more information about social cognitive theory.

In addition, social cognitive theory explains why toddlers and young children will not automatically be able to behave in the same way as adults. This is a source of frustration for parents and practitioners as they might expect that if children have observed them being patient or taking turns in a game, they will be able to do the same. Social cognitive theory suggests that several elements have to be in place at the time of the **modelling**, including an appropriate level of development of the child. Having said this, it

is reassuring that when children repeatedly see others showing attitudes such as kindness, friendliness and thoughtfulness, they seem to eventually model these behaviours as they grow and develop.

Key term

Modelling – an action, gesture or behaviour that a child might observe and later imitate.

Using social cognitive theory

If we model behaviours that are within the developmental grasp of children, they are more likely to be able to show them. This means that simple things such as tidying away toys can be modelled and then children are encouraged to join in. They may not be developmentally ready to do it for a long period of time, but they should be able to join us until their attention wanes. In the same way, if adults model picking up coats or other items from the floor, some older children will also do this.

Children can also learn behaviours from other children. For example, if you identify a child who is showing positive behaviour, it is worth pointing it out to other children. This is likely to encourage them to show similar behaviour, assuming that this is within their developmental grasp.

We also know from Bandura's later work that for children to follow modelling behaviour, it is helpful if they are developmentally ready and have the opportunity to repeat what they have seen soon afterwards.

The advantages and disadvantages of operant conditioning in changing behaviour

Operant conditioning methods of helping children to show positive behaviour can be effective, although it is important that we understand them and only apply them when we are sure that children are developmentally able to show the behaviours.

Link

Go to Unit 1: Section B and C to find more information about operant conditioning methods.

Positive reinforcement

Positive reinforcement should, in theory, encourage children to repeat behaviours. Most settings use the following methods of positive reinforcement:

- praise
- rewards – stickers, certificates, being allowed to choose equipment
- attention – smiles, eye contact, clapping.

Advantages

Positive reinforcers work well if they are used at the time of the positive behaviour that you want to encourage further. Leaving praise or attention until much later is not a problem, but it will not be as effective.

Disadvantages

While toddlers and young children will need positive reinforcement as an encouragement to show positive behaviours, it is also important that children develop an internal model of being thoughtful, kind and aware of others. The danger of continual praise or rewards is that some children show positive behaviour in order to 'get something' rather than for its own sake. It is therefore helpful to encourage children to reflect on the importance of their actions.

Did you know?

Using food as treats for children can cause poor eating attitudes in adulthood. It is thought that where children are regularly rewarded with food treats, they are more likely to eat sugary and other unhealthy foods later – either as comfort foods or because they have developed the attitude of 'being good or working hard = food'.

Intermittent reinforcement

A powerful model of reinforcement is known as intermittent reinforcement. We looked at this in Unit 1 and saw that it can create longer-lasting behaviours in children. This model of reinforcement is useful when praising children, as it means that they do not expect praise every time they show positive behaviours, and so avoids the scenario whereby children stop doing something because they are no longer praised.

Intermittent reinforcements can also be the cause of unwanted behaviours in children. This is worth exploring if you have found that a persistent behaviour is being shown. It might be that the child has had some intermittent reinforcement, which means that their behaviours are now longer-lasting. If intermittent reinforcement is suspected, it is important to maintain absolute consistency as well as talk to the child about their actions.

Changing the script

In some cases, it can be easier to try a strategy that is sometimes referred to as 'changing the script'. This means literally changing the situation so that it is impossible for the child to repeat the behaviour.

Unexpected reinforcers

Adults do not provide all of the reinforcements. Children can have positive reinforcement from sensations that they have discovered. This explains why children love bouncing on sofas, throwing sand and splashing in puddles. Reinforcements from sensations are very powerful for children and they are likely to find it hard not to repeat the actions even when told to stop. This means that at times it might be appropriate to distract children with alternatives and if necessary to remove items that are causing dangerous or inappropriate behaviour.

Case study

Intermittent reinforcement

A day nursery is having difficulty with a 3-year-old child who keeps climbing on the table at lunchtime. The other children laugh when he does this. On some days staff are quick to stop him, but on other days they do not react quickly or decide not to pay any attention.

After a couple of weeks, staff realise this is becoming an issue and that what started as a 'one-off' behaviour has become a daily occurrence and that the child tries to climb even when staff are ready to stop him.

The manager suggests that the staff should use a different approach. She suggests that instead of having lunch at the table, a picnic mat should be put on the floor. The children are all very excited by this and the 3-year-old child is given the job of putting out the plates. Lunch goes very smoothly!

1 How was this child's behaviour being reinforced, and by whom?

2 Why was this an example of intermittent reinforcement?

3 How was 'changing the script' used as an approach and why did it work?

Theory into practice

- What do children in your work placement enjoy doing that needs to be stopped by adults?

- Can you work out what makes it so pleasurable for the children?

- Can you think of other ways in which the children could gain the same stimulation but in a safer context?

Not reacting to children

Operant conditioning suggests that in situations where there is no negative or positive reinforcement, behaviours may disappear. This is the basis of the advice that there may be times when we should not react to children's behaviours but turn away instead. This is effective if children are trying to seek your attention by using inappropriate behaviours such as hitting your arm or threatening to tip a bucket of plastic bricks onto the floor. While this is a very effective method of working with young children, it also takes a little practice on the part of parents and practitioners, as quite often our 'natural' reaction is to respond to the child. This unfortunately gives children eye contact and a reaction, which can ironically act as a positive reinforcement.

Star charts

Star charts are very popular as a way of changing children's behaviour. They can work well, but only if they are used when children are developmentally ready and also if they are designed well.

Ready or not?

Star charts are secondary reinforcers. Children get a small reinforcement by being praised at the time, but the real purpose is that the stars or stickers on the chart build up and at some point are converted into a reward. This is often not meaningful for children until they are 4 or 5 years old. (This is why young children will often prefer a single sticker rather than a pound coin that could buy them a roll of stickers, even when you explain it to them.)

When star charts are used with children who do understand them, they can support a change in children's specific behaviours in a long-term way.

Link

Go to Unit 1: Section B and C to find more information about secondary reinforcers.

The importance of a positive attitude, consistency and collaboration

There are many things that we can do that can help children show positive behaviours.

Positive attitude

A good starting point is your own attitude towards children and also your work. Adults who have a positive attitude are more likely to appeal to children and this makes it easier to form a strong attachment. This in turn can help children to show positive behaviours and seek attention in appropriate ways.

A positive attitude also helps to keep a good pace within the setting. This is important because it stops small incidents from blowing out of proportion and then creating new problems. It also pays to have a good sense of humour and not to take things personally.

Few toddlers and young children plan to show unwanted behaviours. They are normally the result of age-related impulsiveness, frustration or attention seeking.

Consistency

Toddlers and young children need consistency, in many ways. First of all, children need adults to be consistent in the way that they act and in their tone of voice. They also need adults to be calm. All these things make children feel more secure. This is particularly important to remember if you are working with children who have multiple transitions over a week or are facing a significant upheaval within their family structure. The bottom line is that children need to feel that they can depend on adults.

In addition, for children to show positive behaviour, our expectations of them need to be consistent. This is particularly important for children under 4 years of age. 'Exceptions' or 'special occasions' are not helpful for 2- and even 3-year-old children as they struggle with this as a concept. It is easier for a toddler if they know that they always have to put an apron on before painting or that they are never allowed to climb on the furniture.

Case study

Keeping a positive attitude

Fran is having problems in her personal life. She has come into the nursery tired and annoyed with her boyfriend. She has not slept well and is not looking forward to the day ahead. When one of the children arrives and wants a hug, she says in an irritated voice that she is not a teddy bear. The child looks crestfallen. Later when she spots one of the children throwing the knives and forks on the dinner table to the floor, she decides that she can't be bothered to say anything. A little later on during lunch, she spots that one of the children has spilt water onto the table. She shouts that the child is doing it on purpose.

1 How might Fran's attitude affect the children's emotional wellbeing?

2 In what ways is Fran being inconsistent?

3 How might her inconsistency affect the children?

4 Why is it important for practitioners to remain professional regardless of their personal circumstances?

Collaboration with parents and others

As well as consistency within our own practice, it is helpful wherever possible to collaborate with others so that there can be overall consistency for children. We may ask parents to share their views with us and also to explain the ethos of how we manage behaviour in the setting. It is not always possible for all aspects to be consistent, but the aim is to achieve as much consistency as possible.

As well as sharing information about approaches to things such as mealtimes, dressing and sharing, we also need to work with parents to find out what might be happening that may be impacting on a child's behaviour. Working together on any aspects of a child's behaviour that is proving difficult can mean that a consistent approach is taken to things such as biting or mealtimes. Where children are in a range of settings, discussions with others will also be essential, assuming we have parental consent. It may be that practices are different in the various settings and we may need to take these on board when we are working with the child.

Finally, some families will also get additional support from outreach workers, family liaison teams or health visitors. Knowing what has been agreed as an approach at home will be very helpful and again, with parental consent, it is a good idea to contact others who are working with the child and family.

How procedures and policies within settings support effective practice

Every setting should have a policy that describes how positive behaviour is to be promoted as well as procedures for reporting and dealing with unwanted behaviour. It is good practice for such policies to focus on developing children's positive behaviours rather than just on unwanted behaviours.

It is important that you follow the policy and procedures in your setting. These may include guidance as to how adults in the setting should behave, including remaining calm, role modelling thoughtful behaviour and also ensuring that the environment and activities are suitable for each child's stage of development. The behaviour policy should also look at what should happen if specific incidents occur, such as biting, offensive name-calling or swearing.

Research

Find out how your setting handles incidents of unwanted behaviour and whether there are expectations of staff as to their conduct.

Strategies for children at different ages and stages of development

It is important to find strategies to use with children so that they can show positive behaviours that are appropriate to their level of development. There are several strategies that can be used, some of which work best with particular age groups.

Distraction

Distraction is often used to help toddlers and even older children focus on something else. We may, for example, get a puppet out of the bag to distract a toddler who is determined to climb on a table. Distraction works by engaging the child in another activity which is equally or more appealing. As children get older, distraction does not always work, but it is worth considering. If you find that you are relying on distraction as a technique, it may be that the environment, activities or resources available are not sufficiently engaging for children.

Negotiation

Once children are starting to talk, it can be helpful to negotiate with them. Ideally, you should explain the situation and allow children to offer up their own suggestions. This style of working gives children responsibility and makes them feel more involved. The good news is that when children start to set their own rules, they are more likely to follow them as the case study: Negotiating with children shows.

Case study

Negotiating with children

Three 7-year-old children are playing football, but the ball keeps hitting some glass doors. The adult talks to the children. The children are keen to continue playing, although the adult does offer an alternative suggestion. The adult asks them to think about how they can play in such a way that it does not interfere with other children's games or hit the glass doors. The children have a think and then offer to play with a softer ball. The adult considers this and they agree to try it out. A few minutes later, the adult asks them if they are still enjoying the game and congratulates them on coming up with the solution.

1 Explain how the adult gave the children responsibility for setting their own boundaries.

2 What were the overall benefits of this approach?

3 Why was it useful for the adult to acknowledge their behaviour?

Praise

Toddlers and children can be helped to show positive behaviour if they are given sufficient encouragement and acknowledgement. This often comes in the form of praise. Ideally praise should be offered during or shortly after the behaviour as it seems to have more effect. As children develop, it is important to help them learn to acknowledge their own positive behaviour. This might be done through saying to a child, 'Were you proud of yourself?', or 'Did you notice how pleased Daniel was when you let him take his turn?' This is important, as children have to learn to take responsibility and also internally acknowledge their own positive behaviours.

Helping children to develop positive attitudes

Children learn the majority of their social skills through observing adults and being guided by them. This means that early years professionals play an important role in helping children to develop positive attitudes. We should help children learn how to respect and value others, and help them to understand that children are all different. We can do this in a variety of ways, including role modelling thoughtfulness and respect and praising children when they are kind and helpful towards others. We can also share books with children that explore how to respect others and be thoughtful. Books are also a good way of helping children understand that other families may lead different lives to theirs.

Using observations to support positive behaviour and resolve conflict

Observations are useful as a tool to support children's positive behaviour. For some children, we might work out that there are patterns in their behaviour. It might be that a child tends to show unwanted behaviour at the same time each day or in the company of certain children. Wherever possible parents need to work with us on this as they may be able to shed some light on what is happening. We may notice, for example, that on Tuesdays a child's behaviour is different, but then find out from a parent that on Monday nights the child's grandparents come round and on this night they go to bed late.

There are many ways that we might use observations to build up a picture or pattern of a child's behaviour.

Event samples

This is a recording method whereby we keep a note of certain behaviours each time they occur. The time, date and other information needed to find out what is happening is recorded. This way, it is possible to see the frequency of incidents and also if there is a pattern to them. Event samples can also be used to see if any strategies that are being used are helping to reduce the number of incidents.

Diaries

It can be helpful for the setting and parents to keep diaries, day by day or session by day. These can be used as longitudinal records to see if we can notice any patterns and also when and where they occur. Diaries are usually kept over a few days or even months. Diaries can also be used as a way for the setting and parents to keep in touch with each other and make comments about what is happening.

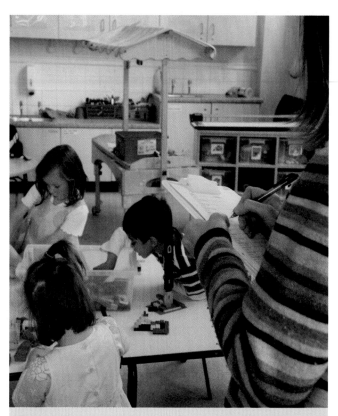

Observations are a useful tool to help us build a picture of a child's behaviour.

Working with families to support positive behaviour

It has often been said that children are not born with an instruction manual. As most parents are not trained in child development, there are times when some parents may run into difficulties when trying to support their children's positive behaviour. There are many ways of supporting parents if this happens. A good starting point is the way that we role model positive interactions with children.

Further reading and resources

Elfer, P., Goldschmied, E. and Selleck, D. (2011) *Key Persons in the Early Years: Building relationships for quality provision in early years settings and primary schools* (2nd ed.), Oxford: Routledge.

Garhart Mooney, C. (2009) *Theories of Attachment: An introduction to Bowlby, Ainsworth, Gerber, Brazelton, Kennell and Klaus*, Minnesota: Redleaf Press.

Lindon, J. (2012) *Understanding children's behaviour 0–11 years*, London: Hodder Education.

Assessment practice 7.4   3D.P7 | 3D.P8
3D.P9 | 3D.M4

You have been asked to write an article for a prestigious early years magazine. The magazine is read by advisory teams and students, as well as early years professionals. The editor of the magazine has asked you to write an article entitled, 'Can early years professionals really make a difference to children's behaviour?'

In order to write the article you should use your own knowledge and experiences of working with children in placement to:

- describe factors that may affect children's behaviour
- explain how early years professionals can model and promote positive behaviours
- give examples of how you have supported children to manage their own behaviour
- show how you have provided support appropriate to children's developmental stages in order to promote positive behaviour.

Ready for work?

Sussana Agresta   Nursery manager

Building up strong bonds and relationships with families is a real focus for our nursery. Our children will often come to us as babies and will stay until they start school. The truth is that we spend more time with some of the children than their parents do, as some children are here for 55 hours a week, 48 weeks of the year. It is therefore our responsibility to make sure that all of the children develop strong bonds with staff. We have a buddy system so that a child is always with a key person that they know. We also try wherever possible to keep staff with children and so when babies move rooms, their key person goes with them. This means that by the end of their time at the nursery, many children and their parents view us as family members. Because of these strong ties, we carry on sending cards and notes to children even after they leave us. We also encourage parents to pop in with their children so that the child does not feel that the relationship is over.

Skills for practice

Promoting positive behaviour

Being able to help children show positive behaviour is an important role of adults working with children. Remember though, all children find it easier to show positive behaviour when they are not tired or hungry.

Tips for helping children aged 1 to 3 years manage their own behaviour

- Give children simple 'at the time' instructions.
- Distract children from situations that are difficult for them.
- Praise children when they show kindness or thoughtfulness.
- Remove temptations, for example, toys children may squabble over or any items of food that may cause them to 'nag'.
- Create an environment and a routine that keep children of this age group busy.

Tips for helping children aged 3 to 5 years manage their own behaviour

- Praise children when they are showing positive behaviour but always tell them what it is they have done well.
- Remind children about the expectations for behaviour, for example, 'Don't forget to tidy up when you have finished playing'.
- Discuss with children the expectations for their behaviour before they start an activity.
- Encourage children to find their own solutions to possible difficulties that might affect positive behaviour, for example, how they are going to share resources or take turns.

Introduction

All children have the right to be kept safe from abuse or neglect. Abuse can seriously affect children's health and wellbeing so all those working with children have a legal duty to protect them. To do this effectively you must be vigilant at all times so that you can recognise and respond appropriately to the signs that abuse may be happening. This unit will help you understand what you should do if you have concerns about a child and ways that children can be supported to protect themselves.

Assessment: You will be assessed by a series of assignments set by your teacher/tutor.

Learning aims

In this unit you will:

A   understand the role of the early years professional in safeguarding and promoting the welfare of children

B   understand types and indicators of child abuse

C   understand how to respond appropriately to concerns that a child has been abused.

> When I first started studying this unit I found it difficult to believe that adults can abuse or neglect young children. I was worried that I would not be able to deal with it if I thought that a child was being abused. Now that I know the signs to look for and the actions that should be taken, I am beginning to feel more confident. I realise that abuse and neglect are not always easy to recognise but if I'm unsure I know where I can go for advice.
>
> Harriet, *a learner on an early years course*

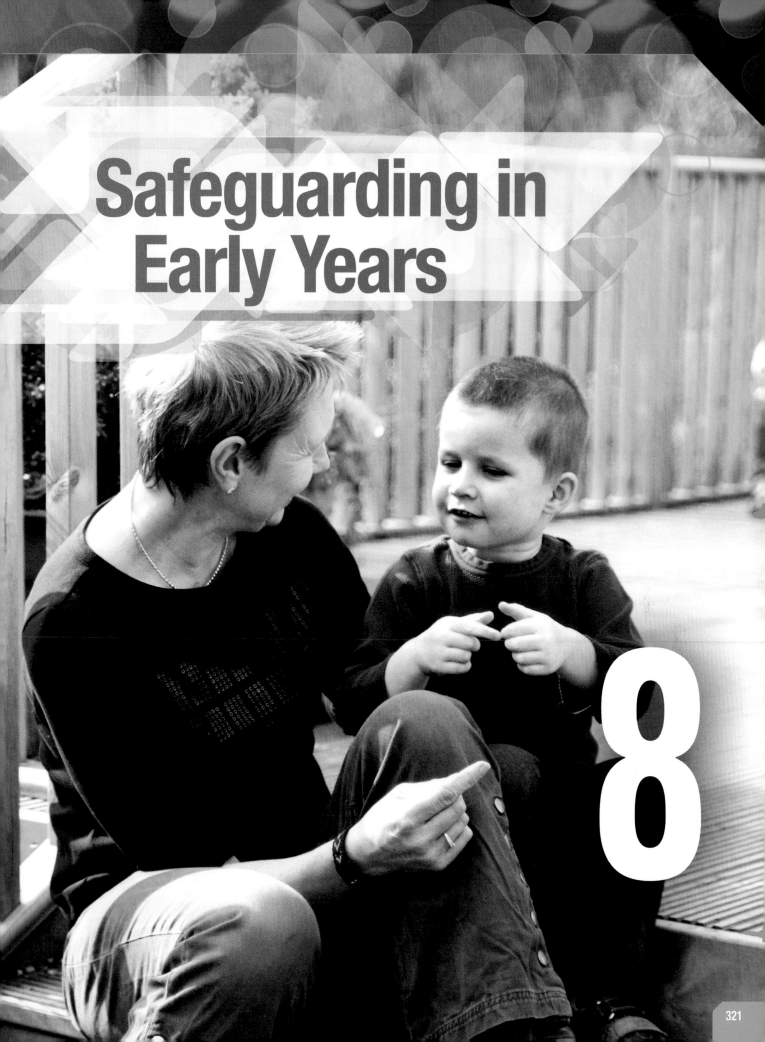

Safeguarding in Early Years

8

BTEC

Assessment Zone

This table shows you what you must do in order to achieve a **Pass**, **Merit** or **Distinction** grade, and lists activities that relate to each learning aim.

Assessment criteria

Pass	Merit	Distinction
Learning aim A: Understand the role of the early years professional in safeguarding and promoting the welfare of children		
3A.P1 Explain how early years professionals must exercise their duty of care effectively, with reference to safeguarding children and promoting their welfare. **Assessment practice 8.1**	**3A.M1** Analyse the role of the early years professional in safeguarding and promoting the welfare of children of different ages. **Assessment practice 8.1**	**3A.D1** Evaluate the ways in which early years professionals can most effectively contribute to safeguarding and promoting the welfare of children. **Assessment practice 8.1**
3A.P2 Explain a child-centred approach toward safeguarding children and promoting their welfare. **Assessment practice 8.1**		
Learning aim B: Understand types and indicators of child abuse		
3B.P3 Explain types of child abuse and their indicators with reference to early years settings. **Assessment practice 8.2**	**3B.M2** Discuss the impact of child abuse on a child's all-round development. **Assessment practice 8.2**	
Learning aim C: Understand how to respond appropriately to concerns that a child has been abused		
3C.P4 English Explain why it is important to follow policies and procedures in safeguarding and promoting the welfare of children in early years settings. **Assessment practice 8.3**	**3C.M3** Discuss, using examples, why it is important to respond appropriately if a child talks about an issue that is of concern. **Assessment practice 8.3**	**3C.D2** Assess best practice in identifying potential abuse and responding effectively in early years settings. **Assessment practice 8.3**
3C.P5 Explain the process in an early years setting for reporting and recording concerns that a child has been abused. **Assessment practice 8.3**		

English   English Functional Skills signposting

How you will be assessed

This unit will be assessed by a series of internally assessed tasks set by your teacher/tutor. Throughout this unit you will find assessment practice activities that will help you work towards your assessment. Completing these activities will not mean that you have achieved a particular grade, but you will have carried out useful research or preparation that will be relevant when it comes to your final assignment.

In order for you to achieve the tasks in your assignment, it is important to check that you have met all of the Pass grading criteria. You can do this as you work your way through the assignment.

If you are hoping to gain a Merit or Distinction, you should also make sure that you present the information in your assignment in the style that is required by the relevant assessment criterion.

For example, Merit criteria will require you to discuss and analyse, and Distinction criteria will require you to assess and evaluate.

The assignment set by your teacher/tutor will consist of a number of tasks designed to meet the criteria in the table. This is likely to consist of a written assignment but may also include activities such as the following:

- producing a reference document including essential information about safeguarding children
- providing evidence of information gained through further reading, examples from practice or discussion with relevant professionals working in the sector
- presenting reasoned conclusions about the extent of the contribution of adults in safeguarding children, based on evidence from case studies, observations or further reading.

Getting started

Talk to the person in your setting who is responsible for child protection to find out what is involved in their role. Before you speak to them, jot down a few questions to ask. Remember that they cannot speak to you about individual children because information must be kept confidential.

Reflect

Advice and support

The issues dealt with in this unit can affect the way you feel. You may have personal experience or knowledge of a child who has been abused. If you are affected by the content in this unit you can receive support from your teacher/tutor, the designated person with child protection

responsibility at your school, college or training centre, or through the voluntary organisations listed below.

- National Association for People Abused in Childhood (NAPAC): 0800 085 3330
- ChildLine: 0800 1111

A Understand the role of the early years professional in safeguarding and promoting the welfare of children

The duty of care of those working with children

A duty of care describes the standards of care that are expected of adults who work with children. A duty of care is a legal obligation of adults to act in a way that promotes the best interest of the children and keeps them safe from harm. It also includes the obligation to do nothing that might harm a child through their actions or through their negligence.

Current legislation

The current key legislation that establishes this duty of care is outlined in Table 8.1. This legislation is for England and Wales. Northern Ireland and Scotland have their own legislation: the Children (Northern Ireland) Order 1995 and the Children (Scotland) Act 1995. These are civil laws that work to safeguard and promote the **welfare** of children and which underpin working guidelines. There are also criminal laws, which deal with people who have abused children.

Table 8.1 Child protection legislation

Legislation	Purpose
Children Act 1989	This Act identifies the responsibilities of parents and established the duty of early years professionals to identify and meet the individual needs of children. It also introduced the concept of welfare of the child being paramount when decisions are made about them.

continued

Table 8.1 (continued)

Legislation	Purpose
	It includes two important sections that focus specifically on safeguarding children. • **Section 47** states that the Local Authority has 'a duty to investigate when there is a reasonable cause to suspect that a child is suffering or likely to suffer, **significant harm**'. • **Section 17** states that services must be put into place to 'safeguard and promote the welfare of children within the area who are **in need**'.
Education Act 2002	This Act sets out the responsibilities of local education authorities, governing bodies, head teachers and all those people working in schools to ensure that children are safe and free from harm.
Children Act 2004	This Act provides the legal framework for Every Child Matters (now referred to as Help Children Achieve More). It also includes the requirements for: • services to work more closely together • a shared process for the assessment of children's needs • a shared database of information that is relevant to the safety and welfare of children • a Local Safeguarding Children Board to be set up in every area (LSCB) • earlier support for parents who are experiencing problems.

Key terms

In need – this refers to children who are unlikely to maintain, or be given the opportunity to maintain, a reasonable standard of health or development, or children whose health could be impaired without the support of local authority services. It also includes children who are disabled.

Significant harm – this refers to the seriousness of the harm or likely harm that a child may suffer.

Statutory – required by law (statute).

Statutory guidance – a legal term that means that settings or an individual have to follow or pay regard to advice.

Welfare – holistic needs including health and wellbeing.

Statutory guidance

Each home country provides **statutory guidance** for agencies and professionals who work with children in accordance with current legislation. In England, there are two key documents: the *Statutory Framework for the Early Years Foundation Stage* and *Working Together to Safeguard Children (2013)*.

Statutory framework for the Early Years Foundation Stage 2014

The framework for the Early Years Foundation Stage (EYFS) gives guidance for working with children aged 0 to 5 years. Section 3 of the document sets out the safeguarding and welfare requirements for early years settings and services, including the duty to:

• provide an environment where children can grow and learn

• keep children safe and secure

• promote good health

• take steps when there are concerns about a child safety and welfare.

Working Together to Safeguard Children (2013)

This guidance sets out the duty of care for all organisations, including those that are voluntary, that provide services for children up to the age of 18 years. This includes, for instance, education services, social workers, health services, leisure services and the police. The document focuses on the importance of shared responsibility and how agencies should cooperate to safeguard children and promote their welfare. It has two key principles:

* safeguarding is the responsibility of all those working with children
* a child-centred approach is essential for services to be effective in keeping children safe and promoting their welfare.

Did you know?

You can download the statutory requirements of the EYFS and 'Working Together to Safeguard Children 2013' from the GOV.UK website or by going to www.pearsonhotlinks.co.uk and searching for this ISBN: 9781447970965.

Children's right to be safe

The United Nations Convention on the Rights of the Child (1989)

The United Nations Convention on the Rights of the Child (UNCRC) treaty sets out the rights and freedoms of all children in a set of 54 articles. Article 19 provides for the right of children to be kept safe from harm and to be protected from all forms of abuse by those looking after them.

The countries that are signed up to the treaty, including the UK in 1991, are legally bound to implement legislation that supports each of the articles.

The responsibility to comply with current legislation

Everyone working with children shares the responsibility to protect them from harm and to promote their welfare. This responsibility includes you, as a student, even if you are not employed by the setting. It is essential, therefore, that you know and understand the policies and procedures of the setting you are working in. Policies and procedures in early years settings are written to help adults protect children and promote their welfare, but they must comply with current legislation and statutory requirements. With particular regard to child protection there are additional requirements that children's settings must have in place:

* a policy for child protection that meets the requirements of the Local Safeguarding Children Board
* a lead professional with designated responsibility for child protection
* a programme of child protection training for all staff.

Figure 8.1 shows early years professionals' responsibilities for child protection.

Safe recruitment

All services and settings that provide early years care or education have a responsibility to recruit staff who are suitable to work with children. When you first applied to work with children you will have been asked to complete a DBS form. This is an enhanced disclosure carried out by the Disclosure and Barring Service (DBS). The DBS accesses information about people that is held by the police. Even with this check in place, abuse can happen and there have been a number of high-profile cases where early years professionals have abused children in a childcare setting. Checks should not be carried out only when a member of staff is recruited. Although checks are carried out when a member of staff is recruited, there must be a system in place for ongoing assessment of the suitability of all those working with children.

Information sharing

In normal circumstances, permission should be sought from parents or carers before passing on information to other professionals. Children and parents must be informed about why you need to share the information, who the information will be shared with and how it will be shared. However, there are exceptions to this rule. When there are concerns about a child's safety, gaining consent before passing on information is not always necessary. Although there is legislation governing information sharing and policies in place, it is sometimes difficult for people

Figure 8.1 The responsibilities of early years professionals for child protection

Research

For more information on safe recruitment, read Section 3.9 of the *Statutory Framework for the Early Years Foundation Stage*, which can be found on the website for the UK government, and a summary of the Safeguarding Vulnerable Groups Act 2006 and subsequent amendments made to the system by the Protection of Freedoms Act 2012, which can be found on the NSPCC website. You can also access these documents by going to www.pearsonhotlinks.co.uk and searching for this ISBN: 9781447970965.

who work with children to decide when information should be shared without consent. It will help you to remember the following.

- The child's welfare is the most important consideration. Ask yourself if, by not passing on information, a child might be at risk of harm.

- If you are given information by a child or adult about concerns of abuse, the information must be passed on. You should also inform the child or adult whom you spoke to that you must do this.

- Information must only be given to those who need to know (the **named person** in the setting with responsibility for child protection, the manager or

children's social services). Information, including data, that is passed on must be accurate, up to date and relevant.

Data protection

Data is any information that can be used to identify a person. The Data Protection Act 1998 is the key legislation that applies to the collection, use of and storage of information. Early years settings must ensure that policies and procedures relating to information about children and their families are in line with this legislation. For example, when collecting data about children and their families it is essential that it is relevant and is used for a specific purpose. Professionals must make sure that information that is written down or passed on verbally is accurate. Information must be reviewed regularly in order to keep it up to date. All data about children and families must be kept safe and secure. It is essential that information is never left on a desk but is immediately locked in a filing cabinet in an office or, if kept electronically, on a safe system that can only be accessed via a password.

Key term

Named person – a person who is the main point of contact.

Research

You can read more about the Data Protection Act on the UK Government website. You can also access this website by going to www.pearsonhotlinks.co.uk and searching for this ISBN: 9781447970965.

Did you know?

In 2009, Vanessa George was found guilty of sexually abusing young children in her care at a nursery where she had worked for three years. Even though she had begun to take children to a separate area to change them in private, none of the staff had raised concerns about her behaviour. During a review it was found that there was no whistle-blowing policy in place in the setting.

You can read about what happened and the subsequent recommendations that were made in the serious case review on the Plymouth City Council website. You can access this website by going to www.pearsonhotlinks.co.uk and searching for this ISBN: 9781447970965.

Concerns about colleagues

If you have concerns that a colleague or professional is abusing a child or that their practice is impacting on a child's welfare, your actions should be the same as if the abuser were a parent, family member or stranger. You must act immediately to protect children by informing the lead professional in your setting who has responsibility for safeguarding, or the manager. If you are unable to approach either person because they are involved in abuse or poor practice, you will need to contact social services.

This type of reporting is known as '**whistle-blowing**'. These are difficult situations, but your first priority must always be the child. It is important that you do not discuss what has happened with others who do not need to know. However, you may need to seek support for yourself from the person within your setting who has safeguarding responsibilities or a professional from an outside agency.

Key term

Whistle-blowing – raising concerns about the actions of an individual, group or organisation.

The child at the centre of care provision

In 2008, an Ofsted evaluation of child protection highlighted that in the majority of serious case reviews, professionals fail to see situations from the child's perspective. This happens when decisions are made by adults who consider that they know what is 'best' for the child without taking the child's own feelings into account. Professionals must remember that every child's experience is different. It is important, therefore, that children are at the centre

of any assessment of their needs. Children who are in need, at risk of abuse or who have been abused are particularly vulnerable, so it is important that any assessments take their holistic developmental and health needs into consideration. To do this, early years professionals must spend time listening to the child and also observing them, as well as speaking to parents and others who work closely with them. The child and their family should also be fully involved in any decisions about the services that will be put in place. This strategy will ensure that targeted and effective support is provided. Where support is provided by different services it is referred to as the 'team around the child'.

Recognising the individual needs of children and barriers to equality

If children are put at the centre of care provision, their individual needs will be recognised.

Every child has their own particular needs. This may be because of their age, stage of development, state of health, culture or family background. These needs may present barriers to children and stop them feeling accepted or included in the setting. These feelings can significantly affect a child's confidence and self-esteem. Knowing about a child's individual needs enables adults to break down these barriers to equality and support the child in an appropriate way. It is important that you recognise where there are barriers and how these can be overcome through inclusive practice.

The importance of listening

Article 12 of the UNCRC states that all children who are able to express themselves should have the right to do so freely. Early years professionals must always take the child's views into consideration. Involving children in decisions about themselves will show them that we value what they say, their opinions and ideas. These may be everyday decisions such as the activity they want to take part in or life-changing decisions about their future. Of course, not all children can express themselves easily. They may be very young or have communication difficulties. If so, they can be helped to communicate by using signing, objects of reference or pictures. In some situations, when a child's family is not able to speak for the child, an **advocate** may represent their views.

> **Key term**
>
> **Advocate** – a person who represents the views of the child.

Routines for active listening

Routines in a setting should include time set aside for individual children to spend time with a key adult when they have their undivided attention. This can happen naturally during mealtimes or when helping children with their personal care. It is important to be receptive to children's chatter during these one-to-one interactions as they often give clues to any worries they may have. Activities should be planned that encourage children to listen and respond to each other. This will help them to understand the points of view of others and to build friendships.

The importance of recognising feelings

Very young children have difficulty understanding their feelings. They can experience a wide variety of emotions such anger, jealousy, frustration, fear or excitement. Without support, children often find it difficult to express or deal with their feelings. Children's emotions can be revealed in different ways, for instance in their facial expressions, body language or behaviour.

Babies can be soothed to reassure and calm them. As their vocabulary expands, children can be helped by giving them the words to use to describe the way they feel. For example, you could say, 'I know you felt sad when Mum left but she will be back soon to take you home for dinner', or 'I know you are angry because James is playing with the car but it will be your turn next.' This will give children the message that it is fine to have these feelings and that you can empathise with them.

At times, children can be overcome by their emotions and this can result in negative behaviour. If they lose control they can become quite frightened. Young children may stamp their feet, scream, cry or have temper tantrums. Sometimes, when angry or jealous, children can display physical aggression towards other children or adults.

Why is it important to reassure a child who is feeling distressed?

It is important that the adult recognises the cause of the child's feelings and supports them to express their feelings in an appropriate way. Physical play can be a safe way for children to release their emotions, for instance, kicking a ball, climbing or playing with soft and flexible (malleable) materials.

Link

Go to Unit 1, Unit 6 and Unit 7 where you will find out more information about children's emotional, social and communication development.

The importance of supporting social and emotional development

Children's emotional and social development involves them having an awareness of themselves and how they relate to others. It is important that children are nurtured in these early years as they develop their personality and temperament. The environment has a direct influence on the way that children feel about themselves; they will thrive when they are made to feel safe and secure. When children are confident, independent and have good self-esteem they are more able to cope with the everyday difficulties they may come across. Children who are independent and self-confident are also more likely to tell an adult when they are unhappy about behaviour being shown towards them. It is important that their social and emotional development is promoted through every aspect of their care. Table 8.2 shows ways to promote the emotional and social development of children and the benefits that this has.

The importance of being an approachable adult

Think about someone you know with qualities that make them approachable. It is likely to be someone who always has time for you and is genuinely interested in what you do and your likes and dislikes. You will be shown respect. They demonstrate active listening because they are keen to hear your views and then take what you say into consideration. They may not always agree with you but they will be consistent and fair.

In an early years setting these qualities are essential. The key person provides for all the baby's or child's needs when the parent is not there. Although it is

Table 8.2 Ways to promote emotional and social development

Ways to promote emotional and social development	Benefits
Providing challenging activities such as climbing, balancing, building a den and exploring new materials.	Gives children a sense of achievement and helps to develop their self-esteem and confidence.
Giving choice in everyday activities such as which jumper to put on or what activity to take part in.	Develops children's confidence in making their own decisions. They will have more confidence in saying 'no' when they feel uncomfortable about an adult's actions.
Developing skills in personal care such as washing and brushing teeth and providing play activities, e.g. dressing a teddy and tying laces.	Helps them to become more independent. Children who are dependent on adults are more vulnerable to abuse.
Building relationships through activities such as games that involve turn taking, role play or circle time.	Helps children to make friends, become more tolerant of others and to respond appropriately when there are disagreements.

important for them to build a strong relationship with the child, the adult needs to remember that this relationship is different from the relationship between a child and their parent. The relationship should always remain professional. Despite this, it is essential that the adult knows the child's background and interests so they can demonstrate a genuine interest in the child. The key person should know and talk about things that interest the child, for example, they could suggest making pink icing during a cake-baking activity if that is the child's favourite colour.

Body language

Facial expressions and body language are very important. They give very clear signals to the child that an adult is receptive to their approach. From a very early age, babies will recognise that an adult is happy to see them. Just a smile will encourage a child to interact. By using eye contact and leaning towards children you show that you are listening to them. Think about how we use gestures in everyday activities. Adults may show a thumb to indicate to a child that it is fine to do something, or they may gesture with their hand to say 'come over and join our activity'.

The role of observation and reflection

Vigilance is crucial in early years settings. It plays an important role in protecting children from harm and neglect, and in promoting their welfare. Being vigilant requires you to constantly observe children in different situations and then use these observations to reflect on, and identify, any changes in their development and behaviour. This in turn means that support can be put in place immediately if irregular changes are noticed. This is critical for children who may have been abused or neglected. Figure 8.2 highlights the role of observation in child protection.

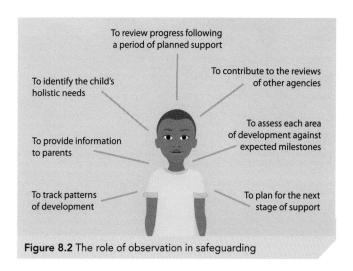

To review progress following a period of planned support

To identify the child's holistic needs

To contribute to the reviews of other agencies

To provide information to parents

To assess each area of development against expected milestones

To track patterns of development

To plan for the next stage of support

Figure 8.2 The role of observation in safeguarding

Empowering children

It is not always possible to prevent abuse, but adults can reduce the risk of abuse happening by providing an environment that helps children to protect themselves. Children will feel more confident disclosing their fears in an environment that encourages supportive relationships and recognises and celebrates individuality.

Games and activities are a good way to help children protect themselves. They can also be used to support children who have been abused. Activities can provide indirect support by developing children's confidence and self-esteem or by helping them to release negative feelings. Activities can also be used to empower children to protect themselves and make safe choices in difficult situations.

Activities promoting confidence and self-esteem

The following types of activities can be used to help to promote children's welfare by improving their confidence and self-esteem.

- Open-ended activities such as construction and water play allow children to succeed at their own level of ability.
- Physical activities involving running, climbing and sit-and-ride toys boost children's energy and feelings of wellbeing.
- Art, music and movement activities help children to release their anxieties and explore their feelings.
- Emotive activities such as reading stories, circle time and the use of emotion cards support children to express their emotions.

Link

Go to Unit 1: Section B and C where you will find out more information about the role of observation and the methods that can be used.

What are the benefits of physical activity for these children?

Research

Research the activities and games that are used in your own setting to empower children and to promote their confidence and self-esteem. You could ask your manager if you can support one of these activities.

Games and activities that empower children to protect themselves

The following types of activities empower children to protect themselves.

- Body-awareness games and activities such as puzzles, matching/identification games, colouring, and songs and rhymes such as 'I've got a body, a very busy body'.

- Activities that teach children to be assertive. For example, teaching children to say no to inappropriate or harmful behaviour by using puppets, stories, drama or body-awareness songs such as 'My body belongs to me'.

- Activities that teach children not to keep secrets by helping them to understand the difference between surprises (e.g. about presents and parties) and secrets (e.g. when children are hurt or touched inappropriately).

- Activities that teach children what to do if they are lost, such as circle time, the use of drama or use of puppets.

- Activities that explore feelings, such as producing anti-bullying or 'group rules' posters. Older children should be given the opportunity to discuss what they understand by the term 'bullying'.

The importance of maintaining accurate and coherent records

Settings must establish a process for recording welfare concerns about individual children. This is called a welfare or safeguarding file and it will be kept separate from non-sensitive information such as a child's contact details. Each separate piece of information, such as a change in a child's behaviour or an injury, helps to builds up a picture of the child's developmental welfare – a bit like a jigsaw puzzle. The person in the setting with safeguarding responsibilities will gain an overview of concerns that have been raised by different professionals. Information may include:

- concerns about health and welfare

- records of discussions about a child's health and welfare including face-to-face conversations, telephone calls or meetings

- formal plans such as an IEP or child protection plan

- copies of letters sent or received about a child's welfare.

It is important that any information entered into the safeguarding file is written accurately and clearly. If information is not clear or does not show accurate dates, for instance, it will be more difficult to make decisions or timely referrals. A key piece of information that is missed out or cannot be deciphered could have serious consequences for a child's safety and welfare. Inaccurate information could even affect the outcome of a court case where there has been abuse.

3A.P1 | 3A.P2 | 3A.M1 | 3A.D1

1 Produce a presentation for your peers that provides information on the role of the early years professional in exercising their duty of care. It should contain reference to protecting children from harm and promoting their welfare. The presentation should include:

- an introduction to the duty of care in early years practice with reference to current legislation and statutory guidelines
- children's right to be safe with reference to the United Nations Convention on the Rights of the Child
- the importance of passing on concerns about the practice of colleagues, professionals or others
- the importance of putting children's needs at the centre of practice, including recognising individual needs and barriers to equality
- the importance of being an approachable adult, including recognising children's feelings, listening to children and valuing their views
- the importance of supporting emotional and social development in keeping children safe and promoting wellbeing

- the importance of observation in identifying needs and recognising changes in behaviour
- the importance of maintaining accurate and coherent records with respect to children's welfare.

2 Produce a handout for your peers that contains four ideas for activities and games for children of two different age groups. The activities and games should include those that will support children's confidence and self-esteem, and empower them to protect themselves.

3 Using information from your presentation, in a small group:

- analyse the role of the early years professional in safeguarding and promoting the welfare of children
- make suggestions for ways that early years professionals can most effectively contribute to safeguarding and promoting the welfare of children
- discuss the differences in approach early years professionals should take to safeguard children at different ages and stages of development.

B Understand types and indicators of child abuse

There are four types of abuse recognised by law: physical, sexual and emotional abuse, and neglect. Bullying is also abuse and can take different forms. Many children who are abused experience more than one type of abuse. For instance, a child who is sexually abused is usually also emotionally abused.

Types of abuse

Physical abuse and injury

Physical abuse happens when a child is physically hurt or injured. Hitting a child with hands or implements or kicking, burning, scalding, suffocating, throwing

and shaking a child are all forms of physical abuse. Poisoning or acts that induce illness in a child are also forms of physical abuse.

Sexual abuse

Sexual abuse happens when a child is forced or persuaded into sexual activities or situations by others. It may involve physical and/or non-physical contact. Physical contact may be penetration (rape) or touching the child's body for sexual gratification. Physical contact also includes masturbation or touching a child inappropriately, even if it is outside their clothing. Non-physical sexual abuse involves forcing or enticing a child to look at sexual materials and sexual activity, or watching a child undress. This is not restricted to adults who are in close proximity to a child; there is a growing problem of sexual abuse happening via the Internet.

Emotional abuse

Emotional or psychological abuse happens when the child suffers persistent ill-treatment that affects their emotional development. It may involve making the child feel frightened, unloved, worthless or in danger. Emotional abuse may happen on its own, but it often takes place with other types of abuse.

Neglect

The legal definition of neglect is the persistent failure to meet a child's basic physical and/or psychological needs. This happens when a child is not provided with adequate food, shelter, clothing or medical care. It also includes not providing for their developmental, educational or emotional needs.

Domestic abuse

Domestic abuse is also a recognised form of abuse. Domestic abuse may be physical, sexual, psychological, emotional or financial and is often a combination of these. This type of abuse happens between adults in the family and is not directly aimed at children. As a result, you may think that it will not affect children in the same way as abuse directed at the child. However, research has shown that when children witness domestic abuse it is likely to have a profound impact on their welfare. It can affect children even if they do not witness the abuse directly and only see the result of the abuse, such as a parent who is upset or injured. Research also shows that children in families where domestic abuse takes place are more likely to be subjected to abuse themselves.

Signs that may indicate abuse

If a child is being abused they may show physical signs and/or changes in their behaviour. Changes in behaviour may not indicate a particular type of abuse, but could indicate that a child has been disturbed by something that has happened to them. A child may make comments that hint that all is not well. For instance, they may mention that they have

watched an 'adult' film or that they don't like being collected from nursery by a particular person.

You may notice that a child:

- becomes clingy
- starts to wet or soil themselves after they have become dry
- rocks their body, or twists or pulls out their hair
- starts to suck their thumb
- is reluctant to play with others and make friends
- becomes aggressive or passive
- has a change in disposition.

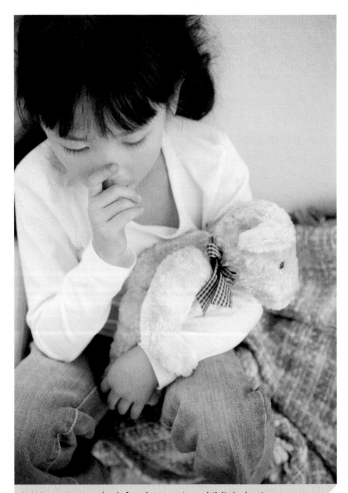

It is important to look for changes in a child's behaviour.

Physical signs of abuse

Young children frequently have bumps or falls and as a result they will have bruises or grazes, often on their knees or forehead. These marks can usually be explained. Physical signs where there is no explanation, or where the reasons given are

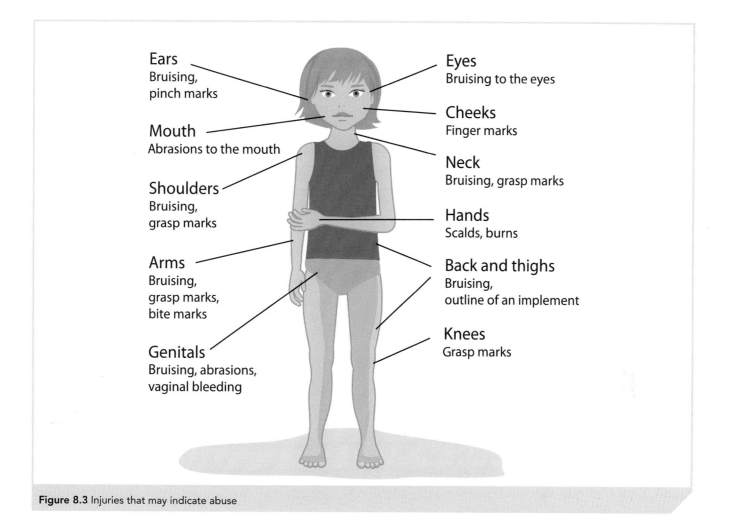

Ears
Bruising,
pinch marks

Mouth
Abrasions to the mouth

Shoulders
Bruising,
grasp marks

Arms
Bruising,
grasp marks,
bite marks

Genitals
Bruising, abrasions,
vaginal bleeding

Eyes
Bruising to the eyes

Cheeks
Finger marks

Neck
Bruising, grasp marks

Hands
Scalds, burns

Back and thighs
Bruising,
outline of an implement

Knees
Grasp marks

Figure 8.3 Injuries that may indicate abuse

contradictory, are a cause for concern. Children may display unusual injuries that would not occur accidentally, such as grasp marks, cigarette burns or bruising to both eyes. Figure 8.3 shows the type of injuries that may indicate abuse.

Signs of neglect

Neglect can show in a child's appearance and behaviour. Signs may include that a child:

- is underweight for their age
- is overweight for their age
- has illnesses that have been left untreated
- is unusually tired
- has poor personal hygiene
- shows they are hungry by eating unusually large amounts, eating quickly or taking food from others
- wears dirty clothing, or unsuitable clothing for the weather.

Behaviour that may indicate sexual abuse

It is important that you are able to recognise when behaviour is inappropriate for a child's age and stage of development. In the early years it is natural for very young children to show interest in their own body parts. They will use personal or childlike terms to describe them. From the age of 3 years they will play games such as mummies and daddies or hospitals. When they reach 5 years old they will become interested in the bodies of their friends. Children do touch or rub their own genitals from time to time.

It becomes a cause for concern if behaviour becomes compulsive or if it is not appropriate for a child's age or stage of development – for example, if they use explicit sexual terms or indicate by what they say, or the way they act, that they may have seen sexual acts.

Being vigilant

The National Society for the Prevention of Cruelty to Children (NSPCC) statistics show that in June 2012, more than 50,000 children in the UK were known to be at risk of abuse. However, this is not the whole picture, as abuse is not always recognised or reported. Research suggests that around half of the abuse of children goes unnoticed at the time it is actually happening. This means that for many children, adults just do not recognise the signs. Each child is unique, so children will show signs of abuse in different ways. It is important that you can recognise changes in children's behaviour, not just the behaviour itself. A child who is usually quiet may become more active, or an active child may become withdrawn. The **key person** role is critical because an early years professional gets to know the child and family very well and, therefore, they are likely to notice even minor changes in behaviour.

The signs identified in Figure 8.3 do not always mean that abuse is happening, as there may be other explanations. For example, what appears to be bruising may be a birthmark, and children are sometimes withdrawn simply because they are unwell. Even so, signs must never be ignored. If you are in any doubt, signs must be reported or a child could be put at risk.

Always seek advice when:

- a child's development has slowed or even **regressed**
- a child lacks interest, for example, they are not taking part in play
- a child becomes clingy and reluctant to leave their key person
- a child appears unusually tired
- a parent raises concerns about their child's behaviour, development and/or welfare
- a child is showing inappropriate behaviour towards adults, such as overfamiliarity.

Children who are more vulnerable

You must be extra vigilant if you work with babies or children who have a disability. Research by the NSPCC indicates that these groups are at a much higher risk of abuse or neglect. It may shock you to find out that children under 1 year old are eight times more likely to be abused than older children, and almost half of the **serious case reviews** are for children under 1 year old.

Babies and children who have a disability are at higher risk because they:

- are dependent on others for all of their care
- are not able to communicate that they have been abused
- require intimate care
- show signs that can be confused with symptoms of a physical or learning disability.

Key terms

Disposition – a child's nature or temperament.

Key person – an early years professional designated to take responsibility for a child's emotional wellbeing by having a strong attachment with them and a good relationship with their parents.

Regress – to move backwards to a previous stage.

Serious case review – a review carried out when a child has died or has been seriously injured as a result of neglect.

Disclosure

Some children may disclose that they have been or are being abused. However, more often, a child may start to say something and then clam up. For example, they may say, 'I've got a secret…' They may just give a hint, for example, 'I don't like Peter coming in my room.' You must be receptive to these types of comments.

Parents or other adults may approach you to tell you that they are concerned a child may be being abused. You must let them know that you will need to share any information with your manager or the person in the setting who has designated responsibility for child protection.

The effects of abuse

The effects of abuse will be different depending on the type of abuse and the child's **disposition**. Each type of abuse can seriously affect children's health and every area of their development: emotional, social, physical and cognitive. Children who have been abused may be underweight or take longer to crawl, walk or talk compared to children of the same age. The early years are critical, so anything that prevents a child from learning may have lasting consequences for their attainment over time.

Physical abuse can cause temporary or permanent injury. Broken bones, scalds or burns affect not only a child's health and physical development but also their self-esteem. Non-accidental head injuries (often caused by shaking) may cause neurological impairment or even death.

Children who have been abused often feel that it is their fault and this feeling causes them to think badly of themselves. In the short term, children will lack confidence and self-esteem. They may find it more difficult to cope with the normal transitions that happen in their lives, such as transferring to primary school.

In the longer term, research suggests that abuse or neglect has serious effects on emotional and social development. Adults who were abused as young children often experience difficulties in building relationships, including sexual relationships. They also suffer from a higher incidence of mental health problems. Abuse can result in self-harm or even suicide.

People who abuse

Anyone who has contact with children can abuse them. There are often preconceptions held about who is likely to abuse children. Common beliefs include that it is men who sexually abuse children or that step-parents are more likely to abuse children than birth parents. These beliefs are unfounded. The abuse we read about in the papers is often carried out by strangers, but this is actually very rare. In most cases, abuse is carried out by people known to the child: a parent, family member or someone who works with the child. Adolescents may also abuse children who are younger than themselves.

Although abuse happens across all sections of society and across all cultures, there are factors within a home that increase the risk of abuse. These factors include:

- domestic violence
- drug or alcohol abuse
- mental health problems
- lack of knowledge about child development/children's needs
- poverty/unemployment.

Assessment practice 8.2   3B.P3 | 3B.M2

It is important that everyone working in early years settings is aware of the types of abuse, the signs that indicate abuse may be happening and the impact that abuse may have on children's development.

1 Plan a training session for new learners that includes:
   - a poster that shows the types of abuse
   - a handout with information on:
     - the physical and behavioural signs to look for that may indicate abuse
     - the importance of being vigilant
     - people who may abuse.
2 In a small group discuss the impact that abuse may have on children's all-round development.

C Understand how to respond appropriately to concerns that a child has been abused

Policies and procedures

A safeguarding policy is a statement that explains the setting's commitment to keeping children safe and promoting their welfare. It also describes how it intends to do this. Procedures should give clear guidance to staff on how to achieve the aims set out in the policy. For instance, the policy may state that the setting has a commitment to maintaining confidentiality and that data relating to children and their families will be kept safe. Procedures will give guidance on when and how information may be shared, how to record and store information and who may access it.

Policies must meet the requirements of the key legislation outlined in Table 8.1 (or the relevant legislation for your home country). Policies state the aims of the setting or service in protecting children and ways to promote their welfare. They should also include procedures for safe working practice that must be followed in different child protection situations.

Recently, as a result of increased use of the Internet and electronic communication systems, children are being put at more risk of harm. Childcare settings are now required to have policies and procedures on e-safety, including monitoring procedures and having filters in place to ensure that children do not access unsuitable materials and information online.

Failure to comply with a setting's policy for safeguarding may put children at risk of harm or abuse.

Figure 8.4 shows the areas of importance surrounding safeguarding.

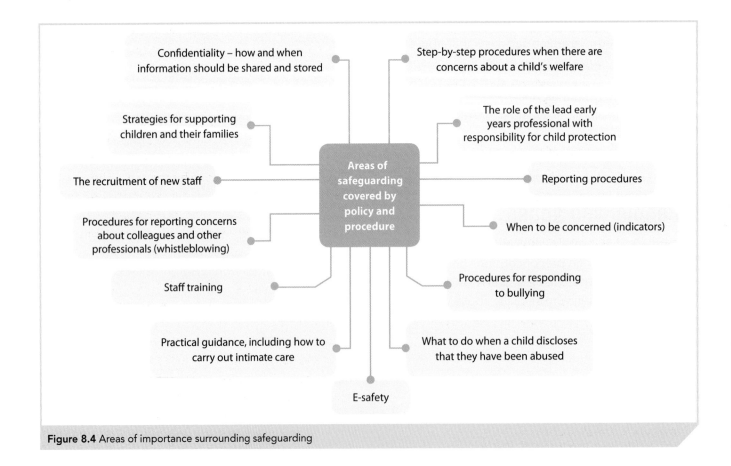

Figure 8.4 Areas of importance surrounding safeguarding

Research

Ask your manager or the person with responsibility for safeguarding for a copy of your setting's policy for safeguarding and child protection (including bullying and e-safety).

1 Read through the policy.

2 Highlight any parts of the policy you are unsure about and ask your manager or the person responsible for child protection about these parts.

3 Read through the policy again to find detailed guidance on each of the areas in Figure 8.4.

Responding appropriately to a child who is disclosing abuse

Although you must avoid jumping to conclusions, you must always respond when you notice typical physical signs of abuse or changes in a child's behaviour. Hints or disclosures of abuse by a child can happen when you least expect them so it is important that you are prepared. You must know what to do and what to say to the child. It is also important to know what you should not do. You must report concerns to the lead early years professional with responsibility for child protection as soon as possible.

Always:

- take disclosure seriously
- remain calm and listen carefully
- avoid using leading questions
- reassure the child that they are not to blame
- tell children that you will have to tell someone who can help them
- write down what you have observed or what has been said as soon as possible
- pass information to the person who is responsible for child protection.

Never:

- promise to keep information a secret
- interrogate or ask further questions, as this could affect later investigations

- make promises to children or adults who tell you about abuse
- discuss what has happened with other colleagues or the child's family.

Activity

Read the three scenarios below. Then:

1 jot down what you, as the professional, should initially say and do in each situation

2 produce a flow chart to show what action you should take

3 share your ideas with two or three peers

4 agree the best action in each situation

5 feed back your decisions to the whole group.

Scenario 1

At the local shops Samirah bumped into a parent of one of the children who attends the nursery where she works. The parent told her that she was concerned about Kayleigh, her daughter's 3-year-old friend. She said that she saw Kayleigh looking out of the window crying late at night and that she was sure that her mother was out. She asked Samirah not to say anything as she was worried that the mother could cause trouble for her.

Scenario 2

Sam is 5 years old. He has recently transferred to Year 1. One day he seemed very reluctant to undress for PE. The classroom assistant, Marc, encouraged him to change his top but, as he removed his T-shirt, Marc noticed bruising on Sam's back. When Marc asked Sam how he had hurt his back he said, 'Mum hurt me 'cause I hit my sister.'

Scenario 3

Jessica is 2 years old. Ellie, a learner working in the nursery that Jessica attends, accompanied her and a group of other children to the toilet area. When Jessica went to the toilet she cried out and said to Ellie that her bottom hurt. When Ellie replied that she would let her dad know when he came to collect her, Jessica looked scared and said, 'No, it's a secret.'

The importance of believing the child

Children will rarely lie about child abuse. It takes a child a lot of courage to tell someone what has happened to them. More often, they will only hint at what is happening because they are afraid of the abuser or may think that they won't be believed. Imagine how a child may feel if an adult just dismisses something they have said as being a lie or exaggeration.

Some adults may feel a reluctance to believe a child because they:

- have assumptions about abuse that makes them less likely to believe some children – for example, they may believe that professionals would not abuse their children
- know and like the adult
- find it difficult to believe that an adult could act towards a child in a particular way
- assume that the behaviour is acceptable in some cultures
- are concerned that they are interpreting what has been said incorrectly and that they are making a fuss.

If we do not believe children it will make them less willing to repeat their fears to us or other adults. This can result in abuse going undetected for some time and putting children at further risk. Remember that it is your duty to pass on concerns using the correct procedures. It is not your role to decide if a child has been abused. Avoid judgements and do not jump to conclusions; you should only share any concerns you may have.

The importance of an appropriate response to concerns

It is always upsetting if we find out that a child has been harmed or neglected but it is important not to show our own emotions. Facial expressions and body language can give mixed messages. If an adult appears shocked, the child is likely to feel that they are in the wrong or even that they 'deserved' the abuse. It is the child's feelings that are important and these feelings should be recognised and acknowledged.

You should also think about how you would respond verbally if a child tells you they are being abused. Your first response is really important and it can affect how well a child copes. Your response should give the message that the child has done the right thing in telling you. For instance, you could say, 'I'm glad that you have told me', or 'You have done the right thing to let me know that you are worried.' You can also show that you understand their feelings. For example, you could comment that the act must have made the child feel scared or unhappy.

Responses should be open to avoid leading the child into giving a particular answer. For example, rather than ask, 'Did your dad hit you with a belt?' you may ask, 'How did you get those bruises?' You may feel angry with the abuser but you should not make comments or pass judgements on the person who has been named. Instead, you should focus on reassuring the child that the action was wrong.

Activity

You should always follow good practice guidelines in your work setting and during off-site visits to prevent concerns being raised about your own behaviour.

Produce a good practice guidance leaflet for staff.

The importance of following reporting procedures

It is important that you know about and follow reporting procedures in your own service or setting. Reports should be passed to the named professional in the setting with responsibility for safeguarding. You must ensure that reports are written clearly, carefully and factually. They should include:

- the child's name and date of birth
- the time and date when signs were noticed or abuse was disclosed
- others who were present
- what happened, including anything that was said
- your own signature and the date.

Remember that the report may need to be used in future reviews, child protection conferences or even court cases. You should always be objective in your comments and avoid making any value judgements. For example, 'Chloe's clothes smelled strongly of urine' is preferable to 'Chloe is always dirty and neglected'. It is also important that you directly report the words that the child used and do not change words, for instance 'he showed me his willy' and not 'she said he showed his penis to her'.

Confidentiality and information sharing

Confidentiality should always be observed. This usually means that information that has been told to you can only be passed on when permission has been given. The exception to this is when you believe that a child is at risk of abuse. But remember, although you have a duty to pass on information, you should only do this to people who need to know, that is, only people involved in the child protection process. Knowing when and how to pass information on is not always clear-cut so it is essential that you get advice from your manager, the early years professional with responsibility for child protection or social services if you are unsure.

▌Child protection procedures

If the person in the setting who is responsible for safeguarding believes that a child may be at risk, they must immediately report their concerns to the children's social care department in the local authority. They may speak to a social worker on the telephone but concerns must be put in writing within 48 hours of the initial report. The social worker will then decide if an early help assessment is required within one working day.

Early help assessment

An early help assessment involves an assessment of the child's developmental needs. It also involves investigating whether the child's family can adequately support the child to meet their needs. Other factors that could affect the family, such as health problems or poverty, will also be considered. A professional, for instance a social worker or key person, will be identified to lead the assessment with other relevant people from different agencies and the child's parents contributing information. Assessments must be completed within 45 days of the referral to social services.

If you have any concerns you must get advice from your manager or the person responsible for child protection.

Where it is considered that a child is 'in need' but they have not been, and are unlikely to be harmed, a Child in Need meeting will be held, which will be chaired by a social worker. This may involve other services but, most importantly, it will involve the child and their parents. This instance may arise, for example, where a parent has been unable to take sufficient care of a child because they are unemployed or have been seriously ill. In these cases, under Section 17 of the Children Act 1989, services must be put into place to ease the problems, reduce the risk of abuse and promote the child's welfare.

Child Protection Conferences

When there is sufficient concern that a child has been harmed or is likely to be harmed, a strategy discussion will take place to decide whether enquiries must be initiated under Section 47 of the Children Act 1989. See Table 8.1 for some information about Section 47. The strategy discussion will then be followed by a more in-depth core assessment of the child's needs. If it is considered that the child remains at risk of harm, a Child Protection Conference will be held within 15 working days of the strategy discussion, led by a manager from children's social care. The Conference will be attended by professionals from a range of relevant services such as health, social care and early years providers. The purpose of the Conference is to review the child's needs and the level of risk of harm or abuse to the child. A child who is thought to be at continued risk will become the subject of a child protection plan and an outline plan will be discussed. If a child is thought to be at immediate risk the local authority can apply for an Emergency Protection Order (EPO) to remove the child from the family or to remove the perpetrator of abuse.

Child protection plan

Once it has been agreed by the conference that the child should be the subject of a child protection plan, there will be a meeting of key professionals led by a named key worker. The purpose of the plan is to keep the child safe from harm. It should address the child's immediate needs and also take their long-term needs into consideration. The plan may also include information on the support to be given to family members to help them to safeguard the child.

The plan must:

- be based on the information learned about the child and their family during the core assessment
- identify the interventions that are necessary to give the best outcome for the child
- identify the services, professionals and the child's parents or carers and their role in supporting the plan
- be regularly reviewed.

A child will no longer be a subject of a child protection plan when a decision is made during a review meeting that the child is no longer at risk of harm.

The role of local agencies

Children's Social Care

Children's Social Care has a key role to safeguard and promote the welfare of children who are in need. To do this it must work in partnership with parents and other agencies. Social workers lead on assessments at each stage of the child protection procedures, recording information and taking decisions (with their manager) on further action. They are also responsible for conducting interviews with children and parents.

Police

The police work closely with Children's Social Care to protect children from harm. The police have a particular role to play. All forces have a Child Abuse Investigation Unit (CAIU), which has powers to take action such as removing the child or the perpetrator of abuse when a child is in immediate danger. They will gather evidence and investigate when it is thought a crime has been committed.

Health professionals

Health professionals, in particular GPs and doctors in emergency departments, may examine children who have injuries they suspect to be non-accidental. They have a duty to alert Children's Social Care when abuse is suspected. Health professionals will carry out medical examinations and, if necessary, give evidence in court.

How agencies work together

The responsibilities for protecting children and promoting their welfare are set out in the Children Act 2004 and we have already covered the roles and responsibilities of some of the key agencies. Although their roles are clear, protection cannot be provided by these individual agencies in isolation. This was highlighted in Lord Laming's report (2009), following the death of Victoria Climbié in 2000, where he concluded that services had failed to share their concerns about her welfare. As a result, the 2004 Act set out the statutory duty for services to work more closely. A document produced by the Department for Education entitled 'Working Together to Safeguard Children' (2013) gives guidance on how this collaboration should be achieved.

Local authorities have responsibility for the welfare and protection of children in their area. Children's social services operate within local authorities and are the main point of contact when there are concerns about child protection. Local authorities are required to coordinate children's services in partnership with a wide range of services. Services may include public services such as the police, private organisations such as specialist health professionals and voluntary organisations, such as advocacy services. In supporting a child who is at risk of harm and their family, it is likely that professionals from different services will be required to assess the child's needs and contribute their own particular area of expertise in the planning and provision of support.

Local Safeguarding Children Boards

In England and Wales, the Children Act 2004 requires there to be a Local Safeguarding Children Board (LSCB) in every local area. Each Board is made up of experts from the range of children's services. The LSCB has a statutory duty to oversee the work of key agencies in the context of child protection. They develop policy and procedures for the recruitment of people who work with children and young people, and for their ongoing training.

An important aspect of their work is to conduct a serious case review when a child dies as a result of abuse or neglect. In some instances, the LSCB may undertake a review in particularly serious cases of sexual abuse and/or when a child has sustained a life-threatening injury.

A detailed report is published following each serious case review. It includes information on what happened to the child, the services that have been involved with the family, how they worked together and recommendations about how to reduce the risk of abuse in the future. You can access reports of serious case reviews on your Local Authority LSCB website.

Research

Read the serious case review report following the death of Daniel Pelka in March 2012. It can be found on the website for the LSCB in Coventry. You can also access this website by going to www.pearsonhotlinks.uk and searching for this ISBN: 9781447970965.

The comparable system in Northern Ireland is the statutory regional Safeguarding Board (SBNI). In Scotland, there are local Child Protection Committees (CPCs) that are responsible for child protection processes in local areas.

The role of outside agencies

The National Society for the Prevention of Cruelty to Children (NSPCC)

The NSPCC is a charitable organisation. Its role, as its name suggests, is to work to protect children from abuse. The NSPCC is the only charitable organisation that has the statutory power, alongside the police and children's social services, to take action when children are at risk of abuse. The NSPCC also:

- provides services to support families and children
- provides a helpline for people to call who are worried about a child
- provides a helpline for children in distress or danger
- raises awareness of abuse through, for example, advertising and training materials
- works to influence the law and social policy to better protect children
- shares expertise with other professionals.

The responsibility of early years providers to comply with current legislation and guidance

The policies and procedures that settings must have in place for safeguarding have been outlined earlier in Section A. They are underpinned by legislation. Staff must comply with them to ensure that children are kept safe and that their welfare is promoted. Consider the implications for children of staff not sharing concerns about them, or of a setting that does not check whether a new staff member is suitable to work with children. Failure to follow policies and procedures could put children at serious risk of harm or abuse and affect their health and welfare. Staff who do not follow policy and procedures may be subject to disciplinary proceedings and may even be dismissed.

Further reading and resources

Websites

The Department for Education: www.education.gov.uk

Publications available from www.education.gov.uk:

'Working Together to Safeguard Children' (2013)

'What to do if you're worried a child is being abused' (2006)

'Safeguarding disabled children' (2009)

The NSPCC: www.nspcc.gov.uk

Barnardo's: www.barnardos.org.uk

Kidscape: www.kidscape.org.uk

Assessment practice 8.3

3C.P4 | 3C.P5 | 3C.M3 | 3C.D2

Read the following case study and then complete the tasks that follow.

Millie is 5 years old. She lives with her mum, dad and two older brothers: Jamie, aged 15 and Sean, aged 12. At school one day, Millie appeared very quiet after an activity that involved the children exploring their emotions. At snack time her teacher, Janet, sat with Millie and asked her why she was upset. Millie was quiet for a moment and then said, 'I don't like Jamie coming into my room, he hurts me.'

1 Produce a flow chart that gives information on the process for reporting and recording concerns about abuse.

2 Explain why it is important that Janet follows the correct procedures and the consequences of not doing so.

3 How should Janet respond to Millie's disclosure?

4 Why is it important that Janet responds appropriately?

5 The head teacher plans to review how staff respond to child protection. What advice should she give to staff about best practice relating to identifying and reporting abuse in the setting?

Ready for work?

Paul Gregos Deputy manager of a children's centre

I have worked at the centre for eight years but for the last three years I have had the role of lead professional for safeguarding, or child protection as it is sometimes known. My responsibility includes all aspects of safeguarding. One of the most important parts of my role is to be the first contact for staff if they have concerns about a child and to pass those concerns to social services.

Although I have this role, all staff in the setting must share the responsibility for child protection. You should remember that even if you are working as a volunteer or if you are a learner on placement, you also have a responsibility.

I ensure that the policy and procedures in the setting are regularly updated in line with legislation and guidelines. I also arrange for staff to undertake training so that I am confident they know the right thing to do if they notice signs that a child may be being abused.

Recently, one member of staff approached me because she had noticed that a child had grasp marks on her upper arms. What she did not know was that another member of staff had already reported that the child had become very withdrawn in the last two days. This incident shows how important it is to pass on concerns, even if you are not sure whether they indicate a child is being abused, because others may also have noticed a sign. When I passed this information to social services, the social worker found that the child's parent had been under considerable financial pressure. It was good that signs were noticed early because support was quickly put into place, which took the pressure off the parent. The child is being monitored now to ensure that they are safe but the outcome might have been much worse.

Skills for practice

Practise the following things related to safeguarding.

1 Become more aware of your listening skills when you are with children. Also consider your own body language. You could ask a colleague to observe your interactions and then and give you feedback.

2 Think of ways you can promote children's confidence and self-esteem. How do you give praise and let children know they are doing well?

3 Develop your own confidence in talking to professionals from outside agencies. You could ask them questions that would help your understanding of aspects of your course.

Introduction

As a professional working with children you will need to observe, assess and plan for their development, interests and strengths. Observing children is quite a skill but, once mastered, it is fascinating and rewarding. By making observations you can begin to understand a child and start to think and plan for their needs and interests. This requires knowledge of both child development and play. It also requires an understanding of the curriculum framework that is being used in your setting.

In this unit you will look at the importance of this process and how to observe and plan learning activities for children, based on the conclusions of your observations.

As observation, assessment and planning is a requirement of early years frameworks, it is important that you read this unit alongside the requirements of the early years framework in your home country. In England, this is the Early Years Foundation Stage.

Assessment: You will be assessed by a series of assignments set by your teacher/tutor.

Learning aims

In this unit you will:

A   understand the importance of observation, assessment and planning in work with children

B   be able to carry out and record accurate observations of children

C   be able to make accurate assessments from observations of children

D   be able to create, implement and review activity plans for children.

> Learning how to observe children has helped me become more aware of their needs and able to plan more effective activities.
>
> Jay, *a student on an early years course*

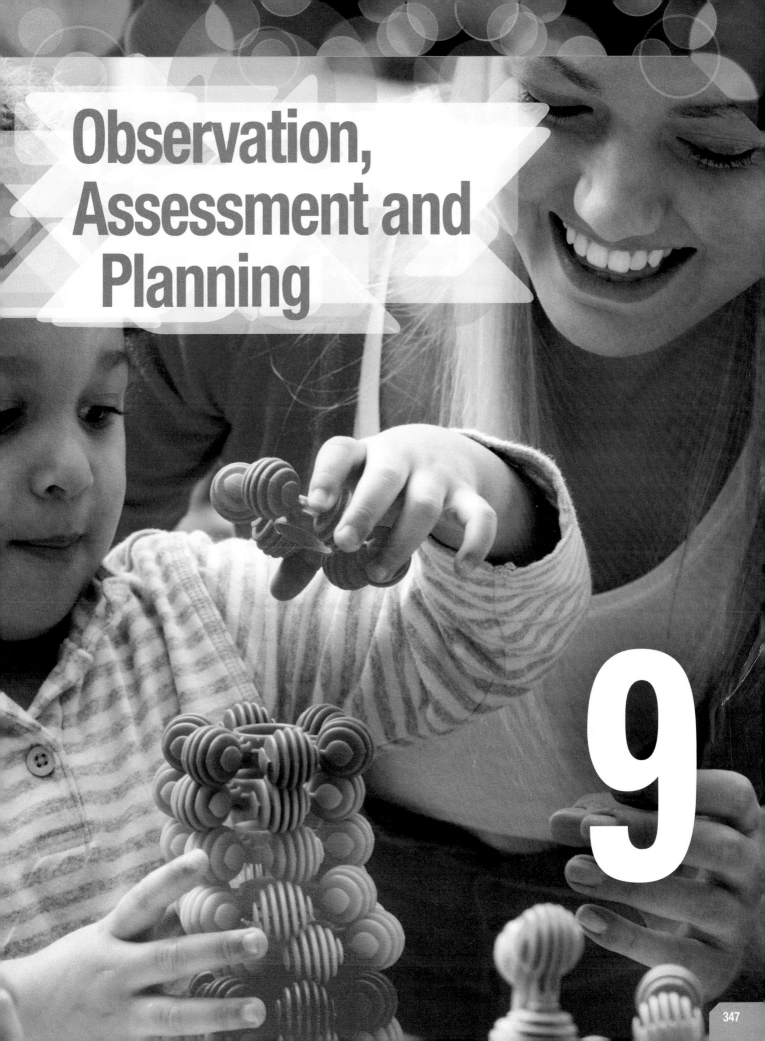

Observation, Assessment and Planning

9

∷BTEC
Assessment Zone

This table shows you what you must do in order to achieve a **Pass**, **Merit** or **Distinction** grade, and lists activities that relate to each learning aim.

Assessment criteria		
Pass	**Merit**	**Distinction**
Learning aim A: Understand the importance of observation, assessment and planning in work with children		
3A.P1 I&CT Explain the importance of observing and assessing children in early years settings to plan how to support their play, learning and development and to meet their individual needs. **Assessment practice 9.1**	**3A.M1** Analyse issues to be considered when observing and assessing children in early years settings. **Assessment practice 9.1**	
Learning aim B: Be able to carry out and record accurate observations of children		
3B.P2 Justify the selection of a set of observational methods to observe the development of a child in an early years setting, giving valid reasons for your choice. **Assessment practice 9.2**	**3B.M2** Analyse the appropriateness of selected observational methods for assessing the play and development of a child in an early years setting. **Assessment practice 9.2**	**3B.D1** Evaluate the validity of the selected observational methods used, making recommendations to address potential weaknesses. **Assessment practice 9.2**
3B.P3 Present full and effective records that show that accurate observation of a child's play and development has taken place. **Assessment practice 9.2**		
Learning aim C: Be able to make accurate assessments from observations of children		
3C.P4 Describe the observed child's stage of development, making use of relevant theories of development. **Assessment practice 9.2**	**3C.M3** Discuss how observation and assessment have contributed to an understanding of the child's development and needs. **Assessment practice 9.2**	**3C.D2** Evaluate how observation, assessment and planning have contributed to the observed child's progress in relation to theories of development. **Assessment practice 9.2**
3C.P5 Select, giving valid reasons, different activities and strategies which could enable the observed child to progress further in their learning. **Assessment practice 9.2**	**3C.M4** Analyse how formative and summative assessment can be used to shape a child's learning opportunities and plan next steps. **Assessment practice 9.2**	

continued

Assessment criteria (*continued*)		
Pass	Merit	Distinction
Learning aim D: Be able to create, implement and review activity plans for children		
3D.P6 I&CT English Present and implement activity plans appropriate for an observed child to support their play, learning and development, linked to the relevant curriculum. **Assessment practice 9.2**	**3D.M5** Analyse the extent to which the plans and implemented activities supported the child's play, learning and development. **Assessment practice 9.2**	**3D.D3** Evaluate own practice in the planning, creation and implementation of activities in terms of how it supported the child's play, learning and development. **Assessment practice 9.2**
3D.P7 English Review the effectiveness of the planning methods, plans and implemented activities in supporting the child's play, learning and development. **Assessment practice 9.2**		

English English Functional Skills signposting   I&CT Information and Communication Technology Functional Skills signposting

How you will be assessed

This unit will be assessed by a series of internally assessed tasks set by your teacher/tutor. They will include practical tasks that will need to be carried out on placement, and that link to your Practical Evidence Portfolio. Throughout this unit you will find assessment practice activities that will help you work towards your assessment. Completing these activities will not mean that you have achieved a particular grade, but you will have carried out useful research or preparation that will be relevant when it comes to your final assignment.

In order for you to carry out the tasks in your assignment, it is important that you check you have met all of the Pass grading criteria. You can do this as you work your way through the assignment.

If you are hoping to gain a Merit or Distinction, you should also make sure you present the information in your assignment in the style required by the relevant assessment criteria. For example, Merit criteria will require you to discuss and analyse, and Distinction criteria will require you to evaluate.

The assignment set by your teacher/tutor will consist of a number of tasks designed to meet the criteria in the table. This is likely to consist of a written assignment, but may also include activities such as:

* observation records of young children
* a report drawing conclusions from observations
* a presentation to your peers and teacher/tutor.

Getting started

Do you know how many different types of observation methods there are and why they might be used? List the methods that you know about already. By the end of this unit, see if you can add to your list.

A Understand the importance of observation, assessment and planning in work with children

Observing and assessing children is key to effective professional working. In this section, we will look at the many reasons why early years professionals and others observe and assess children.

The importance of observing and assessing children

There are many reasons for observing and carrying out assessments on children, shown in Figure 9.1.

Assessments are particularly important as a tool to:

- learn more about children's needs and interests
- track children's progress in relation to normative development
- check children's progress in relation to curriculum outcomes
- plan for next steps and shape learning opportunities for children
- identify when a child needs additional support
- share information with parents about their child
- provide information for other professionals
- help us reflect on our own practice.

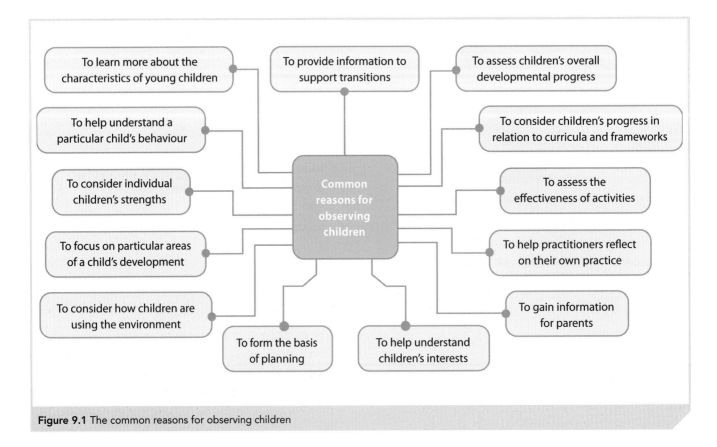

Figure 9.1 The common reasons for observing children

Reasons shown around "Common reasons for observing children":
- To learn more about the characteristics of young children
- To provide information to support transitions
- To assess children's overall developmental progress
- To help understand a particular child's behaviour
- To consider children's progress in relation to curricula and frameworks
- To consider individual children's strengths
- To assess the effectiveness of activities
- To focus on particular areas of a child's development
- To help practitioners reflect on their own practice
- To consider how children are using the environment
- To gain information for parents
- To form the basis of planning
- To help understand children's interests

Children's needs and interests

Observing children helps you learn more about them and so should, in theory, help you to work more effectively. For example, you might spot a left-handed 4-year-old child, so you will need to remember to put out left-handed scissors for them to use; or, when observing another child, you might notice a movement they make that shows when they need the toilet. These are examples of small day-to-day needs, but observing a child might also reveal that they require more significant support, such as speech and language therapy. Identifying a need for this kind of support should happen as early as possible in the child's life, as this has been shown to result in more positive outcomes.

It is useful not to fall into the trap of only observing children when there is a problem or concern. Observations should also tell you about children's strengths and interests, and this information can be used to help plan play and other activities for them.

Tracking children's progress in relation to normative development

Observation and assessments of children are also used to follow children's development in relation to normative or typical development. This is particularly important in the early years where early identification that a child is not showing usual patterns of normative development may indicate that a child needs additional support.

Tracking children's progress in relation to curriculum outcomes

As well as using observations to assess children in relation to normative development, early years settings following frameworks such as the Early Years Foundation Stage (EYFS) are also required to monitor children's progress in relation to outcomes outlined in the framework. A good example of this is the requirement for reception teachers in England to carry out an assessment as to whether children have met the early years goals in the different areas of learning and development within the EYFS.

Planning for next steps

Another reason for observing children is to plan for their next steps. This might mean building on their current interests or recognising that they need additional reinforcement activities so they can become secure in a skill, such as using scissors. In addition, by identifying children's next steps we can also think about how to shape learning opportunities for them. It might be that we have recognised a child needs practice in counting and so we may draw their attention to the number of cars they like playing with. In this way we can shape the learning opportunity to meet the child's needs.

Identifying additional support needs

We know it is important to track children's development against normative or expected development. In addition, we should also be using observations and assessments to consider whether a child has any additional support needs. It may be that the child is lacking confidence and so needs to have planned opportunities that will make him or her feel successful. Alternatively, we might pick up through observations that a child is not responding as quickly as before, which may mean we need to refer the child to an audiologist to check if he or she has any hearing problems.

Sharing information with parents

Working closely with parents is essential in early years practice. Parents have a right to know how their child is progressing and what they have spent time doing.

As we will see later in this section, wherever possible, parents should contribute to the observation and planning process as they will also have knowledge and ideas about their child.

Link

Go to Unit 5 to find more information about how important it is to work closely with parents and other early years professionals.

Providing information for other professionals

Observations and assessments may also be shared with other practitioners and professionals to support any transition. Transitions may include children moving to a new setting, or day-to-day transitions such as children moving between a nursery in the morning and a childminder in the afternoon. Remember though, that observations and assessments can only be shared after parental consent has been gained. You may provide information about how best to help the child settle or ideas for resources and activities that the child enjoys. You may also pass on records about the child's progress in relation to a curriculum framework, where appropriate.

Reflecting on practice

As well as focusing on children, observations should also be used to focus on your practice with children.

The term 'reflective practitioner' is often used here. This means thinking about the impact you have on children's enjoyment, learning and behaviour. By observing children's responses during sessions and activities, you can reflect on how effective you are and consider ways in which you might become more effective.

Link

Look at Student Book 2, Unit 11 to find more information about reflecting on your performance.

Using observations and assessments to inform planning

As you can see in Figure 9.1, observations and assessments are used to help plan activities, resources and play opportunities for groups and individual children. Observations and assessments are also needed to ensure that children are making progress within the curriculum frameworks of their country. For example, a child aged 3 years old living in England is likely to attend a setting that is using the EYFS, while a child of the same age living in Wales is likely to be in a setting using the Foundation Phase.

Types of assessment

It is good practice for settings to observe children during play and adult-directed activities, and to use the information gained to support the planning process.

Two types of assessment are generally used in settings: **formative assessment** and **summative assessment**.

Key terms

Formative assessment – assessment that takes place during the learning process on an ongoing basis, or 'assessment for learning'.

Reflecting on practice – thinking about the way one works in order to make changes, build on strengths and stay up to date with developments.

Summative assessment – assessment of what a child knows and can do at the end of a period of learning, or 'assessment of learning'.

Formative assessment

Formative assessment is where a child's progress is tracked on an ongoing basis. Most settings will do some observations and immediately use the information to consider what the child's next steps might be in particular areas of the curriculum or their development. Formative assessment supports short-term planning.

Summative assessment

Most settings will periodically review a child's progress in all areas of the curriculum. This often takes the form of an overall report. Summative assessment allows for an overview of the child's progress, interests and development. Summative assessments are helpful in long-term planning.

They are also likely to be shared with other settings when the child is due to move, but this can only take place with parental consent. In England, settings following the EYFS are required to produce two summative assessments: one when the child is 2 years old and another when the child has finished their reception year.

Early Years Foundation Stage Profile (England only)

This is a type of summative assessment that is carried out by teachers towards the end of the reception year. The EYFS Profile requires teachers to make judgements about children's progress in relation to the early learning goals. These are targets that have been set by the English government and it is hoped that most children will be able to meet them by the end of this stage. From 2013, teachers will record whether children are working towards, have met or have exceeded the early learning goals. The judgements that teachers make must be based on observations that have taken place throughout the year.

The importance of parental involvement

It is recognised that parents and carers are partners with us in the care and education of their children, so you should involve them in every area of your work. Parents are key to helping you fully understand a child's interests, needs and overall development. They should, if they wish, be involved in the ongoing observation and assessment of their children and you should ensure that you regularly discuss their children's progress with them. It is good practice to find out about what children do when they are at home and what parents have noticed about their children's interests and development. This is important because children often behave differently at home than they do in the setting. At home, children may be more relaxed and also have different opportunities. For instance, they are likely to interact with siblings or other family members. They are also likely to do a range of different activities such as helping in the garden, going shopping or going to the park. Some children may also speak a language at home that is different to that used in the setting.

It is important to involve parents in the care of their children.

The involvement of parents may take different forms according to the age of the child, the type of setting and the parents' wishes. All settings should provide written summaries of the child's progress as well as parents' meetings, but it is good practice to do far more than this. There are many ways in which settings work alongside parents in the observation and assessment process. Table 9.1 shows some of these.

Table 9.1 How settings can work alongside parents

Ways settings work alongside parents	How they are helpful
Sharing photographs, film clips and sound recordings	As children do different things at home, some settings invite parents to share photographs, film clips and sound recordings with them.
Observations in the home	Some parents may be interested in observing their child and looking out for particular milestones when their child is at home.
Sharing observations with parents	It is good practice for settings to show and talk about observations on or near the day they have been carried out.
Observations in the setting	Some settings invite parents to observe their child in the setting. They may give parents some points to look out for.
Summative assessment	Some settings create summative assessments using parental input. Others create specific sections in which parents can make comments about their child.

Issues to consider when observing and assessing children

There are many issues to consider when observing children. It is important to understand these before you begin observing and assessing children. Figure 9.2 outlines the issues.

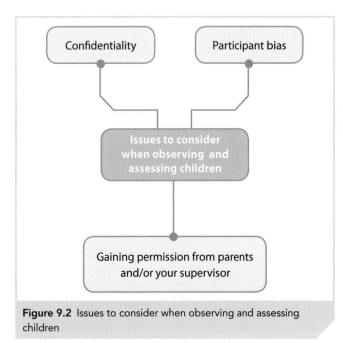

Figure 9.2 Issues to consider when observing and assessing children

Gaining permission

The starting point of any observation is to gain permission. As observation is integral to working effectively with children, settings usually have an agreement with parents that observations and assessments can take place. Digital observation methods such as photography and film are increasingly being used, and parents may sometimes opt out of allowing these methods or may impose strict conditions on how they can be used.

If you are on placement, you should ask your supervisor for permission to carry out an observation. In order that permission can be given, it is helpful for parents or supervisors to know:

- the purpose of the observation
- the method of observation
- how the information gained will be used
- who will have access to the observation.

Confidentiality

Information recorded during observations must be treated as confidential. It is also worth noting that it comes under the scope of the Data Protection Act 1998.

Research

Find out more about the Data Protection Act 1998 and what it means for you and your setting on the UK Government website. You can access this website by going to www.pearsonhotlinks.co.uk and searching for this ISBN: 9781447970965.

It is usual for settings to have policies in place that say who can look at children's records and assessments. This may include the **key person**, the manager and of course the parents. Most settings operate a **need-to-know policy**.

If you submit observations as part of an assignment, it is important to change the names of children and settings. This avoids a child being identified by others who have no direct reason to know about the child. The need for confidentiality is one reason why digital methods, such as photography or film clips, are not likely to be appropriate for observations submitted as part of an assignment.

Participant bias

When you carry out an observation, it can be very hard to remain objective. This is called **participant bias**. There are many possible reasons for participant bias.

Key terms

Key person – a practitioner designated to take responsibility for a child's emotional well-being by having a strong attachment with them and a good relationship with their parents.

Need-to-know policy – a way of making sure that personal information is only provided to those people who genuinely 'need to know'.

Participant bias – where an observer is subconsciously recording information in a subjective way.

Relationship with a child

When an observer has a relationship with a child, they are likely to have subconsciously made judgements about the child based on what they already know. This means they may miss things that do not 'fit' this existing picture. Participant bias is also seen in assessments of children, as someone who knows a child may mark that child favourably or, sometimes, be more critical in their assessment.

Values and beliefs

Observers may have certain beliefs about groups of children, which make it hard to observe them objectively or make accurate assessments. An example of this is gender. If an observer subconsciously believes that girls are more cooperative than boys, the interpretation of a girl answering back to an adult may be different than it would be for a boy.

Information from other adults

You have seen that parents and others are important sources of information in the assessment process. However, observers who have already been given information about a child can find it hard to observe that child objectively. They may pay more attention to information that concurs with what they have been told than to information that contradicts this.

Developmental knowledge

Having a good knowledge of development is important, as without it observers may not pick up on behaviours that are atypical or of interest. On the other hand, if an observer has a particular interest in certain areas of behaviour, they may focus on these to the exclusion of others.

Method of recording

Some methods of recording are 'open', and allow the observer to decide what is of interest and which behaviours to note down. This makes it easier for participant bias to be shown.

Avoiding participant bias

It is difficult to avoid participant bias, but being aware that it may occur is the first step. In addition, it can be useful to choose a variety of recording methods for a clearer overall picture. It is also important to listen carefully to alternative points of view about a child and to consider these when next observing the child.

The need for planning to reflect children's developmental stage, play and learning needs

All settings working with children will have a range of planning techniques. These will depend on the number of children in the setting, the curriculum framework that is being used and also the beliefs of the setting itself. Later in this section we will look at the importance of planning and the range of methods used in settings.

Children can learn a lot from simply playing and being with adults, but it can also be helpful for activities and play opportunities that impart a variety of different skills and knowledge to be planned for them. To ensure this happens, professionals working with children carry out planning based on children's developmental stage, their play and learning needs, as well as their interests. Where a curriculum is being followed, planning will also ensure that any activities meet its requirements.

As well as ensuring that children's needs are met, planning also has other advantages. In group settings, it helps staff to be organised and prevents situations in which the children's needs may be overlooked. Planning can also give everyone, including children, a focus and create a more stimulating environment that aids children's overall development.

The requirements of the curriculum framework for planning

You will need to find out about how the curriculum framework in your country influences the planning process. Most inspectorates that look at how settings implement a curriculum framework will look at the planning in the setting. They are likely to check that all parts of the curriculum are being delivered and that plans are appropriately tailored to meet

Research

Find out about the requirements for planning that relate to the curriculum being followed in your setting.

individual children's needs. To show that this is happening, your setting may have a tracking system in place to help staff plan activities in a balanced way, including between adult-directed and child-initiated activities. You may also find that plans for individual children are drawn up that show how, over a period of time, the setting will support their progress.

Factors that influence planning

There are many factors that influence what we plan in the long and the short term with the children we work with. In some ways, planning is a little bit like a jigsaw puzzle, as there are many pieces to consider. Getting all the pieces in the right order means that children's developmental needs can be met alongside their interests, while ensuring that they make good progress. Figure 9.3 shows the information required in the planning process.

Figure 9.3 Information that supports the planning process

Observations of children

There is little point in planning any activities or play opportunities unless you are sure that they are suitable for children and they will enjoy them. By carrying out observations you can work out what developmental needs children have and what their next steps might be. You can also observe their interests and think about what they enjoy doing.

Evaluations of previous activities

As well as carrying out observations on children, you can also use your evaluations of activities they have been involved in to help you with your planning. For instance, a small group of children who enjoyed playing a particular card game may enjoy playing a similar game.

The curriculum framework

In settings that follow a curriculum framework, planning will be heavily influenced by it. In England, for example, settings using the Early Years Foundation Stage (EYFS) will need to plan activities that cover all of the seven areas of learning, with the aim of helping children reach the early learning goals. In schools, children may be working towards literacy and numeracy goals, depending on the curriculum that is being followed.

> **Research**
>
> Find out more about the Early Years Foundation Stage (EYFS) or the early years framework that is used in your home country, for example, the Foundation Phase in Wales. You can access the relevant website by going to www.pearsonhotlinks.co.uk and searching for this ISBN: 9781447970965.

Discussions with parents and/or carers

Parents and/or carers can often help you in your planning. They may have long-term goals for their child and, wherever possible, you should try to support them. In addition, parents/carers may give you information about what they see their child doing at home and have ideas about how to build on these interests and strengths.

Information from children

You should also involve children in planning as much as you can. You may listen to children's ideas about the equipment, resources and activities they would like to use or do. You can also learn about children's interests and preferences from observations.

Information from other professionals

Where children are receiving support from other professionals such as speech and language therapists or physiotherapists, it is good practice, if possible, for settings to use information about activities or support that the child needs when preparing plans. Information shared by the child's key person, other colleagues within the setting and other early years professionals will also need to be taken into account when planning for children's learning needs.

Plans for children with additional needs

Children with identified additional needs may have individual education plans (IEPs) drawn up with the aim of focusing activities and adult support on specific developmental needs. IEPs should be looked at by settings when they are drawing up their plans.

Link

Go to Unit 19 in Student Book 2 to find more information about children with additional needs.

The ethos of the setting

Some settings have their own very distinct ethos and this is reflected in the curriculum. A Forest School setting might plan to take children out into the woods to support their acquisition of outdoor skills. Similarly, a Montessori setting would follow the methods outlined by Maria Montessori, and their planning would be tailored accordingly.

Planning methods

There are a number of ways in which settings carry out planning, but the one thing they have in common is that they are all based on the planning cycle. As such, it is worth looking at this cycle first.

The planning cycle is sometimes referred to as the Planning, Observation and Evaluation cycle: first you plan an activity or play opportunity, then you observe children's responses to it. The responses will allow you to evaluate the activity, which provides information to help you to plan more effectively in the future.

Early years settings are free to decide how they plan for their children. There is a requirement in the EYFS that settings should plan for individual children based on their needs and interests. As a result, most early years settings create individual plans for children who need additional support as well as plans for the whole group. Many settings will plan a week at a time and adapt these plans over the week. These

plans may show adult-led activities for individual and small groups of children, as well as plans for the environment to support child-initiated play. For example, making sure there is always a range of resources that will provide a sufficient challenge.

Long-term planning – groups

Most settings will have some type of long-term planning. Some settings' long-term planning is done every three or four months, although others may plan for a year at a time. Long-term planning helps settings to schedule in specific activities or topics, outings and festivals. Where a curriculum is being followed, such as those in schools, long-term planning will also be linked to any curriculum expectations for the year group. Long-term planning for most settings centres around the whole group rather than individual children, as it is only very general in nature.

Short-term planning

Most settings will also have some form of short-term planning. This is usually to show what groups and individual children will be doing over a relatively short period of time – for example a week or a day. Short-term planning is likely to show links to curricula frameworks and also to children's developmental needs and interests. Short-term planning often consists of more than one type of plan.

Weekly plans

Many settings will have weekly plans. These show the activities, play and outings planned for that week. They may also include specific activities for individual children as well as for groups of children.

Daily plans

Some settings also produce daily plans. These show the activities, play opportunities and routine for the day in more detail. They may also be used to indicate which adults will be working with which groups of children, and where.

Activity plans

These show single activities or groups of activities and are drawn up to support individual children's developmental needs, or to help groups of children make progress within a curriculum area.

Continuous provision sheets

Most settings offering early years provision will provide a play-based curriculum. The term 'continuous provision' is used to describe the way that resources and activities for play are provided continually both indoors and out. This allows children to choose what to play with and is one way in which settings can provide both adult-directed and child-initiated play simultaneously. As most settings have plenty of toys and resources that cannot all be made available all the time, many will plan what to put out on either a daily or a weekly basis. Resources and activities are likely to be chosen to give children access to several types of play. Settings may also link their provision to the curriculum framework in the planning. Where resources or activities are put out with specific children in mind, this might be indicated on the sheet. An example of a continuous provision sheet is shown in Figure 9.4.

Planning to meet children's additional needs

Planning is essential to ensure children's individual needs are met. Children who may need to be planned for in this way include those who have additional needs such as development delay and those who may need additional reassurance. In some cases, we may also need to plan specifically for children who have English as an additional language and/or are new to learning English.

Activity	Monday	Tuesday	Wednesday	Thursday	Friday
Small-world play	Cars + sawdust	Cars (ML+ST)	Dinosaurs Turf ←——→		
Role play 1	In the living room ——————————————————→				
Role play 2	←—— At the hairdressers'	Develop through week ——————→			
Board games and jigsaws	2 x 4 pieces (ST)				
Sensory materials	Gloop ←——→		Soap flakes?		
Mark-making area	At the printers' ←	Develop through week ——————————→			
Water	Clockwork toys				
Dough	Cake cases + buttons (LT)				
Sand	Buttons				
Construction	Wooden blocks				
Exploration and investigation	Digi microscope (collect things on walk)				
Creative area	Collage + Junk modelling (ST)			Visit to scraps ——→	
ICT	Beebots (BT)	Digi microscope	——————————→		Beebots
Other	Sewing kits ←——→		Marble run		

Figure 9.4 A continuous provision sheet. Many settings only partially fill in the sheet at the start of the week. The sheet is added to and changed based on children's observed interests. These interests can be marked with children's initials.

Planning for children who have additional needs is normally done in the medium and short term. This is partly because children's needs and interests can change quite quickly. For some children who have a learning difficulty or global delay, more specialised plans will be needed. These are known as Individual education plans (IEPs).

Individual education plans

Individual education plans (IEPs) are usually compiled with the input of a Special Educational Needs Coordinator (SENCO) and the child's parents or carers. The plan will show some particular developmental areas that will be the focus of activities, usually over a four- to six-week period. Children's IEPs will help support the setting's short-term plans, so it is important that suggested activities from the IEP are also included in the group planning.

Learning journeys

Many settings have combined observation, assessment and planning for individual children by using 'learning journeys'. The idea behind these is to build up a portfolio of children's progress and interests that can be shared, not only with parents/carers, but also with the children themselves. Most settings that use learning journeys find they are a great way of bringing together observations and planning. Figure 9.5 shows how a snapshot observation accompanied by a photograph is used to record an area of learning. These can form the basis of an assessment, along with some ideas about activities that can be planned as a result of the observation.

Observation	Ayse found her shoes when I said that it was time to go outdoors. It took her a moment, but she was able to work out which shoe went on the correct foot. She managed to fasten the buckles without any support. She was very pleased with herself.
What does the observation mean?	Ayse can now put on most of her clothes and shoes herself.
What next?	• Give Ayse time so that she can get dressed herself. • Show her how to use a zip and find dressing-up clothes that have zips. • Look out for role-play clothes that will help her to practise using buttons, zips and buckles.
Links to the EYFS	PSE Self-care (30–50 months) PD Using equipment and materials (30–50 months)
Notes for the next observation	CLL Look out for examples of mark making and also record speech.

Figure 9.5 An example of a learning journey format

Observations are carried out fortnightly by each child's key person to review the different areas of development. Every six weeks, a summative record is produced to show the child's progress in each of the areas of learning and development based on these observation sheets. At planning meetings, key persons talk about what activities, needs or interests their key children have. These are then incorporated into the weekly plans.

Key term

Learning journey/learning story – a way of assessing and planning for children's development using a narrative approach that can easily be constructed and shared with parents and children.

The importance and value of reviewing plans and planning methods

As with other areas of work with children, it is important for settings to review the effectiveness of their planning systems. This is because when planning systems are working well, children's individual needs are met and activities are sufficiently challenging. This in turn means children are likely to be making good progress. Settings need to consider whether their planning reflects the needs, strengths and interests of the children and also the requirements of the curriculum framework they are using. Children's individual needs should also be reflected within group planning. This can be demanding, as there is often a tension between creating a manageable system, where staff are not spending too long on paperwork, while ensuring planning is sufficiently detailed and robust. This is one reason why settings will often continually review and try to improve their planning systems.

Cultural differences

We know that children are more likely to play and learn when they are relaxed. This is more likely to happen when children can see that their culture and family circumstances are reflected in the play environment and the activities they are taking part in. Therefore, settings need to review plans and planning methods to ensure that they reflect individual children's cultures and family circumstances.

Here are some questions to help you review plans and planning systems.

- Are each child's interests and strengths reflected in the planning?
- Do plans reflect the education requirements of the curriculum being used?
- Are plans used and referred to by adults working with children?
- Do plans take account of children's family circumstances?
- How do plans show what will be happening in the setting on a day-to-day basis?
- How are plans shared with and contributed to by parents?

Assessment practice 9.1   3A.P1 | 3A.M1

You have been asked to write a guide for an early years magazine about the importance of using observations and assessment to plan how to support children's play, learning and development. The publication is aimed at learners who are starting out in their role as an early years professional. Write an article that includes:

- the importance of observations and assessments
- the different methods that can be used
- how to select the appropriate methods according to the information that needs to be collected
- how to ensure activity plans meet children's individual play and development needs
- the issues to be considered when observing and assessing children.

B Be able to carry out and record accurate observations of children

There are many different methods of observing and assessing children. In this section, we will look at several different methods, the reasons why they might be used and their benefits and drawbacks.

Observational methods

Each observation technique has its own advantages and limitations, so it is useful to learn to use several. While there are different techniques, remember that observing children is always about collecting information. Therefore, knowing what you need to learn about the child is important when choosing a technique. There are two broad methods of data collection: closed data methods and open data methods.

Closed data methods

Closed data methods focus our attention very narrowly. A good example of a closed data method is a checklist, which usually consists of groups of statements. The observer reads the statements and then considers whether or not this is what they are seeing while they observe the child. Closed data methods are considered to be less subjective than open data methods. Their major drawback is that they can focus your attention so narrowly that data might be missed; for example, whether children smile as they skip. Closed data methods tend to be good for assessing children's skills and achievements.

Open data methods

Open data methods allow us significantly more freedom, as the observation format is not as narrow. The observer is able to focus on whatever takes their attention. This increases the likelihood of subjectivity, but does mean you might gain more information about children. Snapshot observations are examples of open data recording. In this type of observation, the observer jots down what is perceived as interesting when watching a child.

Figure 9.6 shows commonly used methods of observation.

Figure 9.6 Popular methods of observation

Checklists/tick charts

Checklists, or tick charts, are a popular closed method of observing children, because they are easy to use and understand. Checklists are used in many settings by a range of professionals, and they comprise a list of prepared statements. In some settings these statements relate to the curriculum framework, or they may be compiled to include developmental milestones.

When to use this method

Checklists or tick charts can be used when you need to look at a child's skills or knowledge. This is a good method to use if you want to see how much progress a child has made, as the same tick chart can be used a few weeks later. For example, in the classroom a checklist may be used to see how many letter sounds a child knows. Checklists are often used to compare a particular child's development or knowledge with children of a similar age.

How to use this method

You need to carefully read through the listed tasks or skills before beginning the observation. When you observe the child, note whether or not a child is able to do each with a tick or remark. This is an observation technique that can either be done unobtrusively (by simply watching the child and hoping they will show the skills to be recorded) or by asking the child a specific question or to demonstrate certain skills such as writing their name.

Figure 9.7 shows an example of a checklist.

Advantages of checklists

* It is an easy method to use and you can draw up your own list of skills or knowledge you want to observe.
* Parents can be involved in looking out for skills at home.

Disadvantages of checklists

* Observers who have been working with children may want to demonstrate the child's progress and so find it hard to complete these tests accurately.
* Some statements may not relate exactly to what a child is observed doing, so the observer may have to estimate whether or not the child can perform a task.
* Space for comments may be restricted, so observers may not be able to record whether the child showed a skill or knowledge easily or if they needed prompting, for example.
* Checklists and tick charts do not help us understand children's interests or why they have gained skills or knowledge.

Child			Observer ....
Child's age			
Date of observation			Time ....

Activity	Yes	No	Comments
Puts together three-piece puzzle			
Snips with scissors			
Paints in circular movements			
Holds crayons with fingers, not fist			
Can thread four large beads			
Turns pages in a book one by one			
Can put on and take off coat			

Figure 9.7 An example of a checklist

Time samples

Time samples are interesting and versatile. They provide information about a child's activity at regular intervals (e.g. what a child is doing during a session at 10-minute intervals). Time samples can be structured and written in code form, or they may be freer, with observers simply using a running commentary style as the sample is taken.

Figure 9.8 shows an example of a time sample recording sheet.

When to use this method

This is a useful method to use to look at a child's activity overall or as part of a session. It is less intensive than the target child or the written narrative methods and leaves the observer free to look at other children between samples. It is a good method for observing children's all-round development in a range of contexts. For example, you may observe social interaction while the child is playing indoors with the sand, followed by outdoor play using a range of equipment. Time samples can also be used to observe children's interests and concentration span.

How to use this method

The starting point for this method is to decide how structured the time sample needs to be. A structured recording will mean you need to draw a sheet in advance and familiarise yourself with codes. You will also need to decide how often you will sample the child's activity – this may depend on the length of

Name of child Bryony Matthews			Date of birth	20-08-08
Date of observation 14-9-2012		Start time 10.00 am	End time	11.00 am
Purpose of observation Plays + interaction with other child?				
10.00		Book corner. Alone taking books out of shelves and making piles		③
10.05		Book corner, with adult. Tidying books. Rolling on floor		②
10.10		Book corner. Adult reading story. 2 x other children with BM. BM moves away slightly		⑤
10.15		Book corner. Adult + BM talking. Pointing out pictures. Pushes other child away		⑤
10.20		Sand tray. Standing watching 3 x children at play. Eye contact		②
10.25		Water tray. 2 x other children (ST + TM) Hitting water with hands. Smiling at ST		③
10.30		ST passes BM a funnel. ST smiles, uses funnel, laughs (water tray)		④
10.35		Book corner. Alone. Rolling on floor lifting rug around her		②
10.40		Book corner. Alone. Tapping books on shelves one by one		②
10.45		Snack table. Waiting for turn. Watching 2 x others pour drinks		③

Figure 9.8 A time sample recording sheet. This observer is using a code number to record the intensity of the child's engagement as well as recording what the child is doing every five minutes.

time you intend to observe them for. For example, you may use five-minute intervals for observations that last for less than an hour, or 15-minute intervals for all-day observations. It is unlikely that sample times greater than 15 minutes will be very informative.

Once you have determined the range of the time sample, the next step is simply to record what you see when it is time to observe. While it can be interesting to observe the child in the meantime, it is important only to record at the sample times.

Advantages of time samples

- They provide information about children's activity over a relatively long period.
- They can be used to provide information about children's overall development.
- They can give an indication of children's interests and levels of concentration.

Disadvantages of time samples

- They do not record information about what a child is doing outside the sample time.

Written narrative/running record

This method is probably one of the most straightforward. It requires the observer to put what is being seen into writing. There is a surprising amount of skill required though, as it can be hard to find descriptive language and write it down quickly enough to keep up. The speed at which the observer must write means that only a small amount of information can be recorded and its selection is likely to be very subjective. The language used to record it is also subjective. Observers will not have time to consider vocabulary carefully and may put down the first word that comes to them that they feel fits the situation. For instance, they may use 'snatches', which is more emotive than 'takes quickly'. Most observers using this method find it helpful to pause from time to time to finish off sentences. Afterwards, notes will need to be rewritten so they are legible.

When to use this method

This is a versatile method that is often used as a starting point for future observations. You can choose to record any area of development, or look at a child more holistically and note down things of interest as they occur.

How to use this method

You will need a reliable pen and notepad.

Begin by noting the start time of the observation as well as the context. Then, as you watch the child, write down what you are seeing. This method is sometimes referred to as a 'running commentary'. Most observers find they need to stop after a few minutes, as they are unable to write quickly enough to record everything a child is doing or saying. It is good practice to note the time of each stop and start so that anyone reading it later does not assume that the commentary is continuous. It is also usual for the writing to be in the present continuous tense, for example, 'he is going towards the door' rather than 'he went towards the door'.

Advantages of written narrative

- This is quite an open method of recording, so it can provide quite a lot of information.
- No preparation is required.
- This method provides a 'portrait' of a child and so is popular with parents.

Disadvantages of written narrative

- This way of recording can be quite subjective, as it is impossible to record everything a child does and says while observing them.
- It can be hard to write quickly and to choose words well, so this technique requires practice.

Snapshot observations

This method is a variation on written narrative, and has been used widely by early years settings. The idea is the child is observed very briefly, perhaps a minute or so, because the adult has seen something of interest the child is doing or has decided in advance the child needs to be seen in a particular area of play or showing a particular skill. This short observation is often written on a sticky note. Snapshot observations are also used as the starting point of the 'learning journey' method of assessment and planning.

Link

Go to Section A in this unit to find more information about the 'learning journey' method of assessment and planning.

Advantages of snapshot observations

- They do not take long to write.
- Parents like to see what their child has been doing and these provide accessible information.
- They allow for spontaneous observation and recording.

Disadvantages of snapshot observations

- They are very short and may not provide sufficient, detailed information.
- They may be subjective, as this is an open method of observation.

Target child observations

Target child observations note the actions and responses of a particular child over a continuous period of time. Target child observations require the observer to be very focused and to work intensively. The observer uses codes to ensure they can record what the child is doing minute by minute.

When to use this method

This method is often used to learn about individual children and, while it can be used to provide a holistic observation, it is often used to focus on children's social and language interaction.

Individual child-tracking observation

Name of child Hamza   Observer Steph   Date 22/10/12

Age of child   3 yrs   2 months   No. of adults present 2   No. of children present 6

Free play/structured play/directed activity

Time	Description of activity	Language	Grouping	Level of involvement
10.00 am	TC scooping sand using left hand repeated movements	TC →	P	4
10.02	TC burying r. hand, scooping with other	→ TC ←	I	4
10.03	TC nods head. Other child copies TC, TC smiles	C → TC	P	3

Key

Grouping	Language		Level of involvement
WG = Whole group	TC → A	Balanced interaction between adult and child	1 = No activity
SG = Small group			2 = Frequently distracted
P = Pair	TC → C	Balanced interaction between target child and another child	3 = Fairly continuous activity
I = Individual			4 = Absorbed in activity
	A → C	Adult interacts with more than one child	
	C → TC	Another child interacts with target child	
	→ TC ←	Target child talks to himself/herself	
	TC →	No interaction	

Figure 9.9 An example of a target child observation record sheet

How to use this method

This is an observation method that does need to be planned ahead. It requires the observer to focus on only one child and means the observer is not able to work with other children at the same time.

1 Start by deciding which child is to be observed.
2 Prepare or photocopy a record sheet (see Figure 9.9 for an example).
3 Read through and check that you can remember the codes to use.
4 Write the start time on the sheet and use a stopwatch or clock to keep time.
5 For each minute, record what the child is doing. Use codes to ensure that you can keep up.

Advantages of target child observation

- It provides detailed information about a child's activity over a continuous period.
- Codes are used to enable the observer to write more efficiently. These can be made up by the observer to suit the observation.

Disadvantages of target child observation

- The observer needs to be familiar with the coding system and practise using it.
- It can be difficult for others to understand the notes if non-standard codes are used.

Digital recordings

As technology has become increasingly cheap and easy to use, many settings are now using digital methods to record children. There are many advantages to using these methods. However, as with all methods of recording, it is vital to gain parental/carer consent and ensure all recordings are kept secure.

Good organisation is also required for these methods, as it can be easy to forget when recordings were made. Settings using this method often create a digital folder for each child so that recordings are not lost and can be kept in date order.

Using a camera

Using a camera either to photograph or film children and young people is becoming increasingly popular as an observation technique. Either photography or filming can help you notice details that you might otherwise miss.

When to use this method

This method can be used to film groups of children as well as individual children. If you wish to film children with sound, it is important to choose situations in which there is not too much ambient noise. It is also important to be aware of any children who may wander into view whose parents have not given permission for them to be recorded in this way.

How to use this method

This is a straightforward method, as you only need to decide what to film and then get started. However, it is worth practising first to ensure you can use the equipment easily. Remember to check that the camera has sufficient battery power. It is important to write down the time and date of the observation or to set the camera up so it does this automatically. It is also important to get children used to being filmed first, otherwise they may be more interested in what you are doing than in carrying on with their play or activity.

Advantages of using a camera

- It is easy to review what children are doing and notice details.
- This method is popular with parents, as they can see what their children have been doing.
- Older children can use this as a medium to show us what is important in their lives.

Using a camera is a popular observation technique.

Disadvantages of using a camera

- Confidentiality can be an issue. Children can only be filmed with parental/carer consent. This includes children who are not the focus of the observation but who may stray into the shot.
- Recordings have to be kept secure.
- Background noise may prevent you from hearing what children are saying.
- Photographs only give limited information. It is not possible to know what the child did or said in the moments leading up to the photograph or film, or immediately afterwards.

Sound recordings

It is now easy to record children's speech onto a variety of devices including mobile phones, MP3 players and other gadgets.

When to use this method

Sound recordings work well for recording children's speech. It is particularly useful to make several recordings of the same child over time as a way of checking that their speech is progressing.

How to use this method

Choose a quiet place and note the name of the child and the date, either on a piece of paper or into the recording device. Talk to the child naturally to encourage them to respond as usual. If a child's speech is unclear, either because of their age or stage of development, make sure that you recast what has been said. This is good practice – it is essential that anyone else listening to the recording afterwards can understand what the child was trying to say. For instance, 'We go guirrel?' may be recast as, 'Yes, we are going to see the squirrels later'.

Play back the recording to check it is sufficiently clear, then transfer it into the child's digital folder.

Advantages of sound recordings

- Recordings can be done while you are with the child, which makes this a time-efficient way of recording.
- Parents and carers can hear their child's speech develop if several recordings are made over time.

- Parents and carers can make recordings of their child's speech at home. This can be useful if the child speaks a language different from that used in the setting.
- Where there are suspected speech and language difficulties, recordings can be played to other professionals as part of the referral process.

Disadvantages of sound recordings

- It can be difficult to hear what children are saying in noisy environments.
- It is not possible to see the child's body language or facial expression or to see the context in which speech is taking place.
- If recordings do not specify the time, date and name of the child, it may not be clear later when they were made or who was speaking.

Information from other sources

Strictly speaking, the term 'observation' relates only to what you have actually seen and recorded at a particular time. Having said this, in practice, the term is used more widely and covers information gained in retrospect or from indirect sources; for example, it might include something a parent or carer tells you. Information gained that is not actually seen and recorded at the time is described as **non-contemporaneous**.

> **Key term**
>
> **Non-contemporaneous** – in the context of observing children, this refers to events that are recorded or reported after they have occurred.

Advantages of non-contemporaneous information

Information from others can help you build a holistic picture of a child in a range of situations and over a period of time. This is important, as you cannot be with the child in every situation or for every hour of the day. Other people can also provide additional viewpoints and so potentially counter participant bias.

Disadvantages of non-contemporaneous information

The biggest disadvantage of non-contemporaneous information is, because no direct recording is available, you cannot be sure it is accurate or reliable. For example, a child may tell you what has happened but may not include details that you would have wanted to focus on. You may not be given a full picture of what has happened, or an event might be exaggerated. In addition, parents and others may have different expectations of children and this may colour their reporting. For instance, parents may say their child has shown very difficult behaviour when, actually, the behaviour is quite typical for the child's age range.

Event samples

Event samples are sometimes referred to as 'frequency counts'. The aim of these observations is to find out how often a specific type of behaviour or response takes place and also the context in which it occurs. They are often used when a child is showing unwanted behaviour, but may also be used more broadly. They can help a practitioner to work out the reasons for certain responses, and also provide evidence to show whether responses or incidents are increasing or decreasing. Event samples are non-contemporaneous, as recording takes place after the event or incident has occurred.

When to use this method

Event samples focus narrowly on the particular response of a child. For example, you might decide to investigate how often a child has a tantrum and the context in which this occurs, or you might look at how often a child interacts with other children.

How to use this method

A sheet that directs the user to the type of information to be collected has to be drawn up. There are no standard formats, as the recording columns need to reflect the observer's information requirements. Commonly collected information includes the date and time as well as the context. Figure 9.10 shows an event sample focusing on the number of times a child interacts with other children in a setting. In this situation, it will be important to see whom the child talks to and for how long. It will also be useful to find out whether the child initiates the contact or if the other children do.

Once the record sheet is drawn up, it is only filled in when the specific behaviour or response is noted. In settings where several adults might work with a child, the person who was working with the child at the time could fill in the record sheet.

Advantages of event samples

- They can help us understand the frequency and patterns of a child's behaviour or responses.
- They can be a way of monitoring the success of strategies by providing a baseline.
- They produce detailed information on the behaviour being observed, can indicate events that may trigger the behaviour and confirm if there is the need for concern.

Event	Time	Activity of child	Social group	Language used	Comments
1	11.07	Playing in the water tray	Sam, Katie, Mustafa, Ben	'Look, look! Water fell.'	Sam leaned over and said this to Mustafa and Ben
2	11.16	Playing with two beakers in the water tray, trying to transfer water between the two	Sam, Mustafa, Ben	'Water splash, splash, splash.'	Sam was showing Mustafa, while splashing Ben

Figure 9.10 Part of an event sample showing how often Sam interacts with other children

Disadvantages of event samples

- Others may need to fill in the record sheet if the observer is absent.
- They require the observer to concentrate on one child for a long period of time.
- It is possible that the child being observed will know they are being observed and this could affect the outcome.

Sociograms

Sociograms are used with children from around 4 years old to look at patterns of friendships within groups. By asking children about their friendship preferences, a chart is created that shows which children are frequently named, whether friendships are reciprocated and whether certain children find it difficult to name friends or are not named themselves.

> ### Key term
>
> **Sociogram** – a recording method whereby children indicate their friendship preferences.

When to use this method

Talk to children one at a time when no other children are with them. Ask them to name their friends and, if necessary, use a prompt question such as, 'Who do you like playing with?' Remember to give children enough time to respond, and record the names that are given by each child. Then create the sociogram chart.

This practitioner is talking individually to a child in order to create a sociogram.

How to use this method

It can be interesting to use sociograms as a starting point for further observations. Consider following up with those children who are not named by other children or who had difficulty in naming any friends. It is also important to follow this up with information from parents and colleagues who may have seen children play with each other or who may have heard children talk about other children.

Advantages of using sociograms

- They can provide an indication that some children need more support in making friends.

Disadvantages of using sociograms

- This can be a very unreliable method to use with 4-year-old children, who will often base their answers on whoever they have just played with.
- It can be more reliable with older children, but there is a danger that older children will mention names simply to please the questioner.

Information from parents, carers and others

Parents or carers and colleagues see children in different situations and so may have different views of a particular child's development. Information from parents or carers can be gained from questionnaires, structured face-to-face interviews or informal chats. Some practitioners also encourage parents to observe their children at home using a recording method such as filming.

Advantages of using information from parents and others

- Parents or carers and other professionals will see children in different situations and so may provide information that would otherwise be difficult to collect.
- In the case of other professionals, we may not have the expertise to collect it ourselves while they do.

Disadvantages of using information from parents and others

- Parents and carers may show participant bias, as they want to present their child in the best light or try to second-guess what the setting wants. It may be hard to verify the accuracy of observations or to understand the context in which they have taken place.

How to select appropriate observation methods

It is important to choose the right method of observation, so begin by thinking about what type of information you are trying to collect. For example, if you are focusing on a child's speech and language, you might decide to carry out a sound recording as well as a time sample. This will give information about how the child talks in relation to their age and stage of development as well as whom the child communicates with and how often over the course of a session.

Questions to consider

- What information do I need to collect?
- How focused does the recording need to be?
- How much time do I have to spend recording?
- How reliable must the recording method be?
- Do I need a combination of recording methods?
- Do I want open or closed methods of recording?
- How skilled am I at using the recording method?

How to present records of observation

As observations will be used to support planning and assessment, it is important that they are presented in ways that are easy to understand and refer back to. The following should be considered when presenting records of any observations that you carry out.

Legibility

It is important that records of observations are neat and legible, so that other people can understand them. Observations may be read by parents and/or carers, key persons and other professionals such as inspectors. As part of your course, you may also have to present observations as part of an assignment. These must be neat and legible.

Accuracy and detail

It is important that information is recorded accurately and, wherever possible, in detail. This can take practice, but it is essential, as otherwise there is a danger that inaccurate conclusions will be drawn about a child's interests, needs or development.

Non-judgemental tone

It may be hard, but you should aim only to record what you see or hear – without elaboration and without using words that imply a judgement. You should not state what did not happen, such as 'he did not say thank you', as this was not observed.

Date of observation

It is important to write down the date the observation was carried out. This helps observations to be put in order and allows us to see the progress that children are making. It also helps the observation to be seen as valid.

Age of child

It is usual to note the child's age at the beginning of the observation. This is usually recorded in years and months (for example, 4 years, 3 months). This helps anyone reading the observation to see how what has been observed relates to the typical development.

Contextual information

It is usual to note down information that helps the reader understand the full picture of what was happening at the time. This will include the number of children and adults around the child at the time of the observation. This is important, because children's behaviour changes according to the group size and who they are with. You should also note down the context in which the activity took place and what the type of activity is. For example, what the child was doing or what was happening when the observation began: 'four children were around the sand tray and an adult had just added some more sand'.

Purpose of the observation

It can be helpful to write out the reason for carrying out the observation, as this helps anyone reading it to see what the focus of the observation was meant to be. For example, 'the observation was carried out to determine whether child X talked more when alone with an adult or in a small group'.

Did you know?

Many qualifications require that learners present observations and assessments of children. The reason for this is that it shows whether learners have a good underpinning knowledge of child development. So, what makes a good observation?

- Clear aims and relevant method – the more focused you are as an observer, the more accurate and detailed your observation record will be.

- Open methods of recording – to show your skills, the best methods of recording tend to be open ones. This is because you can collect a wide pool of information about a child. Closed methods, such as a checklist, provide less insight into a child's responses.

- Detail – the more detailed your information, the easier it is to support your conclusions with evidence.

Different observational methods used in settings

We can sometimes use children's varied creations or 'work products' to show their developmental progress. These could include paintings, models, sticky notes and drawings. For example, children's representations in drawings often reflect their cognitive and language development; for instance older children will begin to add more detailed features, such as eyebrows or fingernails, to their drawings of people. Other 'work products', such as models, also help us to see how children's fine motor skills are developing. It is also common in many early years settings to photograph 3D work products or to film children as they are engaged in play to provide evidence of a child's progress.

C Be able to make accurate assessments from observations of children

Observing children is just one part of the process of assessing children and making plans for their play and development. Once you have observed children, you need to interpret what you have recorded. This is an important step, as the conclusions that you draw should influence the short-term planning for the child. Your conclusions will also be used to help parents and others understand the child's developmental progress. Importantly, they might also help to identify when a child may need additional support. This section looks at ways in which you might draw these conclusions.

Identifying a child's stage of development from observations

One of the key reasons for observing children is to check that they are making developmental progress.

Looking at developmental norms may help you realise that a child's development is completely typical for their age group. On the other hand, looking at the normative development may help you realise that the child needs additional support.

Normative development is looked at particularly carefully in children's earliest years. This is because the early identification of needs often makes a significant difference to later outcomes. One of the reasons why early identification is so important is that different areas of development are interlinked. For example, a child with atypical speech and language development may find it hard to control their behaviour and so may not be invited to play with other children.

Checking normative development is especially important when we look at young children's behaviour. A child with a peer group whose behaviour is in advance of expected development may appear to be 'difficult and uncooperative' when, in reality, their behaviour is within the expected range for their age.

Looking at normative development can also help us to be aware of what the child needs to go on and do. This might help in planning equipment and activities and also checking that we are providing sufficient challenges.

How to relate normative development to an observation

When looking at normative development, a good starting point is to check the developmental milestones given for the child's age in reference books, and see how they relate to the skills and knowledge the child showed in the observation. For instance, if the child was busy pouring sand from one container to another, how do these fine motor skills relate to the expected developmental norms or milestones?

Once you have established how the child's fine motor skills relate to the developmental norms, you can then write a conclusion that shows the correlation. This has the advantage of showing the reader how the conclusion was reached. One way of doing this is to start by stating what you have observed and then quoting directly or indirectly what is stated in a reference book or on a trusted website. An example is shown in Figure 9.11, where a learner has made an indirect reference to the author Carolyn Meggitt's work in support of her observation.

> Janie, aged 3 years, repeatedly poured sand from one container to another. She often did this without spilling any. According to Carolyn Meggitt, this is typical of this age group.

Figure 9.11 An example of an indirect reference

Did you know?

Did you know that there are different ways of referencing? To access a helpful website for the Harvard system, go to www.pearsonhotlinks. co.uk and search for this ISBN: 9781447970965.

How to identify children's needs, interests and preferences

Observations can, and should, also be used to look at children's developmental needs, interests and preferences. This will help when planning for the provision of toys, resources and activities. Open recording styles of observation such as filming, written record or target child are particularly useful. When looking at an observation, think about the following:

- With what or whom did the child spend the most time?

This may indicate a friendship preference or a play interest.

- What level of engagement did the child show?

High levels of concentration and perseverance, especially during child-initiated play, are often indicators of interests and play preferences.

- Facial expression

Children may smile, laugh or look intensely interested in things. This may indicate an interest or play preference.

As with development, you should try to show the link between the interests and preferences you have observed and your conclusions. In some cases you may realise that although you have seen the child smile or laugh, you have not recorded it. This is not good practice because, in theory, you are drawing conclusions about something for which you have no evidence. This is one reason why it is important when starting out to keep practising observation. The more you do it, the more skilled you will become. Read the observation in Figure 9.12 by Akbar, an early years professional, to see a good example of an observation record.

> During the observation I saw Michael spend most of the hour playing with a toy shark, which he used in both the sand and the water trays. He also asked if he could take it to the snack table with him.
>
> *Akbar, an early years professional*

Figure 9.12 An example of an observation note

How to record assessments

As we saw in Section A of this unit, there are two types of assessments carried out in early years settings: formative assessments and summative assessments.

Formative assessment

A formative assessment is an ongoing record of the child's development. Formative assessments in many early years settings are often recorded in 'learning journeys'. To record a formative assessment, you need to consider what you feel each observation shows after you have carried it out. This can be quite concise. You should then link it to an area of learning in the EYFS and then consider what the child's next steps might be.

Summative assessments

Summative assessments are literally a 'summing up' of the child's progress, development and interests. Most early years settings will do a summative assessment every 3 or 4 months. In a summative assessment, each area of the child's development is considered and is looked at in line with expected developmental norms. The rate of the child's progress will also be looked at.

Most early years settings have a format for recording summative assessments. Summative assessments are important and so it is important to be accurate and precise when writing them. The format can vary from setting to setting so it is always worth asking a supervisor to show you how the setting in which you work records these assessments.

Relating observations to the planning of activities and experiences

As well as providing developmental information, observations also have to be used to help plan activities and experiences to support the child further. This is often in relation to the curriculum framework being used in the setting. Many settings design observation sheets that include a section titled 'Next steps'. This is where ideas for what could be planned next to support a child's progress or interests may be written.

A good starting point is to look at the information from the observation and then pick out which parts relate to the curriculum framework being used. You may, for example, have observed a child playing a board game. From this observation, there could be several links to the curriculum framework. You might consider their social skills, as the game required them to take turns, and also whether the child understood the concept behind the game.

Once you have identified possible areas to consider, you will then need to look in detail at the curriculum framework and consider what to provide next for the child. It may be that the child would benefit from playing the game again, as they enjoyed it, but would also benefit from further practice in recognising numbers.

Suggestions for next steps

After nearly every observation, you should think about what the observation has told you about the child and what else could be planned to support the child further. You should consider the child's interests when doing this, as well as suggestions contained in the curriculum framework. It can also be helpful to look at the developmental milestones, which may suggest what the child is likely to be working towards. Information and ideas from parents are also important, based on what they know about their children.

Suggestions for activities, resources and play opportunities do not have to be very detailed, but should be sufficient to be followed up in the planning process. It is also good practice to make links to the observation so it is clear what the next steps have been based on. Read the example in Figure 9.13 written by Steven, an early years professional.

> Lorna showed that she enjoyed dropping things and having the attention of an adult. This game could be repeated, but extended by providing other objects for Lorna to drop. The adult could also name the object each time they returned it to Lorna, as this might help her to learn a new word.
>
> *Steven, an early years professional*

Figure 9.13 An example of how to use information to support a child's future learning

Relating theories of play, learning and development to observations

Through observations, you can also think about how a child's play and interests link to theories of play, learning and development. By looking at the information gained from the observations and thinking about the theories, you are more likely to understand the reasons behind the behaviours that children have shown.

This can help you to be more strategic in guiding behaviour. It can also help you see what the child needs from you in terms of planning and further experiences. We have already looked at some key theories of development and play in Unit 1 and Unit 2, and you are likely to be able to see these in action when you watch babies and children.

Link

Go to Unit 1 and Unit 2 to find more information about theories that link to development and play schemas.

The importance of relating theories to what you observe children doing is one reason why you are asked to record this as part of the observations you submit during training.

Theory into practice

Find out whether your setting observes children at play and relates these observations to play schemas.

How to relate theories to observations

As with relating normative development to records of observations, the key is first of all to read through the observation carefully. You should then look in reference books for theories of play or child development and consider whether you can see any links. Record these links by explaining what you saw, which theory of play or development it may link to and why you have made this association. Read the example in Figure 9.14 written by Sarah, an early years professional.

> Hasan repeatedly dropped his spoon on the ground and each time giggled when an adult picked it up for him. I think that the attention he gained from the adult acted as a positive reinforcement and so prompted him to repeat this behaviour.
>
> *Sarah, an early years professional*

Figure 9.14 An example observation note

More than one theory at work

In most observations, you should see that there is more than one theory at work. Children may use objects to symbolise other objects, such as using a cupful of sand to stand for a cup of tea. They may also look for adult support, attention or praise. In addition, the way that they play may give them particular cognitive benefits.

Case study

Analysing observations

Meghan is 18 months old. She has been given a washing-up bowl full of coloured dried rice. She has been dropping toy animals into the rice and covering them over. She has then taken great pleasure in uncovering them and showing them to her key person. She has spent 15 minutes repeating this play.

After looking again at Units 1 and 2, see if you can relate theory to practice by answering the following questions:

1 Why does Meghan repeat these actions?
2 What play schema does this relate to?
3 Why does she keep showing the animals to her key person?
4 What skills is she learning and practising through this hiding and finding?

Atypical development

From time to time, you may work with children whose development does not seem to link to the usual patterns associated with their age group. If you are a learner, you should first raise this with the child's key person. It may be that differences in the child's developmental pattern have already been identified. If, on the other hand, you are working as the child's key person, you should carry out a further observation, perhaps at a different point in the day or where the child is engaged in a slightly different activity. It is very important that you follow the reporting process outlined in your setting, so make sure that you know what this is.

Double-checking that you are not jumping to conclusions is very important, and making sure you have some evidence to support your concerns is also helpful. This evidence, usually in the form of observations, can be used to support other professionals if a referral is needed.

Working with parents and carers

If, after observing the child further, you still feel that there may be potential concerns, you should talk to the child's parents or carers. It may be that they too have a similar concern or that the child behaves differently at home. As there are many factors that can affect children, the next step may be to carry out a series of observations over a couple of weeks, or the decision might be taken after working closely with parents/carers to start the referral process. If a referral is made, it will be important to work closely

with the parents/carers so that information can continue to be shared.

Referring children

If there are concerns about a child's development, the parents or carers must give consent before any referrals can take place. The route to referral will depend very much on the type of concern that is raised and how referrals work in your local area. For many referrals, parents/carers will need to go to their family doctor or health visitor, who will in turn arrange an appointment with the relevant service, although in some areas there are drop-in clinics, for example clinics for speech and language therapy.

Working with other professionals

When a referral has taken place, you may share observations and assessments with other professionals, with the parents' or carers' consent. You may also be asked to observe the child in order to monitor the effectiveness of strategies and the child's developmental progress. In some cases, this may mean using a format given to you by another professional. It is important to remember that information cannot be shared in this way unless parents/carers have given consent.

D Be able to create, implement and review activity plans for children

Activity plans are used in many settings to help promote the acquisition of specific skills and knowledge. Learning how to create, implement and review an activity plan provides us with a valuable thought process that is useful on an almost daily basis. In this section, we will look at how you might create, implement and review plans.

Creating appropriate activity plans for play, development and learning

A good activity plan is really a way of organising your thoughts about providing for children. Figure 9.15

lists the things to think about when creating an activity plan.

Discussion with parents or carers and other professionals

It is good practice when planning activities to get input from others. This should include a child's parents or carers as well as the child's key person, as they will already know about the child's interests and may be able to anticipate the child's likely responses to the proposed activity. It is also important to talk to colleagues to ensure the activity plan does not clash with what they have planned, and also so they can consider whether any of their key children would benefit from the activity.

Activity

Think about what you will call the activity. For example, this could be something like 'bubble painting'. Is an explanation of the activity required?

⬇

Purpose

What is the reason behind the activity?

This could be to develop a specific skill that would support a child's development, extend a child's or a group of children's interest in a particular area, or to develop a skill or knowledge detailed within a curriculum framework.

⬇

Rationale

Give an explanation about why you have chosen this particular activity. We know that children learn best when an activity is interesting and they can be fully involved in it, so you should focus here on why the activity will appeal to children. (At this point, you may realise that your activity is not exciting or interesting enough, and if this is the case you will need to think about planning another activity.)

⬇

Maximum group size

Is the activity going to be carried out by more than one child? If so, is there a maximum number of children that can participate?

⬇

Benefits

What are the overall benefits of the activity for the child or children? Think about developmental benefits and try to make your points as detailed as possible.

⬇

Links to the curriculum

If you are in a setting that follows a curriculum framework, you should state the links between the activity and areas of the curriculum.

⬇

Resources and location

Think about what resources you will need. Resources may include things such as aprons. Think also about whether the activity needs to take place in a specific place.

⬇

Time required for preparation and clearing away

Think about how much time you will need to prepare for the activity and also clear it away.

⬇

Health and safety risk management

Think about whether the resources you need or the activity itself may have health and safety implications. If this is the case, explain how you will manage the risks.

⬇

The role of the adult

Outline what the adult will be doing during the activity. They may take on an active role, showing children how to carry out the activity or guiding them through it, or they could take on a facilitating role where the adult reacts to, and is guided by, the child's interests and play during the activity. If you are working with a child who has an additional need, you should also explain how you will meet this need. For example, if you are working with a child who has a hearing loss you should make sure that you locate the activity in a quiet area.

⬇

Vocabulary

In some settings, you may be asked to write a list of vocabulary that you will need to attempt to use with the child/children during the activity, so bear this in mind when planning your activity.

Figure 9.15 Things to think about when creating an activity plan

Formats for recording planned activities

There is no single format for creating an activity plan. In some settings, paperwork for activity plans is kept to a minimum, while in others more emphasis is placed on this. Whatever format is used in your setting, the process of planning an effective activity remains the same. It is likely that your training provider will give you a sample format to help you get used to the process of creating plans. As you have already seen, you will have a number of things to think about, such as resources, the role of the adult, links to the curriculum and the reason behind the activity. Figure 9.16 is an outline of a sample activity plan that you can use or adapt. If you decide to create your own format, make sure you allow sufficient space for detailed planning.

Research

Find out about the way that your setting plans activities for children.

How to implement activity plans

If you have written a good activity plan or gone through a strong thought process, most of the work of setting up and organising the activity should be straightforward. You should already know what you need in terms of resources, where you might go and, importantly, what benefits the activity is likely to offer the child. All that remains is to implement the plan, which is a skill in itself and depends on a few basic principles.

Activity	
Aim and rationale	
Links to curriculum	
Resources	
Location	
Health and safety	
Individual needs	
The role of the adult	
Additional comments	

Figure 9.16 A sample activity plan

Involving children

Good activities should involve children fully. Their participation is important as we know they are more likely to gain from an activity when they join in and participate. To help children participate, think of ways of involving them early on in the activity. This might include getting them to help set up an activity and encouraging them to make suggestions. It also means the design of the activity should allow for choice, suggestions and plenty of participation by the children themselves. Interestingly in activities such as writing, painting or playing a board game, we know that children are more likely to participate if adults sit and join in rather than just supervising.

Supporting and extending children's learning and thinking

We have seen that children need plenty of opportunities for interaction and, as part of this, children also need opportunities for their thinking to be extended. This means that the style of the adult's interaction should help children to make connections between what they are doing and past experiences, as well as allowing children to reason and predict. This style of working is known as 'sustained shared thinking' and requires great sensitivity and the use of well-timed questions. For example, when we are blowing bubbles we may ask a child to speculate on what size the next bubble may be. We may also experiment with the child to see whether blowing quickly or slowly makes a difference to the size of bubbles. In this way, blowing bubbles becomes an opportunity for the child and the adult to explore an activity together to make meaningful conclusions.

Talking and listening

Children benefit from talking as they are learning. Simply listening to an adult is not likely to help their learning process. If you have planned an adult-directed activity, you will need to make sure that children have plenty of opportunities to talk spontaneously and freely, such as chatting while they are cooking with you.

Learning should be fun

We know that children are most likely to learn, concentrate and persevere when an activity is fun. This means that you should constantly monitor their reactions and reflect on whether they are engaged in the activity. This might also mean you have to adapt the activity or even, in some cases, abandon it.

Allowing for spontaneity

Most experienced early years professionals will tell you that children are very creative and will often find inspiration and have ideas that we had not thought of. It is good practice to be flexible, and not to worry if children learn or discover something other than what you planned or are not as engaged in the activity as you may have thought they would be. In addition to children changing the activity, unexpected events such as the arrival of snow, a rainbow or a hamster on the loose may mean that carrying on with the planned activity may no longer be appropriate. Being ready to adapt and change your plans is therefore important.

How to review plans and planning methods

Reviewing plans and activities is important, as it enables us to improve our planning, and also to think about children's needs and possible next steps. After you have carried out an activity, you will probably have plenty to reflect on, but it is worth spending time thinking about the following.

How engaged were the children during the activity?

This is quite a good starting point. Children who were very engaged and who participated well are likely to have benefited. If this was the case, it may be that you could build on this activity again for a particular child or group of children. On the other hand, you may have found that a child or some children lost interest. This might mean that a different approach is needed with those children in future.

As we know that language is connected with learning, you might also like to reflect on how much speech individual children used and to whom they spoke, or, in the case of babies, vocalised.

Did the activity meet its original aim?

Look back at the plan's original purpose and consider whether you feel that this was achieved. If not, think about why this was and whether other types of activities might have been more suited to the child or children.

How did the activity link to the curriculum framework?

If you made links to the curriculum framework, think about whether these links were correct. It may be that more was covered than you expected. Most settings keep track of the parts of the curriculum that have been covered.

Which aspects of the activity and the plan were successful, and why?

It is important to understand why activities with children work well and how effective the activity was in supporting a child's play, learning or development. This gives us useful insights for future planning. Factors that affect the success of an activity include the type of resources used, the level of challenge or novelty, the way in which the adult was involved and to what extent the activity built on children's interests.

Why is this adult-directed activity working well?

What aspects of the activity could be improved?

While some activities go to plan, others do not. There are a huge number of reasons for this. It might be that the timing or the location was not good. It could be that the number of children was too great or that your style was too controlling. Some activities may not have been sufficiently appealing or challenging for children, or there may not have been enough variety or interest in the resources.

We also know that young children are affected by whom they are with. It may be that your relationship with the child or children is not sufficiently developed for them to feel totally at ease. This is particularly

important to reflect on when you are working with children under 3 years old.

What did children think of the activity?

It is important to take children's views about activities into account when evaluating activities. With older children, you can talk to them directly about what they most/least enjoyed about the activity and which aspects they found the most/least interesting. With younger children such as babies and toddlers, we will need to gain their views by observing their reactions during an activity and reflecting on them afterwards. A good tip is to take some photographs during an activity as this will help you to see how enthusiastic the children were when you reflect on the activity.

▌ Next steps

Next steps for the children

As part of the planning, observation and evaluation cycle, we should always be thinking about the next steps for children following on from activities. It could be that a child really enjoyed the activity and it would be worth repeating it, or perhaps a child struggled with a concept or skill and so adapting the activity or thinking of a new approach might be important. If you spotted that children were keen to use the resources differently, you might think about how to organise this.

It is also good practice to gain input from parents/carers as well as the child's key person and colleagues. This can be done by discussing the child's responses to the activity and what was noticed during the activity with them. This allows parents or carers, key persons and colleagues an opportunity to share their ideas for future planned play and activities. Working together in this way makes it more likely to develop future plans that will meet children's interests and needs. This way of working also encourages parent/carer partnership.

Next steps for you

You should spend time thinking about what you have learned from the activity. Perhaps you have learned about the importance of preparation or about children's interests at certain ages. It may be that you have learned what to do if an activity is not enjoyable for children. It can be helpful to spend time talking to an experienced practitioner about what happened during the activity, as their thoughts might help you gain more insights.

Writing up a review of an activity

It is easy to make statements such as 'all the children enjoyed this activity', but it is good practice to provide a reason for your statement and to make it as detailed as possible. See Figure 9.17 for an example.

> Zoe and Thomas were engrossed in the activity and were disappointed when it was lunchtime. I think that this indicates that this activity worked well for them. Damian, on the other hand, lost interest within five minutes or so and I feel that this activity may not have been sufficiently challenging for him.
>
> *Grace, an early years professional*

Figure 9.17 An example of an observation note

Further reading and resources

Barber, J. and Paul-Smith, S. (2010) *Early Years Observation and Planning in Practice*, London: Practical Pre-School Books.

Tassoni, P. (2012) *Penny Tassoni's Practical EYFS Handbook* (2nd ed.), Oxford: Heinemann.

Walker, M., Hobart, C. and Frankel, J. (2009) *A Practical Guide to Child Observation and Assessment* (4th ed.), Cheltenham: Nelson Thornes.

Assessment practice 9.2

3B.P2 | 3B.P3 | 3B.M2 | 3B.D1 | 3C.P4 | 3C.P5 | 3C.M3 | 3C.M4 | 3C.D2 | 3D.P6 | 3D.P7 | 3D.M5 | 3D.D3

You have been shortlisted for a job in a children's centre. During the interview you need to show detailed knowledge of the observation, assessment and planning processes. On the day of the interview, you will need to carry out observations, assessment and planning, and you will be asked in-depth questions to assess your underpinning knowledge and your ability to self-evaluate. To prepare, you have decided to practise this process and also have a mock interview with your current placement supervisor.

1 Carry out five observations on one child using a variety of observational methods.

2 Present these observations, making sure that the information is complete and accurate.

3 Explain why you used each observation method and evaluate their usefulness, making recommendations about how you could address any weaknesses. Use the observations to analyse the child's play and development using theories of development, play and developmental milestones.

4 Using your analysis of the child's stage of development, interests and play, make suggestions for a range of activities, then produce and implement two activity plans that are linked to the EYFS or other relevant early years framework. Ensure you consider the rationale and role of the adult in these activities.

5 Evaluate your own practice in observing, assessing, planning and implementing activities.

6 Consider the importance of different assessment strategies and how they can be used to shape a child's learning.

7 Analyse the extent to which your plans and activities supported the children's play, learning and development.

8 Evaluate ways in which your observation, assessment and planning linked to theoretical perspectives of children's development.

Ready for work?

Kristie Hannagin Preschool staff member

We are very proud of our observation and planning process. It has taken some time for us to feel it is working well, but I now feel we have a pretty robust system that adults new to the setting and, importantly, parents and carers can understand. This is important because we try to share and involve parents and carers in every aspect of our work and, thanks to the easy-to-use system, they are able to contribute their own observations and ideas. This is normally done with the child's key person.

As a manager who used to work in the National Health Service, I am very keen for staff to be aware of children who are not making the usual developmental progress. I always advise my staff to have a quick look at the developmental milestones before they begin to observe a child, especially if they are new to working with the age group or they have not been with them for a while.

We also try to make sure that information gained from observations is not just put in a child's folder and then forgotten. Each week, when staff are doing their short-term planning, children's key persons will contribute ideas for activities, toys and resources based on what they know their key children need. We also show this on the planning sheet by adding the child's initials in the appropriate place.

Skills for practice

What can I do to stop a child from coming up to me when I am observing other children?

This is quite a common problem. You can try telling children that you are busy but will talk to them or play with them later on. If this does not work, try using closed body language and avoid making eye contact with them.

I have tried to use target child observation, but I keep forgetting the codes.

You can devise your own codes if this makes it easier. Then you can either rewrite the observation substituting conventional codes or you can retain your own, but put a clear key at the bottom. This means that someone else can read what you have written.

I observed that a child who is now 4 years old does not have hand preference. I am not sure what activities I should plan. Help!

Hand preference can be strengthened with activities that require both hands, but where one

hand stabilises an object and the other is active. Unscrewing a bottle or peeling a banana are examples of this type of two-handed activity.

When should you share observations with parents/carers?

It is good practice to share observations with parents/carers as soon as you have carried them out. While some parents/carers may be interested in reading or seeing them, others may prefer you to explain to them what you have seen.

My setting does not write up observations with theories and links to milestones. Why does my teacher ask me to do this?

Learner observations and conclusions are often more detailed than those used in settings. This is because learner observations train you in the process of observing and thinking about children. The idea is that later on you will have these skills and use them to think about children, even if you do not write down everything you know.

Introduction

Learning to read and write is complex, as is the process of mathematical development. Learning to read and write involves various skills: speaking and listening to others, phonemic awareness and deciphering text. Children also need to have fine and large motor skills to be able to write. Mathematics is a broad subject area covering many aspects of learning – including measuring, using money and telling the time. To effectively support children's learning in these two areas, you should consider the range of skills they need to have and the different theoretical approaches to learning. You will also need to be aware of any curriculum area that needs to be followed. You will need to think about stimulating and motivating children and be able to recognise and act on any factors that may affect their progress.

Assessment: You will be assessed by a series of assignments set by your teacher/tutor.

Learning aims

In this unit you will:

A   understand children's literacy development
B   understand how to support children's literacy development
C   understand children's mathematical development
D   understand how to support children's mathematical development.

I always knew reading and writing and using numbers were an important part of our everyday lives, but I had always thought they were skills you just pick up. I never really considered all the different factors that need to come together for it to happen. I have found the different ways in which children can be supported to develop these skills fascinating. I hadn't realised how play and exploration can encourage children's natural curiosity and develop their confidence with using numbers.

Maisie, *a student on an early years course*

Supporting Children's Literacy and Numeracy Development

10

BTEC
Assessment Zone

This table shows you what you must do in order to achieve a **Pass**, **Merit** or **Distinction** grade, and lists activities that relate to each learning aim.

Assessment criteria		
Pass	**Merit**	**Distinction**
Learning aim A: Understand children's literacy development		
3A.P1 Describe experiences and activities that support early reading and writing skills. **Assessment practice 10.1**	**3A.M1** Discuss the role of early reading and writing experiences in children's literacy development, using examples. **Assessment practice 10.1**	**3A.D1** Evaluate the effectiveness of a range of early reading and writing experiences in meeting children's literacy development. **Assessment practice 10.1**
Learning aim B: Understand how to support children's literacy development		
3B.P2 Describe different theoretical approaches to teaching children to read. **Assessment practice 10.2**	**3B.M2** Discuss the extent to which different theoretical approaches may help children to learn to read. **Assessment practice 10.2**	**3B.D2** Evaluate the role of the early years professional in planning provision to support literacy development for children across the age range from birth up until 5 years in an early years setting. **Assessment practice 10.2**
3B.P3 Explain the use of synthetic phonics in helping children to read and write. **Assessment practice 10.2**	**3B.M3** Analyse the contribution of early years professionals in supporting children in experiences and activities that encourage reading and writing skills. **Assessment practice 10.3**	
3B.P4 English Explain how different experiences and activities are used to support children when learning to read and write. **Assessment practice 10.3**		
3B.P5 Explain why it is important to understand the links between learning to read and learning to write. **Assessment practice 10.3**		
Learning aim C: Understand children's mathematical development		
3C.P6 Explain how children's experiences support early mathematical development. **Assessment practice 10.4**	**3C.M4** Discuss the extent to which experiences can impact on the development of children's mathematical skills. **Assessment practice 10.4**	

continued

Assessment criteria (*continued*)		
Pass	**Merit**	**Distinction**
Learning aim D: Understand how to support children's mathematical development		
3D.P7 Maths English Select, with reasons, activities for children aged from 2 years up to 5 years that support development of numbers and space, shape and measures. **Assessment practice 10.5** **3D.P8** Explain how early years professionals can support mathematical development through activities. **Assessment practice 10.5**	**3D.M5** Discuss, using examples, the extent to which activities could support children's mathematical development. **Assessment practice 10.5**	**3D.D3** Evaluate the extent to which early years professionals contribute to the mathematical development of children from birth up to 5 years. **Assessment practice 10.5**

English English Functional Skills signposting   Maths Mathematics Functional Skills signposting

How you will be assessed

This unit will be assessed by a series of internally assessed tasks set by your teacher/tutor. Throughout this unit you will find assessment practice activities that will help you work towards your assessment. Completing these activities will not mean that you have achieved a particular grade, but you will have carried out useful research or preparation that will be relevant when it comes to your final assignment.

In order for you to achieve the tasks in your assignment, it is important that you check you have met all of the Pass grading criteria. You can do this as you work your way through the assignment.

If you are hoping to gain a Merit or Distinction, you should also make sure that you present the information in your assignment in the style that is required by the relevant assessment criterion. For example, Merit criteria will require you to discuss and analyse, and Distinction criteria will require you to evaluate.

The assignment set by your teacher/tutor will consist of a number of tasks designed to meet the criteria in the table. This is likely to consist of a written assignment but may also include activities such as:

- a presentation to peers
- observations
- case studies
- a guidance document.

Getting started

What do you remember about your own experience of learning to read and write? What feelings do you have when you start to think about maths? Thinking about both these things and your own experiences can inform how we present these things to young children. Do you remember being read to as a child or seeing your own parents or carers reading? How were you encouraged in school? What kinds of books were you interested in? How comfortable do you feel with solving mathematical problems or using numbers? Discuss in groups where any feelings you have may have come from, or how your experiences might have affected you in later life.

A Understand children's literacy development

Although children do not start to learn to read and write as soon as they are born, they will start to develop many of the pre-reading and pre-writing skills they need from the earliest stages of development. Children will hear and tune into language as they learn to speak, and this in turn will lay the foundation for their literacy skills.

Link

Go to Unit 6 to find more information about the skills children need to learn to read and write.

The importance of speech and language

As soon as they are aware of others, babies will start to learn to communicate in different ways and pick up cues from those around them. They will gradually learn to tune in to speech and the meaning of words through linking sounds with communication, and be able to hear the way in which conversations take place between one person and another. When children start to learn to read and write, this knowledge will help them to make the link between spoken sounds and written symbols, and also to recognise the structure of sentences.

Speech

Although a high percentage of communication is non-verbal, **speech** is the physical process through

which we can instantly pass on our thoughts to others. Listening to speech enables us to hear patterns in language, such as rhyme or alliteration.

Language

Our home **language** or 'mother tongue' is the medium through which we fine-tune our thoughts and communicate them to one another. As children learn language and extend their vocabulary to include more words, they are gradually able to tell us more about their own thoughts and feelings, as well as being able to understand more about the world around them. Language may be written, spoken or signed (for example, sign language).

Speech and language are, therefore, crucial to the development of children's literacy skills, as they are the basis for the way in which we start to break down sounds and communicate with one another. Through speech and language, children start to make sense of the world and their own place within it. As children become more aware of the written word and start to share books with adults, they are able to extend their experiences, explore worlds outside their own and talk about new ideas. Stories, songs and nursery or

Key terms

Language – the medium through which we talk and communicate.

Speech – the physical act of talking and articulating.

Babies will start to learn basic communication skills from an early age.

action rhymes will also support the development of children's language skills by helping them to identify patterns and alliteration in preparation for learning to read.

Reflect

Look at a nursery rhyme you know well.

In what ways might a rhyme support a child's early language skills? Why do you think this might be important in the context of learning to read and write?

▍Areas of literacy

In order to emphasise the importance of speech and language, the Early Years Foundation Stage (EYFS) framework incorporates both under one **prime** area of learning: communication and language. The following three aspects must be a focus during the early years: listening and attention, understanding and speaking.

As well as two further prime areas of learning, the early years foundation stage framework contains four **specific** areas of learning. One of these areas is literacy and it covers reading and writing skills.

The national curriculum programmes of study for English at Key Stage 1 (when children are in Years 1 and 2) and Key Stage 2 (when children are in Years 3 to 6) breaks literacy down into three areas:

- spoken language
- reading (word reading and comprehension)
- writing (transcription, composition, vocabulary, spelling, grammar and punctuation).

Did you know?

Young children develop their vocabulary very fast. A typical 18-month-old child will have a vocabulary of around 50 words, but by around 30 months the average child will understand around 600 words. Find out how many words this will be by the age of 5 years.

How children develop skills in reading and writing

In order to develop their abilities in reading and writing, children will need to practise a number of different skills regularly and in close succession. They should do this as an adult-supported and also independent activity. These skills will then gradually build up over time. As children like to mimic adults, taught activities will often spill over into their play so that their learning is reinforced.

Case study

Developing skills

Ava and Khavarn are 4 years old and are in the reception class. They have just carried out a large group activity with an adult where they have been practising their sounds. You notice that after the two children go off to play they sit in the corner and Ava tells Khavarn that she is going to test him. She then finds some letter sound cards and holds them up so that he can identify the sounds. As she does this, more children join in and soon there is a large group working together.

1 Why is this kind of play valuable in developing reading skills?

2 What kinds of skills is it developing as well as sound recognition?

Children develop skills in reading and writing by:

- linking sounds and letters
- making marks
- recognising simple words
- understanding simple sentences.

Linking sounds and letters

Children need to be taught that letters represent sounds through focused work on phonics. They will need to spend some time regularly looking at the shapes of the letters with an adult and recognising the different sounds these letters represent. Often early years settings will follow a scheme that outlines the way in which the sounds are taught. This can be helpful for planning and also where different adults are working with the children, as it ensures consistency. Children will then start to build words with the sounds that they know, at first with simple c–v–c (consonant–vowel–consonant) words so that they can learn to blend the sounds together by saying them slowly.

Reflect

Anya is looking at a picture book in the book corner and comes to you saying, 'Look! I have found the word 'pet' in this book! See? P-E-T'.

1 What skill is Anya demonstrating?

2 Why is it important that you listen to and respond to her?

Making marks

As children learn to link sounds and letters, they will need to start to practise mark making so that they can begin to form their own words. This will start simply by using different tools to make marks – for example, paintbrushes in the sand or crayons on paper. They should experiment with as many different forms as possible and you will need to give them opportunities so that they have no fear of 'getting it wrong'. Gradually, as their fine motor skills develop, children will start to attempt to copy the letters that represent the sounds they have been learning.

Link

Go to Section B in this unit to find out more information about the sequence in which children learn to write.

Recognising simple words

At the same time as they develop other literacy skills, children will start to recognise simple, common words without needing to sound out and blend each letter. For example, you may notice when they are reading to adults they will be able to say the word straight away. This often happens quite rapidly as children's skills become more proficient.

Understanding simple sentences

As well as learning to decode when reading, it is important that children are also able to understand what they have read in context. You should, at all stages, ask them questions about the text to ensure they are not just going through the motions of sounding out each word. Children should show that they are using all cues available to them, for example pictures and other clues in the text, to help them make sense of what they are reading.

Engaging children's interest and curiosity in books and written materials

Young children are naturally curious and will want to pick up books and look at them with adults. It is important to harness this curiosity and encourage them to develop this interest, through reading stories with them and making books an enjoyable experience. This will in turn motivate children to value books and enjoy reading.

In order to be ready to learn to read, children will need to have had different experiences so that books and reading have a context. This means that they should have some understanding of where reading fits into their world. Many young children will have been given or shown books from a very early age. This means they will have started to build up their pre-reading skills. Some may have been to story sessions at a local library. They may also have had experience of rhymes, so they will begin to be able to hear patterns in words and start to be able to predict what comes next. Children should be read to as much as possible and should be given plenty of opportunities for speaking and listening. Often, young children will be able to recite whole pieces of text from books long before being able to read, and will 'correct' adults if they get anything wrong.

By being read to, they will start to learn that print carries meaning. It is important that children look at books with adults and learn how to handle them. They will start to understand the way in which we hold a book and how to turn pages. They will also start to understand the way we look at print, both from left to right and top to bottom. To engage children's interest, they could be given access to interactive computer programs that help to encourage and reinforce phonic awareness.

Activity

In two minutes, make a list of all the 'texts' you might read in a typical day. Use this to see if you can come up with your own definition of reading.

The importance of a language-rich environment for literacy development

It is important to expose young children to books and language as much as possible to encourage their natural curiosity and promote their literacy development. Both fiction and non-fiction books should be available to children, as they should be exposed to as much variety as possible. You will probably have seen a reading and/or writing area in your setting, and print used in displays and texts at children's level. Word banks and labels are also good ways to encourage children to look at print in their environment. It is important that these kinds of areas are pointed out by adults and used as much as possible so that children are able to develop their literacy skills.

Figure 10.1 shows examples of how a setting can promote a language-rich environment.

Research

Look for the different places in your setting that encourage children to:

1 be aware of print or to develop their mark-making or writing skills

2 use interactive computer programs that develop their phonic awareness.

What kinds of messages are children encouraged to look at in the environment? How does the setting give them opportunities to try out reading and writing for themselves?

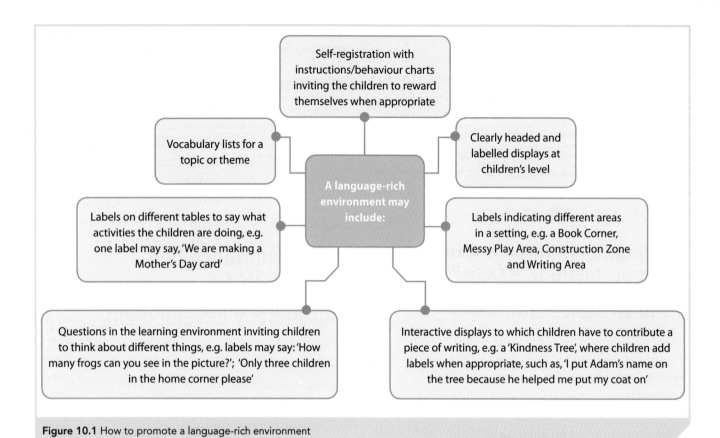

Figure 10.1 How to promote a language-rich environment

The importance of phonemic awareness

As well as looking at books and starting to pick up on different cues, it is important that young children begin to develop **phonemic** awareness as they look at and listen to words. This means that they start to hear individual sounds in words. This will happen if adults start to point at words and relate the print on the page to the sounds and words that they are saying. They should also be taught to listen for sounds within words as they begin to tune in to speech sounds, for example, through being able to hear alliteration or words starting with the same sound. In this way, children will start to understand that what they are looking at relates to what they are hearing. This will make it easier for them to relate **graphemes**, or written representations of sounds, to what they are hearing.

Key terms

Grapheme – individual written symbols.

Phonemes – the smallest units of sound in a language that help to distinguish one word from another. In the English language, for example, 'p' and 'b' are separate phonemes because they distinguish words such as 'pit' and 'bit'.

Assessment practice 10.1

3A.P1 | 3A.M1 | 3A.D1

You have been asked to write a description for preschool parents of some of the different experiences that support the development of young children's reading and writing skills. Using observations or case studies, discuss and evaluate the role of early reading and writing experiences in children's literacy development, using examples, and evaluate their effectiveness. Make reference to activities and experiences such as the role of language-rich environments, hearing stories and rhymes, understanding simple words, sequencing activities and mark-making, and the use of displays, labels, pictures and posters in the environment.

Activities that support reading skills

Reading skills often focus on spoken language activities, which should take place with young children on a regular basis. These include activities such as:

- sharing stories, learning action or nursery rhymes to enable them to hear patterns, rhyming and alliteration in words, and being able to predict what will happen next

- encouraging children to start recognising letter shapes or sounds in the environment (for example, children will often recognise the big 'M' for McDonald's or the name of a favourite shop)

- matching or sequencing activities and sharing books with adults.

Activities that support writing skills

The kinds of activities that support the development of writing skills will be familiar to you from nurseries and preschools, even if they do not immediately appear to be linked to this process. These activities will, among other things, support the development of children's upper body **gross motor skills**. These kinds of activities are very important as they will strengthen the muscles in a child's upper body and arms so that they will have more control when they start mark-making and writing. The activities will also support the development of a child's **fine motor skills** as they start to develop hand–eye coordination as well as control over their arms and hands.

As children develop physically, they will start to become stronger and more skilled in both their fine and gross motor movements, all of which will support the development of their writing skills.

Fine motor skills

Activities that support the development of fine motor skills include threading, cutting, using a knife and fork correctly, using tweezers to pick things up, using playdough, construction or small-world toys, doing puzzles or any other activities that require fine manipulative skills. Children should also have experience in mark-making using different materials and tools such as chalks, paints, brushes, crayons and pencils.

Gross motor skills

Activities that support the development of gross motor skills include throwing and catching, painting, using streamers and hoops, swimming, climbing and any other activities that require children to use upper body strength and develop their shoulder and arm control.

Key terms

Fine motor skills – control of the smaller muscles, such as those in the fingers, to carry out activities such as threading beads onto a necklace, using a knife and fork, or holding a pencil.

Gross motor skills – control of the larger muscles, such as those in the arms and legs, to carry out activities such as running, throwing or kicking a ball.

Activities requiring fine manipulative skills enable children to practise their fine motor skills.

B Understand how to support children's literacy development

Encouraging early reading development

When you are working with children in an early years setting, you will need to know how to support children's early reading development and encourage them to have a love of books. This is one of the most important things early years professionals can do. Children respond to an adult's enthusiasm so you should provide as many opportunities as possible to engage the children in stories and rhymes. Pointing out the pictures and words that are linked to actions that are meaningful to them will help to engage them in the act of reading.

Theory into practice

Carry out or observe an activity with a small group of children during which they are read to or sung nursery rhymes using a book. Look at how the children engage with the book and respond to you as they are being read or sung to. What indications do you have that the children are engaged with the activity? How are the children reacting?

Providing a variety of activities to support development of literacy

Early years professionals should provide children with a wide range of activities so that they have different opportunities to develop their literacy skills. Although they often do this through play, children are very imaginative and will use these skills to develop further. Engaging the imagination of children is an excellent way to encourage them to learn. The kinds of activities you might use include the following.

- Story sacks – children will enjoy using story sacks that contain different elements of a familiar story. For example, a 'Little Red Riding Hood' story sack might include a red cloak, a small stuffed wolf, a basket of fruit, a granny's hat, and so on. Story sacks encourage discussion and develop children's vocabularies as they talk about the text.
- Storytelling – young children love stories and they should start to be able to retell their favourite stories in their own words. This will help them to sequence their ideas.
- Role play – all early years settings should have a role-play area that changes regularly. This will give children opportunities to develop their speaking and listening skills in different contexts as well as their confidence and imagination.
- Puppets – puppets are a good opportunity for children to 'decentre' and think about things from another point of view. They can also help to develop the confidence of children who are more reticent in some situations.
- Story and music CDs – early years settings will usually have a listening corner in which children can sit quietly and listen to stories, rhymes and music.
- Circle time – circle time in small groups with young children encourages them to discuss different topics and listen to one another.
- Small-world play – when children play with small-world toys, such as building blocks and toy towns and other small figures or animals, they are encouraged to use spoken language and their imagination as they 'act' stories out.

Theory into practice

Look around your setting and note down any other activities that are provided in addition to those covered here that might help support children's literacy development. Explain why this is and how they will support children's literacy development.

Delivering curriculum frameworks

The EYFS curriculum relating to literacy is divided into two distinct areas:

- Communication and language
- Literacy.

These two areas are then broken down further into the following areas:

- Communication and language – listening and attention, speaking and understanding
- Literacy – reading and writing.

Communication and language skills run through the whole of EYFS and children who do not have these basic skills will find it hard to make progress in different areas of the curriculum. The teaching of the curriculum relies heavily on children being able to listen to others and respond to them, understand instructions and express themselves effectively. If a child is not progressing in their communication and language skills, you will need to speak to other members of staff and possibly your early years Special Educational Needs Coordinator (SENCO) about how you can support them and work with their parents/carers and other professionals to develop these skills.

For older children, the 2014 national curriculum for England breaks literacy down into the following three areas:

- spoken language
- reading
- writing.

As with the EYFS, these areas of the national curriculum are heavily reliant on children's ability to speak and understand language. They need to be able to articulate what they want to say in different situations and plan their written work accordingly.

Settings should plan learning opportunities for children that encompass a wide range of activities covering all areas of the curriculum. In the early years, planning is usually topic-based. This means you will start from an area, for example, 'mini-beasts', 'houses and homes', 'people who help us', 'transport' and so on. You will then plan to cover different curriculum areas through each of these topics.

To help develop children's reading and writing skills you should provide a range of meaningful practical activities and a language-rich environment. Children should have the chance to practise mark-making and develop their reading skills in different contexts, using different materials. Settings will need to plan their provision so that these opportunities are varied and fit in with different early years topics.

Theoretical approaches to learning to read

Children usually begin to learn to read when they start school between the ages of 4 and 5 years. Different theoretical approaches have emerged relating to how children learn to read, and you should have some understanding of these in order to support children effectively. We already know that before learning to read, it is important that children have been exposed to a language-rich environment and have been able to look at books and share them with adults regularly, as well as taking part in pre-reading activities. This will form a solid basis on which to build their reading skills.

Phonics and phonemes

The **phonics** approach is based on the breaking down and blending of letters so that children learn to link sounds with individual letters and **phonemes**. The sound system is more complex and inconsistent in English than in other languages as there can be a number of different phonemes to represent the same sound (for example, 'f' and 'ph'). Phonics is, therefore, used as a method of teaching sounds as it helps us to look at the different letter patterns together, along with their sounds. There are around 44 different phonemes in spoken English.

> ### Key terms
>
> **Phonemes** – the smallest units of sound in a language that help to distinguish one word from another. In the English language, for example, 'p' and 'b' are separate phonemes because they distinguish words such as 'pit' and 'bit'.
>
> **Phonics** – the name of a method used to teach reading that breaks down different letter patterns into their individual sounds.

There are two main different phonics methods – synthetic phonics and analytical phonics.

Synthetic phonics

Synthetic phonics require the reader to learn individual sounds and blends in a particular order, then put them together to form words. The sounds are taught in a particular way, not to sound like the letters – for example, the sound for 't' would be taught as a short sound and not as 'tee' or 'tuh'. The simpler and most commonly used sounds will be the first to be taught, as these are also straightforward (s, a, t, I, p and n). These can then be put together to form many simple three-letter words, which can be sounded out by children from a relatively early stage.

Analytical phonics

In analytical phonics, blends are taught, rather than individual letter sounds, for example, 'sh', 'th' and 'ch'. Children are encouraged to learn sets of whole words that have a similar spelling, such as 'cat', 'hat', 'mat', 'fat' and 'bat'. A disadvantage of this system is that many words in English are not written phonetically (for example, 'said', 'know' or 'was') and children will still need to learn these words separately.

Whole-language/apprenticeship

Another approach to phonics is the whole-language/ apprenticeship approach. This grew from Noam Chomsky's ideas about language acquisition. Chomsky theorised that we all have an innate ability to learn any language and do not learn it by imitating others.

In 1967, Ken Goodman had an idea about reading that he thought was similar to Chomsky's theory. He described a system for reading by which learners have to use four different cues in order to decipher the words:

- graphophonemic – the shapes of the letters, and their corresponding sounds
- semantic – what you would expect the word to be, based on the meaning of the sentence so far
- syntactic – what word or phrase would make the most sense, based on the context and grammatical

structure of the language – word order, tense and gender
- pragmatic – the function of the text.

The whole-language approach is also sometimes called the 'look and say' approach. It encourages the learner to look at, and recognise, whole words when learning to read, rather than breaking them down into sounds. In this way, the child will be introduced to high-frequency words such as 'said', 'because', 'they', 'were' and 'who', which do not fit into regular phonic patterns. Although the child may take longer to learn this way, they are less likely to make errors than a child who has learned synthetic phonics.

Theory into practice

Read the text below. Can you answer the questions?

'A frotterpat was losping a ticklepup. A binker wootled. The binker wisped "Frimto" to the frotterpat. The frotterpat mantered bentistly.'

- What was the frotterpat doing?
- What wootled?
- What did the binker wisp?
- How did the frotterpat manter?

This exercise is based on Chomsky's idea that sentences can be grammatical without making sense and that we can produce new sentences without ever having heard them before. What do you think the implications of this exercise are for supporting children's reading?

Using phonics and whole-language

Most educationalists agree that a combination of these two main approaches works best, as different children will approach reading in different ways. It is likely that in most settings, although there will be a structured environment for the teaching of reading, you will also find that children are, for example, encouraged to learn high-frequency words as well as learn to sound them out using phonics.

Assessment practice 10.2 3B.P2 | 3B.P3 | 3B.M2 | 3B.D2

You have been asked to write a report for someone preparing a reading course for children. Outline two different theoretical approaches to helping children learn to read and discuss the extent to which they may help children. What further information can you find out? Explain the use of synthetic phonics in helping children to read and write. Evaluate the role of the early years professional in planning provision to support literacy development in children from birth up to 5 years.

The usual sequence by which children learn to read

Even allowing for the different methods used to teach reading, the sequence by which children learn to read will follow a similar pattern. If children have had a positive experience at the earliest pre-reading stages, they will have learned that print is significant and may also have learned to recognise their own name written down, or a few basic letters and sounds. As they start to have more experience of reading, they will be more aware of the conventions of how to handle and use books and that text reads from left to right. Children will start to be taught basic letters and sounds, which will support their reading skills and enable them to use the letters in context. They will begin to learn to recognise the link between the verbal and visual word.

There are different schemes and resources available to support the teaching of phonics, and usually these require the child to learn all the letters and sounds quite quickly so that they are able to start to use them. They will then be revised and extended to form blends and whole words, and children will start to build a visual vocabulary of these.

It is important at this stage for children to have as many different cues available to them as possible when reading, for example, pictures that tell the story and word repetition within the text.

When listening to children read, you should ask them about the text and discuss what they are reading. This may take the form of talking about how a character might be feeling, retelling the story or discussing a point that might be ambiguous within the text. This is because decoding the writing, although important, is only part of reading. As they learn to read, children will also need to develop comprehension skills and be able to relate the text to their own experience to make sense of it.

The need for early years professionals to be reading and writing role models

It is important for young children to make sense of why they are learning to read and write and to be able to put this into context. They should have opportunities to see that adults read books for pleasure, to find out information and write things down to refer to or pass information to others. For this reason, they should have role models who read and write and refer to books as a matter of course. In the setting, there may be limited opportunities for this, but they can still be found; for example, when referring to recipes for cooking activities, or when using books to find out information for a particular topic. Early years professionals should draw attention to the fact that they will need to look at a book to find things out, or make a list so that they remember to do things. They may also refer to books that they are reading at home so that children can relate their own reading to adult experiences.

Remember, children learn all the time from their environment and the adults around them. Praise and encouragement are very strong motivators, as they will support the child in gaining confidence. Children should be exposed to good adult role models so they can see reading skills used and the pleasure that can be derived from reading.

Choosing appropriate books and activities for children

All settings should have a wide variety of books available to children so that different interests and abilities are catered for when learning to read. At the very early stages, books should have simple storylines and vocabulary and contain some repetition. Some early pre-reading books will simply consist of pictures in a sequence so that the adult and child can discuss what is happening. Many early reading books also contain rhymes, which make it easier for children to predict words as they come up.

Some children will be particularly interested in picture books and stories, whilst others may prefer non-fiction and information books. It is important as you get to know children and find out about what interests them that you are able to support them in choosing appropriate books. Many books will display the suitable age or ability level in order to help with this. Whilst some settings will insist on children working through a set reading scheme, others may mix them up so that children experience a variety of different types of text.

Creating stimulating experiences and activities that encourage reading

During the Foundation Stage, and before children start more 'formal' reading activities, there should be a range of activities available that support the development of their pre-reading and reading skills. These may include letter identification and matching activities, sound snap and sound bingo, small-group story time and story sequencing activities among others.

Activity

In your setting, identify the different activities that take place to support early reading skills and feed these back to others in your school/college group. Which activities seem to motivate the children, and why?

Using phonics to decode words

In order to help children to use phonics to decode words, you will need to support them in a non-threatening way so they feel confident to 'have a go' themselves. Large books or interactive whiteboards are ideal for this as you can work with a large group of children and talk them through the process. The more you do this, the more confident they will become as their knowledge develops and increases.

Theory into practice

Look carefully at the way in which your setting teaches phonics to children.

Give a presentation to your school/college group about the way in which the children respond and analyse their progress.

Sharing books with children

When sharing books with children, it is important to ensure that they know they have your support, while at the same time, can develop their independence. You can support children in different ways, as Figure 10.2 shows.

As you hear children read, you will need to help them develop different strategies so that they can identify unknown words and make their own guesses or substitutions if they are unable to decode them. In this way, you will be helping them to become independent readers.

Activity

Carry out a reading activity with an individual child, taking care to include as many of the points in Figure 10.2 as you can. Do you think that you do these things as routine?

You should always have realistic expectations of children's reading. This means the kinds of books you are reading with them will need to be at an appropriate level for them to be able to make progress. You should not give children books that will be too challenging for them to read, or expect them to want to read everything that you present to them. Some children will prefer to look at non-fiction texts and will be less keen on story or picture books, whereas others may like books by a particular author. Children may be happier reading on some days than on others, and as you get to know them you may be able to identify times that are better for them. It can be difficult, for example, to hear them read when you have to ask them to come away from an activity that is particularly holding their interest.

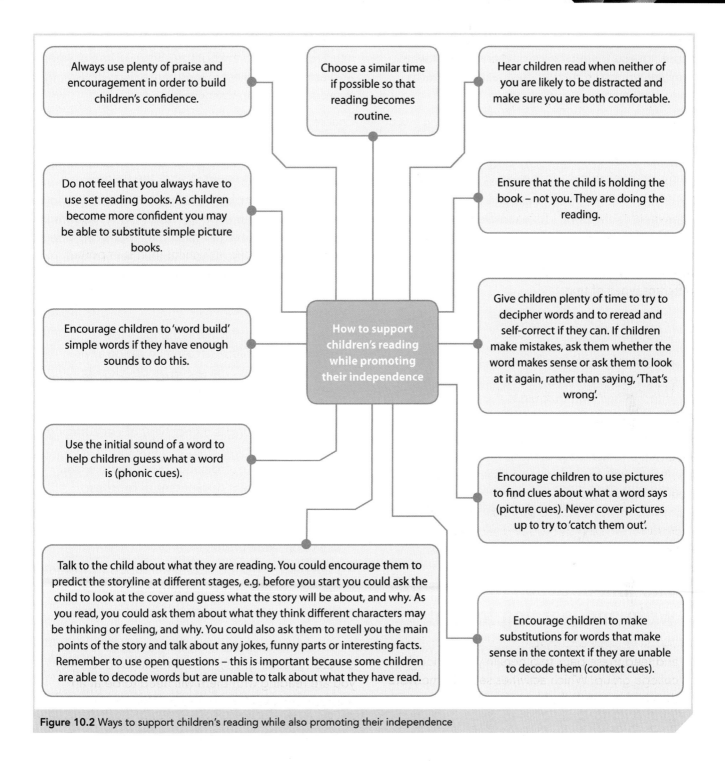

Figure 10.2 Ways to support children's reading while also promoting their independence

Text inside the figure:

Always use plenty of praise and encouragement in order to build children's confidence.

Choose a similar time if possible so that reading becomes routine.

Hear children read when neither of you are likely to be distracted and make sure you are both comfortable.

Do not feel that you always have to use set reading books. As children become more confident you may be able to substitute simple picture books.

Ensure that the child is holding the book – not you. They are doing the reading.

Encourage children to 'word build' simple words if they have enough sounds to do this.

How to support children's reading while promoting their independence

Give children plenty of time to try to decipher words and to reread and self-correct if they can. If children make mistakes, ask them whether the word makes sense or ask them to look at it again, rather than saying, 'That's wrong'.

Use the initial sound of a word to help children guess what a word is (phonic cues).

Encourage children to use pictures to find clues about what a word says (picture cues). Never cover pictures up to try to 'catch them out'.

Talk to the child about what they are reading. You could encourage them to predict the storyline at different stages, e.g. before you start you could ask the child to look at the cover and guess what the story will be about, and why. As you read, you could ask them about what they think different characters may be thinking or feeling, and why. You could also ask them to retell you the main points of the story and talk about any jokes, funny parts or interesting facts. Remember to use open questions – this is important because some children are able to decode words but are unable to talk about what they have read.

Encourage children to make substitutions for words that make sense in the context if they are unable to decode them (context cues).

Encouraging early mark-making and writing development

When it comes to writing, you will need to provide children with encouragement from the earliest stage of development so that they develop confidence in what they are doing. Many children seek reassurance from adults but they should not be afraid of 'getting it wrong'.

Encouragement should begin when children start to make marks as a symbolic representation of their thoughts and experiences. They may at first use either hand (it can take some time for them to decide on a preferred hand), create marks in any direction and use a number of different materials, such as brushes, large markers, crayons, paint or make marks in materials such as sand. However they choose to express themselves, children should be encouraged to develop their control as much as possible. Adults should praise them and ask questions about what they are writing so that children learn that words convey meaning.

For children to develop writing skills, they will need to be provided with a supportive environment. This means that they should have stimulation and resources available when their skills are developing. These may include:

- environmental print – for example, displays with captions and information, key words, clearly labelled areas within and outside the setting in all areas of the learning environment
- dictionaries and topic-based word banks
- adult role models so that children can see the purpose of writing
- a variety of clearly labelled materials and writing areas available so that children can use them to write for their own purposes.

Reflect

Look at your own setting. What kinds of examples does it provide of a supportive environment for the development of writing skills?

The link between learning to write and learning to read

Children in schools and early years settings will learn to read and write at around the same time. It is important to remember that learning to read and learning to write are interrelated and that children will need to have a wide range of literacy experiences in order to support the development of each.

Whereas reading is the way in which we find out about the world and different situations, writing is the way in which we ourselves pass on information and

Did you know?

Until the 1970s, writing and reading were taught completely separately, as there was not thought to be a link between the two.

transfer our ideas to others in different ways. You will need to be able to encourage and motivate children who are in the earliest stages of reading and writing in order to develop their confidence.

Children will need to be provided with a wide range of literacy experiences in order to support their development of both reading and writing skills. These experiences could include the following.

- Sand and water play – children can use sand and water to play and experiment with letter sounds in a different context. For example, adults can hide letter shapes in the sand and ask them to find simple words, or put them in different containers in the water and ask them to match up the same sounds.
- Role play – role-play areas are ideal for encouraging children's communication and imaginative skills. These can be developed through storytelling if the home corner is themed, for example as 'Goldilocks' house'.
- Painting – painting is a good way of encouraging the development of children's fine motor skills and their hand–eye coordination. For example, you could use different thicknesses of brushes.
- Story sacks – story sacks encourage children to think about how a story is constructed through the use of different prompts.
- Print making – print making will support children's handwriting development and coordination.
- Patterns – pattern recognition in rhymes and stories will help children to develop their prediction skills when learning to read.
- Storytelling and poetry – children will need a wide repertoire of stories and poetry read to them so that they can identify the key features and themes that run through them, as well as helping them to look at patterns in language.
- Music and drama – as with storytelling and poetry, children will be able to recognise patterns and rhythms in music, develop their confidence when acting out different situations, for example in the role-play area and predicting lyrics in songs and nursery rhymes.
- Cutting and sticking – cutting and sticking activities will develop children's fine motor skills and control, which will help them when developing the skills that are necessary to write.

The development of handwriting

From the earliest stages, children will begin to develop their handwriting skills through activities that promote hand–eye coordination and strengthen their hand muscles. They should be given plenty of opportunities to develop their fine motor skills through using different media such as brushes, pegs, tweezers, threading or mark making. Children should also be developing gross motor movements in their upper body so that they have the strength needed in their shoulders to be able to write. At this stage, you could be looking out to see whether the child has developed a preference for using a particular hand and support their development of an efficient pencil grip, although children aged 2 to 3 years may still be using a **palmar grip**. Chunky pencils and other writing media are available to help with this, as well as pencil grips that fit normal-sized pencils. Although a tripod grip is best, with three fingers on the pencil, there may be variations on this, and left-handed children in particular may find different grips easier.

> **Key term**
>
> **Palmar grip** – holding an object with the palm of the hand.

Modelling the correct formation of letters and numbers

You should be aware of the handwriting policy in your setting so that you use the agreed method for the formation of letters and numbers. This means that you and other adults should consistently form letters and numbers in the same way so that children will not be confused by different methods. You should also make this method clear to parents and carers so they are able to work with children in the same way at home, for example using lower case rather than capital letters.

The usual sequence by which children learn to write

When learning to write, children will usually pass through different stages as they become more skilled at forming letters and developing ideas. In the earliest stages, they may focus on mark making and forming letters. This will develop into being able to talk about what they have written as they ascribe meaning to marks and gradually into being able to word-build through their phoneme and grapheme knowledge, and write longer sentences (see Figure 10.3).

How to create stimulating writing experiences and motivate children to write for a purpose

During the Foundation Stage, children should be provided with stimulating opportunities to develop their pre-writing and writing skills through activities that encourage them to strengthen and develop their muscle control. They should also be given a variety of media with which to make marks as they start to experiment with this. You should ensure that you talk to children about what the marks mean so they can start to make links between speech and writing. These kinds of experiences may include:

- making marks in shaving foam, sand, dried rice or cornflour and water
- practising using different media such as pens, brushes and water
- using sponges or play-dough to strengthen hand muscles
- threading, sewing and using tweezers to develop fine motor control.

As their control develops, children at this stage should be given opportunities to write for a purpose through play activities – for example, writing appointments in a diary in a role-play area that is a doctor's surgery, or keeping shopping lists. Although they may still be mark making, their writing will have a clear purpose and they will be able to tell you about it. They may also start to practise being able to write their own name.

1 In the earliest stages, children will start to form strings of letters to represent words.

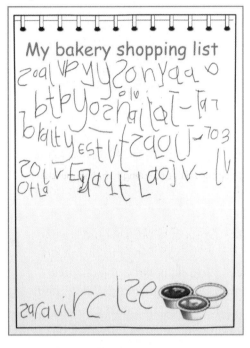

2 Children will start to be able to hear and write individual letter sounds within words – this will usually be the first and last letter of the word.

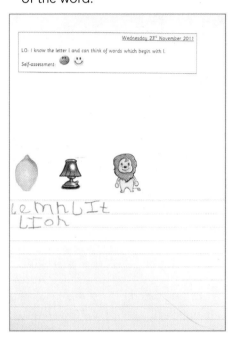

3 Children will start to be able to hear and write several sounds within a word, although letters may not all be correctly formed and spaced out.

4 Words will become spaced out and letters correctly formed with some punctuation. Children may start to use joins if they have not done so from the start.

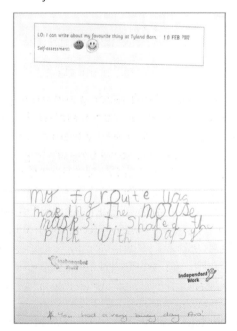

5 As well as continuing to work on punctuation and presentation, the content of children's work will become more involved as they start to use more adventurous and descriptive language.

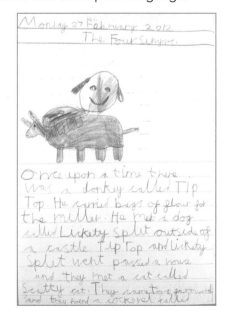

Figure 10.3 Examples of emerging writing skills

Supporting left-handed children

Children who are left-handed may need more support than their right-handed peers. You should make sure you are aware of left-handed children and give them additional attention when they are carrying out activities such as starting mark making, developing their writing skills or using scissors. When left-handed people write they may have a more 'awkward' pencil grip – so when they are starting to write and make marks, encourage them to find a grip that is comfortable, but make sure you support them. It can be difficult for them on a practical level, particularly if they are sitting next to a right-hander who is also trying to write, as they may knock into one another. There are resources available to support left-handers such as scissors and easy-grip pens, and for older children, rulers that read from right to left.

Children should be given opportunities to strengthen their muscle control and make marks.

Key term

Scribe – an adult who writes down what a child would like to say.

Did you know?

The lefthandedchildren.org website offers suggestions and resources for left-handed children. This is a useful resource if you have left-handed children in your setting. To access this website go to www.pearsonhotlinks.co.uk and search for this ISBN: 9781447970965.

Theory into practice

Is scribing used in your setting? How regularly do children write independently and how much of this kind of support are they given?

Scribing for children

In the earlier stages of writing, children may sometimes practise writing through making anti-clockwise rotational marks on a page or learning that we start to write taller letters at the top. In some settings, children may be encouraged to trace over lines or letters in order to support the development of their handwriting skills and you should encourage them to be accurate. There may also be times when children need adults to act as a **scribe** for them, for example, when individual children are starting to learn to write or if they have special educational needs that make pencil control more difficult. Some children who lack confidence in their writing like to copy beneath a line written by an adult, although this method should not be used too often as they can become reliant on it.

Supporting the development of writing in another language

When supporting children's reading and writing skills, early years professionals should remember that a high percentage of children will be learning another language and script at the same time as they are learning to read and write in English. Even though we have to assess them in English, it is important to recognise that learning two languages may initially slow down the development of a child's reading and writing skills, particularly if the language is completely different and they are learning different scripts. We should always encourage and praise the fact that children are learning two (or more) languages, and should value mark making derived from different scripts so that they develop their confidence.

Write a case study about a child whom you are supporting in learning to read and write. What experiences and activities have you provided in order to encourage the child to read and write, and why is it important to understand the links between the two?

Providing examples of the child's writing from the earliest stages, describe the usual sequence of writing development and show how the child has passed through these. How do you see your own role in providing appropriate experiences and activities to support reading and writing?

C Understand children's mathematical development

Activity

What kinds of feelings do you have when you start to think about mathematics? Discuss with a partner why you think you have these feelings and where they come from. What does this tell you about how we should present mathematics to young children?

Theory into practice

Have a look around your setting to see what evidence you can find of mathematics in action over the course of one day. This could be displays and information, activities or adults talking to children using mathematical language.

Why do you think these activities are useful for children's future mathematical understanding?

Links between everyday mathematical experiences and future mathematical understanding

Learning provision for mathematics is important for children, as maths is so much part of our everyday lives. From the earliest stages, children should be developing mathematical skills through practical work that introduces them to aspects of maths such as shape, space, number, measurement, pattern recognition, counting, sorting and so on. Children need to be exposed to numbers in different contexts to explore mathematical language and to think about different ways in which we use measures.

A key aspect of developing skills in mathematics is that children understand its practical purpose and can learn to apply it to real-life situations. You will need to have an awareness of the skills that children in your setting are working towards in order to support them fully and help them to access the curriculum.

The links between continual interaction and communication

Early years professionals should be **continually interacting and communicating** with young children in order to develop their language and communication skills. This interaction is also crucial

Key terms

Continual interaction and communication – in this context, the way in which we talk about maths and use mathematical language so that children learn mathematical vocabulary in different contexts.

Positional language – vocabulary such as 'next to', 'underneath', 'inside', 'outside', 'on top of', 'above', 'around', 'apart', 'middle', 'edge', 'opposite', 'left', 'right', 'across', 'along', 'beside', 'below', 'before', 'after', 'in between'.

to the development of numeracy skills. Traditional and improvised rhymes and counting songs provide a contextual and fun way for children to pick up and recognise patterns in language and number, to recognise **positional language** and also to hear numbers being used in a way that supports their learning.

Link

Go to Unit 1 to find more information about cognitive development.

Reflect

Think about the following nursery rhymes and songs, and how they relate to positional language, pattern recognition and/or the development of number.

- 'One, two, three, four, five, once I caught a fish alive…..'
- Five currant buns in a baker's shop
- The grand old Duke of York
- Five little ducks went swimming one day
- The wheels on the bus

What other rhymes and songs can you think of that would support the development of numeracy though links to positional language, number and pattern recognition?

Reflect

Think about what you know about cognitive development. Before we look at the links to mathematics, what do you think these might be?

Piaget's work was mainly focused on the development of cognitive skills. Piaget believed that we learn more by building on what we know already through **concrete experiences**, and that our learning will progress in this way. His theory of four cognitive stages is also closely linked to mathematical development. Piaget believed that children must pass through each stage and experience at each level in order to have a firm grounding for the next, and that they will not progress to the next stage until they are ready.

Key terms

Cognitive development – the development of the mind and how children learn, reason and understand.

Concrete experiences – practical experiences that make it easier for young children to understand an idea.

Constructivist theory – a theory that states how children learn by constructing their own knowledge through experience and that children pass through specific stages of development.

The theory of mathematical development and its links to cognitive development

In order to understand how children learn mathematics, you will need to have some idea about mathematical theories of development. This will help you understand why maths is taught in a particular way and how different skills build on one another.

You should have some idea about the way in which children develop mathematical skills so that you can support them effectively. The development of mathematical skills is closely linked to children's **cognitive development**. Studies and research have taken place into the way in which mathematical development occurs, but the most influential in this area has been the work of Piaget, through **constructivist theory**.

Piaget's four cognitive stages

1 At the sensory motor stage (0 to 2 years), children will be developing hand–eye coordination and learning to understand object permanence (starting to realise an object is still there, even when moved or hidden). They will start to develop their concept of number, be able to link numbers to objects and have some understanding of counting. At this stage they should be exposed to lots of opportunities to count, such as picture books with numbers, so they are able to make links between numbers and objects.

2 At the pre-operational stage (3 to 7 years), children will have an increasing ability in language and will be starting to understand symbolic thought, as well as some limited logic. This increase in language ability will mean they are able to carry out simple problem-solving activities but will need to be supported by materials such as blocks, cubes, sand, water and other apparatus. These will support their development and should be used in conjunction with plenty of opportunities for questioning and discussion. However, their lack of logical thought means they are unable to transfer what they know to different situations. For example, if they have two identical containers with the same amount of water in each and transfer the contents of one to a third, wider container, they will assume there is less water in the third because the water level has gone down. This is known as conservation. It may also be applied to number – for example, if children are adding two piles of cubes of the same number, they will start counting from the beginning rather than counting on from the first pile. At this stage, children will only use one dimension to judge a task or situation.

3 At the concrete operational stage (8 to 11 years), there is a period of rapid cognitive growth. This is quite a dramatic period and children will now be able to consider two or three dimensions to a task. For example, they will now identify that there is the same amount of water in each container when the water is transferred because as well as seeing that

the level is lower, they can see the dish is wider. At this stage there should also be plenty of hands-on and practical experiences – children will still need lots of support to make links to the abstract and be shown different representations. Their skills at ordering and grouping objects will be increasing.

4 At the formal operational stage (12 to 15 years), children will be able to think in the abstract. For example, in algebra, a child will not need to be given a word problem in order to understand a concept. Their reasoning skills will be increased and they will be able to form their own ideas.

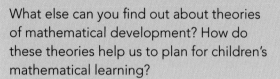

Research

What else can you find out about theories of mathematical development? How do these theories help us to plan for children's mathematical learning?

How mathematics in the early years is broken down into numbers and space, shape and measures

The EYFS breaks the teaching of mathematics down into numbers and shape, space and measures. At the end of a child's Reception year of education, the expectation in terms of 'numbers' is that they should be able to:

- count reliably with numbers from 1 to 20, place them in order and say which number is one more or one less than a given number

- using quantities and objects, add and subtract two single-digit numbers and count on or back to find the answer

- solve problems, including doubling, halving and sharing.

Source: Taken from the Statutory Framework for the Early Years Foundation Stage. © Crown copyright 2012. Contains public sector information licensed under the Open Government Licence v 2.0.

In order to be able to do this, children should have opportunities to use numbers in different contexts, for example counting rhymes, playing board games, going on **maths walks** and playing hopscotch.

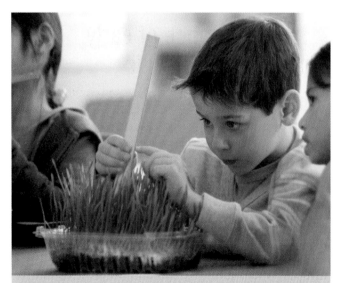

Opportunities should be provided for children to develop through hands-on and practical experiences.

Key term

Maths walk – a walk around a school or setting during which children look for different aspects of maths in the environment, for example numbers and shapes.

Children need to learn not only to count in sequence but to go on to understand what numbers mean and how they can be used, for example by looking at patterns in number. They will then be ready to start simple addition.

To meet the 'shape, space and measures' area of the mathematics curriculum, the expectation at the end of the Reception year is that children:

- use everyday language to talk about size, weight, capacity, position, distance, time and money to compare quantities and objects and to solve problems
- recognise, create and describe patterns
- explore characteristics of everyday objects and shapes and use mathematical language to describe them.

Source: Taken from the Statutory Framework for the Early Years Foundation Stage. © Crown copyright 2012. Contains public sector information licensed under the Open Government Licence v 2.0.

When learning about measures, children should be given the chance to play with measuring equipment and talk about what they are doing. In this way, they will be familiar with equipment when they start to use it more formally in Year 1.

Strategies for developing mathematical skills

You need to be able to use different strategies in order to develop, among others, the following mathematical skills in young children. You can do this through focused activities as well as using the learning environment.

Counting from 1 to 20 and placing numbers in order

As well as counting with young children as much as possible so they are used to hearing numbers in order, numbers should be displayed both indoors and outdoors so that children see them being used. They should also be part of children's play activities or included in class routines. For example, create a 'car park' in the outside play area that contains numbered spaces. Ask children to park toys or bicycles in the correctly-numbered space.

Adding and subtracting single digit numbers

As well as working on very simple addition and subtraction activities, early years professionals should also use day-to-day problems to develop the concepts of adding and taking away. For example, we have enough skipping ropes for six children – how many more would we need for eight children?

Describing the shape and size of 2-D and 3-D shapes

Use a feely bag and ask children to describe what they can feel, encouraging them to think about whether the object has edges, corners, whether it is curved or has straight lines, and whether it is flat or solid and large or small. The focus in this activity should be on mathematical language.

Reflect

Consider how you have used different strategies for developing mathematical skills in these areas and share ideas with others in your school/college group.

The importance of early mathematical skills

The development of early mathematical skills will give children a basis from which to develop their mathematical understanding as they become more familiar with different concepts. Practical exploration is important from the earliest stages of developing mathematical skills because it enables children to have a secure grounding in different aspects of mathematics. Table 10.1 shows basic practical skills that will support children's development of different areas of mathematics.

Table 10.1 Basic practical skills in early mathematical exploration

Skill	Purpose
Matching and one-to-one correspondence	One-to-one correspondence is the matching of numbers within two sets. Children will need to be able to do this in order to count effectively.
Pattern making	Pattern making is important as it enables children to identify simple repeated ideas. This is a good basis for finding patterns in numbers later on.
Matching and sorting	Early sorting activities will help children's understanding of numbers. They should have opportunities to sort as many different materials as possible and in as many different ways as they can. This will also support the development of language – why should these items be put together? Which ones do not belong with the others? Children should also be invited to compare different objects or groups of objects, which will also help to develop language.
Counting and ordering	Children will need to become familiar with the number system. They will do this through counting and ordering numbers and groups of numbers with the same criteria. They should also begin to count in 2s, 5s and 10s.
Recording	Children will start to record numbers, patterns and what they have found out in simple ways, through pictures and simple charts and tallies. This will lead on to later being able to express their ideas through symbols.
The concept of the empty set 'zero'	In maths, a set is a collection of numbers (for example, 2, 4 and 6) that are unique. An empty set simply means a collection of objects with no value – zero, or 'none'. Children will need to recognise that we sometimes need to represent the empty set when discussing mathematical problems and ideas, for example 'There are no balls in this bag – this means there are zero balls in this bag'.

The need for children to acquire mathematical language

When teaching young children mathematical concepts, you will need to remember the importance of language and how problems here can make a big difference to their understanding. There are different ways in which failing to understand mathematical vocabulary may come to light, including if children:

- do not understand instructions – for example, language such as 'find the difference', 'arrange in order' or 'read the table below'
- are not familiar with the vocabulary – for example, vocabulary such as 'pattern', 'in between', 'more/less than', 'greater/smaller than', 'in front of', 'inside' or 'heavier'
- do not understand a mathematical term – for example, 'subtract', 'double', 'match' or 'circle'.

We can sometimes make assumptions about what children understand, particularly in maths. If we focus on the concept rather than the language, some young children, or those who speak English as an additional language, may have difficulty. When carrying out a new topic, a general activity or assessment task, teachers may introduce it by going through mathematical vocabulary to check children's understanding. Words that are used as part of a topic can be displayed on the wall so that children are able to refer to them throughout the topic.

Mathematical vocabulary and language should be displayed in the learning environment. As children work on practical mathematical activities, these displays should be talked about with adults so that children can build up their knowledge of the kind of vocabulary we use in mathematics.

Research

A booklet called the 'Mathematical Vocabulary Book' was produced in 2000 to support the then National Numeracy Strategy alongside the Framework for Teaching Mathematics. It was produced to support the development of children's mathematical vocabulary by identifying words and phrases that children need to understand and use if they are to make good progress in mathematics. You can access it online at the Teachfind website by going to www.pearsonhotlinks.co.uk and searching for this ISBN: 9781447970965.

The importance of building children's confidence

As with all other areas of learning, you will need to build children's confidence when working on mathematical ideas. From an early age, children should be presented with positive and fun methods of working with mathematical activities and experiences in ways that engage all learners. Early years professionals should take care to ensure that tasks are introduced in a way that stimulates children so that they do not think of mathematics as 'difficult'. Occasionally, concepts may be difficult to grasp, and children will find new ideas challenging. Children should be given plenty of opportunities to use games, investigations and other forms of mathematics, which will develop their skills while also encouraging them to be independent.

When children have trouble understanding concepts, you should always give them the opportunity to talk about their understanding and any concerns they have. Group work can be a good opportunity to do this. Children can quickly start to feel they cannot 'do' maths and lose confidence if they find it challenging, and you will need to attempt to build up this confidence as much as possible.

It is also important not to let any of your own possible negative feelings or experiences about maths from the past expose themselves in the verbal or non-verbal language you use around children. Children need to believe maths is 'fun'. Regardless of our own feelings about maths, we need to be able to competently support children in this area by providing positive reinforcement and interactions.

Reflect

Think about how you present mathematical concepts to children and the kinds of language you use. How do you ensure that you build children's confidence and encourage them to develop their ideas?

It is very important for children to have time to carry out practical activities as well as talk about and consolidate what they have learned in an environment that is not pressured. This is because some mathematical ideas are quite complex. If children carry out activities too early, before they have completed the previous stage in their learning, they will be unable to progress to the next stage. For example, if children are still at the early stages of exploring number, counting and combining two groups of objects, they should not progress to recording this until they have had plenty of practical opportunities to develop and become used to the language of number such as 'more' and 'less'.

Assessment practice 10.4   3C.P6 | 3C.M4

Write an account for parents of children who are starting school that explains children's early mathematical experiences. Discuss the importance of these early mathematical experiences for the later development of children's mathematical skills. Include reference to the importance of appropriate early concrete experiences and the effects of lack of confidence.

D Understand how to support children's mathematical development

Supporting children's early experiences of mathematics through play and learning activities

The Early Years Foundation Stage emphasises the importance of play during learning activities. As mathematics is sometimes an abstract subject, it is very important that early years professionals support children's early experiences of mathematics through play by linking mathematical concepts such as number, measurement, shape, space and pattern recognition to practical activities as much as possible to make it meaningful for children. Early years professionals need to ensure that mathematics makes sense to young children so that their experiences provide the basis for understanding these mathematical concepts.

Case study

Supporting mathematics through activities

Anna is working on the concept of weight with a group of four children for the first time. She has two sets of balance scales and a variety of foods on the table as the topic is fruit and vegetables. She starts by asking the children if they know which food will be the heaviest and which will be the lightest before asking them how they can find out if they are right.

1 Is this kind of activity helpful for young children?

2 Give some other examples of how Anna could develop the children's understanding of weight through their topic.

Other ways to support children's early experiences of mathematics

When working with children on mathematical activities, you may need to act as a facilitator for their learning. You may need to support them through talking to them in different ways to encourage them to stay on task. Key methods for doing this include the following.

Commentary

Talk to children about what they are doing as they are doing it in order to reinforce the task. For example, you may say, 'Oh, I see, you are making a pattern with the different coloured pegs'.

Questioning

Questioning is an effective method of encouraging and developing children's experiences, as it can encourage them to think about the task in different ways and extend their learning. You should encourage children to talk about what they are doing, particularly during practical tasks, and question them in a way that encourages them to think about the task differently. Some examples of questioning are shown in Table 10.2, later in this section.

Repetition

Going over or repeating concepts is important with young children, as they will need opportunities to practise what they have learned.

Praise

You should use praise wherever possible as it is an excellent motivator and gives children confidence. Praise can be verbal, but you can also give stickers or rewards, or ask the child to show another adult what they have done or describe it to other children.

How settings might plan and organise their provision to deliver the curriculum framework

In the early years, mathematics will usually be taught through topic work. This means mathematics will be part of a wider study around a subject, such as 'Myself' or 'Toys'.

Topics can last from between two weeks to half a term. In nurseries and reception classes, the curriculum requires the delivery of mathematics will be mainly through practical activities and discussion. Children will carry out a range of activities, including those based on prediction and problem solving. Activities should be meaningful and purposeful, and in the context of the topic they are exploring.

Maths should also be brought into children's routines and should be spoken about, for example by asking questions such as 'How many children are here today?', 'Do we have enough pieces of fruit for everyone?', 'Who will be taller?'. By hearing mathematical language, children will start to develop their own mathematical thinking skills.

In all countries of the UK, when children move into Key Stage or Primary 1, the teaching of mathematics will be taught in different units in blocks of two- or three-week lessons so that children are able to spend some time developing their skills before moving on to the next one. For example, when working on partitioning and calculating in Year 2, the primary framework sets out what should be covered during the year and splits it into three units of two weeks. One of these will then be studied each term.

Can you see how this practical activity is helping to deliver the mathematics curriculum to a group of Reception children?

How to link activities to the child's experience and give direct experience of mathematics

As we know, mathematics is sometimes an abstract subject, so early years professionals need to link mathematical concepts to practical activities to make the concepts meaningful for children. This means, for the youngest children, their introduction to the subject will be mainly through play and exploration. They should be encouraged to recognise numbers and patterns in their environment. Figure 10.4 shows the kinds of activities that they will take part in during the early years that will support mathematical development.

Children may also enjoy being taken on a 'maths walk' in small groups to look at numbers and shapes around the school and outdoor area or in the near environment. Depending on the amount of adult support available, you may like to give them a series of questions to answer, or simply allow them to find out what they can and report back to others.

Activity

Devise and carry out a maths walk for a year group with whom you are currently working. How does this engage the children? How does it support different mathematical areas and build children's confidence?

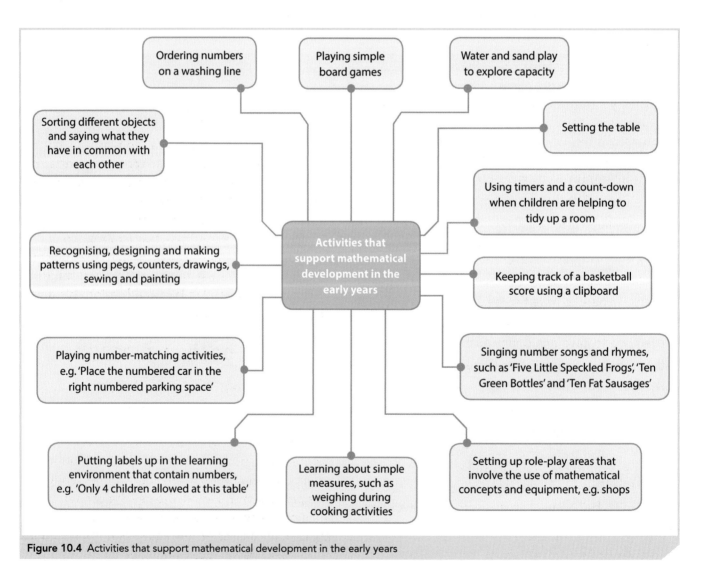

Figure 10.4 Activities that support mathematical development in the early years

Activities shown in diagram:
- Ordering numbers on a washing line
- Playing simple board games
- Water and sand play to explore capacity
- Sorting different objects and saying what they have in common with each other
- Setting the table
- Using timers and a count-down when children are helping to tidy up a room
- Recognising, designing and making patterns using pegs, counters, drawings, sewing and painting
- Keeping track of a basketball score using a clipboard
- Playing number-matching activities, e.g. 'Place the numbered car in the right numbered parking space'
- Singing number songs and rhymes, such as 'Five Little Speckled Frogs', 'Ten Green Bottles' and 'Ten Fat Sausages'
- Putting labels up in the learning environment that contain numbers, e.g. 'Only 4 children allowed at this table'
- Learning about simple measures, such as weighing during cooking activities
- Setting up role-play areas that involve the use of mathematical concepts and equipment, e.g. shops

Central: **Activities that support mathematical development in the early years**

Ways to check children's understanding of the purpose of the activity and help them process information

Sometimes, young children may find it hard to recall what they have been asked to do or why they are doing it. You may need to help them go over what is required. You can do this by first questioning them to check their understanding or by asking them to repeat back to you what they think they need to do next. You may also need to remind them about specific teaching points – this may be because of their own individual learning needs or their ability to remain focused on a task.

Questioning children, modelling and observing their reactions

You will need to constantly observe children's reactions in mathematical situations, so make sure you direct your questions accordingly. This is because it is easy for children to misunderstand mathematical concepts. It is likely that you will use observation, modelling and questioning regularly as children will need to be refocused or asked specific questions to redirect their thinking.

It is important that early years professionals model to children how mathematics is used in everyday life and discuss it with them. For example, when:

- solving problems – are there enough sausages for everyone here to have two each?
- using money – how many pennies would I need for everyone to have one penny each?
- thinking about capacity – is there enough orange juice in the jug to fill six cups?
- counting – count slowly alongside children.

When questioning children, you should make sure that you ask in a way that does not 'lead' them to the answer. Questions should also be open where possible, for example, 'The answer is 5. What could the question be?' Some further examples are shown in Table 10.2.

Table 10.2 Part of an example taken from the 'Mathematical Vocabulary Book', DfES 2000. © Crown copyright 2000. Contains public sector information licensed under the Open Government Licence v 2.0.

Closed questions	Open questions
Count these cubes.	How could we count these cubes?
A chew costs 3p. A lolly costs 7p. What do they cost altogether?	A chew and a lolly cost 10p altogether. What could each sweet cost?
What is 6 − 4?	Tell me two numbers with a difference of 2.
Is 16 an even number?	What even numbers are between 0 and 10?
What are four threes?	Tell me two numbers with a product of 12.

Ensuring children have time to process information

Like any person when introduced to a new idea, very young children will need time to take on board a new mathematical concept or to be able to think through what they need to do. An important part of ensuring children's understanding is making sure you give them this time to process any new information or concepts. Reinforcing learning through questioning and discussion can be a good way of giving children the time they will need to become comfortable and familiar with information.

Having a good command of the English language in spoken and written form

It is very important that early years professionals demonstrate a good command of both written and spoken English when working with children. Early years professionals should also use the correct mathematical terms when explaining activities. It is easy for confusion to arise if activities and instructions are not described or explained correctly.

Case study

The need to have good English skills

Saraya works in a nursery and speaks English as a second language. Although she is having English lessons, there are some gaps in her vocabulary, particularly in her mathematical language. She has been asked to work with a group of children to identify and describe some 3-D shapes and she realises she is unable to identify them herself.

1 What should Saraya do in this situation?

2 Why is it important that she says something about her lack of knowledge to her colleagues?

Supporting children's mathematical understanding through questioning

Children will need to be questioned by early years professionals during mathematical activities to check their understanding and develop their learning. You should encourage children to talk about what they are doing, particularly during practical tasks, and question them in a way that encourages them to think about the task in different ways. Revisit examples of questioning techniques in Table 10.2.

You should remember that the most important part of supporting any aspect of children's learning is to focus on what they are learning and their understanding of it. This is particularly important for mathematics. At the end of an activity, it is more important for children to have understood what they have been asked to do than to have completed the task. The focus should not be on completing the task or getting the correct answer, but instead on children understanding how they should complete the task and what information or resources they will need to do so.

Helping children to obtain and use resources

You may need to prompt children or encourage them to think about resources available to them when working on mathematical activities. These resources may include number lines, measuring instruments, games, computer software and learning programmes. Children may need help if they have been asked to carry out an activity with unfamiliar resources. They

may not have used some items before and younger children should always be given the opportunity to look at and explore what they will be using before starting the activity. If children have sensory support needs, you may need to speak to specialist teachers to find out what additional resources are available.

Reflect

Think about the kinds of mathematical activities you carry out with children. Do you ever rush to complete a task with them rather than focus on their understanding?

Assessment practice 10.5   3D.P7 | 3D P8 | 3D. M5 | 3D.D3

1 Your supervisor has asked you to write a description of three practical activities that you have carried out with children aged between 2 and 5 years to support the development of mathematical skills in number and shape, space and measures.

2 Explain why you chose the activities and how they support children's mathematical development.

3 Evaluate how early years professionals contribute to the mathematical development of children from birth to 5 years.

The role of early years professionals in modelling mathematics

Early years professionals should be able to model mathematics to children as a matter of course through the way in which they interact with them on a daily basis. This could be by, for example, counting aloud in different contexts such as going upstairs, or by giving numbers to children in groups. This should include using and pointing out numbers in the environment as well as using mathematics in a practical way in the setting. For example, when setting up a role-play area as a shop or café, an adult should model to children how money might be used and help them to select coins and make purchases. Early years professionals should also draw children's attention to numbers on resources they may use, such as till receipts, number plates, tickets or signs that indicate how many children are allowed in a particular area in the learning environment.

Explaining and reinforcing the use of mathematical language by providing commentary

You should always reinforce vocabulary that is being used in the setting, extend children's vocabulary and check their understanding of any terms used. Young children, or children who speak English as an additional language, may need you to explain mathematical terms to them. Commentary, or talking through with children what they are doing as they are doing it, enables them to become more familiar with the mathematical language they are using and also encourages them to think through the process as they are working.

Using interactive computer programs

There are a number of interactive computer programs and websites available that encourage and reinforce mathematical concepts. Most children enjoy working with computers and these programs can be useful in engaging them.

Working with parents and carers to encourage enjoyment of mathematics

It is very important for schools and early years settings to work alongside parents to encourage their child's enjoyment of mathematics. However, many parents may have had poor experiences while they were at school and find this hard to overcome. The setting can help in different ways, through running information evenings, giving talks and providing guidelines or booklets for parents on how to support their child when learning mathematics. These may include ideas such as the following.

- Look for shapes and numbers in the environment. Move on to finding odd/even numbers, or numbers higher/lower than.

- Play card and board games, and complete puzzles with children.
- Count up small change with children after going 'shopping'.
- Cook with children to give them experience of weighing ingredients and reading scales. Talk about ingredients being heavier/lighter than others.
- Try not to put too much emphasis on formal 'sums', particularly with very young children. It is more important that they have plenty of practical experience of mathematics.

Parents should be encouraged to come into the setting if possible to see maths in action and to carry out games and activities with children. In this way, they will be able to develop their own confidence as well as gain ideas. There are also plenty of excellent books for parents to support mathematical development.

Research

Many schools now use the Mathletics website to encourage children to enjoy mathematics. The website provides interactive mathematics activities for schools and it encourages children to carry out activities at home too.
Take a look at the website and the service it offers. You can access the website by going to www.pearsonhotlinks.co.uk and searching for this ISBN: 9781447970965.

Case study

Supporting children at home

Andy is a parent of twins who are in Year 2. Although both the children are at an age-equivalent level in mathematics, he would like to support them at home and has approached the school for advice, because apart from working on times tables with them he says that maths is so different from when he was at school, he is worried about 'getting it wrong'.

1 What kinds of suggestions might you be able to give Andy?

2 Why is it important to work with Andy and other parents?

Further reading and resources

Literacy

Letters and Sounds (DFES-00281-2007). This is a government document produced through the Primary National Strategy, which starts in the Foundation Stage and builds up through the different stages.

Goodman, K. S. (1976) 'Reading: a Psycholinguistic Guessing Game' in H. Singer and R. B. Ruddell (eds.), *Theoretical Models and Processes of Reading* (5th ed.), Newark, Delaware: International Reading Association.

Rose, J. (2006) *The Independent Review of the Teaching of Early Reading* (DFES-0201-2006).

Smith, F. (1985) *Reading* (2nd ed.), Cambridge: Cambridge University Press.

Wray, D. 'From Learning to Teaching' in T. Cremin and J. Arthur (eds) (2014), *Learning to Teach in the Primary School* (3rd ed.), London: Routledge.

Mathematics

Boaler, J. (2010) *The Elephant in the Classroom: Helping Children Learn and Love Maths*, London: Souvenir Press Ltd.

Deboys, M. and Pitt, E. (1980) *Lines of Development in Primary Mathematics*, Belfast: Blackstaff Press Ltd.

Donaldson, M. (1986) *Children's Minds*, London: Harper Collins.

Eastaway, R. and Askew, M. (2010) *Maths for Mums and Dads*, London: Square Peg.

Ojose, B. 'Applying Piaget's theory of mathematical development to mathematics', *The Mathematics Educator*, 2008.

Sani, N. (2010) *How to do Maths so Your Children Can Too: The Essential Parents' Guide*, London: Vermilion.

Early Years Foundation Stage document, DCSF 2008.

National Curriculum for England, DfEE 1999.

Mathematical Vocabulary Book, DfES 2000.

Primary Framework for Literacy and Mathematics, DfES 2006.

Websites

Literacy

National Literacy Trust: www.literacytrust.org.uk Advice, resources and case studies.

Mr Thorne Does Phonics: www.mrthorne.com Lots of very useful ideas and clips for supporting the teaching of synthetic phonics. Many of these are also available on YouTube.

The Primary National Strategy for Literacy has now been archived but is still available online: www.education.gov.uk/schools/toolsandinitiatives/nationalstrategies

Mathematics

nrich: http://nrich.maths.org Lots of ideas and resources to support children's mathematical development.

Mathletics: www.mathletics.co.uk A large number of resources for teachers and exciting activities for children. Your setting will need to subscribe to access the full site.

Ready for work?

Wen Lui Teaching assistant

I have been working at St Mary's School for about six months, after working in their preschool for three years. I am based in the Reception class but also spend two afternoons in Year 1. It has been interesting, having come from a preschool, to see how the reading and writing skills that children developed in nursery are carried on when they are in Reception and Year 1.

A good understanding of how children learn to read and write is so important. Knowing about the different stages of learning to read and write also helps identify children who are having difficulties, so that we are able to put in measures to support them as soon as possible. Although all children are different and learn at different rates, I am always amazed when things click into place and they start to make real progress.

I also decided to complete my own maths GCSE, as I did not get a good grade when I was at school. It has been really good to look at maths again and find out some of the fun aspects that can be transferred to my work with the children. I am now full of enthusiasm for it and, as a result, have asked the setting manager if we can run an information evening for parents. My line manager says that it has been great to watch me develop my confidence in this area.

Skills for practice

Support literacy

- When you share books with children, talk to them and develop your relationship.
- Pre-reading and pre-writing skills – use opportunities to develop children's strength in their arms and body as well as fine motor skills.
- Print, label and annotate displays.
- Give children time and repeat back a word correctly if they are wrong, rather than telling them it is incorrect.
- Remember that rhymes and songs also support literacy skills.
- Use props when sharing stories with children to bring books to life.
- Create writing areas with a variety of things to write with and on and encourage children to write by giving them specific topics to write about.
- Have different word lists available for children to refer to.
- Keep up to date with observations and records.

Support mathematics

- Support mathematics in different situations, for example, indoor and outdoor, formal and informal.
- Use as many opportunities as you can to develop children's counting skills and assess their learning.
- Remember that activities such as counting songs and nursery rhymes, puzzles, measuring scores in sports and talking about shapes are all forms of mathematics.
- Use ICT with children to reinforce mathematical concepts.
- Use other activities to consolidate mathematical concepts, for example, cooking, which uses measuring and counting.
- Look for mathematics in the environment, for example, patterns in tiles and shapes. Devise activities and trips that will encourage children to think about numbers in the environment, for example, maths walks.

A

Adolescence – a period of time over which children's bodies develop into sexually mature adult bodies.

Adult-directed play – when adults take a role in planning, organising and leading play.

Advocate – a person who represents the views of the child.

Asthma – a long-term lung disease that inflames and narrows the airways causing difficulty in breathing.

Atelier – a workshop.

Attachment – a special relationship or bond between a child and people who are emotionally involved with them.

Atypical behaviour – behaviour that is not usually associated with a specific age range.

Audiology test – a hearing test carried out with a machine called an audiometer.

Auditory discrimination – the ability to hear and pick out particular sounds amid others.

Axon – the part of the neuron where electricity travels.

Axon terminal – a part of the neuron involved in making a connection with another neuron.

B

Behaviourist – the belief that development is shaped by the environment.

Behaviourist theory – a theory of learning that states that development and behaviour can be conditioned and shaped by the environment.

Block play – play using large wooden bricks of different shapes and sizes.

C

Child-directed speech – speech patterns used by parents speaking to their children, usually involving slow and simplified vocabulary, a high-pitched voice and the use of repetition and questions.

Child-initiated play – when children choose what to play with and how to play.

Chronic illness – a long-term medical condition.

Cognitive development – the development of the mind and how children learn, reason and understand.

Cognitive processing – the way in which the brain processes, retains and makes links between existing and new information.

Concrete experiences – practical experiences that make it easier for young children to understand an idea.

Conditioning – learning to act in a certain way because past experiences have taught us to do, or not to do, something.

Conductive hearing loss – a hearing loss often caused by glue ear.

Constructivist approach – a model to explain children's cognitive development, which considers that children develop their own ideas based on experiences and interactions.

Constructivist theory – a theory that states how children learn by constructing their own knowledge through experience and that children pass through specific stages of development.

Continual interaction and communication – in this context, the way in which we talk about maths and use mathematical language so that children learn mathematical vocabulary in different contexts.

Cooperative – produced by two or more people/groups working together to achieve something.

Cooperative friendship – when children negotiate, play or agree what to do with each other.

Cooperative play – when children are playing with each other.

D

Defecate – excrete faeces (solid waste) from the body.

Dendrite – a part of the neuron involved in making a connection with another neuron.

Development – the skills and knowledge that children gain.

Discrimination – not giving equality of opportunity to groups or individuals because they belong to a particular group.

Disposition – a child's nature or temperament.

E

Emollients – special moisturisers designed to prevent skin from drying.

Emotionally available – the capacity to be able to respond, support and deal with the emotions of others.

Emotionally labile – having emotions that may be strong and fluctuate quickly.

Empathy – the ability to feel or understand the emotions of others.

Encode – the process by which information gained by the brain is stored.

Ethologist – a person who studies patterns of animal behaviour.

Ethos – the philosophy or approach used by a setting that affects the practice.

European Community Directive – a legislative act that countries in the European Union are required to implement in their home country. A directive does not specify the method that should be used to implement the act, so countries are given a certain amount of freedom to decide how they achieve the intended outcome of the act.

F

Facilitate – the action of supporting children rather than leading their actions and play.

Fine motor skills – control of the smaller muscles, such as those in the fingers, to carry out activities such as threading beads onto a necklace, using a knife and fork, or holding a pencil.

Formative assessment – assessment that takes place during the learning process on an ongoing basis, or 'assessment for learning'.

Foster care – temporary care in foster families for looked-after children who are not with their parents.

G

Gestation – the period of time between conception and birth.

Gloop – a sensory mixture made by mixing cornflour with water.

Glue ear – a condition in which fluid builds up in the auditory (Eustachian) tube in the ear, preventing sounds from being heard properly.

Grapheme – individual written symbols.

Gross motor skills – control of the larger muscles, such as those in the arms and legs, to carry out activities such as running, throwing or kicking a ball.

Growth – the process by which cells subdivide.

H

Health and Safety Executive – an independent national body that regulates health, safety and illness in the workplace.

Hyperglycaemia – when there is too much glucose and insufficient insulin.

Hypoglycaemia – when there is too much insulin and insufficient glucose.

Hypothesise – to speculate or propose an idea or theory.

I

Immunisation – the process by which someone is protected against an infectious disease.

Indiscriminate attachments – when babies and children do not seem to have formed special relationships with other people.

Infant mortality – the rate of death in the first year of life.

Informal care – when parents make childcare arrangements with friends or family who are unregistered.

Innate theory – behaviours/actions that children do instinctively.

In need – refers to children who are unlikely to maintain, or be given the opportunity to maintain, a reasonable standard of health or development, or children whose health could be impaired without the support of local authority services. It also includes children who are disabled.

Inspectorate – a body that makes sure regulations relating to a particular activity are obeyed.

Interpersonal skills – the skills required for building relationships.

K

Key person – an early years professional designated to take responsibility for a child's emotional wellbeing by having a strong attachment with them and a good relationship with their parents.

L

Language – the medium through which we talk and communicate.

Learning journey/learning story – a way of assessing and planning for children's development using a narrative approach that can easily be shared and constructed with parents and children.

Longitudinal observations – information gained about a child from a series of observations that are carried out over a period of time.

Looked-after children – when the local authority has responsibility for the care of children.

M

Malnourished – having a lack of proper nutrients.

Makaton – a UK language programme where signs and symbols from British Sign Language are used to help children with specific difficulties understanding the spoken word.

Maths walk – a walk around a school or setting during which children look for different aspects of maths in the environment, for example numbers and shapes.

Mean length utterance – the average number of words used in a sentence.

Microorganisms – living organisms, including viruses and bacteria, that are too small to be seen with the naked eye.

Modelling – an action, gesture or behaviour that a child might observe and later imitate.

Morbidity – the rate of incidence of ill health within a population.

Motherese – the language patterns of parents speaking to their children, which are often simplified and repetitive. The term is usually used in reference to mothers.

Mouthing – exploring items by putting them in the mouth.

Multiple attachments – when babies and children have many specific attachments to other people.

Myelin – the substance that coats the axon.

Myelination – the process of myelin coating.

N

Named person – a person who is the main point of contact.

Nativist – the belief that development is predetermined.

Need-to-know policy – a way of making sure that personal information is only provided to those people who genuinely 'need to know'.

Neural growth – when neuron cells increase in size.

Neural pathway – an established route for signals within the brain.

Neurological development – the growth and development of the brain, including the formation of new neurological connections.

Neuron – a brain cell.

Neuroscience – the study of how the brain grows and works.

Non-contemporaneous – in the context of observing children, this refers to events that are recorded or reported after they have occurred.

Norovirus – a common stomach bug that causes severe diarrhoea and vomiting.

Notifiable disease – a disease that has to be reported to authorities.

O

Object permanence – recognition that when objects are out of sight, they have not disappeared.

Onlooker play – when young children are watching other children play and are copying their actions from a distance.

Operant conditioning – a theory that suggests that the environment 'operates' on and thus influences a child's learning using reinforcers.

P

Palmar grip – holding an object with the palm of the hand.

Parallel play – when young children play next to each other using similar actions and materials. They are aware of each other but are not playing with each other.

Participant bias – where an observer is subconsciously recording information in a subjective way.

Pedagogy – an approach to the teaching of children.

Perceptual skills – the ability to judge objects in relation to their shape, size and/or motion.

Phonemes – the smallest units of sound in a language that help to distinguish one word from another. In the English language, for example, 'p' and 'b' are separate phonemes because they distinguish words such as 'pit' and 'bit'.

Phonics – the name of a method used to teach reading that breaks down different letter patterns into their individual sounds.

Physiological effects – changing or influencing normal bodily functions.

Picture Exchange Communication System – a system that helps children with communication difficulties to learn about the two-way nature of communication through the exchange of pictures.

Positional language – vocabulary such as 'next to', 'underneath', 'inside', 'outside', 'on top of', 'above', 'around', 'apart', 'middle', 'edge', 'opposite', 'left', 'right', 'across', 'along', 'beside', 'below', 'before', 'after', 'in between'.

Positive reinforcement – an action or object that acts as a reward to reinforce a desired behaviour.

Predisposition – an increased likelihood of showing a skill, trait or developing a condition as a result of genetic inheritance.

Prelinguistic phase – the first phase of language learning, which comes before the production of first words.

Preventer inhaler – an inhaler that is used to control the symptoms of asthma with the aim of preventing or reducing attacks.

Psychological effects – changing the pattern of behaviour or thinking.

Purposeful play – play that allows children to concentrate and also may permit the learning or practice of new skills or concepts.

Q

Qualitative data – information that is collected by informal methods and cannot be scientifically replicated.

R

Reciprocal friendship – when children take equal or similar pleasure in being in each other's company.

Reflective practice – thinking about the way we work in order to make changes, build on strengths and stay up to date with developments.

Reflexes – automatic movements that do not require a conscious decision.

Regression – to move backwards developmentally to a previous stage.

Reinforcers – positive or negative experiences used to strengthen children's behavioural responses.

Reliever inhaler – an inhaler that is used during an asthma attack. It works by enlarging the airways, so helping to facilitate breathing.

Resilient – being able to recover quickly from different or difficult situations.

Respiratory disease – a condition that affects the lungs or a person's ability to breathe.

Retrieve – the process by which memories can be activated.

Rickets – a bone disease caused by lack of vitamin D.

S

Scaffolding – a term used to describe a style of working with children in which the adult helps the child to acquire information.

Schema – a repeated action, way of doing something or way of thinking/reasoning that can be specific or generalised.

Scribe – an adult who writes down what a child would like to say.

Selective mutism – where a child is unable to talk although they have the ability to do so.

Self-efficacy – the understanding that you are able to do things for yourself.

Separation anxiety – a set of behaviours and actions that occur when a child is distressed as a result of the person or people they are attached to being absent.

Serious case review – a review carried out when a child has died or has been seriously injured as a result of neglect.

Significant harm – this refers to the seriousness of the harm or likely harm that a child may suffer.

Small-world play – play with toys such as sets of farm animals, trains, cars and play people.

Social constructivist – a model that explains children's cognitive development by suggesting that their logic and reasoning is developed through experiences, but also by interactions with and questions from adults and older children.

Social interactionist theory – behaviours/actions that children learn to do as a result of gaining information and feedback during interaction with adults and other children.

Sociogram – a recording method whereby children indicate their friendship preferences.

Specific attachments – when babies and children have formed special bonds with other people.

Speech – the physical act of talking and articulating.

Spurt – a short period of intense growth.

Statutory – required by law (statute).

Statutory guidance – a legal term that means that settings or an individual have to follow or pay regard to advice.

Summative assessment – assessment of what a child knows and can do at the end of a period of learning, or 'assessment of learning'.

Sustained shared thinking – sensitive interactions between adults and children over a period of time that support children to develop their thoughts about a topic or concept.

Synapse – the gap between two neurons; electrical impulses pass across this gap from the dendrite of one neuron to the axon terminal of the other neuron.

T

Taboo – a custom that prevents discussion of a particular practice or association with a person, place or thing.

Theory of mind – children recognising their own conscious mind and understanding that other people will have different thoughts to them.

Topical corticosteroids – prescribed creams that are used in the treatment of eczema.

Trait – a set of characteristics.

Transitions – changes in children's lives, especially in relation to adults who may be looking after them.

Treasure basket play – a collection of natural materials and objects put in a basket to support babies' play.

V

Vaccine – a very weak dose of an infectious organism that is injected into someone in order to prevent a disease.

Variables – factors that may be involved in development.

Virtuous errors – logical mistakes made by children that suggest they have some understanding of sentence structure, for example, 'I runned' and 'I wented'. Although the tenses are used incorrectly, the errors are logical.

Vocalisations – sounds that are made by babies either for communication or as a means of exploration. Sounds may include words.

W

Welfare – holistic needs including health and wellbeing.

Whistle-blowing – raising concerns about the actions of an individual, group or organisation.